Blackwell N. A.

W9-BQL-976

Political
and Social
Thought in the
Contemporary
Middle East

Political and Social Thought in the Contemporary Middle East

Revised and Enlarged Edition

edited by
Kemal H. Karpat

PRAEGER SPECIAL STUDIES • PRAEGER SCIENTIFIC

Wingate College Library

Library of Congress Cataloging in Publication Data
Main entry under title:

Political and social thought in the contemporary
    Middle East.

    Includes bibliographical references and index.
    1. Political science—Near East—History.
2.   Near East—Politics and government. I. Karpat,
Kemal H.
JA84.N18P64 1982   320.5   81-11877
ISBN 0-03-057609-1   AACR2
ISBN 0-03-057608-3 (pbk.)

Published in 1982 by Praeger Publishers
CBS Educational and Professional Publishing
a Division of CBS Inc.
521 Fifth Avenue, New York, New York 10175 U.S.A.

© 1982 by Praeger Publishers

All rights reserved

23456789   145   987654321

Printed in the United States of America

088726

PREFACE TO SECOND EDITION

The first edition of this book was sold out in a very short time, despite reprintings that followed its publication. It was used extensively both by specialists as a reference book and by teachers as a textbook or supplementary reading in Middle East courses both in the West and in the area proper. The book's wide acceptance can be attributed to its original approach, concepts, and methodology.

I have felt all along that the Western student and the general public must have direct access to the ideas, thoughts, and aspirations of the Middle Easterners as they are formulated, expressed, and diffused by the very people in the area. Any effort to interpret and reformulate the Middle Eastern thought solely within the framework of Western values, modes of expression, and ideological tendencies can lead easily to distortion and misrepresentation. One can pass only qualified judgments on the Middle Eastern ideology, since ideology by its very nature is subjective and attuned to the specific conditions that engendered it or made its borrowing necessary. This basic philosophy has been maintained throughout the second edition.

In order to make the book more useful I undertook a number of significant changes. The section on Iran has been thoroughly revised and enlarged. A new section dealing with Israel that did not exist in the first edition has been added. The section on thought in the Arabic-speaking countries has been updated and a special section on the Palestinians added. The section on Turkey has been updated and revised to reflect current developments. The introduction to each section has been revised in such a way as to include information on basic historical and political developments. Extensive bibliographies have been added to each section. The purpose of these changes and revisions was to make the book more suitable for class use, both for lecture and paper writing. At the same time I have been also careful to provide some in-depth analysis of various currents of thought and their social and political environment in order to interest the student in further reading and research on the subject. Since I consider Muslim fundamentalism the harbinger of basic changes in the Middle East I have provided extensive information on the issue.

As usual a number of people have provided valuable assistance in revising this book. My thanks go to Jacob Landau, Aryeh Shmuelevitz, and to Mehrdad Kia for their help. I would like to express my gratitude to the editors of the *Journal of Palestine Studies, Jerusalem Post, The New Outlook* (the Middle East), the Mizan Press, Random House (Vintage Books), and Macmillan Publishing Company for permission to reproduce from their publications.

PREFACE*

    This book is basically intended to provide students of Middle Eastern affairs with direct access to contemporary political and social thought in the area. A correct understanding of the Middle East requires close familiarity with the ideas that prepare the ground for political action and that justify it. The study of writings by Arab, Turkish, Iranian, and Israeli intellectuals that appear in reviews and books is the best means to gain this familiarity. These writings, in addition, help the outside observer to gain a better understanding of how Middle Eastern intellectuals view events and issues in their own countries and in the world at large. Understanding is a two-way communication. Westerners need to know the thoughts and aspirations of other peoples at the same time that people in the rest of the world must know the thoughts and aspirations of the West.

    Although some books and articles by Middle Eastern intellectuals have been translated into Western languages, mainly since World War II, they have not provided the means for a comprehensive, comparative study of major contemporary currents of thought in the Middle East. Consequently, this book attempts to present a broad, comparative view of Middle Eastern thought through a selection of appropriate writings. With a number of exceptions, none of the extracts have previously been published in English.

    In preparing a book of this kind, an editor is faced with various methodological possibilities. He may, for example, classify the currents of thought into various categories with well-determined characteristics and select texts accordingly. Or he may follow a historical approach and choose material to indicate, step by step, the evolution of a particular current of thought. Both approaches, however, are guided by the compiler's understanding and interpretation of what he regards as the main current of thought at a given time. Moreover, an editor may be persuaded to accept a text as important because of its clarity and comprehensiveness rather than because of its actual place and impact in the society from

---

*The preface to the first edition, though partly updated, is preserved as it comprises the basic methodological and conceptual views.

which it derives. Contemporary writing in the Middle East cannot be classified in well-determined categories because there is much overlapping of ideas of nationalism, socialism, modernism, cultural reformation, and other subjects. Some writings are so comprehensive that they can be fitted into almost any category, while others require a special category of their own. Although the historical approach is relatively sound, the tendency in the Middle East to ignore many writings of the past renders the element of thought continuity rather tenuous. The Middle Eastern intellectual reveres history but rarely reads it.

I have followed an entirely empirical method in selecting the material for this book. First, from various sources, I accumulated a list of authors and texts related to Middle Eastern political and social thought. My courses at New York University and a preliminary reader compiled for a summer seminar at Columbia University served as preparatory steps. Subsequently, I spent several summers in the Middle East interviewing newpaper and magazine publishers, politicians, writers, scholars, and students. I asked these people to define the main political and social issues of public interest and to name the most influential writers and, if possible, some of their principal works. My ultimate choice of texts was determined primarily by issues and only secondarily by the personality or style of the authors. My purpose was to accumulate texts that would give a broad picture not only of the major political and social currents in the area but also of various social groups, self-interpretive opinions, causes of change, and the like. Texts by a few important writers associated with Middle Eastern thought were omitted either because their writings had lost their current appeal or were too didactic. Yet, writings by several men no longer alive, such as Hasan al-Banna and Antun Saadeh, were included mainly because their ideas continue to exert an influence. Articles by relatively unknown writers were selected either because they were by dissenters from generally accepted views or because they expressed a viewpoint that may become significant in the near future. Moreover, since public opinion in the Middle East, as elsewhere in the world, is formed by a mixture of propagandistic writings and carefully formulated thoughts, I did not hesitate to include examples of both. A few of the authors casually paraphrase or quote passages, often from memory, from Western writers. It is tradition, in Islam, to back a statement by referring to, or quoting from, an authority. But by not giving full references, some contemporary authors make it virtually impossible to locate their sources. Consequently, such quotations should be regarded as part of the writer's ideological argument rather than as accurately representing the thought of the original author.

The texts have been arranged for convenience according to topics that correspond approximately to what may be considered as the principal currents of thought in the Middle East today. The arrangement, however, is not based on, nor does it establish, well-defined categories, since the contemporary ideology of transition in the Middle East defies precise classification.

The book consists of a general introduction and four major sections. Each of these sections—Arab, Turkish, Iranian, and Israeli—is preceded by an introductory survey of thought development, and each selection by a brief biography of the author and, if his ideology is at all influential, by an analysis of it and suggestions for further reading. Thus, there are relatively long analyses—and annotations—of the Muslim Brotherhood, the Ba'ath, and various other important issues or groups. Although the translations of the texts have been somewhat simplified and adapted to English usage, the original style has been preserved as much as possible. The titles of some of the extracts have been changed. The Arabic transliterations are adapted from the system used by the *Middle East Journal*; the Turkish and Iranian transliterations are the compiler's.

Compiling a work of this kind requires the cooperation of a great number of people and entails many years of tedious toil and frustrations that are well known to those who have worked on similar projects without the aid of sophisticated bibliographical tools. The main reference available in this case was Fahim I. Qubain's very useful *Inside the Arab Mind* (Arlington, Va.: Universal Printers and Lithographers of America, 1960). Meanwhile, an excellent new bibliography that has appeared is George Atiyeh, *The Contemporary Middle East 1948–1973: A Selective and Annotated Bibliography* (Boston: G.K. Hall, 1975).

My thanks go to the many people who contributed to this book in various ways. Don Peretz and Ward Morehouse of the Area Studies Program of the University of the State of New York sponsored the project and provided its main support. Tarif Khalidi, of the American University of Beirut (AUB), rendered invaluable assistance in translating Arabic materials; Frank Tachau of Rutgers University and the late Sakina Berenjian helped to translate the Turkish and Persian texts. The advice of Nicola Ziadeh, Nabih Faris, and Constantin Zurayk of AUB and the work of Adnan Bakhit greatly facilitated my selection of Arabic texts. Yusuf Ibish and Walid Khalidi of AUB kindly contacted many leading politicians and writers in Beirut, allowed me extract pasages from their valuable source book *Arab Political Documents 1963*, and put at my disposal the secretarial facilities of their office. For their advice and time, I am grateful to the editors and staff of *al-Akhbar, al-Amal, al-Ba'th, al-Hayat, Hiwar, al-*

Jumhuriyya, al-Nahar, al-Yawm, Ruz al-Yusuf, and others; to many leaders of political groups and to writers too numerous to mention; and to various Arab information offices. Thanks also are due to the librarians of AUB, Mr. Bekhazi and Linda Sadaka, and to the librarians of the Turkish National Library. For information and advice, I extend my thanks to Sina Akşin of Robert College of Instanbul, Kenan Bulutoğlu of the University of Istanbul, Yaşar Nabi, the editors of *Yön,* and various newspaper editors in Turkey. The editors of *Middle East Journal* and *Middle Eastern Affairs* graciously permitted me to reproduce texts. Barbara Stowasser skillfully transliterated and clarified Arabic terms and nomenclature and established the basis for an index. The editors at Frederick A. Praeger rendered various gallant services. Whatever errors occur—despite all this competent assistance—are entirely my own.

CONTENTS

PART THREE: POLITICAL AND SOCIAL THOUGHT IN TURKEY

INTRODUCTION

Sources and Functions of Ideology

The Middle East, like other developing areas, is in ideological ferment. The political and social ideas expressed in the various nations of the Middle East are an inseparable part of the general process of modernization. Primarily action-oriented, they are, in fact, the intellectual justfication for material developments as well as an attempt to incorporate empirical acts in an intellectual framework. Ideology in the Middle East thus embodies the values associated with modernization and is as important in understanding it as the material forces that triggered modernization.[1]

Middle Eastern political thought comprises, in varying degrees, the four elements accepted as general characteristics of ideology: a philosophy of history, an analysis of man's present stage of development, a projection into the future, and a plan of action.[2] Each characteristic assumes peculiar forms according to the historic cultural, social, and political conditions specific to the area. A brief analysis of the rise of modernist thought in the Middle East may explain the political and social functions of ideology in the area.

The principal source of ideological upsurge in the contemporary Middle East is the social dislocation caused by the breakdown of the traditional social and political order. Traditional society was divided basically into four social groups or estates: men of the pen, men of the sword, merchants and craftsmen, and food producers. Each social group had its assigned role, status, and function, and developed a philosophy of life, manners, expectations, modes of expression, and general attitudes according to its place and function in society. The traditional organization thus produced a division of labor each of which had a specific culture. The functions of government were determined by the needs of the community and the religious principles underlying the social structure. Government and religion—that is to say, authority and legitimization—in the traditional Muslim society of the Middle East had developed in intimate association with each other. Islam came to accept this social arrangement, despite contradictions with some of its basic monolithic principles and the fact that the social system originated in Greek thought and Persian practices. In other words, Islam incorporated in its social and political system elements of other cultures which it reinterpreted and adopted to its own dogma.

Government maintained this social arrangement by keeping each group in its assigned place. Numerous social conflicts, appearing in the form of heretical religious movements, created divisions within the existing order, but did not alter its basic structure and philosophy.

Since the social and political order was considered divinely prescribed, it was natural that the laws governing the order were also immutable. Consequently, man gained a certain sense of emotional security, inner contentment, and serenity in the belief that his place in society and the government that ruled him were determined by divine will. The disintegration of the traditional social order in the Ottoman Empire shook man's view of his role in society and his relation to the government, and eventually compelled him to create a new social and political order. The roots of modern ideology lie in this search for a new social and political order—that is, the modern state.

The economic and social basis of the old Ottoman system was the land system, which was organized to provide obedient support for the upper level of the social structure. The *sipahi* (cavalryman) administered the *timar* (land unit), supervised its cultivation, and maintained its legal status and that of the peasant, thus indirectly assuring social stability in the rural areas of the empire. The disintegration of the timar system—that is, of the government's military and bureaucratic organization supervising a large segment of the rural economy—created the conditions for a new social mobility.[3]

The emergence of the *ayan* (notables) in the Ottoman provinces, chiefly after the seventeenth century, marked the beginning of class differentiation based on wealth and communal authority. The ayan were originally communal leaders, who gradually acquired tax collecting privileges, and in some areas replaced the sipahis as administrators of state lands. Eventually, in the eighteenth and nineteenth centuries, they challenged the power of the central government. In that period, the increase of trade with Europe, the introduction of manufactured goods from the West, and the government's need for revenue and its consequent search for new sources of income created patterns of social and economic relations unknown in the past. These relations intensified in the second half of the nineteenth and the beginning of the twentieth century and irrevocably disrupted the traditional concepts of social organization and government and their legitimizations based on Islam.

The disruption of the old social organization created a crisis of identity and political purpose, which first manifested itself among the ruling groups in the form of dissatisfaction with, and criticism of, the government system. The so-called modernization reforms in the Ottoman Empire, Egypt, and Iran in the nineteenth century aimed to reestablish political and social cohesion by simply reorganizing government institutions. The reforms failed to achieve the desired results, not only because of foreign interference, but also because the theory and practice of the reforms did not adequately take into account the causes of the changes. The new ruling elite (bureaucracy, military, and intelligentsia) monopolized power within the "modernized" government structure, justifying it largely on the basis of political tradition, as in the past. They disregarded the essential fact that the lower social groups supporting the new political edifice were undergoing a process of political and social awakening similiar in the long run to that of the "modernized" ruling groups. In due time, the wealthy agrarian, commercial, and other elite groups capitalized on the social discontent among the masses and used them to further their own ambitions. Thus, the forces that caused the disintegration of the old order also determined the nature of the emerging currents of thought.

The sources of ideology in the Middle East are, as stated, on the one hand in social dislocation and the crisis of identity—a new pattern of social differentiation and stratification—and on the other in the need to establish a new cohesive social and political order with an identity of its own, capable of reaching the material and intellectual standards of contemporary civilization and of solving the conflicts in the social body. Modern ideology began to develop in the Middle East as a search first for a collective identity and then for modernist goals. The search was conditioned by the society's own historical sense of identity and by the political goals of the modern states in which the new social arrangement took place. Each ethnic group glorified its own national characteristics. Turks, Arabs, and Iranians reinterpreted history to prove that they preserved their national identity and creative genius, which were not destroyed by alien influences, but only prevented from keeping abreast of modern civilization. Turks and Iranians did not hesitate to blame religion for the backwardness of their society. Arabs, being intimately identified with Islam, accused the Iranians and Turks of imprinting on Islam their authoritarian concepts of government and rigid class differentiation. In reality, less than a century ago, Turks and Arabs shared a common Islamic affiliation under the Ottoman Empire.

Ideology strove to reinterpret history, to create pride in the past and confidence in the future, and to identify an ethnic group with a geographic region. It also operated in the field of social reconstruction, attempting to redefine the relations among social groups, to establish new

divisions of labor, and to assign responsibilities, with the ultimate purpose
of achieving social cohesion and national solidarity. Moreover, ideology
sought to relieve social tension by introducing the idea of social justice,
which became, in fact, the most powerful motive for political action.

Ideology in the Middle East also performed an intellectual function
within the general framework of modernization. It introduced new ideas
by adapting them to indigenous forms of expression and values, and
eventually claimed to have created a new—albeit eclectic—national
ideology. The claim to possess a national ideology strengthened newly
acquired political identities and facilitated further borrowing of ideas and
values from other cultures without risking internal opposition. Ideology
broke the limitations imposed by the old culture on the freedom and scope
of thought. It added new dimensions to thought by introducing to it
economic, social, and political elements. Thus, it helped achieve a sort of
intellectual liberation, a renaissance (as it is often referred to in the
Middle East), and a recognition of man's empiricism, on which the
humanist edifices of modern culture and science could more easily be
built. The idea that change, progress, better living—in a word, modernity—were induced scientifically by man was popularized through
ideology.

All currents of thought in the Middle East had a common background
and, as different aspects of the same continuous process of change, they
remained related to each other. The successful execution of the course of
action advocated by the ideology required some sort of directing authority. This authority turned out to be the government. Consequently, state
intervention in economic, social, and cultural activities was advocated in
one form or another by all major ideologies and became a common
characteristic of Middle Eastern political thought. In this respect, all
Middle Eastern ideologies may be considered statist. The state thus
became the "source of inspiration and of authority for action . . . [and]
built up [its image] as a source of power, knowledge, wisdom, [and]
resourcefulness."[4] When the state espoused radical methods, it was able to
justify them as necessary for the creation of the new life.[5]

In summary, ideology in the Middle East performed at least three
basic functions. First, it strove to create a political identity, which served as
the foundation of modern nationhood. In this capacity, ideology was
nationalistic. Second, ideology attempted to consolidate the social content
of the political state through a series of economic and educational
measures. In this functon, it was socialistic. Third, ideology attempted to
enlarge the cultural and intellectual horizon of Middle Eastern society in
conjunction with nationalism and socialism. The modernizing functions of
ideology are embodied in nationalism and socialism.

Modes of Expression

The emotional, subjective, and unsystematic writing emanating from the contemporary Middle East has baffled Western observers. Some Westerners have, in fact, been insultingly critical, without bothering to seek the significance of this writing. Current Middle Eastern writing is, indeed, far inferior to the accomplished style and crisp expression of traditional Arab, Persian, and Turkish poetry. Avnery found Hebrew to be a harsh language reflecting the hard conditions of life and climate. One must, however, place this writing in its proper context. It has caused revolutions, affected government policies, and produced mass movements. It is, in the last analysis, a powerful factor for political change, and must be studied as such.

An Arab, a Turk, an Iranian, or Israeli writes for a domestic audience and must convey his thoughts intelligibly and effectively to that particular audience. The writer must conform to native patterns of communication, using words and symbols with specific psychological effect, to persuade his readers. The most frequent form of persuasion in the Middle East is an appeal to the emotional and the personal, rather than to logical reasoning. Societies such as that of the Middle East—with a strong literary tradition and historic attachment to mysticism and religion, but forced to accept the changes imposed by progress—develop their own intricate processes of persuasion, through which they assimilate changes without acknowledging them. This process of assimilation is deeply rooted in the literature of the area. Many Middle Eastern political writers have been poets and novelists. The most successful modernizing poets and writers were those who could articulate modern ideas through the traditional forms of expression. Ahmet Mithat Efendi's educational novels in the Ottoman Empire were popular because he used the folk story genre. Political writing makes use of many literary techniques, such as metaphors, analogy, and allegory. The poet thus performs the function of social philospher by using the traditional methods of persuasion to root new ideas. In fact, during this stage of intellectual development in the Middle East, any political writing was ineffective if the author disregarded the traditional forms of expression and that subtle mixture of myth and emotion with reality.

The writing of the Middle East is, nevertheless, changing rapidly. Rational, logical, and consistent thought and expression are a matter of intellectual training as much as the result of environmental influences. A transitional society, with all its traditional forms of organization disrupted and perverted, can produce only a fragmented, organically unrelated thought process. Many of the forms of contemporary ideology in the

Middle East do not stem from the direct social experience of society, but are borrowed from abroad. Middle Eastern intellectuals agonize over the application to their own society of ideas and concepts developed in the West through centuries of consistent intellectual development. Arab intellectuals refer continually to a crisis of thought and spirit caused by the struggle between the past and the future, between materialism and spiritualism. The crisis will be resolved, many feel, through the discovery of an ideology that will galvanize all the dormant virtues of the Arab soul.

The stabilization of social and political life and the advent of a regular process of change may produce in the Middle East intellectual responses accordingly. The Middle East is experiencing a literary revolution, especially in novel and short story writing. Prose is largely a modern import. Through prose, the Middle Eastern intellectual learns to organize his thoughts and relate them in an organic fashion to life around him. The present relatively advanced level of political writing in Turkey occurred only after one generation of writers developed through literature an organic, consistent thought process, capable of conceptualizing and expressing the intricacies of modern life. The same development occurs in the Arab world.

The Middle East swept in less than a century from a predominantly oral system of communication to the mass media of the twentieth century—the newspaper, radio, and television. Governments used these media to mobilize the masses politically and inadvertently, perhaps, to imbue them with the idea of change. The effect of the communications media and of the audience on the content of communications cannot be ignored. Contemporary Middle Eastern writing can be better understood if judged in the perspective of the above conditions—that is, the need of a cohesive political and social doctrine and the availability of modern mass media.

The Rise and Evolution of Nationalism: Arab, Turkish, and Iranian

The development of nationalism in the Middle East was intimately associated with efforts to create a modern political system, the national state. Through the idea of the national state, the concept of the territorial state revolutionized traditional Middle Eastern thought. The true political modernization in the Middle East occurred within the framework of national statehood.[6] Thus, it resembled the process of national formation in Eastern Europe in the nineteenth century. It emphasized language, history, and culture. On the other hand, the struggle for liberation from Western domination made the process of nation formation in Arab countries resemble in some respects that of the African countries after World War II.

The Arab nationalist movement for separation and independence from the Ottoman Empire in 1908–16 was not identical in motivation and ideology with the anti-Western nationalist movement in Egypt after 1882 and in the Fertile Crescent after 1920. The Arab provinces of the Ottoman Empire did not have colony or mandate status. All provinces were equal within the framework of the Empire until the central government, failing to produce a successful, modern organization based on the universalist ideas of Islam, resorted to a nationalist, secularist political organization based on the supremacy of the Turkish ethnic group.

The early advocates of modernization, the Young Ottomans (1865–76), attempted to lay the theoretical foundations for a political organization that would preserve the basic Islamic characteristics of the Empire and incorporate into it the ideas of Western liberalism. They reached larger audiences with the press and literature in their attempt to create a new Ottoman identity and attachment to the fatherland.

Ottomanism, however, was essentially a legal concept. It ignored economic interest, ethnic and social origin, and language. It could not forego the reliance on Islam, since religion was still the only force capable of achieving social cohesion and loyalty to the state. The ideology of the Young Ottomans thus became an Ottoman nationalism rooted psychologically in Islam. It had no appeal, therefore, to the various Christian groups in the Empire, such as the Greeks, Bulgarians, and Maronite Arabs, whose commercial middle classes and Western-educated intellectuals had laid the ideological foundations for their independence and nationhood.

Though temporarily successful among the Muslims, Ottomanism eventually proved to be powerless. New solutions were needed. Some thirty years later, Yusuf Akçura (Akçoraoğlu) accurately analyzed the dilemma of political modernization in the Ottoman Empire. In his classic *Üç Tarz-i Siyaset (Three Political Ways)*, first published in Cairo in 1904, he pointed out that Pan-Islamism and Ottomanism were no longer suitable as bases of a modern political organization. Ottomanism rejected the idea of an ethnic nation—or a true nation, as he described it—and Islamism could not appeal to Christians. Akçura advocated Turkish nationalism, since this ideology could bring together all Turks and make them the foundation of the new state. This became the policy of the Young Turks (1908–18). It is understandable that the political ideas of the Young Ottomans, developed to correspond to social realities in 1865–76, did not appeal to the twentiety-century Young Turk movement. The Young Turks adopted from the Young Ottomans only those precepts—such as loyalty to fatherland and nation—that had lasting practical value.

The Young Turks, stressing Turkish national characteristics, departed radically from the Islamic universalism and expressly anti-Turkist policy of Ottomanism. The divisive impact among Muslims of this nationalist policy was dramatically illustrated in the poems of Mehmet Akif (d. 1936), the author of the text of the Turkish national anthem. In his "From the Rostrum of Suleymaniye," he cried in 1912: "Is it the devil that put into your mind the idea of nationalism? Nationalism shall destroy from its foundations Islam which keeps under one nationality so many different national groups."[7] Obviously, if ethnic origin, language, and territory were given priority, and the state was reshaped accordingly, religious ties and a sociopolitical system based on religion lost their importance. The Young Turks' glorification of Turkish national history and character, their attempt to introduce Turkish in schools, and the secularist thought implicit in all these attempts were the initial factors in the undermining of Islamic unity in the Middle East. They carried out their ideas by instituting practical measures intended to establish a central administration and to bring under its control the various areas and groups that had preserved semiautonomous administrative status, e.g., the Muslim holy lands in the Hijaz.

The economic and social changes in the Ottoman empire at the beginning of the twentieth century created new social and economic aspirations which were eventually included in the general term populism. Indeed, populism emerged at the turn of the century as a new dimension of modernization and included nascent economic and social aspirations in the form of a unique egalitarianism. It proposed to bridge the gap between the elite and the masses, spread education, establish a national economy, and reform government institutions to serve society's needs. Thus, nationalism began to derive part of its force from social demand. (Many studies of the Middle Eastern nationalism, however, tend to overlook the social foundations of this ideology.)

The Young Turks' nationalism, with its secular orientation, threatened to reduce the Muslim Arabs to the status of a secondary ethnic group. Consequently, the nationalist ideas of the Ottoman Empire's Christian Arab subjects, expressed in various forms toward the end of the nineteenth century, began to appeal to the Empire's Muslim Arab subjects. The Arab students' convention in Paris in 1913, often cited as the first formal expression of Arab nationalism, claimed allegiance to the Ottoman Empire, but demanded decentralization and local government. Those reforms, if granted, would have jeopardized the integration the Young Turks rightly considered a prime condition of nationhood.[8] Foreseeing the downfall of the Ottoman Empire in World War I and fearing that the Young Turks, if victorious, might pursue their nationalist policy, the Arab leaders eventually decided to support the British. The exchange of letters between Sharif Husayn of Mecca with the British, in which the British agreed to independence for the Arabs, was followed by the Arab Revolt of 1916, which cut Arab links with the Ottomans.[9]

The results of the Arab and Turkish nationalist efforts were thus determined by World War I. The defeat and disintegration of the Ottoman Empire in 1918 was not only an international event, but the beginning of an important transformation of the area internally. The Middle East as a whole, after existing for thirteen centuries under imperial forms of government, finally entered the age of modern nationhood.

The modern unitary (national) state in the Middle East began to emerge after the religiously legitimized sociopolitical organization of the Ottoman Empire broke down. This "emergence" was, in fact, a continuous process, operating at several levels. Politically, it called for integration around a new political authority exercising effective control over the people and territory that comprised the nation. At this stage, however, there was no nation in the cultural and historical sense of the word. The state consequently assumed the responsibility for creating a nation with an identity and national consciousness of its own, as other empires did when they broke up into nations. It developed a nationalist ideology and used it to define its own future goals. These goals became a unifying factor among the various social groups and a form of legitimization for the state authority. The state strove to identify itself with the nation by describing its actions in terms of their benefits to the nation. At the social and cultural levels, the modern state attempted to integrate all social groups into the new system by developing a national identity and a new sense of community, not necessarily by destroying the traditional values and loyalties, but by incorporating them, when feasible, into the value system of the new political structure. It stressed the cultural and linguistic characteristics of the dominant majority group, and claimed a geographic area to which it could be historically related.[10] It fought at the same time against the imperialist and colonialist policies of England and France, which ruled most of the area.

After 1918, one cannot speak of a commonly shared Middle Eastern ideology or political aspiration. Henceforth, one must deal separately with Arabs, Turks, and Iranians, as each country or group of countries tried to fashion its own nation-state. Iran had preserved its national bondaries, which had begun to be formed in the sixteenth century, but it, too, strove to create a modern, integrated national state. After achieving independence in a bitter struggle with the occupying Allied powers in 1919–22, Turkey embarked under an authoritarian regime onto a vast program of nation-building. The Arabs, exchanging Ottoman rule for the French and English mandate, fought for national independence. After World War II, the Arabs finally gained their independence and began to build a modern Arab national state. Whether this would be unitary or federal, socialist or democratic, was secondary to the creation of Arab national consiousness. Constantin Zurayk pointed out as early as 1938 that no Arab national renaissance was possible without a national philosophy that would establish goals and methods of achieving those goals. A national revival could succeed only by

> considering carefully the means and the ends involved, by defining the meaning of nationhood and nationalism, establishing the special traits and characteristics of the Arab nation and making manifest its special place among the nations and the role it has fulfilled in the past ... and [will] fulfill in the future ... through the creation of a comprehensive, clear and systematic national philosophy.[11]

This still remains a central problem.

The foreign policy of the Middle Eastern countries had a profound effect on the course of nationalism and on the very concept of modernism. After World War II, Arab nationalism adopted an anti-Western stand. It stood for nonalignment and neutralism and often rejected Western civilization, even though in practice it continued to emulate its achievements. The creation of Israel, with the support of the West and on the Western model of political organization, exacerbated Arab opposition to the West and its culture.

In Turkey, after 1923, there was little question that modernization necessitated a wholesale adaptation of and identification with Western values. However, the Cyprus dispute chilled Turkey's relations with the West after 1963 and stimulated an anti-Western cultural reaction. The socialists and Marxists led the anti-Western drive, using, in a new social context, many of the ideas originally put forth by the Islamists and conservative nationalists. Iran achieved a revolution based on the same ideas.

Nationalism and Secularism

Nationalism must have an emotional content in order to generate enthusiasm and loyalty on behalf of its goals. In other words, nationalism must also be viewed as a system of values. In the Middle East, Islam is considered the mainstay of culture and the binding force among all social values. One must, however, distinguish between the original values and culture stemming from Islam proper and those that were already in existence and were gradually incorporated into the belief system of Islamic society. The physical environment, the family, the community, historical experience, and tradition formed the bases of subcultures, which in turn created value systems of their own. The Islamic belief system, however, superseded them in terms of scope and loyalty. The coexistence of a purely religious culture with a nonreligious subculture is possible only to the extent that the prevailing system of thought does not recognize their separate sources or functions. In practice, the religious and nonreligious cultures follow their own pattern of development. Thus, in the Middle East the subcultures developed under the impact of geographic, economic, and social forces not related to religion. Religious culture answered spiritual needs, and nonreligious cultures responded to worldly needs, although the distinction was never formally made.

Nationalism relied essentially on various nonreligious subcultures within a specific region, and eventually tried to integrate these subcultures into one dominant national culture. The religious culture in turn became a subculture—although, in some places, a major one in the new national political system.

In practice, however, this cultural operation was neither clear nor easy. The Muslim's only loyalty was to his religion. Consequently, modern Middle Eastern statesmen had to find the means to transfer to the national culture the various loyalties previously perpetuated by Islam, without destroying the social cohesion and solidarity built by the religious culture. The conflict for loyalty between politics and Islam was actually a matter of separating the subcultures from the purely religious culture and of creating a new secular loyalty to the modern state. The formal institutional separation of religion from politics could be accomplished only by a similar success in the field of culture.

The policies adopted by Middle Eastern statesmen toward this difficult social-psychological problem have differed in method but not in substance. A comparison between the policies of Atatürk in Turkey and Gamal Abdel Nasser in Egypt may illustrate the point. Although both adopted a secularist approach to the consolidation of the state, they accepted the importance of religion. Both came to power partly through the support of religious groups: Atatürk made wide use of the religious leaders of Anatolia in 1919–22; the Muslim Brotherhood supported the officers' revolution in 1952 that brought Nasser to power in Egypt. Both leaders turned against their former religious supporters because the religious hierarchy posed a challenge to the establishment of the modern national state. Both blamed the religious leaders for opposing the "true" spirit of Islam, which Atatürk and Nasser reinterpreted according to nationalist ideas.

Atatürk and Nasser differed, however, in their methods of action. Aware of the symbolic power of organized institutions, Atatürk methodically destroyed the political-educational institutions of Islam. He tried gradually to incorporate into the fabric of nationalism the political values, loyalties, and sense of identify promoted by Islam. Turkish nationalism had from the very beginning substituted itself for all feelings, values, and loyalties expressed through religion in the past. The years between 1930 and 1960 in Turkey may be considered a period of nationalist assimilation of subcultures and of Islam as well. A certain separation also occurred. The religious system began to acquire certain spiritual characteristics that conformed, to some extent, to the Western understanding of religion, and some now claimed independence from state control because religion had acquired these spiritual features and could no longer impair the government's worldly tasks. Nasser, on the other hand, maintained Islamic institutions almost intact in Egypt and gradually incorporated them into his modernist state. Without challenging the existence of the religious establishments, he tried to invest them with some modern functions on behalf of Arab nationalism, which came to be synonymous with the religious definition of Arabism. Islam in Egypt was formally affiliated with, although subordinated to, the state. Coexistence between state and religion, however, was possible only to the extent that the religious hierarchy believed state actions conformed basically to Islamic precepts. Modern national statehood—that is, nationalism, whether Turkish or Arab—cannot act forever in consensus with organized religion, especially in view of the political system's need to justify its deeds sooner or later in secular terms. Nationalism inevitably made secularism a condition for its own survival.

The conflict between the state and Islam soon became evident in Egypt. Some members of the faculty of al-Azhar University in Cairo timidly rejected the separation of state from religion as an artificial concept borrowed from the West. They advocated a state policy that would attempt to fulfill the commandments of Islam. Consequently, some Arab intellectuals with a predominantly religious viewpoint rejected the idea of Arab nationalism as formulated by Nabih Faris, Fayez Sayegh, Hazem Z. Nuseibeh, and other early nationalists, who claimed that Arabism, as it is understood by the Islamists, is not nationalism. In their view, nationalism was an ideology exclusive of religious affiliation while Arabism was an integral part of Islam.[12] By the late 1960s, this nationalism came under attack as too conservative.

Socialism in the Middle East

In its politically meaningful phase, socialism developed in the Middle East almost entirely after World War I and, especially, World War II. Its birth was preceded and conditioned by the rise of nationalism and statehood, usually after monarchy or foreign rule were toppled by political revolution.[13] The beginnings of socialism may be traced to the nineteenth century, when all nationalist thinkers and movements had social purposes. The Young Ottomans, the 'Urabi revolt of 1882 in Egypt, the Young Turks, the workers' strike of 1908–9 in Turkey's Balkan provinces and of the socialist parties of the Ottoman Empire in 1908–11, and a series of scattered writings expressed social discontent of some sort.[14] But these lacked a rationally formulated, comprehensive scheme of social organization, possessed little understanding of the forces causing social unrest, had limited popular following, and ignored economic development and political action as means for attaining social goals.

Socialism in the Middle East is an extension of nationalism. It aims to consolidate the power of the modern state through an internal reorganization of the productive forces and a reassignment of roles and responsibilities, with the idea of creating a participant society. It proposes to create social consciousness, responsibility, and dedication to ideas above individual interests and loyalties. It strives to arouse mass enthusiasm on behalf of its goals by appealing to the social ethics rooted in the native culture and by creating desires and expectations. Socialism in the Middle East has two facets. It may appear as a rejection of the Western economic system (capitalism), of excesses of individual economic power, and of class differentiation. Socialism may also appear as an egalitarian movement to eradicate differences of wealth and position and thus pave the way for the social integration necessary for the survival of the modern state.

Socialism is also a kind of a modern moral system. It draws much of its ethical-moral strength from Islam and the West. The Islamic ideas of charity, social justice and responsibility, mutual assistance, and communal solidarity, reinterpreted in the light of contemporary needs, provide powerful bases for socialist action. Even some conservatives in the Muslim Brotherhood, such as Mustafa al-Siba'i, used the teaching of Islam to develop an Islamic brand of socialism. Other social-minded Muslim scholars, such as Mahmud Shaltut, the former head of al-Azhar, relied on Islamic ideas to justify the social and economic policies of his government. In Turkey, too, many contemporary Socialists strive to prove that there is no conflict between modern socialism and the social purposes of Islam.[15] Eventually the reliance on Islamic social ethics led to the rise of a powerful leftist Islamic fundamentalism that demanded full social justice and egalitarianism as well as the abolition of monarchies and other forms of personal rule. The issue will be discussed at length in the relevant sections.

The other source of socialism was the West. Indeed, the secular understanding of man and justice, of man's enlightenment achieved through education and science, which occupies such a central position in Middle Eastern socialism, came from the West. Middle Eastern intellectuals became acquainted with various versions of Western socialism after the turn of the century. They borrowed social ideas rather indiscriminately from Fabianism, Darwinism, Bergsonism, welfare socialism, and Marxism. Western socialism appeared at this stage as a condemnation of the unjust aspects of Western civilization, while simultaneously demonstrating that the same civilization had preserved humanitarian and altruistic ideals. Some early Middle Eastern Socialists, such as Salama Musa, admired Western intellectual achievements and advocated emulating them, at the same time that they condemned Western imperialism. Although they occasionally had roots in Islamic belief, socialist arguments in favor of social justice, egalitarianism, and elimination of class differences were based primarily on the writings of Western socialists.

Participation in the production of wealth became the outstanding feature of socialism after World War II. The basic purpose of this approach was to create national economic self-sufficiency, which appeared to be the principal condition for progress in all areas. After World War I, Atatürk expressed the idea in the form of a call for all social groups to create wealth; Nasser strove constantly to convince the masses that the chief benefits of socialism would come only if they applied themselves to its tasks.[16] At present the overwhelming majority of Socialists in the Middle East have accepted the idea that economic development is essential to the success of their doctrine. The idea of building a just social system on the material foundation of economic efficiency was socialism's major contribution to Middle Eastern thought.

The acceptance of economic development as the vehicle of social progress transformed socialism into a method of action and returned to the government primary responsibility for drawing up and enforcing plans for economic development. Thus, the government became the ideological-organizational nucleus around which postwar Middle Eastern socialism developed. Statism would, in fact, be a more appropriate name for this kind of socialism.[17]

Middle Eastern socialism rejects class struggle, even though it does not hesitate to condemn the former regimes for having been dominated by feudalists, capitalists, and agents of the West. Socialism stresses unity at all costs and condemns any opposition—regardless of whether it is led by Communists or ordinary dissatisfied citizens—as divisive and subversive. Middle Eastern socialism is promoted mainly be intellectual elites who are supposed, as Nasser expressed it, "to build a mighty structure for their homeland ... direct their country toward a specific goal ... and gain insight into the people's hopes and aspirations."[18] This is the socialism of the elites, which has not yet faced squarely the challenge of populism.

In terms of political action and economic reorganization, Middle Eastern socialism has turned its back on the West. It has borrowed planning, administration, and industrialization techniques from the socialist countries of Eastern Europe. While firmly anti-Communist and pro-Western in its internal and external policies, even Turkey in the 1920s adopted many ideas on economic development and organization from the Russians. Yugoslavia served as a model for Egyptian socialism after 1956, and enjoys considerable popularity among Middle Eastern Socialists for its successful combination of nationalism and Marxism, but also freedom, measured in practical terms as the ability to achieve national independence and economic development.[19] Some Marxist ideas on history and social classes and Leninist views on imperialism have entered into the stream of Middle Eastern socialism, chiefly since World War II. But Arab socialists have firmly rejected communism. Middle Eastern socialism is also anti-Western, antiimperialist, and anticapitalist. National independence is its major foreign policy goal. Consequently, it is only as friendly to the Soviet Union as is necesary to safeguard national independence.

Middle Eastern socialism belongs in a special category. Use of the term socialism is inaccurate, since the socialism of the Middle East describes chiefly the social goals of modernization. One may divide socialism in the Middle East first according to the country and second according to its ideological characteristics. Egypt advocated Nasserite or Arab socialism; Syria, Ba'th socialism; Algeria, Algerian socialism; various groups in Lebanon promote progressive socialism; while Islamic and Marxist socialism are found among small groups throughout the Middle East. Only Islamic and Marxist socialism have international goals or look beyond their own national boundaries. Although it was victorious in Syria and Iraq and enjoyed some popularity among intellectuals in Jordan and Lebanon, Ba'th socialism seems to be limited in scope and appeal.[20] The Arab nationalist movement, advocating Arab socialism, follows Nasser's social and political views on unity. It is still active in several Arab countries, but its success has thus far been only moderate. It accepts class struggle to the extent necessary to defeat the Arab monarchies, which are allegedly supported by feudalists, capitalists, or the middle classes, created through association with the West and largely supported by the oil industry.

Of the various Arab secular socialist schools of thought, only the Ba'thist possesses a fairly broad doctrine. The Ba'thists have a Marxist view of social classes, rely on a political party to achieve revolution, accept secularism, and court social reconstruction and economic development as essential conditions for development. The Ba'th philosophers Michel 'Aflaq, Salah Bitar, and Nureddin Atasi claimed that their ideology was original and corresponded to the social and spiritual characteristics of the Arabs. In reality, however, the core of their doctrine rests on Marxist materialism, while the remainder of their teachings are syncretic and oratorical additions to this base.

Nasser's socialism rejected class struggle, accepted the petite bourgeoisie as "national capitalists," and strived to associate itself with peasants and workers through the Socialist Union. Nasser's Arab socialism emerged fully in 1961, well after the military took power in 1952, while the Baʻth developed its doctrine and organization simultaneously in the early 1940s, and then tried to acquire power. The Baʻth claimed that Nasser borrowed many of its socialist and nationalist ideas in his bid to assume the leadership of the Arab world. Nasser won the race for this leadership, primarily because he had behind him a relatively well organized govern-ment and because he succeeded in winning over the Arab masses through modern communications media. Both types of socialism are becoming inadequate to meet the sophisticated demands of a modernized, complex Arab society. Both are challenged on the one hand by extreme Marxist socialism and on the other by the timid requests of some intellectuals for a more liberal democratic regime.[21]

Nationalism and socialism in the Middle East are ideologies of transition. Their basic functions are to establish a modern political organi-zation and rejuvenate society, thus completing the transition to a new phase of life.[22] The ideologies of transition in the Middle East enabled society to acquire a modern identity and to adapt itself to new forms of modern organization. These ideologies are bound to disappear or to change in form and content once the main phase of the transition is completed. Subsequently, after the emergence of differentiated social, political, and economic systems, one may expect Middle Eastern ideolo-gies to reflect more accurately the views of various social groups, rather than those of the government elites.[23] Further structural differentiation in the Arab world coupled with freedom of thought may stabilize the ideologies.[23]

Indeed, nationalism and socialism were also essentially part of the drive for decolonization and the search for identity. The first objective was to rid the native culture of the accretion of foreign elements imposed from the top or "voluntarily" adopted under the pressure of outside forces alien to the native society and its culture. Once this initial goal was accomp-lished, the thrust was toward changes as indicated by the conflicting meanings given the terms "reform," "civilization," and "progress" until about the 1950s and thereafter. In the first phase, "reform" meant chiefly borrowing institutions, ideas, and manners from the civilization of the West. In the second phase "reform" was changed to "revolution," and revolution included also the rejection of the social arrangement that made possible the penetration of ideas and attitudes from the West. For instance, *inqilab* in Turkish and in Arabic meant basically "reform." The initial "revolutionary" dimension given the term *inqilab* at first consisted merely of the rejection of the old regime and to some extent of the repudiation of certain Islamic and traditional features of the native culture associated with regression, and the replacement of these with Western counterparts. But in the 1960s and 1970s, the term *devrim*, which replaced *inqilab*, meant chiefly "revolution" aimed at rejecting the contemporary social "bourgeois" order and its economic values, most of which had come from the West. In Arabic *thawra* has been normally translated as "revolution," although the term implied a violent outburst to unleash the hidden forces of society and individuals; now it is commonly taken to mean a change in the order of things.[24]

The basic purpose of nationalism was to remove the obstacles—that is, the foreign political domination and the social and cultural accretions that had produced alienation—that stood as barriers between the authentic personality and identity of the native masses and their aspirations for the future, which were to be formulated in accordance with their own cultural yardstick.[25] The intellectual elites acquired a key role in deciding what to retain or acquire in order to achieve the goals of nationalism. It is essential to point out that this process, which was called also a revitalization or revivalist movement, borrowed its theoretical arguments from the very West it was rejecting.

The new concepts that sprang out of nationalism and moved it toward Marxism in the late 1960s and 1970s were anticolonialism, antiimperialism, populism, and violence. The anticolonist and antiimperialist literature had already been instrumental in the 1940s and 1950s in mobilizing the masses to push the British and French from the area. The former colonialist and imperialist regimes established directly by the West or by natives following Western models were accused now not only of having dominated the area politically and exploited its economic resources but also of having undermined and destroyed the native social order and caused the degeneration of its culture. This interpretation, different from that of the early nationalists who attributed the Western domination chiefly to cultural or historical motives, laid the emphasis on economic and social factors. Whereas the early thinkers saw imperialism and colonialism as the continuation of the crusades and the animosity between Islam and Christianity and as the consequence of the irreconcilable ways of East and West, the new nationalists saw it as the result of concrete forces, such as the West's need of raw materials and markets in the East. It is in this context that Marxism began to find wide acceptance throughout the Middle East, not in the form of classical Marxist parties but as a new approach and method for understanding and evaluating the society's transformation. Indeed, most of the reformist, nationalist, and even socialist movements in the Middle East had paid scant attention to the question of the material bases of their society or analyzed its social and economic structure using inductive methods and empirical evidence gathered on the spot. Rather, they had relied on the general, a priori postulates of dialectical materialism. For instance, Michel 'Aflaq's Ba'thist nationalist ideology began by citing concrete economic and social forces to explain the background of Arab history, but eventually it adopted general cultural postulates that conflicted with the earlier premises. In the 1960s Marxism penetrated Turkey to such a degree as to produce profound disturbances as well as ideological confusion; knowledgeable sources estimated that in 1979 there were over 50 different groups that called themselves Marxist. The Arab Nationalist Movement itself found out, after 1967, that the old Nasserite nationalism was powerless to achieve the aims of the Palestinians. Consequently, its early leader, George Habash, became a Marxist, as did several of his associates, and established eventually two of the more powerful groups in the Palestine Liberation Organization (PLO)—the Popular Front for the Liberation of Palestine (PFLP) and the Popular Democratic Front for the Liberation of Palestine (PDFLP). In Iran, Marxism nourished the revolutionary Fedayi and to a lesser extent some of the Mujahedin. Populism acquired a new dimension under this brand of Middle East Marxism. The early nationalist and some socialist movements in the Middle East aimed at healing cultural alienation and at overcoming the dichotomies that had divided the population into elites and masses, traditionalists and modernists, Westernists and Orientalists. This could not be achieved in the past, despite formal acceptance, such as in Turkey of populism as a constitutional principle, because the enforcers of populism —those advocating the equality of the masses and the elites—were themselves elites who ruled and exploited the masses. Marxism, on the other hand, claimed that differences between social groups and classes resulted from the fact that the rich classes possessed the means of production. Of course, the idea of ruling classes had long existed in the Middle East, but the sustaining economic basis of this group was seldom explicitly explained and linked to historical forces. The neo-Marxists claimed that real equality depended on achieving social and economic equality, which in turn was the precondition and essence of populism. It is in this context that the native middle classes, which came to be increasingly referred to as "bourgeois," became the target of devastating criticism and condemnation similar to that aimed at the monarchies and the imperial elites who had been the chief targets of the early nationalists and socialists. After the mid-1960s the bourgeois classes, which included practically all the entrepreneurial groups produced by or involved in the existing market economy, came under attack. State-run economies became the alternative to the capitalist Western economic system. By 1970 most of the landlords, who had been portrayed as the symbol of economic and cultural backwardness, feudalism, and reactionism in the 1950s, had been liquidated or neutralized in most countries.

The "bourgeoisie" was described not as a real social class, created by economic forces following the laws of history as in the West, but as the product of political and economic subservience to Western capitalism and colonialism. They were considered a "comprador" bourgeoisie, produced by the "dependent" economic system of their countries—a dependency that continued even after political liberation and the establishment of national statehood. The continued existence of the bourgeoisie thus appeared to be the continuation of colonialism, imperialism, and national oppression, and the chief obstacle to achieving equality and populism. Consequently, this group had to be liquidated or recast in a new and revolutionary mold. This view may explain why violence was used as much against natives refusing to follow the revolutionaries as against foreigners. The violence, which had a redemptive effect in rehabilitating native self-esteem, enabled the new group to ascend to power and became a respectable method of struggle, at least under certain conditions.[26] It is essential at this point to point out that the Marxist and pseudo-Marxist interpretation of native history superseded national and international boundaries. The analysis outlined above was evident in Turkey as well as in Iran and the Arab countries, and was similar to the Latin American and African view of the social history of their responsive continents. The Palestinians played a major role not only in radicalizing Middle Eastern thought but also in helping it break away from national confines. The issue is of fundamental importance to understand the evolution of the Middle East thought.

Palestine was an Arab issue from the very start. It was the rallying force, a reminder of national failure, and the justification for the emerging Arab nationalist-socialist elite's defeat and liquidation of the monarchical regimes, as is well illustrated by the victory of Nasser in Egypt. But the war of 1967 proved that the new elites with their sustaining nationalist ideology were as ineffective in settling the Palestinian claims against Israel as their predecessors had been. Eventually Nasserism, which had flourished in the 1950s and 1960s, lost its appeal and was replaced by a series of leftist ideologies. The Palestinians portrayed their efforts to return to their homeland as a struggle against colonialism and imperialism and hence became the rallying force for practically all the leftist, and also nationalist, groups in the Middle East. Nationalism, whether secular in form or as the political extension of the traditional religion—or political religion[27]—joined forces with leftism under the Palestinian banner.

The above may induce the reader to believe that the Middle Eastern society started in the 1970s to move irrevocably toward full acceptance of Marxism and, possibly, of a Soviet-type regime. Actually the Middle Eastern leftist ideology deviated from Marxism as much as it did from the Western-nationalist and socialist models used earlier. Most of the neo-leftists did not seek a total transformation of society but, rather, a change in orientation and outlook. They would, for instance, criticize the native bourgeoisie class for its subservience to the West but would rehabilitate it if the bourgeoisie accepted the revolutionary ideology, including the supremacy of the people, i.e., of the community, and returned to its brotherly fold. In effect this was a "return to self" through the rejection of the West, using the West's own logic and argument, and a search for authenticity of identity, living, and feeling in the fountainhead of native history and culture.[28] The transformation of fundamentalist Islam, chiefly among its lower class followers, from a search for theological purity to a movement of social equality and justice aided greatly the rise of neoleftism in the Middle East. The social ideal of the early fundamentalist Islamic community was a classless society based on justice and piety, and this was also the social ideal of the neoleftists, although their materialistic philosophy and secular outlook was different (see the introduction to the Arab section).

The secular leftists and the Muslim Socialists agreed on an initial aim: restoration of the physical and cultural integrity of the community. Marxist social ethics and methods seemed acceptable to the extent they could help achieve this goal and did not shatter further an already alienated society. Muslim social thinkers claimed that the model of the classless society was embodied in the concept of people or al-nas, that is, the masses living in a Muslim egalitarian community as redefined by Ali Shariati in his reinterpretation of Islam. Many neo-Marxists who sought a classless society found acceptable the Muslim fundamentalists' ideal of creating a society without class differences by returning to the absolute egalitarianism of the umma in the spirit of the Kharajites. Both Marxist revolutionaries and Muslim fundamentalists were united in their rejection of the Western economic, social, and political system, and they eventually produced their own Islamic revolutionary doctrine of political liberation and social change. In Algeria (this revolution was characterized by some as the outcome of the Koran and Das Kapital) and in Iran the merger of Islam and Marxism produced results, and it is being tested elsewhere in the Middle East.

I have explained in some detail, in the sections dealing with the Muslim Brethren and with Iran, that the Muslim fundamentalism that emerged in the 1970s was different in many ways from the early movements. First, it sought to create a new, truly Islamic society through social engineering rather than merely being a defensive movement against, or a partial rejection of, the West; second, it had the potential to regenerate itself from within through perpetual dialectic interaction; third, it established a certain degree of ideological unity between the elite and the masses; and, fourth, it brought about a revolution not through military coups or other elite action but through the mobilization and participation of the masses in action. One should stress the fact that the Algerian and Iranian revolution, as well as the mini–civil war in Turkey, were carried out essentially by countryside people or their descendants who were newcomers to the city. The rural migration and the folk Islam, with its egalitarian features, were instrumental in the success of the new socialist Islamic fundamentalism. This in turn stimulated many intellectuals to develop new social theories based on Islam. After all, the classical Muslim thinkers had produced a great variety of theories that could explain the social order and its relation to the political system, and these were based on the Koran as much as on the Greek philosophers. There was no reason why contemporary Muslim intellectuals could not do the same, interpreting the Koranic precepts in a new and dynamic fashion. Muslim fundamentalism did not manifest itself in the same way or produce identical results everywhere.[29] The degree of preparation, the existing power structures, the level of organization of the society at a given moment, and so forth, all contributed to speeding up, delaying, or diverting the intensity of Muslim fundamentalism. For instance, in Turkey the National Salvation Party had the effect of absorbing, channeling, containing, and reconciling with the system many of the fundamentalist forces, while in Saudi Arabia the movement took a sectarian form. The differences between Shiite and Sunnite fundamentalism were also important, although these differences should not be overemphasized, for the developments mentioned above narrowed at least for a while the gap between these two branches of Islam; for example, Khomeini permitted the Iranian Shiites to follow the prayers conducted by Sunni prayer leaders in Mecca, certainly an important unifying act. (A number of other Iranian religious leaders, on the other hand, have advocated a Shiite crusade in the rest of the Islamic world and have isolated themselves both from the rest of the Muslims and from the world at large.)

Most of the leftist ideologies rejected collaboration with the Soviet-oriented Marxist parties and the view of history put forth by these groups. In some places Marxists showed their rejection of Soviet Marxism by adopting the Chinese, and even the Albanian, model. In Turkey the Aydınlık group, which established the Workers and Peasants Party of Turkey, has advocated essentially a national communism, as have other groups. The Mujahedin and a section of the Fedayi in Iran are vehemently critical of the Soviet Union and of their own Tudeh (Communist) Party. Many Middle Eastern Marxists tend to regard their established communist parties as mere tools of foreign powers and not different from bourgeois parties that supported the West. One can go one step further and say that the national leftism of the Middle East seemed to accept the views of early nationalist Communists such as the Muslim Marxist Sultan Galiev (1880–1937) in Russia and Li Ta Chao (1888–1927) in China. These looked at the social revolution through the eyes of the oppressed peoples of Asia and saw both the capitalist and the worker as belonging to a dominating national group and as the oppressors of the dominated group, exploitation being as much national as class oriented.[30]

It must be mentioned that the influx of oil money into a few selected countries, such as Saudi Arabia, Kuwait, and the Gulf emirates, in amounts far beyond their needs, while other countries with large populations and more developed economies, such as Turkey and Egypt, depended on foreign aid, produced new power alignments and increased the tendency to view the world in economic terms. The oil income gave to Iran and Iraq, the only countries with relatively large populations, a sense first of independence and then of power, the latter manifesting itself in vast purchases of arms and, eventually, in war. The social imbalance created by the influx of oil money has stimulated the rise of leftist thought, but only to a limited degree. Some Western Marxist scholars, such as Maxime Rodinson, have become depressed by the loss of progressive drive toward basic change in the Middle East and by the drift into capitalism, especially in the Arab world, caused by the oil wealth and the rise of conservative new centers of power such as Saudi Arabia.[31] Rodinson has rejected the view that Islam is an autonomous political ideology, despite strong religious feelings among the population. Needless to say, he does not recognize an autonomous, non-European type of ideological sphere in the Islamic world.

Leftism in the Middle East, as repeatedly implied, instead of being a definitive commitment to a specific regime is, rather, a method for coming to grips with and explaining the economic and social bases, that is, the material components of the national statehood. The old subjective and passionate nationalism, with its infatuation with history, has lost much of its rhetorical fervor, while attachment to the land, to language, and to one's cultural identity and opposition to imperialism in all forms have intensified.

The return to Islam is not so much a return to religion for the sake of piety as a search for an interpretation of the immense political, economic, and social changes that have occurred in the past 30 years and for the acceptance of these changes within the framework of traditional values and in accordance with the society's own ethos. In sum, nationalism has not disappeared or decreased but, since decolonization, has evolved, coming into a new and more mature phase through its acquisition of economic and social dimensions and a populist orientation. The result has been, relatively, internal political stability, especially in the Arab world during the past 15 years, as indicated by the decreased rate of military coups.

The ideological developments in the Middle East indicate that a changed view of the world, a new self image, and a more sophisticated view of native history and society have emerged or are about to emerge. The writings published throughout the Middle East during the past 15 years manifest the growing tendency to reject the old European images and cliches about Islam and the Muslim society; they strive to present, instead, their own interpretations of history and society. The Orientalists' approach, views, and methods, already criticized and rejected, have come under attack both in the Middle East and abroad. The controversy created by Edward W. Said's timely book *Orientalism*, which dared to attack some of the assumptions and preconceived images of the Western scholars, illustrates best the Middle Easterners' search for a more authentic interpretation of themselves and their history.[32]

In conclusion, one can say that the political and social thought in the contemporary Middle East has acquired new social and economic dimensions and has harmonized itself in varying degrees with the traditional values and modes of thought of its own civilization. A full understanding of the various types of ideologies and their peculiar forms and manifestations can be achieved by reading carefully the introduction to each major section and the excerpts therein.

Notes

1. Since we consider ideology primarily within the framework of political action, we have used the terms "ideology" and "currents of thought" as synonymous. It is impossible to speak of philosophy in the Middle East in the Western sense of the word. Speculative, pure philosophy has enjoyed limited popularity in the Middle East since thought has been predominantly concerned with the organization and behavior of society.
2. L. H. Garstin, *Each Age Is a Dream: A Study in Ideologies* (New York: Bouregy & Curl, 1954), p. 3.
3. Discussed in Kemal H. Karpat, "Social Structure, Land Regime and Modernization in the Ottoman Empire," in *Beginnings of Modernization in the Middle East*, ed. William R. Polk and R. L. Chambers (Chicago: University of Chicago Press, 1968). For background information, see Charles Issawi, *Economic History of the Middle East, 1800–1914* (Chicago: University of Chicago Press, 1966) and Kemal H. Karpat, *Social Change and Politics in Turkey: A Structural-Historical Analysis* (Leiden: E. J. Brill, 1973).
4. Yusif A. Sayigh, "Development: The Visible or the Invisible Hand," *World Politics 13* (July 1961): 573. See also Malcolm H. Kerr, "Political and Ideological Aspects of Economic Development in the U.A.R.," paper presented to the Princeton University Program in Near Eastern Studies, May 14–16, 1964.
5. On this point, see Malcolm H. Kerr, "Arab Radical Notions of Democracy," in ed. Albert Hourani, *Middle Eastern Affairs Number Three*, (St. Antony's Papers, No. 16 (London: Chatto & Windus; Carbondale, Ill.: Southern Illinois University Press, 1964), pp. 9–40; see also Munif al-Razzaz, *Ma'alim al-hayat al-'arabiyya al-jadida* [Foundations of New Arab Life] (Cairo: Dar Misir, 1953).

6. Bernard Lewis, *The Emergence of Modern Turkey* (London and New York: Oxford University Press, 1961), and Bernard Lewis, *The Middle East and the West* (Bloomington, Ind.: Indiana University Press; London: Weidenfeld & Nicolson, 1964).

7. Cevdet Kudred, "Mehmet Akif," *Yön* [Direction], no. 196, Istanbul (December 1966): 8. On Akçura see François Georgeon, *Aux Origines du Nationalisme Turc* (Paris: Editions ADPF, 1980).

8. See C. Ernest Dawn, "From Ottomanism to Arabism: The Origin of an Ideology," *Review of Politics* 3 (1961):378–400; and H.Z. Nuseibeh, *The Ideas of Arab Nationalism* (Ithaca, N.Y.: Cornell University Press, 1956), pp.49 ff. The classic book on Arab nationalism–George Antonius, *The Arab Awakening: The Story of the Arab National Movement* (London: Hamish Hamilton, 1938; Philadelphia: Lippincott, 1939)–overemphasizes the role of the Lebanese Christians in the development of Arab nationalism and distorts the course of events.

9. Zeine N. Zeine, *Arab-Turkish Relations and the Emergence of Arab Nationalism* (Beirut: Khayat's, 1960), pp. 137–38.

10. I am aware of the fact that many scholars may not share my viewpoint. For instance, Gustave E. von Grunebaum, *Modern Islam: The Search for Cultural Identity* (Berkeley, Calif.: University of California Press, 1962), p. 221, rejects the idea that the Arab Middle East in engaged in nation building. In support of his view, he quotes a work by Rashid Rida (1865–1935) to prove that the Arabs placed religious above national allegiance. "Problems of Muslim Nationalism," in *Islam and the West*, ed. Richard N. Frye (The Hague: Mouton, 1957), pp. 7–40; and E. I. J. Rosenthal, *Islam in the Modern National State* (Cambridge, England: Cambridge University Press, 1966).

11. Constantin Zurayk (Qustantin Zuraiq), *al-Wa'y al-qawmi* [National Consciousness] (Beirut: n.p., 1940), pp. 19–22. Quoted in Shimon Shamir, "The Question of a National Philosophy in Contemporary Arab Thought," in *Asian and African Studies* (Jerusalem: Israel Oriental Society, 1965), p. 1. See also Hasan Sa'b, *al-Wa'y al-'aqidi* [Ideological Awareness] (Beirut: Dar al-'ilm lil-malayin, 1959).

12. See Isma'il Ragi A. al-Faruqi, *On Arabism: 'Urubah and Religion–A Study of the Fundamental Ideas of Arabism and Islam at its Highest Moment of Consciousness* (Amsterdam: Djambatan, 1962). The following bibliographical articles provide an excellent view of currents of thought in the Arab world until the early 1950s: Nicola A. Ziadeh, "Recent Books on the Interpretation of Islam," *Middle East Journal* 5 (1951): 505–10, and "Recent Arabic Literature on Arabism," *Middle East Journal* 6 (1952): 468–73; Nabih Amin Faris, "The Arabs and Their History," *Middle East Journal* 7 (1954): 155–62; Nissim Rejwan, "Arab Nationalism in Search of an Ideology," in *The Middle East in Transition: Studies in Contemporary History*, ed. Walter Z. Laqueur (London: Routledge & Kegan Paul; New York: Frederick A. Praeger, 1958), pp. 145–65.

13. See *President Gamal Abdel Nasser's Speeches and Press Interviews* (Cairo: Information Department, 1962), p. 177.

14. For the history of socialism in the Arab world, see Nicola Haddad, *al-Ishtirakiyya* [Socialism] (Cairo: Dar al-hilal, 1920); Kamel S. Abu Jaber, *The Arab Ba'th Socialist Party* (Syracuse, N.Y.: Syracuse University Press, 1966), pp. 1–7; and his *Judhur al-Ishtirakiyya* [Roots of Socialism] (Beirut: Dar al-tali'a, 1963). For Turkey, see Huseyin Avni (Sanda), *Bir Yari Müstemleke*

Oluş Tarihi [The History of Semicolonialism] (Istanbul: Sinan Matbassi, 1932); L. Erişçi, *Türkiye' de Işçi Sınıfının Tarihi* [History of the Workers' Class in Turkey] (Istanbul: Kutulmuş Basimevi, 1951); and Mete Tunçay, *Türkiye' de Sol Akimlar* [Leftist Currents in Turkey] (Ankara: Sevinç Matbaasi, 1967).

15. Mehmet Emin Bozarslan, *Islamiyet Açısından Seyhlik-Ağalik* [Sheyhs and Agas from the Viewpoint of Islam] (Ankara: Toplum Yayinevi, 1964); and A. Cerrahoğlu, *Islamiyet ve Sosyalizm Bağdaşabilir mi?* [Can Islam and Socialism Be Reconciled?] (Istanbul: B. Kervan, n.d.).

16. Fayez Sayegh, "The Theoretical Structure of Nasser's Socialism," in *Middle Eastern Affairs Number Four*, ed. Albert Hourani, St. Antony's Papers, No. 17 (London and New York: Oxford University Press, 1965), pp. 20 ff.

17. The extensive authority acquired by governments, first on behalf of nationalism and then of socialism, conforms, according to some scholars, to the traditional concepts of the state in the Middle East.

18. *President Gamal Abdel Nasser's Speeches and Press Interviews*, p. 178.

19. Malcolm H. Kerr, "The Emergence of Socialist Ideology in Egypt," *Middle East Journal* 16 (Spring 1962): 127–44. See also Hisham Sharabi, "The Transformation of Ideology in the Arab World," *Middle East Journal* (Autumn 1965): 471–86. An excellent survey of Arab political development is Charles F. Gallagher, "Language, Culture and Ideology: The Arab World," in *Expectant Peoples: Nationalism and Development*, ed. K. H. Silvert (New York: Random House, 1963), pp. 199–231.

20. George Lenczowski, "Radical Regimes in Egypt, Syria and Iraq: Some Comparative Observations on Ideologies and Practices," *Journal of Politics* 28 (1966): 29–56; Charles Issawi, "The Arab World's Heavy Legacy," *Foreign Affairs* 43 (1965): 501–12.

21. See Leonard Binder, *The Ideological Revolution in the Middle East* (New York: John Wiley & Sons, 1964).

22. Albert Hourani, "Near Eastern Nationalism Yesterday and Today," *Foreign Affairs* 42 (1963): 123–36.

23. See, on this point, Charles Issawi, "Social Structure and Ideology in Iraq, Lebanon, Syria, and the UAR," in *Modernization of the Arab World*, ed. J. H. Thompson and R. D. Reischauer (Princeton, N.J.: Princeton University Press, 1966), pp. 141–49.

24. Shimon Shamir, "Arab Socialism and Egyptian-Islamic Tradition," in *Socialism and Tradition*, ed. S. N. Eisenstadt and Y. Azmin (Atlantic Highlands, N.J.: Humanities Press, 1975), pp. 193–218. For the usage of old terms to connote new meanings, see Bernard Lewis, "On Some Modern Arabic Political Terms," *Orientalia Hispanica* 1 (1974): 465–71.

25. Menahem Milson, "Medieval and Modern Intellectual Traditions in the Arab World," *Daedalus* 101 (1972):17–37. The author sees the problems in terms of alienation.

26. Elie Kedouri, "Revolutionary Nationalism in Asia and Africa," *Government and Opposition* 3 (1968): 453–55. For a critical, and at times disparaging, view of ideologies in the Arab world, see Moshe Zeltzer, *Ideologies in the Middle East 1946–1972* (New York: Vantage Press, 1975).

27. Anthony D. Smith, "Nationalism and Religion," *Archives de Sciences Sociales des Religions* 35 (1973): 23–43.

28. Fauzi M. Najjar, "Nationalism and Socialism," in *From Nationalism to Revolution*, ed. A. Jabara and Janice Terry (Willmette, Ill.: Medina University

Press, 1971), pp. 3–14. The author claims that nationalism and socialism in the Middle East, although of Western origin, cannot be dissociated from their Islamic roots. See also Mahmoud Hussein, *Class Conflict in Egypt, 1945–1970*, Trans. M. and S. Chirman (New York: Monthly Review Press, 1973).

29. The relation of Islam to the Left has been debated in Arab intellectual circles. See, e.g., *The Rightist and Leftist Currents in Islam* by Ahmad 'Abbas Salik in Egypt and *Leftist Studies on the Rightist Thought* by 'Afif Farraj in Syria (both books are in Arabic). Mustafa al-Sibai's *Socialism in Islam*, mentioned elsewhere in this anthology, is still the main work on the subject. The manifestations of Muslim fundamentalism in various countries has been studied by several Muslim scholars. See *al-Ittihad* 15, no. 4 (October 1978), published by the Muslim Students Association of the United States and Canada.

30. Some related views have been put forth by David Kimche, *The Afro-Asian Movement, Ideology and Foreign Policy of the Third World* (Jerusalem: Israel Universities Press, 1973).

31. Maxime Rodinson, *Marxism and the Muslim World*, trans. Michael Pallis (London: Zed Press, 1979). This book originally appeared in Paris in 1972; it contains the author's various articles on the subject. The English edition has a new concluding chapter.

32. Edward W. Said, *Orientalism* (New York: Vintage Books, 1979). Useful reference to works in Western and Middle Eastern languages are in George N. Atiyeh, *The Contemporary Middle East 1948–1973: A Selective and Annotated Bibliography* (Boston: G. K. Hall, 1975). See also the introduction to the section on Arab thought in the present volume.

PART ONE

Political and
Social Thought
in the Arab Countries
of
the Middle East

I.   INTRODUCTION TO POLITICAL AND SOCIAL THOUGHT IN THE ARAB COUNTRIES OF THE MIDDLE EAST

Virtually no independent school of Arab political thought existed until nationalism emerged as an ideological force toward the end of the nineteenth century. In the past, practically every Muslim intellectual in the Middle East, regardless of his ethnic origin, had tried to interpret changing social and political conditions according to Islamic notions of government and authority. It was mainly the Christian Arabs of Lebanon and Syria–notably the Maronites and, to a lesser extent, the members of the other Eastern churches–who had developed an interest in their local history and language as early as the eighteenth century.[1] Muslim Arabs, however, did not experience a truly nationalist awakening until the end of the nineteenth and the beginning of the twentieth century. (A large proportion of the educated Arab elite, "particularly in Syria and Iraq, received their education not so much from French and American schools and colleges, the importance of which has been overstressed, as from the educational institutions set up in the successive phases of the Ottoman reform. Consequently, many developments can only be fully appreciated in this larger context.")[2] The Wahhabi Movement, founded by Muhammad ibn 'Abd al-Wahhab (1703–87), was not a nationalist but a religious movement. Even the early nationalist writings, such as the manifesto of Faris Nimr and the poem of Ibrahim al-Yaziji addressed to the Arabs (c. 1879), were not so much nationalist appeals as exhortations to reject fanaticism and embrace a new outlook on life. The secret society established (c. 1882) in Beirut to evict the Ottomans attracted no support among the Muslims and dissolved itself.[3]

The nationalist endeavors of the Christian Arabs had a major handicap that Christian groups in the Ottoman Empire's Balkan possessions were spared: The overwhelming majority of the Arabs were Muslims. The language and culture used as bases for nationalism by the Christian Arabs had developed in intimate association with Islam and were consolidated under Ottoman rule. The Ottomans had masterfully used the Islamic concepts of government and social organization to build and justify their own political system, which in turn became an inseparable part of Islam itself. Even though the separation of government and religion was greatly accelerated in the nineteenth century, the religious justification of the political system did not change. The empire continued to guarantee in theory the fundamentals of the *umma* (Islamic community)–its universality, faith, and integrity–against outsiders. Consequently, "modernist" political thought in the nineteenth century developed mainly in Istanbul, the Ottoman capital, and concerned itself chiefly with the adaptability of Islamic political concepts to Western representative institutions. The Young Ottoman school of political thought (1865), represented chiefly by Ibrahim Shinasi, Ziya Pasha, Ali Suavi, and Namik Kemal, along with nineteenth-century statesmen such as Hayreddin Pasha,[4] attempted unsuccessfully to reconcile modern and traditional concepts of government within the framework of the imperial-religious state.

Beneath the entire process of political and ideological transformation lay the basic changes that had gradually shattered the economic and social foundations of traditional Muslim society and its universalist government. A mere change in Ottoman political institutions could not solve the social and economic problems resulting from the disintegration of the traditional sociopolitical order. Broader measures were necessary. The eventual solutions were centralization (introduced after 1839) and nationalism, which provided administrative and ideological bases for a new sociopolitical reorganization. Turkish nationalism and secularism–promoted by the Young Turks in 1908–18 as principles of reorganization–undermined the political foundations of Islamic universalism and stimulated the rise of nationalism among the Muslims of the empire. Albanian nationalism, which resulted in the creation of an independent Albanian state in 1912, is an excellent measure–better than Arab nationalism–of the impact of the Young Turks' nationalist policies.

The efforts of the Turkish political elite to improve the economic and social situation of its own ethnic group could only strengthen the determination of the Arabs and other ethnic minorities to establish their own states. The social transformation in the Arab lands was propitious for such a political endeavor. Although this transformation occurred much later, it was not essentially different from the social transformation in the Western sections of the Empire that led to the establishment of independent states in the Balkans. The Arabs had their own derebeys, ayan, middle classes, ulama, and governors—such as the Shihabs and Jumblats in Lebanon, Zahir al-'Umar in Galilee, and Baban in Kurdistan—who extended their hold over surrounding areas and aspired to national independence.[5]

Although they provide some social basis for the eventual evolution of Arab nationalism, these developments cannot be separated from the transformation of the Middle East as a whole that occurred within the Ottoman Empire. The rise of Egypt as a separate political system in open defiance of the Sultan at the beginning of the nineteeth century had far-reaching effects on the Ottoman government and eventually on the Arab world. It is important to note that Egypt, despite occasional appeals to the Arabs, developed essentially as a national state. It took up the banner of Arab nationalism mainly after World War I. New currents of thought, occasionally stressing Arab nationalism, developed within the context of Egyptian nationhood and the slowly emerging Egyptian political system. Current works by Arab nationalists, however, aimed at preparing the ground for Arab unity, tend to stress the more universal Arab character of Egyptian nationalism rather than its particularist aspects.

Mehmet Ali (Muhammad 'Ali) (d. 1849), the founder of modern Egypt, was of either Albanian or Turkish origin. He came to Egypt at the time the Ottoman armies were fighting the French, who had invaded the country in 1798. Mehmet Ali remained there as a governor, seized power, and was recognized as a viceroy by the Sultan in 1805. He eventually embarked on an ambitious military, administrative, and economic program designed to establish a strong state and thus to ensure his position against possible attack by the Sultan. Mehmet Ali probably could not have risen to power without the defeat inflicted by the French on the Ottomans. One may ask whether Mehmet Ali could have established relatively modern political and military structures if his efforts had not been preceded by a series of internal social changes that prepared the ground for his reforms. A study of Egypt before 1800 could furnish rather edifying answers to this basic problem. Mehmet Ali was, after all, an ayan,[6] without a popular following. He defeated the ruling Mamluks by taking advantage of increasing popular dissatisfaction with them, liquidated the old feudal order, and established his own state in which a new landowning class and a small bourgeoisie became the dominant social forces. He was able to carry out these reforms because Egypt was prepared internally to move to a higher level of political organization. The French invasion was meaning-ful not because it demonstrated the inability of the Sultan to defend a Muslim territory–the Sultan had already lost many territories considered Muslim, including the Crimea and sections of the Balkan Peninsula, without impairing his religious authority–but because it facilitated the liquidation of a disintegrating social order and the subsequent establish-ment of a new political system.

The Ottoman government imitated some of Mehmet Ali's most successful reforms and used Egypt, an orthodox Muslim country, as an example to prove that innovation and change did not undermine Islamic faith. The Egyptians, in turn—still recognizing formally the suzerainty of the Sultan and regarding him as the representative of the Islamic com-munity—borrowed freely the ideas developed by the Young Ottomans. Indeed, the modernizing influences exerted on each other by the Otto-man and Egyptian intellectuals could provide new insights into the process of change in the Middle East and place the Western impact on the area in its proper perspective. The most important contribution of Egypt to ideological development in the Middle East was its political system, which conditioned a new pattern of socioeconomic and cultural relations. These relations, developing in a relatively rational and secular spirit and amidst increasing social differentiation, provided the material bases for future ideological development. Consequently, Egypt provided the most fertile soil for the emergence of a new type of thinker.

The first thinker of renown, Rifaʻa Badawi Rafiʻ al-Tahtawi (1801–73), belonged to an ancient landowning family that lost its fortune becasue of Mehmet Ali's tax policies.[7] Al-Tahtawi was inspired by classical Islamic ideas, but he also adopted a rational view of reality, possibly because of ideas acquired during his stay in Paris (1826–31). He pondered the idea of geographically limited communities and the theory that "the rise and fall of states was due to causes," and he related them to Egyptian society. Several of his writings deal specifically with Egyptian history and society and the type of economic activity necessary to restore Egypt's lost power. By stressing any given section of the body of ideas he developed, al-Tahtawi may be described as the precursor of nationalism or even of socialism.[8] While adhering closely to Islamic views, al-Tahtawi implied that changing conditions had altered both the nature of society and the function of government.[9]

Al-Tahtawi's philosophy was comprehensive enough to provide sound foundations for intellectual development, but modern Egyptian and Arab thought was not able to mature along these lines, largely because of European involvement in Egypt. The British occupation of Egypt in 1882 stimulated the rise of anti-Western nationalism and distorted the positive aspects of al-Tahtawi's philosphy. It eventually compelled nationalism to revert to Islam as the only ideological force capable of preserving the integrity and identity of Egyptian society. Hence, any effort by the British to modernize Egypt's social or political structure could easily have been interpreted as likely to undermine the society's culture and identity. This situation affected the entire process of change and modernization in the Arab world.

The independent states of Iran and Turkey had the illusion that they decided freely what to take from the West. Assured of political sovereignty and a corresponding national identity, they could play down the Islamic heritage and forestall the objections of Muslim theologians to imitation of institutions from the non-Islamic world.[10] Egypt, deprived of such assurance, had to use Islam to mobilize popular support. It is quite understandable, therefore, that the Islamic Reformation—which had profound political consequences in the Middle East—found fertile ground for development in Egypt. The revolt of al-ʻUrabi precipitated the British occupation of Egypt in 1882 and strengthened the rise of an anti-Western nationalism.

British policy in Egypt, although far less motivated by considerations of cultural domination than, for example, French policy in Algeria and elsewhere, still seemed to pose a threat to Egypt's cultural identity. The profound impact on Egyptian development of Jamal al-Din al-Afghani (1839–97) can be explained chiefly by the potentiality of his ideas on Islamic reform to awaken the Muslim community and to strengthen its political opposition to the British. Al-Afghani's Pan-Islamism, constitutionalism, and opposition to the ruling Khedive (who was ready to give in to foreign demands) stemmed from his religious-political convictions. Muhammad 'Abduh (1849–1905), a close friend and follower of al-Afghani, while firmly dedicated to safeguarding the integrity of his community, tried to visualize the threatening West not in terms of material power but as a "challenge of the intellectual, social, and ethical dynamism underlying that power to an Islamic superstructure no longer suitable to the present age."[11] Later in his life, 'Abduh, who was already known to disapprove of violent action, including Urabi's methods, dealt with philosophical questions and detached himself from politics.

The ideas of al-Afghani, 'Abduh, and the latter's pupil Rashid Rida (1886–1935), Qasim Amin (1849–1905), and several other thinkers are usually referred to as forming the core of the movement of Islamic Reformation.[12] They stressed in various degrees the necessity of free inquiry and reasoning (opening the ages of Ijtihad), free will, reinterpretation of Islamic teachings in the light of new conditions, and they debated the questions of faith and science, always upholding Islam's ability to adapt to modern conditions. Their efforts were directed toward delivering Muslim countries from backwardness and toward restoring them to moral and material vitality through positive effort. The movement of Islamic Reformation opened the door to serious thinking among small groups of upper-class intellectuals, but without visibly penetrating the masses. It remained relatively without effect among Turks and Iranians, chiefly because, in the case of the former, reformations were secured by political action and open acceptance of positivist scientific ways of Western thought.

In the Arab world, 'Abduh's ideas created continuous interest and debate. Rashid Rida left his native Syria and came to Cairo, in 1897, where he published the review *al-Manar* (The Beacon) until his death, in 1935. In addition to expanding 'Abduh's ideas, Rida wrote numerous articles and books and became involved in a variety of religious organizational activities. 'Abd al-Rahman al-Kawakibi (1849–1903), a Kurd from Syria who opposed the despotism of Sultan Abdulhamid, contributed to *al-Manar* and also wrote two books—one on the future of Islam and the other on despotism. His major political contribution was his demand that the power in the Islamic community be taken by Arabs, whom he considered to be better people than the Turks, and that a caliph be chosen from among them, possibly the ruler of Egypt.[13] The reformist ideas of 'Abduh found positive support among some religious men; 'Ali 'Abd al-Raziq, for example, claimed in 1925 that Islam was free of political and social preoccupations and pointed out the nonreligious basis of the caliphate, and in 1950, Khalid Muhammad Khalid directed a bitter attack on religious dogmatism and conservatism.

The counterpart of the Islamic Reformation, the Muslim Brotherhood (*Ikhwan al-Muslimun*), demanded a return to the original form and spirit of Islam, while initiating practical programs of economic and social development. Spokesmen for the Muslim Brotherhood included Hasan al-Banna, the founder, Muhammad al-Ghazzali, Sayyid Kotb (Qutb), and Mustafa al-Siba'i.

Guided by Muhammad 'Abduh's fundamentalist philosophical views, the Islamic Reformation lost its active interest in practical politics. A new militant generation turned nationalism into a vehicle for mobilizing public support in the struggle for independence from the British. The leaders of this movement were the 'Urabi group, 'Abdallah al-Nadim (1843–93), the journalist Mustafa Kamil (1874–1908), and Sa'd Zaghlul, the leader of the Wafd Party. Members of the lower class intelligentsia, they were interested primarily in political action. Their polemically oriented writings lack depth and do not have much intellectual value. Yet, this kind of militant nationalism—represented so well by Mustafa Kamil—later became generalized.

At the end of the nineteenth and the beginning of the twentieth century, Egypt witnessed the rise of another group of intellectuals that formed the backbone of the liberal nationalist and humanist school of thought. The best-known members of this group are Ahmad Lutfi al-Sayyid (1872–1964), Taha Husayn (b. 1889), Muhammad Husayn Haykal (1889–1956), Ibrahim al-Mazni (1889–1949), Tawfiq al-Hakim (b. 1889), and the "socialist" Salama Musa (1887–1959). It may be said that the intellectual aspects of modernization found their way into Egypt and eventually into the Arab world through the publications of this group.[14] Members of the group debated basic issues such as constitutionalism, liberalism, secularism, modernization, and Islamic reform, largely within the framework of Egyptian culture, history, and identity. They viewed Egyptian nationalism not in a limiting political light, but in a broad philosophical and human context, and strove in many cases to identify Egypt with Western civilization. This group, however, represented the views of a minority. Many of its members belonged to the upper wealthy groups. In some cases they supported the monarchy and, by implication, the British.

The formal independence granted to Egypt in 1922 and the constitution promulgated in 1923 did not change the dual character of Egyptian thought. The Wafd nationalist movement lost many of its progressive features in the struggle with the British, but it increased its militancy. The liberals, in turn, became less influential, and were gradually estranged from the mainstream of political life.

Paradoxically, the British occupation stimulated modernization of the Egyptian economy and administrative system by establishing a communications network and reorganizing the civil service and education. All these reforms later gave Egypt an organized power base from which to advance claims to the leadership of the Arab world. Until World War I, ideological developments in the Arab world were thus concentrated chiefly in Egypt and centered on Egyptian nationalism.

Well-formulated ideologies did not appear in the Fertile Crescent until the end of World War I. Despite its appeal to an Arab consciousness, Arab nationalism—promoted by Christian Arabs such as Butrus al-Bustani, Khalil Ghanim, Jurji Zaydan, and Nagib 'Azuri—found relatively little response among Muslims. As early as 1904–5, the Christian Arabs demanded independence for a Muslim-Christian Arab nation, and blamed the Turks for having caused the backwardness of the Arab lands. The Christian Arabs eventually came to think more in terms of an independent Syria and, especially, Lebanon, with ties to the West, rather than a single large Arab state with its center at Damascus. With the exception of a few, such as al-Kawakibi, operating out of Cairo, Muslim Arabs in the Fertile Crescent had shown little interest in disengaging themselves from the Ottoman Empire until the Young Turks' policies—designed to transform the empire into a centralist, nationalist, and secularist Turkish state— became evident in 1908. The Arab reaction manifested itself in the form of a series of societies founded after 1908 to defend Arab interests.[15] Eventually, an Arab congress was held in Paris in 1913 to demand a degree of autonomy and decentralization for the Arab provinces. Secret societies, such as al-Qahtaniyya and al-Fatat, formed mostly by army officers after 1908, seemed to be oriented toward Arab independence, although even in these cases some officers still wanted to preserve Muslim unity within the Ottoman Empire.[16]

These activities led to Sharif Husayn's agreement with the British and subsequently to the revolt of 1916, which severed the Arabs' ties with the Ottoman Empire and supposedly paved the way for the independence of the Arab lands after the downfall of the Ottoman state. The Fertile Crescent did not win its independence, however, and was not united under one Arab state except for a very short time in 1920–21. The area was divided between the French and the British: The French established a mandate over Syria and Lebanon; the British gained full control of Egypt and established mandates over Palestine, Transjordan, and Iraq. The British promised to facilitate Jewish migration into Palestine and to establish a Jewish National Home. Only Hijaz, the desert heartland of the Arabian Peninsula, was free. Thus "betrayed" by the West, the Arabs in the Fertile Crescent were placed politically in the same subordinate position as Egypt and eventually forced to shape their ideologies in the light of the struggle for independence and opposition to Jewish immigration to Palestine, rather than in terms of internal conditions. The Arab leadership in the East was in the hands of a small group of officers and bureaucrats educated in Ottoman schools, who often borrowed the Young Turks' ideas on nationalism. This tendency is particularly evident in the writings of Sati' al-Husri.

The present ideological features of Arab nationalism began to appear after 1919. The basic idea of the nationalist movement was that Arabs constituted one single nation, a political entity with a common culture and language that prevailed in an area stretching from the Atlantic Ocean to the Indian Ocean. Islam, in turn, had an Arab character, and, in fact, was an inseparable part of the Arab national identity. The reliance on history, the glorification of the past and of everything even slightly related to Arabs, and the wholesale Arabization of the Muslim heritage, were the inevitable results of this nationalism. Among the better known exponents of Arab nationalism were Sati' al-Husri and 'Abdallah al-'Alayli, who even engaged in polemics with Egyptian intellectuals in their efforts to downgrade local and regional nationalism in favor of the emerging broader concept of Arabism. They stressed the political role of Islam in the formation of the Arab nation but defended also the reformist principles necessary to modernize Arab society. The Muslim Brotherhood, on the other hand, accepted Islam and the return to its original principles as its cardinal doctrine and rejected the idea of an Arab nation with a nationalist and functionally differentiated political system. Secularism, which formed an indivisible part of Turkish nationalism, was dismissed by Muslim Arabs as incompatible with their nationalism, although it was enforced in practice. A secular, regional nationalism, represented chiefly by Antun Saadeh (Sa'da) (1904–49), developed in Syria and Lebanon parallel to the development of Arab nationalism in the other Arab lands. Saadeh's nationalism emphasized the common culture and history of the ethnic groups that had inhabited Syria and Lebanon for thousands of years, and proposed to establish an independent country based on an indigenous culture.

In comparison with nationalism, the Socialist and Communist movements, promoted by small urban groups, were relatively unimportant in the Arab world in 1918–52.

Most of the Arab lands won their independence after World War II. The boundaries of the new states were determined chiefly on the basis of the administrative divisions that had been imposed by the mandatory powers. The new though feeble local identities (such as Iraqi and Jordanian) fostered by the occupying powers were reinforced by group alignments and by the national, educational, and bureaucratic systems that had developed in 1920–45. These tended to strengthen separatist tendencies in the Arab world. The West, according to the Arabs, had calculatedly thwarted the aims of Arab nationalism. It had left the Arabs disunited and weak so that, at the first opportunity, it could re-establish its domination. The British-French-Israeli attack on Egypt in 1956 reinforced that belief.

The establishment of Israel as a national state in the former mandate of Palestine and the Arab defeat in the war of 1948–49, followed by Western efforts to drag the Arabs into military pacts (such as the Middle East Defense Organization and the Baghdad Pact, which later became CENTO), increased Arab suspicion of the West. The Arabs believed that a strong, unified Arab state, capable of preserving its independence and of forging a modern society, could not only oppose foreign encroachment but also play a leading role in world affairs.

The failure of the Arab League (1945) to achieve lasting unity increased the insecurity and sense of frustration felt by the rapidly growing Arab intelligentsia. The revolution that resulted in the overthrow of the Egyptian monarchy in 1952 was one of the most dramatic results of these political and psychological frustrations. At the beginning, the revolution was not very different from other Arab military coups. It entered a new phase after the withdrawal of the British, the nationalization of the Suez Canal, and the abortive British-French-Israeli expedition in 1956. Overnight, Gamal Abdel Nasser (Jamal 'Abd al-Nasir) was transformed into an Arab hero capable of avenging all past humiliations and of restoring Arab national self-confidence and pride. All other Arab leaders rapidly lost their stature, especially after Nasser asserted his position as one of the three leaders of the neutralist bloc.

The rise to power of Nasser and his associates was also a social change of great magnitude. The sons of government clerks and small merchants, they represented the lower social level of the intelligentsia and displayed religious attitudes similar to the pietism of the masses. Reinforced with ideas on social, economic, and educational development, this pietism could mobilize the masses to share the leaders' political ideas and condemn their opponents.[17] The social and political changes wrought by the Egyptian Revolution gave a new orientation to Arab nationalism (which was aimed at independence), transforming it into Arabism (oriented toward internal modernization and unity) and making Egypt its spokesman.

Arabism stresses the similarities of culture, history, and ideals among Arabs and minimizes their differences. It draws heavily on Islam as the emotional link among Arabs, but without using it as a principle of political organization. As it was defined by a variety of groups in Egypt, Arabism gradually absorbed or replaced Islamism and the various forms of regional and local nationalism.

Egypt adopted national economic plans and launched a completely socialist development program in 1961–63. Consequently, Arabism, without losing its nationalist features, broadened its scope to include socialism. Arab socialism was essentially a radical form of statism, relying mostly on the bureaucracy and the intelligentsia, rather than the workers or peasants, to enforce its program. It opposed communism and remained a tool of its goal of establishing an advanced society unified in one Arab state. Socialism was used by Nasser to achieve throughout the Arab world the uniform social structure and political regime considered prerequisites of unification.

The influence of the United Arab Republic was chiefly a result of Nasser's charisma and the nation's relatively well-organized government, internal cohesion, and integration, achieved during the 150-year effort to develop a modern state. Indeed, modern nationhood gave to Egypt the material basis to launch its ideological drive for unification and, incidentally, domination of the other Arab lands.

In the period from 1956 to 1967 Egypt became once more, as it has been in the past, the intellectual and ideological center of the Arab world, whose thought now revolved around Arabism-Nasserism. The nationalization of the Suez Canal in 1956 was both a symbolic and a real declaration of national independence, and it permitted Nasser to elevate Arabism, with its nationalist and socialist components, into a potentially general ideology for all Arabs. Yet, the main thrust of the ideology was the "search for self," with modes of expression altternating between *indifaiya*, *L'afziya*, and *narjisiya* (impulsivity-explosiveness, verbalism, and narcism), as Jacques Berque noted.[18]

Meanwhile, economic development, notably by means of plans put out by various state planning agencies that directed expenditures toward investment in industry, education, and social services, increased the size not only of the bureaucracy but also of the professional classes, first in Egypt and then in other Arab countries. Technicians, school teachers, and a variety of other trained personnel from Egypt began serving all the other Arab countries, replacing many Western experts. Egypt thus became the source not only of political leadership and ideology but also of technical know-how and labor for the rest of the Arab world. Nasserism appeared to work as a unifying force at various levels, despite the existence of several centrifugal forces; for example, the Ba'th in Syria and Iraq were opposed to Nasserism and its brand of Arabism, but the impact of this party's disapproval was limited, as was that of the left-wing Palestinian organizations.

The relative ideological unity provided by Nasser's Arabism was shattered by the crushing defeat and loss of territory suffered by Egypt, Syria, and Jordan in 1967. The war, as explained elsewhere, undermined Nasserism and permitted a variety of other ideologies to assert themselves. Two currents of thought appeared as contenders to supersede the brand of nationalism and socialism promoted by Nasser: left radicalism and Muslim fundamentalism. Algeria and the PLO played the leading role in this ideological development. The Algerian revolution, which gained the country its independence from France on July 3, 1962—in part with the aid received from Nasser—produced in fact an alternate and more radical model of revolution and social transformation than Nasserism.[19] The victory of Houari Boumedienne over Ben Bella, the original leader, in 1965 replaced the semi–secularist-socialist approach of the latter with a new interpretation of the Algerian revolution based on the mujahedin Islamic viewpoint. The Algerian revolutionary ideology acquired also a self-redeeming philosophy of violence, as developed by Frantz Fanon in his *The Wretched of the Earth*, a book that was widely read and accepted in radical Arab and African circles.

The war of 1967 permitted also the rise of al-Fatah and enabled it to achieve the control of the PLO, as described in some detail elsewhere. Al-Fatah, controlled by Sunni Muslims, became close to the Algerians, as did the Marxist Palestinian groups, PFLP and PDFLP, that favored socialist internationalism over Arabism and nationalism; the leaders of the last two had already become disenchanted with Nasserism and with Nasser himself as early as 1966. The Libyan version of Islamic fundamentalism, as described by Muammar Qaddafi in his *Green Book*, was ideologically closer to that of the Algerians than to that of Nasser, whom the Libyan leader regarded as his model. The overthrow of the monarchy in Libya in 1969 and the establishment of a republic there produced a new center of ideological influence in the Arab world. These developments indicated that ideological evolution in the Arab world had completed the *etape nationalitaire* (nation-building stage), as Anouar Abdel-Malek called it:[20] it was now moving toward a social stage, shifting attention from the Arab nation (*qawmiyya*) to the Arab society (*ijtimaiyya*).[21]

The war of 1967, accepted almost by most scholars as a watershed in the political and ideological history of the Arab world, undermined the

Wingate College Library

subjective premises of greatness and invincibility embodied in the old nationalism and permitted a more objective and dispassionate analysis of the weaknesses and strengths of the Arab society.[22] The first step was to adopt a more critical view of the Arab world and of nationalism itself, as already demanded by leftist writers such as Ilyas Murqus, who had criticized Sati al-Husri, the father of Arab nationalism, for his subjective views on the issue. Meanwhile, Sadiq Jalal al-Azm, in a book which created considerable debate, advised the Arabs to seek the explanation of the defeat in the war of 1967 in their own faults instead of placing the blame on others.[23] For the first time Israel was studied as a modern state with a strong army and an established society rather than as an historical aberration. Rakah, the Israeli Communist Party, which was dominated by Arabs, claimed that Israel was a national state and that this fact had to be adequately considered.

The war put also an end to the anguished, feverish, narrow, and often superficial preoccupation with the self (as distinguished from "return to self") and forced many Arab writers and thinkers to "unwrap" and relate themselves to the outside world.[24] They began to discover the Iranians, the Turks, and other Muslims in the world whom they had long ignored or belittled while at the same time usurping from these other Muslims, on behalf of Arabism, their intellectuals and their artistic contributions to Islam—which they had represented for 1,000 years during the Arab eclipse. Finally Arabs began to see that their problems did not stem solely from the struggle with Israel or from Western colonialism but also from myriad elements rooted directly in the structure and organization of their society.

These discoveries spurred the development of scientific socialism, or Marxism, on the one side, and of Islamic socialism, or fundamentalism in its new, dynamic form, on the other. Marxism was promoted mainly by the Palestinian organizations' radical Marxist wings.[25] The views put forth by leaders for these groups, George Habash and N. Hawatmeh, was that nationalism and Islamic reformism as expressed in the past by Afghani and others helped continue the old class system and preserve its privileges. The new socialism had to start with the fact of the division of society into classes and to rely on rational, critical, truly socialist ideology. Some neo-Marxists claimed that social reformism actually hindered the development of true socialism as much as did Stalinism; and the Arab communist parties called for emancipation from Soviet influence so as to develop their own strategies.[26] According to the neo-Marxists, Nasserism and Ba'thism were the continuation of Islamic modernism. These were, in effect, the views of what came to be known as the New Arab Left, which expressed the strong secular tendencies of the PLO and specifically, of the Christian leaders of the PLO who spoke on behalf of Marxism—namely, Habash and Hawatmeh. Paradoxically, the Palestinian Marxists have been criticized by some Arab Communists for trying to achieve socialism and national, or patriotic, liberation simultaneously and for failing to follow the historical stages of Marxism. The majority of the PLO, represented by al-Fatah under Yasser Arafat, remained uncommitted to Marxism and, in fact, closer to the Algerian and, possibly, the Iranian view of Islamic revolutionary socialism. The criticism of the conservative Arab nationalism and socialism on the part of the New Arab Left became more extreme after the Palestinian radical wings of Habash and Hawatmeh precipitated confrontation and suffered heavy losses in their fight with the Jordanian army in 1970.

The Ba'th also drifted to the Left; its ideologue, M. Aflaq, regarded the Palestinian struggle as the means by which Arab unity could be established, a view which was actually contrary to the PLO policy of not involving the Palestinians in Arab politics. Hence, the relations of the PLO with the Ba'thist regimes have been ideologically rather cold, despite their close political and military collaboration (Syria and Iraq have their own Palestinian commando groups). Meanwhile, a dissident Marxist group in the Ba'th, under Yasin al-Hafiz, showed definite dissatisfaction with the party and led the Ba'th to accept a more leftist program; but this did not satisfy the Ba'th Marxists, who went on to establish the Hizb al-ummal al-arabi al-thauri (Revolutionary Arab Workers Party) and declare themselves totally separate from Ba'th. Al-Hafiz claimed that Nasserism had a Marxist orientation (Nasser's Charter of National Action of 1962 included some Marxist views), attempting thus to draw the Nasserite parties, especially in Lebanon, into the mainstream of Marxist thought.[27] Meanwhile the Arab Socialist Union was formed in Lebanon in 1974 through the merger of five Nasserite organizations including the Nasserite Socialist Union, The Union of Nasserite Forces, and others, thus giving the surviving Nasserism a leftist orientation.

The New Arab Left soon became involved in discussing peripheral topics and ideas, such as the Cuban revolution, Vietnam, and Africa, and lost touch with the realities of the Arab world. The real issues of the Arab world, as Abdallah Laroui observed, came to be debated not in universities or other established institutions but in the peoples' daily encounters and in the newspapers.[28]

The main body of the Ba'th, however, after moving to the Left in 1966, began to split apart after Assad took over the power in Syria and adopted a more moderate ideological position. The Iraqi branch followed its own path, continuing an outwardly radical stand. Other socialist parties modeled on European social democracy showed little activity.[29] Egypt, on the other hand, after the death of Nasser in September 1970 and the rise of Anwar Sadat to the leadership of the country, shifted dramatically to a middle-of-the-road, liberal economic policy, dismantling much of the socialist-statist edifice created by Nasser.

Two additional unrelated events gave a new direction to Arab ideological developments. First, the rise in oil prices allowed small peripheral states hitherto only marginally involved in Arab politics to acquire a growing influence that affected the Palestinians as well as other established states. It is not wrong to claim that after Egypt's expulsion from Arab politics in 1978, Saudi Arabia became the chief spokesman for conservative Arabism and Islamism. The Saudis began to give grants and loans to other Arab and Muslim states. This aid, plus the remittances of workers employed in the oil-producing countries, produced a substantial increase in income as well as in the size of the middle classes in many Arab countries.

The second event was the October war of 1973 and the use of oil as a weapon against the United States and other countries. The initial success of the Egyptian and Syrian armies against Israel not only rehabilitated the Arabs in their own eyes but created also a new self-confident Arab, as M. H. Haykal has put it.[30] The demonstrated efficiency of the oil weapon increased the prestige and the self-confidence of the established middle classes and sanctified the leadership position of Saudi Arabia. The oil money became also a subject of ideological debate, for the Left regarded the money deposited in Western banks as outside the control of the Arabs and as serving non-Arab interests.

The rise of Saudi Arabia and Anwar Sadat's abandonment of Nasserism and disassociation from the Soviets seemed to shift the ideological balance in the Arab world in favor of social conservatism and Muslim pietism. Marxism was described as totally incompatible with Islam by the conservative Islamists and came under sharp attacks, despite the fact that it was partly accepted and promoted by intellectuals in Algeria, Syria, and Iraq.[31] The Muslim Brethren in Syria engaged in a struggle against the Ba'thist regime, which they accused of undermining Islam through a secularist policy and the political supremacy of the ruling Alawite minority. Yet, the Ba'th parties in Syria and Iraq have restricted greatly the activities of the local communist parties. However, they did not hesitate to collaborate occasionally with Marxist intellectuals and parties, either to please the USSR or to seek ideological guidance; for example, Assad of Syria included the Communist party under the veteran leader Bakdash in the National Progressive Front dominated by Ba'th (eventually the Communist Party split in two). In Iraq the Communist Party secretary general, Aziz Muhammad, is in the Progressive National Front but has had no success in expanding his party. In fact, the Iraqi regime has increased the surveillance of the Communists since the Soviet invasion of Afghanistan. In Lebanon the party is active and a member of the Leftist Front but, having lost its Christian support in the civil war of 1975–76, is now powerless. In Egypt the Communists are few but influential and are represented by Khalid Muhyi al-Din in the National Progressive Party, which received 200,000 votes in 1976; they are often allied with the Nasserites and have some support in the trade unions and universities. Only in South Yemen is the Yemeni Socialist Party following closely the Marxist-Leninist line of the Soviet Union.

The polarization of ideology in the Arab world around Islamism, which included in varying degrees nationalism and Arabism, and leftism, both Islamic and secular, was accelerated by the sharpening of class differences caused by the influx of petrodollars into the Arab world and by Anwar Sadat's liberal economic policies in Egypt. At the same time, Sadat's trip to Jerusalem in 1977 and his signing of the peace treaty with Israel in 1979 undermined the power of the informal conservative axis formed by Egypt and Saudi Arabia since 1973 and separated the two countries from each other. The breakdown of the conservative axis, although by the logic of necessity a temporary rift, gave free vein to a variety of conventional and radical Islamic social ideas long in the making. Already various non-Marxist Arab writers had emphasized the need for a more scientific approach to the study of their society based on Muslim concepts, notably on Ibn Khaldun; for example, Nasif Nassar and Ali al-Wardi discussed the establishment of a "communal society," that is, of a sociocultural structure based on confessionalism.[32]

The paradoxical situation created by the growing interest of secular-minded Arab intellectuals in Marxist ideas and the rejection of Marxism by the liberals and the radical Islamists is one of the most intriguing contradictions in the Middle East and Arab thought. At the same time, some Marxists have openly acknowledged their failure to indoctrinate the masses and have found the explanation in their basic inability to produce significant arguments drawn from Islamic history and Muslim thought. The issue, interestingly enough, was debated at length in Egypt in 1975 by rigid conservative Islamists led by Abdul-Halim Mahmud (Sheikh al-Azhar) and Marxist intellectuals.[33] Sheikh Mahmud adopted the view that one is either a Muslim or a Marxist, but some of the lesser *ulema* inclined toward the Islamic class view set forth by Mustafa Sibai, Syrian leader of Muslim Brethren. Indeed, Sibai's views, attacked when first presented, have become extremely popular during the past few years. A pious Muslim, Sibai saw the conflicts and class contradictions in the Muslim society from a dialectical viewpoint, but his point of departure is the Koran and the Sunna. He included in his methodology Marxist ways of social analysis without being himself a Marxist and probably without having even read Marx. In effect, Sibai's method is similar to that of Ali Shariati in Iran.

The ideological polarization in the Islamic social thought is best symbolized by the emergence of a militant radical wing, the Takfir Wa al-Hijra
founded in 1971, in the Muslim Brethren (Ikhwan al-Muslimin) in Egypt.
It carried out armed attacks against Egyptian military installations and
officials. Its leader, the Palestinian Salay Sareya, who was executed,
belonged originally to the Iraqi branch of the Ikhwan, and after coming to
Egypt he established relations with high-ranking members of the organization (see section on Ikhwan and Sadatism).

I have mentioned in the general introduction that probably the most
important ideological development in the Middle East was the convergence of Marxist and Islamic fundamentalist thought toward certain
common views on the social situation, despite the irreconcilability of their
basic philosophical stands. Thus Muslim socialism, or the Muslim Left,
succeeded in coming to grips with the social problems of the time without
formally departing from or contradicting the tenets of Islam. This development preempted many of the arguments and much of the power of the
secular Marxists, or scientific Socialists. Some Islamists have gone so far as
to claim that there is no contradiction in being a Communist and a Muslim.
In fact, there is an attempt in Egypt to reinterpret many works by early
Arab and Muslim writers, including Afghani and Sayyid Kotb, as the
precursors of the Muslim Left.[34] This, it should be mentioned, is being
undertaken by some groups in the Muslim Brethren. In sum, Arab social
and political thought is at a crossroads and appears to be ready to take the
road that will bring it into harmony with development in other Muslim
countries in the Middle East and with its own history and social development. The excerpts on Muslim fundamentalism in the Arab section should
therefore be read together with those in the sections on other countries in
the area.

Notes

1. Albert Hourani, *Arabic Thought in the Liberal Age, 1798–1939* (London and
    New York: Oxford University Press, 1962), pp. 55 ff.
2. Bernard Lewis and P. M. Holt, eds., *Historians of the Middle East* (London
    and New York: Oxford University Press, 1962), p. 17.
3. Sylvia G. Haim, ed., *Arab Nationalism: An Anthology* (Berkeley, Calif.:
    University of California Press, 1962), p. 5.
4. Hayreddin Pasha (Khayr al-Din Pasha), prime minister of Tunisia, wrote a
    treatise on government in 1867.
5. Leading families, such as Tannus al-Shidyaq, claimed that the Lebanon
    should be a separate independent nation. On the other had, a new middle
    class emerging in the market towns of Syria, Lebanon, and even Palestine,
    fought against the old feudal structure and in some cases even caused civil
    war (e.g., the civil war in Lebanon in 1860). Hourani, p. 235. See also
    Malcolm H. Kerr, *Lebanon in the Last Years of Feudalism, 1860–1864*
    (Beirut, Catholic Press, 1959), pp. 3 ff.

6. A notable, or a man of influence. *Ayan* (Arabic *a'yan*, the plural of *'ain*) is the form of the world generally used in English for the single and the plural.
7. Anouar Abdel Malek (Anwar 'Abd al-Malik), *Anthologie de la littérature arabe contemporaine* (Paris: Éditions du Seuil, 1965), p. 34, describes al-Tahtawi as an humble *kuttab* (secretary) in order to show that rational thought and socialism arose among the lower classes. Hourani, however, points out that the al-Tahtawi had a conventional Islamic view and stressed the supremacy of the Shari'a (Islamic law) over the ruler. Hourani, pp., 73–74. See also Ibrahim Abu-Lughod, *Arab Rediscovery of Europe* (Princeton, N.J.: Princeton University Press, 1963), pp. 42–62, 166–67.
8. This seems to be the case of Abdel Malek, who opens his anthology with an excerpt from al-Tahtawi's writings on the value of labor.
9. Hourani, p. 76.
10. The involvement or noninvolvement of Islam in nationalist movements among Muslim peoples was determined largely by the political status of those people. Iran and the Ottoman Empire (and later Turkey), enjoying independence, could adopt secularist policies, since their national identities were determined essentially by the political considerations of a national territorial state. The Turkic peoples in czarist Russia, however, had no independence and had to rely on Islam to develop a sense of national identity, while trying to reform and enlighten their respective communities from inside. This question of political independence goes a long way to explain the rise of Muslim reformist movements (which did not appear in Iran and Turkey) in the Islamic world. Serge A. Zenkovsky, *Pan-Turkism and Islam in Russia* (Cambridge, Mass.: Harvard University Press, 1960), p. 9, writes that "the Turkic national revival was preceded by a Moslem cultural revival."
11. Nadav Safran, *Egypt in Search of Political Community* (Cambridge, Mass.: Harvard University Press, 1961), p. 63.
12. Malcolm H. Kerr, *Islamic Reform: The Political and Legal Theories of Muhammad 'Abduh and Rashid Rida* (Berkeley, Calif.: University of California Press, 1966).
13. Haim, pp. 26–29; Hourani, pp. 271–72.
14. The works of Safran and Hourani and Jamal M. Ahmed, *The Intellectual Origins of Egyptian Nationalism* (London and New York: Oxford University Press, 1960), deal mostly with these writers and thinkers.
15. Zeine N. Zeine, *Arab-Turkish Relations and the Emergence of Arab Nationalism* (Beirut: Khayat's 1958), p. 80.
16. Majid Khadduri, " 'Aziz 'Ali Misri and the Arab Nationalist Movement," in *Middle Eastern Affairs Number Four*, ed. Albert Hourani, St. Anthony's Papers No. 17 (London and New York: Oxford University Press, 1965), pp. 140–63
17. For instance, in a speech attacking the Ba'thists as atheists, Nasser declared: "The Revolution is of the people. The Revolution leaders are from the people. Religion forms the frame which limits the action of everyone. This particular thing can be done because it is right, while that other thing cannot be done because it is sinful. Piety is the basis of religion. On these bases, the Revolution has made its way bringing together the hearts of the people and working for the elimination of exploitation, for the elimination of tyranny, for the removal of class differences and in order to render everyone free, with a free will forging along his own way and finding honest and honourable work. . . . If those who dominate Syria today believe that religious ideas are rotten, we tell them that it is the atheist ideas that are rotten. It is by no means possible that a religious people would respond to atheist leaders."

President Gamal Abdel Nasser's Speeches and Press Interviews, January-December, 1963 (Cairo: Information Department, 1964), pp. 187–88.

18. "Vers une culture arabe contemporaine," *Cahier d'Histoire Mondiale* 14 (1972): 783 ff. General views on Arab thought may be found in Abdallah Laroui, *L'ideologie Arabe contemporaine* (Paris: F. Maspero, 1967). A good survey by Michael Kamel, which appeared first in *Al-Adab* (January 1973) has been translated into French, "Dialogue entre l'heritage culturel et le modernisme dans la pensée Egyptienne contemporaine," *Travaux et Jours* 461 (1973): 53–71.

19. Some have found strong European socialist and Marxist influences in the Algerian revolution; see Rouchdi Fakkar, *Reflets de la sociologie marxiste dans le Monde Arabe* (Paris: P. Geuthner, 1974).

20. *La Pensée politique arabe contemporaine* (Paris: Seuil, 1970), p. 17. For an inside view of the Algerian revolution, see Moufoud Feraoun, *Journal, 1955–1962* (Paris, 1962).

21. An excellent analysis of Arab nationalism is in Bassam Tibi, *Nationalismus in der Dritten Welt am Arabischen Beispiel* (Frankfurt: M. Europaïsche Verlag-sanstalt, 1969). There are also excellent passages on nationalism in Tibi's book dealing with the Arab Left; see *Die arabische Link* (Frankfurt: Europaische Verlagsanstalt, 1969). For a comparison of nationalisms, see Sholomo Avineri, "Political and Social Aspects of Israeli and Arab Nationalism," in *Nationalism: The Nature and Evolution of an Idea*, ed. Eugene Kamenko (Canberra: Australian National University Press, 1973), pp. 100–22.

22. See Robert Springborg, "On the Rise and Fall of Arabism," *Australian Outlook* 31 (1977):92–109. For a general view of nationalism, see Anthony D. S. Smith, *Nationalism in the Twentieth Century* (Oxford: Martin Robertson, 1979).

23. *Al-naqd al-dhati ba'd al-hazima* [Self Criticism after the Defeat] (Beirut, 1968). In another book al-Azm criticized the religious currents of thought and was then ousted from Lebanon.

24. Arnold Hottinger, "The Depth of Arab Radicalism," *Foreign Affairs* 51 (1972–73):491–504.

25. See an excellent, comparitive article by Olivier Carré, "Evolution de la Pensée Politique Arabe au Proche-Orient depuis Juin 1967," *Revue Française de Science Politique* 23 (1973): 1046–79.

26. See Bassam Tibi, "The Genesis of the Arab Left, A Critical Viewpoint," in *The Arabs Today*, ed. Edward Said and Fuad Suleyman (Columbus, Ohio: Forum Associates, 1973), pp. 31–42; and Walid Kazziha, *Revolutionary Transformation in the Arab World: Habash and His Comarades from Nationalism to Marxism* (New York: St. Martin's Press, 1975).

27. An extensive treatment of these problems is in Tareq Y. Ismael, *The Arab Left* (Syracuse, N.Y.: Syracuse University Press, 1976). Ismael analyzes the birth of leftism in relation to nationalism and presents excerpts from ideological writings. For an earlier, more general and traditional view of Arab thought, see Majid Khadduri, *Political Trends in the Arab World* (Baltimore: Johns Hopkins Press, 1970).

28. *La crise des intellectuels arabes: traditionalisme ou historicisme* (Paris: F. Maspero, 1978), pp. 105 ff.

29. For further details, see sections on the Ba'th; see also Sami A. Hanna and George H. Gardner, eds., *Arab Socialism: A Documentary Survey* (Leiden: E. J. Brill, 1969) and Abdel Moghny Said (with a section by M. Samir Ahmed), *Arab Socialism* (London: Blandford Press, 1972).

30. The situation of the Arab world after the war of 1973 was discussed by Arab intellectuals Munif Razzaz (Ba'th founding member), M. H. Haykal (former editor of *al-Ahram*), and A. Yusuf (PFLP representative) at the Annual Convention of the Arab-American University Graduates held in Chicago, October 17–19, 1975. Excerpts of the talks appeared in *Race and Class* 17, no. 3 (1976): 253–80.

31. See Shimon Shamir, "Marxism in the Arab World: The Cases of the Egyptian and Syrian Regimes" in *Varieties of Marxism*, ed. Shlomo Avineri (The Hague: Nijhoff, 1977), pp. 271–78.

32. Nasif Nasser, *Nahwa mujtama jadid, Muqaddimat asasiyya fi-naqd al-mujtama' al-taifi* [For a New Society, Introduction to the Fundamental Ideas of Ideas of Communal Society] (Beirut, 1970). See also Carré, p. 1970.

33. See Adel Hussein, "Islam and Marxism: The Absurd Polarization of Contemporary Egyptian Politics," *Review of Middle East Studies* 2 (1976): 71–82; the issue was debated in *Akhir sa'a* and *Rose al-Yusef* (both weeklies) in August and September 1975.

34. For further views on marxism, see Ilias Murqus, *Al-Marksiya wa al-mas'ala al-qaumiyya* [Marxism and the National Question] and *Al-Marksiya wa al-sharq* [Marxism and the East] (Beirut: Dar al-talia, 1968). On communism see M. S. Agwani, *Communism in the Arab East* (New York: Asia Publishing House, 1969); see also a report presented to the Central Committee of the Italian Communist Party by Gian Carlo Pajetta, *Socialismo e Mondo Arabo* (Rome: Editori Riuniti, 1970).

II. THE BACKGROUND OF ARAB NATIONALISM

1. The Historical Roots of Arab Nationalism[*]

'Abd al-'Aziz al-Duri

After studying at the University of London's School of Oriental Studies, al-Duri returned to Baghdad and taught at the Higher Training College there. He served as dean of the University college (1949–60) and as professor of Islamic history at Baghdad University. In 1963, after the revolution, he became dean of the University. He had published several serious books on the early history of Islam. In the book from which these excerpts have been taken, al-Duri traces the origin of Arab nationalism to its pre-Islamic roots

[*]Extract from 'Abd al-'Aziz al-duri, *al-Judhur al-tarikiyya lil-qawmiyya al-'arabiyya* [The Historical Roots of Nationalism] (Beirut: Dar al-'ilm lil-malayin, 1960), pp. 10–14, 41–42, 85, 91–92.

"in the move toward formulating a unified literary language" and finds a continuity in Arab nationalism after the emergence of Islam.

If we examine the beginnings of Arab consciousness, we find that the first vague stirrings occurred prior to the rise of Islam. During that pre-Islamic period, the Arabian Peninsula was threatened by two powers, the Sassanians in the east and Byzantium in the west, each of which tried to dominate the civilized borders of the Peninsula.

The civilized principates and other states collapsed one after another and either came under direct foreign domination (as in Iraq, Syria, and the Yemen) or relapsed into tribal chaos. This wave of tribalism spread into the more civilized regions. The Peninsula suffered from internal conflicts and fragmentation and passed through a period of religious anarchy.

Amid this total chaos, Arab consciousness first appeared. It made its presence felt in politics, society, and culture and prepared the way for a total renaissance. Here, we are concerned with only a few of these aspects.

Arab consciousness began with the move toward replacing the many dialects with a unified literary language—a language that appeared first in poetry and crystallized in the Qur'an. Historically, therefore, the Arabic language was the first common denominator.

Arab consciousness also coincided with a kind of political renaissance, which originated when tribes living on the edges of the Peninsula began individually to fight with the Eastern and Western power. (The Battle of Dhu Qar[1] and its consequences in the northern part of the Peninsula are an example.) This renaissance was further manifested in attempts to create a limited political sovereignty—as, for instance, in the principality of Kinda.[2]

Commercial activities, which involved a certain measure of independence, enhanced the development of this social [i.e., national] consciousness. This in turn produced a certain degree of unity and the diffusion of common social norms and conventions. This consciousness was also apparent in a religious tension, religion being an important social and ideological substructure. The Arab worship of individual tribal gods was transformed into the worship of more universal gods and into communal prayers at holy sites. With the development in the Yemen and Hijaz of a form of early monotheism, there also arose a type of monotheism that was connected neither with Byzantine-supported Christianity nor with Judaism, which enjoyed some protection from the Sassanians. The believers in this creed looked toward a sublime God transcending the local deities and called Allah in the western Peninsula. They considered the various deities as intermediaries between the people and Allah, and regarded the Ka'ba, to which pilgrimage was made from all parts of the Peninsula, as the House of Allah. Thus, the pilgrimage was another unifying factor among the Arabs.

Hence, we observe a renaissance, not devoid of anxiety, but containing a common consciousness and a new self-awareness—an awareness that lacked clarity, organization, and guidance.

With the appearance of the Prophet and Islam, the Arab spirit burst forth and the common consciousness reached its climax. The Prophet provided the leadership and the total framework for this consciousness, and Islam furnished Arab consciousness with a clear content and a well-defined direction. The movement was therefore Arabic in language, habitat, and message-bearers. In essence, it expressed a comprehensive Arab spirit. It rejected tribalism and all its attendant values and ideals, and it provided a barrier against social and ideological anarchy. It sought political unity, rejected fragmentation and servility, tended to evolve unified values and ideals, and adopted a secular attitude toward life.

The Qur'an was revealed in Arabic. It struck a blow at all other dialects and provided the Arabs with one language, the language of the Qur'an. This important foundation of the nation was fixed. We can go even further and say that this new movement guaranteed the perpetuation of linguistic unity when it added a new and common dimension to the Arabic language. Arabic became the greatest common denominator and [those who spoke it had] the proof of belonging to the Arab race. The Arabs did entertain certain vague notions about a common stock and descent, and this feeling of a unified origin crystallized in the well-known distinction between Bedouin Arabs, genuine Arabs, and naturalized Arabs. But the new movement did not encourage the perpetuation of vague lineage to old ancestors. It emphasized the language, considering it as a total framework within which people might truly belong. Thus, the Arab came to be distinguished from the non-Arab, and the most Arab of all peoples were regarded as those whose languge most closely resembled that of the Qur'an. Coming out into the world [i.e., out of the Peninsula], the Arabs carried this distinction with them.

The Arabs were unified through the Islamic movement and became "one nation." Although the term "nation" in this context may possess a religious connotation, in fact it included only Arabs. Thus, we can say that in that period the nation was an Arab nation. Islam provided this Arab nation with a humanistic message that it carried throughout the world, and it gave the Arabs a comprehensive foundation for the creation of a new society and a new civilization.

Thus, Arab consciousness and the Arab renaissance acquired significance through Islam: one nation, one language, a historic message, and a common destiny. For the first time, the Arabs emerged united onto the stage of history out of chaos, fragmentation, and the conflict between the Sassanian East and the Byzantine West. . . .

We are concerned here with understanding how the Arabs met the challenge to Arab consciousness and the Arab idea.

The attacks [of the Shu'ubiyya] against the Arab heritage caused the Arabs all the more tenaciously to embrace this heritage of wisdom in prose and poetry.[3] They took care to collect this heritage and to base Arabic culture upon it. Gone was the old attempt to divide Arab history into Islamic and pre-Islamic periods, to ignore all pre-Islamic culture, and to regard Islam as the starting point that superseded the dark ages. Thus, both al-Jahiz (d. 869) in his *al-Bayan wal-tabyin* [Book of Eloquence and Exposition, a treatise on rhetoric] and Ibn Qutayba (d. 889) in his *'Uyun al-akhbar* [Choice Histories, a medley of citations and reminiscences from poetry, history, and traditions] presented a vivid picture of pre-Islamic Arabic culture in the form of elegant and attractive selections. They did so in order to refute the anti-Arab charge that the Arabs did not possess a literature and a heritage to compare with those of the Persians. The two verse anthologies *Diwan al-Hamasa* [Anthology of Fortitude, by Habib ibn Aus al Ta'i Abu Tammam (d. 845)] and *al-Mufaddaliyat*[4] offered easy access to the grandeur of Arabic poetry (including pre-Islamic poetry) for the benefit of the younger generation and the educated classes.

For the first time, the idea of the cultural continuity of Arabic before and after Islam made itself clearly felt in the life of the Arabs. We can feel that at that period they came to realize that they possessed a rich pre-Islamic heritage, contrary to the charges of the anti-Arabs. This outlook was not confined merely to men of letters but appeared also among historians. In his *Kitab al-ma'arif* [Book of Knowledge], Ibn Qutayba dealt at length wih pre- and post-Islamic Arab cultural history. This book was in fact a short literary, historical, and Islamic encyclopedia, in which he intended to provide the writer or literate gentleman with brief information on these topics. . . .

In our study of the historical roots of nationalism, we must distinguish between Arabism and Islam. Although Islam appeared as an Arab revolt, and although the Islamic and Arab movements were identical in the heyday of Islam, the two movements diverged when Islam began to expand, when it was used as a weapon to attack the Arabs, and when the Arabs were led, in the name of religion, to accept a foreign domination, against which they later rose. The pride we take in our heritage and the proper attention we pay to its values do not mean that we must forge a political union out of Islam or base our Arab state upon it.

The Arab contact with the West, first as a culture and then as an imperialist power, was very important in clarifying the historical roots of Arab nationalism, in consolidating these roots, and in establishing their true import. The Arabs welcomed the implications of freedom and tried to imitate the West in bettering their way of life and their economy. But they were not prepared to forsake their heritage or deny their identity. In their anxiety that this heritage and identity should not disappear, they took great pains to emphasize these [national] characteristics. . . .

The study of the historical roots of Arab nationalism is valuable in helping us to establish and clarify the content of nationalism on a firmer level than that of the emotions. It also enables us to lay down the philosophical foundations for Arab nationalism.

We have seen that Arab nationalism is essentially cultural. It is not based on a racial concept, since the conception of the Arab nation was drawn from the language, the process of Arabization, the cultural heritage, and the historic role of the Arabs.

The Arab nationalist idea is neither ephemeral nor borrowed. It is the result of the development of Arab consciousness, which blazed forth 1400 years ago, was gradually unraveled and defined through the course of Arab history, and finally emerged in modern times in a self-awareness which is manifested in a new vitality that seeks to reactivate the Arab nation and build up its own state. This is the modern Arab nationalist consciousness.

We have seen that Arab consciousness began by being comprehensive and popular but, because of certain ideological and political factors, was somewhat weakened in the course of history. The Arab intellectuals stoutly defended Arab consciousness when it came under attack during the ʿAbbasid period; it again became comprehensive and popular when other peoples overran the Arabs. Finally, in modern times, it reappeared among the intellectuals but has developed until now it is again popular and comprehensive.

We have also seen that Arab consciousness was [universally] humanistic in character, since it carried its message of religion and civilization throughout the world. When it reappeared in the guise of nationalist consciousness, it stood up against tyranny and foreign domination, and sought to liberate the Arabs and create a new Arab society. Thus, this movement is essentially peaceable and constructive in its aims. It emphasized the revival of the Arab cultural heritage and the proper understanding of the path of the Arab nation in history. It views this as a means of understanding the Arab character.

Notes

1. The Battle of Dhu Qar took place near Kufa in 610 and resulted in a decisive Persian defeat. Despite the small number of troops involved, the victory by the Arabs is seen as the beginning of a new era, since it gave the Arab tribes a new confidence and enthusiasm.
2. One may take issue with the statement that the principality of Kinda truthfully

reflected an attempt to express Arab consciousness. Kinda was one of the many examples of a tribal leader's briefly establishing his personal supremacy without any clear political aim.

3. At least two major movements in ancient Islam were known as *Shu'ubiyya*. The word, derived from *shu'ub*, meaning "peoples" or "nations," and referring mostly to non-Arabs, is derived from the Qur'an XLIX, 13 ("Men, We have created you from a male and a female and divided you into nations [*shu'uban*] and tribes that you might get to know one another"). The purpose of this passage from the Qur'an was to create brotherhood among Muslims. The first Shu'ubiyya movement rose from among the Kharijites (about A.D. 657), who claimed that no race or tribe was inherently superior to others, and therefore rejected the claim of the Quraysh (the Prophet's tribe) to the caliphate. The second Shu'ubiyya, a sociopolitical-literary movement of the second half of the eighth century, represented the efforts of the urban middle classes, especially in Iraq and Persia, to achieve political and social equality with the Arabs. The Shu'ubiyya in this sense was an egalitarian movement. Ignaz Goldziher, *Muhammedanische Studien* 2 (Halle, 1888–90), Part I, pp. 147 ff. Sir Hamilton Gibb has stressed the special role played by secretaries (*kuttab*) at the 'Abbasid court, who were involved in the Shu'ubiyya. They used the Persian language and tried to frame Islamic political and social institutions according to Sassanian forms. Representatives of the Shu'ubiyya rejected the view that the Arabs were pure of race and descent (Abu 'Ubayda) and resented the Arabs' emphasis on the close relation between the Arabic language and the Qur'an. The Shu'ubiyya's development of certain anti-Islamic tendencies led to repressive measures by the state and prepared the ground for the emrgence of the *Mu'tazila*, a movement of rationalists who defended the orthodoxy of Islam. The other important reaction to the Shu'ubiyya referred to by al-Duri was a literary movement that sought the primacy of the Arabic language. Al-Jahiz (Abi 'Uthman 'Amr ibn Bahr, d. 869) and Ibn Qutayba (Muhammad ibn Muslim al-Dinawari, d. 889) borrowed some Persian forms, adopted a more common language and expressions, and thus widened the range of Arabic literature to cover most aspects of life. Thus, the Shu'ubiyya ended with a compromise by which Arabs borrowed forms, expressions, ideas, and approaches, mainly from Persian, and in exchange assured respect for Arabic as the language of the Qur'an. In later days, the term implied divisive tendencies. See H. A. R. Gibb, *Studies on the Civilization of Islam*, ed. William R. Polk and Stanford Shaw (Boston: Beacon Press, 1962), pp. 12–13, 66–72; and R. A. Nicholson, *A Literary History of the Arabs* (Cambridge: Cambridge University Press: 1961). For other forms of the Shu'ubiyya see Sami A. Hanna and George H. Gardner, "Al-Shu'ubiyya Up-Dated." *Middle East Journal 20* (Summer 1966): 335–51. See also 'Abd al-'Aziz al-Duri, *al-Judhur al-tarikhiyya fi al-shu'ubiyya* ([The Historical Roots of the Shu'ubiyya Movement] (Beirut: Dar al-tali'a, 1962).

4. The title bears the name of the compiler, Mufaddal al-Dabbi (d. 786). The original title was *al-Mukhtarat* [Selections].

2.   The Qur'an and Arab Nationalism[*]

'Ali Husni al-Kharbutli

'Ali Husni al-Kharbutli is a professor of Islamic history at the University of 'Ain Shams in Egypt. In al-Quawmiyya al-'arabiyya min al-fajr ila al-zuhr *[Arab Nationalism from Its Dawn to Its Fulfillment] (Cairo: Mu'assasat al-matba'a al-haditha, 1960), al-Kharbutli claimed that religious and national unity are distinct questions. Another book of some interest by al-Kharbutli is* al-Mujtama' al-'arabi *[The Arab Society] (Cairo: Mu'assasat al-matba'a al-haditha, 1960). In the following extract, al-Kharbutli emphasizes the religious sources of Arab nationalism.*

The Qur'an is a holy book that was revealed to Muhammad. It is an Arab Qur'an, revealed to an Arab prophet on Arab soil and transmitted by the Prophet to the Arabs, who have conformed to it and preserved it. Not surprisingly, therefore, the Qur'an is considered a factor in the manifestation of Arab nationalism. . . .

The Qur'an was revealed in the language of the Arabs, according to the Arab manner. The words it contains are Arab words, except for a few rare words that were borrowed from foreign languages and Arabized. The Arabs made them their own and applied their grammatical rules to them. The Qur'anic expressions are the expressions of spoken Arabic. We find in the Qur'an the etymological sounds, as well as the metaphor and metonymy, of the everyday language of the Arabs. That is quite normal, for the Qur'an existed first of all to call the Arabs to Islam and it therefore had to be written in a language they could understand. "Each apostle We have sent spoke in the language of his own people, so that he might make plain to them his message" (Qur'an, XIV, 4).

God chose Muhammad from among the Arabs in order that he might set seal to the succession of the prophets. The miracle concerning Muhammad necessitated two conditions: first, that he possess the qualities most admired and appreciated by the Arabs, for the miracle of any

---

[*]Extract from 'Ali Husni al-Kharbutli, *Muhammad wa-al-qawmiyya al-'arabiyya* [Muhammad and Arab Nationalism] (Cairo: Mu'assasat al-matba'a al-haditha, 1959), pp. 67–75. Here and elsewhere, the translations from the Qur'an follow the version of N. J. Dawood, trans., *The Koran* (Harmondsworth and Baltimore, Md.: Penguin, 1956).

particular people is the miracle in which they most excel; second, that this miracle remain eternal and that it last as long as the Law by which God wished to close the series of all other laws, since God desired that all laws be brought to an end by the Prophet chosen to transmit the Law. These two conditions have made the Qur'an the miracle of the Prophet.

The words and style of the Qur'an were widespread among all the Arab tribes, and the Arabs used them when they made speeches or wrote poems. The Qur'an therefore became a common language for the Arabs, unifying their tastes and forming among them a power of imagination with common affinities and a common ideal.

The Qur'an was revealed in a style comparable to no other. It is written neither in verse, nor in free prose, nor in measured rhyming lines. It is a composition that pleases, whose words have an agreeable ring and that express lofty thoughts. All the literary figures of speech and all styles of rhetoric are encompassed there. The Arabs found in the language of the Qur'an and in its beauty and style an object of admiration and wonder. They began to imitate it. Their admiration for the Qur'an and the wonder it inspired led certain of them to abandon poetry, as was the case with Labid ibn Rabi'a, one of the authors of the *Mu'allaqat*.[1] Each time he was asked to recite one of his poems, he would reply, "God has given me something better instead," and he would recite a sura of the Qur'an.

The Qur'an is considered the most literary book the Arabs have ever possessed. Without it, they would have neither the arts and humanities nor law: It is "a Book of revelations well-expounded, an Arabic Koran for men of understanding" (Qur'an, XLI, 3).

Although famous for their literary debates, and although literature was always honored among them, Arab literary men have been incapable of producing a book equal to the Qur'an. After long discussions, they had to admit that by its composition and the diversity of its methods, the Qur'an differs from all other compositions conceived up to now, treads a different path, and possesses a style of its own that distinguishes it, in its expressions, from other styles that are generally used. . . .

The Arab Qur'an was the miracle of the Arab Prophet. It is through him that God has challenged the Arabs. Muhammad himself stated that the Qur'an was an exceptional work and that it was impossible to produce anything like it. And that is why the believers turn to him so faithfully.

In their eyes, the different elements of which it is composed are not differentiated in value. The Arabs consider the Qur'an in its entirety as a divine miracle achieved by the Prophet; they even see it as the greatest of all miracles that prove the sincerity of the Prophet's divine mission.

The Qur'an launched its challenge to the Arabs in this Verse: "Bring down from Allah a scripture that is a better guide than these [the Qur'an and the Torah] and I will follow it" (XXVIII, 49). We find in the Qur'an a clear and precise challenge: "If men and Jinn combined to write the like of this Qur'an, they would surely fail to compose one like it, though they helped one another" (XVII, 88). These two verses constitute the last challenge contained in the Qur'an. It finishes as it began, by demonstrating clearly to the Arabs their inability to produce a comparable work. The reason for their inability is contained in two factors: first, that the Qur'an is a book of direction and guidance; second, that it was composed in an Arab manner. These two factors cannot help forming a part of any challenge to produce anything comparable to the Qur'an.

The inability of the people of Quraysh to take up the challenge considerably influenced their attitude toward the Prophet. They were the most cultivated of the Arabs in science and knowledge, and the most able in literature and rhetoric, to the point that poets allowed them to judge their recitals. They gave up opposing the Qur'an by speech and finally took up opposition by arms. The Prophet was obliged to confront them armed, but he had recourse to the sword only thirteen years later.[2] During the time he spent among them at Mecca, he had called them to Islam by persuasion, then had challenged them by a divine miracle in order not to close the door to reflection but to lead them gently and with indulgence toward faith.

They refused, and left it to arms to judge between him and them. There was then a succession of wars, through which the infidels aimed to distract attention from the miracle that they had been challenged to accomplish, and to camouflage their own weakness in the eyes of the public.

The Qur'an is a mirror that reflects certain images of the life of the Arabs and of the call that was addressed to them to come to Islam. There also exist archives in which may be found writings about the events that occurred at Mecca and Medina during the time of the Prophet.

Goldziher says that among the 114 suras of the Qur'an, one can clearly distinguish those of Mecca and those of Medina. This chronological distinction is absolutely justified by a critical and esthetic examination of the Qur'an. Dating from the Meccan period are the sermons in which Muhammad presents in a fantastic, impetuous, and spontaneous form the images suggested to him during his passionate exaltation. There is no clanking of swords; he addresses himself neither to warriors nor to subjects. He reveals rather to those who contradicted him the conviction that dominates his soul, the infinite omnipotence of God—creator of the world and his sovereign—and of the approach of the terrible Day of Judgment. He tells of the punishment of peoples and tyrants who paid no heed to the warnings of God that were sent to them by His Messengers and His Prophets. . . .

We know that the sole aim of this miracle was not the Arabic language itself; it aims at political unity, even if this unity is based on language. In effect, the Qur'an represents for Arabs the very essence of the language, for by its style and perfection it has torn down the barriers and wiped out the language differences among the Arabs.

Such was the policy of the Qur'an about uniting the Arabs; there was a realization that their language influenced their spirit. They were led, therefore, by means of their language. That is why it [the language] became second nature for them, the victorious nature that prevails in all people and endows them with intelligence and makes them derive from this intelligence the key [knowledge] to open the door to their destiny.

It is the Qur'an that purified the instincts of the Arabs and softened the asperity of the Arab spirit, to the point that the sense of the divine manifested itself therein as if they themselves had produced it.

Why, then, have the Arabs emerged so stormily from their history after Islam, as though coming out of their skin, although Islam offered them tranquillity and the inherited moral qualities of their earlier times, traditions to which they were naturally drawn, and practices that were known to them?

By impressing its miraculous aspect on the Arab nature, the Qur'an has left its imprint on the Arabs as time does. He who revealed it by His knowledge, and who in His wisdom gave it this power, is the creator of all Time. What He destroyed in the hearts of the Arabs, He built anew. That is the difference between the human and the divine, between what is possible and what is impossible.

One of the impossibilities that the Qur'an achieved was to unite those who over the centuries had remained divided, by a racial bond in which there was no sectarianism except that of the spirit. The Qur'an touched the intimate side of their nature and brought together their hearts to establish equality between them. It made of them a nation ready and capable of embracing all other nations from wherever they might come, for this nation looked only toward God. Between it and God there was everything under the sky. It is this aptitude that led to the blossoming of the Arab race. The Qur'an began this work by fusing the various primitive dialects. It then united their hearts in a single religion, and finally gave to Arabs the chance to understand the languages and feelings of other peoples, by a good and wise method which no science or education could improve.

If nations do not have a linguistic bond to unite them, religion or anything else will unite them, except in artificial union of the kind made in business while buying and selling.

The fact that the Qur'an has preserved its Arabic aspect means that, as regards society and in their own eyes, all Muslims—no matter what race they belong to, red or black—become one single body expressing themselves in the language of history, in one single language, and all racial particularities disappear.

Notes

1. "The *Mu'allaqat* are prize-winning poems which traditionally date back to the period just preceding the Qur'an, and are generally supposed to have been written in the language spoken in Mecca. The common belief is that these poems were all written in the dialect of Mecca because poetical competitions were held there during the pilgrimage season, and the winning poems were attached to the walls of the Ka'bah; hence the name *mu'allaqat*, i.e., things that are hung, or attached to something." E. Shouby, "The Influence of the Arabic Language on the Psychology of the Arabs," *Middle East Journal*, 5 (Summer 1951):284–302.
2. Presumably this indicates the period between 610—the date of the first divine call (*laylat al-qadr*, or Night of Power)—and the attack on a Meccan caravan that resulted in the Battle of Badr in 624. In 628 and 630, the conquest of Mecca was completed. The "thirteen years" may also apply to the period between the first revelation (610) and Muhammad's flight from Mecca to Medina (Yathrib) in 622 (the Hijra or Hejira).

3. The Foundations and Objectives of Arab Nationalism*

Darwish al-Jundi

Since literary Arabic is used by intellectuals throughout the Arab world, whereas the vernacular, in a variety of dialects, is spoken by the lower classes, there are profound barriers of communication between the upper and lower strata in all the Arab countries. Arguing that the literary language is "the ideal self of the Arabs" and that colloquial Arabic is "the monopoly of the practical functions of the real self," E. Shouby, a noted student of Arabic, has claimed that the differences between the "ideal" and "real" language also create deep repercussions in the Arab personality structure. (See E. Shouby, "The Influence of the Arabic Language on the

*Extract from Darwish al-Jundi, *al-Qawmiyya al-'arabiyya fi al-adab al-hadith* [Arab Nationalism in Modern Arab Literature] (Cairo: Maktabat nahdat misr, 1962), pp. 36–43, 141.

Psychology of the Arabs," Middle East Journal 5 *[Summer 1951]:284–302.)*
Darwish al-Jundi, however, like Sati'al-Husri, stresses the importance of
language in creating a bond of unity. Al-Jundi is an Egyptian with a Ph.D.
degree in Arabic literature. Despite his gross errors of history and interpre-
tation, al-Jundi gives a fair picture of the ideas and spirit of nationalism. His
argumentation is typical.

The Foundations

Arab nationalism possesses all the foundations and contituents that
appear in the various definitions of a nation. Perhaps no other nation can
compare with the Arabs in the numerous, deep-rooted, and continuous
links that bind its various groups to each other. We shall first mention the
constituent features of the Arab nation. . . .

(1) A common land. The lands inhabited by the Arab nation span
two continents, Asia and Africa. But these lands are by nature very closely
tied to each other. Indeed, they constitute a region by themselves,
independent of the two continents. This region stretches from Persia, the
Arabian Gulf [Persian Gulf], and the Indian Ocean in the east to the
Atlantic Ocean in the west, and from the Taurus Mountains and the
Mediterranean Sea in the north to Central Africa in the south. The region
is bounded by such natural frontiers as oceans, plateaus, and mountains.
For the sake of accuracy, we ought to mention that two natural barriers
separate the Arab land mass. They are: (a) *the Red Sea,* but this sea is a
narrow inlet of little importance as a barrier, since it ends with Sinai in the
north, where land communications exist, and with Bab al-Mandab in the
south, where the straits are very narrow; (b) *the Western Egyptian Desert,*
which, although constituting a natural barrier, does not prevent communication and the movements of peoples from that region to another.

This means that the fragmentation of Arab lands at the hands of
imperialists following World War I goes against the natural features of this
land mass and that the frontiers erected thereafter are all artificial. It also
means that the creation of Israel in the midst of Arab lands is equally
unnatural. Israel, however, cannot prevent Arab unity since the Arabs
encircle it on all sides. Israel exists amid an Arab world that has vast
potentialities, and the day will come when Arab nationalism will wipe out
this foreign body from the Arab map.

Certain enemies of Arab nationalism attempted to create geographical entities that are non-Arab in character, such as an Eastern or Mediterranean league of nations, basing themselves on mere proximity and

neglecting the national bonds. But proximity alone is not enough. If there exists a certain measure of sympathy among the group of Arab nations called "Eastern," this is because they fought imperialism in a common front and not because the national links binding them together are stronger than elsewhere.

France attempted to keep Syria and Lebanon under its tutelage and so championed a Mediterranean league, aiming thereby to convince the Syrians and Lebanese that they were nearer to France than to the Arab world. . . .

Arab sentiment is what binds together the inhabitants of this region where the Arab nation first appeared. This nation first arose in the Arabian Peninsula, then in Syria, Lebanon, Palestine, and Iraq. From the earliest times, the nation spread westward across the Red Sea and the Sinai Peninsula and mingled with the races that inhabited North Africa. A racial mixture occurred, and the result was a nation that was patently Arab in its descent, customs, way of life, language, and general outlook on life.

(2) A *common economy*. The wealth of the Arab lands is complementary. If the Arab nations were freely allowed to draw up a single economic policy, the ensuing economic self-sufficiency would be unparalleled. We all await the day when this Arab region finally rids itself of the imperialism that has exploited its riches and prevented the Arabs from having a unified economic policy capable of ensuring propserity to the Arabs.

(3) A *common race*. Although . . . racial unity exists nowhere among the peoples of the world, yet the Arab nation is the most racially homogeneous group of all. The story of the Arab race goes back to the days when the inhabitants of the Arabian Peninsula spread out in search of water and pastures. When the Peninsula could no longer contain them, they moved out into neighboring regions. It is well known that the first Semitic race was the Arab race and that this stock was originally located in Najd, Hijaz, 'Arud, and Yemen. From there, the first Semitic advance was made into the northern Peninsula, where the Jewish Arabs lived. Thereafter, the Arabs advanced into Palestine, Syria, Iraq, Ethiopia, and the Nile Valley. The Arab exodus from the Peninsula increased with Islam. The Arabs came to live and mix with their neighbors until the Arab stock spread as far east as Central Asia and as far west as Spain. Racial purity varied. It became more pronounced as one moved closer to the [Arabian] Peninsula. . . . Thus the central region of the Islamic world was stamped with the Arab conquest, which has now come to form the Arab nation.

The Arab man, despite the various types appearing in the various countries, can be easily recognized through his spiritual make-up. He undoubtedly differs from both Europeans and Far Easterners, since, historically his life has given him certain traditions and a particular view of virtue and goodness.

The Arab is courageous, but despite his great courage in war, he is very humane. He is generous, enlightened, tolerant, faithful to his promise, averse to all illusions and superstition, and protects the weak. He is eloquent and is enchanted by sublime literature.

(4) *Religion.* Religion is a factor in Arab national sentiment. God has favored this spot by making it the origin of divine revelation and of messages that are similar in doctrine and essence. These religions teach men to be tolerant and to reject fanaticism, which breeds injustice and tyranny. Although Muslims are a majority in the Arab world, their religion enjoins them to be tolerant and to live in peace and good will with non-Muslims, as appears from the following verse in the Qur'an: "There is to be no compulsion in religion." Muslims in many periods of their history gave us noble examples of their treatment of the People of the Book [*ahl al-kitab*; or the Protected People, *ahl al-dhimma*], which helped to strengthen the bonds between Arabs of various religions. . . .

(5) *Language.* The Arabic language is the strongest foundation of Arab nationalism. It has drawn together the Arabs of the various countries and has been the means of communication of both their mind and spirit since the emergence of Islam. The Arabic language is a record of Arab creativity, a symbol of their unity, and the expression of their intellectual and technical achievements. The Arabic language has displayed a tremendous vitality in its meticulous structure, its wide extension, and its flexibility, which has rendered it a fitting vehicle for the transmission of the arts and sciences.

The imperialists were aware of the influence of the Arabic language in drawing the Arabs together, in binding their past to their present, and in consolidating Arab nationalism. They fought it and tried to replace it with their own languages. They also attempted to develop colloquial and regional dialects, hoping thereby to stamp out classical Arabic, tear the links between Arabs, and weaken Arab sentiment, which is everywhere nourished by the language.

In fact, the history of classical and colloquial Arabic is closely linked with the imperialist policies of France and Britain. In the beginning, these two powers encouraged adherence to classical Arabic, since they wanted to stamp out the influence of Turkey. When the Arabs were no longer in the British, French, or Italian spheres of influence, the imperialists everywhere fought classical Arabic and helped to strengthen the colloquial dialects, in order to sever the common Arab link for the communication of sentiments, ideas, and opinions. . . .

This view is echoed by Salama Musa, who was the most prominent champion of colloquial Arabic. . . .

The ideal language is one whose words are not forced, whose meanings are neither blurred nor closely similar but are sharply differentiated as five is from six. It must be a rich and fertile language that can supply the multitude of words needed by civilized men and can absorb the new words coined to suit the increasing requirements of modern life. . . . In Egypt, a class of writers has been trying to use the Arabic language as a literary means to recapture the past. Indeed, we have certain linguists who speak about Arabic in much the same way as European Orientalists discuss Sanskrit, but with this basic difference, namely, that the latter are not trying to revive dead Sanskrit words, whereas the former are trying to revive ancient Arabic words. Had they been in touch with the modern age they would have been well advised to bury such words. Most of this class is found among teachers of Arabic in our schools. . . .

Nothing in the world is more valuable than a good language. Our feelings and actions are determined by words. Our behavior at home, in the street, in the fields, and in factories is above all a linguistic behavior, since the words of the language determine our ideas and reactions and dictate our behavior. We can even say that the British domination of India and civilized domination over barbarians is, to a certain extent, linguistic, i.e., a rich and comprehensive vocabulary of knowledge and morals, artistically creative and ethically oriented, which leads to domination and, sometimes, to aggression. . . .

Since our language lacks the vocabulary of modern culture, our nation is denied the benefits of modern life. We still use the language of agriculture and have not yet acquired an industrial vocabulary. Therefore, our mentality is stagnant and anachronistic and looks always to the past. We occupy ourselves with writing about Mu'awiya ibn Abi Sufyan while we should be writing about Henry Ford, or the significance of industry in our age, or Karl Marx and the meaning of futuristic thought.

The call for a modern language is in effect a call for a modern life, since the writer who adopts foreign words as they are, without attempting to translate them, is in fact adopting the civilization of science, logic, and industrial progress instead of the civilization of literature, dogmas, and agriculture. . . .

(6) A common history. From its earliest times, this Arab nation has lived through common historical experiences. We in the Arab world have all faced the invasion of Alexander the Great, and been subjected to Roman injustice, Mongol barbarity, Crusader violence, and Turkish ferocity.

Today, we face various forms of imperialism and we all suffer from the tragedy caused by Zionism. We are all equally exposed to the machination of our common enemy who lies in waiting for us.

A common history gives rise to common sentiments and aspirations, a common memory of past glories and tribulations, and similar hopes for a renaissance and a bright future. A common history does not involve a mere outlook on the past but expands to the future and embraces a common destiny. Thus interpreted, a common history and a common destiny are both included in the definition of Arab nationalism.

The Objectives

Since Arab nationalism embraces the common destiny of the Arab nation, common objectives and a common pursuit of these objectives follow of necessity.

Every nation desires what is in conformity with its basic structure and the conditions of its own existence and current world events. Hence, the objectives of Arab nationalism are confined to the achievement of our political and social revolution, to laying the foundations of an Arab society which is free from all foreign influence of every description, and to internal stability, through the destruction of feudalism, reaction, opportunism, and the predominance of capitalism. Our nationalism seeks complete and total liberation, where the Arabs would be sovereign in their own land and sole beneficiaries of its wealth and riches. It also seeks to destroy Israel, which is an imperialist bridgehead, erected on Arab soil. It seeks to achieve a better and more dignified social life for all Arabs.

President Nasser has sketched the broad outlines of nationalist objectives under the following heads:

1. Arab nationalism means dignity and construction.
2. It spells the end of foreign occupations and exploitation.
3. It casts out agents of all foreign powers.
4. It emplies unity, strength, and stability....

4. A Summary of the Characteristics of Arab Nationalism[*]

'Abd al-Rahman al-Bazzaz

'Abd al-Rahman al-Bazzaz, a former Iraqi teacher and Iraqi ambassador to Egypt, became his country's Prime Minister in 1962. He was known first for a lecture given in 1952 in Baghdad, in which he expressed the view that there was no contradiction between Islam and Arab nationalism. This talk, al-Islam wa-al-qawmiyya al-'arabiyya [Islam and Arab Nationalism], was translated by Sylvia G. Haim, Die Welt des Islams, III (Leiden, 1954), pp. 201–19, and is reproduced in her Arab Nationalism (Berkeley, Calif.: University of California Press, 1962), pp. 172–88. Al-Bazzaz asserted in his lecture that those who considered nationalism as essentially secular had adopted the Western view of nationalism. Arab nationalism and Islam, according to al-Bazzaz, were intimately connected. Islam was a kind of national religion; its inner core was truly Arabic, but its Arabic purity was destroyed by other nations who came into its fold .The Prophet was an Arab, the language of the revelation, the Qur'an was Arabic, and Islam retained many of the customs of the Arabs. Therefore, notwithstanding its universality, Islam had an inner appeal to the Arabs and, through its language, formed the core of Arab nationalism.

Al-Bazzaz' views on the relation between Islam and Arabism are not new. Rashid Rida (1886–1935), another famous exponent of Arab nationalism, had similar ideas, but he placed priority on Islamic solidarity, condemning racism and local or regional nationalism. This partiality shown to the Arab origins of Islam and the sense of superiority with which it was expressed caused adverse reactions among the non-Arab Muslims. Since the turn of the century, Turkish nationalists and secularists have contended that, with its Arab characteristics, Islam jeopardized the development of Turkish national culture and identity. Both Arabs and Turks had thus come to view religion, though for different purposes, in purely particularist, nationalist terms. Consequently, they had overlooked the historical fact that Islam became a truly universal religion after it renounced its Arabic racism in the 'Abbasid period (750–1258). Thereafter, it was possible for Arabs, Turks, Iranians, and other nationalities to live together for centuries by giving their allegiance to the universally binding precepts of Islam. In the age of

[*]Extract from 'Abd-al-Rahman al-Bazzaz, Buhuth fi al-qawmiyya al-'arabiyya [Studies in Arab Nationalism] (Cairo: Ma'had al-dirasat al-'arabiyya al'aliyya, Jami'at al-duwal al-'arabiyya, 1962), pp. 320–23.

nationalism, however, the Middle Eastern Muslims were committing an error that Western nationalists were able partially to avoid, namely, using religion to further nationalist claims.

It may be useful to summarize in a few paragraphs the salient features of Arab nationalism, some of which we have already discussed at greater length elsewhere. Our nationalism is "comprehensive," in the sense that it believes in the whole of the Arab nation and embraces the entire Arab homeland and all concepts connected with Arab life. At the same time, it is not a fossilized dogma that dispenses with man's humanity or denies his individuality.

It is also "fixed," in the sense that it is neither a temporary nor a transitory phase that nations pass through on their way to a wider internationalism. Nevertheless, and despite its fixed foundations, our nationalism is neither stagnant nor reactionary nor hostile to the noble ideals of humanity.

It is also "democratic," in the sense that it believes in the right of the Arab nation to decide its destiny and to govern itself, for the benefit of all its sons. Its democracy is based on open deliberation *[shawra]*, which is averse to tyranny and dictatorship. At the same time, it does not feel obliged to cling obstinately to certain types of democratic practice. It is concerned, above all else, with the democratic spirit, as it understands it and as guided by its own democratic experience and development.

Furthermore, it is "socialist," in the sense that is socially oriented, serving the public interest before individual freedom and seeking to achieve social justice and cohesion and fruitful cooperation among all citizens. It works to develop the Arab economy on the basis of planning that aims to create a just and healthy economy and to achieve prosperity for all. But its socialism is not Marxist and its economic beliefs are based solely neither on the material things of life nor on the domination of one class by another.

Our Arab nationalism is "cooperative," in the sense that it propagates a spirit of cooperation, not of conflict and hostility among the citizens in all sectors of life. But its cooperative character does not entail the total subjection of the economy to a system of cooperatives, of which it makes only a limited use. It regards coopertion, with its wide horizons, as extending beyond the realm of the merely economic.

It is "progressive" and forward-looking, and believes in renewal and creativity. But it pursues its clearly defined objectives with perspicacity. Its progressive character does not make it deny its past, and it moves forward, not for movement's sake, but in order to achieve its unalterable nationalist objectives.

It is "revolutionary"; it believes in, propagates, and adheres to the demands of the revolution. But it distinguishes between constructive revolt and negative destruction that leads to chaos and fails to achieve reform.

It is "positive," for it cooperates with all nations, exchanging its ideas with all modern ideas consonant with its philosophy. But despite its positive character, it does not aim at dissolving itself into internationalism or at losing its distinctive character by attaching itself to leagues and treaties. At the present juncture in particular, it prefers to adhere to a policy of positive neutrality and nonalignment.

It is "mobile," in the sense that it actively pursues its objectives. But its constant advance does not blind it to its ideals. It does not wish to lose sight of its path by indulging the wishes of one group or another who attempt to pull it in various directions.

In addition to all this, our nationalism, despite its belief in the importance and necessity of the material things of life, places its faith in the spiritual aspect of life, holding that the souls of men are in need of high ideals and creeds, and that noble spirits cannot be satisfied by bread alone but require a certain nourishment which exemplifies the genuine dignity of existence.

To sum up, then, Arab nationalism is an eternal message emanating from the character of the Arab nation and is inspired by Arab history. Historical inevitability calls upon it to achieve its material and spiritual purposes, both present and future.

It is the mission and the rallying point of Arab nationalists who have faith in its requirements, believing it to be the only road to salvation, dignity, peace, justice, and stability.

5. The Historical Factor in the Formation of Nationalism*

Sati' al-Husri

Since the mid-1950s, Abu Khaldun Sati' al-Husri (b. 1879) has been the most influential contemporary writer on Arab nationalism. Born in Aleppo, al-Husri studied in Istanbul before World War I and became an official in

*Extract from Sati' al-Husri, Hawla al-qawmiyya al-'arabiyya [Concerning Arab Nationalism] (Beirut: Dar al-'ilm lil-malayin, 1961), pp. 104–5, 108–10.

the Turkish Ministry of Education. After the war, he associated himself with the Arab nationalist movement, as represented by King Faysal, whom he followed from Damascus to Baghdad, where al-Husri became the head of general education. Banished from Iraq because of his involvement in Rashid Ali's pro-Nazi coup of 1941, al-Husri went to Beirut, then to Cairo. In 1947, he became the head of the cultural section of the Arab League, a position he held until his retirement.

Al-Husri believed that nationalism is a question of belonging to and identifying with a group, and that history and especially language create such conditions. Departing from his early views, he increasingly advocated the fusion of the individual into the nation, even if this meant sacrificing the individual's freedom. It is interesting that al-Husri's friend, Ziya Gökalp, a prominent Turkish nationalist, arrived at more or less the same conclusion, following not the logic of free thought but the rise and evolution of the political state capable of acting on behalf, and fulfilling the ideals, of a nation. (Al-Hursi differed from Gökalp on the purposes of education.) This identification of the individual with his political group has a religious mystical significance that is rooted, as Sylvia G. Haim remarked, in the "union of the worshiper with the Godhead" of the Islamic mystics (Arab Nationalism: An Anthology [Berkeley, Calif.: University of California Press, 1962], p. 44). *Haim claims that using a religious concept for a secular purpose is al-Husri's great innovation. Actually, Ziya Gökalp, a mystic in his own right, had stated this even earlier, and far more explicitly, than al-Husri. Gökalp discussed the obligations stemming from life in a community and stated that "one must develop a will powerful enough to overcome individual ambitions. In short, the individual must 'negate' himself in the community before he may 'survive' in it. . . . In this way a self-seeking being becomes a sacrificing citizen." (See translation in Niyazi Berkes,* Turkish Nationalism and Western Civilization [New York: Columbia University Press, 1959], p. 188.)

Both al-Husri and Gökalp present similar arguments about the differences between their respective nationalisms and Islamic universalism and about the place of language in nationalism. With his convincing style and argumentation, al-Husri has continually and successfully argued against the views of those Arab writers who excluded Egypt from the proposed Arab state or did not consider it Arabic. The emergence of Egypt as the center of Arab nationalism and her advocacy of the union of all Arabs have greatly facilitated the popularization of al-Husri's ideas. Their popularization was also possible because of al-Husri's sense of political realism and his ability to distinguish between the practical and the utopian. These characteristics resulted not only from al-Husri's being "marginal to the process he was describing" (as Albert Hourani puts it) but also from his knowledge of the history of European nationalism and his keen understanding of the Turkish experience in building a national state.

On al-Husri, see L. M. Kenny, "Sati' al-Husri's Views on Arab Nationalism," Middle East Journal 17 (Summer 1963), 231–56, and Albert Hourani, Arab Thought in the Liberal Age, 1798–1939 (London and New York: Oxford University Press, 1962), pp. 311–17. Unfortunately, the scanty Western writings on al-Husri ignore his intellectual activity in Istanbul and the Rumelian provinces and his many publications in Turkish, including his basic articles on education published in the review Muallim (Teacher) in 1915. For al-Husri's activities in Turkey, see Hilmi Ziya Ülken, Türkiye'de Çağdaş, Düşünce Tarihi [History of Contemporary Thought in Turkey], vol. 1 (Konya: Selçuk yayinlari, 1966), 269–92. The best source on al-Husri is William L. Cleveland, The Making of an Arab Nationalist (Princeton: Princeton University Press, 1972).

Al-Husri's writings on nationalism have been reprinted several times. Mention should be made of Ara' wa-ahadith fi al-wataniyya wa-al-qawmiyya [Views and Speeches on Patriotism and Nationalism] (Cairo: Matba'at al-risala, 1944), and Muhudarat fi nushu' al-fikra al-qawmiyya [Lectures on the Origins of the Nationalist Idea], 3d ed. (Beirut: Dar al-'ilm lil-malayin, 1956). In Ma hiya al-qawmiyya [What Is Nationalism?] (Beirut: Dar al-'ilm lil-malayin, 1959), and in the following extract based on his prior writings, al-Husri restates his views on the foundations of Arab nationalism and on who is an Arab.

A young man once relayed to me a criticism he had heard over the radio of my book *What is Nationalism?* The critic apparently said that, in the concluding sentence of my book I wrote that "The basic factor in the formation of the nation and nationalism is the unity of the nation and of its history." The critic added that, in a book of 250 pages, I had not touched upon the unity of history prior to this phase.

I was astonished. I opened the book and read the following sentences. . . .

A common descent cannot by any means be considered as among the distinguishing characteristics of a nation. . . .
　　In fact, the sons of a single nation consider themselves as kinsmen and brothers, as though they descended from a common stock. In general, they call their ancestors 'grandfathers' [ajdad]. But the relationship that they feel toward their ancestors is spiritual. It is a relationship that is born of various social bonds, especially a common language and history, but that in no way denotes a relationship of blood or descent (p. 45).

It may be noted that I have here mentioned history together with language. Furthermore, having explained this spiritual relationship, I wrote: "In any case, a common descent must form no part of any definition of the nation. It would be more appropriate to substitute a common history instead. The importance of a common history in the formation of this spiritual relationship and in the creation of the widespread myth of a common descent is paramount" (p. 46). Here again I wrote about history, citing it as one of the most important constituents of this spiritual relationship, and urging that it should occupy a special place in the definition of a nation, instead of a common descent and blood, which must be discarded from such a definition.

Thus, it is patently false to claim that I did not discuss the question of a common history until the concluding sentence of my book. As a matter of fact, I did not revert to a discussion of the two passages quoted above, because this problem was never a subject for debate among scholars. My book *What is Nationalism?* was devoted to a critical review of the various theories. Furthermore, in my other works—especially in my *Patriotism and Nationalism* [al-Wataniyya wa-al-qawmiyya]—I have explained the role of history in the formation of nationalism.

Who Is an Arab?: A Reappraisal

In my book *Views and Speeches on Arab Nationalism* [i.e., *Views and Speeches on Patriotism and Nationalism*], I described an argument that took place in the lecture hall of the Society for Arab Unity concerning the question, "Who Is an Arab?"

The lecturer who opened the discussion said, "An Arab is a man who speaks Arabic and wants to be an Arab." I objected to the latter part of his statement. "Suppose," I said, "a fellow is an Arab but ignores this fact— what then?" The lecturer replied, "If he does not want to be an Arab, how can you consider him as one? Would it not be better to make the will a condition for being an Arab?"

This is how I answered: "When we find a man who disowns, and takes no pride, in the fact that he is an Arab, even though he is Arabic-speaking and belongs to an Arab nation, we must discover the reasons for his attitude. It may be out of ignorance, in which case we should tell him the truth. It may be that he is deluded, in which case we should direct him to the true path. It may be that he is too selfish, in which case we must work to curtail his egoism. Whatever the reason, we must not say he is not an Arab as long as he does not wish to be an Arab but disowns and despises his Arabism. He is an Arab, whether he likes it or not, whether he accepts it or not—at the present time. He may be ignorant, stupid, ungrateful, or treacherous, but he is an Arab all the same—an Arab who has lost his sensibility, his emotions, and maybe even his conscience" (pp. 65–66).

It appears that the view I briefly outlined above escaped the notice of some and did not alter the opinions of others. Some writers and scholars still claim that an Arab is "a man who speaks Arabic and wants to be an Arab." This has led me, on several occasions, to reopen the controversy and to express my views on the matter in greater detail. A man once put forward the following objection: "I say very frankly that I cannot consider a person to be an Arab when I see him disowning his Arabism and unwilling to be an Arab." I decided to adopt a new approach in the hope of convincing him, so I said, "I would like to know what our attitude would be toward someone who, having previously disowned his Arabism, says 'I am an Arab.' Should we say, 'He was not an Arab but then became one' or should we not rather say, 'He was not conscious of his Arabism, but when he discovered his true Arab identity, he recognized this fact'?" Having put this question to him, I followed it up with references to factual examples: "Two years ago," I said, "I read an article by Ahmad Bahaeddin [Baha' al-Din], in which he admitted that he was once very far from Arabism. He then related the particular circumstances and events that made him change his mind and become conscious of his Arab identity. Last year, I read an article by Salah 'Abd al-Sabur in which he eloquently and candidly described the development of his inner self and the change that came upon his views and emotions and restored him to Arabism.

"Here then," I continued, "we have frank confessions from two of our ablest younger writers. Given these circumstances, should we say about them that they were not Arabs but then became Arab at the moment when they published their confessions and explained the change that had come over them? It is obvious that this would be absurd. Faced with such circumstances, we are, logically speaking, obliged to say that the fellow was unconscious of his Arabism but then came to discover his Arab identity."

I noticed that the objecter was impressed by this argument. Nevertheless, not wishing to abandon his former position, he added: "But these are exceptional cases. Should we base our judgment on exceptions?" "No," I said, "they are not exceptions. I mentioned these two confessions because they appeared in print. But I assure you that I heard similar confessions in conversations with many writers and thinkers. Furthermore, if we closely examine these articles by 'Abd al-sabur and Bahaeddin we shall find that they mirror, not only the writer's own feelings, but the feelings and sentiments of a whole generation."

III. REGIONAL AND LOCAL NATIONALISM

6. The Shu'ubiyya and Arab Nationalism*

'Abd al-Hadi al-Fikayki

'Abd al-Hadi al-Fikayki, a Shi'ite from Baghdad, was closely associated with the Ba'th Party in Iraq. Representing current thought among the extreme nationalists, his writing expresses resentment against liberal nationalists, Fabian socialists, and Westernists. Al-Fikayki finds it difficult to explain the conflict between Egypt's attachment to her own past and her leadership role in the drive for unity based on an Islamic interpretation of Arabism. Consequently, he adopts the expedient viewpoint of the polemicists—that Egyptians were Arabs who came out of the Arabian Peninsula thousands of years ago and established the Pharaonic civilization. The racial implications of this view are too evident to warrant further discussion. It is also interesting to note that al-Fikayki refers to the Shu'ubiyya (discussed in Chapter II) as a disruptive movement as it was understood by the orthodox in the past. The Shu'ubiyya is considered an attack on the Arab aspect of Islam and on Arab nationalism.

Local Communism: The Climax of Anti-Arabism and Its Extension

No sooner had the Arabs cast off Turkish domination and the danger of Pan-Turanism than they fell victim to the great imperialist powers, following the Sykes-Picot Treaty of 1916 which divided the Arab world into several weak states.

At that time, Communism was still new in the Arab world. The anti-Arabs wanted to use it for their own intrigues as they saw in it the best cover for their malice against the Arabs. Communism was encouraged and supported by them. In support of our view, we notice that the leaders of the Arab Communist parties were, for the most part, non-Arabs who bore a bitter grudge against Arab nationalism and unity.

Local Communism proved, in effect, to be more than a continuation of the anti-Arab movements that had plagued the Arabs ever since the

*Extract from 'Abd al-Hadi al-Fikayki, al-Shu'ubiyya wa-al-qawmiyya al-'arabiyya [The Shu'ubiyya and Arab Nationalism] (Beirut: Dar al-Adab, 1961), pp. 97–98, 100, 102–11. (The titles of subdivisions in the extract have been added.—ED.)

emergence of Pharaonic language, and an "Egyptian nationalism" divorced from Arab Egypt and its stuggle for Arab nationalism. Thus we see Salama Musa calling upon the Arabs of Egypt to substitute Latin in place of Arabic characters in the Arabic language.[1]

He went so far as to advocate, quite openly, the abandonment of Arab society, when he wrote, "Let us turn our faces toward Europe." Either becasue he was ignorant of, or (what is more likely) because he ignored Egypt's Arab character, he considered Egypt a part of Europe, justifying this astonishing claim on the basis that Egypt is situated on the shores of the Mediterranean Sea. In his book *Today and Tomorrow* [*al-Yawm wa-al-ghad* (Cairo: al-Mat-ba'a al-'asriyya, 1928)], we find him, in the chapter entitled "The Search for the Egyptian Nation," casting doubts on Egypt's Arab character and mounting an exaggerated attack an Arab civilization, preparatory to his advocating closer ties with the West. To those who call Salama Musa's thinking "progressive," we answer that it is precisely the theories of Musa and like-minded writers which have retarded the progress of Arab consciousness in Egypt, helped to keep the Arab youth of Egypt away from their Arab society, and erected a cultural barrier between them and Arab culture and revolutionary movements elsewhere in the Arab countries.

The theories of Salama Musa and other writers of his school concerning Arabism are indeed reactionary. They obstinately propagate error and give currency to ideas that are dangerous to the Arab revolutionary movement. We do not deny Musa's deep influence on youth and on the intelligentsia. But we cannot also deny that his call, for example, to replace the tarboosh [or fez] with the European hat is an absurd mimicry of inessentials. Can we really believe that Musa was unaware of the strong nationalist bond between Egypt and the rest of the Arab countries? Is it possible that such a prominent writer never came across those nationalist bonds, those spiritual, literary, historical, and social links that bind Egypt to the Arab world? Did he ever stop to think why Egypt was called the sheath [literally, quiver of the Arabs (*kinanat al-'arab*)]? He and his followers should have championed an Arab, not a European, league. He should rather have taught the Egyptians about their genuine Arab character and about the close national link that binds them to their Arab brethren, instead of waving the European hat in place of the Turkish tarboosh. Had this school of writers that talked about "Egyptian" and "Pharaonic" nationalism not included some of Egypt's leading men of thought, we might have found excuses for them, such as their misunderstanding of Arabism or perhaps their lack of culture or knowledge of Arab history. Those champions of "Egyptian" nationalism, those enemies of Egypt's Arab character, went so far as to hold a conference in Asyut and Cairo in 1911, in order to clarify their theories and propagate their teaching. Their message was an anti-Arabist movement in disguise. Thus 'Abd al-'Aziz Jawish . . . made a distinction between the Arab and Egyptian nations, . . . [and] Muhammad Magdi . . . regarded the Egyptian nation as comprising Egypt's Pharaonic population only.[2]

Had these scholars merely been ignorant of Arabism and upholders of a narrow regionalism, the harm engendered would have been mild. Not content with this, they proceeded, like other anti-Arabs, to attack the Arab national liberation movement. Muhammad Farid, in an article published in the magazine *The Sciences* [al-'Ulum], describes Arab nationalism as "trivial" and "the work of devils."[3] In another article, Ahmad Lutfi al-Sayyid, in his usual argumentative, conservative style, denied both the merits and the future of Arab endeavor.[4] He even denied the existence of an Arab problem. He protested against the concern some Egyptians had shown regarding the Italian attack on Arab Libya and took them to task when they collected donations for the benefit of the Arab victims. On May 5, 1950, *The Illustrated Magazine* [al-Musawwar] published an interview with Lutfi al-Sayyid, in which he said:

> I was always a firm upholder of the Egyptian character of Egyptians. Some of them claimed that they were Arabs, others that they were Turks of Circassians . . . We Egyptians must hold fast to our Egyptian character and must belong to no other nation save the Egyptian, irrespective of our Hijazi, Syrian, Circassian, or other origin. We must preserve our nationalism, honor ourselves and our fatherland, and belong to no other nation . . .

'Abdallah al-Nadim in the magazine *The Teacher* [al-Ustadh] once described the fighters for the Arab cause as "stupid."[5] Among other writers who held similar views in their writings were Dr. Taha Husayn and Fathi Radwan, who championed a revival of the Phoenician language in *The Journal* [al-Majalla].

I may add here that I do not personally object to pride being taken in Pharaonic civilization, nor would I attempt to denigrate it. What is truly regrettable is that the enemies of the Arab liberation movement have hit upon this current as a means for disseminating their evil propaganda and justifying their anti-Arab views. Indeed, I personally consider the Pharaonic to be a part of Arab culture.

In answer to those who strive to conceal their anti-Arabism under the false pretense of preserving the Pharaonic heritage, let me quote the words of Sati'al-Husri:[6]

> Egypt has forsaken the Pharaonic religion without destroying the Sphinx. It has abandoned the Pharaonic language without destroying the Pyramids . . . The Pyramids, along with all other Pharaonic monuments, have not prevented Egypt from achieving a total linguistic union with the rest of the Arab countries . . . The deep nationalist currents that have swept over Egypt during the past centuries, creating new movements in their path, have effaced its old religion and language—despite the Pyramids and the Sphinx.

> Egypt does not need either to destroy or to conceal any of its old monuments prior to adopting the policy believed in by supporters of Arab unity.
>
> The champions of Arab unity have not called upon the Egyptians, either implicitly or explicitly, to abandon their Egyptian character. They have merely required them to add a comprehensive Arab sentiment to their own peculiar Egyptian one. They ask them to work for the Arab cause in addition to working for the Egyptian one. They have not and will not tell Egypt, "Forget yourself," but rather, "Enrich yourself by working to unite those who speak your own language."

This anti-Arab current will never be able to efface the Arab character of Egypt or to shake the faith in Arabism that has swept the hearts of the Arabs of the United Arab Republic.

Despite the anti-Arab inclinations and campaigns of certain writers against Arab nationalism and unity, Egypt (the U.A.R.) has now become the standard bearer of Arab nationalism and of the struggle to achieve freedom, unity, and socialism for the Arabs. This is the best proof of Egypt's Arab character and the secret of its progress.

Those regionalists who do not wish to look beyond Egypt's frontiers to the wider Arab world and who, in their dogmatism and their ignorance of Arabism, declared that "Egypt is for the Egyptians" and "Egypt comes first"—those men must now admit, if they are sincere, that Egypt is for the Arab cause and that Arabism comes first. They must come to recognize that the Egyptians are Arabs by language, culture, history, religion, and common nationalist sentiment and will. Furthermore, there is abundant historical evidence for the Arab origin of the Pharaohs, which can silence all dissent and deception. The Arabs of ancient Egypt, the Pharaohs, belonged to an Arab-Semitic stock whose original home was the Arabian Peninsula. There is evidence to prove that they settled in Egypt after a migratory wave stretching from Chaldea to the Nile Delta. Indeed, the majority of the Arab peoples living in the Arab world are descended from a single stock, the Semitic or ancient Arab. In this context, the famous French Egyptologist Maspero has written, "The ethnic ties linking the ancient Egyptians, Arabs, Phoenicians, and Chaldeans are very close. The ancient Egyptians were Semites who moved away from their original home before the others."

Lebanese Nationalism, the West, and Charles Malik[7]

In Lebanon, the imperialists chose an anti-Arab idol, whom they called a philosopher, and trained him to be hostile to Arab nationalism, Arab history, culture, and civilization. This was the man [Charles H. Malik] about whom Dr. Muhammad Majdhub wrote, "The West picked upon a mouthpiece who would serve their purposes. He was chosen as a purveyor of poisonous ideological and political views and an agent for their designs upon the free nations. The West loaded him with gifts, conferred titles and decorations upon him, and exalted him."

When the imperialists had made him a cabinet minister, he issued a statement that is replete with malice against Arabism, Arab history, thought, and culture. He wrote:

> Our ideal is to enter seriously into the positive Western heritage of thought. In this heritage we find the complete truth . . . This heritage is the sole historical arbiter of existence . . . It represents the living, active, and ultimate entity and every entity outside it inclines either to nothingness or to being connected with it in a master-slave relationship. To enter upon this heritage means to adopt it without qualification so that we can become parts of it and vice versa . . . One of our noblest ideals, then, is to arrive at a time when Arab thought will be perfectly at home in Oxford, Freiburg, the Sorbonne, and Harvard.

We do not object to the Arab intellectual's acquaintance with the honest intellectual heritage of the West or to his adoption of knowledge useful to the Arab nation. Indeed, we call upon all Arab intellectuals to acquaint themselves with Western thought, on condition that they embrace only what is essential and useful to the Arab peoples, whose culture and outlook would thereby be broadened and would contribute to the Arab intellectual renaissance.

But we cannot possible tolerate the boasts of an anti-Arab, who uses this cultural exchange as a means of attacking Arab thought and culture and of making the Western heritage of thought the sole origin for the culture of the Arab man.

This new anti-Arab movement aims not so much to serve the Arabs as to create a generation who would disown their Arab character and Arab civilization, and deny the splendid Arab intellectual heritage, which was itself a rich source of inspiration for the Western culture that Malik raves about in Lebanon today.

It may be noticed, in conclusion, how all anti-Arab movements, both ancient and modern, have adopted a common policy in attacking Arabism—a policy which differs only in methods, in accordance with the circumstances and the degree of Arab consciousness.

If we were to summarize the objectives of anti-Arabism we would find that it concentrates upon attacking Arab nationalism, perverting Arab history, emphasizing Arab regression, denying Arab culture, being hostile to everything Arab, and being in league with all the enemies of Arab nationalism. In all its various roles, anti-Arabism has adopted a policy of intellectual conquest as a means of penetrating Arab society and combatting Arab nationalism. At the same time, these anti-Arab movements, at all stages of their existence, unwittingly helped Arab consciousness to appear. The Arabs rallied around their Arabism, defended and took pride in their civilized heritage, and obstinately withstood the attacks of anti-Arabism and imperialism. Anti-Arabism produced a reaction among the Arabs and was partly responsible for their literary and intellectual renaissance.

Notes

1. Salama Musa (1887–1959), a Christian Copt, is well known for his advocacy of anti-imperialist socialism and of Egyptian nationalism inspired by the Fabians as well as by liberal thinkers. Salama argued in favor of reforms that would accompany independence. His autobiography, *Tarbiyat Salama Musa* [The Education of Salama Musa] (Cairo: Mu'assasat al-Khanji, 1949), which has been translated into French and English (see L. O. Schuman, *The Education of Salama Musa* [Leiden: E. J. Brill, 1961]), gives an excellent picture of educational and cultural conditions in Egypt at the end of the nineteenth century and at the beginning of the twentieth century. Salama repeatedly criticized the "purist" attitude of Arab intellectuals, the difficulty in writing Arabic, and the obsession with the linguistic past. He advocated the introduction of Latin characters as the possible avenue for a basic change in the Arab outlook. See his article "Arab Language Problems," translated in *Middle Eastern Affairs* 6 (February 1955), and reproduced in Benjamin Rivlin and J. S. Szyliowicz, eds., *The Contemporary Middle East* (New York: Random House, 1965) pp. 325–28. See also K. S. Abu Jaber (Jabir), "Salama Musa: Precursor of Arab Socialism," *Middle East Journal* 20 (Spring 1966), 196–206, and Mohamed-Saleh Sfia, "Egypte: Impacte de l'idéologie socialiste sur l'intelligentsia arabe," in *La Deuxième Internationale et l'Orient*, ed. Georges Haupt and Madeleine Reberioux (Paris: Editions Cujas, 1967), pp. 409–38.
2. These authors belong to an earlier period, almost at the beginning of the twentieth century, when local liberal and Western-oriented nationalism was on the rise. The fact that they are still remembered indicates that their influence persists.
3. Possibly Muhammad Tal'a Farid, who was Minister of Education in the Sudan in 1962.
4. Ahmad Lutfi al-Sayyid (1872–1963), member of a rich landowning family in Egypt, began his political career as a nationalist but soon adopted a moderate nationalism opposed to Pan-Islamism. He was founder and editor of *al-Jarida* [The Daily], 1907–16, which expressed the viewpoint of the Umma (Nation) Party. It was the party of the upper social groups who wanted to stay on good terms with the British, as opposed to Mustafa Kamil's extreme nationalists, who fought the British. Al-Sayyid was, with the exception of short periods, the head of the state university in Cairo from 1924 to 1941. He was instrumental in shaping the Egyptian intellectuals' viewpoint through books and especially through newspaper articles. Al-Sayyid believed that freedom—meaning chiefly freedom from state control—was the natural condition of man. He

regarded utility as the foundation of all sentiments, actions, and human society. His main purpose in gaining freedom was to free reason from imposed authority and to liberate the individual from the uncritical acceptance of thoughts and ideas on authority. Al-Sayyid rejected Pan-Islamism as well as attempts to deprive the Egyptians of their national identity. Since this identity had a Pharaonic core on which were grafted various influences, Egyptians would not lose their national personality by borrowing from the West. These ideas were expressed by al-Sayyid as early as 1913–14. See *al-Munktak-habat* [Selections], 2 vols. (Cairo: Maktabat al-Anglo-Misriya, 1937–45). As late as 1950, as al-Fikayki resentfully states, Lufti al-Sayyid still defended the Egyptians' own national personality.

Taha Husayn (b. 1889), a leading Egyptian novelist, essayist, literary historian, and educator, as well as defender of the Pharaonic past, was brought up under al-Sayyid's influence and shared his views. In fact, in 1926, when Husayn published a book on pre-Islamic poetry in which he upset some Islamic dogma, al-Sayyid, as head of the university, defended Husayn against the attacks of conservatives and religious leaders. Taha Husayn's abandonment of Egyptian nationalism in favor of a broader Arab nationalism seemed to have al-Fikayki's attention. For background developments, see Marcell Colombe, *L'Evolution de l'Egypte, 1924–1950* (Paris: Maisonneuve, 1951).

5. 'Abdallah al-Nadim (1844–96), born in Alexandria, joined revolutionary movements in his early life. He published several reviews supporting the nationalists and promoted programs of social and educational development. After the revolutions of 1882, al-Nadim eluded the authorities for nine years by hiding in villages and towns: he thus acquired first-hand information about the life of the lower classes. Beginning in 1892, his writings were often published as social satire, especially in the review *al-Ustadh* [The Teacher]. Later, he was invited to Istanbul and left Egyptian politics.

Al-Nadim was both an Egyptian nationalist and a populist intellectual. He wanted Egyptians to understand Europeans but also to appreciate their own values, rights, language, and religion. Whether Muslim or Christian, Egyptians were tied together by national bonds superior to religious allegiance. "Preserve Egypt for Egyptians" was his motto. His chief writings are collected in *Sulafat al Nadim* [The Choicest Wine (or, The Drinking Companion) of *al-Nadim*], 2 vols. (Cairo: Amin Hindiyya, 1897–1901).

6. For a discussion of Sati' al-Husri, see section II–5.

7. Charles Habib Malik (b. 1906) was a well-known Lebanese teacher, statesman, diplomat, and liberal thinker whose generally pro-Western attitude has earned him the enmity of extreme Arab nationalists. Malik's rather liberal recognition of Islam's place in present-day Arab nationalism was short of the total surrender desired by Islamist Arab Nationalists.

7. The Principles of Syrian Nationalism and Its Party*

Antun Saadeh

Antun Saadeh (Sa'da) (1904–49), the founder of Syrian regional national-ism, was the son of a physician of Greek Orthodox faith who migrated to South America. Saadeh returned to Lebanon in 1929, and for a time tutored German at the American University of Beirut. He developed the idea that the Syrian nation differed from the Arab nation and consisted of a unique historical synthesis of Arabs, Phoenicians, and other groups who lived in Syria, Lebanon, Iraq, Jordan, and part of Palestine and who therefore must be united under the flag of a Greater Syria. This nation would form a homogeneous society in which traditional group loyalties, feudal land relations, and capitalism would be abolished and religion separated from the state. These ideas, which Saadeh regarded as a scientific national philosophy and made mandatory learning for his disciples, were embodied in a program (reproduced here) that formed the ideological basis of the Syrian Social Nationalist Party † (SSNP) and had a lasting impact on the thinking of some Arab intellectuals. The party began as a secret organization in 1932 and was discovered by the authorities in November, 1935. Saadeh and his lieutenants were arrested, charged with plotting against the state, and sentenced to prison. The SSNP attracted both Muslim and Christian Arab intellectuals, for its prime purpose was independence and the assertion of national identity.

Saadeh left for America in 1938, but came back to Lebanon in 1947 and engaged in politics. In 1949, after attempting an unsuccessful coup in Lebanon, he fled to Syria. The Syrian dictator Husni Za'im received him well at first, but then handed him over to the Lebanese authorities, who, within a twenty-four–hour period in July, 1949, tried and executed him. (The Lebanese Government tried to justify its hasty and much criticized action in Qadiyat al-hizb al-qawmi [The Case of the Nationalist Party] [Beirut: Ministry of Information, 1949]).

After 1945, the idea of a Greater Syria, which was the backbone of Saadeh's nationalism, no longer appealed to the Christians of Lebanon, who

*Extract from *The Syrian Social Nationalist Doctrine: The Principles and Aims of the Syrian Social Nationalist Party* (Beirut: n.p., 1949), pp. 21–33.

† Also known as the Syrian National Party.

rightly feared that they would be lost in the Muslim majority. Nor did the idea appeal to Muslim Arab nationalists, who had begun to think in terms of a union of the entire Arab-speaking world. Thus, Saadeh's brand of totalitarian, corporative, antireligious nationalism was overwhelmed by the rising tide of Arabism. Unlike the Egyptian nationalism defended for long and then abandoned (e.g., by Taha Husayn) in favor of Arabism, Saadeh's Syrian nationalism is still effective. It appeals to those groups who are interested in maintaining Syria's national existence and making it the center of a large Arab political entity. It also appeals to extremist secularists, including some Christian Arabs, who feel that neither Islam nor any other religion should be made the basis of nationalism, since they consider national bonds, such as language and history, stronger than religion.

It may rightly be said that Saadeh's condemnation of feudalism and his call for economic progress and social justice formulated within the context of secular nationalism and corporatism have been preserved and reshaped under the new ideology of Arab socialism. There is a striking similarity between the principles of the Syrian party and the writings of some contemporary socialists. Finally, in his paradoxical manner, Saadeh's missionary appeal on behalf of independence left its imprint on all subsequent Arab revolutionary movements. Many of Saadeh's followers joined the Ba'th; and then, after Arab nationalism began to lose its secular character, supported President Nasser, or joined other socialist parties. In recent years the party was legalized and moved to populism and revolutionism.

Saadeh's continuing influence is well illustrated by the repeated publication of his writings and the continuation of political activities inspired by his writings. SSNP was active in Syria until 1955, when it was banned and its rank and file driven underground. Many of its leaders came to Lebanon and continued to work as the Parti Populaire Syrien. The well-organized and trained groups of this party provided vital armed assistance to the Lebanese Government in preventing a takeover by Pan-Arabists in 1958, and the party was allowed to act freely. But its almost successful coup on December 31, 1961, led to its being banned. The prosecution's case presented to the military tribunal in 1963 showed clearly that the party had preserved its original Greater Syrian ideology. See al-Hayat, October 8, 1963; sections translated in Walid Khalidi and Yusuf Ibish, eds., Arab Political Documents, 1963 (Beirut: Slim Press, 1964), pp. 415–20.

A fairly complete list of Saadeh's writings may be found in Fahim I. Qubain, Inside the Arab Mind (Arlington, Va.: Universal Printers and Lithographers of America, 1960), pp. 45–48. For background, see Stephen Hemsley Longrigg, Syria and Lebanon Under French Mandate (London and New York: Oxford University Press, 1958), and Albert H. Hourani, Syria and Lebanon: A Political Essay (London: Oxford University Press, 1946). The best and most comprehensive treatment is Labib Zuwiyya

Yamak, The Syrian Social Nationalist Part: In Ideological Analysis (Cambridge, Mass.: Harvard University Press, 1966). Antun Saadeh's works continue to be published. A new edition was published in Beirut, in 1972. See also a work by his disciple Abbud Abbud, Falsifat Nushu' al Hizb al-Suri al gawmi al-ijtimā-i [Birth Philosophy of the SSNP] (Beirut: al-Kulliya Hizbiyya 1973).

The principles of the party reproduced here were written by Saadeh and published in 1932; they were translated into English in 1943 and revised and enlarged in 1949.

Syria represents to us our character, our talents, and our ideal life; it signifies for us an outlook on life, art, and the universe; it is the symbol of our honor, glory, and final destiny. This is why to us Syria is above every individual consideration, above every partial interest.

The Reform Principles

The First Principle: *Separation between religion and state.*

The greatest obstacle in the way of our national unity and our national welfare is the attachment of our religious institutions to temporal authority, and their claim that there is sufficient justification for the religious centers of influence to exercise sovereignty within the state and to dominate, wholly or at least partly, the functions of political authority. But the truth is that the great struggles for human liberation have always arisen between the interests of nations on the one side and the interests of religious institutions on the other, the latter claiming the divine right to rule and to exercise the judiciary functions. This principle of divine right is a dangerous one and has enslaved many peoples to the point of exhaustion. It was used not only by the religious institutions but also by the sacred royalty, which claimed to derive its authority from the will of God and the sanction of the religious institutions, but not from the people.

In the state where there is no separation between the state and the church, we find the government ruling in the place of God, and not of the people; but wherever the excessive dominance of the state by religious institutions is diminished, we find the latter always trying to preserve themselves as civil authorities within the state.

Theocracy, or the religious state, is opposed to the principle of nationhood, because it stands for the dominance over the whole community of believers by the religious institutions, as do the papacy and the caliphate. The pope, for example, is the prince of all the believers wherever they may happen to be, and the same is true of the caliph. Religion as such recognizes no nation and no national interests because it is concerned with a community of belief dominated by a central religious institution. It is only from such a point of view that religion can become a temporal, political, and administrative affair, monopolized by the sacred religious institution. This is the temporal aspect of religion, and religion was suited for it when mankind was still in his savage stage or close to it, but not in our modern civilization.

It is against this aspect of religion that the Syrian Social Nationalist Party fights, not against religious or theological thoughts and philosophies which deal with the mysteries of the soul and immortality, the Creator and the supernatural.

The concept of pan-religious political community is opposed to nationalism in general and to Syrian Social Nationalism in particular, because the adherence of the Syrian Christians to a pan-Christian political movement makes of them a group with special interests discordant with the interests of other religious groups within the country and, on the other hand, exposes their own interests to the danger of dissolution in the interests of other peoples to whom they are tied by religious bonds. In the same way, the adherence of the Syrian Muslims to a pan-Islamic move- ment exposes their interests to coming in conflict with the interests of their countrymen of other faiths and to becoming lost in the interests of the greater community, over which they have no control, and which is always in danger of disintegration in the struggle for political power on the part of the constitutive nations, as has happened in the 'Abbasid period and in the Turkish period. The call for pre-religious movements can lead only to the disintegration of national unity and to failure in the struggle for national existence.

Neither nationalism nor the national state is based on religion. This is why we find that the two greatest religious communities in the world, Christianity and Islam, did not succeed in being temporal or political communities as they did in being spiritual and cultural communities. A religious spiritual community is not a danger nor need have any fear; as for the religious temporal-political community, it is a great danger to the existence of nations and to the interests of their peoples. This was clearly demonstrated by the last Turkish regime.

National unity cannot be attained by making the national state a religious state, because in such a state the rights and interests are religious rights and interests, enjoyed exclusively by the dominant religious com- munity. Where rights and interests are the rights and interests of a religious group, there can be no realization for those national rights and interests which are common to all the children of the one nation. And without the unity of interests and of rights there can be no unity of duties and no unified national will.

With this legal national philosophy the Syrian Social Nationalist Party has succeeded in laying down the foundations for national unity and in bringing about its actual realization.

The Second Principle: *Prohibition of the clergy from interference in political and judicial matters of national concern.*

This principle is implied by the previous one, the only reason for stating it explicitly being due to what we have already stated concerning the surreptitious ways by which religious institutions attempt the attainment or preservation of temporal authority even where the separation between church and state is admitted in principle. It is meant to put an end to the indirect interference by religious institutions in the course of temporal and political affairs with the hope of directing matters in favor of their interests.

This principle specifies what is meant by separation of church from state, so that the meaning of that principle may not remain ambiguous and subject to false interpretations; because the reform must not be restricted to the political sphere alone but must extend to the legal-judiciary sphere as well.

It is not possible to have well founded national civil status and common rights when a varied and discordant judiciary is based on, and divided among, the different religious sects. This is an evil which stands in the way of unifying the laws that are necessary for the following of one national order.

It is necessary, therefore, that the Social Nationalist state have a unified judiciary and one system of laws. For this unity makes the citizens feel and know that they are all equal before the law.

We cannot possibly have one and the same mentality and at the same time act according to different and conflicting conceptions which are incompatible with the oneness of our social community.

The Third Principle: *Removal of the barriers among the different sects.*

Undoubtedly there are, among the different sects and denominations of our nation, traditional barriers not necessitated by religion. These discordant traditions derive from the organizations of our religious and denominational institutions and they have exercised a tremendous influence in weakening the social and economic unity of the people and delaying our national revival. As long as these traditional barriers remain, our calls for freedom and for independence will continue to be cries of pain and sighs of ineptitude. It is not proper that we should know the illness and continue to ignore the cure. We the Syrian Social Nationalists are not like the quacks who call for union while ignoring the true ties of union and who shout for unity while concealing a different purpose in their hearts.

Every nation which wills to live a free and independent life in which it can realize its ideals must be a nation with a strong spiritual unity. And a strong spiritual unity cannot develop while every one of the religious groups of the nation leads a secluded existence within a separate social-legal circle making of it a mentality independent from the mentalities of the other groups, hence leading to variance in purposes and aims.

National unity cannot be realized except by the removal of all causes of dissension. And the social-legal barriers between the sects and denominations of the same nation obstruct the realization of a material-spiritual national unity.

Unity is something real, not fictitious, so replace not reality with a fiction.

As a nation we must stand one and united under the sun, and not as separate groups and heterogeneous factions of discordant mentalities. The existence of the present social and legal barriers among our different sects means the persistence of this incurable sectarian cancer in the body of the nation. We must break down these barriers in order to render social unity a deep-rooted fact, and to set up the Social Nationalist order which will bestow health and power upon the nation.

The Fourth Principle: *The abolition of feudalism, the organization of national economy on the basis of production, the security of the rights of labour, and the protection of the interests of the nation and of the state.*

Is there in Syria a feudal order? In one sense one could say that there is no feudalism in Syria, because feudalism is not legally recognized; but in another sense we find that there exists in different parts of Syria a feudalistic state, both from an economic and from a social point of view. There are in Syria real feudal estates which involve a considerable part of the national wealth and which cannot be considered as private property in any sense of the word. These estates are under the disposal of Beks, or feudal lords, who manage these properties or neglect them as they choose, without any consideration for the national interests. Some of them neglect their feudal properties and go to such excesses in their mismanagement as to lead to financial difficulties which end by reducing the land to the possession of foreign banks, foreign capital, and foreign plutocracy. The Syrian Social Nationalist Party considers it very necessary to put an end to this state of affairs, which threatens national sovereignty.

On some of these feudal lands live hundreds and even thousands of peasants in a miserable state of slavery. Such a state of affairs is not only inhuman, but also endangers the safety of the state, because it leaves a large section of the laboring and fighting people in a state of weakness, and a considerable part of the national wealth in a state of underdevelopment. The Syrian Social Nationalist Party cannot keep silent with regard to these matters.

As for the organization of national economy on the basis of production, it is the only way for the attainment of normal balance between the distribution of labour and the distribution of wealth. Every member in the state must be productive in some way or other. Production and the producers must be classified in such a way as to insure cooperation and the participation in labour to the widest possible extent and the attainment of a just share in the produced goods, and to insure the right of labour and the right to its proportionate share. This principle puts an end to absolute individualism in labour and production, which entails great social damage, because every form of labour and production in society is a form of common cooperative labour or production; hence if absolute freedom were left to the capitalist in his dealings with labor and production, it is inevitable that great injustice would fall upon labour and upon individual workers. The common wealth of the nation must be subject to the common interests of the nation and to the control of the national state. It is impossible to develop all the resources of power and progress in the state to the highest possible level except by this principle and this way.

The Syrian Social Nationalist Party wants to realize a strong national unity in which the Syrian nation may be enabled to persist in the struggle for life and progress. This national unity cannot be realized within a bad economic order, just as it cannot be realized within a bad social order. Therefore, the realization of social-legal justice and economic-legal justice are two necessary prerequisites for the success of the Syrian Social Nationalist Movement.

Social production is a common and not a private right. Capital, which is the resultant of production and the guarantee of its continuity and increase is, in principle, a common national property despite the fact that individuals acting as trustees utilize it for the sake of production; and active participation in the process of production is a condition sine qua non for the participation in the common right.

On the basis of this economic organization we will insure our economic revival, better the lot of millions of workers and farmers, increase the national wealth, and strengthen our Social Nationalist state.

The Fifth Principle. *Preparation of a strong army, which will have an effective role in defending the country and in determining national destiny.*

The competition for the resources of life and supremacy among nations is a question of a struggle between national interests. The vital interests of a nation cannot be protected in the struggle except by force in its two manifestations, the material and the spiritual. Now, spiritual power, no matter how perfect it may be, is always in need of material power. In fact, material power is itself an index and manifestation of an advanced spiritual power. Hence, it follows that an army and the military virtues are essential bases for the state.

National rights are not asserted in the struggle of nations except to the extent to which they are supported by power in the nation. For force is the decisive factor in the assertion or denial of national right.

By the armed forces we understand the Army, the Navy, and the Air Force. The art of war has reached such an advanced stage of development that it becomes incumbent upon us to be in perfect military readiness. Indeed, the Syrian nation in its totality must be powerful and well armed.

It is our own power that we trust in attaining our rights and in defending our interests. We intend to persevere in the struggle for existence and for supremacy in life, and life and supremacy shall be our reward.

The Aim and Program of the Party

The aim of the Syrian Social Nationalist Party is the creation of a movement which will realize its principles and revivify the nation, and the establishment of an organization which will lead to the complete independence of the Syrian nation, to the affirmation of its sovereignty, the setting up of a new order capable of protecting its interests and raising its standard of living, and the endeavor for the formation of an Arab front.

It is plainly manifest from the wording of this article that national revival is the center of attention for the Syrian Social Nationalist Party. The rise of the Social Nationalist Movement involves the realization of nationhood in Syria, the protection of the life and interests and means of progress of the Syrian nation, and equipping it with the power of strong union and true national cooperation. Thus, the Party seeks a distant aim of the highest order of importance because it does not restrict itself to dealings with some political form but rather involves the foundations of nationhood and the basic trends of national life. The purpose of the Party is to orient the life of the Syrian nation toward progress and success and to activate the elements of national power in Syria. This national power, once developed, will crush the force of tradition, liberate the nation from the chains of sluggishness and acquiescence to antiquated beliefs, and place an impregnable obstacle in the way of foreign ambitions threatening the interests of the millions of Syrians and their very existence.

The aim of the Syrian Social Nationalist Party is a comprehensive view which involves national life from its very foundations and from all its aspects; it includes all the basic issues of the social community—social, economic, political, spiritual, moral—and the final aims of life. It involves the national ideals, the purpose of independence, and the establishment of a true national society. This implies the founding of a new moral mentality and the establishment of a new basis of ethics. Consequently, the fundamental and reform principles of the Party reveal a new and a complete philosophy of life.

A complementary part to the foreign policy of the Party is the realization of an Arab front from the Arab nations. This front will become a strong barrier in the way of foreign imperialistic ambitions and a power of considerable weight in deciding the major political questions.

Syria is one of the Arab nations, and indeed it is the nation qualified to lead the Arab world, as is proved decisively by the Syrian Social Nationalist revival. It is obvious that a nation with no internal cohesiveness to insure its own unity and progress is not the one that can help revive other nations and lead them in the way of progress and success. Syrian nationalism is the only true and practical way and the first prerequisite for the awakening of the Syrian nation and for enabling it to work for the Arab cause.

Those who believe that the Syrian Social Nationalist Party proclaims Syria's withdrawal from the Arab world, because they do not distinguish between the Syrian national awakening and the Arab world, are in great error.

We shall never relinquish our position in the Arab world nor our mission to the Arab world. But we want, before everything else, to be strong in ourselves in order to convey our mission. Syria must be strong in its own national revival before it can undertake the realization of its greater task.

The comprehensive idea which was conceived by the Syrian Social Nationalist Party constitutes an idealistic mission in national life. The Party does not intend to restrict this fine concept and its great effects to Syria alone, but it intends to carry it to our sister Arab nations by way of cultural activities, exchange of opinions, and mutual understanding, not by way of the destruction of the nationalities of these Arab nations and the imposition of these principles on them.

As to the political aspect of the Party's aim, the Party, from the interior point of view, considers that the Lebanese question has arisen because of justifications which were acceptable when the concept of the state was still a religious concept. But the principles of the Syrian Social Nationalist Party have established the national social-legal basis for statehood. By the realization of the principles of the Syrian Social Nationalist Party, those justifications for the separation of Lebanon are removed.

As to what concerns the Arab world, the Party is in favor of following the road of conferences and alliances, as being the only practical way of leading to the cooperation of Arab nations and to the formation of an Arab front of considerable weight in international politics.

8. The Teaching Book of the Syrian Social Nationalist Party[*]

Antun Saadeh

Antun Saadeh's execution in 1949 by the Lebanese Government did not prevent his followers from perpetuating their leader's ideas and engaging in political activity. The Syrian Social Nationalist Party (SSNP), founded by Saadeh in 1932, continued to fight underground or to work openly for the ideal of a Greater Syria. Postwar developments, however, forced the SSNP to think in terms of Arab unity and devise a role for Syria accordingly. Consequently, Saadeh's original ideas were emphasized in those aspects that advocated a greater role for Syria among the Arab nations. Moreover, based again on Saadeh's writings, his followers tried to reconcile local differences in favor of the ideal, a single unified Arab nation and social progress. This extract is taken from a relatively new edition of Saadeh's writings, issued on behalf of the party.

The Syrian nation represents the unity of the Syrian people with a long historical past stretching back to prehistoric times.

This principle evolves from the theory of progression. It defines the nation as mentioned in previous articles, and requires, from the ethnic point of view, a closer examination. The principle is not meant to assign the Syrian nation to one common stock, Aryan or Semitic, but aims to describe the reality. This latter constitutes the final outcome of a long history comprising all nations that have settled in these countries and mingled therein, from the Late Stone Age, prior to the Chaldeans and Canaanites, down to the Amorites, Arameans, Assyrians, Hittites, and Akkadians, all of whom eventually became one nation. Thus, we see that the principle of Syrian nationality is not based upon common descent but upon the social and natural unity of a mixture of stock [i.e., of various stocks]. This is the only principle that embraces the interests of the Syrian people, unifies their aims and sublime ideals, and safeguards the national ideal from bloody and barbaric conflicts and national fragmentation.

---

[*]Extract from al-Hizb al-suri al-qawmi al-ijtima'i (Syrian Social Nationalist Party), *Kitab al-ta'alim al-suriyya al-ijtima'iyya. Mabadi'al-hizb mashruha bi-qalam al-za'im* [Teaching Book of Socialist Syria. The Principles of the Party Interpreted by the Leader] (n.p., 1955), pp. 17–20, 77–82.

Those who know nothing about sociology or their nation's history challenge these facts, claiming purity of blood and common descent and refusing to admit the mingling of blood. These people are commiting both a philosophical and a scientific mistake. To ignore the reality, which is the basis of our temperament and our psychic make-up, and to erect an illusion in its place is a sterile philosophy, akin to saying that it would be preferable for a body revolving around an axis to leave it because this would improve its motion! As for the claim of purity of stock or blood, it is a myth that obtains nowhere among the civilized nations and is rare even among savages.

All nations at present are a mixture of species of flat-heads, round-heads, and long-heads, and of several historic peoples. The Syrian nation is a mixture of Canaanites, Arameans, Assyrians, Chaldeans, Hittites, and Akkadians, while the French nation, for example, is a mixture of Ligurians, Franks, etc., and the Italian nation a mixture of Romans, Latins, Samnians, Etruscans, etc., and so on for other nations. "Saxons, Danes and Normans, that is what we are," says Tennyson about the English.

As for the superiority of the pure stock and descent over the mixed stock (especially among homogeneous and civilized stocks), this myth, too, has been exploded. The genius and mental superiority of the Syrians over their neighbors and others is a self-evident truth. It was they who civilized the Greeks and laid the foundations of Mediterranean civilization in which the Greeks joined them later. Greek genius flowered in Athens, a city of mixed stock, not in Sparta, which was proud of its descent and preserved its purity of blood.

Nevertheless, we must accept the fact that differences among stocks do exist. Some stocks are civilized and others are degenerate. We must also recognize the principle of homogeneity and diversity, both of blood and of stock. This principle will enable us to understand the reasons for the psychological superiority of the Syrians, which is not the result of unconstrained mixture but of the superb quality of homogeneous mixing, perfectly in harmony with the type of environment....

The Objectives and Plan of the Party

The aim of the Syrian Social Nationalist Party is to effect a Syrian national social renaissance capable of achieving its ideals and restoring to the Syrian nation its vitality and power. The party also aims to organize a movement that would lead to the complete independence of the Syrian nation, the consolidation of its sovereignty, the creation of a new system to safeguard its interests and raise its standard of life, and the formation of an Arab front. This article makes it perfectly plain that national resurgence is the party's main concern. National social renaissance embraces the establishment of the concept of the nation, the preservation of the life of the Syrian nation, and the means for its progress, furnishing it with the power of unity and proper national cooperation and creating a new national social system.

The party's objectives are long-term and of paramount importance. They are not limited to the treatment of political questions but deal with the very roots of nationalism and the trend of national life. The party's aim is to guide the life of the Syrian nation toward progress and virtue. The party desires to activate the various elements of national strength in order to destroy the hold of outdated customs, to liberate the nation from lethargy and submission to antiquated beliefs, to stand firmly opposed to foreign rapacity which threatens the interests and the sovereignty of millions of Syrians, and, finally, to establish new traditions that would institute our new attitude to life and our national social dogma.

Thus, the objectives of our party embrace a comprehensive view of the roots of national life in all its aspects. They include all the social, economic, political, spiritual, and methodological questions of national society, together with the larger problems of life. They incorporate the sublime national ideals, the objectives of independence, and the creation of a just national society. Implied in these objectives is the formation of a new ethical outlook and a new ideology, which is to be found in the basic principles and reforms of the party, constituting, as they do, a comprehensive outlook on life and a complete philosophy.

The formation of a front of Arab nations in order to stand as a barrier against imperialist designs and as a force of considerable importance in deciding major political issues is indeed a complementary part of the party's foreign policy. Syria is one of the nations of the Arab world and is fitted for the leadership thereof. In fact, the Syrian national social renaissance is the conclusive proof of its fitness to lead. It is obvious that a nation that does not possess a spirit of unity ('asabiyya) capable of self-regeneration, is not one that can be expected to lead other nations into the path of virtue. Syrian nationalism is the only practical method and the basic prerequisite for Syrian regeneration and the consequent participation of Syria in Arab affairs.

Those who believe that our party teaches the abandonment by Syria of Arab questions plainly do not understand the difference between the Syrian national social renaissance and the Arab question, and are greatly mistaken.

We shall not abandon either our position in the Arab world or our mission to it. But we must, first of all, strengthen ourselves so that we can fulfill our mission. Syria's national social renaissance must itself be powerful before it can achieve its major tasks.

The comprehensive outlook of our party raises a problem of ideals in national life. The party does not wish to restrict this noble ideal and its momentous consequences to Syria but wishes to carry it forth to sister Arab states, by means of cultural activity and the exchange of opinions. We do not advocate the dissolution of the various Arab nationalities or the imposition of theories upon them by force.

From the internal political point of view, the party considers that the Lebanese question [i.e., the existence of a separate Lebanese state] originated from side-issues that were justifiable when the conception of the state was a religious one. But our party's principles have created a social, legal, and national foundation. When our principles are put into effect, the isolation of Lebanon would no longer be justifiable.

As for the Arab world, the party considers that alliances and conferences are the only practical method for achieving cooperation among Arab nations and for creating an Arab front that can wield international authority.

But national sovereignty is a principle that must be safeguarded in all agreements and alliances.

9. Spiritual Materiality is a False Theory That Exists Neither In Man nor in the Universe[*]

Kamal Jumblat

Kamal Jumblat, an influential Lebanese politican who has held ministerial positions, was a writer and thinker and a chief of the Druzes. He was the founder and leader of the Social Progress Party (Progressive Socialist Party), which has attracted many former members of the SSNP, and a humanist and a democratic socialist, familiar with the West; he was educated in France. Jumblat had often been associated with men who represented a liberal viewpoint in Lebanon, such as former President Camille Chamoun (Sham'un), the late Emile Bustani, and Ghassan Tuwayni, the editor of al-Nahar [The Day]. Beginning in 1952, Jumblat cooperated with these men in the Socialist and National Front, which

[*]Extract from Kamal Jumblat, Adwa' 'ala haqiqat al-qadiyya al-qawmiyya al-ijtima-'iyya al-suriyya [Light on the Real Issue of Syrian Social Nationalism] (Beirut: n.p., 1962), pp. 9–12, 43–48.

achieved a bloodless, reformist revolution, and then eventually faded away. In the Lebanese civil war in 1975–76, Jumblat was the head of the leftist front, which was eventually defeated after the Syrian army intervened to defend the rightist or the Christians. Jumblat was assassinated in 1977 and his place as the head of the Druze community was taken by his son Walid. The passages below criticizing Antun Saadeh's social nationalists represent Jumblat's general views on ideology, religion, nationalism, and Arab socialism.

"Spiritual materiality" [*Madrahiyya*] is a term that Saadeh coined from spirit and matter, attempting with this new theory to put an end to the traditional dispute between the philosophers of matter and the philosophers of spirit.

The latter maintain that the absolute eternal spirit is itself the whole of existence and that the world of appearances is transitory and nonessential, and exists only in as much as it participates in spirit which creates all matter. We believe that the oldest prototype of this philosophy can be found in Plato's theory of ideas.

The former maintain that the eternal absolute spirit does not exist, that matter is itself the whole of existence, and that spirit is the reflection of matter upon itself, as is claimed for instance by Marx and the Marxists.

We suppose that Saadeh intended that his theory of spiritual materiality would reconcile these two theories of existence. That intention is apparent in the following extract from [an article by Antun Saadeh] in *al-Nizam al-jadid [The New System]:*

> The world has now realized, after World War II, the extent of the damage wrought by the emergence of fragmentary philosophies—the selfish philosophies that thrive on destruction, such as suffocating capitalism and violent Marxism, which have finally united in their denial of spirit; and other philosophies like fascism and National Socialism, which appropriate spirit to themselves and aim to dominate the whole world thereby. This world of ours stands today in need of a new philosophy that would rescue it from the falsity and confusion of such philosophies. This new philosophy—the philosophy of the unifying interaction of all the human forces—is the one represented by the renaissance." (*al-Nizam al-Jadid*, March, 1948, p. 5.)

Instead of turning to science and to the empirical method for a foundation on which to build the philosophy of his party (even though science would not be able to clarify everything), Saadeh turned to the German social thinkers and to Durkheim and his followers and modeled his theory of spiritual materiality after them—a theory that is nonempirical and has roots in neither Greek nor any European cultural tradition. Saadeh's theory was incomplete, confused, false, and out of date, since

Durkheim and his school had neglected to base their theories on modern science. Thus, his theory may have suited men of the late nineteenth or early twentieth centuries, but it is of no use to us today. It is a theory rejected by both science and history. Those who make of this theory their object in life are like students who fail in a modern medical school and revert to the study of Galen, Hipprocrates, Avicenna, and others and content themselves with ancient knowledge and satisfy themselves that these ancient books contain all that is to be known about medicine. They may then prescribe remedies that would prove fatal to patients. Furthermore, Saadeh in his spirtual materiality confuses "spirit" as defined by the traditional idealist philosophies with "social consciousness" as defined by the German social school and Durkheim, a consciousness that is a mere perpetuation of the "mana" of primitive African tribes.

Spirit, according to Saadeh, is sometimes the spirit of society—every society, whether German or Syrian, possesses a spirit, so how can he speak, as he does earlier, of "appropriating the spirit"?—and that is all he means when he says that "justice, virtue, and beauty, inasmuch as they are absolute values, are the values of society." Saadeh confesses that such values as justice, virtue, and beauty may be absolute—i.e., fixed, final, and comprehensive—for all societies at the same time, for all individuals in the same society, and for the whole of humanity as well. He does not realize that these values cannot, at the same time, be absolute for every single society without also being absolute for all societies. If the values of justice, virtue, and beauty were at the same time absolute in the German, British, and Syrian societies, absolute chaos would ensue.

Every nation and every state would rise and struggle for what they consider absolute relative to themselves but what would not be absolute relative to the others. Might, rather than correct belief, would then make right. This theory of "absolute international chaos" entails the extinction of the human race or at least their dispersion into various societies which cannot agree upon any value and which hold their own peculiar opinion concerning justice, virtue, and beauty. It would in effect mean the end of the world, the end of civilization, and the end of men as human beings.

At other times, we find Saadeh using the word "spirit" to mean the individual soul of each human being. He says, for instance, "The values of justice, truth, virtue, and beauty are not material. They are human and personal" (meaning the values of the human being and his personality which form the essence of all creatures that belong to the human race). But he corrects himself later by writing, "They are social values."

Saadeh, then, is either contradicting himself or mixing man's social and human attributes. If the latter is what he means, then we may rightly conclude that, as certain species of insects (e.g., ants and bees) possess social instincts, then they must also be human. Saadeh does not realize that man's human rather than social attributes make him man. His social attributes he shares with many animal species.

Saadeh also means by "spirit" the individual soul of each human, the basic essence in us as used by the idealist philosophies. Thus he claims, for example, that justice, truth, virtue, and beauty are "the values of the soul's triumph, the triumph of the strong and beautiful personality." Saadeh is at his most confused stage when he illustrates to us this conflict in his thinking between the concepts of the individual and the social spirit. Thus he says, "We should not believe that justice, virtue, and beauty require us to relinquish our genuine soul [sic]. What would it profit us if we gain the whole world and lose ourselves?" (This last sentence he has taken from the Bible.)

In this passage, the contradictions in Saadeh's thought become evident. He attempts therein to reconcile the individual human spirit with the social spirit. He believes that the social values of justice, virtue, and beauty need not entail relinquishing our genuine soul and that it would not profit us to gain the whole world but lose ourselves. This means that the social values of justice, virtue, and beauty conform with our genuine personal desires for justice, virtue, and beauty. They are, indeed, identical. If the essence of the individual soul differs in various persons, we would not be able to talk about the human race. Thus, Saadeh implies that the absolute values of justice, virtue, and beauty are themselves the values of the private soul which are called by the common people the values of the conscience. Saadeh should have reached this conclusion by himself, especially since he had already declared that we need not "relinquish our views of life, the universe, and art or abandon the ideals entrenched in our soul." He means here that this view of life, the universe, and art (our own personal view) conforms to and joins with the social values of justice, virtue, and beauty. Similarly, our own private ideals are identical with the ideals of society, just as the private conscience is reflected in social relations.

Surely, no one can argue that man can possess two sets of ideal views (one social and the other individual) or two views of life, the universe, and art (one social and spiritual-materialist and the other individual). Such ideals and such views are themselves comprehensive and absolute. Man cannot harbor within himself two theories both of which are absolute and comprehensive. Saadeh's mistake—and it is also the basic error in his theory of spiritual materiality—is that he relied in constructing this theory upon a purely rational a priori hypothesis, namely that "Throughout the world, there exists no unanimity concerning the interpretation and the absolute understanding of these values except where the variety and conflict of opinion and interests in human societies are negated."

In Saadeh's language, this means that the values of justice, virtue, and beauty are subject to the division of mankind into groups and societies, since the interests of the group, in his view, do not conflict within a single society but do conflict between one society and another.

Herein lies Saadeh's misunderstanding of man's true social existence, which does not involve the whole of man and his essence but provides only a field for man's activities and is the product of such activities. Saadeh also displays here his ignorance of the true foundation for the values of justice, virtue, and beauty and his misunderstanding of the function of these values in society.

These values, which are to a certain extent abstract, have been formulated and have become manifest because of the diversity of opinion and interests and the conflict between individuals and societies. These values are the fixed criteria to which people resort when they clash or quarrel. Without a diversity in views and interests, and without conflict between varying societies, these values would not have emerged among societies and individuals.

These values emerge from the conflict of individuals belonging to the same society, and thus is born the science of personal ethics, of constitutional, civil, and criminal rights, all of which regulate the relations among the citizens. In the field of international justice, these values reappear in common definitions of concepts like science, thought, philosophy, and civilization in general. In private and public international law, which regulates the relations of states and citizens with other states and citizens, these values are also felt. Just as the citizens of one society have observed in the course of history the growth of public institutions that provide greater guarantees for their rights, so, for the last twenty-five years or so, we have all witnessed the growth of public international institutions and laws that protect the rights of private and public societies. . . .

Egocentricity and Other Political Cheaters

The cheating social nationalists, the "worshippers of the state"—this new idol—have failed everywhere, having filled the world with malice, wars, ruin, ignorance, and sorrow. They shall inevitably fail in the East as they have failed in the West, since they tell mankind things that are not consonant with human nature. They have produced their magic lantern and told mankind, "You are only a potentiality, you have no real existence." This selfish nationalism with its malicious and disruptive spirit makes distinctions between one race and another, between one human being and another, and treats men not according to the dictates of justice and fair-dealing but in accordance with the private, selfish interests of the people and in accordance with personal whims and the thirst for power.

Machiavellism remains unchanged; in the past, the justification offered was the interest of the Prince; now it is the interest of "society." But the ignorant nation soon perceives, behind this new idol of society, the men who hold the reins of power as they manipulate man, who, according to them, has become a social animal, an ape. Thereafter, the nation rejects those cheaters who had for long screamed in its face, "You are social animals. We want to liberate you from every trace of humanity."

These national social theories are in origin drawn from the writings of Hegel about the state and society and from Durkheim, Lévy-Bruhl, Bougle, Halbwachs, and other social thinkers of the German and French school in the last half of the last century.

The other sort of cheaters are those who tell mankind, "Economics is the basis of everything, of society, the family, the fatherland, philosophy, public morality, and religion. Man is nothing but the reflection of matter upon itself"—as if matter can, by itself, reflect itself upon itself and at the same time be conscious of such reflection! Economics implies the exploitation of a country's resources by a certain class of people. Salvation lies in changing the economy by handing over the means of production from the owning classes to the non-owning ones. All men would then become employees and workers in a state that is administered on a class basis by a new class of people, even if such administration were to be achieved by force for a certain period of time.

These cheaters also claim that both reform and salvation lie in adopting and casting upon the world a materialist and socialist outlook— an outlook that takes no account of spiritual morality—as if a change of systems would suffice to reform mankind or as if justice, virtue, and love were confined only to one class of people who, once in power, would bring about the Golden Age which has been the dream of mankind since the world began!

All these theories misapprehend the truth. It is not enough to substitute one class for another, one system for another, and one law for another, in order that justice, virtue, and love may prevail.

Justice and love are aspects of the reflection of self as revealed in the apparent dualism in man. Reform must come from both within and without the human being. A virtuous socialism that believes in man's influence on social systems and their implementation is alone capable of guiding us to the true way. Otherwise, we would be like machines without fuel and bodies without soul.

Indeeed, if mankind is able to reform itself, to eradicate is egocentricity, and to allow its true self to appear, it would have no need to reform its social systems and enact legislation.

10. Lebanese Nationalism and Its Foundations: The Phalangist Viewpoint*

Pierre Gemayel

Pierre Gemayel (Jumayyil), a Maronite Lebanese who has served in several national cabinets, is the leader of the Lebanese Phalanx (al-Kata'ib al-Lubnaniyya), or Lebanese Social Democratic Party, founded in 1936. It publishes the daily al-'Amal [Action]. The party was organized to foster Lebanese nationalism, but, as it turned out, it relied chiefly on the support of the Maronite community for the purpose of maintaining the supremacy of that community. The census of 1932, according to which the Christians formed a majority, serves as the basis for Lebanon's present constitutional regime, the President being a Maronite, the Premier a Sunni Muslim, etc. Gemayel's party (about 60,000 members) is determined to preserve the system, which is based on the assumption that Christians still constitute a majority of Lebanon's population, and the party therefore considers all Lebanese living abroad (mostly Christians) as permanent citizens of Lebanon. In 1953, the restive Muslim groups published in English a pamphlet—which was later banned—Muslim Lebanon Today, written by Mustafa Khalidi. In it, Khalidi proposed that a census be held and criticized the priority given to Christians in government jobs. The speech reproduced here, addressed to President Chamoun, constituted an answer to Khalidi's pamphlet. It was preceded by a memorandum. Both the memorandum and the speech were published in English in a party pamphlet as indicated.

The Lebanese nationalism defended by Gemayel's party differs radically from Antun Saadeh's Syrian nationalism—first, in that it is limited to Lebanon; second, by its recognition of democratic freedoms and by its representation of the political views of the Maronites (Saadeh rejected all local interests). See also the following section.

Memorandum

Lebanon, small as it is, constitutes an irreducible entity. None can question its tradition of independence. If it were absorbed by a larger

---

*Extract from *Al-Kataeb Al-Loubnaniat* [i.e., *al-Kata'ib al-Lubnaniyya*]: *"Phalanges Libanaises"* [The Lebanese Phalanx] (Beirut: Parti democrate social libanais, 1956), pp. 22–25, 25, 26–36, *passim.*

neighbor, it would create insurmountable difficulties for this neighbor, so great is its capacity for resistance and its faith in its own mission.

Lebanon is "a soul, a spiritual principle." It would be materially possible to absorb it into a Syrian or Arab empire temporarily; it is spiritually impossible to unite it to a world which does not share its state of soul, its spiritual principles.

Lebanon is a "mission." And this mission is incompatible with that which the Arabs aspire generally to realize. A Syrian or Arab empire in which Lebanon would be swallowed would not be on a human level. From the start, it would find itself divided against itself, in its view of life, in its intelligence, in its soul, and in its being.

Undermined by diversity and by antagonism, it would be unable to realize the common good and it would not be long before it would give birth to troubles, to discord, to havoc.

Since far antiquity, Lebanon has marched with giant's feet on the road of civilization. Even while they were only Phoenicians, the Lebanese aleady showed their sense of the universe, their attachment to liberal traditions, and a generosity of spirit and heart so great that it enabled them to love and understand even the most distant peoples.

It is thus that they have contributed to the blossoming of Mediterranean civilization in the domain of art, science, religion, and material progress. Western humanism, a tributary of Rome and Athens, owes to them its first foundations.

The faithfulness of Lebanon to its mission and to its heritage had never been denied over the last six thousand years of history. A small land, ten thousand square kilometers in size, it remains at the crossroads of human civilizations which it always seeks to know and to assimilate.

Traditionally, Lebanon is both of the Orient and of the Occident. This explains why it is periodically the object of attacks; these attacks are made by those who have been unable to follow the royal path of universal humanism, who have not shared its vision of the world, and who are, in fact, permanently against the idea it embodies and wish its liquidation.

In the Middle Ages, Lebanon affirmed its personality with even more marked vigor with the adhesion of a part of the population to Christianity. Thus, the physical, social, and political geography of this country have naturally placed it in the heart of the Eastern Question.

Heirs of Byzantine and Sassanian caesaropapism, the Muslim caliphs imposed on their lands a theocratic regime involving a state of discrimination against non-Muslim religious minorities. Class distinctions and inequalities were established. The Christians, called *dhimmis* or the protected, were not equal to the Muslims in regard to rights.

This situation continued into the period of the Ottoman Empire until after the 1914–18 war. If it has generally disappeared in the documents, it has persisted in customs. Moreover, the constitutions of seven members out of eight of the Arab League provide that Islam is the religion of the state or that the head of state must be a Muslim.

It is against this theocratic system that Lebanon (Islamo-Christian by its social structure) has always stood with firmness.

Settled in their inaccessible mountains, the Lebanese first won a *de facto* autonomy, which extended itself under the government of the quasi-independent dynasties of the Ma'an and of the Shihab. This autonomy received legal consecration in 1864, with the promulgation of the organic stature guaranteed by the seven powers of the European Concert, and in 1920, with the establishment of Greater Lebanon. In 1943, Lebanon became fully independent; finally, in 1945, it was admitted to the United Nations Organization and it participated in the establishment of the Arab League.

It is because it was constituted in protest against imperialism of all sorts that Lebanon has served, in the course of the centuries, as an asylum and a refuge for ethnic minorities and those persecuted because of their religion. It is thus that it has given hospitality successively to Mardaites, Maronites, Druzes, Shi'ites, Armenians, Kurds, Assyrians, Syriacs, and Chaldeans. Today still, it ofen provides an asylum for political personalities of the Arab world who are harassed by their compatriots.

Thus, while still remaining in the center of the Arab world with which it shares language and certain elements of cultural heritage, Lebanon maintains a character to which it remains fiercely attached, because its instinct for survival dictates this to be categorically imperative.

Lebanon is of the Orient and of the Occident. It intends to continue to serve as a link between the two worlds without being absorbed by either, for then it would fail its mission.

Lebanon is liberal and humanistic. It is the only Arab country where all citizens without distinction as to religion enjoy real equality and public liberties of the sort intended by modern constitutionalists. It is more particularly the only Arab country that applies the provisions of the Universal Declaration of the Rights of Man especially in matters of personal status and liberty of conscience, the latter being understood in its broadest sense and including the right to change religion. Indubitably, it is to its liberalism that Lebanon owes its spiritual and material impetus.

Lebanon considers itself to be a modern and secular state. It repudiates any theocracy that produces discrimination and inequality. As it is the fatherland of all cultures, it is also that of all religions and does not hold any cult as official to the exclusion of the others. Secular authority is distinct from religious authority without the two being in conflict. No opposition, but rather separation and cooperation. Lebanon is the only Arab state in the Arab League which practices "A free religion in a free state."

Lebanon is neccessary to the West. It is the interpreter of its culture, of its ideas, its spiritual values, to the Arabs. It provides full guarantees to Western material interests. Nowhere else is foreign capital so safe.

Lebanon is culturally necessary to the Arab East. The latter owes to the former its intellectual renaissance in the nineteenth century. It was the Lebanese, and the monks in particular, who, in their convents, according to the Muslims themselves, protected the literary heritage of the Arabs. The greatest journalistic enterprises in the Arab world are still, in Egypt and elsewehere, directed by Lebanese.

Lebanon is politically necessary to the East. It is a factor for balance and reason. It is listened to by Christian nations with which it has long had friendly relations. For the Arabs, it is an incomparable lawyer in the West. For the West, it is an irreplaceable interpreter to the Orient. For both, it is a center of meeting and exchange.

Thus, national and international considerations militate strongly in favor of maintaining Lebanon free and independent.

Conscious of these needs, the Lebanese are determined to spare no effort to repulse any attack that would constitute a formidable peril for both this little country and the civilized world. If Lebanon disappears someday, it is not Lebanon, but the West, and secondly the Arab world, that will bear the stamp of defeat.

Lebanon refuses to consider such a possiblity. It will never resign itself to it. It will mobilize all of its resources against any combination of evil forces united against it.

Beirut, February 25, 1955

PIERRE GEMAYEL
President of the Lebanese Phalanx

We Want Lebanon To Be a State, Neither a Church nor a Mosque

Mr. President,

It would have been my desire to avoid this discussion of a complex and boundless problem, but I feel forced to deal with it because of a tendency which, if it finds free expression and is followed to its logical conclusion, threatens to confront our country with an imminent catastrophe. . . .

In spite of the declaration of the "Preparatory Committee for a General Muslim Conference," with all its surprising foolishness—and in spite of the pamphlet *Muslim Lebanon Today* with all its false accusations and preparatory intrigues, all of it constituting and instigation to open troublemaking—we have always believed that these opinions and actions were no more than the passing fancies and boastfulness of ignorant men imbued with an odious fanaticism, which deserves no attention.

Today, however, when we see people and organizations who bear the burden of leadership, and who comprise doctors, lawyers, journalists, politicians, intellectuals, and notables, associating themselves with these ideas, it becomes clear that this question is more profound and of wider scope than it would have been if it had been created only by ignorant troublemakers. It is obvious that silence concerning this bitter fact will bring about a grave and general danger.

It might have been possible for us to say nothing about this problem, as some Pharisees, both Christians and Muslims, would have wanted us to. . . .

But silence at this time and in these circumstances, now that this problem of Muslim-Christian relations in Lebanon has taken such an evil turn, would be synonymous to crime. And it would indeed be nothing but crime, and treasonable crime at that. . . .

Al-Kata'ib, which was founded as a national patriotic organization and the aim of which has been the establishment of Lebanon as a secular state founded on freedom—an aim testified to by its actions even more than by the mere statements of its supporters—is happy to be the only organization to warn against the grave dangers constituted by these fanatical sectarian movements which are supported by some groups in Lebanon. *Al-Kata'ib* is happy to be the one organization to assume this national patriotic duty, for one one can assuse *al-Kata'ib* of being a bargainer among the bargainers, or an appeaser among the appeasers, or of acting with hypocrisy and deceit.

And I, Pierre Gemayel, a Christian proud of my Christianity and a dutiful observer of its doctrines, am happy to interpret the thoughts of the majority of the Lebanese and the basic ideas we are now presenting.

I am happy to be such an interpreter because of the general recognition that in national politics I have never acted as a religious "doctrinaire," and that in all my activities I have endeavored to be guided by the most general principles of humanity and exclusively by the interests of the country as a whole. . . .

All of us are acquainted with the difficult problem of the Christian minorities in the Muslim states of the East, including the Arab states.

All of us know that these states, in another era, used to pervert the Muslim religion—a noble, generous and idealistic religion—into a narrowly fanatical doctrine which caused some Muslim majorities to persecute non-Muslims in a way that conscience and honor can never have condoned. . . .

The state of affairs described above lasted until the dawn of the blessed Arab National Renaissance. Christians were the first to support this progressive movement, and they did so with all their strength. Their sacrifices on behalf of this movement and their services, in the East and in the West, cannot be denied even by the most extremist of the ignorant fanatics.

In Lebanon, the seeds of this movement fell on good soil, and we, of *al-Kata'ib*, were the first the proclaim it and to fling away the conception of majority and minority. We were the first to demand that the policy of Lebanon be national and patriotic, that is, nonsectarian. We were the first to make the people of Lebanon accept the belief that Lebanon must be a nation and a fatherland, and not a church or a mosque.

We, of *al-Kata'ib*, fought for this idea. We struggled against the foreigners with all our strength, not like so many others whose struggling was done around cocktails in drawing-rooms.

In our struggle, we opposed many Christian groups who were suspicious and hostile to our ideas, many sincere people with good intentions, because they were afraid of a new movement and of new catastrophes which might have made the old catastrophes seem less dangerous, if this new movement were to fail. . . .

The Muslim organizations claim to desire "the realization of social justice, and the distribution of offices on a basis of equality. . . ."

And we, too, want this demand fulfilled, and that within the next 24 hours; on condition that it be based on justice and truth, which means that offices must be allocated according to character, training, and productivity, regardless of sectarian origins. This means that equality implies obligation as well as rights.

Accordingly, Christians would not be compelled to pay 80% of the taxes, while non-Christians pay only 20%.

It also means that the national treasury would not give money to one sect and take it away from other sects. . . .

The Muslim organizations demand a "general census and the application of Lebanese laws to all those who apply for Lebanese citizenship. . . ."

We are happy to see eye to eye with these organizations. We, too, insist on a general census—on condition that we do not consider the

Lebanese immigrants unclean, who should be excluded from our Lebanese community.

And on condition that the government makes good its shortcomings by registering the hundreds of thousands of immigrants in an appropriate period of time. . . .

Are those fighting the registration of the immigrants spokesmen for these immigrants? Why are they acting against the immigrants instead of supporting their rights, when they know that the immigrants are the shields of our Lebanon, its staunch defenders, and the guarantors of our happy life? . . .

The Muslim organizations want "the realization of economic union with Syria."

In plain language, this means that Lebanon should show the white flag and surrender unconditionally to a Syrian union that would destroy its freedom and sovereignty, and reduce it to a mere satellite of Syria, whose ambitions with respect to Lebanon are a matter of notoriety.

How can the Muslim organizations reconcile these two opposites: union with Syria, and the preservation of Lebanon as a free and independent state?

If the Muslim organizations are really sincere in their desire for the economic recovery of Lebanon on behalf of Arabism, why do they not join with us in demanding an economic union with all the Arab states together, and not Syria alone? . . .

The Muslim organizations wish "to abolish sectarianism."

This is exactly what we long for, and what we are striving to achieve in a practical way. The total abolition of religious sectarianism, or at least of some of it, can be achieved only through the liquidation of the legal personal courts and by making the Lebanese Republic a secular state in toto. Thus, all Lebanese citizens would have to submit to a civil legal code that would apply uniformly to everyone in Lebanon.

Here we ask: Are the Muslim organizations really prepared to go along with us toward total secularism, or do they have a hidden objective in demanding the abolition of sectarianism? Are they aiming at putting a certain definite group of people into power? . . .

The Muslim organizations wish to "amend the constitution."

The aim of this is clear. It is either to put a stop to the power of the President of the Republic, or to distribute the power between him and the Prime Minister equally. It is obvious that the only reason for this is that the President is a Christian and the Prime Minister is a Muslim.

This is the real objective, and as for what they say by way of argument, it is all a fraud and an attempt to hide the truth.

This demand, with its accompanying agitation, has increased the suspicion of all Christians and put them on their guard. They are afraid that this demand for an amendment to the constitution may turn out to be a step imperiling the existence and future of the country. . . .

All sincere Lebanese view this problem as one of their personal security, menaced and compromised by a destructive emergence of fanaticism. It is a problem that must be solved if Lebanon can fulfill its mission and help in the solution of the problems confronting all Arabs. This can only be done in an atmosphere free of suspicion and the threats arising from an upsurge of ignorant dictatorial egotism.

If these Muslim organizations were sincerely devoted to Arabism, as they pretend, they would have exerted every effort to preserve the special quality for which Lebanon is celebrated. Lebanon, impregnated with Christian civilization, is regarded as holy, and is dedicated to the human values, though it is not ourselves who regard this as "Christian," but these Muslim organizations themselves. Hence, Lebanon can only serve Arabism if it remains national, and not religious, and it would fail altogether if it were transformed into one more Muslim theocracy which is what these deluded and short-sighted dreamers want it to become.

But if Arabism is Islam, and the religion of Islam has a lofty, spiritual source and is not based on vulgar egotism, how can we ask Christians to be Arabs when they know the sinister designs of these ignorant fanatics?

And if the ultimate goal of all this agitation is to make Lebanon part of a Syrian, Arab, or Muslim state, then we say firmly and unequivocally to these Muslim organizations: In that direction we will not go with you one single step.

We, of *al-Kata'ib*, want Lebanon to be a country of freedom, untainted by any sectarianism, independent of the East and of the West, and cooperating fully with the Arab states; but we do not want Lebanon to be a "province" in some other unit, and we will never allow it to become a "district" of a union with anyone else. . . .

At a time when civilized nations are laboring ceaselessly to raise the living standards of their people through the exploitation of all their natural resources, while they are struggling to wipe out ignorance, disease, and poverty, and while Lebanon urgently needs to exploit its potential capital of water and electricity on the model of the TVA in the United States and the Volga project in the Soviet Union, it pains us to see our people diverting themselves with delusions and planting a wind to harvest the tempest, and seeds of strife to reap the evil of destruction. . . .

If these evil movements, which aim at the destruction of sovereign Lebanon, call for a strike in support of what they call "some demands," we, of al-Kata'ib, can only oppose such a strike by another one of our own, in the interests of our country.

And if demonstrations are made, we will make our own, in order to prevent our house from crumbling according to the wish of the sinister forces opposing us.

If the Government fails to do its duty in safeguarding our laws and our security, then the youth of Lebanon [the al-Kata'ib youth branches] will do its duty by providing security and tranquility on its own terms.

And if the state fails to rule according to civilized standards, then the Lebanese people will have to reconsider its option of this state! We feel compelled to do this, in order to preserve our beloved country, Lebanon. . . .

Let us assume for a moment that the sectarian struggle for which some egotists are carrying the banner has achieved a Muslim victory over the Christians.

Let us suppose that the road was made easy for the demented sectarianism of the mob, as we saw at the end of July, 1954.

Let us suppose that Lebanon has succumbed to such a catastrophe, sinking to the status of other countries backward in civilization and culture.

Let us suppose that all this has happened.

Do those who wish this to happen to the Christians imagine that the Christians will fall asleep over their grievances, and humbly and obediently submit without conjuring up a flame that will enable the "foreigners" to enter Lebanon at will and harm Lebanon itself and every other Arab state?

Would this be a service to Lebanon or the Arab states, to lean backward so violently while the nations of the world are gradually awakening to progress. . . .

To the Muslims in Lebanon particularly, and to the Arabs in general, we say: You must never forget one thing, and that is that the paramount interest of the nation demands that you never make the Christians suspicious of your aims. Never let them lose the feeling of security and tranquility, even if you, the Muslims, must sacrifice something of your own rights and interests. The Christians will rise to defend their interests and those of the Arabs only insofar as they have confidence in you. And, on the other hand, just as far as you make the Christians suspicious, and disgusted with you, just so far will this lead to calamity for the cause of Lebanon and the cause of the Arabs together. . . .

11.   The Clash of Ideologies in Lebanon, 1975–76: Five Views

Lebanon emerged in 1860, through French pressure, as a semiautonomous unit limited to the area around Mount Lebanon. The arrangement was designed to protect the Maronites (Catholics) and to establish through them a foothold for the French in the area. In 1920 France gained mandatory rights over Syria and Lebanon and promptly created a greater Lebanon by adding to it Syrian territories. The Christians, especially the Maronites, were given a series of social and political privileges. They maintained these privileges through the National Pact signed in 1943, which established the constitutional regime and also declared Lebanon free of the French mandate. The National Pact gave the Christians the right to elect the president and to hold a majority of seats in the Parliament on the basis of a 1932 census that gave them a slight numerical majority; all calculations rely still on that census, long outdated by demographic changes. Indeed, the situation changed drastically after 1946. The number of Muslims grew rapidly, as did numbers of the urban population, due in part to the higher birth rates, migration of poor Shiites from the south, and the influx of the Palestinians (although the latter, living mostly in camps, remained separate). Meanwhile, Lebanon became a major commercial center, attracting considerable investment both from the Arab and Western countries. The discrepancies of wealth increased, as did the tensions between the poor and the rich, who happened to correspond roughly, but not exclusively, to Muslims and Christians, respectively. Yet, Lebanon remained relatively quiet, due to her confessional and clannish structure under the rule of the Zaim, or the leader of the clan. Lebanon's constitutional basis was confessional in the sense that each Muslim (Shiite, Sunni) and each Christian group (Maronite, Greek Orthodox, Armenian, and so forth) was represented in the Parliament according to its numerical strength. In the 1950s and 1960s Lebanon was described admiringly as a political miracle and an example of democratic goodwill, although the arrangement was beset by gross social and political inequities; see, e.g., Leonard Binder, ed., Politics in Lebanon (New York: Wiley, 1966). There was a warning in 1958 when Nasserite groups attempted to change the status quo by staging an upheaval in Beirut. It fizzled after the American marines landed; the marines were pulled out soon afterward.

The situation deteriorated rapidly after 1970 when the Palestinian commando groups pushed out of Jordan settled in Lebanon, which already sheltered several hundred thousand Palestinians (see section on Palestinians) living in squalid camps around Beirut. The commando groups had already been relatively active in Lebanon and had been able to secure, through what is known as the Cairo Agreement of 1969 signed by the Lebanese leaders, the right to bear arms and engage in action against Israel. After 1970 the guerillas increased their activities in southern Lebanon, causing strong Israeli military retaliation that compelled many Shiite Muslims to leave their villages and go to Beirut, increasing further the ranks of the underprivileged. This situation aggravated further the conflict between the privileged minority—made up mostly of Christians but also of some small groups of rich Muslims clinging to the status quo—and the majority of poor Muslims, who were attempting to change the situation in their favor. Initially the Palestinians were not interested in involving themselves in Lebanese internal affairs; but in the end they could not avoid involvement as, unwittingly, they had become the crucial element in the internal balance of power. Pierre Gemayel, the leader of the Phalangist party (Hizb al-Kata'ib al Lubnaniyya), the political arm of the Maronites, initially regarded the Palestinian commandos as a possible protection against the Communists, especially against the Ba'thists from Syria, and therefore acquiesced to their presence in Lebanon. He changed his position as the PLO shifted to the Left after 1967 and drifted ideologically speaking, closer to the Lebanese Socialists and Nasserite nationalists, as well as Marxists, all of whom were demanding a change in the situation in Lebanon. A number of non-Maronite Christians also looked hopefully toward a secular regime that would permit the emergence of a true Lebanese national identity above confessional and clan loyalties, and these also tended to look with sympathy on demands for change in the status quo. The Palestinians ideologically sided with the Left and, well-armed and trained as they were, they posed potentially the main challenge to the Phalangist militia, which otherwise could have easily defeated the armed forces of any of its local rivals. Meanwhile the Israeli attacks on South Lebanon caused considerable damage there and raised the specter of occupation of that part of the country, which contained the headwaters of the Litani River, coveted by the Israelis. The Maronites described the Palestinians as the source of Lebanon's problem and demanded that they be disarmed and confined to their camps. Then, in a provocative act without any apparent reason, in 1975 they killed a number of Palestinian workers, triggering a civil war between the leftist and rightist forces—or between Muslims and Christians, as the Western press distortedly reported the strife. The Lebanese army meanwhile had disintegrated, as soldiers and officers joined one or the other group and left the government powerless. The leftist *forces, led by Kamal Jumblat, were nearing victory when the Syrian army intervened in order to protect the Phalangists, fearing that their final defeat would cause a variety of political complications and ultimately lead to the disintegration of Lebanon. The Syrian army ultimately prevailed and, after heavy casualties, pushed back the Palestinians, saving the Phalangists from sure defeat and allowing them to maintain the upper hand. Syria then became the dominant factor in Lebanese politics. The Syrian army has remained in the country as an Arab peacekeeping force that includes token forces from other Arab states. The civil war came to an uneasy halt late in 1976; but the situation has remained very precarious, for Lebanon does not have a strong government or a sufficiently large army to enforce its will. The civil war has not changed formally the status quo but has undermined substantially its economic and social foundations and left in shambles this once flourishing country. Meanwhile the situation in southern Lebanon deteriorated further, due to the occupation of a narrow strip along the border by a so-called "rebel" army of Major Sa'ad Haddad, armed and supplied by Israel. A United Nations peacekeeping force is in the area, separating the Palestinian military units from Haddad's troops and the Syrians in the north from the Israelis further south.*

For additional information on the Lebanese political and ideological situation, see John P. Entelis, Pluralism and Party Transformation in Lebanon: al-Kataib 1936–1970 *(Leiden: E. J. Brill, 1970); and Michael C. Hudson,* The Precarious Republic *(New York: Random House, 1968). On the civil war, see M. Kamal Salibi,* Crossroads to Civil War, Lebanon 1958– 1976 *(Delmar, N.Y.: Caravan Books, 1976); P. E. Haley and L. W. Snider,* Lebanon in Crisis *(Syracuse, N.Y.: Syracuse University Press, 1979); and John Bulloch,* Death of a Country: Civil War in Lebanon *(London: Weidenfeld and Nicolson, 1977). There are also many articles in various scholarly journals; they are too numerous to be listed here.*

The excerpts below indicate the views of various leaders and parties in Lebanon about the internal situation of the country, and civil war of 1976, and the Syrian intervention. The writings appeared originally in the Lebanese press, al-Nahar, August 17 and September 2, 1976, and in al-Safir, September 11, 1976; the excerpts are from the version translated and published in the Journal of Palestine Studies *5, nos. 3–4 (Spring-Summer 1976): 266–81 passim; and 6, no. 2 (Winter 1977): 184–87 passim.*

A Christian View on Lebanon:
Maintain the Status Quo

The formula for religious coexistence in Lebanon is still a tender plant, a human experiment that has not yet been completed.

It also happens that the Muslim Lebanese have up to now been influenced by so-called Arab nationalism, in which religion is an essential element and a preponderant factor. They are also influenced by the allurements of unity or Arabism, which they see as an instrument for the unification of the countries and peoples of this area. Finally it so happens that Lebanon has become the confluence of the tributaries of the Palestinian torrent flowing from the neighbouring countries and that this country, because of its prevailing atmosphere of freedom, has become their temporary homeland and almost their only road to their original usurped land.

Could world communism be expected to stand idly in the face of all these temptations and openings without exploiting them—or trying to do so—to the greatest possible extent? And this is what it has done, with all its energies, expertise and resources.

Its first step was to embrace the Palestinian resistance and to try to persuade it that in Lebanon it could only rely on communism, suggesting that anyone who was not a Marxist or at least a fellow-traveller, was either the enemy of the Palestinian revolution or subject to American, Western or imperialist pressures. . . .

While Lebanon was trying in vain to build sound relations with the Palestinian resistance, the communist movement chose a new approach, concentrating on religious differences between the Lebanese establishing them more firmly in men's hearts and minds and using all the ploys at its command, whose "revolutionary" effectiveness is so well attested. . . . They had started to hold meetings to discuss the system. Sincere attempts were being made on both sides to advance gradually beyond the stage of political confessionalism, with slow but sure steps. The Chamber of Deputies had taken up the question of the so-called "Muslim demands," acceded to some of them and started to consider the rest. When it abolished the principle of confessional succession in certain key posts and offices, the Phalangists were the first to support this move and give it their blessing. . . .

This was a few months before the present crisis. What made it necessary to precipitate the explosion on the pretext of changing the system? . . . The reason is that, just as in the case of our relations with the Palestinian resistance, international communism did not want to let us build up our future with our own hands and cure our maladies with love and mutual confidence.

Here too it hastened to rectify its omissions and proceeded to seize on and monopolize the "Muslim demands." It made out that the safeguards given to the Christians in the forties were monopolies of power, responsibility, the future and destiny. It even made use of the Palestine problem to incite the Muslims against the Christians until it had succeeded in establishing a broad front grouping the Muslims, Palestinians, Marxists and fellow-travellers to combat the Christians of this country, heaping them with abuse and violating all that was most sacred to them on the pretext that they were monopolizing all benefits, blessings and power in the country.... When we recall that the political system in Lebanon is a result of agreement and understanding between the Christians and the Muslims, we see clearly how evil is this determination to change it by violence, and the force of arms. What is evil about it is that it firmly convinces the Christians that the formula of partition to be firmly established in their hearts and minds as the only escape hatch and their last card....

To be honest with the Muslims ... Christians are now psychologically and intellectually incapable of surrendering what they were ready to discuss before this civil strife began. It is no exaggeration to say that the continued pressure on them aimed at extracting certain concessions from them will indubitably destroy their last hopes that the formula for coexistence can be saved or carried on.

If you ask me what the solution is, I should say that the only way is through restoring calm and stability and rebuilding the confidence that civil strife has destroyed....

View of Ibrahim Qulailat,
Secretary-General of the Lebanese
Independent Nasserist Movement

1. Lebanon's Arab character cannot be the subject of doubt or discussion. Her Arab affiliations are not a piece of merchandise to be bartered....

2. Our movement rejects the nonsense about sovereignty that the leaders of the isolationist parties and the highest official in the country have been repeating for so long and regards it as a prelude to liquidationist thinking calling for the destruction of the Palestinian resistance....

3. The existing regime, with its decayed institutions based on political confessionalism, which has made Lebanon a country of privileges for the Maronite community, is utterly unacceptable. In pursuit of its scientific and democratic line, our movement calls for the modernization and development of the regime. In this, it is in agreement with the broad lines of the nationalist and pro-gressive movements and forces as regards the programme of political reform proposed by the progressive parties....

Here mention must be made of the minimum or common denominator demands necessary for reaching a settlement about which there has been so much talk in the last few days. Superficial though they are, and though our movement does not believe they can do any good, these minimum demands have been rejected by the isolationists [Maronites and other groups opposed to change] on the other side. This in itself shows how determined they are to hang onto their confessional privileges and to reject even a semblance of reform. What would their attitude be to the real modernization and reform of the state?

The isolationist groups' rejection of the superficial and fatuous solutions that have been called "common denominations" is a slap in the face for the traditional Muslim leadership, which has tried to ride the wave of the popular mass upsurge, firstly in order not to lose their position of leadership, and secondly in order to ensure that the demands made [by the progressive parties] are not granted. The isolationists' rejection of the common denominators has deprived the traditional Muslim leadership of all justification for their existence and their continued political activity. It also confirms our movement's view that the crisis of confidence between the traditional leadership and the mass movements is the result of the former's inability to comprehend the variables and equilibriums of Lebanese politics. In place of this comprehension, their thinking has continued to rotate around the crumbs of privileges which have been allocated to them by the regime, and, but for such a regime, they would have disappeared from the political scene and been brushed aside by the masses . . . .

4. The independent Nasserist Movement absolutely rejects partition and refuses to be intimidated by the daily threats of it.

Statement by Phalangist Party Leader Pierre Gemayel
on the Differences between
the Two Sides to the Lebanese Conflict

A certain confusion has occurred in Muslim quarters as a result of the war. One sign of this is the attempt made by certain outside power groups, or groups enjoying foreign support, to occupy positions of leadership among the Muslims and to behave thereafter in a manner that may well be termed arbitrary and exploitative. Understanding and free choice in these circumstances is impossible. In my view, this is one of the major reasons why we do not have the peace which we all want and hope for. The nation's will is not only divided. It is occupied or has fallen under occupation. This will was not split because one-half believes in Marxism, for example, while the other half rejects it, but because Muslims held a different view of the Palestinians and of other issues relating to their own representation in government than the Christians. The difference between the two views is itself the sectarian difference or one of its manifestations. And if the Palestinians and communists have been able to manipulate this difference and use it for their own purposes, this does not mean that they have become the spokesmen of Lebanese Muslims. We do not recognize this attribute of Muslim representation except as expressed by the [traditional] Muslim leadership. For if these leaders have been ejected by force from their positions, this does not mean that their authority has been abolished nor does this forceful ejection have any binding effect on us, of course .... We believe that the formula worked out in the 1940s broke up only because some of us practiced it by adhering to Arabism as the melting pot idea for all the Lebanese while others warned against this melting pot idea. They viewed Arabism as a direct threat to Lebanese sovereignty and independence and a real threat to the freedoms of Christians and to freedom in general. For this reason, the formula began to totter and disintegrate.

The problem is, first and foremost, a problem of freedom. To say that it is a sectarian Christian reaction is false, or at least incorrect. In any case, the Christians do not constitute any danger or tyranny to Muslims or to Arabism. Tyranny comes instead from Arabism and from the Muslims. It is not fair to view the rejection of this tyranny or the rebellion against it as a sectarian reaction. In my view, the tyranny is itself sectarian; this is what Christians also think and feel. It is not fair to interpret Christian caution with respect to Arabism as sectarian either, so long as Arabism itself remains nothing but a sectarian prejudice. As proof of this, I will cite only two instances: the first is the Arab aid which is reportedly being sent to Lebanon. This was sent to the Muslims—Lebanese and Palestinians—not to the Christians. What does this mean except that the Arabs regard Christian Lebanese as outsiders and foreigners? Are the Christians not victims of this war also?

The second instance is the Arab interference in the conflict, both positive as well as negative. From the negative viewpoint, our voices became hoarse calling for Arab League intervention to separate the two sides to the conflict. All our appeals were in vain. We did not hear one word of protest when Christians were being evicted from 'Akkar, Damour and the Biqu'a and subjected to acts of terror. It was only when Syria clashed with the Palestinian resistance that the Arab League intervened.

In the view of the Christians, the League intervened only because Syria had recognized the truth about the conflict and became aware of the injustice done to the Christians, so it quickly began to treat them like the other Lebanese. It is because of this that we feel comfortable with the Syrian position and not with the others who, had they been able, would have forced President al-Assad to withdraw. I do not know whether or not this campaign against al-Assad's Syria is further evidence that Hafez al-Assad wants to purify Arabism of sectarian prejudice but the rest of the Arabs or Arabism itself do not want this to happen.

View of the Palestinians
(Salah Khalaf-Abu Ayyad)
on the Lebanese Conflict°

... We are opposed to this war raging in Lebanon which has no rhyme or reason. It is a war which no sane person can believe resulted from some acts of excess or certain violations. For if we were to compare these Palestinian excesses committed form 1969 until April 1975 with the massacres that took place in the last seventeen months, these would be a drop in an ocean. Let us not deceive ourselves by saying that the war was a result of these excesses. The war was the result of a conspiracy against the Palestinian revolution which then exploded certain issues among the Lebanese .... With all this as background, I tell you that we are prepared to carry out all that is required of us irrespective of all the propaganda we hear from the Phalange and Amchit radio stations and the campaign against the Palestinians, to whom are sometimes added the communists. But this is erroneous. The war is not between Palestinians and communists on the one hand and Christians on the other, nor between some who want to liberate Lebanon and are anxious for its sovereignty as they cheer the Syrian occupation. They say that we are an occupying power.

We were forced to seek refuge in this country and in others under the well-known circumstances in 1948. We are not an occupation force. The fact is that a revolution arose among this nation and it carried arms wherever it was possible. We carried arms in Jordan. It is true that a conspiracy was carried out against us but we are still present in Jordan in one form or another. The world will realize that we are still present in Jordan, even though not in the form of an open revolution. In Syria too we were present. It is true that our presence may be passive in one form or another but we do have an armed presence in Syria despite the battles in Beirut and elsewhere. I know this presence is passive. But this is not our fault; the fault is that of the Syrian regime ....

Once this war against us ends, the greater danger will come from

°From an interview.

Israel which is preparing things for us in the South [of Lebanon] in order to engage us in a long war. I will repeat, therefore, that in spite of all this we are ready to facilitate the task of President Sarkis and to do all he asks, provided this is proportionate to other concessions made by the other parties to the conflict, and specifically the isolationists.

Q.   What you have just said leads us to ask about the nature of current relations between Syrians and Palestinians. Are any serious efforts being made to reconcile you to Damascus?

A.   Relations have neither progressed nor regressed. Efforts are of course being made and we are concerned with the well-being of Syria and the Syrian army. This is why we demand the withdrawal of Syrian troops from Lebanon despite the fact that this demand annoys our brethren in Syria. We must, however, put an end to this nightmare which has descended upon certain regions in Lebanon. This is why we are anxious for Syrian army withdrawal, but if this withdrawal does not take place, this strangulation will continue . . . . After having followed the same line as Syria, there are now people trying to mediate between us and the Syrians. Others threaten either a political or a military show-down. I would like to state that we are not afraid, no matter how loud or violent these declarations are . . . for we have nothing to lose in Lebanon except the Cairo Agreement . . .

Q.   There is talk of a proposed confederal union between Syria, Jordan and Lebanon. Since you as Palestinians are present in all three states, this proposal concerns you, too. What is your opinion of this union?

A.   We, in principle, are for any Arab union. Would that Arab unity be attained! But any unity founded on a suspicious basis, namely with the object of achieving a settlement with Israel, we shall oppose to the very end. So far, all talk of union has been linked with a settlement. Any union bound by one united front against the enemy we would welcome with enthusiasm and help to accomplish. But any form of union which comes into being in order to absorb the Palestinians and their cause or to restrain the Palestinian people and harness the revolution for the sake of signing a settlement whereby the West Bank would be the Palestinian state proposed for a confederation with Syria, Jordan and Lebanon—that sort of union we are opposed to because it has no content as a force for struggle. Any other union which has a potential for struggle, we are ready to join.

Interview with Kamal Jumblatt, Leader of the Lebanese Nationalist and Socialist Movement

Q. On the eve of September 23, 1976 the Lebanese war enters a new phase. Do you think President Sarkis will really assume office?

A. The problem of Sarkis assuming office is not created by the nationalist forces. On the contrary, the nationalist forces believe that his assumption of office is a starting point, at least for preventing the continuation of Arab and international conspiracies. You know that, as a result of the initiatives of the nationalist movement and of contacts with the various factions and following the pressure applied by the Americans while [Dean] Brown was here, the constitution was amended and the Chamber met to elect a president and elected Sarkis. Therefore, we are working within a plan whose aim is to restore some form of legality to the country. But the problem is the other side, who still play upon the Syrian presence and exploit it. Were it not for this presence, the position of the isolationists, as is well known to all Lebanese and to Syria itself, would have been on the verge of final collapse, especially after the occupation of Metin and Sannine. It seems they still want to use the Syrian presence to the full, even though the isolationist faction has begun to be apprehensive about the Syrian presence, since the bill presented to the isolationists by the Syrian regime for services rendered will be very costly in the end.... They have begun to talk about a confederal union and a security pact and are asking the isolationists to accept this. It appears this issue has caused division. Chamoun, former president and leader of the Liberal Party, who was opposed to the Phalangists but in favor of the *status quo*, wants to go on to the bitter end, not caring whether he wins or loses since all he cares about is material gain and cheap victories over the Kata'ib. There is also a group in the Kata'ib who follow Chamoun in principle and take his orders, as well as a number of smaller factions. In addition, there is a Kata'ib group which wants to finish [the war] and to provide the proper atmosphere for a new Lebanese unity. In general, however, they are expecting what they call a European force which will balance the Syrian army if Syria changes its policy or if there are any changes in the Syrian regime. They believe that the fighting must go on until this is achieved, in addition to other reasons that have to do with the Palestinian presence ....

Q. There is a certain lack of clarity regarding the American-Israeli scheme. At times you state they are after a confederal union. At other times you say they want to break up the region into sectarian states, including a national Maronite home. What in your view is the truth about their intentions?

A. What one is afraid of is that the proposed confederal union might be a prelude to partition. Within this union, there might occur what once took place in Syria during the French mandate: the State of Damascus, the State of Jabal-Druze, the State of the Alawites, the State of Aleppo. Hence we fear that talk of a confederal union may ultimately prepare for the rise of an Alawite state in Syria, a Maronite state in Lebanon, a Shi'ite state, a Druze state and this may then become enlarged to include a Kurdish state. Hence, the proposed confederal union may have two aspects: one, as a safeguard for the unity of Lebanon as well as the unity of Syria, Jordan and the Palestinian people, and, two, as an instrument for partition. Thus the scheme runs in two directions. The plan of partition may be more important than the plan for unity according to the Israeli-American-Syrian scheme . . .

Q. At what point then do the wishes of the Syrian regime intersect with this scheme? Are they complementary to it or is the Syrian regime involved in a conspiracy and hence part of an American plan directed at dissipating the power of the Arab confrontation states?

A. This scheme, if we look at it from the viewpoint of nationalistic commitment and the Arab future, does not safeguard the interests of Syria. I think Syrian policy was very imprudent to have fallen into this trap and to have retreated from its nationalist objectives. I do not see what interest Syria has in collaborating with this scheme except perhaps it wishes to prove that the Syrian regime can solve the Palestine problem by giving it one form or another which may not be reconcilable with the Palestinians' right to recover their land and reestablish the Palestinian state within the 1947 borders. On the international level, the Syrian regime has demonstrated its daring by accepting to act as a tool in this scheme. All this is in reality highly complex and contains many contradictions. In the end, it does not serve Syrian interests. Al-Assad, on the other hand, likes to appear as the man of peace in Lebanon. He has a strange theory. He wants to "contain" the isolationists and make them veer towards Damascus. But this will not work because the isolationists have not put their trust in Syria, nor in any Syrian regime, nor in the Arabs either, to whom they refer in their broadcasts as "the nomads." Just as Israel does not trust the Arabs, so Maronite Zionism is similar in this respect to Israeli Zionism. Perhaps, however, the Maronite variety is more fearful of its future whichever Arab side they turn to. They know how to exploit the Arab states to their advantage and then turn their back to them. This is because the isolationists among the Maronites look only to the West. They are in truth the new Crusaders of the East, and this very expression was attributed to a Kata'ib leader. Hence between the Syrian, even Ba'athist, mentality and that of the isolationist Maronites there can be no bridge and no mutual trust. This is why I described Syrian policy as irrational because it did not recognize its true interests. One day, Syria will have to change its policy or else the Syrian people, the army and the regime itself will force a change of leadership so as not to be carried away any further in this idiotic policy from which there can be no gain. The isolationists have rejected the security pact as well as the federation. Syria will not gain anything, not even the loyalty of the isolationists .... Even now, the isolationists are calling for a European force, preferably French according to their plans, in order to face the Syrian army. You know that the Syrian army has not been accepted in a single Christian village or town and has not dared to enter any of them because the isolationists have opposed this vigorously.

Q. You have laid down certain conditions for accepting a confederal union and a defensive security pact against Israel. Some say that if you were to take a plane to Damascus and meet al-Assad, you might make the Syrians concede and matters would then end.

A. I do not think so. A change must take place in Syrian policy and the Syrians must make us feel that they changed their policy and are willing to follow a new one. Naturally, this cannot occur unless they withdraw from the regions from which they have promised to withdraw and thus fulfill their promises and demonstrate their good intentions. As for my taking a plane to Damascus and meeting al-Assad, this is just a traditional Lebanese mode of thought which may be the result of an underdeveloped political mentality in Lebanon as compared to the West ....

IV. ISLAM, FUNDAMENTALISM, AND MODERNISM

Islam is both a religion and a social, economic, and cultural system. Its ethical and moral system reflects the religion and the socioeconomic foundation on which it is based. Consequently, the Islamic societies evaluate every sociopolitical event, change, and innovation from thier own particular viewpoint. In practice, the implication of this is that a development, event, or a social change viewed in one fashion in the West may be seen in a totally different light by an Islamic society. On the other hand, these Islamic societies have changed continuously, like other societies, because of internal forces and/or foreign influences. Many Western scholars who call themselves "experts on Islam" have claimed that Islam remained passive and lethargic after the "closing of the gates of *Ijtihat*" in the twelfth to the fourteenth century. *Ijtihat* in a general way means intellectual inquiry, innovation, and speculation. The truth is that the Islamic societies have continued to develop in a dialectical fashion until the present day, but the intellectual appraisal of these developments has not always corresponded to the material change itself; there was therefore some discrepancy between the actual events and the appraisals and explanations of these events.

The so-called "ossification" of the thought process was due essentially to a social and political synthesis, reached after centuries of evolution, and to the resulting equilibrium, which created a long period of social and political stability beginning in the twelfth century. This stability began to be disturbed in the eighteenth century by the increasing penetration of the West, first through peaceful trade relations and then through aggressive economic and political policies of colonialism and imperialism. Consequently, the old relationship between Christian West and Muslim East underwent a substantial qualitative change from one in which the Islamic society was equal to the West to one in which it was subservient, dominated, and exploited. The results of this change were felt by every Muslim social group in every walk of life. Reaction to the political subservience and economic exploitation, and to the resulting social and cultural alienation, was expressed in religious terms for, as explained, the conceptual framework of Islamic society made it inevitable that all developments taking place within it would be evaluated in Islamic terms.

"Islamic" to the Westerner had a mainly religious connotation, as he was used to regarding "Christianity" and "religion" as synonymous. For a Muslim, "Islamic" meant not solely or necessarily "religion" or "religious" but the whole life and ethos of the Muslim society. It is true that any intellectual explanation, acceptance, or repudiation of a particular event had to be formulated in "Islamic" terms, but often the substance of the argument had only a formal relation to Islam. Consider, for example, the case of Jemaleddin Afghani, who is considered by some as one of the first major Muslim reformers. Many scholars, especially Nikki Keddie, have engaged in much discussion of whether Afghani was a "true believer" or merely used Islam as a vehicle to express his anticolonialist political views. The answer is that Afghani had no other way to express his views so as to make them relevant to the Muslim audiences except by reference to Islam. Afghani was known also as the promoter of Pan-Islamism. This ideology, known generally—and incorrectly—solely as a movement to unite all Muslims against the West and initiated and promoted to large extent by Sultan Abdumhamid II, in reality comprised a variety of ideological aspirations, which, short of secular channels of expression used the traditional-religious ways to exteriorize themselves. Thus Pan-Islamism, besides being an anti-imperialist movement, also expressed the social grievances of the lower class produced by the gradual introduction of the Western capitalist system into the Middle East. It also expressed the populist yearnings of some sections of the old traditionalist elites as well as of the modern elites arising among the lower classes in the fast-growing port cities and administrative centers. Consequently a correct understanding of the ideological developments in the Middle East demands a new and thorough evaluation of Pan-Islamism in order to distinguish its purely religious aspects from its secular, political, social, and economic dimensions. This is an essential task because some of the nationalist, populist-socialist views embodied in Pan-Islamism came to be expressed chiefly after World War I in the form of independent ideological currents of thought.

The first Muslim reaction to the Western domination apeared in a variety of forms and at all levels of society (Tahtawi, Young Ottomans, and so forth) but Western scholars chose only those that suited their theological understanding of Islam. Hence, Afghani, Abduh, Rida, and others received enormous attention, while others received but scant mention. Even the changes in the Ottoman Empire in the nineteenth century, considered "reforms," did not escape one-sided evaluation. There is a basic qualitative difference between the earlier and the later reforms: the widespread changes introduced by Mahmud II (1808–39) conformed to the Islamic traditions and were successful, while those imposed by the West after 1839, and particularly after 1856, had no relation to the social and political traditions of Islam and led rapidly to the disintegration of the Ottoman state. Yet all these reforms have been defined as "Westernizing" endeavors.

One can almost safely state that, for the most part, the views on reform, change, and so on expressed during the second half of the nineteenth century by Muslim thinkers on behalf of Islam, however genuine and well meaning, embodied in varying degrees Western views of social organization and change borrowed from a variety of Western sociologists and historians. In other words, this "reformist" thought did not take its essence from the Koran or even the Sunna, that is, from the genuine sources of Islamic life and thought, but contented itself with adopting contemporary thoughts and views through formal reference to Islam. (This method of change may be inevitable, but it cannot be discussed further here.)

Real Islamic fundamentalism, meanwhile, was expressed in diffuse ways, first among the masses in the form of a rejectionist current that took its essence directly from the Koran. The rejectionists repudiated much of the thought and the institutions and practices borrowed from the West by intellectuals or governments, although many religious leaders also demanded change. The fundmentalist thought, which began to take a more systematic shape in the late nineteenth century, was quite different from the so-called Wahhabi fundamentalist movement of Arabia of the late eighteenth century. The Wahabbis envisaged fundamentalism as a life of prayer and devotion, as this was how they knew Islam in their isolated, poor tribal area of Central Arabia. They did not and could not envisage Islam in a changing society challenged continuously by forces from within and without. Recent Islamic fundamentalism developed both as a formal movement and as a current of thought that saw the salvation of Islam not in a return to the rigid formalistic rituals of the Wahabbis but in a dynamic interaction between the Koran and the Sunna (some would accept only the Koran) and the contemporary sociopolitical world. Exponents of this movement sought, in other words, both a return to the fountainheads of Islam and an accommodation, in the spirit of Islam, with the existing order of things. Implicitly they rejected much of what had been accepted in the name of change and modernity.

The practice, as usual, followed a different course. There is no question but that the antiimperialist struggle after World War II, which led to the liberation of many Islamic countries from colonial rule, was affected deeply by Islamic fundamentalism. Algeria and Egypt are two prominent examples. But after liberation the Islamic policy of these countries was substantially different from the rigid, formalistic fundamentalism of Saudi Arabia and Libya (which, incidentally, had to fight little or not at all for their liberation). It appears that until about 1970 Islamic

fundamentalism was extremely useful in sharpening Muslim consciousness and mobilizing public opinion against foreign domination but was less
successful in assuming control of government and instituting a truly
Muslim way of life through the force of law and authority. The first marked
departure from this pattern occurred in Pakistan in 1977, after General
Zia ul-Hak ousted the secularist-minded Zulfikar Bhutto and instituted a
policy of Islamization. A number of people ignored the fact that Zia ul-
Hak, whatever the merits and the ultimate outcome of his Islamic policy,
did not act through sheer personal inspiration but followed in many ways
the teaching of Maulana Sayyid Abdul A'la Maududi (1903–79). Maududi
was one of the greatest Muslim fundamentalist scholars of our time. Born
in India and self-taught, he was active in journalism and politics until about
the mid-1930s when he began to study the major social and political
problems of Muslim India from an Islamic viewpoint. In 1940 he launched
the organization known as Jama'at-Islami (Muslim Community); then, in
1947, he emigrated to Pakistan, where he continuously advocated the
Islamization of the country. He was condemned to death, partly because of
his views, in 1953; this led to riots, and he was subsequently released
because of the popular pressure. His main thesis was that the Koran and
the Sunna embraced the entire life of man, and that Islam was a complete
way of life rather than a mere set of rules governing relations between
man and God. He also criticized the tendency to cling to everything from
the past as if it were sacred. His greatest work is *Tafhim al-Qu'ran*, written
in Urdu over a period of 30 years. It has already been translated piecemeal
into many languages and is rapidly becoming one of the most widely read
Muslim writings of our time. Some of Maududi's works have been
translated into English and edited by Ahmad Khursid; see *Fundamentals
of Islam* (Lahore: Islamic Publications, 1975), *Guide to Islam* (Lagos,
Nigeria: John West, 1969), *The Islamic Law and Constitution* (Lahore:
Islamic Publications, 1960), and *Towards Understanding Islam* (London:
The Islamic Foundation, 1980).

Fundamentalist Islamic movements have appeared in our day in all
the Muslim countries. In some places, such as Turkey, Jordan, Pakistan,
and Indonesia, they have taken the form of associations or political parties,
while elsewhere, such as in Syria, Egypt, and Sudan, they have acted as
small informal underground groups. The only country in which Islamic
fundamentalism took control of the government through revolution is
Iran. (That event is discussed at length in the section devoted to Iran.)
Currently the fundamentalists are engaged in a major movement of
resistance aginst the Ba'thist regime of Syria.

The most important fundamentalist Islamic organization, which has
influenced in a variety of ways the Muslim thought throughout the world
and affected many of the political events in the Middle East, is the Muslim

Brethren, or *Jam'iyat al-Ikhwan al-Muslimin*. Born in Egypt and defined by itself as "a universal Islamic body which strives to attain the objectives for which Islam arose," the organization has survived pressures and persecutions and has increased its influence, especially among the masses. The works of the founders of the movement, especially of Hasan al-Banna, have been translated into several languages and disseminated throughout the Islamic world. The basic principles of the Muslim Brethren, as ratified in 1945, are the following: To provide a precise explanation of the Holy Koran by interpreting it and by referring back to its origins and its universal elements, by completely revealing it in the spirit of the age and by defending it from falsehoods and suspicions; to unify Egypt and other Islamic nations on the basis of Koranic principles; to assure the growth of national wealth; to expand and make available to every Muslim social services; to liberate all Islamic lands from foreign assistance and to help Muslim minorities through the establishment of a Muslim League; and to promote universal peace and a humanitarian civilization through the universal principles of Islam. This of course necessitates the establishment of a Muslim religious government to supervise all these activities. The philosophy of the Muslim Brethren can be understood best through a study of the life and teachings of its founder, Hasan al-Banna.

The literature on the Muslim Brethren is rather rich. See for further reference *The Muslim World Book Review* (published in London by the Islamic Foundation) 1, no. 1 (1980); Richard P. Mitchell, *The Society of the Muslim Brothers* (London: Oxford University Press, 1969); G. E. von Grunebaum, "Some Recent Constructions and Reconstructions in Islam," in *The Conflict of Traditionalism and Modernism in the Muslim Middle East*, ed. Carl Leiden (Austin: University of Texas Press, 1966), pp. 146–50. On al-Banna, see *al-imam al-shahid Hasan al-Banna yatahuddatu ilā shahab al-'alām al-Islami* [Martyr Imam Hasan al-Banna Speaks to the Youth of the Muslim World] (Damascus: Dar al-qalem, 1974); and Abd-al-Halim Mahmud, *Manaj al-islah al-islami al-mujkma* [Method of Islamic Reform in Society] (Cairo: Dar al-shaab, 1972).

12. Renaissance in the Islamic World[*]

Hasan al-Banna

Hasan al-Banna (1906–49), the founder of the Muslim Brotherhood (or Muslim Brethren), was born in the village of Mahmudiyya in the Nile Delta province of Beheira, Egypt. His father, a respected scholar and a follower of the fundamentalist Hanbalite Sunni school, greatly influenced his son. Al-Banna received a religious education and teacher training, the latter at Dar al-'Ulum in Cairo. Early in life, he became a member of various orthodox religious organizations and took part in anti-British activities; and his dedication to Islam, to teaching, and to missionary work was evident. His nationalist feelings were aroused by the British occupation of Egypt. While teaching in Isma'iliyya, the administrative center of the Suez Canal, he was constantly aware of the relatively easy life enjoyed by British troops and French officials, whose standard of living was far better than that of the average Egyptian. He was also opposed to the missionaries' evangelical activities. Al-Banna founded the first nucleus of the Brotherhood in Isma-'iliyya in 1928.

Officially established in 1929, the Jam'iyyat al-ikhwan al-muslimin *(Society of Muslim Brethren) became the most powerful Islamic organization since the heyday of the Wahhabi movement. Al-Banna came eventually to Cairo, where he taught from 1934 to 1946 while leading the organization. Endowed with a prodigious memory, inexhaustible energy, oratorical skill, and personal charm, he was a born leader. He had a keen knowledge of various Sufi, heretical, and subversive movements in Islam, as well as of their techniques, which he combined with modern notions of organization and propaganda.*

The secret organization soon spread throughout the towns of Egypt, and then to Sudan, Syria, Lebanon, Jordan, Palestine, and North Africa, and al-Banna became known as Murshid al-'amm *(the Supreme Guide). The organization advocated a return to orthodox Islam but also devoted attention to education, community development, training in industrial skills, and social welfare, and it even owned commercial companies. In 1948, it was estimated that the membership amounted to 2 million, most of whom were from the lower classes. Al-Banna reportedly defined the Brotherhood as a Salafi movement, an orthodox way, a Sufi reality, a political body, an*

---

[*]Reprinted, with a new title, from Hasan al-Banna, "Min al-qadim: Ittijah al-nahda al-jadida fi al-'alam al-islami ["Of Old: The Direction of the New Renaissance in the Islamic World"], *al-Muslimun* [The Muslim], Damascus, February 1958, pp. 55–60.

athletic group, a scientific and cultural society, an economic company, and a social idea.

Beginning in 1939 and during the war years, the Brotherhood came into conflict with the government. The Brethren advocated independence for Egypt, unity of the Nile Valley, and eventually a government with a caliph at its head, but also reforms, which, if not forthcoming, they argued might cause revolution. Later, they urged a jihad (holy war) against the Zionists, and pressed for full return to the laws of Islam. The Brethren were implicated in the assassination of two Egyptian Prime Ministers, and consequently many members were arrested and persecuted. Al-Banna made futile attempts to extricate the movement from politics, but he was assassinated on February 12, 1949, probably by order of King Faruq, and the Brethren were outlawed. In 1950, however, their freedom was partially restored, and the Brethren again engaged in politics under a director general, Hasan al-Hudaybi, a former judge attached to King Faruq, assumed this position in 1950, after the position had been filled by several people, including Ahmad Hasan al-Baquri, who became Minister of Waqfs (Foundations) from 1952 through 1953. Hudaybi remained supreme guide until his death in 1973.

The Brotherhood supported all independence movements. It was one of the principal forces that contributed to the success of the officers' revolution of July 1952, and immediately afterward enjoyed full freedom. Even before 1952, in fact, the officers' secret organization had established relations with the Brotherhood through Anwar al-Sa'dat, and even Nasser (Jamal 'Abd al-Nasir) was thought to have been a member for a short time. But after the revolution, the Brotherhood's ideal of a theocratic state based on Islamic principles clashed with the more practical aims of the officers, who, although faithful to Islam, believed that the renewal of the social, political, and economic systems called for a secular approach. The Brethren tried to impose their viewpoint on the Egyptian Government and even interfered in the negotiations with the British. Finally regarded as a political party, they were dissolved on January 12, 1954, briefly restored, and then abolished again. The military found it necessary to explain at great length their repressive action. See "Dissolution of the Muslim Brotherhood—Statement of the Council of the Revolutionary Command," Middle East Affairs 5 (March 1954): 94–100 (a translation of the original statement, which appeared in al-Ahram, January 15, 1954: "Mu'amarat kubra li-iqsa' al-'ahd al-hadir yudabbiruha al-ikhwan al-muslimun ma'a rijal al-safara al-baritaniyya fi al-Qahira. Hajama'at al-ikhwan al-muslimin wa-ghalq markazaha wa-furu'iha fi anha' misr" ["Great Plot for Overturning the Present Regime Prepared by the Muslim Brethren and the Men of the British

Embassy in Cairo. Dissolution of the Muslim Brethren Group and Closing of its General Headquarters and Branches in Egypt"].

The dismissal of Muhammad Naguib (Nagib), the nominal head of the Egyptian Revolution, brought Nasser to power and sealed the doom of the Brethren. The final rift with the Revolutionary Council, which had wanted to retain friendly relations with the Brethren, came after the evacuation agreement was signed with the United Kingdom on October 19, 1954. The evacuation was to take place in 1956. The Brethren opposed the terms of the agreements and accused Nasser of collaborating with the British, but also criticized the fact that all these decisions were made by the government without the consent of a freely elected parliament and without freedom of expression. An abortive attempt to assassinate Nasser on October 26, 1954, led to the trial and execution of six Brethren and the imprisonment of many others.

The Egyptian ouster of the Brethren dealt a deadly blow to the organization. Many of its followers were won over by Nasser's economic and social policy as well as by his ability to gain the support of al-Azhar, the citadel of Muslim orthodoxy. The movement, however, remained active in Syria, Iraq, Jordan, Lebanon, and Sudan. Mustafa al-Siba'i, the head of the Syrian organization, reportedly was elected director general. The Brethren's publication Majallat al-ikhwan *[Magazine of the Brethren]*—generally known as al-Muslimun *[The Muslim]*—continued its publication in Damascus in 1955, under al-Siba'i's editorship, and was transferred to Lebanon in 1958, after the emergence of the United Arab Republic. Later, the organization moved to Geneva, which became its propaganda center. It continued its underground activities. As late as the summer of 1965, the organization planned to assassinate President Nasser and take power. It was a rather massive plot involving university students, upper class intellectuals, and engineers, who provided the explosives. More than 400 plotters were arrested. For the official view of this plot, see Arab Observer (an English weekly published in Cairo), September 13, 1965, pp. 7–12. By 1975 it began to publish al-Daawa, a daily which had a circulation of over 100,000 copies.

Aided by special temporary conditions, the Brotherhood spread into practically every Arab country. Its importance as a truly international movement with genuine popular support cannot be summarily dismissed. Appealing to their common religious feelings, the organization mobilized the Arab masses against foreign domination. It emphasized the primacy of Islam while stressing in theory and practice the need for economic, social, and educational progress. It also successfully organized the masses for political purposes. Thus, in all these fields, it prepared the psychological and organizational ground on which the later regimes established their own *power and were forced to abide by some of the ideas of the Brethren. However, it failed politically for it was unable to remold the classical Muslim idea of government and state and to adapt it to modern requirements. In fact, it became a partisan movement by competing with the government. It also adopted an unrealistic view of international relations and was utterly inflexible on matters of law.*

Al-Banna was certainly aware of the threat to Islamic values posed by modernization and by identification with the West, especially in matters of economic and social organization, and he therefore tried to incorporate them into Islam or at least to redefine them according to the Muslim ethos.

Sayyid Qutb, an influential member of the Brotherhood and first editor of some of its journals, tried to interpret social justice, a dynamic idea in the present drive for socialism in the Middle East, from an Islamic viewpoint. See his al-'Adala al-ijtima'iyya fi al-islam *[Cairo: Lajnat al-nashr lil-jami'iyyin, 1954]; in a translation by John B. Hardie, it was published as* Social Justice in Islam *(Washington, D.C.: American Council of Learned Societies, 1953). In the 1970s the Ikwan gained additional strength but also split into factions such as Takfir al-Hijra, which advocated an extreme form of Islamic socialism and engaged in armed attacks against the government installations in Egypt. In 1981 the principal spokesmen for the organization were Omar al-Talmasani and Salah Ashmāwi, who published the monthly* al-Daawa *(The Cause) that was closed and then allowed to reappear.*

Many publications in Arabic about the Brotherhood represent both positive and negative points of view. The best book in English is Ishaq Musa al-Husayni, The Moslem Brethren: The Greatest of Modern Islamic Movements, *translated by John F. Brown and John Raey (Beirut: Khayat's, 1956). The original appeared as* al-Ikhwan al-muslimun: kubra al-haraka al-islamiyya al-haditha *(Beirut: Dar Bairut, 1952). Christina Phelps Harris,* Nationalism and Revolution in Egypt: The Role of the Muslim Brotherhood *(The Hague: Mouton, 1964) is based largely on Husayni's book. A good article summarizing the basic principles of the movement as expressed in al-Banna's pamphlet* Da'watuna *[Teachings] is Franz Rosenthal, "The 'Muslim Brethren' in Egypt,"* The Muslim World 37 *(October 1947):278–91. See also Francis Bertier, "L'Idéologie politique des frères musulmans,"* Orient, 8 *(1958):43–57; and Kenneth Cragg,* Islamic Surveys: Counsels in Contemporary Islam *(Edinburgh: Edinburgh University Press, 1965), pp. 110–21.*

Al-Banna's writings and speeches have been repeatedly issued in various editions. The article reproduced here extolls perfection in Islam and points out that the Brotherhood arose because of the West's failure to provide spiritual nourishment.

When we observe the evolution in the political, social, and moral spheres of the lives of nations and peoples, we note that the Islamic world—and, naturally, in the forefront, the Arab world—gives to its rebirth an Islamic flavor. This trend is ever-increasing. Until recently, writers, intellectuals, scholars, and governments glorified the principles of European civilization, gave themselves a Western tint, and adopted a European style and manner; today, on the contrary, the wind has changed, and reserve and distrust have taken their place. Voices are raised proclaiming the necessity for a return to the principles, teachings, and ways of Islam, and, taking into account the situation, for initiating the reconciliation of modern life with these principles, as a prelude to a final "Islamization."

Causes

This development worries a good number of governments and Arab powers, which, having lived during the past generations in a state of mind that had retained from Islam only lessons of fanaticism and inertia, regarded the Muslims only as weak drudges or as nations easily exploitable by colonialism. In trying to understand the new movement [the Brotherhood], these governments have produced all sorts of possible interpretations: "It is the result," said some, "of the growth of extremist organizations and fanatical groups." Others explained that it was a reaction to present-day political and economic pressures, of which the Islamic nations had become aware. Finally, others said, "It is only a means whereby those seeking government or other honors may achieve renown and position."

Now all these reasons are, in our opinion, as far as possible from the truth; for this new movement can only be the result of the following three factors, which we will now examine.

The Failure of the West

The first of the three is the failure of the social principles on which the civilization of the Western nations has been built. The Western way of life—founded in effect on practical and technical knowledge, discovery, invention, and the flooding of world markets with mechanical products— has remained incapable of offering to men's minds a flicker of light, a ray of hope, a grain of faith, or of providing anxious persons the smallest path toward rest and tranquility. Man is not simply an instrument among others. Naturally, he has become tired of purely materialistic conditions and desires some spiritual comfort. But the materialistic life of the West could only offer him as reassurance a new materialism of sin, passion, drink, women, noisy gatherings, and showy attractions which he had come to enjoy. Man's hunger grows from day to day; he wants to free his spirit, to destroy this materialistic prison and find space to breathe the air of faith and consolation.*

Perfection of Islam

The second factor—the decisive factor in the circumstances—is the discovery by Islamic thinkers of the noble, honorable, moral, and perfect content of the principles and rules of this religion, which is infinitely more accomplished, more pure, more glorious, more complete, and more beautiful than all that has been discovered up till now by social theorists and reformers. For a long time, Muslims neglected all this, but once God had enlightened their thinkers and they had compared the social rules of their religion with what they had been told by the greatest sociologists and the cleverest leading theorists, they noted the wide gap and the great distance between a heritage of immense value on one side and the conditions experienced on the other. Then, Muslims could not but do justice to the spirit and the history of their people, proclaiming the value of this heritage and inviting all peoples—nonpracticing Muslims or non-Muslims—to follow the sacred path that God had traced for them and to hold to a straight course.

Type of Development

The third factor is the development of social conditions between the two murderous world wars (which involved all the world powers and monopolized the minds of regimes, nations, and individuals) which resulted in a set of principles of reform and social organization that certain powers, in deciding to put them into practice, have taken as an instructional basis. These principles have become the prey of change and transformation, in fact subject to disappearance and ruin. Muslim thinkers looked on, observed, and returned to what they already possessed in their own right—the great Book of God, the brilliant manifest example of their Prophet and their glorious history. There was nothing of value they could accredit to any existing regime that could not be already found inspiring their thought and conduct and already inscribed in Islamic social organization. There was no blemish against which the social organization of a

---

*This argument has been put forth in various forms by Muslim writers since the end of the nineteenth century, and it is continually stressed by various other writers included in this anthology.

watchful Islam could not guard [its people] by showing them its fearful consequences.

The world has long been ruled by democratic systems, and man has everywhere glorified and honored the conquests of democracy: freedom of the individual, freedom of nations, justice and freedom of thought, justice for the human soul with freedom of action and will, justice for the peoples who became the source of power. Victory at the end of World War I reinforced these thoughts, but men were not slow to realize that their collective liberty had not come intact out of the chaos, that their individual liberty was not safe from anarchy, and that the government of the people had not in many cases freed society from camouflaged dictatorship that destroyed responsibility without limiting jurisdiction. Quite the contrary, vice and violence led to the breaking loose of nations and peoples, to the overthrow of collective organization and family structure, and to the setting up of dictatorial regimes.

Thus, German Nazism and Italian Fascism rose to the fore; Mussolini and Hitler led their two peoples to unity, order, recovery, power, and glory. In record time, they ensured internal order at home and, through force, made themselves feared abroad. Their regimes gave real hope, and also gave rise to thoughts of steadfastness and perseverance and the reuniting of different, divided men around the words "chief"and "order." In their resolutions and speeches, the Führer and the Duce began to frighten the world and to upset their epoch.

What happened then? It became evident that in a powerful and well-knit regime, where the wishes of the individual were based on those of their chiefs, the mistakes of the chiefs became those of the regime, which shared also in their acts of violence, their decline, and their fall; then, everything was at an end, all had been cut down as in a single day, but not until the world had lost in a second war thousands of men, the flower of her youth, and masses of wealth and material.

The star of socialism and Communism, symbol of success and victory, shone with an increasing brilliance; Soviet Russia was at the head of the collectivist camp. She launched her message and, in the eyes of the world, demonstrated a system which had been modified several times in thirty years. The democratic powers—or, to use a more precise expression, the colonialist powers, the old ones worn out, the new ones full of greed—took up a position to stem the current. The struggle intensified, in some places openly, in others under cover, and nations and peoples, perplexed, hesitated at the crossroads, now knowing which way was best; among them were the nations of Islam and the peoples of the Qur'an; the future, whatever the circumstances, is in the hands of God, the decision with history, and immortality with the most worthy.

This social evolution and violent, hard struggle stirred the minds of

Muslim thinkers; the parallels and the prescribed comparisons led to a healthy conclusion: to free themselves from the existing state of affairs, to allow the necessary return of the nations and peoples to Islam.

The Three Regimes and Prayer

In a whimsical moment, I happened to say to my audience at a meeting—which, thanks to God, was a complete success—that this Islamic prayer which we perform five times a day is nothing but a daily training in practical social organization uniting the features of the Communist regime with those of the dictatorial and democratic regimes. Astonished, my questioners demanded an explanation. "The greatest value of the Communist regime," I said, "is the reinforcement of the notion of equality, the condemnation of class distinction, and the struggle against the claim to property, source of these differences." Now this lesson is present in the mind of the Muslim; he is perfectly conscious of it and his spirit is filled with it the moment he enters the mosque; yes, the moment he enters, he realizes that the mosque belongs to God and not to anyone of his creatures; he knows himself to be the equal of all those who are there, whoever they may be; here there are no great, no small, no high, no low, no more groups or classes. And when the muezzin calls, "Now is the hour of prayer," they form an equal mass, a compact block, behind the imam.° None bows unless the imam bows, none prostrates himself unless the imam prostrates himself; none moves or remains motionless unless following the imam's example. That is the principal merit of the dictatorial regime: unity and order in the will under the appearance of equality. The imam himself is in any case limited by the teachings and rules of the prayer, and if he stumbles or makes a mistake in his reading or in his actions, all those behind him—young boys, old men, or women at prayer— have the imperative duty to tell him of his error in order to put him back on the right road during the prayer, and the imam himself is bound absolutely to accept this good advice and, forsaking his error, return to reason and truth. That is what is most appealing in democracy.

How, therefore, can these regimes by superior to Islam, which astonishingly unites all their merits and avoids all their sins? "If this message came from some other than God, many contradictions would be found in it" (Qur'an).

°The imam referred to here is a leader of prayer, and should not be confused with the Shi'ite Imam, who is the supreme head of the community.

No Incentive for Trouble

As I have said, [the people of] the West—and with them those who are blind—are worried by this development, which they consider serious, since they see themselves forced to combat it by every means, being less accustomed to finding themselves facing such a situation than to seeing the success of their reactionary principles on the less developed nations, in contempt of all the rules of civilization followed by cultivated and orderly peoples; judgment steeped in error and the flagrant suppression of rights can be seen as clearly as daylight.

Here, our intention is to demonstrate to the West two points:

(1)   Demonstration of the excellence of Islamic principles of collective organization, and their superiority over everything known to man until now, these principles being:
  (a)   Brotherly love: condemnation of hatred and fanaticism.
  (b)   Peace. Error is committed by the misguided thinking on the legitimacy of the Holy War.
  (c)   Liberty. Error is committed by those who suspect Islam of tolerating slavery and interfering with liberty.
  (d)   Social justice: obvious character of the Islamic theory of power and class structure.
  (e)   Happiness: manifest error in the appreciation of the reality of abstinence.
  (f)   Family: matters concerning the rights of women, number of wives, and repudiation.
  (g)   Work and profit: matters concerning the different kinds of profit, and error in the appreciation of the fact of relying on God.
  (h)   Knowledge. Error is committed by those who accuse Islam of encouraging ignorance and apathy.
  (i)   Organization and determination of duties. Error is committed by those who see in the nature of Islam a source of imperfection and indolence.
  (j)   Piety: the reality of faith, and the merit and reward attached to it.
(2)   Demonstration of the following facts:
  (a)   For the good of man in general, Muslims must move toward a return to their religion.
  (b)   Islam will find in this return her principal strength on earth.
  (c)   Far from receiving impetus from a blind fanaticism, this movement will be inspired by a strong regard for the values of Islam which correspond fully to what modern thought has discovered as most noble, sound, and tested in society. It is God who says what is true and who shows the way.

13. Islamic Socialism[*]

Mustafa al-Siba'i

Mustafa al-Siba'i (b. 1910 in Homs, Syria) is one of the best known leaders and writers of the Muslim Brotherhood. He occupied several high positions in the Brotherhood—as controller general, head of the Syrian branch, and then, reportedly, as director general. Al-Siba'i began publishing al-Manar [The Beacon] in Damascus in 1946. He became the editor of al-Muslimun [The Muslim] after it began publication in Damascus in 1955, and he gave intellectual tone to the Brotherhood. Al-Siba'i is definitely more socially and politically oriented and farther to the left than was al-Banna. He considers himself a Muslim socialist and a republican. In the Constituent Assembly of 1949, al-Siba'i had made common cause with Akram Hawrani, the leader of the Syrian Arab Socialist Party, in support of a republican regime. The Muslim Socialist Front (al-Jabha al-ishtirakkiya), headed by al-Siba'i and representing essentially the views of the Muslim Brotherhood, had four seats, and the Ba'th Party had three. During debates in the Assembly, al-Siba'i proposed a social program on behalf of the Front. He declared that he would work for a true Islamic socialism. Al-Siba'i claims that some of the socialist principles of his movement—in particular, the limitation of land property—were introduced in the constitution of 1950 (Art. 22) as measures of social reform. He clashed with the Syrian Social Nationalist Party (followers of Antun Saadeh) and later with the Ba'th Party. His group was so powerful in Syria that it forced the Egyptian Government to ask the Syrian authorities for written guarantees that the Brotherhood's actions would be brought under control. After 1955, however, al-Siba'i and his group associated with forces trying to oppose the leftists and thus indirectly pushed the Ba'th Party into a coalition with the Communists.

Al-Siba'i wrote articles for reviews and published several books, among which is al-Ahzab al-siyasiyya fi suriyya [The Political Parties of Syria] (Damascus; Dar al-rawwad, 1954). An article proposing Islam as the state religion of Syria ("Islam as the State Religion: A Muslim Brotherhood View in Syria," translated by R. Bayly Winder) appeared in The Muslim World *44 (July–October 1954):215–26; the original had appeared in al-Ayyam, March 9, 1950, and in al-Samir, a New York daily, March 9–14, 1950. Al-*

---

[*]Extract from Mustafa al-Siba'i, *al-Wahda al-kubra* [The Great Union], Damascus, October 29, 1961. A French translation, "À propos du socialisme de l'Islam," appeared in *Orient*, no. 20 (1961):175–78.

Siba'i's views on socialism are expressed in al-Ishtirakiyya al-islam *[Islamic Socialism] (Cairo: Dar al-qawmiyya lil-tiba 'a wal-nashr, 1960), in which he suggested that practically all major economic and social problems could be solved by the socialism of Islam. Reprinted several times, the book met with the approval of some of the 'ulama' but, since al-Siba'i had opposed nationalization and the type of socialism enforced in Egypt, the Voice of Arabs and Cairo radios, both controlled by Nasser, attacked it as having distorted Islam and socialism. Today Sibai has become a major source for ideological guidance for the left-wing Islamic fundamentalism in Syria and Egypt. Al-Siba'i rejected Egyptian accusations in a series of speeches and articles. The following article summarizes al-Siba'i's book on socialism; the pages cited refer to the book.*

Islamic socialism rests on five fundamental rights that must be guaranteed to all its citizens:

1. The right to live and, as its corollary, the safeguarding and protection of health and illness (p. 59).

2. The right to liberty in all its forms, and particularly to political liberty (p. 75).

3. The right to knowledge: This right extends to all the knowledge the nation needs, both spiritual and material (p. 59).

4. The right to dignity, in all its aspects (p. 113).

5. The right to property, subject to certain conditions (p. 124).

I have also mentioned in my book the most important principles on which property is based in Islam:

1. Work—the most important way of acquiring property. All work leads to possession; it is legal if it involves neither fraud nor injustice (p. 132).

2. Private property is an indefeasible right. The state guarantees it and punishes those who interfere with it (pp. 133–35).

3. Property is a social function: the state forbids its utilization as a means of oppression and exploitation (p. 134).

4. Wealth involves social duties: legitimate charity, pensions for relatives, mutual social aid (p. 136).[1]

5. Inheritance is a legitimate right protected by the state (p. 136).

Nationalization can be applied to goods and articles necessary to society only if their possession by one or several individuals involves the exploitation of society, on condition also that economic experts agree that it is in the obvious interest of the nation (p. 163).[2]

Henceforth, when the state has recourse to nationalization in cases of social or economic necessity, it is obliged to afford adequate compensation to the dispossessed proprietors (p. 164).

The principles of Islam, our social situation, and the obligation placed upon us by our religion to wipe out oppression and give human dignity to the peasants—all this renders the limitation of landed property legal in the eyes of the law and makes it one of the duties of the state (p. 170). Nevertheless, it must be applied in all fairness and in conformity to the general interest, and not merely to satisfy rancor and vengeance.

Moreover, the seizure of private goods should be carried out only under certain conditions, especially in cases of extreme danger, invasion, public disaster, famine, flood, or earthquake..Only if the state treasury and the funds held by the authorities are inadequate to guard against any danger is it lawful to deduct from people's wealth what is strictly necessary to meet such necessity, as proclaimed by the 'ulama' of Islam, such as al-Nawawi,[3] al-Ghazzali,[4] etc. (pp. 194–96).

I have then cited the rules of mutual social aid. Numbering twenty-nine, they guarantee the fulfillment by the state of this obligation vis-à-vis its subjects, thus assuring them as well as their children a decent life in case of incapacity, illness, or unemployment.

Briefly summarized, such is the conception of Islamic socialism that I have set out in my book. I have then compared it with the socialism of the extreme left.

1.   In recognizing the lawful character of private property, Islamic socialism allows those with talent to participate in constructive competition, an essential condition for the expansion of civilization and the development of production (p. 259).

2.   This socialism encourages and leads to cooperation and friendship, not to class struggle (p. 260).

3.   It is a moral socialism based on sound morals, of which it makes a foundation in its doctrine (p. 261).

4.   All that concerns man comes under the care of this socialism: religion, morals, education, clothing, food, and not only the material aspects of life (p. 264).

5.   It is an integral part of the credo of the Muslim, who can but apply it. It constitutes a more rapid and more effectual method than any other socialism for the reform of our society (p. 266).

As for the socialism of extreme left, this is what I wrote: "Its roots are not in the depths of the human soul; it is not based upon religion or human nature or conviction. It cannot therefore be applied except by force and in an atmosphere of terror" (p. 267).

Such are the aspects and characteristics of socialism in Islam. Without doubt, it is totally different from the type of socialism that attaches no importance to religious values, relies on the class struggle in society, seizes private property without good reason, nationalizes industry and economic concerns that contribute to the national economic prosperity, paralyzes initiative and competition in the individual as well as the community, impoverishes the rich without enriching the poor, originates from hate and not from love, claims to work for the people while it terrorizes them, impoverishes them, and humiliates them. A socialism of this kind is as far removed as possible from Islam and has nothing in common with it. Moreover, Islam foresees in it the inevitable ruin of any society where it reigns and exercises influence.

Finally, since our revolutionary order [the Syrian revolution] and our government have agreed on socialism as a social regime, and since they have published a detailed program which is in no way contrary to Islam,[5] it is good—and I say this in all sincerity and frankness—that the cause of Islamic socialism should be encouraged, because of its profound influence on the minds of the masses and its facility for building a worth-while society, unique and advanced in its economy and its social relations. It is also desirable that this socialism should be embraced by every zealous defender of our nation who is anxious to avert the danger of extreme left-wing socialism.

In fact, Islamic socialism conforms to human nature. It satisfies the dignity of all citizens as well as their interests. To the workers, it grants a decent standard of living and an assured future; to the holder of capital, it opens up wide horizons as regards production under state control. Finally, it applies to all citizens without discrimination, and is not the prerogative of the followers of one religion to the exclusion of those of another.

Notes

1. This principle forms the key difference between the voluntary personal concepts of social aid or charity defended by al-Siba'i and the institutionalized, state-controlled social welfare system enforced by Egypt.
2. According to al-Siba'i and the doctrine of the Muslim Brotherhood, nationalization is limited to movable goods and items—that is, to the products of labor. This provision applies more to handicrafts and to small plants than to industry as a whole.
3. A Shafi'i jurist known for his high erudition, al-Nawawi Muhyi al-Din Abu Zakariya Yahya al-Hizami al-Dimashqi (1233–77), was also famous for his opposition to Sultan Baybars' confiscatory policies and tax exactions.
4. The greatest Sufi theologian of Islam, Abu Hamid al-Ghazzali (1058–1111) was also a great jurist who dealt extensively with questions of property. Works on al-Ghazzali are extensive; see *Encyclopaedia of Islam*, new edition.
5. These views were put forth in October 1961, apparently just before Syria decided to pull out of the union with Egypt. The decision was prompted by the Syrian reaction to the overwhelming domination by Egyptians of Syrian

life as well as by the nationalization decrees of July and August 1961, which threatened to liquidate the upper- and middle-class enterprises in Syria. The government that was established after the revolution considerably softened the soialist measures, but in 1963 the Ba'thists and the military introduced their own brand of socialism, which led almost to the annihilation of private enterprise.

14.   Socialism and Islam[*]

Mahmud Shaltut

Long known for his reformist views, Shaykh Mahmud Shaltut was dismissed as a member of the faculty of al-Azhar in the 1930s, but he was appointed wakil (rector) of al-Azhar in 1958. In 1961, when religious and administrative authority in al-Azhar were separated, Shaltut retained his office as religious head and Dr. Muhammad al-Bahi became the head of the administration. Although it has often been described as the citadel of resistance to oppression and strong government, al-Azhar actually has associated itself more often than not with the policies of the ruling governments. In the 1930s and the 1940s, al-Azhar had a progressive group of teachers, who eventually (in the 1950s and 1960s) came to support President Nasser's social and economic policies. These teachers, representing the weight of religious sanction, provided one of the main channels for winning over the population to these policies. In this article, which is also an indirect rebuttal to Mustafa al-Siba'i's work, Shaltut invokes various Qur-'anic citations to prove, in effect, that Egyptian socialism conforms to Islamic laws. In many respects, his views about the universality of Islam; are similar to those put forth by the Muslim Brotherhood; Shaltut, however, suggests that the state's extensive role is implicit in the idea that all the social obligations of Islam can be met by increased production or wealth. He insists on the need for increasing wealth and gives the government a unique role in achieving it. The position of Shaltut was reaffirmed by Shaykh Ghazali in 1979 in a dispute with the Egyptian Marxists who claimed that there was a similarity between Islam and Marxism.

---

[*]Extract from Mahmud Shaltut, "al-Ishtirakiyya wa-al-islam" ["Socialism and Islam"], *al-Jumhuriyya*, Cairo, December 22, 1961. A French translation, "Le Socialisme et l'Islam," appeared in *Orient*, no. 20 (1961):163–74.

Social solidarity proceeds from men's feelings of responsibility toward one another. Each individual bears the faults of his brother; if he does ill, he does it both for himself and for his brother; if he does good, he does it for himself and for his brother.

Islam and Society

Islam is not only a spiritual religion, as some wrongly imagine, thinking that it limits itself to establishing relations between the servant and his Lord, without being concerned with organizing the affairs of the community and establishing its rules of conduct. On the contrary, Islam is universal in character. Not only does it determine the relations between man and his Lord, but it also lays down the rules that regulate human relations and public affairs, with the aim of ensuring the welfare of society.

Islam's sole desire has been that men shall accept this organization, that their attitude in this regard should stem from the fear they feel for the one who created Islam, from the veneration they have for His power, and from their conviction that He knows the secrets of their hearts; so that there may be ingrained in their minds the principles of clemency, love, cooperation, mutual help, and unanimity. Each man then considers himself as a stone in the structure of society, and becomes an integral part of society, paying for it with his person and his property.

Mutual Social Aid Among Muslims

Members of human society cannot be considered independent of one another. On the contrary, as a result of their existence in this world and the very conditions of their lives, they render each other mutual service and cooperate to satisfy their needs.[1]

Nevertheless, as regards relations between individuals who constitute human society, Islam has not limited itself to the necessities and conditions of life. Above all, it has taken upon itself the task of strengthening the very nature of social life, of preventing deterioration, breaking up, and the consequences of the psychological factors and personal tendencies that often make men exceed the limits of moderation necessary to tranquility, happiness, security, and stability. That is the reason why Islam wants to establish emotional bonds that unite men in their orientation and in their aims, and that make of them a strong, united force, soundly organized, with love as the thread, the common good as the chain, and as their aim happiness in this life and in the life hereafter. This bond is one of faith and belief, which are linked to the source of all good—that is, to God.

This bond is, in Islam, the "religious brotherhood" among Muslims. It is in the "brotherhood" that rights and social duties are expressed in the most sincere fashion. It is this that constitutes the most powerful factor leading toward clemency, sympathy, and cooperation, and giving a sense of the idea; it leads society toward good and banishes evil.

Islam has established this "brotherhood" among Muslims. "The believers are a band of brothers" (Qur'an, XLIX, 10), and the Prophet said, "Muslim is brother to Muslim." Moreover, Islam has raised the religious brotherhood over and above the blood relationship.[2]

Muslims have attained social solidarity to a unique degree in their Islamic society, which God has immortalized in His Book, which says, "Prize them above themselves, though they are in want" (LIX, 9).

Although the word of today may proclaim social solidarity between its members and society, it nevertheless assigns it only a limited objective— simply to ensure the material needs of those who are in need of food, clothing, housing, etc. For fourteen centuries, Islam, for its part, has not contented itself with these objectives. It has given to man five rights, the loss of a single one of which means the loss of all happiness and dignity. Then turning to the fate of those whom circumstances have prevented from enjoying these rights, it has called on society to make these rights available to them.

Social solidarity in Islam, therefore, is conceived in the widest and most complete sense. In effect, it is not limited to the needs of food, housing, and clothing; it stretches still further to the five rights of man:

To preserve his religion
To preserve his life
To preserve his children
To preserve his possessions
To preserve his reason

Thus, the Muslim conception of mutual social aid extends to all the aspects of life, both material and religious.

Mutual social aid in Islam exists in various forms, each of which must be achieved. These are:

1. Moral mutual aid: Desire for another man what you desire for yourself.
2. Mutual aid regarding knowledge: "When our guidance is revealed, those who accept it shall have nothing to fear or to regret; but those that deny and reject Our revelations shall be the

heirs of Hell, and there they shall abide forever" (Qur'an, II, 154-55).

3. Political mutual aid: Muslims are equal in blood; the most humble of them will give his word. They form a solid block in the face of others.

4. Mutual aid regarding defense: "Whether unarmed or well-equipped, march on and fight for the cause of Allah with your wealth and your persons" (Qur'an, IX, 41).

5. Mutual aid with regard to crime: In Islam, blood cannot be shed with impunity. It will be paid for, either by retaliation ("Believers, retaliation is decreed for you in bloodshed" [Qur'an, II, 173]) or by payment by kinsmen of the author of the crime, by those who refuse to swear the oath [qasam] five hundred times, or by the public treasury. The price of the blood will be sent to the family of the victim.

6. Collective mutual aid: This is fixed by legal provisions that define "collective obligation"; individual mutual aid corresponds to this; it is fixed by the provision of individual duties, such as prayer and fasting.

7. Economic mutual aid: Do not squander your possessions. "Do not give to the feeble-minded the property with which Allah has entrusted you for their support" (Qur'an, IV, 4).

8. Moral mutual aid: Let him among you who witnesses a reprobate act change it by his hand; if he is incapable of this, let him do so by his tongue; if he cannot, with his heart; that is the minimum of faith. Those who revolt against the sanctions of God and those who apply them are like the people who share a ship—some have the top, others the bottom. When they need water, the latter must cross the territory of the former. They decide to make a hole in their part, without harming their neighbors up above; if the others prevent them, all are saved.

9. Mutual aid as a product of civilization: "Help one another in what is good and pious, not in what is wicked and sinful" (Qur'an, V, 3). . . .

[In the following sections, Shaltut discusses the benefits and conditions of mutual assistance and the sources necessary to finance the assistance. Among the latter, he cites the alms (zakat) which can be collected by force; the religious foundations (awqaf)[3]; the voluntary help of the rich; the voluntary distribution of property in case of inheritance; booty; mines; and a variety of other sources.]

Social Solidarity Among Muslims

Social solidarity among Muslims is of two kinds—the moral and the material. Moral solidarity derives from two factors. The first is recognizing good and virtue and inviting one's neighbor to conform to it with sincerity and fidelity. "You are the noblest nation that has ever been raised up for mankind. You enjoin justice and forbid evil. You believe in Allah" (Qur'an, III, 106).

The second allows one to hear the Word of God and receive it with gratitude and acknowledgment. "Give good news to My servants, who listen to My precepts and follow what is best in them. These are they whom Allah has guided. These are they who are endued with understanding"(Qur'an, XXXIX, 19–20).

The interaction of these two forces makes cooperation between members of a Muslim society more sound.

Material solidarity consists of meeting the needs of society, of consoling the unfortunate, of helping to achieve what is in the general interest, i.e., whatever increases the standard of living and serves all individuals in a beneficial manner.

It is not to be doubted that all those foundations on which life rests, such as perfection, happiness, and grandeur, matters of science, health, greatness, dignity, civilization, power, and strength, cannot be attained without wealth.

In its attitude toward allowing man to assure his needs, Islam considers wealth realistically. Islam has made wealth an "ornament" of this life (Qur'an, XVIII, 44). It also qualified it as the "support of man." Wealth is not an end in itself. It is only one of the means of rendering mutual service and procuring what one needs. Used thus, it is a good thing, both for the one who possesses it and for society. Considered as an end in itself, and with the sole aim of being enjoyed, wealth becomes for its owner the cause of great harm, and at the same time sows corruption among men. . . .

That is why the Qur'an regards wealth as a good thing, on condition that it is acquired legally and spent for the good of others, and that it remains not an end in itself but simply a means.

Agriculture, industry, and commerce, on which the material life of society depends, are the sources of wealth. Society needs agriculture for the foodstuffs that are produced by the soil. It also needs the various industries that are necessary to man. Clothing, housing, agriculture, machinery, roads, waterways, and railways are also necessary for the protection and defense of the state. All these can be acquired only through industry.

Agriculture, industry, and commerce must therefore be developed as much as possible. That is why the men of Islamic religious learning [*'ulama'*] teach that it is a collective obligation to learn to make all that one cannot do without, and that if this obligation is not fulfilled the sin that falls back on the whole nation can be effaced only if a part of the nation discharges the obligation.

There is no doubt that this obligation consists in working for the achievement of the principle that Islam imposes on its followers, i.e., the autarky [or establishment of self-sufficiency] that allows the Muslim community itself to meet all its needs. Henceforth, the other industrial and mercantile nations have no means of interfering in the affairs of this community, which thus safeguards its existence, its glory, its internal order, its traditions, and its natural wealth. This interference has, in fact, often been utilized to introduce foreign states into our countries, culminating in the occupation and exploitation of the industry and commercial wealth of the country.

It cannot be doubted that agriculture, commerce, and industry are the pillars of the national economy in all nations that wish to live an independent, enlightened, and worthy life. These three realms of activity must be coordinated so that the nation can reach the aim which Islam has assigned to it with the sole aim of preserving its existence and its governmental and administrative independence.

Now history teaches that a nation's lack of the means for self-sufficiency in agriculture, commercial, and industrial matters constitutes the first cause of colonialism.

Whoever holds authority in the Muslim community and influences its interests must therefore take steps to see to it that the nation draws the greatest profit possible from agriculture, commerce, and industry by coordinating the three sectors of activity so that, in the matter of investment, one does not develop at the expense of the others—even if this means transforming agricultural land into capital or industrial concerns, according to the country's needs as dictated by its interests. The country is therefore organized in such a way as to be self-sufficient. Foreign countries can then no longer interfere in its affairs, except in the course of the usual general exhanges between states. The government is therefore an organization that benefits the country and preserves it from all foreign interference. . . .

[*After citing instances of limitation of land property in Islamis history, Shaltut continues:*]

Muslim jurists are unanimous in recognizing the right of authorities to expropriate [land] in order to enlarge the place of prayer [i.e., the jurisdiction of Islam] until the whole world becomes mosque. They also have the right to act likewise to enlarge a street or any other public service, in the interests of both individuals and the community. . . .

[Continuing, Shaltut claims that to be rich is a social function and to be poor is a social ill.]

Worldly possessions are the possessions of God, given by Him to His servants for the benefit of the universe. God sometimes claims possession of these goods: "Allah gives without measure to whom he wills" (Qur'an, XXIV, 38). At other times, He attributes them to their previous owners: "Do not give to the feeble-minded the property with which Allah has entrusted you for their support" (Qur'an, IV, 4).

God has clearly established that the possessors of goods, who are the holders after Him, must preserve, increase, and spend them in a manner laid down by Him: "Give in alms of that which He had made your inheritance" (Qur'an, LVII, 7). God also has put his wealth at the disposal of all men equally: "Allah created the heavens and the earth to reveal the truth and to reward each soul according to its deeds. None shall be wronged" (Qur'an, XLV, 12).

If worldly possessions are the possessions of God, if all men are the servants of God, and if the life in which they toil and do honor to the possessions of God belongs to God, then wealth, although it may be attributed to a private person, should also belong to all the servants of God, should be placed in the safekeeping of all, and all should profit from it. "Men, serve your Lord, who has created you and those who have gone before you, so that you may guard yourselves against evil; who has made the earth a bed for you and the sky a dome, and has sent down water from heaven to bring forth fruits for your sustenance" (Qur'an, II, 19–21).

Thus, to be rich is a social function whose aim is to ensure the happiness of society and satisfy its needs and interests.

So that all men may profit from worldly goods and their souls be free from all greed in this regard, Islam has opposed all who hoard and jealously watch over their wealth. . . . "Proclaim a woeful punishment to those who hoard up gold and silver and do not spend it in Allah's cause. The day will surely come when their treasures shall be heated in the fire of Hell, and their foreheads, sides, and backs branded with them. Their tormentors will say to them: 'These are the riches which you hoarded. Taste then the punishment which is your due' " (Qur'an, IX, 36).

Similarly, Islam has fought the stupidity that leads to the squandering of goods uselessly: "The wasteful are Satan's brothers" (Qur'an, XVII, 29).

Islam has fought luxury, which has created hatred among the social classes, which menaces a peaceful and stable life, not to mention corruption and anarchy. . . .

Islam has traced the straight path of the ideal society; it is a path of solidarity by which the nation lives and which ensures the strength of society. With this end in view, Islam has abolished from the minds of owners [of property] and capitalists such vices as meanness, the taste for squandering the luxury. It has employed all means to encourage men to give generously and to be afraid of appearing miserly and of neglecting the right of the people and of society, to such a point that it has raised liberality to the rank of faith. . . .

"The true servants of the Merciful are those who walk humbly on the earth and say 'Peace!' to the ignorant who accost them; . . . who are neither extravagant nor niggardly but keep the golden mean; who invoke no other God besides Allah . . . " (Qur'an, XXV, 64–66).

For Islam, avarice similarly is one of the traits that condemn the infidel: " 'What has brought you into Hell?' They will reply: 'We never prayed or fed the hungry . . . ' " (Qur'an, LXXIV, 43–44).

Islam has maintained this view for so long that it considers it a denial of the Judgment not to encourage giving to the needy: "Have you thought of him that denies the last Judgement? It is he who turns away the orphan and does not urge others to feed the poor" (Qur'an, CVII).

Briefly summarized, such is the doctrine of Islam regarding the relation among men from the point of view of the solidarity of members of society. It contains in detail all the solid foundations necessary to make our nation a magnificent stronghold, a haven of happiness for those who shelter there.

The doctrine also contains a clear statement of what the socialism of Islam is, for adoption by those who wish to adopt it. Can man find a more perfect, more complete, more useful, and more profound socialism than that decreed by Islam? It is founded on the basis of faith and belief, and all that is decreed on that basis participates in the perpetuation of life and doctrine.

Notes

1. The idea that human society originated in man's practical need for help has been the cornerstone of Islamic social thought. The idea may be traced to Aristotle's view that "every polis (or state) is a species of association and . . . [that] all associations are instituted for the purpose of attaining some good." *The Politics of Aristotle*, trans. Ernest Barker (London: Oxford University Press, 1958), p. 1. Muhammad ibn Muhammad ibn Tarkhan Ab Nasr al-Farabi (*ca.* 870–950) states in his work *al-Siyasat al-madaniyya* [Political Economy] (Hyderabad text; 1346 [1930]) that "man belongs to the species that cannot

accomplish their necessary affairs or achieve their best state, except through the association of many groups of them in a single dwelling place." Quoted from an edition in preparation by Fawzi M. Najjar, in Ralph Lerner and Muhsin Mahdai, eds., *Medieval Political Philosophy* (New York: Collier— Macmillan—Free Press of Glencoe, 1963), p. 32. Finally, in his *Muqaddima (Prolegomena)*, 'Abd al-Rahman ibn Khaldun (1332–1406), states that "Human society is necessary. Philosophers express the truth by saying that man is social by nature, i.e., he needs society or a city as they call it. The reason for this is that . . . it becomes necessary for him to unite his efforts with his fellow men." (Charles Issawi ['Isawi], *An Arab Philosophy of History: Selections from the Prolegomena of Ibn Khaldun of Tunis [1332–1406]* [London: John Murray, 1958], p. 99.) There are, however, basic differences between Aristotle and Muslim thinkers about the nature and source of laws that govern human society.

2. Elsewhere, the author defines in detail the features of his brotherhood.
3. Generally given in the anglicized plural form *waqfs*.

V. ARAB SOCIALISM AND ITS RELATION TO NATIONALISM, COMMUNISM, AND CAPITALISM

15. Communism and Ourselves: Seven Differences Between Communism, and Arab Socialism[*]

Muhammad Hasanayn Haykal

Muhammad Hasanayn Haykal (b. 1924), the former editor of al-Ahram, was a close friend of President Nasser. Covering a wide range of topics, his articles in al-Ahram have expressed the government's viewpoint on current problems and have varied according to changes of opinion or policy in the ruling circles. His views have regularly been reproduced by other Egyptian

---

[*]Reprinted, in a slightly abbreviated form, from Muhammad Hasanayn Haykal, "Nahnu wa-al-shuyu'iyyah: 7 fawariq bayn al-shuyu'iyyah wa bayn al-ishtirakiyya al-'arabiyya. Al-Tarikh la yasir fi tariq masdud" ["Communism and Ourselves: 7 Differences Between Communism and Arab Socialism. History Does Not Unfold on a Closed Parth"], *al-Ahram*, Cairo, August 4, 1961.

newspapers, as well as by Nasserite publications throughout the Arab world. After the death of Nasser, he opposed the liberal economic policies of Sadat, the new president of Egypt, and lost his editorship of al-Ahram. He was even forbidden to write. Nevertheless he published several new books defending Nasser's legacy. See The Cairo Documents: The Inside Story of Nasser *(Garden City, N.Y.: Doubleday, 1973). The article reproduced here appeared during the first major phase of socialism in Egypt. After the decrees of July 1961, which nationalized more than 80 percent of the economy, the country seemed to move to the extreme Left. Haykal's purpose was to assure both the moderate Egyptians and the Western world that Nasser's socialism was not communism. Moreover, the ruling circles were concerned with the growing ideological tension between the intellectuals with Marxist tendencies and the nationalists and liberals. Haykal's other aim, therefore, was to stress the special national characteristics of Arab socialism as practiced in Egypt in order to achieve a common viewpoint among the intellectuals.*

My aim is to analyze the contents of Arab socialism and of Communism, in order to compare these two doctrines and highlight their differences. As preamble, however, I wish to indicate that my intention is neither to disparage Communism nor to vilify Communists, for several reasons:

The first is that our experience in socialism rose from nothing, but from now on is open to debate and confrontation....

The second is that we believe in the right of the people to choose their own system. If the American people choose capitalism, it is their right, and if the people of the Soviet Union choose Communism, that is also their right.

The third is that no one can deny that Communism as experienced in the Soviet Union has achieved great results for the people of that country, even though the price they paid under the terror of Stalinism was tremendous. In fact, the Soviet Union has taken a great leap forward in the course of the last forty-three years, and together with the U.S.A. it has become one of the two great world powers as regards scientific progress and production.

Finally, the fourth reason is that the existence of a Communist world opposite the capitalist world has created an extremely important international balance, which has allowed many colonized and conquered people to rise up against their masters.

1.   The first difference between Arab socialism and Communism lies in the conception of class by each. The existence of classes and their conflicting interests and the class struggle from which the movement for

social progress stems are accepted facts. It is here that the first difference appears between Arab socialism and Communism; it lies in the solution proposed by each of the two systems to the problem of conflicting contradictory class interests.

The solution proposed by Communism is proletarian dictatorship represented by the Communist Party, whereas Arab socialism proposes the fusion of the differences that exist between all the classes. Communism asks the dispossessed to revolt and transform all the possessors into dispossessed. It also asks them to get rid of all property owners, by any means, if necessary by massacre—all such owners being in its eyes exploiters.

The Communist solution is therefore the final elimination of all classes by a single class. Arab socialism asks the dispossessed to revolt so that they may have access to property and take their rightful share of the national wealth. For Arabs, it is a question of eliminating the contradictions between the classes within a framework of national unity and revolutionary plotting, while society evolves to form only one class in which each member occupies a place commensurate with his work, without the impediment of any class barrier.

Thus punishment and vengeance mark the first steps of Communism, the class struggle inevitably assuming, in the eyes of the Communists a bloody character. As to Arab socialism, its origins are in justice and equality. Revolutionary intrigue is carried out in a peaceful manner, unsoiled by bloodshed, and without the specter of the gallows in the background.

2. The second difference, which derives from the first, concerns the ideas of the two systems regarding private property. As far as Communism is concerned, every property owner is also an exploiter, hence it is necessary to eliminate him in order to eliminate exploitation itself.

For Arab socialism, with its different point of view, property is of two kinds—that which exploits and that which results from work. Communism affirms: Whoever possesses exploits; he must be eliminated. Arab socialism says: There are proprietors and proprietors. In fact, there is a kind of property that represents the result of work and that cannot be used by the owner to exploit or dominate others. This property is an essential right. It is a right that should be extended to that as many as possible can share in it and benefit equally from it. As for the exploiting proprietor, Arab socialism continues: Do not kill him. Take from him rather the means that make him an exploiter, then allow him to live in the new society. It does not matter if he enters with anger and bitterness the society that is capable of educating him, since it is capable of educating its children and initiating them into a new way of life.

3. The third difference emerges from this logical chain of thought. Communism says: It is necessary to expropriate. Arab socialism says: It is

necessary to compensate. This difference is the inevitable consequence of the two former differences. Arab socialism has as its aims justice and equality, not punishment and vengeance. Private property is a right—even an aim, one may say—on condition it does not end in exploitation. The system of nationalization with compensation, as was practiced by Arab socialism in its attempt to increase the people's share in the national wealth and its revenues, is not only a guillotine that operates automatically, rising and falling to cut up and destroy. On the contrary, nationalization is carried out in a responsible, patriotic manner. This explains the apparent difference in the procedure employed with regard to certain firms affected by these measures. Total nationalization has struck first at all the international monopolies, starting with the Suez Canal Company, which was dominated by Britain and France. Then came the Company of New Egypt, a simple façade behind which lay Belgian interests, followed by banks and insurance companies, so as to prevent money's becoming the weapon of exploitation. Nationalization was then extended to public services closely linked to the public interest, such as the Tramway Company, for example, and the Lebon Company, and took in the heavy industry that exercised a direct influence on the national economy.

In other cases—altogether ninety-one cases affected by the revolutionary measures—nationalization has not been total but partial (50 per cent). Such is the case, for example, with the works of Yasin the glass manufacturers. Muhammad Sayyid Yasin, their founder, has made a real effort in a new productive bid. He has succeeded, and in his success lies a whole history of struggle and experience . . .

4. Let us turn now to the role of the individual in society. In the Communist society, the state possesses everything. The individual is a tool; he receives what is necessary for his essential needs. . . . In Arab socialism, the state is an instrument of the people for achieving justice and guaranteeing its application.

While the individual in the Communist society feels he is only a small cog in a huge machine, the individual in the Arab socialist society feels that his capacities for invention are not subject to limitation or hindrance, so long as he does not indulge in exploitation.

In Arab socialism, the individual is the very basis of the social structure. There is nothing is it that fetters ambition. . . . Arab socialism desires that workers in the factories shall be coproprietors, concerned with profit not only from the viewpoint of production but also from a personal point of view. . . .

[*In the passage omitted, Haykal alludes to his visit to the U.S.S.R. and to the talk he had with various Soviet citizens.*]

One, for example, named Stephanovsky, was an employee in one of the government services. I asked him this question: "What is your ambition?" Perplexed, he replied, "Ambition . . . ambition . . . I don't understand you." I asked him, "For example, do you want to have a car some day?" He replied sharply, "No, no. I am too ordinary to own a car. I dream only of owning a motorbike." Even dreams have limits that must not be exceeded. . . .

The underground stations [in the Moscow subway system] were very elegant and luxurious. The contrast was particularly striking between the clothes of the travelers in the trains and the imposing marble walls and sparkling lights suspended from the ceiling. . . . The real tragedy, however, was the enormous contradiction between the different aspects of present-day life. The difference between the trains and the travelers is hard to imagine.

In short, the difference and the points of conflict between the Communist point of view and the point of view of Arab socialism on this question are as follows: Communism says that the present does not interest us; we look only toward the future. Arab socialism says, on the contrary, that the present does interest us. . . . If the present loses all love of life, the future cannot be created from nothing.

Communism says: It is important to sacrifice everything now in order to gain everything tomorrow. Arab socialism says the sacrifice must not exceed its limits, otherwise it will kill the sense of liberty and humanity in the individual.

> We proclaim the necessity for work . . . but we refuse slavery. We aim for production . . . but we want a society where well-being reigns. We are working to produce . . . but we do not forget the necessity of providing employment for all. We build factories . . . but we build houses as well. We are building dams and power stations . . . but we have a special budget for hospitals and schools.

It is because of this, for example, that, at the outset, Communism had no fixed working hours. On the contrary, these hours grew longer and longer, in the sole interest of production, with no increases in wages. Even to this day, the workers in Communist China have no annual holiday.

Arab socialism reduced the number of working hours right from the start. There is no doubt that present circumstances help Arab socialism to follow this line of action. First of all, there has been enormous progress in the means of production. The Soviet Union, for example, at the outset, did not have the same success as we have had. We start with the most up-to-date achievements of modern science. Our factories and tools are the most modern yet produced. Progress in the means of production permits us to decrease working hours, and consequently helps us to insure the welfare of the individual, without this being at the expense of production as regards quality and quantity.

The basis of the disagreement concerning the individual in Communism and Arab socialism is that Communism regards the individual as a simple historical result. ... Arab socialism considers that the cycle is complete and that there is a balanced relationship between the individual and history. Man is a result of history, but at the same time he is one of the causes of history. Man is molded by history, but he also molds history.

5.   Thus another difference appears between Communism and Arab socialism. Communism was founded on the sacrifice of several generations of men in order to arrive at a growth of production. Especially during the Stalinist period, it put these ideas into practice by confiscating all national resources and mobilizing the total work force toward production. The extreme cruelty of the conditions in factories and on collective farms, the coercion and oppression, could only be justified to the generation of that time by looking toward the future.

Arab socialism has another view on this question. To achieve an increase in production and eventually the highest level of production necessitates a general national mobilization of all resources, but the present generations have the right to live . . . .

6.   We come to a sixth difference between Communists and Arab socialism. It is the difference between abject servility and free initiative. Above all, it is the difference between immobility and dynamism, or rather between blind fanaticism and free thought. Even though it undertakes to conform to Marxist dialectic, Communism cannot depart from the well-defined paths without being accused of deviationism, as was the case with Tito, who was attacked when he tried to transform, modernize, and free himself and to become independent.

The Arab socialist feels that all the richness of thought throughout the world is available to him. He can benefit from it and explore its possibilities. Above all, he feels that he is capable of adding something to it and sharing in its growth. He adds to it his own national experience, and he helps it grow by his historical heritage.

In his speech made on the eve of the celebration of the revolution, Gamal Abdel Nasser expressed this idea in these words: "We do not open books to find all the answers, but we open the book of our reality [time] and try to find the solution of its problems."

That is the difference between the Communist and the Arab socialist. The Communist is a pupil who remains faithful to the words of Marx, Lenin, Stalin, Khrushchev, and Mao Tse-tung crammed into his head. Even though these words are in many cases divergent and remote . . . .different and contradictory . . . , the Communist must listen and obey. The Arab socialist is a pupil who remains faithful to the history of his nation, to his national heritage, to the problems of his people, and to their hopes.

It is possible that this is the reason for the failure of Arab Communists to achieve the least following among the people, particularly in the United Arab Republic. The Arab masses have heard nothing from the Communists but stiff foreign slogans. They see in the Communists only puppets, worked by string from behind their frontiers.

7.   Communism believes that political organizations should be confine to the Communist Party alone. For this reason, that supreme and unchallenged authority is exclusively in the hands of the Party. No revolution can be lawful unless the Communist Party is the instigator and the master. Arab socialism considers that the organization encompassing political acitivity must extend to the whole nation.

To achieve democracy, Communism sees no way other than the dictatorship of one party, the Communist Party, which permits the existence of no other party. Arab socialism proclaims the idea of national union to organize political action on the basis of the whole nation so that the meaning and foundation of democracy may extend to all the people.

National union, it is true, still needs to be more clearly defined and developed, so that it may achieve all that is expected of it. However, these are only details, although they have a very great importance.

But what is important is that Arab socialism has succeeded in finding a means of organizing political action in accordance with its now national circumstances—and even international circumstances. In effect, the powers that face each other on the international scene [i.e., the United States and the U.S.S.R.] are ready to penetrate the country by manipulations and to divide it so that each can secure the support of a group or interest and use it for its own designs.

16.   Our Socialism in Relation to Capitalism and Communism[*]

Fathi Ghanim

Fathi Ghanim belongs to the Egyptian leftist group (whose members range from Fabian socialists to Marxists) that publishes the influential ideological review Ruz al-Yusuf[Rose of Joseph]*in Cairo. Basically, this group supported Nasser's economic policy, and many of its members, after*

[*]Extract from Fathi Ghanim, "Ayn ishtirakiyyatune min al-ra'smaliyya wal-shuyu'iyya" [Our (Superior) Socialism in Relation to Capitalism and Communism"] Ruz al-Yusuf [Rose of Joseph], Cairo, February 13, 1961, pp. 8–9.

oscillating between Egyptian nationalism and Arab nationalism, now solidly support the latter. (The Marxists seem more interested in Egypt's pre-Islamic past.) The publishers of Ruz al-Yusuf and Sabah al-Qahira (a more popular type of publication) have studied and publicized the writings and ideas of the Arab nationalists. They have also tried to propagate the ideas of a democratic, cooperative socialism based on the idea of consumer interest. But because of their weak ideological foundations, they have been forced to lean more and more on Marxism. This article, one of the many that tried to define the ideological tenets of Egypt's cooperative socialism, is critical of both capitalism and communism. See also Fathi Ghanim, "Dimuqratiyyat al-ishitirakiyya" [The Democracy of Socialism], Ruz al-Yusuf [Rose of Joseph], Cairo, October 26, 1959, p. 1.

There are two well-defined but completely opposed methods of ensuring the progress and development of a nation—one in the West, especially in America, the other in the East, particularly in the Communist countries. It is worth while to examine the inherent characteristics of these two methods before reviewing the characteristics of our own regime.

In the West, economic progress results from the activities of individual businessmen, heads of industry and commercial establishments, etc. These businessmen do not plan their projects with public interest in mind; profit is the prime motive behind their activities. When he builds a factory, forms a company, or constructs a block of flats, a businessman is not thinking of the needs of the community. He has only one aim: to sell to whoever has the money to buy, and to make a profit on the deal . . . . The industrialist does not select his industry with regard to the over-all interest of the nation; he prefers to manufacture spirits rather than set up a foundry or a steelworks. The same goes for the capitalist who may prefer to invest his money in a night club rather than use it to prospect in the desert . . . In effect, for the businessmen as for the capitalist, what counts is profit, by whatever means . . . .

On the other hand, flooding the market with consumer goods creates a special mentality among buyers—the selfish mentality of the individual who thinks only of himself and of his own welfare.

The individual who is used to devoting the whole day to the choice of an elegant tie . . . is likely to be highly selfish; by his very nature, he rejects all efforts to persuade him to sacrifice a little of his well-being for the sake of the general good. He is not concerned about the "general good" and ignores the millions whose standard of living is very low. He regards them as foreigners, treats them as though they were a different kind of creature, unconnected with himself, as though they were living in a different world and not in the same country . . . .

All this is reflected in the political regime of this individualistic society; businessmen claim absolute political freedom and refuse to admit that they can be restricted in any way. They have only one aim: to prevent any state intervention that might restrain the activities by which they hope to enrich themselves and exploit the other classes of society.

Western economists believe that private enterprise, despite many imperfections, does not completely supress the freedom of the individual, ensures economic development, and raises the standard of living without resorting to compulsion; economic growth develops naturally and finally expands to cover all the needs of the people.

But what is this freedom of which the West is so proud? It is that of the businessmen and the monopolies, whose influence dominates the press and the radio, and who takes pains to hide the reality of a situation that is contrary to the interests of the majority. Besides, this individualistic philosophy is of no advantage to a nation that desires rapid progress and improvement and is impatient at the thought that its standard of living might remain very low for many generations or for many long centuries.

We find in the Communist countries the second method of ensuring development and progress. The exact opposite of Western methods, it suppresses private enterprise and private control, and aims to carry out only projects that are in the general interest. Heavy industry has priority over consumer goods. Individuals live as if they were in a huge factory, with no prospect except work. They have sacrificed their well-being and cannot choose their own living accommodations or clothes. Sometimes the family lives in one or two rooms; the wife has only one kind of shoes; the materials from which she makes her dresses are available only in certain qualities or colors. The superfluous is unknown. The import of perfumes, spirits, and automobiles is absolutely forbidden.

Individuals are swallowed up in the mass. Their productive work is supervised by a group of directors and technicians linked to political chiefs, whose aims—for the interest of all—are well understood.

This means that one generation or more is sacrificed completely for the sake of future generations. Consequently, those in political power must maintain a strong regime extending its control to every sector of life to ensure that the wheel of productivity turns without hindrance and that no negligence prevents the carrying out of schedules as planned.

Experience has shown that, in the Communist countries, the political power group can keep all the reins well in hand. It is helped by the clarity of its line of conduct, despite its tight hold over the individual. It is helped also by the individuals themselves, who in the heat of work forget their egoism, which in any event receives little or no encouragement in their current way of life. They do not have the leisure to choose ties, gaze in shop windows, and ponder over a restaurant menu.... Everything is prepared and clearly defined in advance, and their minds are geared to productivity and work.

This kind of life runs into a crisis as soon as the state, with the majority of its projects achieved, begins to expand the consumer market. From this moment, men begin to acquire the consciousness of their personality.... In actual fact, the average man in the cities of Russia then sees opening before him the possibility of choosing goods—a situation that changes his mentality and consequently the political regime itself.

Consumers represent an enormous force. They run into millions, and their numerical force has an influence on the directors, technicians, and politicians, who judge it wise to be in harmony with the feelings of the force which the consumers represent.

We in the U.A.R. adopt neither private control nor collective control which totally paralyzes private initiative. We favor a midway solution which does not merely try to maintain a balance between the two regimes. It is in fact a unique system, whose essential characteristics are as follows:

> a desire to hasten economic development with the least possible delay; a determination not to sacrifice the special interests of the individual, except within reasonable limits, and not to destroy man's feeling of individuality.

On the first point—i.e., our wish to catch up as rapidly as possible in our economic development—there can be no dispute; this desire is solidly anchored in the minds of the whole Arab nation.

The second point—where private interest stops and general interest begins—is far from clear to the majority of the middle class. This confusion results from our desire to foster both individuality and a sense of the general good in the individual. That is a difficult ideal to achieve. Although man can easily accept that which emphasize his individuality, he finds it difficult to accept the idea of toil for the general good.

In the towns today, the average person is always in a position to choose what he intends to buy, and all the efforts of the state to limit his choice—or to suppress it—come up against solid opposition. It is enough for the state to forbid the importation of English wool, silk ties, perfumes from Paris, or records and record players and it clashes immediately with the frantic desire of the individual to buy these objects and get them for himself by any possible means. Every day the U.A.R. Customs continue to intercept travelers arriving from abroad laden with these goods; their joy at having procured them is such as to verge on madness.

The important thing here is not to find means of forbidding the entry of goods, but rather to understand the mentality of the buyers of these goods; their individualism and their own particular interests always take precedent over their consideration for the general interest.... We are expected at the same time to concentrate on work and the application of the five-year plan so as to raise the standard of living of the poor majority.

Today we come up against a sharp contradiction when we ask consumers to be both consumers and producers and demand that they consume the least while producing the maximum. The Communists tell us that in order to resolve this contradiction it is necessary to establish an authoritarian regime and accustom people to privation and sacrifice in the interests of future generations ... We reject this opinion, which in effect does not coincide with the nature of our people ....

We cannot forget that the Arab nation had an ancient civilization and that it is deeply ingrained in the souls of the people. Although he may be poor and illiterate, the ordinary man retains the pride and the glory of belonging to an ancient race. That is why he refuses completely to sacrifice his individuality, and why he refuses also to merge himself totally with the mass.

That is why it is wise constantly to try to reconcile the pressing need to hasten development in the interest of society with the no less pressing need to preserve man's individuality, in spite of the contradiction that this effort entails. The way to achieve this is to consider the contradiction not as shameful but rather as a fact of our life. It follows from this that rather than suppress the contradiction we must try to overcome it by being conscious of it and understanding it in its reality. We must take it into account when, as ordinary citizens, we consider our political regime. We must take it into account when we prepare our final constitution ....

By persuading the individual that his interests and those of the nation can coincide, we can assure the success of our democratic, socialist, and cooperative regime. It is not a difficult thing to achieve, for each of us, no matter what our particular interests, is a noble, good hearted citizen, capable of limiting his individuality.

17. The Crisis of the Arab Left*

Clovis Maqsud

Clovis Maqsud, (b. 1925) of a Maronite family, was a member of the
Lebanese Phalanx and subsequently joined the Arab National Bloc, a group
that wanted to maintain a democratic, independent Lebanon rather than to
support the interests of a specific group. Ideologically, Maqsud was for a
time the principal theorist for Kamal Jumblat's Popular Socialist Party. In
1956, however, he opposed Jumblat because of the latter's pro-American
attitudes and drifted closer to association with the Ba'th. In the late 1970s
Maqsud became the Arab League representative at the United Nations.

Maqsud is one of the most original Arab thinkers. He has expressed
himself searchingly, with clarity and force, on all major problems confronting the Arab world, In Ma'na al-hiyad al-ijabi [The Meaning of Positive
Neutrality] (Beirut: Dar al-'ilm lil-malayin, 1960), he defined the nonalignment of the Arab world as a consequence of international forces rather
than as an organic growth of Arab nationalism. (See Leonard Binder, The
Ideological Revolution in the Middle East [New York: John Wiley and
Sons, 1964], pp. 242 ff.) However, the main problems dealt with by Maqsud
have been ideological. In 1960–61; he was a member of the Arab Socialist
Association presided over by Colonel Kamal Rifa'a of Egypt's Revolutionary
Council, who had been active in various Marxist organizations in 1947–51.
The history of this association (whose members came from several Arab
countries) is basic to understanding not only Maqsud's views but also the
ideological problems confronting the Arab world generally. The key issue
was to determine the role of the intellectual in the new revolutionary
national and socialist framework of the Arab republics.

Ideology in the Arab world, from the turn of the century to World
War II, had developed relatively freely within a broad spectrum of ideas
that ranged from extreme Marxism to Islamic. There were no national states
whose political philosophies relied exclusively on one of the existing ideologies. Even if certain ideologies seemed stronger than others, the lack of
national independence prevented a full ideological confrontation, since none
of the ideologies could determine the final form of a regime. The period
before the 1950's therefore, could be called relatively liberal.

The Egyptian revolution of 1952 produced new conditions. The revolution had certain goals but no ideology, except broad but vague democratic

---

*Extract from Clovis Maqsud, Azmat al-yasar al-'arabi [The Crisis of the Arab Left]
(Beirut: Dar al-'ilm lil-malayin, 1960), pp. 9–21.

social attitudes. The ensuing permissive atmosphere in Egypt in 1952–58 stimulated an intensive intellectual activity whose depth and scope are still to be determined. Leftist or socialist currents mushroomed, and the Marxist groups occupied an important place among them. Meanwhile, the military regime had secured full national independence and acquired authority, prestige, and influence, both internally and internationally. A state with a sustaining bureaucratic structure had fully emerged. The crucial problem faced by the Egyptian regime was to define its base of political power and to make it harmonize with the changing social structure, with the underlying currents of thought, and with the country's future social an cultural goals. The key issue, therefore, was to define ideologically the relationship of the existing military leadership with the emerging socioeconomic structure and the new philosophy of life stemming from it.

The Marxists posed the strongest ideological challenge to Nasser's ruling group. They regarded the military's role in the transformation of Egypt as short and transitional. The rise of Marxist thought had been greatly aided by the fact that Egypt's antiimperialist and anti-Western "neutralist" policy had undermined the force of sociodemocratic ideas of the West and of their intellectual representatives. The Marxists critically questioned the social bases of the military regime. They felt that the military was socially and ideologically unqualified to carry out the full modernization of Egypt. For them, the military was a power group whose range of thought and action would be confined, in the long run, to the concepts of the anti- imperialist, nationalist bourgeois class to which they belonged. True, the struggle against imperialism and the urgent need for development had engendered in the military a certain revolutionary dynamism, but this would exhaust itself soon after independence and national statehood were firmly secured. Consequently, the Marxists felt that they alone were emi- nently qualified to bring Egypt into the new age.

The clash between the organized political power and the leftists occurred in 1958–59. Many intellectual were dismissed from universities and government positions, and the militant Marxists were imprisoned. These measures were hailed in the West as proof of Nasser's anticommunism. (There was truth in this belief.) But the measures also betrayed a certain intellectual insecurity on the part of Nasser's group and marked the beginning of a severe intellectual crisis. Nasser followed up the anti- Communist measures with efforts to devise a new social philosophy that would incorporate the main currents of thought in the Arab world. A variety of institutes and associations were formed, consisting of intellectuals and professionals, and even al-Azhar was subjected to reform in order to bring it into the twentieth century, according to the dreams that Muhammad

'Abduh had formulated at the end of the nineteenth century. Yet, all these measures and the socialism they engendered in Egypt, suffered from a basic contradiction, which defeated their purpose. The Marxists were silenced chiefly as enemies of democracy and as agents of a foreign power, just as the Muslim Brotherhood had been disposed of as the enemy of progress. (Some members of the Brotherhood were rehabilitated.) The revolutionary government had, therefore, disposed of Marxists in order to protect democracy and freedom, which in this case meant simply freedom from being forced to accept a certain ideology.

But in initiating his subsequent ideological measures, Nasser did not scruple to violate the same democracy and freedom in reorganizing and directing from the top the intellectual life of Egypt in a manner decided by his own group. Anwar Sadat would do the same in 1980–81.

The result was intellectual apathy, servility, and forced formal political loyalty. There burst into the open a struggle between the organized authority, conscious of its identity and purpose, and the society at large, which refused to be regimented into a preconceived scheme. This "intellectual crisis" was discussed in a series of articles in al-Ahram in March, 1961, and in two debates in June of that year. The articles were published in a volume by Muhammad Hasanayn Haykel, Azmat al-muthaqqafin [Crisis of Intellectuals] (Cairo: al-Shirka al-'arabiyya al-muttahida lil tawziyya, 1961). The discussion, largely stimulated and controlled by the government, explained the background of intellectuals in Egypt and in the Arab world generally but did not diagnose the real cause of the intellectual crisis. Yet, the cause was obvious: Directed from the top, the discussion had been aimed ultimately at enlisting the support of the intelligentsia for Nasser's socialism generally and for the forthcoming nationalization decrees of July-September 1961, specifically. The Arab Socialist Association, to which Clovis Maqsud belonged, was part of the Egyptian Government's endeavor to combine socialist ideas with the ideas of Arab nationalism and to use them to prepare the ideological ground for Arab unity. This was to be the Arab ideology, a unique blend of progressive ideas, human freedom, and national aspirations, opposed to both communism and capitalism. As indicated by his previous writings on the subjects of socialism and nationalism, Maqsud was uniquely qualified for the task. See, for example, al-Mahiyya al-ishtirakiyya al-'arabiyya [The Nature of Arab Socialism] (Baghdad: Maktabat al-nahda, 1959), and Nahw ishtirakiyya 'arabiyya [Toward Arab Socialism] (Beirut: Dar Munaymilna, 1957). The formulation of general socialist principles did not, however, attract unanimous consent, especially since the Marxists continued to pursue their own policy. Maqsud, therefore, was forced to answer some basic and difficult questions—how to preserve freedom and

democratic values—the very spirit that made social thoughts attractive,
without destroying them in the web of the organization established to
implement them; and how to distinguish the humanist philosopher Marx
from pragmatic masters of power such as Lenin. The issue has an ever
present value.

The extract is taken from a book in which Maqsud tries to find an
answer to the foregoing questions.

The left in the Arab world is undergoing a severe crisis—a crisis with
roots that are implicit, on the one hand, in the historical circumstances
that created the Arab left itself and, on the other, in the crisis of the left in
general.

What do we mean by the left? The "left" is a political term that
denotes those classes who work for an ever-widening participation of the
masses in the various economic, political, and cultural fields, on the basis of
ever-decreasing class differences. The left includes all the elements who
are determined to liberate man from all conditions that cause him to live
on the periphery of life and events and who are determined to make him
an active agent in determining his future and achieving his dignity and
prosperity. The various ideologies that have attempted or are attempting
to translate these wishes and endeavors into practical programs have not
faced the same problems. Furthermore, the motives that led some ideologies to work within the general framework of the left have not been the
same. Therefore, diverse ideological and political schools of thought
inevitably arose within the left, and it has become necessary to reappraise
the criteria for determining whether or not a group of people belong to
the left.

Despite these obvious or latent differences in the currents of the left,
certain ideological presuppositions act as a common denominator in
determining belongingness to the left. In addition to the brief definition
cited above (which constitutes the practical foundations of the left),
certain ideological commitments must be satisfied if we desire the left to
keep to its progressive path. Several groups can work together for
temporary or short-term objectives that are of the essence of leftist
planning and strategy, but such groups cannot continue to work indefinitely to strengthen the means for safeguarding the progressive participation of the masses in national life.

In order to follow a progressive path and to clarify and foresee its
results, we must accept certain basic philosophical theories. We must
admit, for example, that mind emanates from matter and that evolution is
the genuine expression of the inner spirit of our existence. The conjunction of theory and practice is a basic prerequisite for finding a method

of dealing with affairs that conform both with the requirements of our modern age and with the objectives whose achievement would solve the problem of man and lay the foundation for human and social happiness.

In view of these definitions, which, as a whole, constitute the ideological and practical legacy of the left, diverse socialist groups, with their diverse policies, and certain progressive elements were all termed "leftist." Although some radicals have denied that certain progressive elements were leftist, the term "left" covers anyone who works for reform (being convinced of its value), but no one who accepts partial reform as a barrier to prevent the completion of the social revolution. Some conservatives submit to partial reforms which are carried out either under pressure from the left or as a result of the dire need to protect capitalism and exploitation. In such cases, their reforms act as an opiate on the increasing consciousness of the people, and as an attempt to keep the initiative for directing economic progress with those classes who believe in, and work for, the preservation of class differences and the denial of the ownership of the means of production to the people and their representatives.

Is Communism within or outside the pale of the left? The over-all impression is that Communism and the Communists are of the core of the left. The capitalist bourgeoisie in its propaganda has attempted to isolate the left and to picture Communism as the "extreme" left. This being so, the remaining left would appear to be ranged under this "extreme." In this manner, spokesmen for capitalism would place Communism within the left and make of it the logical end of the road for any leftist movement. In this manner, capitalism aims at striking a blow at the left and at creating a polarity between itself on the one hand and Communism on the other. When this polarity is achieved, discontent and antagonism within the capitalist camp would be limited, since, in accepting this polarity, one would have to admit that Communism is the only alternative to capitalism. But so that it should not fall into a severe crisis of conscience because of the cessation of ideological development, capitalism resorts to partial concessions calculated to reduce the tension in its structure and the struggle against its very foundations. A psychological atmosphere is created wherein revolutionary secession from capitalism would be rendered impossible, since a revolutionary drive would become the mere tool of Communism. The net result is that Communism and its leaders would see in this distorted logic a perfect proof of the contradictions inherent in capitalism and, in such contradictions, the perfect tool to serve their own purposes. For capitalist mentality regards any secession from capitalism as a deliberate move toward Communism. If this revolution against capitalist exploitation and the tradition of dissent against the ideological and psychological atmosphere created by capitalism gives birth to a deep-rooted revolutionary challenge independent of Communism, the dualistic structure of capitalism is quick to impeach and to suffocate this challenge. Therefore, the basic problem facing such a genuine challenge is that the left should persevere in the face of this capitalist siege and attack its dualistic structure by clarifying its own independence and the basic revolutionary impulses that gave rise to it. The crisis of the left in general lies in the fact that the left is unable to rise to the occasion and to its responsibilities in our modern age.

This crisis, which has resulted from the dichotomy between what exists and what is required, has led to two erroneous attitudes among leftists vis-à-vis the Communists. (1) The men of the left feel inferior to the Communists and submit to the logic that maintains that Communism is the highest form of socialism. (2) These men often react negatively to Communism. Let me now explain these attitudes in detail.

1. There is no doubt that the efficiency of Communist organization, its apparent ideological wholeness, and the fact that certain Communist parties have assumed power in certain countries, doubtless have led socialism to feel inferior to Communism. Socialism appears to lack unity and has no ideal model that socialists can point to. Almost all states that have achieved a socialist program have been small, like Sweden, where socialism was no more than a logical development of a certain historical and social evolution. Since such socialist systems were not exposed to internal or external setbacks, they have not invented methods and means that can be applied at various times and circumstances. Thus, socialism, without an international, self-sufficient status, becomes a mere movement, parts of whose socialist program may be adopted by capitalist regimes without thereby endangering any of the basic existing nonsocialist systems. Because of socialism's lack of appeal—which has resulted from the absence of ideological, philosophical, and practical homogeneity—various men of the left have been attracted to Communist political strategy (without necessarily joining the Party), although they can plainly recognize the failings and irrationality of Communism and the Communist parties. Among them are such groups as the Peace Partisans, the Women's Rights societies, the groups for Democratic Rights, and the Democratic Youth movements. These people are not necessarily Communists but they feel somewhat inferior to them. Grasping the situation, the Communists often conceal their true intentions by coining slogans calculated to draw to them elements of public opinion that are ordinarily far removed from Communism. Even when these elements discover the truth about such slogans as "Peace and Democracy," which denote something that the Communists themselves do not accept, the leftists continue to work within these Communist-organized fronts. They believe that Communists must not be denied access to public life and that the non-Communist left,

because of its weakness, must obtain the support of what is even more to the left and is more efficacious, both politically and internationally. Despite their dangerous policy, such leftist elements are potentially the supporters of a clear and positive leftist movement. Thus, one must not ignore or refuse to deal with them but must constantly work to draw them back to their natural sphere of action. These men have erroneously drifted toward Communism not because they are unaware of Communist violations of man's rights at various times and places but because they feel an urgent desire to quicken the transition to the socialist society and man's liberation from the exploitation of both men and machines. This sense of urgency masks a revolutionary spirit of which the Arab left stands greatly in need.

2. Another danger to the left resides in a negative reaction to Communism and Communists. Much Communist activity at various levels doubtless constitutes a provocation and a threat to man's dignity, liberty, and prosperity. At various periods in the history of the relations between the left and the Communists, the latter concentrated on the destruction not so much of the forces of reaction and capitalism, as of the forces of socialism and progressive liberalism. The history of Communist parties contains many instances where the forces of reaction were placated and even strengthened so that the Communists could strike at the left. To the Party's rank and file, Communism justifies such contradictions on the basis that these leftist, non-Communist movements are attempts to waylay the "labor movement" or that they are "an extension of capitalism." Such false charges leveled at the left, especially after the left has offered the popular movements all it had by way of sacrifices, inevitably create a negative reaction, often akin to a sense of emotional outrage. When the Communists plan to make themselves the only active revolutionary and progressive agents (even to the extent of suppressing leftist movements that are more sincere and radical than they are), and when their plans become manifest, a natural reaction to this great lie sets in. It soon becomes apparent that Communism pursues objectives that are diametrically opposed to the slogans the Communists bandy about. The Communist Party, it is seen, seeks to usurp power.

This strategy, which becomes progressively more obvious as the Party increases its power, is coupled with the Communists' other stratagem in time of weakness. They lie low when they are not influential and when they are trying to organize their ranks. Members of the left inevitably recall how, with a view to infiltrating the basic social scene, the Communists exploited the left's adherence to freedom and its consequent readiness to support the Communists' individual, social, and labor problems. The left then recognizes such a strategy of exploitation for what it really is and knows that, according to Communism, adherence to absolute freedom is a mere throwback from the traditional bourgeoisie and a sign of the vacillation and weakness of the non-Communist left. The left then discovers that Communism treats it on two different, contradictory levels. At certain times, and on the public level, Communism uses the left as a façade and as a mere tool for its activities. At other times, Communism treats the left as including "all honest citizens"; at still other times, it describes the left as the only enemy of the people's national and class struggles. What is important to the Communists is that the left should remain ideologically fragmented and incapable of independent revolutionary control.

When it discovers these facts, the left reacts either violently and rashly or by attempting to strengthen and clarify its own revolutionary message. In the first case, a gap appears in the left through which various nonrational elements penetrate and lead the left away from its objectives, hinder its unity, and pervert its essence. The result is that the left comes to ignore or pardon certain [conservative] policies and tendencies which are diametrically opposed to the values and the ideals for which it is working.

Owing to this often shameful acquiescence of the part of the left, traditional modes of thought have restored vitality to the forces of reaction, after the left had already challenged them vigorously and had, at various times, become capable of destroying them. It [refrained] and was set back because of emotional attitudes. This attitude also causes the left to stray from its revolutionary path and to yoke itself to a reactionary policy which tolerates it only as long as it needs to regain the energy of which the left had once deprived it. This attitude also implies that the left comes acquiesce in Communism as the product of the socialist revolutionary tradition, despite Communism's deliberate perversion of this tradition. It also implies that the left must concentrate its energy on rectifying and combating this perversion.

This is what we meant by the left's straying from its revolutionary path. The left's reason for existence is that it should combat reaction, protect evolution, and define its nature. What is needed to protect the left from perversion is a deeper, more comprehensive commitment to the values and ideals for which it is striving, not a total preoccupation with rectifying errors and fighting Communism. This means that the left should concern itself only with consolidating its independence, but also with strengthening its own ideological foundations. It presupposes that Communism must not be combated except in order to protect and ensure progress, i.e., to protect socialism and the advancement of the masses. It is futile to fight Communism as such if the power that is fighting it is neither positive nor revolutionary. We can go even further and maintain that persistent opposition to Communism is in fact wrong, even if it proceeds from conviction that such opposition would protect the gains of the left, since this persistence would eventually rob the left of its effective humanistic outlook and would disfigure the left precisely as the Communists are attempting to do.

It appears, therefore, that a comprehensive ideology and a total commitment to socialism are of paramount importance so that no gap may be created in the left and so that no emotionalism develops toward Communism. This emotionalism in the left breeds exhaustion and a lack of self-confidence, so that no new ideas to deal with new problems and requirements are forthcoming. It is possible that it will not lead to the ignorance of the major issues facing man, but it will certainly render the left incapable of solving these issues in a radical manner for fear that such solutions might be similar to Communist or non-Communist [i.e., rightist] solutions. At certain moments in history, this timidity has been responsible for the vacillation of the left. The left has often lost the initiative or has placed itself in a general political framework created by the reactionary regimes or has accepted liberal capitalistic standards for determining the propriety of its own revolutionary path. With the loss of the ideological and practical initiative, the masses have lost confidence in the leadership of the left. The result is that Communism has not become the punishment [the alternative solution] for the left's timidity and vacillation.

This analysis leads us to a fundamental question the answer to which may clarify the nature of the crisis in the left. The question is: Is Communism a part, or does it lies outside, of the left? The answer, very frankly, cannot be either a categorical yes or a categorical no. This is not because one is afraid of committing himself to a certain viewpoint or because it is difficult to define the left, but because, over the past few years, a certain confusion has arisen. In answering this question, we must, to begin with, clearly distinguish between Communism and Communists and, again, between Communists and Communists. To do so is sometimes rather difficult, and this is why the answer to the question cannot be categorical. Thus, the left must now define the criteria according to which certain Communists might be accepted or rejected as clearly belonging to the left. This, again, means that the left must define its own standards, which it can only do if it attains a deeper understanding of what it wants and how it can achieve it.

Communism as a philosophical doctrine and as a comprehensive outlook on life and existence emerged as a fundamental challenge in the modern world when Marx and Engels laid down its scientific foundations. To a considerable extent, therefore, the left and Communism hold common theoretical and philosophical positions. To that extent, Marxism may be considered a living part of the left. Inasmuch as Communism directly adopts fundamental Marxist theories, by that much can it be asserted that Communism is of the core of the left. But is modern

Communist known to be merely Marxist or is it more? If Marxist Communism were to stand still, it would thereby be doing violence to Marxism itself. It would be closed in upon itself and would lose its vitality and its ability to develop in accordance with modern progress. Therefore, modern Communism is not merely Marxist, but is Marxist-Leninist, as the Communists themselves admit. Therefore, it is not purely Marxist but embraces the Leninist interpretation of Marxism. (Many major socialist schools of thought regard Marxism as a starting point without considering it as the end of the road.)

Thus, modern Communism has confined itself, and adhered, to the Leninist interpretation of Marxism, thereby excluding from its ideological development any other interpretations of Marxism, of some of which the left might approve. It has rejected all liberal and progressive tendencies that were not Marxist but were complementary to Marxist doctrine. This deliberate exclusion has introduced another element into Communism, namely, its wilful isolation, which has become part of Communist dogma. In confining Marxist interpretation to Lenin, despite Lenin's considerable revolutionary and ideological contribution to the development of Marxism, in excluding all other interpretations, and in making of this the measure of loyalty through strict party organization, modern Communism has been led to adopt a limited outlook on life and to become incapable of absorbing man's complex problems. Communism has now become a certain program of action whose characteristics are seclusion, blind discipline, and a separation between means and ends, both ethically and philosophically. This is a philosophical part of Communism that is influenced by Stalinism. Therefore, we find that modern Communism is the narrow Stalinist program for the implementation of Lenin's interpretation of Marx. The resolutions of the Twentieth Party Congress [of the Communist Party of the U.S.S.R.] constitute a departure from Stalinism and a step beyond the monistic interpretation of Lenin. There are certain signs pointing in that directon, but they are not sufficiently clear to allow us to assert that the present Soviet regime is a leftist society, simply because of this new urge for freedom.

Furthermore, the break with Stalinism has thrown wide open the possibility that Communism may become a vast potential of the left. Thus, we can assert that Communism in Yugoslavia has, in our view, become a part of the international left, as a result of laying itself open to progressive tendencies in the world. But Communism is, by and large, still in the grip of an ideological restlessness that places it at a crossroad. It can either revert to Stalinism or continue to open itself out. If the first path is chosen, as has recently happened in China, then Communism is outside the pale of the left. If it chooses the second path of liberation, it can become a part of the left, and then the conflicts within the left will become secondary and concerned only with side issues. This tremendous development, whose results will be very important to the future and the evolution of humanity, must be treated by the left in a manner that would enable it continuously to attract Communism to the path of liberation, despite the psychological difficulties within the ranks of both parties. It is possible that Communism will change. The manner in which this change is accomplished will determine whether or not Communism is to belong to the left.

We conclude, then, that there is a conflict raging in the international Communist movement and within the regional Communist parties. Those Communists who work from conviction to develop this freedom drive are potential members of the left. Others, who follow the Stalinist line, i.e., who assume that it is futile to interact with leftist tendencies, are decided enemies of the left and may be considered to be a part of the reactionary and nonrational elements who want to arrest the movement of history and of evolution. It may well be that political life will, in the future, consist of a struggle between a stagnant reaction and a stagnant Communism on the one hand pitted against the vital forces that work for progress. Events have proved that certain Communists are potential members of the left and that certain others are, potentially, the left's most bitter and most dedicated enemies.

If we decide that the left embraces all those who work for an ever-increasing participation of the masses in all walks of life, we shall find that the left's axis is socialism. This does not mean that modern socialism embraces the whole of the left. Furthermore, the crisis in the left in general is caused either by an absence of mature consciousness among the masses that renders them incapable of supporting leftist policies, or by an absence of cohesion and harmony among the various parties of the left.

However, our view that socialism is the axis of the left may not meet with unqualified support, even from certain quarters in the left. Some leftists claim that Communism, by being the "extreme" left and the most comprehensive and influential of the doctrines of the left, has a better title than socialism to be considered the axis of the left. But for Communism to belong to the core of the left, it must meet the basic requirements of the left. Thus, while some Communists do meet these requirements and others do not, discussion of Communism on our part will not be in the traditional manner of political commentators, which treats international Communism as a homogeneous whole.

It appears, therefore, that the basic problem facing the left is to define the relations between Communism and socialism in general. We have maintained above that the leftist, and especially the socialist, attitude must rid itself of two complexes as regards Communism. The first is the inferiority complex and the second is emotionalism. But freeing the left from these complexes is not sufficient: It is far more important to clarify, in a comprehensive manner, the left's theoretical and practical position as regards Communism. This is not to deny that there are other problems concerning the relations between socialism and the progressive and national freedom movements that still need clarification and settlement, but, compared to the major problem, such issues are secondary. In addition, the problem of the relationship between socialism and the liberals and radicals, in general, is to some extent determined by the problem of the relationship between socialism and Communism.

VI.   SOCIALISM IN THE DOCTRINE OF THE BA'TH

18.   The Socialist Ideology of the Ba'th*

Michel 'Aflaq

Michel 'Aflaq is a co-founder (with Salah al-Din Bitar) of the Ba'th al-'arabi al-ishtiraki *(Arab Socialist Resurrection) movement. As both a theory and a political organization, the Ba'th has played a crucial part in the contemporary history of the Arab world, particularly in Syria, Lebanon, and Iraq.*

'Aflaq was born in Damascus in 1912, to a Greek Orthodox Arab family that dealt in grain. He studied in Paris, where he became a Communist, but after he returned to Syria and became a secondary school teacher he turned against Communism. Unlike most other Arab politicians, 'Aflaq was an ineffective public speaker, yet he early achieved great popularity among Arab intellectuals. He was almost ascetic in his living habit, and he generally refused to accept high office. 'Aflaq's early success, and that of the Ba'th generally, stemmed chiefly from the timing of the movement and its ability to place within an ideological framework the major problems facing Syria and the Arab world.

°The first excerpt in this work dealing with a general definition of Ba'th's socialist ideology and its differences from other types of leftist and rightist socialisms is taken from Michel 'Aflaq, Fi sabil al-ba'th [For the Sake of the Ba'th] (Beirut: Dar al-tali'a li al-tiba'a wa-al-nashr,1959), pp. 96–100. The sections dealing with Islam, capitalism, and class struggle are taken (titles slightly altered) from a new edition of the same work (2d ed.; Beirut: Dar al-tali'a li al-tiba'a wa-al-tiba'a wa-al-nashr, 1963), pp. 122–24, 135–36, 219–23.

The Ba'th was launched in 1940. It emerged into the open in 1943, when Syria gained formal independence, began publishing the journal al-Ba'th in 1946, and held its first congress in 1947. Those years corresponded to Syria's gaining of independence and its attempts to devise for itself a new role and a new identity within the Arab world. The nationalist currents that had developed in Syria since the turn of the century made it clear that Syria would become a fountainhead of the Arab renaissance and a natural leader in future developments.

Syria's economy—a fairly balanced one—was dominated by an urban commercial middle class in which Christian groups occupied a large place, although they made up only 14 percent of the total population. This trade-oriented economy seemed unsuited, by both mentality and organization, to meet the immediate problems of mass economic development and extended social welfare posed by conditions after World War II. Divided into various religious groups, subgroups, and national minorities, and without well-defined natural boundaries, Syria lacked the conditions necessary for establishing strong internal unity. The large investment in land undertaken by business groups after the war was initially successful in increasing agricultural production, but socially and politically it proved to be a liability because it led to sharper differences in wealth. These conditions provided fertile gound for the emergence of socialist ideas in the form of reformist measure as early as March, 1949, when Colonel Husni Za'im led a coup and took over the government. The next dictator, Adib Shishakly, opposed Syria's union with Iraq in a kingdom, launched a series of development measures and worked closely for a time with Akram Hawrani and his Socialist Party, which was founded in 1950. Private enterprise was still recognized as the chief element of the economy. Deteriorating relations with the West and the struggle within Syria between small but dynamic leftist and rightist groups striving to dominate a large but unorganized conservative center led to economic stagnation and, at the same time, increased demands for economic reorganization. The rapprochement with the USSR, which was greatly accelerated by the French-British-Israeli attack on Egypt in 1956, led to the public expression of pro-leftist sentiments.

Alongside these developments was the political mobilization of the lower classes, as well as an increased sense of economic and social expectation, which seemingly could be fulfilled more easily by a revolutionary regime. The Ba'th's fortunes and ideology closely followed these development. The nationalism preached by 'Aflaq adopted social goals, which were generally defined as socialism.

Meanwhile, 'Aflaq had overcome the most difficult ideological hurdle—the definition of Islam's place and role in his nationalist theory. Almost from their very beginnings in the 1920's, the nationalist movements in Syria and Lebanon had two major aspects that were in fact contradictory. One *nationalist current, backed somewhat by popular groups, envisaged nationalism mainly in Islamic terms, but many intellectuals seemed to lean toward a secular nationalism and thus were able to soothe the fears of the Christian Arabs, who were afraid of being absorbed in a state that had a huge Muslim majority. Another nationalist current, promoted chiefly by Lebanese Christians, defended the idea of an independent state protected by European powers.*

As early as 1943, 'Aflaq had described Islam as part of the foundation of Arabism and a response to the Arab soul's permanent search for noble and higher spiritual pursuits. True, 'Aflaq had taken religion out of the narrow limits of orthodoxy, but at the same time he indicated that Muhammad and Islam expressed the best of Arabism and helped recast the Arab society into a new form. Consequently, the relation of Arab nationalism to Islam was unique, and Islam could be considered, even by Christian Arabs, a national culture. This interesting view was in part a preparation for further identifying Islam with Arab nationalism and thus removing the popular distrust shown by the masses toward secular nationalism and secular socialism. The distrust naturally was toward socialist theory itself and not toward its fruits. In expressing his views on socialism, however, 'Aflaq seemed to be far more secularist than he might have intended. The constitution of the Ba'th Party, after introducing sweeping nationalist principles (one Arab nation forming an indivisible political-economic-cultural entity with an eternal misson of renewing human values and increasing progress and harmony), defines its economic and social policy. This policy aims at achieving social justice through redistribution of wealth and nationalization of industries, participation by workers in management of industries, limitation of land and industrial ownership, and economic development. The Ba'th constitution unequivocally proposes measures to control the economy through state intervention, but it is too general in its plans for development. Yet, the great service rendered by Islam to Arabism in the past could not be repeated in the twentieth century since the problems challenging Syria were not essentially religious but political and social. The measures in the social and political fields were envisaged strictly in secular terms and this in practice was a radical departure from the spirit of Islam and its socio-economic concepts. Thus, in the last few years—that is to say, since the Ba'th's coming to power—'Aflaq and the Ba'th in general have often been described as godless and as enemies of religion. The Ba'th's nationalism gave a dominant place to the state, which, by necessity, was to be limited to a small ruling group backed chiefly by the military. This became an elite group without popular roots.

In the political field, 'Aflaq's ideal of Arab unity made the Ba'th appear as its natural instrument and Syria as its center. The union with Egypt in 1958 collapsed in 1961, and the second union undertaken with Iraq and

Egypt in 1963 remained on paper. The chief cause for the failure of the union was Ba'th's insistence on preserving its organization and freedom of activity and its implicit refusal to surrender completely to Egypt Syria's potential leadership of the Arab world, even though Egypt seemed to be politically more capable of achieving unity.

Moreover, the activities of 'Aflaq and of the Ba'th Party in Syria, leading to the latter's accession to power in 1958 and 1963, did not appear as a process of assimilation of other groups but as a twisted maneuver to subdue and eliminate parties and groups that disagreed with the Ba'th.

In the elections of 1949, the Ba'th had suffered a heavy defeat, and in 1953 it had united with Akram Hawrani's Arab Socialist Party; in 1954–55, it had begun to collaborate with the army and had entered the government by assuming some ministerial positions. The Ba'th finally succeeded in eliminating Antun Saadeh's Syrian Social Nationalist Party, and then collaborated with the Communists, spreading its control over the press and the government. After it had eliminated the conservatives, the Ba'th was threatened by the Communists, whose well-knit organization and ideology proved to be far stronger than anything the Ba'th had to offer. Having destroyed the regime's democratic, constitutional bases, despite lip service to a democratic system in its constitution, the Ba'th appeared unable to control the government or to find popular support. Consequently, it engineered the union with Egypt in 1958, lest the Communists take over. But the party then did its best to undermine the union. The zenith of the Ba'th's and of 'Aflaq's popularity came in 1963, when the Ba'thist wing of the military in Iraq acquired power. But the Ba'thist National Command, established over parties in both Syria and Iraq, was torn apart by successive coups led by officers in each country. Aflaq and Bittar were in the National Command. But the power struggle in Syria and then the Israeli-Arab war of 1967 had a negative impact on Aflaq's career and on the integrity of the Ba'th as an ideology and a movement. A coup by a left-wing group led by General Saleh Jadid in 1966 toppled the government (National Command) of Amin Hafez and Bittar and led to the arrest of prominent Ba'thists including Aflaq. Relations with the USSR improved and Communists were included in the government. It was at this point that the paths of the Syrian and the Iraqi Ba'thists began to diverge.

The war with Israel cost Syria the Golan Heights and further radicalized the regime. The new government refused to participate in the Khartoum conference of August 1967, in which the Arab leaders agreed on a political solution instead of war to solve the conflict with Israel, if the latter gave back the territories captured. Instead, Syria led the 9th Congress of the National Command of the Ba'th and adopted sweeping radical measures concerning the entire range of Arab and international affairs. Meanwhile the struggle within the ruling group—between those who placed priority on *the military security of Syria and collaboration with Arab states and those who advocated revolutionary socialistic change—deepened. The dispute was solved in 1970 through the elimination of Saleh Jadid, who had made the mistake of invading Jordan in order to retaliate against King Hussein's attacks on Palestinians and had suffered heavy casualties. Hafez Assad, the Minister of Defense and Air Force Commander, took over the government and eliminated the left-wing Ba'thists. On March 7, 1971, he established the National Front, in which the Ba'th, although retaining the main position, shared some of its power with the Arab Socialist Movement, the Socialist-Unionists, and the Communists. Assad made some other moves toward installing some sort of parliamentary constitutionalism. He also departed from the old, extreme secularist view of Ba'th by making it mandatory to have a Muslim as the president of the republic. But Assad, like most of the officers, belonged to the Alawi minority, while the country is overwhelmingly Sunni. He met with accusations that the Ba'th was used to achieve supremacy of the Alawis (Nusairi) and with a growing armed resistance from the orthodox Muslims, especially the Muslim Brethren. Nevertheless, Assad managed to maintain good relations with the other Arab regimes, including Egypt, until Sadat's visit to Israel in 1977. Assad's regime, although much more moderate than his predecessor's is still considered too socialistic by most Arabs.*

Iraq meanwhile underwent several changes of government. Eventually the civilian faction of the Ba'th prevailed through the emergence at the top of Saddam Hussein, the leader of the civilian group. The Ba'thists in Iraq adopted a much more radical attitude on internal and international relations but remained ideologically more moderate than the Syrians. Consequently, the two Ba'thist regimes in Syria and Iraq denounced each other for betraying the Ba'thist ideals and have come to the brink of war, despite sporadic periods of close relationship.

After his release from jail in Syria, 'Aflaq and his close followers found refuge in Iraq; but soon he left for Brazil, complaining that he was the only true Ba'thist left. He returned in 1969, but his influence has been declining, although he enjoys respect in Iraq. Meanwhile Syria, which on one occasion condemned 'Aflaq to death in absentia for involvement in a plot to overthrow the government, had discovered the "real" founder of the Ba'th. He is Zaki al-Arsuzi, who was a nationalist leader in Alexandretta and established in 1940 the al-Bath al-Arabi (the Arab Resurrection). Al-Arsuzi eventually learned of 'Aflaq and Bittar's party and joined it; however, in 1966 the Syrian Ba'thists declared that al-Arsuzi, not 'Aflaq, was the spiritual father of the movement. Thus the two main branches of the Ba'th—that is, the Regional Commands in Syria and Iraq—have followed a different path since 1966, despite occasional collaboration.

On the Ba'th and its founders, see John F. Devlin, The Ba'th Party. A

History From Its Origin to 1966 *(Stanford: Hoover Institution Press, 1976);
Kamel S. Abu Jaber,* The Arab Ba'th Socialist Party, History, Ideology and
Organization *(Syracuse, N.Y.: Syracuse University Press, 1966); Zaki al-
Arsuz,* al-Mu 'allafat al-kamila *[Complete Works] (Damascus: n.p., 1972).
On the Iraqi Ba'th, see Majid Khadduri,* Socialist Iraq: A Study in Iraqi
Politics since 1968, *(Washington, D.C.: The Middle East Institute, 1978);
R.E. Thoman, "Iraq Under Ba'this Rule,"* Current History 62, *no. 365
(January 1972): 31–41. On the controversies in the Syrian Ba'th, see the
memoirs of Munif al-Razzaz,* The Bitter Experience *(Beirut, 1967) and
Sami al-Jundi,* al-Ba'ath *(Beirut, 1969), both in Arabic, and also Nabil M.
Kaylani, "The Rise of the Syrian Ba'th, 1940–1958"*International Journal of
Middle East Studies 3 (1972):3–23.

*Following the separation from the Syrians, the Iraqi Ba'thists published
a series of booklets in English on party affairs; see* Pertinent Problems and
Questions *(Madrid: Litografia Eder, 1977);* A Survey of the Ba'th Party's
Struggle 1947–1974 *(Madrid: Fareso, 1978);* About the 1973 October-
War, *Report adopted by the Ninth Regional Congress* (Florence: Coopera-
tive Lavoratori, 1977); Michel Aflak *(sic),* Choice of Texts from the Ba'th
Party Founder's Thought *(Florence: Cooperative Lavoratori, 1977). For
further reading see Gordon H. Torrey,* Syrian Politics and the Military,
1945–1958 *(Columbus, Ohio: Ohio State Univesity Press, 1964). Partial
treatment is given in Leonard Binder,* The Ideological Revolution in the
Middle East *(New York: John Wiley & Sons, 1964), pp. 156–92; in Nicola A.
Ziadeh (Ziyada),* Syria and Lebanon *(London: Ernest Benn; New York:
Frederick A. Praeger, 1957); and in Muhammad Shafi' Agawni, "The Ba'th:
A Study in Contemporary Arab Politics,"* International Studies 3 (1961–
62):6–24 *(reprinted in Benjamin Rivlin and Joseph S. Szyliowicz, eds.,* The
Contemporary Middle East: Tradition and Innovation *[New York: Random
House, 1964], pp. 452–60). The constitution of the Ba'th Party is printed in*
Middle East Journal 13 *(Spring 1959): 195–200, with corrections in*
Middle East Journal 13 *(Autumn 1959): 487–89. It also appears in Sylvia
G. Haim, ed.,* Arab Nationalism: An Anthology *(Berkely, Calif.: University
of California Press,1962), pp. 233–41. The latter includes a passage from
'Aflaq's writings. See also Jubran Majdalani, "The Arab Socialist Move-
ment," in Walter Z. Laqueur, ed.,* The Middle East in Transition *(London:
Routledge & Kegan Paul; New York: Frederick A Praeger, 1958), pp. 337–
50. See also Hisham B. Sharabi,* Nationalism and Revolution in the Arab
World *(Princeton, N.J.: D. Van Nostrand, 1966), p. 161. Extracts from Ba'th
ideology may be found on pp. 111–12, 135–39. See also Gordon H. Torrey,*
"Arab Socialism" in ed. H. Thompson and R.D. Reischauer, *Modernization
of the Arab World* (Princeton, N.J.: D. Van Nostrand, 1966), pp. 178–96.

'Aflaq's chief writings have been published under the title Fi sabil al-
Ba'th. *A general statement on Ba'th ideology and socialism may be found in*

a joint work by Michel 'Aflaq, Akram Hawrani al-Razzaz, and Jamal al-Atasi, Hawl al-qawmiyya wa-al-ishtirakiyya *[On Nationalism and Socialism] (Cairo: al-Matba'a al-'alamiyya, 1957). Seven volumes published in Beirut by the Syrian Government—*Nidal al-Ba'th fi sabil al-wahda al-huriyya wa-al-ishtir-akiya *[The Struggle of the Ba'th for the Sake of Unity, Freedom, and Socialism] (Beirut, Dar al-tali'a, 1963–65)—cover the period from 1943 onward. These books contain party communications and declarations and speeches by leaders and are excellent primary sources.*

The Philosophy of the Ba'th and Its Differences from Communism and National Socialism

The Arab Ba'th is a unique movement that undertakes neither to disguise problems nor to treat them superficially; it sees itself as reflecting the soul of the nation and her various needs. When we say that this is revolutionary movement must first of all forge the essence of the nation and rekindle in the Arab personality its strenghth to fight and to shoulder the responsibilities of life, we also have in mind the recovery by Arab thought of its aptitude for seeing things directly, freely, without artifice or imitation. Arab thought will then be in line with the laws of nature and of life; it will be able to understand problems in their true perspective and organize its work in a creative manner. In saying this, we have in view our great mission which is to lead the Arabs, individually and collectively, toward this healthy state of thought and mind.

To philosophize on the society of tomorrow is contrary to our ideas. What we are trying to do is to forge a society that will find within itself its means of existence and elements of survival. It is hardly necessary to be a great prophet to predict that certain unchanging and tangible facts such as socialism compel our attention. The Arab nation is socialist and one cannot conceive of a healthy society within this nation without socialism. Ba'th socialism is in perfect accord with present Arab society, a society whose past, present, and future are linked to the soil. This uncompromising and courageous socialism differs from the socialist name and label behind which the leaders and politicians shelter.

Theoretical Differences Between Our Socialism and That of the Communists

Socialism in the Communist system is not limited only to the organization of the economy; it must obey the ends and aims of the Communist system. Communism, as a universal doctrine, aims in effect at world-wide revolution and can only henceforth be applied if this revolution is an entire success. On the other hand, as long as the revolution is not at an end, the economic system of a Communist country will remain subject to the aims and directives of the policy of the Communist movement, including preparation for war and competition with other countries. It is for this reason that Tito was considered a defector from objective Communism because he did not agree that Yugoslavia should be made to serve the general aim of world revolution. Tito refused to submit the production and resources of his country to a Communist general policy under the direction of Moscow.

Arab Ba'th socialism, on the contrary, limits itself to organizing the economy so as to redistribute the wealth of the Arab world and to establish a basis for an economy guaranteeing justice and equality among all citizens, and also to promote a revolution in production and the means of production.

Communist socialism is impregnated with Communist philosophy. This philosophy emanates from a specific group with its own particular requirements, characteristics, and conditions. Our socialism is impregnated with our philosophy. This philosophy emanates from an Arab group with its own special needs, its own historical conditions and characteristics.

Communist philosophy is based on belief and materialism. It explains historical and social evolution solely and wholly by economic factors, which results in its changing its philosophy and spiritual beliefs. The philosophy of the Arab Ba'th does not agree with this materialistic conception. On the contrary, it considers that the "spiritual" factor plays a very important part in the evolution of history and human progress. Consequently, it considers that the spiritual influences that have appeared in the Arab world, such as Islam, are in no way strange.

Being materialistic, Communist philosophy accords only little importance to the individual; it does not respect him and it scorns his freedom. It is concerned only with the mass. This conception leads to dictatorship and the creation of a materialistic society completely lacking in spirit. This philosophy similarly results in a lack of balance between the individual and society and between Arab societies and others. Our socialism, on the contrary, is based on the individual and his personal freedom; it does not allow his individual liberties to be scorned and considers all individuals as equal and a tyrannical dictatorship unnecessary.

Practical Differences Between
Our Socialism and
That of the Communists

Communist socialism has gone too far in the direction of nationalization; it has abolished property rights and consequently has killed all individual initiative. Ba'th socialism, on the contrary, believes that the main strength of a nation resides in individual initiative which encourages action; it is careful not to abolish private property, therefore limiting itself to the creation of strong impediments to abuse.

Communism does not recognize the right of succession. Our socialism, on the contrary, recognizes it and believes that a citizen cannot be deprived of it. Nevertheless, to prevent the wrongful use of the national wealth and exploitation of labor, we have imposed certain changes that make this right in certain cases almost theoretical and that reduce it in other cases to a simple moral right.

Criticisms of Communism

Communist socialism is limited. It is based, in effect, on an economic philosophy, Marxism, whose economic and historical conceptions nowadays cannot stand up to true scientific criticism. In addition, we observe that this Communist socialism is difficult to achieve and does not correspond to the reality we know. In fact, it can only succeed through world revolution. Ba'th socialism is flexible and is not tied by artificial economic laws. In addition, it can be easily achieved and corresponds to reality, for it consists simply in a fair and healthy economic reorganization of Arab society. This socialism will be achieved when Arabs take charge of their own destiny and free themselves from imperialism and feudalism.

Russia may not have broken with Communism as her first leaders saw it, but she has nevertheless abandoned the theory of world-wide revolution. She has restricted herself to aiding expansion of revolution and the propagation of a Communism conforming to the interests and aims of Russia.

Theoretically, Communism is a universal party without geographical limits and does not constitute a state. Nevertheless, we observe that Russia, like the other great powers, has it own civilization, aims, and relations, and tries to be a center from which her strength and civilization may radiate. This is a contradiction of Communism as it was conceived by the first philosophers.

We consider that the Communist Party is a destructive force, for two reasons. The first resides in its deceptive socialism which promises the Arab people all they direly need, at the same time trying to drag it into the clutches of another state, Russia. The second reason is its internationalism.

When Our Socialism Succeeds . . .

If we come to power in Syria, we will abolish the differences between the privileged classes and the others; we will ensure justice, at the same time preparing ourselves to perfect our work. Perhaps we shall not be able to give the people all they desire; perhaps even we shall take a part of what they need, in order to equip the army and ensure the success of the *coups d'état* in all the Arab countries. Socialism cannot be achieved in Syria alone, for Syria is a small state with limited resources. It cannot be achieved, because imperialism and the pressure exerted by all the other Arab countries make the total success of socialism just as difficult there. That is why our socialism will only be able to gain definite recognition in the framework of a single Arab united state—that is to say, when the Arab people are freed, and when the impediments that oppose the success of socialism, such as imperialism, feudalism, and the geographical frontiers created by politics, are removed. This does not prevent certain Arab countries from putting this doctrine into practice before others, although perhaps only in part.

Differences Between our Socialism
and National Socialism

Theoretical differences.   The National Socialism of Germany and of Italy is linked to Nazi and fascist philosophy, based on the idea of racial superiority and on the difference between peoples, i.e., on the superiority of one kind over another and their right to dominate the world. These philosophies likewise establish differences between nationals of the same nation, which leads to the dictatorship of an individual or of a class. True socialism cannot succeed in such a system.

Ba'th socialism is inspired by its own philosophy, does not despise other nations, and does not aim at domination. It is an end in itself, to procure economic and social benefits that are easily achieved. It does not cloak political or denominational ambitions.

Practical differences.   Subjected to Nazi and fascist regimes, National Socialism in Germany and in Italy is closely linked to their aims; expansion and colonialism. These aims can only be achieved, therefore, by territorial expansion. Thus, National Socialism is only a means to imperialism. Ba'th socialism, on the other hand, does not aim at expansion. Its sole aim is to create a fair economic system in the Arab world. It supports all that tends toward the liberation of peoples still under colonial rule. It desires that other peoples may practice socialism and follow an economic policy that gives justice to all and a higher standard of living for all peoples, at the same time conserving the individuality of each.

The Ba'th Attitude Toward Religion

Before we discuss the policy of the future Arab state and the place of religion in the life of nations in general and of the Arab nation in particular, I would urge you, at this stage of liberation and reawakening, to acquire a solid culture and always to make use of it. Without freedom of thought, you will never arrive at the truth or be able to formulate the correct solutions for your own and your nation's problems.

Religion Is a Basic Factor in Human Life

From the earliest times to the present, religion has been a basic factor in human life. We would like, at the outset, to reject the callous, contemptuous attitude to religion prevalent among certain superficial young men. Religion is a serious subject and it cannot be dismissed with a few superficial comments. But we must distinguish between the essence of religion and its objectives, and religion as it becomes manifest under certain circumstances.

The problem, then, is to distinguish between the genuine and the apparent character of religion, because religion encompasses both. The problem arises when a wide gulf separating the genuine from the apparent content of religion creates a contradiction. When appearances are dia-metrically opposed to the genuine character and objectives of religions, crises arise among men. Such crises assume various forms in accordance with the intellectual level of men and the extent of their interest or lack of interest. The issue is a complicated one, involving science, thought in general, passions, and private interests. Arab youth must take a calm view of the situation and must pronounce a dispassionate judgment. They must come to recognize the part played by emotions and private interest in this issue, and only in this manner can the matter be settled with approximate accuracy and to the public advantage.

Islam Is a Revolution
That Can Only Be Understood
by Revolutionaries

A momentous event occurred in our national life, an event of both national and human significance, namely, the rise of Islam. I do not believe that the Arab youth give it enough importance and I do not find them concerned to study it in depth. I believe that Islam possesses a magnificent moral experience and a tremendous human experience which can enrich them and their culture, in both theory and practice.

Does our youth consider the fact that, when it arose, Islam was a revolutionary movement that rebelled against a whole system of beliefs, customs, and interests? Can they not perceive that Islam can only be properly understood by revolutionaries? After all, this is only natural, since all revolutions are identical and eternally unchangeable. All revolutions, past, present, and future, have the same psychological conditions and, to a great extent, the same objective circumstances. It is very strange, there-fore—and this you must ponder—that those who seem to be the staunchest defenders of Islam are themselves the most unrevolutionary elements. It is inconceivable that such men really understand Islam and, at the same time, very natural that those who are closest to Islam in sentiment and spirit are the revolutionary generation who are presently rebelling against the old and the corrupt. Nevertheless, we find that not all, and not even most, of this revolutionary generation acknowledge this link with Islam, while those who pretend to maintain this link are themselves the enemies of revolution and the upholders of a corruption that must be overcome before the Arab nation can progress.

You undoubtedly know certain elementary things about Islam, and I hope that you will come to know everything. The first thing you know about Islam is that it was first preached by one individual, who was able gradually to atract a few, mostly uninfluential, converts. Those men suffered a great deal of harm and persecution for thirteen years in Mecca before the *Hijra* [to Medina, A.D. 622]. After the *Hijra*, Muslims became relatively more powerful. They were no longer a limited number surrounded by a sea of enemies but a band of faithful and dedicated men.

Does anyone who has not known persecution and has never fought in the ranks of the few who have right on their side against the deluded majority—does such a person have the right to speak in the name of Islam? Does he have an exclusive title to Islam? I personally do not think so, nor do I believe that anyone has this right except those who are persecuted, who have principles and courage, and who preach their faith to all since it is of benefit to all—even when the majority of men and the circumstances are against them and work to destroy them. Such men have this right because all messages and calls, whether social or religious, should be judged by action and not by talk. It is always easy to talk or to write since the energy expended is minimal, but the value of principles can be assessed only by the test of action. If we accept this standard, we shall be able to see our path more clearly and shall discover much falsehood and deception, ignorance and vanity among those who fancy themselves as, or claim to be, men of principles. We shall find that these men have chosen the easy way out and decided to back the winner. They have contrived to acquire all means of comfort and protection in society and to safeguard their private interests, their comfort, and their vanity. We shall discover that these men are not those who are best suited to fight for their principles. . . .

The Ba'th Party member must satisfy very rigorous conditions which are almost contradictory. He must fight all deception and all attempts to prevent progress and liberation that are made in the name of religion for the purpose of preserving corruption and social regression. But at the same time, he should be able to understand the true religion and the genuine human spirit which is, in essence, positive, possessed of faith, and intolerant of recusancy and stagnation. He must recognize the people as friends, whose confidence must be won, and not as enemies. It is true that the people are deluded, but we cannot show them how they are deluded unless we understand them, react with them, and share their life, their emotions, and their mentality. Every step we take in their direction gives us hope that they will move closer to us. Thus, the Ba'thist is always exposed to danger: If he follows this path, there is danger that he will reacquire the reactionary mentality against which he had formerly rebelled. If he follows an opposite path and declares an open war against erroneous beliefs, he is in danger of becoming a negative person, of losing the positive aspect of Ba'thist teachings, and of moving closer to the negative Communism which we have rejected. He may also find himself allied to one form or another of a sham liberalism which is mere show and empty boast. In fighting reaction and resisting its challenge, its slander, and its provocations, the Ba'thist must constantly bear these positive, spiritual principles in mind and must remember that he is fighting not the ideals themselves but their perversion by reaction. He must not forget that, in guiding the people to the proper level of consciousness without hurting their feelings, he is a revolutionary who does not accept, either for himself or for his nation, a cheap and reactionary interpretation of beliefs and spiritual ideals. He must bear in mind that he defers to the people only temporarily and only for the sake of preparing them to understand more difficult matters. The faith of the Ba'thist in man generally and in the Arab man in particular must constantly compel him to be more audacious in combating erroneous and outdated beliefs. Since the Arab nation is fertile and holds within it the experience of centuries of misery, regression, and injustice, he must not suppose that it cannot support so much revolution and liberation. Thus, it is ready to surge forth and to attain a spiritual level of great intensity. . . .

Ba'th Views on Capitalism and the Class Struggle

I do not suppose it would be necessary to explain in detail that the party's views and its publications over the years have stated that we have, from the beginning, categorically rejected the capitalist outlook. Nor need I emphasize our rejection of any creed that gives the object more importance than the man, since our party believes that man is himself the highest value, while capitalism believes the contrary.

Capitalism is not a philosophy but an existing situation: It represents man's submission to the objects that he has created or produced. If by capitalism we understand unlimited individual freedom of possession with all its consequences, if it is said that such a freedom is sacrosanct and that neither society nor the state has the right to interfere with it, then we say that no one, not even in the capitalist countries, would be found ready to defend such a view. For these capitalist countries and societies have recently come round to the view that unlimited individual ownership is not sacred, does not always yield the desired results, does not always conform to the public interest and that the state must interfere to safeguard this latter. But if capitalism is understood by some people to mean a system which opposes all others that do not recognize man's absolute freedom, then we might here recognize a certain positive element. But in reality, this is not capitalism but the socialism that we and many other nations advocate: a socialism that is vital, that is genuine and not artificial, and that does not seek to substitute one disease for another or to destroy the idol of capitalism in order to erect the idol of a society which enslaves men and represses their healthy initiative. Our socialism is one which, as we stated, considers man to be the highest value and to be a master of all that he creates. Therefore, we believe that a genuine, far-sighted, and wise creed must evolve in order to destroy exploitation in all its forms without suppressing individual freedom. This, in turn, leads me to ask whether our party believes in class structure and struggles.

There is no theory of class structure in the Marxist sense in our ideology but we do recognize class structures without accepting their Marxist interpretation. Marxism was right in stating that the great struggle of our age was between classes, thus making the class struggle a law of historical evolution. The Marxist analysis of the characteristic features of our age is accurate. Therefore, we cannot possibly ignore the class struggle.

But Marxism greatly exaggerated its importance, erected it into an international conflict, and almost completely ignored the vital historical development of nationalism. Marxism falsely believes that the links between exploiters and exploited throughout the world are much closer than those linking one particular class to its nationalism. Events have proved the falsity of this view since international proletarian solidarity did not evolve in the manner and to the same powerful extent that Marxism predicted.

There is no doubt that within the same nation there is a struggle between those who own the means of production and those who do not. But even within the same nation, it is not possible to view this struggle in the literal and arbitrary manner proposed by Marxism. To begin with, we have rejected internationalism in the Marxist sense and have advocated a free cooperation among independent socialist countries. Hence we accept the links binding us Arabs to other nations and we admit the possibility of meeting together on equal terms, not under the orders of an organization like Communism. This latter course has led, as you know, to the subjection of all the working classes to the Soviet Union, where they act as mere agents of Soviet policy.

Hence, our advocacy of free cooperation among independent socialist countries is more realistic and appropriate. Within the Arab world, we have tackled the problem in a manner that differs from Marxism: We have postulated the national problem as an indivisible whole and have not, like the Marxists, merely isolated the economic aspect, namely, the conflict between the owners and those who do not own. Our problem is much more extensive than this: It is a problem of a nation that is fragmented and partly colonized. Fragmentation is the major obstacle in its path of progress. It is also a problem of a backward nation—in mentality, in its economy, in politics, and in everything. We must build everything anew. Thus, we have placed the Arab nation to one side and all who attempt to retard its progress, to another. The capitalists and feudalists are not the only enemies of the Arabs; there are also the politicians who cling to this state of fragmentation because it serves their own interests; there are, in addition, those who submit to the imperialists, in one form or another, and finally, those who fight ideas, education, evolution, enlightenment, toleration, and the independence of our homeland. All these men we have placed on one side and the Arab nation on another. Therefore, we do not claim to have divided our nation into two or more classes, on the Marxist pattern. We maintain that a man of religion, for example, who sows the seeds of religious fanaticism and is poor, is as detrimental to society as the capitalists and feudalists who exploit workers and peasants.

Nevertheless, our comprehensive national outlook which elevates our problem and transcends the purely economic must not make us forget that the economic problem is essential. If we are to justify our leniency toward exploiters and reactionaries by using nationality as an excuse, we would deprive our struggle of its vital nerve. This conflict between the masses who are deprived of ownership and the exploiting class, which hinders all development and is deaf to all appeals to the national interest, is in fact beneficial and should not frighten us, since it will lead to national resurgence. From the liberation of the poor masses will issue forth the virtuous Arab citizen who is capable of understanding his nationalism and of achieving its ideals, since nationalism loses all its significance if it exists alongside injustice, poverty, and privation.

The matter is not as easy as you might suppose. We must preserve this tension between the two aspects of the problem and must constantly warn against the loss of the nationalist idea or its identification with criminal class interests. We must guard against the deceptive boasts of interested men who falsely advocate the national interest and merely wish to protect their skins when, in attempting to influence us, they ask: "Are we not all of one nation?" The Ba'thists must be on their guard against such guile. Nationalism as currently understood in our homeland or in the West is, for the most part, a negative and illusory concept permeated with reactionary and exploitationist beliefs. It is our duty to strip away this mask of negativism and deception. Nor need we be afraid of this, because a core will always remain after we have purified the nationalist ideal. This core may be something very simple and insubstantial but it is nevertheless essential. Nationalism, in truth, is not vanity, is not fanaticism vis-à-vis other nations, is foreign to all material interests of a certain class, and is, in fact, humanism itself manifested and realized in one living reality: the nation.

Therefore, we accept only the positive aspects of nationalism, having cast aside all fanaticism and superficialities. Nationalism is the spiritual and historical bond between members of a nation, whom history has stamped in a special manner and has not isolated from the rest of humanity. History gave those members of a nation a distinctive character and a distinctive personification of humanity so that they might become active parts of this latter, creating and interacting with the whole. This, then, is our nationalism. It is not built upon malice toward other nations or toward our fellow-citizens. The struggle we have created within our nation is not vicious but beneficial. Love, in reality, is a hard thing. For when we love our nation and our fellow-Arabs and wish them a prosperous future and a dignified life, we do not shrink from the use of force against all who attempt to hinder our progress and our evolution.

Those rulers and others with vested material or moral interests who obstruct the nation's unity must be fought decisively by the people. But they must be combatted in a spirit of love, since the struggle of the people against them does not issue from greed or envy or spite but from the love of life itself, which these men are trying to suffocate and retard.

19. The Iraqi Ba'th Party's View of Events in the Arab World

The schism between the Syrian and Iraqi Ba'th parties and their views about the founder of the movement is well illustrated in the passages reproduced below. The Iraqi, as well as the Syrian, Ba'th are maintaining relations with Ba'thist groups in various Arab countries, as the excerpts indicate. However, these groups have limited influence and power.

The following excerpts are taken from the Arab Ba'th Socialist Party, A Survey of the Ba'th Party's Struggle 1947–1974 *(Madrid: Fareso, 1977), pp. 105–16, and from M. Aflak (sic),* Choice of Texts from the Ba'th Party Founder's Thought *(Firenze: Cooperative Lavoratori, 1977), pp. 188–89.*

After the 8th Congress [1974], Iraq began to play a more effective part on the Arab and international scene. Its leaders made frequent visits to the progressive Arab countries and to friendly countries throughout the world. . . . As a result of the considerable increase in revenue following the increases in the price of oil, Iraq in 1974 made enormous progress in her economic and social development. Laws were passed on February 7th, which increased salaries and reduced the price of services with a consequent rise in the standard of living, especially for the working class. Iraqi and Arab scientific specialists were invited to serve Iraq and were provided with ample facilities.

During the same period, the country became more involved in Arab common economic projects, regarded as being one the solid bases for unity. The decision to finance industrial projects in common with Egypt, Syria, and other Arab countries was the best way by which Iraq could express its vision of unity and the maturity of the Party in its Arab policy, without being concerned with the differences between the regimes. . . .

The revolution of July 17th and 30th in Iraq was the most spectacular Party action on the Arab and international political scene, and an example of its militant existence on the pan-Arab level. In other countries, however, the militants were no less active in continuing the struggle, in deepening the roots of the Party among the masses and in pursuing their national mission of confrontation with imperialism, division, exploitation and the dictatorial and reactionary regimes.

In Syria, despite the difficult conditions facing the Party as a result of the repression and confusion instigated by the regime which continued to use falsely the name and slogans of the Party, the militants pursued the struggle against the dictatorship which had surrendered the country's rights. In May 1970, the regime began a wave of arrests of militant civilian and military members of the Party, and forced others to leave the country. They were brought before so-called courts, in August 1971, accused of plotting against the government. The sentences went from the death penalty to life imprisonment or imprisonment for a period for a large number of militants, the elite of the Party, including the founder and General Secretary, comrade Michel Aflaq . . .

When it became clear that the regime was collaborating with the imperialist plans to force capitulation on the Arabs, people's hopes in

Syria, were placed more and more in the [Iraqi] Party. Arab and international public opinion discovered daily the long term aims of the plot which had been hatched against the Party ever since February 23rd, 1966. . . .

In Jordan, the Party went into retreat for a time as did the majority of the national movement following the September massacres and the liquidation of the Resistance in 1970 and 1971. The impact of its ideas and programmes remained, however and the authorities from time to time arrested militants and accused them of being members of the Party's secret organisation. Other operations were mounted to isolate the Ba'th youth both materially and psychologically. . . . It should be mentioned here that it was difficult, and in the Lebanon also, to distinguish between the struggle led by the Ba'th and that of the Arab Liberation Front. The latter had been founded at the beginning of January 1969 on the Party's initiative and in accordance with the 9th National Congress resolutions. Its aim was to intensify its activities by resorting to a people's armed struggle, and to widen the Arab national dimension of the Resistance which sometimes became extremely localised.

The Arab Liberation Front [Iraqi-backed Palestinian commando group] appeared on the battlefield in April 1969, and began its first operations on the anniversary of the Party's foundation. It thus became a vehicle through which the Ba'th could participate in fedayeen operations and attempt to influence certain errors of theory, practice and organisation of these operations . . .

The Front collaborated closely with the Party in preparing the Palestinian and Lebanese people for the fight by training and arming them. The Front and the Party were therefore able to play an important part in resisting the plots hatched against the Resistance after it had become established in the country, notably in April 1969, March 1970 and May 1973.

After several years of struggle, the Front held its foundation congress in August 1972. Questions of military and political organisation were discussed and a Central Committee elected. This was the beginning of a new phase and was a reflection of the Front's growing importance on the Palestinian scene. At the beginning of January 1973, the National Palestine Council even adopted a project put forward by the Front, which meant that it was fully integrated into the Resistance's institutions. . . .

Young Ba'thists were the pillars of support for the many student agitations in the Lebanon at this time, taking part in the national organisation. . . . The uprising in the American University in 1974 was an extension of its long struggle against imperialist cultural institutions. In its famous manifesto, in the name of the Youth of the American University in March 1967, it had demanded its Lebanization. . . .

In the Sudan, during this period, the Ba'thists successfully disseminated the Party's ideas on socialism and unity amongst the working people, the students and the intellectuals. Their activities were carried out under difficulty and demanded many sacrifices. They played a noteworthy part in organising the demonstrations at the time of the Arab Summit Meeting in Khartoum after the 1967 defeat, in the many fights for democracy with the reactionary regime which preceded the military movement of May 1969, and in their continuous activities to make this movement more democratic and progressive. . . .

In Tunisia, the Party had become a growing political force while leading the student protests of the spring of 1968 against the sentences of their comrades who had led the June demonstrations. As a result, the Tunisan authorities arrested many Party members and started a defamatory campaign in the mass media. . . .

The Party had reorganised itself in many countries, both Arab and foreign, after the disturbances and splits caused by the serious crises which had shaken it on a national level. It was the Party in the Yemen which regained most influence in the country's events. It resisted the reactionaries linked with Saudi Arabia, and constantly moved in the direction of national democracy. For this reason it was the object of a wide reactionary conspiracy to arrest and persecute the Party militants. . . .

Following the 10th [1970] Congress, the National Directorate, in addition to its work with the Party organisations, established and developed relations with the people's movements and parties in the Maghreb and the Mashreq and also with the organisations of the Palestinian Resistance. It made contact with all of them and their leaders and encouraged them to unite and put up a stronger front for Palestine vis-à-vis the proposals for liquidating it.

At the beginning of 1974, the National Directorate made an agreement with the People's Liberation Front in Oman, underlining the need for unity and cooperation. The comrade General Secretary visited Democratic Yemen once again to reinforce Party links with the Nationalist Front. The Directorate effectively supported the revolution in Eritrea so that it could face up to all the traps which threatened it.

The National Directorate has established close links with all world socialist parties and liberation movements. It has attended their congresses and expressed sympathy with their struggles.

The experiment of the Baath in Iraq is a starting point for the Arab revolution . . . .

'Aflaq's View of the Ba'th in Iraq

We must express our faith in our nation, in our Party and in our revolution by determination by increased activity, sacrifice, effort, and by envisaging life as a continuous attack. The mentality of defence does not suit the mentality of revolution: continuous attack means initiative, it means that man surpasses himself by exerting his utmost efforts. It means that we always explore new areas to exploit for the enrichment of this revolution, the revolution af the Party [and] to increase the power of this revolution and its invincibility. We must increase the power of this revolution and its invincibility; we must give it light, a light that can later illuminate the whole Arab land and construct this experiment. . . .

Yes, it is an extraordinary experience, that of the Party in Iraq. It is the experience of the Party which is not going to be surpassed. Not because we have reached all our aims for we are at the beginning of the road. But this genuine beginning is the only one which will take us to the victorious end. Some minutes ago I said to our dear Comrade Saddam that the idea of the Party was from the start a rigorous idea that required a rigorous revolutionary standard as you know from the writings in the early life of the Party. I told him that the conditions of Syria where the Party emerged were not of the same degree of difficulty and cruelty. It was natural that Arabic Iraq, with its tragic and cruel conditions, be the starting point for a serious realisation of this idea.

VII.   NASSERISM

20.   The Principles That Guide Egypt's Political Life*

Gamal Abdel Nasser

The political and social ideas of Gamel Abdel Nasser (Jamal 'Abd al-Nasir), derived basically from the practical needs of a changing society, have had a strong impact on the entire Arab world. Nasser's social origins and background help explain his ability to understand the spirit of the Arab masses, to identify himself with them, and to manipulate them for his political purposes.

Nasser was born in Alexandria on January 15, 1918, the son of Abdel

*Extract from *Address by President Gamal Abdel Nasser at the Meeting of the National Assembly's Ordinary Session, Cairo, March 26, 1964* (Cairo: Information Department, 1964), pp. 3–7, *passim.*

Nasser Husein ('Abd al-Nasir Husayn), a postal clerk, and Fahima, a coal merchant's daughter. He attended primary school in Cairo, and secondary school in Helwan and Alexandria, studied law for six months, and received a lieutenant's comission from the Military Academy in Cairo in 1937. He served in the Sudan, was an instructor in the Military Academy, and participated in the Arab-Israeli war of 1948. The defeat of the Arabs crystallized his thoughts about the need to remedy the corruption in the Egyptian Government and to restore Egypt's pride and self-confidence. His revolutionary activity, which began after 1948, brought him into contact with the Muslim Brotherhood and various other groups that were likely to support the overthrow of King Faruq's regime. He formed a Free Officer's committee, out of which grew the Council of Revolutionary Command, which overthrew Faruq in July, 1952; and in 1954, Nasser emerged as the leader of the revolution after General Muhammed Naguib, its nominal leader, was ousted. He was elected president of Egypt in 1956 and he was re-elected repeatedly, in uncontested elections, most recently in 1965. After the Israeli forces defeated those of the U.A.R. in June, 1967, Nasser resigned the presidency but, on popular demand reassumed the office the following day.

Friendly to the West and not quite certain of his policy at the beginning, Nasser gradually adopted a radical foreign policy, which was soon reflected n his internal rule. The arms deal with Czechoslovakia, the Bandung conference, the final departure of the British from Egypt, the seizure and nationalization of the Suez Canal, and the abortive British-French-Israeli attack on Egypt—all in 1955–56—made Nasser a world personality and a champion of nationalism, nonalignment, and anticolonialism.

Although Nasser originally was not against political parties, eventually he banned them as representing only minority views and strove to create an organization that would embrace the entire nation. The Liberation Rally (1953–56), the National Union (1958–62), and the Socialist Union (1962) derived from his efforts to create a mass party. Nasser, as leader (ra'is), has dominated them, but the idea that the leader must be able to interpret the people's wishes remained a cardinal principle in his thought. The union of Egypt and Syria in the United Arab Republic in 1958 was a great victory for him, and the collapse of the union when Syria withdrew was a severe defeat. This experience enabled Nasser to estimate better the practical obstacles to unity, as well as the different views of other Arabs about political parties and government.

Nasser's political thought was determined on the one hand by the very nature of Egyptian society, which he described in The Philosophy of the Revolution as "not yet crystallized, which continues to ferment and be agitated, which has not yet settled down and taken on its final shape, which in its development, has not yet caught up with the nations that have preceded [it] on the path." On the other hand, it was determined by the potential role Egypt could play in international relations. This was described in terms of three circles or zones: Arab, African, and Islamic. The Islamic and African circles eventually coalesced and shrank considerably, while Arabism, composed of nationalism and Islam, became the core of Nasser's thought.

The political and social ideas included in Nasserism, it has been said, were suggested by his own countrymen and by intellectuals elsewhere in the Arab world. But it was Nasser who assembled disparate ideas into cohesive plans of action and translated them into concrete realities. Aware of the political role of ideologies, as the extract from the unity talks in 1963 indicates (see Chapter X, Subchapter 34), he has used them to justify and legitimize his policies.

A composite ideology whose content varies considerably, Nasserism may be divided into three closely related segments: foreign policy, nationalism, and socialism. Nasser's foreign policy toward the other Arab countries can be regarded as born out of protest against the artificial division of Arab lands into several states and against their backward economic, social, and political systems which consist of both monarchies and socialist republics. The ultimate goal of this view was a Pan-Arabism that would lead eventually to unification and integration in the form of one Arab state. To a large extent, nationalism and socialism have become the means for fulfilling this unity. The main conditions for unity are free choice by people seeking union, consolidation of internal unity by each Arab state, willingness of a majority in a country to live in a union, and adoption of socialism. In its global foreign policy, Nasserism opposed colonialism, neocolonialism, imperialism, spheres of influence, foreign military bases, and alignment with the Great Powers, despite the fact that Nasser's own policy in Yemen contradicted these principles. One may, in fact, refer to the Arab world as Nasserism's sphere of influence, even though in many cases this influence was perpetuated by domestic groups sympathetic to Nasser's views on unity, nationalism, and socialism. The outcome of Nasserism as an ideology was indeed determined by the course of the U.A.R.'s foreign policy.

Aside from its manifestations in foreign policy, nationalism was described by Nasser as love and solidarity among Arabs, as a movement and philosophy for political, social, and economic mobilization, and as a struggle for the unity, freedom, integrity, and dignity of Arabs. The bases of Arab nationalism are unity of language, culture, and hope, and strategic necessity. These are manifest in unity of thought, conscience, and feelings, community of future goals, and the need to oppose foreign powers who want to control the oil and strategic areas of Arab lands.

Nasser's early socialist views—especially those on equality—were sentimental yearnings rather than rationally conceived plans. He visualized the *middle classes—professionals, small shopkeepers, and middlemen—as nonexploiters, and regarded capitalists and feudalists—whom he usually identified with building and landowning—as economically harmful. Instead of changing his basic orientation, Nasser gradually altered his social views according to the need for economic development and unity. First, about 1955, he spoke about closing the gap between classes and referred to this measure as socialism; later, he set up a series of planning organizations.*

In 1961, he adopted a series of laws to nationalize large enterprises according to the six principles of the revolution. This was part of his attack on imperialism, feudalism, monopolies, and the domination of capitalism. It aimed also at establishing social justice, a truly democratic system, and a powerful army to guarantee the achievements of the U.A.R. Despite Nasser's professed wish to make the workers and peasants its social foundation, this socialism came to rest on the bureacuracy and the intelligentsia. Nasser's nationalist and socialist views acquired their final form in the National Charter of 1962, which is a cogent analysis of the U.A.R.'s political and social revolution and an ideological appeal to Arab intellectuals. It described revolution as "the only way that enables the Arab struggle to abandon the past and orient itself toward the future" and move out of the regression that was the natural consequence of oppression and exploitation. The Arab revolution, according to the Charter, would arm itself with three values: a scientific and free conscience (thought), a rapid adaptation to circumstances in line with the final objectives and moral principles of the struggle, and a perfect understanding of these objectives or goals—freedom, socialism, and unity. Freedom, both individual and national, meant liberation from feudal domination and colonialism. Socialism was a means and a goal—that is, both sufficiency and justice. Unity was the restoration to its natural state of "the same and unique nation torn apart by its enemies against its own wishes and interests." The Charter analyzed the situation of the Arab world generally, political democracy (a natural part of social democracy based on freedom from exploitation, on equality of opportunity, and on security for the future), and proposed ways to reach the ultimate goals. The Charter remained the foundation of Nasser's internal and external policy, but its fulfillment depended more on the outcome of international factors and relations among Arab states than on its ideological force.

The death of Nasser of a heart ailment in 1970 was preceded by his gradual demise as a world statesman and as the most influential Arab leader. The war of 1967 was precipitated by Nasser's misinterpretation of Israeli intentions and motives and his provocative military moves, despite his belated attempt to pull back from the brink of war. The defeat in that war demonstrated in a way the inability of Nasserism to overcome the basic weaknesses of the Arab society. Consequently, many socialist and nationalist Arab intellectuals who had espoused Nasser's views drifted to the Left in search of a new ideology capable of galvanizing and rapidly modernizing Arab society. Nasserism now appeared to them as the ideology of petty-bourgeois nationalist groups that relied chiefly on the army to gain power rather than on the revolutionary fervor of the masses. For instance, many of the leaders of the Arab Nationalist Movement who had been the followers of Nasser adopted Marxism. It is true that Col. Muammar Qaddafi, who overthrew the monarchy in Libya in 1969, was a disciple of Nasser, but his successful revolt did not prevent or delay the downfall of Nasserism as indicated by the policies adopted by Anwar Sadat in Egypt—policies just the opposite of those followed by his predecessor, as discussed elsewhere.

Yet, it would be wrong to dismiss Nasserism entirely. There are in practically every Arab country, especially Lebanon, Syria, and Egypt, a number of people who adhere to his ideas or appreciate the basic role played by Nasserism in speeding up the liberation of the Arabs from imperialistic domination and in better defining the political and social problems of the Arabs and their national identity. Nasserism was a necessary transitional stage. It could unnecessarily have lasted far longer if it had been headed by a leader without Nasser's commitment to the independence, integrity, and progress of the Arab world. The literature on Nasserism is abundant. We cite only some of the relevant sources: Raymond William Baker, Egypt's Uncertain Revolution Under Nasser and Sadat (Cambridge: Harvard University Press, 1978); Jean Lacoutre, Nasser, trans. D. Hofstader (New York: A.A. Knopf, 1973); M. Hasanayn Haykal, The Cairo Documents: The Inside History of Nasser and his Relationship with World Leaders, Rebels, and Statesmen (Garden City, N.Y.: Doubleday, 1973); Nisim Rejwan, Nasserist Ideology, Its Exponents and Critics (New York: John Wiley and Sons, 1973); C. Aulas, L'Egypte d'aujourdhui: permanence et changements (Paris, 1977); Gad Silbermann, "National Identity in Nasserist Ideology, 1952–1970" Asian-African Studies (1972); 49–85; Anouar Abdel-Malek, Egypt: Military Society, trans. Charles Lam Markmann (New York: Random House, 1968); and R. Dekmejian, Egypt Under Nasser (Albany, N.Y.: SUNY, 1971).

For additional information on Nasserism, see Gamal Abdel Nasser, The Philosophy of the Revolution (Cairo: Information Department, 1964); President Gamal Abdel Nasser's Speeches and Press Interviews (issued by the Information Department, Cairo); Jean and Simonne Lacouture, Egypt in Transition (London: Methuen, New York: Criterion, 1958); Wilton Wynn, Nasser of Egypt: The Search for Dignity (Cambridge Mass.: Arlington Books, 1959); Keith Wheelock, Nasser's New Egypt (New York: Frederick A. Praeger; London: Stevens & Sons, 1960); Charles D. Cremeans, The Arabs and the World (New York: Frederick A. Praeger, 1963); Benjamin Rivlin and J.S. Szyliowicz, eds., The Contemporary Middle East (New York: Random House, 1965); Tom Little, Modern Egypt (London: Ernest Benn;

New York: Frederick A. Praeger, 1967); Middle East Forum, *April 1959 (special issue on Nasserism); Fayez Sayegh, "The Theoretical Structure of Nasser's Socialism," in* Middle Eastern Affairs Number Four, *ed. Albert Hourani, St. Antony's Papers, No. 17 (London and New York: Oxford University Press, 1965); and George Lenczowski, "The Objects and Methods of Nasserism,"* Journal of International Affairs 19, *no. 1 (1965): 63–76. On the impact of the Israeli-Arab war of 1948, see Constantin K. Zuryak (Qustantin Zuraik),* Ma'na al-nakba *(Beirut: Kasnaf Press, 1948), translated into English by R. Bayly Winder as* The Meaning of the Disaster *(Beirut: Khayat's College Book Cooperative, 1956).*

The elected popular Assembly is a serious and decisive event in the life of the Arab nation. The revolutionary popular will has opened the road and prepared for it this major role. The will of the popular revolution has paved the way for what it was able to achieve with God's help, namely, the defeat of imperialism, the overthrow of reaction and exploitative capitalism [which are] partners [in an] unholy alliance against the people, [and which] wish to terrorize and subjugate the people so that they may be able to proceed in the spoliation of their wealth and labor and ensure their own luxury and wealth at the expense of the blood and sweat which flow unlimited from millions of workers....

This Assembly which stems from the will of the masses must always stay with them. It cannot afford to raise itself pompously above their demands; nor can it forgetfully drop behind their aspirations. It must always keep abreast of the masses and must never forget to light up their life. This Assembly has ... grown out of a revolution and it must march along the path toward the revolution to the end. It has grown out of hope and it must carry this hope all the way [to] fruition. It has grown out of the will for drastic change and it must attain the broad objectives of change, the objectives of unbounded sufficiency and justice, of unrestricted social and political democracy, of a society with equal opportunities for all and no class differences, and of new vistas in which the Arab individual can do honor to life and life can do honor to the Arab individual....

The six principles [that guided Egypt's political life in 1952–64] ... were as follows: the elimination of imperialism and its traitorous Egyptian agents; the eradication of feudalism; the destruction of monopoly and of the domination of capital over the government; the establishment of social justice; the establishment of strong national Army and the establishment of a sound [democracy] ...

What happened to each of these six principles? How did each one of them turn into a weapon bringing victory and sovereignty to the Egyptians over the few years which have elapsed since then?

First: the first principle—the elimination of imperialism. I do not think we need much effort to prove that this nation today is foremost among the independent countries of the world after having been a foreign-occupied base firmly gripped for more than 70 years and terrorized by 80,000 armed British soldiers on the banks of the Suez Canal. . . .

Second: the second principle—eradication of feudalism. The ownership of the greater and more fertile part of the agricultural land was in the hands of a small number of big landlords, besides other vast areas held by agricultural companies that were owned by foreigners, though they tried to conceal their real identity behind Egyptian façades. In accordance with the socialist laws, including the Agrarian Reform law, the area of lands that has been expropriated for distribution to farmers amounted to 944,457 feddans. . . .

Through [regulation] of the rental of agricultural land, which was a part of the Agrarian Reform [Law]; through the consolidation of cooperation and [availability] of interest-free financing, as well as [reorganization] of agricultural land on the largest scale, there came about a transformation in the conditions governing the productivity of the agricultural land, besides the transformation which took place in connection with its ownership. . . .

Third: the third principle is the abolition of monopoly and the domination of capital over the government. . . . the public sector . . . consolidated itself through the complete domination of capital . . . in banks, insurance companies, foreign and internal trade companies which were nationalized and which became public property. It [i.e., the consolidation of the public sector] was followed by the socialist decrees of July, 1961, which ensured the public ownership of the larger part of the means of production, particularly in the industrial field. Clear limits for public ownership were then drawn so as to include the main skeleton of production, such as railways, roads, ports, airports, motor power, the means for land, sea, and air transport, then the heavy, medium, mining, and [the] building materials industries, the effective part of the consumer industries, in a manner which would leave no room for exploitation. This was connected with the realization of complete popular supervision over foreign trade, the breaking of any monopoly in internal trade which was thrown open to private activity. . . .

Fourth: the fourth principle—the establishment of social justice. Experience has proven that social justice cannot be attained except upon the two bases of sufficiency and justice, neither of which could attain the objective without the other. Indeed, each of them without the other would take a course contradictory to the objective.

Sufficiency—that is, increased production—without justice means a further monopolization of wealth. Justice—that is, the distribution of national income without increasing its potentiality—ends only in the distribution of poverty and misery. But both together—that is, sufficiency and justice—hand in hand [they] reach their objective. . . .

In the field on international action: The final step lay in the liquidation of the ruling alliance between reaction and imperialism as well as the liquidation of their inherited privileges. There was no enmity toward any individual or family . . .

Although I consider that this class has been liquidated, I find it important here to make two remarks:

First: To see with tolerance that we were not against individuals. We were opposed to class distinction. It was our right to eliminate its effect but it was not our right to destroy the dignity and humanity of individuals. Therefore, a new page should be opened in front of all without distinction.

Second: We should not, at any cost, permit the emergence of a new class which would believe that it is entitled to inherit privileges from the old class. . . .

We moved from the domination of one class which monopolized all privileges, to a position which, for the first time in our country, allows for the establishment of a social democracy on the basis of sufficiency and justice and social democracy.

The old picture of a state of princes, pashas, and foreigners has disappeared and [has been] replaced by a state of farmers, workers, intellectuals, soldiers, and national capital—the working popular powers and its leading alliance. . . .

In the stage of the great upsurge which followed the stage of the great conversion, there are three major objectives which we have unlimited capacity to achieve if we arm ourselves with sincerity to both the experience and to the hope.

First: There is the objective of continuous development, a comprehensive plan preparing for another comprehensive plan, a doubling of the national income followed by another doubling based on the result of the first doubling. . . .

Second: There comes after development the objective of democracy and the continuous expansion of its framework and deepening of its concept. In the next stage, there are interactions which we should allow to have full effect on life in our society.

We have to complete the structure of the political organization of the

Socialist Union. Though the general structure of this Union is now perceptible before us, this structure should be full of effective and creative life . . .

But we should not allow ourselves to get entangled in lengthy philosophical discussions on the role of the Socialist Union.

The Socialist Union, in short, is the political organization of the working popular powers through which they work to ensure that authority shall, at all times, remain in their hands and shall not move into other hands.

This is the aim of all political organizations, including parties. But whereas a party represents a certain interest in any country or class, the Socialist Union does not represent a group or a class but expresses the political will of the active popular powers allied within its framework. . . .

Third: There follows the stage of upsurge with development and democracy, the objective of realizing over-all Arab unity.

Although we cannot, as yet, give this inevitable unity its final shape, the success in realizing the aim of development and the aim of democracy in this country, which we consider to be the base and vanguard of the Arab nation, will bring nearer the day of unity, define its final form, and mold it in accordance with the will and requirements of national conscience. . . .

21. Statute of the Arab Socialist Union*

Since the July 23, 1952, Revolution committed itself to its six principles and the struggle of people was transferred by the socialist conversion of the July, 1961, laws, the stages of the struggle [have] dictated establishing a popular formation, that is, the Arab Socialist Union. This would be capable of safeguarding the six principles of the Revolution and would give the Revolution impetus toward its greater goals defined in the National Charter.

The Arab Socialist Union represents the socialist vanguard which leads the people, expresses their will, directs national action, and undertakes effective control of the progress of such action, within the framework

---

*Extract from *Statute of the Arab Socialist Union* [December 7, 1962] (Cairo: Information Department, n.d.), pp. 3–12.

of the principles of the National Charter. The Arab Socialist Union is the meeting place of the demands and requirements of the people.

The Arab Socialist Union, as a strong popular formation, includes the active powers of the people. The alliance of such powers is represented in the Arab Socialist Union.

Objectives

–To realize sound democracy represented by the people and for the people, so that the Revolution will be by the people insofar as its methods are concerned, and for the people in its objectives.

–To realize a socialist revolution, that is, a revolution of the working people.

–To give revolutionary impetus to the potentialities for advancement in the interests of the people.

–To safeguard the guarantees embodied in the National Charter, which are:

–To safeguard the minimum representation for workers and farmers in all popular and political formations at all levels, thus guaranteeing that at least 50 per cent of the membership of the Arab Socialist Union itself is made up of workers and farmers, as they are the overwhelming majority of the people deprived for a long time of their fundamental rights.

–To safeguard the right of criticism and self-criticism.

–To realize the principle of collective leadership.

–To strengthen cooperative and labor union formations.

–To transfer the authority of the state gradually to elected councils.

Duties

–To become a positive power behind the revolutionary action.

–To protect the principles and objectives of the Revolution.

–To liquidate the effects of capitalism and feudalism.

–To fight against infiltration of foreign influence.

–To fight against the return of reactionism which was eliminated.

–To fight against infiltration of opportunism.

–To resist passivity and deviation.

–To prevent haphazard work in the national action.

Work Principles

The Arab Socialist Union is the comprehensive political structure of national action. Its formation embraces all powers of the people—farmers, workers, soldiers, intellectuals, and holders of national capital—with the understanding that they bind themselves to national action in close solidarity at all levels, from the base of the organization to its collective leadership.

To ensure that this popular organization attains its objectives, relations between the members themselves, and between them and their formations, must be based on values and principles ensuring positive momentum for the ASU in the direction of its revolutionary goals.

Most important of these principles are:

–Respect by the minority of the will of the majority, so that there may be no scope for the emergence of dictatorship within the . . . Union.

Gaining the confidence of the people through conviction. This confidence, which is the means for the people's obedience of their leaders, is not the product of fear but of conviction, and does not impart to leaders at any level acquired rights, leading to the creation of dictatorships within the formations of the Union.

–Observance of order and obedience in relations between the leaders and the socialist vanguard. There must be readiness to give and to sacrifice. The people must be convinced.

–Striving to establish sound relations between the Union and the working people.

–Striving to solve the problems of the people.

–Striving to maintain the revolutionary drive among the people.

–Facts must be revealed to the people.

–Overbearance, or any form of haughtiness, must not be shown toward the working people.

–Mistakes must be acknowledged and quickly corrected.

–The Arab Socialist Union, the authority of the people, assumes the action of leadership, guidance, and control in the name of the people. The labor unions and popular councils, on the other hand, implement the policy drawn up by the ASU while the National Assembly, which is the supreme authority in the state, implements, conjointly with the syndical and popular councils, the policy laid down by the ASU.

The ASU does not replace labor unions, cooperatives, or youth formations, but strives to discharge its mission and realize its objectives with the help of these formations in the manner set in the Charter.

In the light of the ASU formations at all levels, the Charter becomes the proper theory of our Revolution and the revolutionary ideology for the application of our socialism.

In assuming its role of leadership, carrying the responsibilities of the vanguard, guarding the guarantees safeguarded by the Charter, practicing its functions in a democratic manner [and] its upsurge from within the population and representation of their aspirations and expression of their will, the ASU establishes the principle of sovereignty of the people and a fundamental concept of political and democratic organization—that sound democracy becomes, in socialist logic, a means and an end for national struggle.

22.   Arab Nationalist Movement[*]

Muhsin Ibrahim

The Arab Nationalist Movement (ANM) appeared first at the American University in Beirut in 1954 as a protest by students and teachers against the general situation in the Arab world. It published a weekly, al-Raay, under the editorship of George Habash in Amman Jordan, and then in Damascus. In the beginning it stressed the need for unity and opposed class struggle and communism. It established relatively strong organizations in Lebanon, Kuwwait, and Jordan and a weak one in Syria. By 1961, after Egypt adopted a socialist program the ANM came under the strong influence of Nasser to the extent that it merged in 1965 with the Arab Socialist Union, the ruling party of Egypt (UAR at the time). By this time a group within ANM headed by Muhsin Ibrahim demanded assimilation with Nasserism while another group under George Habash wanted to preserve the movement's independence and its nationalist orientation against the more radical views of the first group, which hoped to radicalize the Nasserite organization from within. However, the incorporation into the Arab Socialist Union proved unworkable both ideologically and organizationally, and consequently Muhsin Ibrahim's group drifted apart and became critical of certain aspects of Nasserism as expressed in the movement's newspaper, al-Hurriyah [Freedom]. After the Arab-Israeli war of 1967, the movement began to disintegrate as the leftists moved toward Marxism, especially the Palestinian factions under N. Hawatmeh, and formed the Popular Front for the Liberation of Palestine. Muhsin Ibrahim and Mohammad Kishly went on to establish the Organization of Lebanese Socialists. Each group called itself leftist and accused the other of rightist deviation. The main body of the Arab Nationalist Movement, however,

---

[*]Extract from Muhsin Ibrahim, "Arab Socialism in the Making," *Arab Journal* 1, nos. 2–3 (Spring–Summer 1964):15–25. The article appeared originally in Arabic. Reproduced by permission.

remained under George Habash and gradually shifted toward Marxism-Leninism and reorganized itself as the Arab Socialist Action party or Hizb al- amal al-Ishtiraki al-arabi. The ANM died but not before giving birth to at least ten factions of which three—Popular Front for the Liberation of Palestine (PFLP), The Popular Democratic Front for the Liberation of Palestine (PDFLP), and the Revolutionary Popular Front for the Liberation of Palestine (RPFLP)—represent the Marxist wing of the Palestine Liberation Organization (PLO) discussed further in the appropriate section. Other groups such as the Arab Socialist Action Party and the Organization of the Lebanese Socialists have played a major role in the Lebanese politics and the civil war of 1965–76. For further information on the ANM see Tareq Y. Ismael, The Arab Left (Syracuse: Syracuse University Press, 1976), pp. 62–77.

Muhsin Ibrahim played a crucial role in the establishment and demise of the movement, especially after he became the editor of al-Hurriyah and attempted to maintain his allegiance to Nasserism while preaching a policy of leftist radicalism—a viewpoint maintained until now. The article below presents Muhsin Ibrahim's view about the debates on ideology in 1964–65 that led to the movement's disintegration.

The Main Characteristics of the Present Phase in the Development of Arab Socialism

Chief among the issues of today's Arab socialism is that which relates to the emergence of the "scientific approach." This looming phenomenon seems to be the major contribution of the present phase. Confronted with a number of problems, Arab socialism, in ideology and practice, is now re-examining its theoretical foundation. The problems that have prompted this self-appraisal are the following:

1. The problem of "transition" into socialism. Up until the beginning of the present phase, the question of "transition" had been submerged in vague notions and obscure concepts of socialism which predominated in the debate. Basically, the "transition" was thought of to be one of developing the "national struggle" into a "socialist struggle"; that from the latter, a progressive economic and social transformation will then evolve.

On the other hand, this theory of transformation of the "Arab national struggle" into a "socialist struggle" had, for a long period of time, been stated with a premise that ruled out the necessary recourse to class struggle. The relatively long life this theory enjoyed had been due mainly to its having adopted a type of analysis that drew its power by appealing to notions such as the "special circumstances of Arab society" and to political objectives such as "national unity." The analysis goes like this: The "special circumstances" of Arab society will enable it to "transform itself into socialism within the framework of national unity and the eventual peaceful reconciliation of existing contradictions." In other words, the experiences of European societies where capitalism could not be defeated without a class struggle are due mainly to the peculiar nature of European society; Arab society is shaped in such a way that neither the existence nor the emergence of such a struggle will be permitted.

These vague conceptions of "transition" into socialism in Arab society have now given way to the development of a more mature approach which emphasizes the real issues involved in the "transition." Class struggle is now recognized as inevitable if Arab society is ever to achieve a successful "transition" into socialism.

In the past, as we have seen, analysis of Arab society ruled out the need for class struggle because of the "special circumstances" of this society. Present analysis emphasizes that these "special circumstances," different though they are, give us a society with merely a different balance of power structure. For an effective "transition," the potentialities of this structure should be fully realized; this can be done by a thorough exploration of this structure and an accurate determination of the alternatives it offers.

But the fact remains that transition into an Arab socialist society cannot be achieved without first defeating exploitative capitalism and feudalism; that only by revolution can these institutions be defeated; and this would consequently allow the productive members of society to assume full power. These members unmistakably are neither the feudalists nor the capitalists. They are the peasants, the workers, the educated, and the soldiers.

Only this way can the avenues for a socialist revolutionary transformation be opened. And this, clearly, is a class struggle.

2. *The objectives of transformation into socialism.* Previous phases in the development of Arab socialist thought were characterized by vagueness and contradictions. Into this conglomeration of uncertainty the so-called "reformist" elements were allowed to infiltrate under the banner of "Arab socialism." These elements were in fact neither socialist nor revolutionary.

Even these elements in Arab socialist thought varied in their definition of "socialism." Some said, "Socialism is not necessarily nationalization, for the latter is a means not an end. The end is 'economic growth' and 'social justice.' As long as these are possible to achieve by recourse to other means, it follows that nationalization is not inevitable."

Others saw the realization of "socialism" through "progressive taxation," "social securtiy," and the assurance of an "adequate standard of living." These ideas stemmed from the concept of the "welfare state," which, this group alleged, was "the same as the modern concept of socialism."

Another group claimed that one could draw a line between economic development and the reconsideration of wealth distribution and the ownership of the means of production. From this assumption they concluded that "socialism" at this stage in the development of Arab society was exemplified by economic development; and, therefore, it was too early to consider the question of ownership and distribution!

Finally, there were those who advocated the concept of a "mixed (socialist) economy." For it, they envisaged a public sector with a limited ownership of some basic public utilities and some of the large means of production. On the other hand, they envisaged a private sector which would assume various types of important patterns of growth. In other words, "socialism," as seen by this group, was "based on the co-existence of the principles of individual and public ownership."

But these obscure concepts of objectives, with which Arab socialism was flooded, have also given way to a new understanding that rejects the concept of a "welfare state," the concept of a "mixed economy," etc. In this new concept of socialism one can see a precise definition of objectives. It clearly states that socialist transformation has the objective of establishing the material foundation for a progressive society and the setting up of public ownership for the means of production. It further states that the latter is fundamental for the emergence of a socialist society.

Fundamental though it be, public ownership does not deny the existence of small private businesses, crafts, and a limited private agricultural land. These forms of private enterprise will, however, remain partial and limited in a socialist society. Furthermore, development in the transformation process will inevitably accelerate the shrinkage of these forms of private enterprise.

3. *The socialist revolution in the realm of social relations and political institutions.* In this area too, lack of perception was evident in previous phases of Arab socialist thought. What seemed to have been missed was no less than the very essence of socialist approach whether in analysis or in thought. At times, "Arab socialism" was conceived of as an "economic revolution" whose sole objective was to organize the economic life of society. At other times, "Arab socialism" was conceived of as the "economic aspect of Arab nationalism," etc.

These conceptions cleared the way for ideas such as a "socialist remedy for an economic problem" and a "democratic remedy for a political problem." This erroneous way of thinking made it possible for some to consider the revolutionary transformation of society as two distinctly separate processes: an economic process through socialism, and a political process through democracy.

This line of reasoning was clearly an attempt to retain the capitalist tools of analysis and apply them to the so-called "political problem" i.e., the question of political rights and political institutions. This was un-mistakably "liberal capitalism" disguised under "socialism."

The advocates of this approach must have had one thing in mind, i.e., the artificial separation between the political and the economic aspects of society where it would not be permissible in the process of change to advance "socialism" at the expense of "democracy," and vice versa. Put in a different way, the entire revolutionary process of change was reduced to "ingredients of reconciliation whose ultimate success lay in mixing the proper measurements of democracy and socialism."

These shaky concepts (envisaging a revolutionary process with sep-arate components partially advancing) have now retreated in the face of an advancing ideological force. The position of this new force on matters of ideology is clear. It rejects the concept of an amputated "economic revolution.' It also rejects the concept of social life as one made up of two distinctly separate fields of endeavor. It further rejects the artificial separation of the question of socialism and democracy.

The emerging concept of socialism sees in the socialist process not merely a material change in the economic life of society, but (by virtue of public ownership of the means of production) also the elimination of exploitation and contradictions in social relations. Only by freeing these relations from undue pressure can true democracy flourish, where dem-ocracy means the emergence of political institutions that represent the real productive members of society, on the one hand, and their ability to exercise their political rights, on the other.

4. *Transferring state-owned means of production into direct social ownership.* One of the most pressing issues facing contemporary socialism is the question of state—vs. direct—ownership of the means of production. Arab socialism in its turn and in line with its dynamic nature has also begun to consider this important question.

Arab socialism views this problem by first stressing that socialism is not fully achieved by mere nationalization and state control of the productive means. Nationalization is only a step in the direction of socialism. For exploitation to be removed, for social relations to be freed, and for democracy to be reinforced, the foundation of socialism must be completely established. This, Arab socialism asserts, can be achieved by transferring the productive means from state into direct social ownership, thus transferring the actual control into the hands of the real producers. This, by definition, means 'self-management." By supporting self-management, the necessary guarantees against the problems of bureaucracy have been provided and the freedom in social relations has consequently been furthered. This then is the favorable environment for the true exercise of democracy.

5. *The question of unifying the Arab socialism movement in the Arab homeland.* In the process of their growth, the Arab socialist revolutionary movements have acquired new dimensions and their achievements have focussed the debate on the question of "one Arab socialist movement."

The debate has actually revolved around a number of issues that have a direct relationship to the Arab socialist revolution. These issues are the following:

(a) Given that the socialist revolutionary movements in the Arab homeland are independent of one another, could we conclude that that is conducive to Arab unity simply because the [separate] socialist program of each revolution is assumed to be oriented toward this unity?

(b) Or, if we are to await a total Arab revolution which would then provide the true basis for Arab unity, how could we then expect the fulfillment of this revolution without the emergence of a united Arab movement in all parts of the Arab homeland?

(c) If the latter is true, i.e., if a united Arab socialist movement should emerge, *how* could it emerge? What are its possibilities and what form shall it take? And finally, what avenues are open to it?

These, then, are five major problems that we had to become acquainted with in order to perceive the main characteristics of contemporary Arab socialism. Evidently, Arab socialist growth stands at the threshold of a significantly major development. It remains for us to show, however, what constitutes the "Arab socialist camp" and who is responsible for the theoretical and practical development of Arab socialist growth.

Who Is Responsible for the Development of
Arab Socialism in the Arab Homeland:
The Role of the July 23 Revolution

The objective historian who sets out to trace back the historical development of Arab socialism will inevitably find that this development was carried out by three major pioneering forces: the July 23 [1961]

Revolution in the U.A.R., the Algerian Revolution, as well as the Arab unionist forces and popular movements who were determined on marching forward and interacting with this progressive trend. To verify this statement, let us subject it to some historical analysis.

In the preceding discussion of the major issues that have confronted "Arab socialism," we discovered that at the outset this concept was very vaguely defined. The revolution of July 23, being the first of its kind, had, therefore, the task of subjecting the concept to its first practical test.

To carry this responsibility, the revolution of July 23 had two circumstances in its favor: First, it had already completed the political liberation and economic independence and, second, it was endowed with a specific type of leadership which, by virtue of its dynamic nature, had the capacity to perceive the real historical meaning of the step, to rise to the level of the event, and to foresee the successive stages involved in the struggle.

This revolution was, therefore, partly a natural outcome of an already completed preparatory stage (between 1952 and 1961) that involved, besides political liberation and economic independence, the initiation of a "guided" economic set-up. It was these steps that had set the stage for the July, 1961, socialist revolution which was conceived to be the only process capable of transforming society.

The union of Syria and Egypt placed the July 23 Revolution at the helm of a new historical force. New horizons opened; but also new requirements emerged. We should, therefore, ask: "What fruits did the union bear?"

In the first three years of the union and those which preceded the July Revolution of 1961, a major question was longing for an answer: "Should the building of the new state be confined to an agrarian reform, a guided economy, and social security? Or does it require the search for far more promising horizons through the socialist approach?"

Not before the middle of the fourth year (July, 1961) was the answer found. It was symbolized by the socialist resolutions of July, 1961. Not only did it put the revolution on the right track of socialist growth, but [it] also brought about an era of clarity for the objectives of Arab socialism. The nature and meaing of the socialst process also gained clarity.

From this, the idea of public ownership grew and began to crystallize. Consequently, the public ownership came to be understood as the fundamental principle for the emergence of a socialist society and the establishment of its progressive material foundation.

Though marking a major turning point in the history of Arab socialist growth, the July resolutions were far from being a complete answer. To be sure, they were merely partially socialist. They were also very dangerously obscure. And in this area of obscurity the following theoretical and practical questions remained unanswered:

1. To have understood the July resolutions in their true context, it was essential to have provided full verification of the objectives of the socialist process. While, for example, the principle of public ownership may have been understood from the said resolutions, other vital questions remained unanswered. Such is the question of "private ownership." Could the socialist process accommodate the co-existence of two such basic principles?

2. It is to be conceded that the enactment of the July laws was a step in the direction of socialist transformation. But what is the underlying theoretical basis for such a step? It was clear that the July resolutions were based on the assumption that transformation was possible without recourse to class struggle; that class differences could be eliminated peacefully within the framework of "national unity" represented in a political organization (National Union) encompassing all classes. But this deprived the leading revolutionary movement of the alliance of the productive popular classes who, alone, were capable of guarding the revolution against subversion by the forces of exploitation.

3. Furthermore, the July resolutions lacked the clear conception of what was really involved in the process regarding social relations and political rights and institutions.

In themselves, these resolutions did consitute a tangible basis for the liberation of social relations from exploitation, pressure, and contradiction. They did also aim at enabling the struggling masses to control society's political institutions and exercise their political rights. Nevertheless, they fell short of bringing this about to its fullest extent. Why? Because instead of taking a clear and positive form, the change in social and political institutions was made to depend on passive forms of criticism directed against the evils of the bourgeois system. It was essential also to have provided the necessary tools that could bring about transformation. Such a tool would be an organized revolutionary movement which would lead the allied productive classes of society in the direction of democracy and ultimate control of political institutions.

It has become clear from the preceding why the July resolutions were considered only partially socialist and that this type of socialism remained vague and dangerous. It is to be stressed, however, that this objective appraisal is in no way intended to underestimate the historical value of these resolutions. On the contrary, what took place in July, 1961, will remain a significant turning point in the history of Arab socialism. It is to be recalled that these resolutions were the first serious action Arab socialism ever achieved.

Furthermore, the vagueness and obscurity that accompanied these resolutions were justifiable on the ground that Arab socialism itself, in theory and in practice, was still in its infancy. And this partially socialist approach to social transformation did ultimately lead, being correctly oriented, to the inevitable confrontation with the basic issues involved. But before these issues became discernible to the revolutionary forces, the reactionary forces were faster to recognize their implications. They thus moved faster and made their surprise attack by breaking the union of Syria and Egypt.

The secessionist movement in Syria was, therefore, an attempt at burying the July socialist resolutions before they could fully materialize as a completed socialist program capable of bringing about the full revolutionary change in the economic, social, and political structure.

The Second Major Development
as a Reply to Secession

The secessionist blow which was dealt at the U.A.R. was definitely a setback in the struggle for Arab unity. There was, nevertheless, a positive aspect to this setback: It alerted the unionist forces in the Arab homeland to the reality of class differences and brought to light the difference between the nut and the shell in political slogans. Consequently, two distinctly opposite Arab camps emerged.

On the ideological level, the developments instigated a dialogue in which the U.A.R. revolutionists and other Arab unionist forces became fully involved. The dialogue centered on the meanings offered by the union and those which evolved from secession. It actually led to new frontiers in Arab thought and was, in the final analysis, a second major achievement in the development of Arab socialism. To be sure, the "National Declaration" of the U.A.R. embodied the results of this specific dialogue which opened new horizons in Arab socialist thought and revolutionary struggle.

Chief among the achievements of this development in Arab socialism was that it provided what the July resolutions had left out. Instead of avoiding the issue of a class struggle, the new development recognized its inevitability and equipped itself in order to face it. This realistic approach strengthened Arab socialism and give it the power to plough deep into the heart of existing problems instead of pretending their nonexistence, or, at best, skimming over their surface.

When the question of transformation into socialism was now raised, all its fundamental elements were spelled out. It became evident that class struggle in Arab society was an unavoidable element in the transformation

process. Objectively analyzed, class differences were seen as a phenomenon that actually existed. It came to be recognized as a serious stumbling
block obstructing the Arab revolutionary movement. To overcome it was
to face it and to crush it, not to avoid it by deviating from the main path
and following a detour.

Transformation into socialism, therefore, was seen to hinge on the
defeat of the feudalist-bourgeois alliance through a revolutionary process.
It was also seen to hinge on the complete assumption of power by the
productive classes of society. It thus became clear that the responsibility
for transformation could not be carried through a political structure whose
theoretical foundation was based on the concept of "peaceful dissolution"
of basic social contradictions (between the forces of exploitation and the
real productive classes).

From that, it followed that only by allying the real productive sectors
of society together and by defeating the forces of exploitation can
transformation into socialism be achieved.

It was this clarity in the revolutionary concept of transformation that
gave this phase of Arab socialism a special significance. It was this clarity
also which enabled the nationalist revolutionary struggle to transform
itself successfully into a socialist revolutionary struggle.

Besides this clarity in the nature of Arab socialist revolution there was
also clarity in the objectives of socialist transformation. This made it
possible for the "National Declaration" of the U.A.R. to embody both the
methodology for the achievement and the precise definition of objectives
of its socialist revolution, whether in the field of "national product,"
industry, trade, capital, or real estate. The definition of objectives in these
areas strongly emphasized the fundamentality of public ownership of the
means of production as the only basis for a truly socialist society.

Having started from a correct premise and having equipped itself
with the right tools of analysis, the new ideological force arrived at
similarly sound conclusions regarding socialist change in the realm of
social relations and political rights and institutions. The original negative
criticism of the bourgeois social structure and its [products of] forged
political rights and political institutions now developed into positive
socialist thought. This was necessary for the understanding of democracy
in its revolutionary context. We thus saw "liberal bourgeois concepts"
(which artificially separate between democracy and socialism) give way to
a concept which states forcefully that "democracy and socialism are one
inseparable extension to the revolutionary struggle." In other words,
socialist transformation was conceived to be the only gate that leads to the
liberation of social relations and political rights and institutions—that is, to
liberate them from undue pressure, exploitation, and forgery.

If negative criticism was to develop into a positive attitude, it was not sufficient to merely speak of the organic unity of democracy and socialism and their relationship to the revolutionary struggle. It was essential to come up with a positive formulation for a process of achieving democracy and for a method of reinforcing it within the framework of socialist transformation.

The debate actually led the U.A.R. to adopt some basic principles in its "National Declaration." The most significant of these principles were that the "Arab Socialist Union," which emerges from the alliance of society's productive classes, is the representative authority of the people and that which enhances the capabilities of the revolution; that the political organizations of the people which are based on direct free elections shall inevitably represent the forces of the majority; that authority of elected assemblies over the executive branches of the state shall be continuously emphasized; that it is of the utmost necessity that, within the framework of the "Arab Socialist Union," a new political organ be created to mobilize and embrace the benevolent elements of leadership and organize their efforts; that it is essential for group leadership to be guaranteed; that popular organizations are capable of playing an influential and effective role in preserving the elements of true democracy; and that criticism and self-criticism are some of the most important guarantees of freedom, etc.

From the point of view of ideological thought, the greatest value these general principles carry lay in that they put the search for democratic reinforcements on the right track. As we said earlier, public ownership of the productive means, considered objectively, became a fundamental principle for the socialist transformation in both the social and political realms. Public ownership became, therefore, a clear objective for the revolution.

The search for democratic reinforcements went even further. It manifested itself in more sophisticated arguments such as that which related to the question of state vs. direct social ownership of the means of production. It revolved around the meaning of this transference and the process it should follow. In other words, Arab socialism, in its search for democratic guarantees started to examine such progressive socialist theories which favor the placing of the productive means under the direct control of producers, and the achievement of self-management.

In practice, the effects of the ideological trend appeared in the U.A.R. when workers were actually allotted a share in profits and representation on the boards of directors. Of course, it would have been meaningless to have taken these measures if they had not been based on a clear understanding of the issues—that is, to have had a clear differentiation between "state ownership," which does not completely preclude exploitation and contradiction, and "direct ownership," which is the true corrective device in social relations and reinforcement of political democracy.

There has been still another development after the secessionist setback of September, 1961. Earlier in the discussion a statement was made to the effect that a new outlook is now being sought regarding relations between the various Arab revolutionary movements. This became a necessity because one of the major contributing factors to secession was the partial contradictions in the relations of these movements. To be sure, it was the deepening of these differences that provided the reactionary forces with an appropriate climate to reactivate their power and consequently subvert the unity of Syria and Egypt.

It was, therefore, natural for the postsecession period to have been witnessing numerous attempts which aimed at laying down the groundwork for the establishment and solidification of ideological and practical relationships between these movements. These trends found expression in the slogan which called for "the meeting of all Arab revolutionary forces" in a single front. As to the development of this "front," two alternatives were seen: Either it would remain a "front" which will continue to embrace numerous revolutionary forces, or it would evolve into a united revolutionary movement.

In the United Arab Republic, this development found expression in the "National Declaration" of July 23. The "Declaration" stressed the belief in the "inevitability of a unified progressive popular movement in the Arab world which would assert itself in the subsequent stages of Arab struggle."

To conclude this section, let us reiterate the main points: Besides familiarizing ourselves with the main characteristics of this stage, we discovered that it was the second most important in the postsecession period. It has been made clear that this stage was held in reverence because it offered constructive and brave criticism, perceptive debate, and genuine interaction that won it a unique historical significance. These elements entered the ideological bloodstream of Arab revolutionary movements who were able to perceive the meaning of unity and discover new horizons which secession uncovered.

But again it was an open debate because a number of basic questions remained without definite answers. These questions and the debate that grew around them will be the subject matter of the following final section.

Features of the Third Major Development
in Arab Socialism

It is evident from the preceding discussion that the achievements of Arab socialism after secession marked a fundamental turning point in the history of this movement. Divided into two phases, the July, 1961, resolutions were the backbone of the first phase; in the second phase, or in "postsecession socialism," the achievement was mainly in the area of crystallizing the concept of socialism. The latter, significant and historically important though it was, left a number of questions without definite answers.

First, the question of a leading socialist revolutionary movement. This question was closely related to the meaning of transformation into socialism, the implications and workability of the process itself. In other words, it was not sufficient to state that the productive class was the only qualified revolutionary force which is capable of overthrowing the feudalist-bourgeois alliance and consequently effecting socialist transformation. People's capacity to revolt hinged on the emergence of a leading revolutionary movement which was capable of crystallizing their motivations and helping to launch them in the direction of socialist struggle.

It was also insufficient to state general principles which emphasize the importance of a socialist economic structure as the fundamental principle for socialist transformation in the realm of social relations and political rights and institutions. The instrument which could translate these general principles into action should have been specified and provided as well.

From this, we could discern a fundamental difference between popular organizations, which were set up by election, and leading socialist revolutionary movements which "mobilize and organize the efforts of benevolent elements that are capable of leadership." Organizations that come by popular vote are unquestionably important if society's productive classes are to be represented in a political body that reinforces their alliance and if they are to become the source of power for the state. However, before these organizations become truly "representative authorities which enhance the capacities of their revolution and safeguard democratic values," it is imperative that a leading socialist revolutionary movement emerge to embrace and organize the efforts of selective "benevolent elements that are capable of leadership." This movement would then inspire elected popular organizations and inject in their bloodstream the ability to exercise their authority. This movement is, therefore, the backbone of socialist revolution.

This fundamental question did not escape the dialogue which revolved around socialist growth in the postsecession period. As a matter of fact, some results of this dialogue were actually presented in the "National Declaration." It emphasized "that there is a (clear) need for the creation of a new political body within the framework of the Arab Socialist Union which will mobilize and organize the efforts of benevolent elements that are capable of leadership. It will also crystallize the revolutionary motivations for the public, feel their needs, and help find right answers for these needs."

On the other hand, the dialogue did not reach its fullest extent regarding the question of a leading socialist revolutionary movement. Nor was an answer found to the question as to whether one or a multiplicity of such movements should lead the revolution.

The second fundamental question which remained unanswered was that concerning individual (private) ownership. In postsecession socialist growth, transformation was clearly working on the principle of public ownership for the means of production. However, obscurity continued to engulf the question of individual ownership. This allowed rightist elements to exploit this issue for the purpose of distortion.

It was clear that the idea of permitting "unexploiting individual ownership" did not mean that a socialist society could be established on two equally fundamental principles: Public ownership for some means of production, on the one hand, and individual ownership, on the other. In fact, the idea of allowing "unexploiting individual ownership" was put forward originally in the general context of public ownership of the means of production; the latter was by far the more fundamental principle for transformation in a socialist society, and objectively and ideologically, the process of transformation will carry with it an accelerated growth in the weight and extent of public ownership. Correspondingly, an accelerated shrinkage in the extent of individual ownership will take place. Ultimately, this "unexploiting individual ownership" would be transformed into small and limited forms within a general basic framework called the "public ownership of the means of production."

As we said earlier, some rightist elements took advantage of this obscurity and began to speak a language quite foreign to socialism. The need thus arose for Arab socialist growth (after secession) to acquire greater clarity. It should do that if it were to silence the rightist elements and if it were to bring to an end their ability to capitalize on this issue on the ideological level.

Thirdly, there was the question of transferring the means of production from public to "direct social ownership." It is to be conceded that postsecession socialism was not far from grasping this matter. Allotting to workers a share of profits and a representation on the boards of directors were themselves indications of awareness in the U.A.R. Yet the matter did not gain enough clarity in conception or regarding methodology to enable the transformation in this area to be carried to its fullest extent. Instead, this lack of clarity led to greatly confused meanings of expressions such as nationalization, state ownership, and public ownership.

Fourthly, there was the question of unifying the Arab socialist movement. Here, too, clarity in postsecession socialist thought was not sufficient. This insufficiency led to incomplete formulation of the structure of relationships between various elements and forces in Arab socialist struggle.

It is obvious, therefore, why the debate remained unclosed. It is precisely this lack of answers which set the stage for the third major development in Arab socialist thought. On the practical level, the events of the year 1963 paved the way and provided the proper circumstances for the execution of the third stage in the development of Arab socialism . . .

The year 1963 witnesses the fall of a separatist regime in Syria and a dictatorship in Iraq. The collapse of these two regimes made it possible for the initiation of a historical dialogue over the tripartite unity of Egypt, Syria, and Iraq. To be sure, unity was not the only subject matter of that dialogue. Unity was merely the proper gate. Having entered this specific gate, the parties concerned then stood in a spot in which they came face to face with fundamental Arab socialist problems, whether in ideology, in struggle, or in application.

It turned out that the same forces that crystallized "postsecession socialism" have now carried out the third step: The socialist revolution of July 23 and the unionist popular movements were able to extract full conclusions from current events.

VIII.   SADATISM

23.   Anwar Sadat: The Man and His Policies

Anwar Sadat claims that his life "like every man's life, [is] a journey in search of identity" and that events in Egypt have paralleled the events of his own life. Born in the village of Mit Abul-Kum in 1918, he moved to Cairo at an early age and went to elementary school there; he graduated from the military academy in 1938. He became involved in anti-British revolutionary movements and was one of the founders of the secret military organization that ousted King Faruq in 1952 and established the Republic. Sadat was a close confidant and supporter of Gamel Abdel Nasser in the Revolutionary Command Council, which ruled Egypt after 1952, although in his memoirs he criticizes some of Nasser's personal characteristics (mistrust of others and secretiveness) and his statist policies. From 1954 to 1961 Sadat was the

Secretary General of the Islamic Congress, which sought to replace the disbanded Muslim Brethren (with whom Sadat had close relations in his early youth) and to establish closer relations with Muslim writers. Sadat achieved prominence as a world figure after he became president of the Egyptian National Union in 1957 and chairman of the Afro-Asian Conference held in Cairo in 1958.

Sadat is known in general to be an ardent Muslim believer but also an Egyptian patriot who puts the interest of his country above other considerations. He dropped the title UAR—United Arab Republic—adopted after Egypt established a union with Syria in 1958; the present name is the Arab Republic of Egypt. A practical-minded, pragmatic individualist, Sadat has a special regard for the values and comforts of contemporary civilization. He has been able to preserve and also to refine, enlarge, an harmonize the pragmatic philosophy of life and the deep wisdom of the Egyptian peasant with the realities of contemporary life. Sadat's own life and personality have been shaped by the two cultures of Egypt. He was first married to a simple village girl who bore him children and raised them in the traditionalist, rural Egyptian culture. After his divorce from his first wife, Sadat married his present wife, Jihan, a dynamic, sophisticated urbanite by whom he had other children who have been raised in the culture of modern Egypt.

The political career of Sadat took a new turn after the death of Nasser in 1970. As second to the rais he became, naturally, Egypt's president. From the start he faced the challange of Aly Sabry and his leftist group in the Central Committee of the ruling Arab Socialist Union and had to make a choice between two available options: whether to continue the statist-socialist policy of Nasser and tighten even further the reins of power or to opt instead for an open society, democracy, and free enterprise. He chose the second alternative, beginning with the neutralization of Aly Sabry and his group and the gradual dismantling of the regime erected by Nasser. Sadat abolished political controls, scaled down economic statism, and encouraged private enterprise and foreign investment. He took far-reaching decisions in foreign policy also. Sadat seemed to accept the view that the Arab-Israeli conflict and the Palestinians' grievances underlying it could be settled more easily by relying on American help rather than Soviet support. He seemed to believe that America's long-range interests in the Middle East would be better served by friendship with the Arab world. Thus Sadat's foreign policy views were just the opposite of those defended by Nasser—i.e., support for Arabism and the Palestinian cause coupled with animosity toward the United States. Sadat's change of outlook on Egypt's foreign policy began with his ousting of the Soviet advisers in 1972. Then he proceeded to change the frozen situation in Arab-Israeli relations through the well-planned Yom Kippur, or Ramadan, War of 1973, through which the Egyptians regained the Suez Canal and restored Arab self-confidence in their military capabilities. Sadat was thus able to repair the heavy damage to Arab prestige caused by Nasser's policies and the disastrous war of 1967. His own prestige and influence soared throughout the world, especially in the Arab countries.

In the middle of the 1973 war, when he had the upper hand, Sadat called on Israelis to evacuate the Arab lands occupied in 1967 and to do justice to the Palestinian claims. In return he offered Israel peace and secure borders and thus turned a new page in Arab-Israeli relations. Yet the relations did not improve. Sadat felt that psychological barriers of mistrust and suspicion prevented the solution of the Arab-Israeli conflict. Consequently, on November 20, 1977, defying opposition from most Arab leaders, he took the dramatic step of flying to Jerusalem and addressing the Knesset. In the speech to the Israeli legislature Sadat again proposed peace and security for Israel in return for the Arab lands occupied in 1967 and justice for the Palestinians. The visit was followed by the Camp David Agreements and finally by a peace treaty signed by Egypt and Israel on March 26, 1979. Immediately following the Camp David Agreements of 1978 the Arab states met in Baghdad and rejected the agreements, thus establishing in effect a common front against Egypt. The other Arab states accused Sadat of compromising their strongest card against Israel, i.e., nonrecognition, and of breaking their united front and jeopardizing the solution of the Palestinian problem merely in order to secure peace and economic benefits for Egypt. Most cut off diplomatic relations, and Egypt was ousted from various Arab and Muslim organizations. Egypt meanwhile established diplomatic relations with Israel and improved her relations with the Western world but has not been able to reach an agreement with Israel concerning the status of Palestinian lands and people under Israeli occupation since 1967. The key issue is the degree of self-determination to be accorded the Palestinians on the West Bank and Gaza. Israel proposes a limited administrative autonomy that would enable her to retain control of the areas, while Egypt interprets self-determination in liberal terms as leading all the way to the establishment of a Palestinian state. Sadat has not changed his position on this point. Meanwhile he has been dangerously isolated in the Arab world while the opposition in his own country is gaining some strength; the opposition is born as reaction to both his domestic policies and relations with Israel. It is essential to note that even Jordan and Saudi Arabia, known as moderates, have opposed Sadat's policies and indirectly have strengthened the hand of the more radical regimes.

Sadat's promise to establish democracy has failed to materialize. He silenced much of the opposition and amended the Constitution to remain president to the end of his life. He is the chief of the National Democratic Party, created by him in 1978 to replace the Socialist Union, the earlier *government party. In May 1980 he named six deputy prime ministers who are expected to carry out his policies. The economic policies of Sadat have created a small group of rich and influential entrepreneurs comprising just about 5 percent of the population and known as* infitah—*an allusion to their dependence on trade with the West. Sadat's two daughters married the sons of two of the most prominent members of this group, Sayed Marei and Osman Ahmad Osman.*

Internal opposition to Sadat comes from the university, the Communists, and especially from the leftist Muslim fundamentalists, among whom the Takfir Wa al-Hijra, an armed goup established in 1971, is an important faction. It was this group, which enjoys middle-class support, that kidnapped and executed in 1977 a former minister of religious affairs. Another faction of the militant fundamentalists attacked Heliopolis Military Academy near Cairo in 1974 with the purpose of acquiring arms to oust Sadat. The agreements with Israel, which cost Egypt the $2 billion of development aid coming from the Gulf Organization, spurred growth of the opposition. Eventually, in 1980, Sadat suspended all associations promoting extremism, that is, the Muslim fundamentalists and other similar secular organizations. It is obvious that if the talks with Israel to not soon lead to a solution favorable to Palestinians and if Sadat's isolation from the Arabs and the Third World continues, Sadat may not last long. The Arab leaders, however, are keenly aware of the pivotal place and function of Egypt in the Arab world and would welcome her back if Sadat changed his policies toward the Israelis and, indirectly, the United States. Sadat in turn believes that the rest of the Arabs will ultimately follow Egypt's lead.

(Just as these galley proofs were being corrected there came the news of Sadat's assassination on October 6, 1981, by members of the Muslim Brotherhood during a military parade to celebrate the anniversary of the Ramadan War of 1973, the event which opened the way for Sadat's rise to international fame and led to peace with Israel.)

The literature on Sadat is not very extensive. The Yom Kippur (October) War, on the other hand, has been extensively studied. See the bibliography by Michael Rubner, The Middle East Conflict from October 1973 to June 1977: A Selected Bibliography *(Los Angeles: California State University Press, 1977) and Sadat's own* In Search of Identity: An Autobiography *(New York: Harper and Row, 1978) and* Revolt on the Nile *(London: Alan Wingate, New York: John Day, 1957). The first extract below represents Sadat's views on peace with Israel, as expressed in his speech in Jerusalem. The next extract is a Marxist evaluation of Sadat's economic and social policies.*

24. Speech by Egyptian President Anwar Sadat to the Knesset, November 20, 1977*

I come to you today on solid ground to shape a new life and prepare a peace. We all on this land, the land of God, we all—Muslims, Christians, and Jews—we all worship God and no one but God. God's teaching and commandments are love, sincerity, purity, and peace. . . .

As I have already declared, I have not consulted, as far as this decision is concerned, with any of my colleagues or brothers, the Arab heads of state, or the confrontation states. Those of them who contacted me following the declaration of this decision spoke of their objection because the feeling of opposite mission and absolute lack of confidence between the Arab states and the Palestinian people on the one hand, and Israel on the other, still surges in us all. . . .

There are moments in the life of nations and peoples when it is incumbent for those known for their wisdom and clarity of vision to overlook the past with all its complexities and weighing memories in a bold drive towards new horizons. Those who, like us, are shouldering the same responsibilities entrusted to us, are the first who should have the courage to take fate-determining decisions which are in consonance with the circumstances. We must all rise above all forms of fanaticism, above all forms of obsolete theories of superiority. The most important thing is never to forget infallibility is the prerogative of God alone.,

If I said that I wanted to avert from all the Arab people the horrors of shocking and destructive wars, I must sincerely declare before you that I have the same feelings and bear the same responsibility towards all and every man on earth, and certainly toward the Israeli people.

Any life lost in war is a human life, be it that of an Arab or an Israeli. A wife who becomes a widow is a human being entitled to a happy family life whether she be an Arab or an Israeli. Innocent children who are deprived of the care and compasion of their parents are ours. They are ours, be they living on our lands or Israeli lands.

Well, I have come to you carrying my clear and frank answer to this big question so that the people in Israel, as well as the whole world, might

---

*This excerpt, from the speech in the Knesset, is based on several texts appearing in the *Jerusalem Post*, November 21, 1977, and the *Journal of Palestine Studies* 7, no. 2 (Winter 1978):186–95 *passim*.

hear it . . . The first fact: no one can build his happiness at the expense or the misery of others. The second fact: never have I spoken or will ever speak in two languages. Never have I adopted or will ever adopt two policies. I never deal with anyone except in one language, one policy, and with one face.

The third fact: direct confrontation and a straight line are the nearest and most successful methods to reach a clear objective.

The fourth fact: the call for permanent and just peace, based on respect for the United Nations resolutions, has now become the call of the whole world.

The fifth fact, and this is probably the clearest and most prominent, is that the Arab nation, in its drive for permanent peace, based on justice, does not proceed from a position of weakness or hesitation, but on the contrary, it has the potential of power and stability which tells of a sincere will for peace. The Arab declared intention stems from an awareness, prompted by a heritage of civilization that, to avoid an inevitable disaster that will befall us, you and the whole world, there is no alternative to the establishment of permanent peace based on justice—peace that is not shaken by storms, swayed by suspicion or jeopardized by ill intentions. . . .

You [Israelis] want to live with us, in this part of the world. In all sincerity, I tell you we welcome you among us, with full security and safety. This, in itself is a tremendous turning point, one of the landmarks of a decisive historic change.

We used to reject you. We had our reasons and our claims, yes. We refused to meet with you anywhere, yes. We used to brand you as "so-called Israel," yes. We were together in international conferences and organizations and our representatives did not—and still do not—exchange greetings with you, yes. This has happened and is still happening. . . .

Yet today, I tell you, and I declare it to the whole world, that we accept living with you in permanent peace based on justice. We do not want to encircle you, or be encircled ourselves, by destructive missles ready for launching, nor by the shells of grudges and hatred. I have announced on more than one occasion that Israel has become a fait accompli, recognized by the world, and that the two superpowers have undertaken the responsibility of its security and the defence of its existence.

As we really and truly seek peace, we really and truly welcome you to live among us in peace and security. There was a huge wall between us which you tried to build up over a quarter of a century, but it was destroyed in 1973. . . .

Yet, there remains another wall. This wall constitutes a psychological barrier between us. A barrier of suspicion. A barrier of rejection. A barrier of fear of deception. A barrier of hallucinations around any action, deed or decision. A barrier of cautious and erroneous interpretation of all and every event or statement. It is this psychological barrier which I described in official statements as constituting 70 percent of the whole problem....

Once again, I declare clearly and unequivocally that we agree to any guarantees you accept, because in return we shall obtain the same guarantees. In short, then, when we ask what is peace for Isreal, the answer would be that Israel live within her borders with her Arab neighbours in safety and security, within the framework of all the guarantees she accepts and which are offered to the other party. But how can this be achieved? How can we reach this conclusion, which would lead us to permanent peace based on justice?

There are facts that should be faced with all courage and clarity. There are Arab territories which Isreal has occupied and still occupies by armed force. We insist on complete withdrawal from these territories, including Arab Jerusalem.

I have come to Jerusalem, the City of Peace which will always remain as a living embodiment of coexistence among believers of the three religions. It is inadmissible that anyone should conceive the special status of the City of Jerusalem within the framework of annexation or expansionism. It should be a free and open city for all believers....

Complete withdrawal from the Arab territories occupied in 1967 is a logical and undisputed fact. Nobody should plead for that. Any talk about permanent peace based on justice, and any move to insure our coexistence in peace and security in this part of the world, would become meaningless while you occupy Arab territories by force of arms. For there is no peace that could be in consonance with, or be built on, the occupation of the land of others. Otherwise it would not be a serious peace. Yet this is a foregone conclusion, which is not open to discussion or debate—if intentions are sincere and if endeavours to establish a just and durable peace for ours and the generations to come are genuine.

As for the Palestine cause, nobody could deny that it is the crux of the entire problem. Nobody in the world today could accept slogans propagated here in Israel, ignoring the existence of the Palestinian people and their legitimate rights are no longer ignored or denied today by anybody. Nobody who has the ability of judgment can deny or ignore it....

I have chosen to set aside all precedents and traditions known by warring countries, in spite of the fact that occupation of the Arab territories still exists. Rather, the declaration of my readiness to proceed to Israel came as a great surprise that stirred many feelings and astounded many minds. Some even doubted its intent. Despite it all, the decision was inspired by all the clarity and purity of belief and with all the true expression of my people's will and intentions.

And I have chosen this difficult road, which is considered by many and in the opinion of many the most difficult road. I have chosen to come to you with an open heart and an open mind. I have chosen to give this great impetus to all international efforts exerted for peace. I have chosen to present to you and in your own home the realities devoid of any scheme or whim, not to manoeuvre or to win a round, but for us to win together the most dangerous of rounds and battles in modern history—the battle of permanent peace based on justice.

It is not my battle alone, nor is it the battle of the leadership in Israel alone. It is the battle of all and every citizen in all our territories, whose right it is to live in peace. It is [a] commitment of conscience and responsibility in the hearts of millions. . . .

25.   Views of the Egyptian Communists on Sadat's Policies*

Nagib Kamal

Upon assuming the office of president, Sadat adopted a stance on many issues that signified a departure from the patriotic policies of Nasser. His first year in power was marked by the drafting (in February 1971) of a bilateral phased settlement, armed intervention against the Hashim al-'Ata [leftist] movement [which temporarily replaced Numeiri] in the Sudan, and a virulent propaganda campaign against the "communist threat." Sadat hastened to consolidate relations with Iranian and Arab reaction, chiefly with Saudi Arabia, in preparation for an active part in the attacks on the Arab and African national liberation movements. A crucial step in this direction was the dismissal of some progressive personalities [Sabry Aly], from the political leadership [May 1971]. The regime took steps to

*Nagib Kamal, a member of the Egyptian Communist Party (one of four communist parties) and a critic of Sadat, offers extensive information on Sadat's internal politics. It appeared originally in the *World Marxist Review* (March 1979) and was reprinted in the *Journal of Palestine Studies* 8, no. 4 (Summer 1979): 130–135.

alter the class structure of various Egyptian institutions. After progressive patriotic elements were arrested, tried and deprived of political rights, elections were held to the leading bodies of the Arab Socialist Union and to the People's Assembly. This substantially enhanced the weight and influence of the rural bourgeoisie, numerically the largest class, which grew stronger with the intensification of capitalist exploitation and spread its activity to commerce, contractural work and other fields. The merchant bourgeoisie, holders of real estate and entrepreneur-contractors also won increasing influence. Progressive patriotic elements were weeded out in ideological and cultural institutions, press media, the public sector and the trade unions. . . .

Legislative backing for socio-economic structural changes was given soon after Sadat came to power. These changes consisted of the following:

1. In September 1971 laws were promulgated to encourage foreign and Arab (non-Egyptian) investments. They granted privileges to investment companies and banks, commercial banks, and foreign and mixed insurance companies. All were exempted from control by the Central Bank and the fiscal authorities. They were given the right to use local currency for transactions in all fields of investment, including agriculture, transport, mining and real estate. They were exempted from income and profit taxes, customs duties and payment of interest on loans. They were allowed to export profits and given other privileges.

2. On the pretext of ensuring justice and equality, the Egyptian bourgeoisie received the same tax benefits as were granted to foreign investors. The action programme adopted by the People's Assembly noted that the "open door" policy in foreign trade should be accompanied by an analogous policy at home that would encourage private enterprise. Moreover, it was stressed that "economic democracy requires limiting the sphere of state activity to the main enterprises, which function for the common weal and cannot be taken over by the private sector." The restrictions on "free" foreign and domestic trade were lifted. Private Egyptian capital substantially widened its activity, particularly in trade, the services industry and contractual work. Within a few years there were 50,000 import and export companies and bureaus, while the number of contractors, according to official statistics for 1976, topped 30,000.

3. The public sector was gradually undermined. Profitable state enterprises were denationalized. Multinational monopolies were permitted to invest in the cement, mining, textile and other industries. Norms operating in the private sector were spread to those industries—general meetings of shareholders were introduced, workers were no longer allowed to participate in managerial councils, and the payment to them of the established share of profits was discontinued. In agriculture the

cooperative sector was abolished through the dismantling of the Organization for Cooperative Development and the General Administration of Agricultural Cooperatives and their replacement by a "farmers" bank. . . .

4. Major amendments were introduced in labour legislation. In 1971 it was decided to abolish trade union branches at factories employing less than 200 persons, i.e., at most factories in the private sector. Owners and managers of factories were given the right to transfer or dismiss factory or office workers without control. . . . So-called social mobility developed among the bureaucratic bourgeoisie [managers and technocrats]. Its links and interests interlocked more closely with the merchant bourgeoisie, particularly those engaged in import and export operation and wholesale trade, and with entrepreneurs in contractual work and real estate speculators, i.e., with those groups of the "business" bourgeoisie through which the main channels of "cooperation" between foreign and local capital passed. . . .

With the coming of Sadat to power the ruling coalition acquired the following make-up: agrarian, merchant, finance and industrial bourgeoisie, owners of real estate, owners of contractual and services companies, and the higher strata of the right-wing intellectuals and bureaucracy. The agrarian and bureaucratic bourgeoisie played the most conspicuous role at the beginning, but the bitter rivalry in the ruling coalition later brought into prominence the finance and merchant bourgeoisie, and also entrepreneurs of an undisguisedly parasitical trend in the sphere of contractual work and the services industry. In the course of these mutations the conditions ripened for an open alliance with imperialism and Zionism. . . .

When the evolution of the soci-economic conditions that led the Sadat regime to direct cooperation with imperialism and actual surrender to the Zionist rulers of Israel is analysed, there can be only one assessment of the behaviour of the Egyptian bourgeoisie. Its main strata take dependence on the capitalist market and the multinational monopolies for granted. However, they do not wish to submit to Israeli political and economic domination and link themselves with Israeli capital. . . .

Egypt's economic potential and industrial base are relatively developed, and its bourgeoisie is quite mature and experienced. The Egyptian bureaucracy and technocracy have likewise accumulated considerable experience and influence. All this makes it difficult for Israel to establish its economic supremacy. Even with new "peaceful" relations, the Zionist state and Israeli capital will have, in order to achieve this aim, to strike a "crushing blow" at the Egyptian economy so as significantly to undermine and not simply subordinate it.

It is from this angle that one can explain the seemingly complex and contradictory phenomenon that while some segments of the Egyptian bourgeoisie have totally capitulated to imperialism and the multinational monopolies, they continue to retain a certain "patriotism" relative to relations with Israel. . . .

This apprehension of the Egyptian bourgeoisie has been intensified by the fact that the settlement—from their standpoint—has proved to be "more Israeli than American" and that Washington "took no steps" or was "unable" to bridle Israel's expansionist ambitions. The hopes for American "protection" against Israel's expansionist claims have not justified themselves, and this is compelling the Egyptian and other Arab bourgeoisie to oppose not only Israel's maximalist military-backed economic lust but also the onerous military terms of the agreement.

Further, the alliance with Zionism is coming into conflict with the national patriotic feeling of the masses. . . . The Egyptian working class, which is the most developed and mature in the Arab world, is in the centre of the present and future social battles. It has played a prominent part in the history of the liberation movement, and at some of its stages was able to undertake the role of leading force.

. . . The determination of the working class to win ideological, political, and organizational independence, and play the leading role in society was subsequently demonstrated in various ways. With this are linked the prospects for a fundamental solution of the nation's long-standing and steadily aggravating problems which, time has shown, obviously cannot be resolved by the bourgeoisie.

IX.   ARAB THOUGHT AND CONTEMPORARY WESTERN CIVILIZATION: INTERPRETATIONS

26.   The Individual and Society*

'Atif Ahmad

This article represents an effort by Professor 'Atif Ahmad of Cairo University to explain the relations between society and the individual in a rational manner by taking man's environment as the conditioning basis of his social behavior. Inspired by Marxist theories, Ahmad's approach contrasts sharply

---

*Extract from 'Atif Ahmad, "Bayn al-fard wa-al-mujtama' " ["Between Individual and Society"], al-'Ulum [The Sciences], Beirut, September 1960, pp. 56–58.

with Islamic traditions of thought, and his arguments are intended to justify Egyptian socialism.

The relation between the individual and society is a contemporary question that has attained special importance in the conditions of the present world civilization of capitalism and socialism. It has become a major problem facing thinkers everywhere, and the traditional question they now ask is this: The individual or society?

From the replies given, three distinct trends can be observed; the advocates of each are convinced of having discovered the secret of human happiness.

The first consider society as superior to the individual, the value inherited from our forebears tipping the balance; they believe that conduct regulated by particular individual values is at the bottom of the human misery here on earth.

The second group sees things quite differently. According to them, the self is the true reality. The individual represents the authentic being, and a predominance of social values would only have one result—slavery. That is why individual liberty, as they understand it, is the most precious thing man possesses.

The third group, the moderates, consider that neither the individual nor society should have an advantage over the other, and that a compromise is preferable.

Thus, the question is posed and the possible solutions outlined. According to the ideas of the theorists, all we have to do is to choose one of the solutions.

Nevertheless, if one goes deeper into the matter, one quickly rejects the replies given on realizing their deficiencies. These deficiencies relate to a philosophy of a unique nature concerning the understanding of society, which wins over the doctrinaires by pretending to forget—through ignorance—that they are forever harping on the same wrong idea, namely, that there is a division between the individual and society and that it is their faith in this division that dictates the question: The individual or society.

The first thing to be done is to put the problem in its proper place, to verify the facts, and, finally, to discover the right way of solving it. And in this case, what is the actual bond, therefore, between the individual and society? One feels that, in the history of humanity, man never has lived without society, and never will do so. In the dawn of history, in the most distant times, when the human species was still in its primitive stage, the first men lived in the forest in separate groups. They did not live alone.... When the group evolved into a primitive community, the individuals grouped together in a society and became associated collectively in work. The individual did not feel himself imprisoned by the others—quite the contrary. He considered being separated from the others as a kind of death sentence. After this came slavery, feudalism, and exploitation . . . represented at various stages in the evolution of human society. Despite the savage brutality of those systems, no member of a society withdrew from it and went off to live on his own in the forest or in the desert. Why?

The conclusion is quite simple: It is that man is a social being, and can live only among others. . . . The aim of life is life itself, i.e., the satisfaction of human needs. These cannot be supplied completely by natural and spontaneous manifestations. Thus, man who lives by nature must, by a kind of human obligation, inescapably engage in production, i.e., struggle against the natural order of things, conquer it, and exploit nature to satisfy his needs.

From the very first, his life is crystallized in his mode of production, which is the direct expression of his way of life. Of necessity, life is fashioned according to the laws of production that govern it, and production cannot be an individual operation. In their struggle against nature, which they exploit to meet their needs, individuals are not in the least isolated or cut off from one another. They participate socially in production as amalgamated groups or committees. Thus, production is always and in all circumstances a social matter. . . . °

Consequently, society constitutes a human necessity, imposed by the laws of production as well as by those of biology. Does the symbiosis between the individual and society mean that no individual or private existence is any longer possible? . . .

The reality of today acknowledges productive, creative hands and their part in the great scientific achievements, and sees the question of personal existence in a different light. . . . The integration of each man into a specific society has two sides—a general and a particular one. The first comprises the general conditions that surround man, whose specific possibilities are influenced according to the very nature of these conditions, linking his individual existence to that of others to constitute a unique entity—society. The second comprises the biological conditions, the personal potentiality of each individual as such, even though he has not yet reacted to contact with society.

However, as soon as the inescapable confrontation of the individual and society occurs, the two aspects combine in each individual to constitute a straightforward manifestation of his social existence, since he lives in society.

°The author refers to his source, Jean Baby, *Les Lois fondamentales de l'économie capitaliste.*

What are the general conditions that relate the individual existence of each human being to others? Once again, these relate to production, by which I mean the laws governing the relationship of production to men and to society, for through production a well-defined relationship grows between people—a relationship defined by the nature of the productive force and by other natural conditions. This relationship to production shows the degree of response among men and determines the value they derive from their experience. I mean by this that it determines their way of life and, consequently, their position in society.

If we were to question the validity of this statement in the light of past history, the answer would be in the affirmative. In primitive communities, the concept of production was based in effect on collective ownership of the means of production—in this case land for the purpose of hunting— and the conditions of those barbarous times compelled men to work together in large communities. Thus, one finds in primitive communities that everything—including sexual relations—was shared, and that all values reflected this form of ownership; food, shelter, and all the necessities of life were shared in a spirit of mutual aid. The individual, therefore, perceived his own existence only through his relations with the group.

In a slave society, where relationship to production was based on ownership of the available means of production (i.e., slaves), this gave rise to two contradictory points of view, one for the free man and the other for the slaves. The individual was either a master of slaves or a slave himself.

The slaves—the majority of the people—were treated as tools of production and deprived of all humanity, for no other reason than the enslaving nature of the production, which enlisted human existence in the service of profit for the individual and made slaves of men.

In a feudal society, where the relations of production were based on ownership of land and on the products of nature which were monopolized by the feudatories, individuals were similarly divided into different groups—that is to say, opposing groups. . . .

In all human societies, the individual's way of life was determined by the relations of production. The decisive factor conditioning the life of the individual certainly did not come from his individual existence, even though specific circumstances played an important part in establishing the final characteristics of this existence. This indicates that members of a specific society were the products of particular social conditions determined by specific factors. These factors were distinctly reflected by individuals and their particular characteristics.

Every individual constitutes a shade or a definite color in the total picture that we call society. An organic unity exists between the two—the individuals being the various features of society. Perhaps each nuance has its own particular significance, but in the long run the human face emerges as a type of its own. . . . If we examine carefully the face of socialist society, the charm of symmetry dazzles us and begins to give us a sense of human perfection, while if we endeavor to do likewise with regard to capitalist society we are soon overwhelmed by the tragedy of the exploitation of man by man. . . . [This is] the tragedy of a savage struggle, of intellectual poison, [promoted] always with the purpose of glorifying exploitation and surrounding it with bright colors, so as to capture forever the life of all productive individuals. . . .

In a class society where a capitalist regime holds the upper hand, there is a contradictory relationship in individual existence; i.e., all realization of individual existence is at the expense of another human being. Whenever the capitalist's profits increase, the wages of the workers decrease; and whenever the workers' wages rise, the capitalist's gains decrease.

Each rise in the profits of a capitalist diminishes the gains of another. Whenever new workers are engaged in a factory, the level of wages for the old workers is endangered; and whenever an individual rises in importance, others fall.

There is a conflict in the capitalist society because unity and exploitation exist at the same time. The class system is based on the exploitation of labor by a handful of individuals, and from this results the sharp contradiction between the different needs of individuals. Hence is also born the contradiction between the individual and society which takes a specific intellectual form in individualist philosophies, the natural outcome being self-centeredness and feelings of hostility toward others.

At their height, the individualist philosophies result in existentialism, and they are a true expression of the crises of man in a capitalist society and the expression of man's inability to resolve this contradiction scientifically.

Whenever the individual feels the hostility of others toward himself, he withdraws into himself. But he cannot resign himself to living alone, and thereafter he is caught in a vicious circle, with himself as the center, eventually losing contact with others as well as with himelf. His whole life becomes loneliness, anxiety, violent internal disturbance. . . . If he had been aware of the reality of the link between the individual and society, he would have understood that his individualistic philosophy is nothing but a social phenomenon stemming from an internal bleeding at the heart of organized class society.

The situation is entirely different in socialist society, where production is oriented not toward attaining the maximum individual profit but, on the contrary, toward guaranteeing the lives and future of men and satisfying their physical and cultural needs. We find here—but not in capitalist society—a unity of view regarding improvement and close coordination in the existence of individuals. Each improvement in the life of an individual corresponds, at the same time, to an improvement in the lives of others; and each time production increases, general prosperity increases also. No more exploitation, no more interest at the expense of the work of others, but a close and conscious cooperation toward a worthwhile human life. Socialist society is simply the realization of the existence of individuals, the expression of their lives both on social and human levels.

27.   East and West—Shall They Meet?*

Anwar Sadat

The decision to nationalize the Suez Canal [1956] is a turning point in the history of humanity, and heralds a new era, with a new evolution and a new history.

Today—or to be more exact, since the nationalization of the Suez Canal—whoever reads the English, French, or American press, or that of other Western powers, realizes that in each line there is some hesitation over the words West and East; the reader remarks differing trends: Sometimes the West is afraid of the East, and sometimes it provokes it. Now, through this distrust or provocation, there shines a glaring, obvious truth—namely, that in the West, all the ideas about understanding the East and associating with it have flourished only under the harsh light of distrust and watchfulness, hostility, and provocation.

For my part, I do not use the terms West and East in the sense in which they are normally used today—as referring to the two big blocs that divide the world—East meaning Russia and her allies, and West meaning America and her allies. On the contrary, when I use these terms, I revert to their original meaning, in keeping with the times and with history, and the nearest interpretation to my own is that of Kipling, the poet of colonialism, in his famous poem: "East is East, and West is West, and never the twain shall meet."

---

*Extract from Anwar Sadat, *Qissat al-wahda al-'arabiyya* [Story of Arab Unity] (Cairo: Dar al-Hilal, 1957). It appeared as "Orient et Occident" in *Orient*, no. 6 (1958):145–54. For biography of Anwar Sadat, see Chapter VIII on Sadatism.

As soon as we try to define boundaries between East and West—which are precise enough to allow us to classify the countries by study and analysis consistent with history and reality—we come up against numerous difficulties.

For example, are the frontiers in question geographical in origin, or are they a fact of civilization, in the sense that the characteristics of this or that civilization, taken in the light of its history, permanent features, and common origin with various peoples, represent the true boundary—as in the case for what we include under the name East on the one side and West on the other?

Or, again, are the boundaries determined by race, so that we may say that, race being the specific factor, certain races constitute essentially the West and others the East?

If, by adhering to geography, we were to repeat, as did the scholars of the nineteenth century, that the dividing line between West and East roughly follows a line from north to south touching the eastern shores of the Mediterranean—the countries situated to the east of the line constituting the East and the countries to the west the West—we would be committing a grave error, indeed; in effect, Egypt, Palestine, Libya, Tunisia, Algeria, and Morocco would all be ranged in the West, although they are linked to the East by the ancient bonds of history and civilization. The same goes for all institutions involving purely Eastern peoples, who would find it impossible to assimilate with the West, from which they remain as far removed as possible.

An error of the same kind might be made with regard to Australia and New Zealand, which, on the lines of the division in question, form part of the East, although their history, civilization, and institutions do not bind them to the East, from which they are separated to a maximum degree both in spirit and by natural inclination. We shall no longer take race as a criterion, for China unites in a single people innumerable races, as do also America and Russia.

The only sound criterion that remains to us, therefore, is civilization, defined as a common spirit and inscribed in the institutions that provide the very basis on which we can distinguish between East and West. We can thus define as Eastern the group of peoples whose civilization and history belong to the East, a similar definition being likewise applied to the West.

We shall thus avoid mistakes: Tunisia, Algeria, and Morocco form part of the West according to the map, but in reality they are bound by their civilization and their history to the East. The same reasoning applies, in reverse, to Australia and New Zealand, which, according to the map, are situated in the heart of the East, while in reality, by civilization and history, they are attached to the West. . . . As I have already said, and as the present world situation proves, we are engaged in a battle that concerns not only Egypt but that began many long centuries ago between East and West, and the fate of which was definitely sealed by the nationalization of the Suez Canal. That is why we see the Western press and governments since the proclamation of today immersed in a fear and terror that strongly resembles mass hysteria, to the point where the Western powers assemble their fleets, equip their troops, and proclaim to the whole world that they are preparing for hostilities, and thus provoke the opinion of the free world. The Western press can no longer disguise the truth; it proclaims its fear of the East, at the same time provoking it; it weeps and laments over the fate of the West, since the East can no longer be humiliated.

The Western view of the East springs from two sources: Either it is mistrust, giving rise inevitably to precautionary measures and incessant preparations against an Eastern plot, or it is provocation aimed at humiliating the East and thwarting its aspirations. In both cases, what the West has in view is the acquisition of the resources of the rich East, for the enrichment of the Western community and its sons, and the suppression of all progress, instruction, and power, so that this same East may be reduced to weakness and ignorance, and kept underdeveloped under the yoke of the Western protectorate.

How can we define the role of the nationalization of the Suez Canal in the progress of this struggle? That is what we shall now examine.

The Facts of the Struggle

Let us go back to what I just said about the Western view of the East. What is this struggle, in fact?

In order to uncover this truth, we must treat as historical events all the signs that came from the West during the Battle of Suez. We are going to dig into the facts of this struggle, which marks, in a way no less real, the end of the tragedy of the domination of East by West.

[The following] is a symptom whose appearance is of exceptional importance: In an unguarded moment, the French Premier declared that Muslims should have confidence in the help of France, which would look after the common good of Islam and the Muslims. The responsible English did not waste their time.

The Western press, however, proclaimed with more frankness that the struggle was between Islam and the Arabs on the one hand and the West and the Christians on the other. A certain section of the press went so far as to declare that the Muslim East wanted to annihilate the Christian

West. It is here, in this premeditated confusion, that the heart of the problem lies.

The East, which today confronts the West in the battle for the Suez Canal, extends from China to the Atlantic Ocean. China has a population of 600 million, and the Chinese of all stations are rising to brave the West... In India, 380 million men likewise are rising to brave the West....

The problem, therefore, is not that of a Muslim East; it is that of an East deceived, an East colonized by a West that has sucked its blood. That East wishes to avenge itself, but not in the Western manner by hostility and usurpation. All it wishes is to live freely and independently, that each nation shall make her own destiny, exploit the riches of her soil for the benefit of her own children, and respect the independence of other nations, whether they be Eastern or Western.

Thus, Egypt can be aided by 1,500 million men, of all stations in life, of different religions and instruction, but all united in the same resolution and the same faith.

Western propaganda, according to which the Islamic East is seeking to destroy the Christian West, sows confusion and flagrantly contradicts the facts. But it constitutes a symptom of the struggle that is destined to continue between East and West before one story ends and another begins. For if the conflict for the Suez Canal had involved India and the West, we would have heard similarly, from the voice of the Western press, that the Hindu East was seeking to destroy the Christian West. If the conflict for the Suez Canal had involved Burma and the West, we would have heard similarly, from the voice of the Western press, that the Buddhist East was seeking to destroy the Christian West.

What I want to say in conclusion is that the West-East struggle is as real and as old as the civilization of the East and the designs of the West. This struggle will last as long as the East is rich in resources and treasures brought from the depths of its soil, from the goodness of its earth, and the abundance of its various products; this struggle will carry on as long as the West persists in its present view of the East, founded on entirely mistaken and unjust principles that are in total contradiction with earthly and divine principles.

What are these mistaken principles? How have they been able to develop and assume enough importance to menace, by the Suez affair, the security of humanity and inspire the repulsion of all that is just, true, and generous? How has the West sought to involve, in these demonstrations of hostility and hatred, religions that counsel only love and peace? That is what we are now going to examine.

Mistaken Principles

The West sees in the East only swarming millions of starving, naked, and ignorant people, toward whom it has the duty to assume the role of tutor according to the principles of humanity, the Christian religion, and European civilization!

There again, the West runs counter to truth, to history, and to human values. Has it, in effect, the prerogative of carrying the Christian message? Has it the right to interpret it in a manner contradictory to its fundamental principles, to enlist it in the colonial adventure founded on hate and discord between the sons of humanity? No, that is one thing we do not accept, we in the East, for we know Christianity and its principles: The Christians are people like ourselves; our land is the cradle of this religion; it is from our soil that the new message went forth to conquer pagan Europe!

The diversity of our beliefs and our laws does not prevent us in the East from recognizing Christianity, from respecting it and separating it from all the West would add to it. The Buddhists, the Hindus, the Muslims, the Confucians, the Christians of the East, and the Copts know Christianity better than the West knows it or claims to know it.

In pronouncing the puerilities about Christianity, the West forgets that the millions of orientals, whom it sees naked and starving, knew civilization, religion, and wisdom while Europe was still wandering in the blackness of ignorance and living under the influence of witchcraft and myth. The East, the cradle of Christianity, knows that it is founded on the two principles of faith and charity. Do these figure in what the West calls Christianity?

The East, the cradle of Christianity, knows that the basis of its message is not to separate men, but to urge them to love one another for all time. If, then, a man of black or yellow race should approach a Christian to ask him to cure him, the Christian will treat him exactly as if he were white. Does the West really understand Christianity as we understand it in the East?

No, for the West wallows in the materialism that penetrates all its principles and shames the letter and the spirit of Christianity. It is the West that has created the myth of the white man and his superiority over the "colored"; it is the West that undertakes the killing of the innocent, assuming the right to determine the destiny of their countries; it is the West that calls piracy courage, for whom the stripping and subjugation of man are established rights.

That is the fundamental point of conflict between East and West. For us orientals, religions are a spiritual refuge where our souls find peace from the cares of this world. The West, on the other hand, enlists religion in its plans for domination.

For us orientals, Christianity has a universal message of mercy which in principle does not differ from other religions and beliefs that we practice, for they all teach love, brotherhood, and peace. The Westerners, on the other hand, consider themselves as the privileged guardians of Christianity, and those who are not Christians as illiterates, sorcerers, and barbarians.

It is thus that the West has gone astray, that Christianity and its principles are mixed with the acts of this sinful world, forgetting that the East is the cradle of Christianity and the source of all religions. [Sadat describes the battle for the Suez Canal as the encounter of the forces of East and West and mentions again that some Europeans asked that Western civilization be safeguarded.] . . .

But Western civilization and its heritage, for which Europe and America fear so much, live only on the debris of the East and would not flourish if they had not sucked its blood. That is the astonishing truth.

Western civilization is not today a civilization [*hadara*] as the term is understood by science and theory, but only a way of life [*madaniyya*], and there is a big difference between a civilization and a way of life. A civilization, in fact, is characterized, above all, by its ideals and spiritual principles, and material institutions come only in second place; we see therefore, that it is not concerned with appearances but is above all founded on the spirit.

A way of life, on the other hand, is not concerned with ideals or spiritual principles, and in the life of the individual or of the group, it presents only a purely material and readily artificial face, as if life itself were as mechanical as machines or pushbuttons. There is no value in a way of life that ignores the very essence of human life.

Civilization, therefore, is defined and will always be defined by the highest human values, while a way of life interprets human values in terms of material progress. By virtue of this argument and what we see all around us, we can appreciate the distance that extends between a civilization and a way of life, and can identify the so-called civilization of the West as the Western way of life. And there, as I see it, is another conflict between West and East: The West claims the right to impose its present way of life; it claims that the basis of the new message is to make the Eastern peoples receive only some examples of this Western "civilization" in well-defined and restricted form—for example, when the West introduces a democratic system to an Eastern people it is not in the same form as in the West. Westerners content themselves with imposing on the people [of the East] a system designed to ensure Western authority and domination, finally baptizing it democracy and calling it the outcome of modern Western civilization.

When the West introduces modern science to an Eastern country under the yoke of colonialism, this knowledge is not transmitted by natural stages, for the Western concept of civilization is that the East should not have more than the outer shell of Western science, the preservation and usages of knowledge being reserved for the white man.

Hence many peoples, victims of colonialism, have thus far been suffering and have been incapable of growth, since they have neither medicine nor geometry—these skills being reserved, in the Western theory of civilization, for the white man, the chosen man. That is how the West ensures its domination. One last illustration of this state of affairs: England invites military missions to come to England from various Western and Eastern states. It happened that in 1950 some Egyptian officers formed part of one of these missions. On their return, they told how the main meetings were barred to them and to other delegations from Eastern countries, because those meetings dealt with military secrets reserved for the English and the Europeans. . . . These examples illustrate what is understood in the West by civilization, or, rather, way of life.

The Eastern idea of civilization differs radically. The East is proud of the fact that the greatest civilizations known to man were nurtured on its soil: the Chinese civilization, which discovered wisdom and light; the pharaonic civilization, which astonished and continues to astonish the world by its brilliant past in science and the arts; the Indian civilization, which, since antiquity, has plumbed the secrets of the spirit and of matter and presented to humanity a philosophy and science whose glorious heritage will remain until the end of time.

The East, therefore, interprets civilization as founded on spiritual rather than material values. We believe that the Chinese, Egyptian, or Indian civilizations invented ethics and humanities and arts, honored the family, organized the relationships of individuals with one another, and the relationships of individuals to society or to the government—the Chinese civilization remaining unsurpassed in its theory of power and the applications of power, on the one hand, and of subjects and their essential politeness, on the other.

But the sole result of these civilizations has not been the establishment of human values. Science, art, mathematics, and architecture remain as testimonials to the permanence of the superiority of these civilizations over thousands of years. The East conceives civilization as an edifice where coexistence reigns for the good of all, and that is why it is proud of its civilization, which it deems superior to the Western way of life.

Everything was therefore abundantly clear to the East when it threw off the vestiges of colonialism and Western domination. It now desires to make up for lost time. It feels an ardent desire for the civilization which is part of its lifeblood and which will devour it like a fire; and the civilization engrained in it burns with a flame which cannot be extinguished.

The West finds itself—with its "civilization" built by the sword, by fire, by piracy, and by violence—faced with people who possess a pure and genuine civilization, faced with people who would live honorably and rescue their spiritual strength from the grip of Western "civilization."

The struggle will continue until the true civilization triumphs over the false—in other words, until supreme values replace base methods of force.

28.   The Arabs and the Civilization of the Century[*]

Muhammad Wahbi

Muhammad Wahbi is a Lebanese whose writings on Arab intellectual and philosophical problems are both critical and detached. In his first book, Azmat al-tamaddun al-ʿarabi [The Crisis of Arab Civilization] (Beirut: Dar al-ʿilm lilmalayin, 1956), *Wahbi argued for a more basic revolution within Arab society to absorb modern civilization in all its aspects, instead of concentrating solely on gaining independence. In a later book, he discusses, among other ideas, the clash between conservative and revolutionary tendencies and stresses a basic problem of the Middle East: Is there one civilization, or is the Middle East divided into Western and Eastern civilizations? Is the first materialistic and the latter spiritualistic, as claimed by Anwar Sadat in Egypt (see previous section) and many other in the East? Or is there just one civilization with many cultural aspects? Wahbi claims that there is one civilization—the contemporary one to which all mankind belongs. (A similar idea was put forth by Dr. Abdullah Cevdet, a Turkish thinker, at the turn of the century. "If you speak about civilization," he said, "there is just one, and that is in the West. Consequently, one is either in or out of it. There is no other alternative to being civilized." Abdullah Cevdet's thoughts exercized a profound influence on Atatürk and were expressed in his reforms.)*

Today there are two opposing currents of ideas in the Arab East. In

°Extract from Muhammad Wahbi, ʿUruda wa-insaniyya [Arabism and Humanism] (Beirut: Mansharat ʿUwaydat, 1958), pp. 13–20.

fact, since Western civilization overwhelmed this region, two main trends have come to light; one is conservative in character, the other revolutionary. The first is the color-bearer of the opposition to that civilization; it stands against it. Its supporters [the conservatives] are convinced that this civilization is purely materialistic and that material things are all that matter to it; it is the source of all aggression in the peoples who are influenced by it. The East, on the other hand, is spiritual in nature, and must in no way renounce its spirituality.

To justify this extreme thesis, some go so far as to say that this [Western] civilization carries within it the germ of all wars, which, in their eyes, is proof of its extreme materialism. . . . They also maintain that this civilization came to us via colonialism, which it embodies and which it serves; we must therefore reject it and avoid it. They affirm that it is in great part the work of Zionism, which penetrates its web and directs it; we must therefore beware of its misdeeds and its depravity. It is clear that these arguments are fallacious, and have no logical connection.

The supporters of the second trend [i.e., the revolutionaires] nourish such admiration for this civilization that they launch an appeal in favor of its complete adoption. They also believe in the materialism of the West and the spirituality of the East, and this influences their attitude, although their admiration does not prevent them from proclaiming their great disappointment in spiritualism and their blind attachment to materialism. There is another so-called intermediate trend between these two extreme, exclusive, and opposing trends, and this invites comparison. The supporters of this consider it appropriate to adopt only one part of Western civilization—that which refers to science, which is indispensable to progress, the rest being discarded, especially as regards morals. This theory is also founded on the belief that Western civilization is materialistic, while the East is spiritualist.

Thus, if we examine the ideas of the supporters of these three trends, we note they agree in affirming the materialism of the West and the spirituality of Eastern thought. Frankly, I do not see how such a "consensus" has been achieved and on what logical foundation it is based. Is it because Western civilization abounds in achievements of a material nature, although these are but the expressions of a spiritual force? And what is spirituality, then, if not the close relationship of all absolute values with the sole aim of dominating nature and utilizing it, rather than fleeing from it in order to shelter in a sterile world of sentiment and fancy? And what do Eastern morality and spirituality represent with regard to the behavior of the really civilized man, whose behavior is so full of love for truth and fulfillment of duty, so rich also in profound respect for the liberty of others?

None of these theories is right; all are constructed on false bases. There is no spirituality today in the East. It is in the West that one must look for spirituality, which is the prime cause of all evolution.

Although these three concepts are completely valueless, there is nevertheless one that we should qualify as dangerous, and that is one called "intermediate." In appearance moderate, it is hypocrisy itself. More than the other two, it exercises an evil influence on the mind, for it is more convincing by its moderation, although it is founded on a basic contradiction. In fact, in Western civilization, no knowledge is born or developed except on a moral basis, and it would be nonsense to wish to adopt scientific progress while rejecting its foundations. This proves that this civilization is one and indivisible, that its different branches are nourished by the same spirit, and to dismember it would lead to its losing all value and usefulness. Such a conception can only be qualified, in effect, as cowardice and weakness; it derives from an inability to discover truth, which leads to fear and hesitation.

In fact, it matters little whether we align ourselves with one or the other camp. Whatever we do, the course of things will not be changed. In fact, the influence exercised by Western civilization is effective and spontaneous because of the constant contact of modern life and the multiplicity of the means of communication. There is nevertheless another important fact that is indisputable: Not only do we derive no value from this influence, but it threatens to endanger Arab thought if it remains linked to a wrong conception of the spirit of this civilization. In fact, if we stick to this conception, we will derive absolutely no profit from this influence, but, on the contrary, will suffer its ill effects and serious consequences.

Consequently, if we wish to keep ourselves as much in the background as possible regarding the essence of the things we are ourselves adopting, then we are working toward our own ruin by isolating ourselves and shutting ourselves up in the poor sphere in which we circle today with our false ideas and opinions.

It is of prime importance to us to revise the conception we have built up about Western civilization; to convince ourselves, subsequently, that it is necessary to adopt this civilization as a whole, voluntarily and openly! It is, in fact, the civilization of the century for the whole world. There is no other alternative for a people who wish to live and do not desire to become fixed in a past which is over, but to accept it and assimilate it in its totality.

The expression "Western civilization" is nevertheless somewhat exaggerated; it is important now to examine its meaning and define it. It seems to indicate that this civilization is uniquely that of the West; in reality, it is the civilization of the whole of mankind.

In fact, one of the characteristics of the present time is that it cannot allow the existence of several separate civilizations, man's situation being far different from what it once was. In the past, a particular civilization appeared, then crumbled or disappeared under the influence of political events or as a result of the appearance of another civilization and its contact with it. It sometimes happened that different civilizations existed in widely separated regions of the world. But man's life today is no longer what it was yesterday.

Humanity has profoundly changed. Having once lived isolated from one another, as in sealed vases, the nations of today lead the same collective existence. This is the result of the growth of all forms of communication and their extraordinary rapidity. These communications have facilitated the diffusion of ideas and news. Geographical frontiers and great distances no longer play any role, with the result that humanity as a whole lives as one single family under the same roof. As a result of this evolution, humanity has been entrusted with a unique mission—that of carrying the torch of a civilization that cannot but be unique. It is difficult for this civilization not to be the synthesis of what the human spirit has produced in the course of time. It cannot, in fact, forget the past even in part, because it is the path that led to the present, and do not all people today collaborate in this common effort which bears the mark of each? Similarly, this civilization cannot remain fixed on all or part of the past; the law of evolution does not allow it.

The present civilization is that of all humanity, and although Europeans have played a considerable role in its creation and have stamped it with their seal, that does not imply that it can be considered basically as European.

This civilization, in fact, is only the result of a convergence. It was formed in the melting pot of former civilizations and what they engendered—the essential contributions of the human spirit in the course of its evolution, the transformations and improvements demanded by progress.

To carry the torch of modern civilization is today the mission of all nations that are to participate in its expansion, each according to its possibilities. It is no longer possible today to make a distinction between the mission of one nation and that of another. It carries with it responsibilities of which each nation bears a part. The value of a nation is measured according to the importance of the responsibility it assumes and carries out effectively. It is measured also according to the importance of these responsibilities with regard to the common good. We note, when we consider the spirit of this civilization, that it represents the highest degree of civilization in man, as such. Among its various elements, we must note the scientific spirit, with all the intelligence it implies; the result of a wide culture; the constant and disinterested search after knowledge.

This scientific spirit has allowed industry to develop, and has transformed the conditions of life. It is distinguished also by a social spirit, which includes a growth in cooperative movements, and the birth of a large number of practices that have helped in the development and progress of social life. Finally, it is distinguished by the existence of international public opinion, which is now a powerful force in politics.

Nevertheless, when we examine all these elements more closely, we can see that they all stem from one source—freedom. Freedom is, in fact, the soul of all endeavor, whether scientific or social. That is why the manifestations of national liberation are the most important consequences of this civilization in the political sphere.

As to the aggressive colonialist tendencies that still exist, they are not important and only survive in a minority of politicians who are not the representatives of the will of their people, as events prove.

That freedom should be considered the soul of present-day civilization is a fact that proves that we are at the summit of human evolution, for freedom is the essence of man. Civilization has allowed him to discover this, and to identify himself closely with it, but not without meeting many obstacles on the way. That is why we can say that the destiny of each nation depends on the way in which it fulfills its mission in the service of this civilization.

29.   The Causes of the Crisis in Arab Thought[*]

Ishaq Musa al-Husayni

Dr. Ishaq Musa al-Husayni, a Palestinian living in Cairo, is the author of The Moslem Brethren: The Greatest of Modern Islamic Movements *(Beirut: Khayat's, 1956), published originally in Arabic as* al-Ikhwan al-muslimin: kubra al-haraka al-islamiyya al-haditha *(Beirut: Dar Bairut, 1952). In the book from which the following excerpts are taken, he deals with the broader cultural problems that confront the Arab world.*

The crisis is, in origin and essence, a crisis in thought from which proceed all the other crises that arose from time to time. This crisis has five manifestations.

---

[*]Extract from Ishaq Musa al-Husayni, *Azmat al-fikr al-'arabi* [The Crisis in Arab Thought] (Beirut: Dar Bairut, 1954), pp. 15–24. (A review appeared in *Middle East Journal* 13 [Winter 1959]:97–98.)

The first is uncertainty. We are uncertain where we are going, like a man leaving his house in the morning with no clear idea of what he intends to do. He sees many paths before him and dashes into one of them without knowing where he will end up. He may achieve something or he may not. It might take a short time or a long one, and he may find what he wants or he may not. In other words, we inhabit cities with nameless streets and numberless houses. If we had clear foresight, we would have planned our cities so that, before leaving our houses, we can specify the street and the destination we seek. Because of the widespread faith in destiny, in the over-all ordering of the universe, and in the total foreordinaton of all our comings and goings, it may be that this has led to our complete reliance on God and to the absence of planning which would do away with uncertainty. A poet has expressed this sentiment by saying: "To seek your fortune when your fortunes have already been allotted is a crime that would lead to ruin." Another poet has written: "Our destiny is foreordained. Thus activity and inactivity are both futile. It is sheer madness to seek your fortune, since the fortune even of the unborn child is determined in advance." I need not emphasize, however, that Muslim thinkers have drawn the real moral from this belief. They have distinguished it from true submission to God and have defended the Almighty from charges of injustice, often quoting the words of the poet: "He is bound and thrown into the sea and is told, 'Don't get soaked!' "

The second manifestation is extemporization. Where there is uncertainty and absence of planning, there will always be extemporization. Our literature defines rhetoric as speech consonant with the requirements of the situation. An Arab proverb says, "The proper words for the proper occasion," and another says, "The best oratory is extemporaneous." But it often happens that we are faced with situations for which we are not prepared. We view the problems of life so closely that they become blurred. When these problems arise suddenly, we improvise solutions that are often wrong.

The third manifestation of this crisis of thought is the absence of reason: correct and logical thinking based on study and meditation. The men of thought have not participated effectively in building our modern society, and have not been given the chance to do so. We do not possess institutions that include scholars working each in his own specialized field. We have no writers researching and studying our various problems, recording their opinions, and transmitting their knowledge to successors in order to evolve a scholarly heritage embracing all walks of life. We have no specialized books in such fields as economics, sociology, agriculture, etc. If we are forced to do some research, we borrow, quote and make a show of approximating what is written by foreign authors. We have no conferences to discuss and debate various problems that would require the knowledge of experts and scholars. We have no intellectual societies that expound and uphold various ideas. We have given our whole attention to politics, and have emptied it of all its real content, so that now politics is merely tinkering with words. True political thought, which embraces economic, social, industrial, and other questions, has not been sufficiently studied.

The fourth manifestation of the crisis is the absence of courage, ideological freedom, and self-criticism. Our sense of collective responsibility is not strong enough to lead to the disinterested expression of truth, for the sake of God and the fatherland. The thinking man among us is suspect. If he departs from the ordinary, he is accused of hypocrisy or unbelief. Thus, freedom of thought is imprisoned within us, where it tortures our conscience, and the crisis becomes worse from one generation to the next. The modern life enjoyed by other men is an object of envy for us when we visit the West. This modern life, in both its spiritual and material aspects, did not descend from on high, nor was it evolved suddenly, but it was made possible by the participation of scholars and men of thought. In this context, I would like to draw attention to the work of the Fabian Society, founded in England in 1883, which prepared the ground for the creation of the democracy we presently witness in England and elsewhere in the West. The activity of this society was purely rational. It tackled social problems individually and, in its successive pamphlets, enlightened the public and the various governments. Its studies were based on freedom of thought, pure science, and specialization, with the ultimate aim of service to society. The members of this society refused to join the government, since their aim was not to get into power but to lay the scientific foundations for good government and to support the government by offering sensible opinions. They were afraid that if they were to join the government they would be distracted from the original aim for which they labored.

The fifth manifestation is our obsession with the past and the respect, bordering on worship, for ancient laws, repeating all the while this vague and magical incantation, "We can remedy the present only with the remedies of the past." This in effect means that we must go back to live in deserts and caves, ride on camels, wear our traditional baggy robes, treat diseases by cauterization, allow epidemics to decimate us, content ourselves by reading incantations, and suffer the resources of the earth to remain buried.

It is undeniable that Arab history witnessed periods of great power and dominion, intellectual eminence and concern for experimental knowledge that was of great service to humanity. The Arabs may be justly proud of this heritage. But all this has passed away. Neither regret nor negative adulation nor imitation can bring it back. Two things only can do so: One is to seek for the true causes of that intellectual eminence and material prosperity, in order that we may benefit therefrom in building our modern society and restore our waning morale by recalling past glory. Nations possess peculiar characteristics which render them susceptible to grafts that are taken from their own stem, so to speak.

The second requirement must be our determination to link the ancient with the modern. Of modernity we have nothing at all at present, so we must adopt it unhesitatingly wherever we find it. It is wrong to suppose that modernity begins where antiquity has left off. Between ancient and modern there is a vast chasm that we cannot bridge, whatever our might or resources. We must therefore begin at the stage reached by civilized nations. This entails the adoption of a different attitude than the one we adopt today, or at least that some of us wish to adopt, toward modern civilization in general. This latter, with its experimental science, its industry, its studies that are based on statistics, its attitude toward the value of the individual in society, its application of modern methods of government, and its social justice—this civilization is the only bridge that can link our past with our present.

These, then, are the manifestations of the crisis in thought that we experience today. Other and similar manifestations do undoubtedly exist, and my own treatment has naturally been too generalized. I must now turn to some detailed examples. I shall cite three basic problems: (1) the form of the state that has not yet crystallized; (2) our turbulent material life; and (3) our moral or spiritual life, which contains many flaws.

The Form of the State

Writing about governments and their influence on shaping the minds of the peoples, Bertrand Russell said: "Give me a well-equipped army backed by an authority which would provide it with a higher salary and more food than most people can obtain and I will guarantee that within thirty years, I will get most of the citizens to believe that two and two makes three, that water freezes when boiled and boils when frozen or any other absurd notion that may be of service to the state."

In point of fact, however odd in form, the state is capable of directing the people in any way it desires. A proverb that is born of experience says, "The people follow the religion of their kings." And yet, Arabs still differ as to which form of state should exercise power. There are three conflicting schools of thought: The first calls for a religious state that derives its authority from canonical legislation. The second calls for a sectarian state that derives its authority from the wishes of the various sects. The third calls for a secular state that derives its authority from the public interest which in turn follows the development of the people and renders all the citizens equal in rights and obligations. This last is the form chosen by most nations, both Eastern and Western, after having undergone severe trials and painful calamities.

In our part of the world, people have misunderstood the term secular state, supposing it to mean a nonreligious state that works to undermine religion. That is a false notion. Linguistically and historically, the term implies a modern state that pursues two aims: (1) absolute justice and complete equality among individuals, irrespective of their creed, and (2) civic legislation that is based on the discoveries of modern knowledge about material and moral problems in society, and that develops so as to suit the changing circumstances of the various nations. These two aims, far from negating religion or battling against religious creeds, are, in fact, derived from the sublime ideals advocated by all religions. There is a difference between separating religion from the state and separating religion from society. Religion can no more be severed from society than the soul from the body. Religion, in its own ways, treats of the life of the soul, while the social, political, and economic sciences treat of the life of the body in accordance with their various and developing methods. After a long period of unity, psychic and physiological medicine have finally drawn apart. This is because life is of more value to man than anything else and, in order to preserve it, man has had to sacrifice some of his religious vanity. But there are some who still live in an era when the two medicines have not yet parted and are thus exposed to grave danger.

Thus, to link religious and secular remedies would result in rival inclinations, diversity in the distribution of authority, and the conflict of sects and classes at the expense of the state itself. Throughout the course of history, we have seen that whenever secular and religious authority were combined, one would suffer at the expense of the other. Therefore, and after long experience, men in most countries of the world have come to agree that the two authorities should be separated so that each can proceed along its natural course and each can develop for the benefit of both and of humanity at large.

I must here mention that Islam, which has been unjustly accused of stagnation, has prepared the ground, through such doctrines as analogy [qiyas], individual interpretation [ijtihad], consensus [ijma], and public interest [al-masalih al-mursala], for this development of secular and religious affairs. Had it been otherwise, Islam, at its early stages, would never have contributed so generously to human civilization, both materially and spiritually. In the age of decadence, and to some extent even today, the Muslims blocked all these avenues to progress for fear of their consequences. But such suppression was worse in its effects than the emancipation of thought. Indeed, one has only to look at most of the Islamic world today, and to compare it with the past or with the conditions prevalent elsewhere in the modern world, in order to perceive this truth.

Moreover, secular legislation has been adopted by most Islamic countries. Modern jurists have been able to reconcile this with Islamic law, despite opposition varying in intensity in various countries. I would like to quote here a respected modern jurist, 'Abd al-Rahman Badawi, a judge at the International Court at The Hague. While addressing a committee entrusted with the drawing up of a constitution for independent Egypt in 1922, he said: "Whereas the minorities tend to remember the past with its record of persecutions, it is a fact that both the majority and the minority lived under an authoritarian regime where both were equally persecuted. We do not wish or contemplate the revival of the past within our modern system. Religious differences, even with us, are beginning to fade away and it will not be long before they totally disappear from our social relations. We must therefore allow this spectre to overshadow us. Indeed, I greatly fear this problem, especially in an age where religious differences have weakened and where the factor of common interest, irrespective of creed, has become the binding link among men in society. I hope to see the day when all our activities, even marriage, divorce, etc., are unified under one well-organized civic system of life. We want a purely nationalist policy, which pays no regard to religions and sects but works always for the interest of the nation."

Turning now to some Arab countries that live under a sectarian system, we find that there is much complaint therefrom. If my guess is correct, such a system is inevitably on its way out, since divided loyalties and conflicting hopes weaken the structure of the state. . . .

It is high time that the Arabs must take account of three considerations: The first is that constructive nationalism is founded upon complete justice among the citizens and works to unite them by all means, especially through legislation. The absence of justice breeds grievances and, in the end, allows the enemy to break through our lives. The second is that constructive nationalism inevitably entails the adoption of the ways of modern civilization. This latter has arrived at a scientific solution for the various economic, social, and political questions of state. We must adopt, understand, and use these solutions. The third is that the adaptation to world civilization is a matter made imperative by modern developments in the various means of transport and communication. Such adaptation demands unification, cooperation, and the rejection of all forces pleading for isolation and individual action. If this is necessary internationally, it is much more so on the home front and among the various groups that make up a nation.

X. ARAB UNITY AND IDEOLOGY

30.   Greater Syria and Arab Unity*

The question of unity in the Arab Middle East was alive as early as 1941. In that year, Anthony Eden declared that the British Government would support closer ties among Arab countries. Soon afterward, in 1942, Nuri al-Sa'id of Iraq published a Blue Book proposing a federal union in the Fertile Crescent linking Syria, Lebanon, Palestine, and Transjordan to Iraq. In reaction, the Jordanians proposed a Greater Syria under the monarchy of Jordan. The unity scheme displeased the Sa'udi dynasty, which did not want its rival Hashimite crowns of Jordan and Iraq to be strengthened. Syria and Lebanon, in turn, rejected the proposal since, as independent democratic republics, they could not be united under an absolute monarch. The Syrian answer, in the form of a book supposedly written by a group of educated Syrians—Kalimat al-suriyya wal-'arab fi mashru'at suriyya al-kubra [Views of the Syrians and the Arabs on the Greater Syria Plan] (Damascus, 1947)—apparently emanated from the government. Meanwhile, the Egyptian Government had submitted to a General Arab Conference, in 1944, its own scheme of unity—a loose organization in which each of the seven participating states would preserve its independence and political regime. The League of Arab States was subsequently formed on March 22, 1945. In any case, from the very beginning, political differences constituted a major obstacle to unity. The controversy over unity continued, largely as a reaction to the idea of a Greater Syria under a monarchy. (See the speeches and letter of King 'Abdallah in the next section.) The extracts indicate that, even

---

*Extracts from Kitab al-urdunn al-abyad: al-watha'iq al-qawmiyya fi wahdat suriyya al-tabi'iyya [Jordanian White Book: The National Documents Concerning Natural Syrian Unity] (Amman: al-Matba'a al-wataniyya, 1947), pp. 75–77, 104–8.

before independence was achieved, there were tensions between monarchies and republics.

THE APPEAL OF H.R.H. PRINCE ʿABDALLAH TO THE SYRIAN PEOPLE AND THE ARAB WORLD

People of Syria, both city and country dwellers, from the Gulf of ʿAqaba to the Mediterranean and the Euphrates.

All men have come to know that the Arabs, during their great revolt,° did not sow civil discord or attempt to usurp power, but were champions of justice, freedom, and national sovereignty who believed in their right to a free life. They rose up in arms to defend Arabism and Islam. Their leaders defined the borders of their homeland as stretching from the Arabian Peninsula in the south to Syria and Iraq in the north. This was the objective of their revolt and of their national aspirations. In this, they manifested their belief in their glorious heritage and their faith in the promises made to them by the Allies, especially Great Britain, who undertook to support their claims, respect their desires, and guarantee their independence.

The Great War ended, and the rights of the Arabs were sealed with the blood of their heroic martyrs.

The military and political leaders of the Allies were fully cognizant of the importance of the Arab revolt to the outcome of the war. They lavished praises on the Arab leaders. As a result, Iraq, the Hijaz, Najd, and Yemen all obtained their independence.

Only the Syrian lands were kept fragmented and anxious to reunite within their natural borders, in one land united by nationality, geography, and history and irrigated by the water of the Euphrates, the Orontes, and the Jordan. If the conflicting foreign interests had led to the fragmentation of its unity, the principles of international justice, the natural rights of life, and the promises made to Syrians in particular and Arabs in general were all factors acting against the disruption and fragmentation of the same land and the same family.

People of Syria!

Now that the call for Arab unity has become definite, it is essential to this blessed call that we openly advocate the necessity of uniting the Syrian regions, basing this upon the express will of the nation ever since

---

°In 1916.

the last war and upon the vital, natural, and legitimate interests of the people.

Today, we attempt, through political channels and trusting in certain rays of hope contained in the promises of the Allies and in our past endeavor and our present position of authority in southern Syria, to defend your will as expressed in the resolution of the General Syrian Congress of March 8, 1920, which, together with the McMahon correspondence, placed its faith in the Hashimite house.

The charter of the Syrian Arab nation and its call for total unity have always been our charter and our call. Although circumstances have made us tarry for a while in a certain region of Greater Syria, we work today in the light of a new democratic charter, supported by past and future promises to implement the national will for union with the rest of Syria. We firmly believe in our country's rights and our nation's support, drawing, in all this, upon our past history, our past struggle, and our sacrifices. We do not forget the friendship of the Allies, and the prominent role played by Great Britain in supporting the Arab cause. We are also grateful to the Free French representative, who, with characteristic French magnanimity, declared last year the termination of the French mandate over Syria and Lebanon and the proclamation of their sovereign independence, as guaranteed by the British and other governments.

People of Syria!

Our sister state Egypt has responded to the principles enunciated by the great Arab revolt. Its Prime Minister has called for an official Arab conference that would attempt to remove the obstacles and make a *rapprochement* easier. We must thank Egypt for this gesture. We call upon Iraq also to respond to this invitation by Egypt, which we ourselves welcome. We hope that this conference will support the charter for a united Syria so that Greater Syria can occupy its proper place alongside a Pan-Arab union.

At the same time, we call upon the leaders of public opinion [*ahl al-hall wal-'aqd*; literally, men who bind and deliver] to rally to this project for a total Syrian union. Let them debate the issue at a special Syrian conference, which we would welcome here in our capital whenever they choose. Or let all classes, sects, leaders, and scholars examine the implications of this project carefully and give it their support.

The truth is clear as daylight, and now is the time for serious endeavor. The future beckons the Arabs to retrieve past glory and achieve unity. God helps those who help themselves, and in Him we trust.

Amman, April 8, 1943

THE PROJECT OF GREATER SYRIA AS IT FIGURED IN THE DISCUSSIONS OF
ARAB UNITY [CONFERENCE OF ALEXANDRIA, 1943] AND IN THE CHARTER
OF THE ARAB LEAGUE [CAIRO CONFERENCE, 1944]

During the discussion of Arab unity [the Alexandria Conference], the
subject of Greater Syria was reviewed. Both the Syrian and the Jordanian
delegations concurred in the necessity of creating a natural Syrian unity.
However, the form of government in this state was left undecided. Jordan
expressed its adherence to the original plan of a constitutional monarchy,
in accordance with the resolution of March 8, 1920. This resolution was
framed by representatives of Greater Syria and was considered by all the
Syrian regions to be their common national charter at that time. No Syrian
region had the right to abrogate it unilaterally.

The Syrian delegate, however, expressed his attachment to recent
developments in northern Syria, the emergence of the Republic, and the
desire to impose the republican system upon Greater Syria as well. It was
the opinion of Jordan that the only natural and legitimate solution of the
probem would be to hold a free plebiscite througout the Syrian regions
and to acquiesce in the over-all will of the nation.

Reference was later made to the possibility of a federation between
the governments of the independent Syrian regions. This federation
would be created by a special charter and would possess its own council,
without disturbing the form of the regional governments. It was intended
to hold a special conference for regional Syrian governments in order that
this problem could be tackled naturally and within a legal framework. But
this was not to be, and the questions of both union and federation have
been suspended without justification, although such suspension is detrimental to the national interests of this one Arab country.

In order to clarify the facts, we shall quote the observations made by
the delegate of northern Syria concerning natural Syrian unity, together
with other remarks made by the delegates of Egypt and Iraq. These words
prove that the strengthening of relations between two or more states of
the Arab League, far from constituting a breach of the League Charter as
was rumored, is in fact an affirmation of the aims of the Charter itself. Here
are some random remarks, recorded in the official minutes, made by H.E.
Sa'd Allah al-Jabri, the delegate from northern Syria:

> The fragmentation of Syria went against its political and geographical nature.
> It was the result of certain foreign agreements and interests, both open and
> secret, which were imposed on the people by force.
>
> Syrians, like all sincere Arabs, desire unity, especially in this era, which
> witnesses the gradual dissolution of small nations.
>
> The Syrian problem is the concern of four regions: Syria, Lebanon,
> Palestine, and Transjordan.

There are basic factors that make for unity in these regions, irrespective of the nature or form of this unity. This unity is the objective we have sought in the past and have worked to achieve unconditionally and in the face of all obstacles. But, twenty years later, each country has become used to its own particular manner of life and its own character, and this development has necessitated a change in our policy. We must now attempt to compromise with and to persuade each other. With Damascus as the capital and the republican system as a basis, we insist upon unity but leave the choice of the particular form of unity to the citizens.

The inhabitants of Lebanon, including many Christians and all Muslims, especially in the parts added to Lebanon after the Great War, desire to join Syria unconditionally.

We are therefore anxious to create Greater Syria and do away with the fragmentation imposed on us by force, foreign interests, and political rivalries. We want to arrive at this objective by any means chosen by the countries that were carved out from Syria. We do not deny that there are many obstacles to be overcome. This program of cooperation between us and Lebanon may be taken as an example of how the affairs of regions cut off from their mother country may be handled, until the union is achieved and this unjust fragmentation of Syria is ended. Indeed, this fragmentation has retarded Syria's growth and removed it from its rightful place. While desiring that this unity should be effected through peaceful persuasion and mutual understanding, we wish to reaffirm the necessity of retaining Damascus as capital and the Syrian republic with all its republican institutions.

The Opinion of the Jordanian Delegate

THE CHAIRMAN (EGYPT): What form will this unity between Syria and Jordan assume?

H.E. ABU L-HUDA PASHA (THE JORDANIAN DELEGATE): The form of this unity will be determined by majority opinion.

THE CHAIRMAN: But what is your own opinion?

ABU L-HUDA PASHA: I believe it should be a monarchy.

THE CHAIRMAN: But Syria is a republic.

ABU L-HUDA PASHA: A republican system may be replaced by a royalist regime. I say this because I know that many Syrians prefer a royalist regime. I also believe that the present leaders of Syria are genuine patriots who will not allow this question of monarchy vs. republic to stand in the way of their country's prosperity. If they find that it is to the interest of their country, I am certain they will change their form of government.

The Possibility of Syrian Unity or Federation
as Discussed in Debates Centering on
Article 9 of the Charter of the Arab League

Following is the text:
"ARTICLE 9. Member states of the Arab League desiring to strengthen their common ties and cooperation among them in this Charter may enter

upon any agreements they like in order to achieve this purpose. Treaties and agreements, both past and future, between one member state of the League and any other state shall not be considered binding upon the other members."

'ABD AL-HAMID BADAWI PASHA: "I would like to stress that closer ties between two or more member states would by no means be considered contrary to the Charter. Indeed, they would underline the basic aims of the Charter itself."

'ABD AL-RAHMAN 'AZZAM PASHA: "I do not consider this article to be framed in a negative sense. I believe it was put in in order to emphasize the rights of member states to conclude whatever agreements they like that are broader in scope than this Charter."

The Attitude and Reservation
of the Iraqi Government

H.E. The chairman of the subcommittee in charge of the projected Charter of the Arab League,
Dear Sir,
I have the honor of informing your excellency that due to the delay in the signature of the minutes of the sessions of the political subcommittee of the Preparatory Committee of the Arab Conference, caused by a motion to add to and amend the projected Charter of the Arab League, certain League states had not yet consulted their governments. Therefore, to remove any possible misunderstanding and to inform my government accordingly, I would like to present to your excellency the Iraqi Government's view that the following points should be made clear:

One—Article 12. League states must not, either collectively or individually, interfere in any quarrel of any kind arising between Iraq and any state or states within or outside the League, except at the request of Iraq and the other state or states.

Two—Article 14. This article gives the League the right to establish a more extensive cooperation among League states than is specified in the Charter, providing such states agree to this. It is obvious that this mandate is really a confirmation of the right at present enjoyed by League states. Therefore, it must be made clear that no state of the League can object for any reason at all if other League states decide to increase cooperation between them.

Three—Article 15. It is the right of the citizens of each state of the League to choose their own form of government. Since Article 15 does not make this principle clear, it is necessary to explain that Iraq cannot possibly forsake a principle that has been adopted throughout the civilized world.

I would be grateful if your excellency would acknowledge receipt of this letter so that I can inform my government before March 15.

[Signed] Tahsin ʿAskari
Minister-Delegate of Iraq.

31.   Islam and Arabism and the Unity Plan of King ʿAbdallah of Jordan*

King ʿAbdallah of Jordan

The drive for unity or a Greater Syria was renewed after Transjordan attained independence from the British in 1946 and the proclamation of the ruler (amir) *as king seemed assured. Actually, the title Hashimite Kingdom of Jordan was not conferred until 1948 or recognized internationally until 1949. From the start, the incumbent King ʿAbdallah faced the opposition of Egypt and especially of his bitter enemies, the followers of Hajj Amin al-Husayni, the former Mufti of Jerusalem. The latter was supported by Egypt, Saʿudi Arabia, and Syria, all of which were opposed to the expansion of Jordan. Deprived of an economic basis (it added the eastern section of Palestine in 1948–49), Jordan sought to increase its influence—possibly through a merger with Syria. King ʿAbdallah therefore revived the idea of a Greater Syria. He regarded Jordan as part of Syria, and described unity as a necessary measure for assuring national security. He justified his own claim to the throne of Greater Syria as a natural consequence of his royal family's contribution to the Arab cause. It is interesting to note that, despite the Pan-Islamic, Pan-Arabic aims of his movement, Hasan al-Banna, the leader of the Muslim Brotherhood, opposed the idea of a Greater Syria under the Jordanian monarchy.*

Some insights into the background of these developments may be found in Philip Graves, ed., Memoirs of King ʿAbdallah of Trans-Jordan, *trans. G.*

---

*Extract from al-Maktab al-daʾim lil-muʾtamar al-qawmi al-urdunni (Permanent Secretariat of the Jordanian National Conference), *Suriyya al-kubra aw al-wahdat al-suriyya al-tabiʿiyya: haqiqa qawmiyya azaliyya. Radd ʿala kitab "Kalimat al-suriyya wal-ʿarab fi mashruʿat suriyya al-kubra"* [Greater Syria or Syrian Natural Unity: An Eternal National Truth. Answer (Rejection) of the Book "Views of Syria and the Arabs on the Greater Syria Plan"] (Damascus: al-Mashur fi Dimashq, 1948), pp. 61–65 (King's speech), 36–38 (letter to Hasan al-Banna).

Khuri (London: Jonathan Cape; New York: Philosophical Library, 1950).
    The first extract is a speech delivered by King 'Abdallah at the opening of the Islamic Cultural College in Amman on September 19, 1947. The second extract is an answer to Shaykh Haasan al-Banna's request to King 'Abdallah to end his call for a Greater Syria. (For al-Banna's views, see Chapter IV, Subchapter 12.)

SPEECH OF KING 'ABDALLAH

It gives me pleasure to announce the opening of the Islamic Cultural College, which has been founded on national and Islamic bases in order to disseminate true knowledge and faith. I have also noted with appreciation the sentiments expressed by the various speakers, and it is my dearest wish to see my beloved people striving for the right causes, endeavoring to be constructive, and calling for unity rather than fragmentation. I hope and pray that our religious and educational institutions will continue to preach this message and to create a new, vigorous Arab generation which is possessed of all virtues and ideals that give it mastery over the earth and make it fit to receive God's light and the divine messages of justice, freedom, and human dignity.

However, with reference to what certain speakers have said about Islam and Arabism, and to the resolutions of our national congress held last week as regards unity—I would like to comment on the speech of the President of Syria, broadcast two days ago from Damascus, in the course of which he made some unfounded allegations about this faithful Syrian Arab land. Let me first say, May God forgive him! In paying homage to Islam and to Arabism within the precincts of this College, I send my best wishes to the Syrian nation throughout its homeland and greetings to the Syrian President in the northern region of our beloved homeland. I pray that God will help me to bear with patience and to forgive and forget. But we must continue to work for our national rights and to try to make those who bitterly oppose us see the truth. The Syrian President has seen fit to perpetuate national fragmentation and intensify this animosity among brothers. We, however, can do no more than bow to the nation's free and unified will, without either forcing its decision or doubting its judgment. This is why I call for a general plebiscite of the Syrian nation, in order that a common decision be taken regarding its unity or its federation. No honest man can possibly take us to task for such a view. No honest man can conceivably see in this policy any ground for alarm or for declaring it to be detrimental to Arab problems or the unity of Arab ranks—provided there is good faith. But I believe that prevarication in such a problem is far worse and far more dangerous, especially as our call genuinely serves our countries' common interests, has always been honest and fraternal, and has never violated the nation's charter and the unanimous national resolutions. Our nation shall never forsake its natural right to unity or federation, no matter what lies are propagated or what charges are made against its national charter, as, for example, that it is inspired by Zionism and imperialism. The truth is that the nation has framed this charter in defiance of Zionism and imperialism and of the attempt to fragment our homeland. Furthermore, the nation shall implement its own charter of its own free will after it shall have framed it in a way that would guarantee the national rights specified in the Charter of the United Nations.

Therefore, our call is no mere desire on our part for an increase of royal power, but is rather the task entrusted to us by the nation. We thank God that our family has never pursued power for its own sake. Our struggles for our country and people are of greater value than any royal power.

Al-Daylami in the *Masnad* of Firdawsi records the following saying of 'Ali ibn Abi Talib: "Whoever does not, by knowing more of this world, grow more abstemious, draws further away from God." As for the President's claim that my recent message to him entails his having to break the oath he took to be loyal to the constitution, I have really no comment to make.

Our message to him was in reality a cordial invitation freely to come to an agreement. It could not possibly be interpreted as implying the breaking of the oath that he took on two occasions, namely, on March 8, when Syria's independence was declared together with its natural borders; and when the regional Syrian republican constitution was proclaimed. This latter calls, in any case, for comprehensive unity.

However, the President still works to preserve this state of fragmentation. He and his friends have gone so far as to invent a quarrel among Arabs of the same region. He has perverted the Arab League Charter by interpreting it as antagonistic to any free unity of our countries, although he knows very well that that Charter has, both explicitly and implicitly, called for stronger bonds between League states and for the encouragement of national aspirations. "Syrian unity" is very much a national aspiration, not solely because of natural and national rights, but also by reason of common regional interests. It is strange that the President should feel it is his right to impose a republican regime upon our kingdom—a regime which arose accidentally—and should deny to us the right to ask for a united national plebiscite where the nation's will can be determined. Is he not really advocating a dictatorship in the guise of a republic? It is very strange that he should justify this fragmentation indefinitely by arguing that there can be no unity between a free man and an unfree man, although he knows perfectly well that Jordan is fully independent and has treaties and alliances with major powers. He also knows that the present world situation does not allow for isolation and that a federation where each party retains its rights would create a unified power which would benefit all parties concerned. There can be no room for denial that Jordan is a part of the Syrian entity and that to abandon or renounce this entity is to renounce the national charter and to submit to the solution imposed by foreign imperialism and the consequent fragmentation of the same land. It is indeed regrettable that a fighter for Arab causes [i.e., the Syrian President] should consider this call for Syrian unity or federation a violation of international law and of the U.N. Charter. This charge is unjustifiable, not only from the national but also from the international point of view, since the U.N. Charter has explicitly recognized the right of self-determination. Furthermore, common geographical, historical, and national considerations are recognized in international law. With all due respect to the present regimes in the regional Syrian states and to their independence, we do not see that this state of affairs necessarily precludes any free call for the restitution of our natural right to unite or federate. Nor can this call be considered as an intervention in the regional Syrian state since the Syrian people in all the regions have already accepted the principle of natural Syrian unity in its general charter of 1920. Besides, the constitution of the regional Syrian Republic does not admit accidental national fragmentation and, indeed, stipulates that Jordan should be united or federated to Syria. The constitution in fact states that any other course of action would be tantamount to a denial of the will of the one nation and of its rights and interests. Non-Syrian states do not, of course, have the right to defy the will of the Syrian people within their own homeland as a whole or to interfere in their internal affairs. The safeguarding of independence and the repulsion of the Zionist menace are not grounds for bombastic talk within the one nation. In any case, Jordan is closer to Palestine, and any threat to the latter is a direct threat to the former as well. Jordan has always been the first to answer the call of duty in Palestine. Indeed, the father of the Arab revolution [i.e., King Husayn of Hijaz], who is the dearest man to our hearts, lies buried in the Aqsa Mosque in Jerusalem, ever present in our hearts and a symbol of the vow we have taken to God.

Although Syria does not belong to any ruling family, as the Syrian President has said, it does owe something, without the need for gratitude, to a family that, in two world wars, has answered its call. This family is in duty bound to oppose Syrian fragmentation or the renunciation of its common charter. Syria, in its natural borders, and not just in one of its regions, belongs to all of itself and is the legacy handed down by its martyrs and heroes. Those who fought for it are its own sons, whose rights and obligations are those of the nation itself. Its will shall remain entire and unfragmented. Peace be upon this land of freedom and dignity, from the Gulf of 'Aqaba to the Mediterranean and the Euphrates.

REPLY TO H.E. SHAYKH HASAN AL-BANNA, DIRECTOR-GENERAL OF THE MUSLIM BROTHERHOOD, EGYPT

Greetings. I received your letter on August 30 [1947], delivered by your messenger, Mr. 'Abidin. My answer will be as one Muslim brother would address another, neither shunning the truth nor avoiding blame.

Our call for the unity of the Syrian countries has itself been expressed by the first Syrian National Convention. It is also the call that was pronounced by our now legislative assembly, whose decisions we are bound to accept. We cannot possibly betray the trust of our people whom certain dissenters are endeavoring to isolate from our one homeland. Such a betrayal would be detrimental to their national rights and their moral and material welfare. No Muslim and no Arab would want to inflict this upon another Muslim or Arab.

Therefore, we mean to achieve a common Syrian charter by freely advocating it. We have no desire for personal glory or private gain, but look solely to the interests, the prosperity, and the future of the Arabs. We advocate the unity of the Syrian region in a manner that would safeguard the national interests of the Syrians and be brought about by their own free will and choice.

In our latest statement and in our message to H.E. the Syrian President may be found ample proof of this. There is no justification for this hostility against us. Rather, it is those who brought upon us the enmity of brothers and strangers alike that stand most in need of good advice. What is so reprehensible in our call for a preparatory national congress that would include representatives of the peoples and governments of a single nation, so that they can, of their own free will, create a union or a federation? Is this sufficient reason for antagonizing a fellow-Arab who has not forced them to do his bidding but simply asked for an open deliberation [shawra] of national leaders and who is prepared to abide by whatever decision they think fitting?

This hostility, if it has been the work of some sowers of discord who have succeeded in deceiving our coreligionists and in disseminating their false propaganda in the Arab world, is truly reminiscent of the schemers of the Quraysh tribe who failed to exhaust the Prophet's patience or to make him abandon his mission. It grieves me that Your Excellency seems to have been taken in by those liars who distort an innocent call for a common national charter into alleged "treason." These men aim to keep our one homeland fragmented, implementing in this a certain policy of which you yourself are aware. In this, they are also at one with certain fanatics in Lebanon. Their purpose is ultimately to undermine Arabism and Islam. It also grieves me that Your Excellency should make a distinction between Syrian unity and the call for the unity of Egypt and Syria. This one homeland cannot survive in its present state of national, political, and economic fragmentation.

If truth is truth at all times and places, then why can we not debate the issue on the basis of open deliberation and the common interests of an unfortunate Arab country? Why should this be detrimental to the Egyptian problem? Our Egyptian brethren are the Arabs who care most for their country's unity. No honest Egyptian would accept the fragmentation of his country into governments and states in the north and south without rising up in arms to safeguard the unity of his homeland.

Our attitude to the Egyptian problem, which we sincerely regard as our own, is no mere propaganda. We consider this to be our duty. As for your objections against Syrian unity, we believe that our general statement and our cordial message to the Syrian President contain an ample refutation. We need only add that a federation and a union, where some regions would enjoy a certain measure of autonomy, are not really open to the sort of objections you have cited. Thus, we hope that the Muslim Brotherhood will come round to our point of view, namely, an exchange of opinions among governments instead of the present campaign of slander. We believe that this is the most equitable solution of the problem. Our call for an open deliberation among Muslims, as is commanded by God, is not in defiance of the Arab League. Indeed, the reverse is true. We have pledged ourselves and all we own for the Arab cause. Having been turned out of our country, we have not been humiliated or brought low, and God Almighty can grant us the victory.

32. The Characteristic Features of Union and Federation[*]

'Abd al-Rahman al-Bazzaz

'Abd al-Rahman al-Bazzaz, a former teacher and ambassador, became prime minister of Iraq in 1965. In the book from which this extract is quoted, al-Bazzaz proposes a union of Arab states under a federal form of government, which he considers the most suitable system for the Arab world.

Having reached this stage in our discussion, we should mention briefly the most important characteristics of these two types of states. Each, undoubtedly, possesses distinctive features and advantages.

In a union, complete harmony is achieved between the members of society, and all differences are, as much as possible, removed. Authority is concentrated in a single body wielding power over all the affairs of state— over questions of higher policy, of sovereignty, of peace and war, or those concerned with internal affairs and ordinary everyday problems, such as public health, culture, the arts, entertainment, municipal affairs, supply, and reconstruction. In a unified state it is highly unlikely, although not impossible, for one region to secede and become independent. This type of government is usually suited to small or medium-sized states where a particular form or organization has been traditionally handed down through the course of many centuries. In some states it might conceivably be the final stage of a long evolution toward total unification.

The federal system, on the other hand, is more suited to vast countries that have different geographical regions, that possess varying political systems, and where the social classes are not in total harmony. Furthermore, the federalism comes nearer to the spirit of our modern age, since it implies specialization. In other words, the federal state concerns itself with the major problems relating to its over-all structure, its foreign policy, its defense, its finance, and its economy in general. Regional governments are left to deal with local or regional problems, such as health, culture, city planning, roads, and other problems that have become increasingly important in modern life. The functions of the present-day state have multiplied in a way that no nineteenth-century thinker would have

[*]Extract from 'Abd al-Rahman al-Bazzaz, *al-Dawla al-muwahhada wal-dawla al-itti-hadiyya* [The Federal State and the Unitary State], 2d., (Cairo: Dar al-'ilm, 1960), pp. 89–94, 99–102.

thought possible. The federal system, too, is appropriate for large nations that have lived under different forms of government and diverse social and economic conditions. It provides a practical solution midway between submission to fragmentation and the idealism calling for "complete fusion and total union."

This was perhaps the intention of the men who framed the national charter in Iraq after World War II. In discussing the political system of the future Arab state, they wrote, "Arab unity is a national necessity, required by their [the Arabs'] very existence, imposed by their will to life, which is the natural right of the Arabs. Arab nationalism considers unity a national objective to be attained through all possible means, such as a federal system which seems a practical step toward this unity."

The Ideal System for the Arab Countries

One might now ask: Which of these two systems is better for the Arab countries? Before giving an answer, we must first define these countries or, rather, think about them realistically.

They stretch across a vast land mass between two great continents. They are made up of regions with very different climates. Some are Mediterranean by location and climate, others are tropical. Some are among the world's mildest and most beautiful spots and resorts. The population, too, of this Arab world varies greatly in culture, economy, and lineage. The inhabitants of seaports like Alexandria, Beirut, and Latakia live differently from those of San'a', Riyadh, Mecca, or Rabat, while the city dwellers of Damascus, Aleppo, and Mosul, with their inherited culture, differ greatly from the Bedouin and the lake [Hor] dwellers in southern Iraq. Among the Arabs there are some who have attained high academic distinction in the greatest universities of the world, while millions of others cannot even write their own names.

Have we carefully considered the actual area of this one homeland in order to judge the best form of government suited to us in this age? Perhaps the following geographical facts may be helpful in elucidating the problem.

The area of the Arab world is more than 4 million square miles, greater than the whole of Europe, including Russia. The area of Switzerland, which is a federation, is less than 16,000 square miles, and the Arab world is 250 times larger.

India, often referred to as a subcontinent, has an area of only 1.25 million square miles; that is, the Arab world is three and a half times larger. In fact, the whole of the United States is a little more than 3 million square miles, about one-third less than the Arab countries.

These figures, I believe, suffice to give us a clear idea of the vast domain of the Arab world, We must, therefore, give serious thought to the question of choosing the right form of government for this great territory.

The countries of the Arab world are, politically speaking, a most curious amalgam. Some are completely independent, others are semi-independent. Some are inferior to colonies in status, others are still protectorates of one state or another, while others are, at least theoretically, constitutional. There are also shaykhdoms, principalities, and so forth.

Our homeland, then, is vast in area, with diverse regions, political systems, and social standards. All this leads us to declare that a federation would be the best form of government for this one people, which still possesses, despite all divergences, the basic constituents of a single nation.

There are also other factors that we must neither ignore nor over-emphasize—as, for example, the presence of ethnic and religious minorities. Therefore, a federal system apears to be the most suited to our needs, especially at the present time. If we add to these considerations the fact that a total union of the whole Arab world would necessitate the destruction of all monarchies and that certain countries, because of their present situation or of the services rendered them by their kings, do not wish to change their status, it becomes perfectly obvious that a federal system is the most practicable solution under the circumstances.

General Principles

I suppose it would be valuable if, at the end of my discussion, I attempt to lay down some general principles to be seriously considered when the federal constitution is drawn up.

1. Emphasis must be placed upon the one Arab nation. This fact is the cornerstone of any general Arab entity to be created. The attempt by certain groups to weaken nationalist sentiment by strengthening local and regional tendencies is the greatest threat to our future entity. It should be clear that when we call for a federation, we are not renouncing faith in our one nation but merely choosing the best governmental system for it under the present circumstances.

2. It must be stressed that choosing any one of the many systems of government is only a means to an end, not the end itself. Our real end is to "achieve the greatest possible measure of prosperity and happiness for the greatest number of Arabs." This prosperity and happiness can be properly and finally achieved only if "a general political entity" is created that unites the Arabs in their various countries, protects them from all internal and external aggression, and seeks to establish social justice. In pursuit of

these goals, we must not be led astray by phraseology and other technicalities of this sort.

3. The world is constantly progressing. It behooves us to choose a system of government which would be capable of renewal and progress. Our laws and institutions must be flexible and must allow for development, avoiding the extremes of rigidity or impetuous change, the latter being resorted to only by men to whom a gradual and reasonable evolutionary progress is denied.

4. When, on the other hand, we call for a comprehensive Arab federation, we do not mean to deny the possibility of the creation of stronger bonds between some regions of the Arab world.

We are here concerned with the whole rather than with the parts. In other words, total union is a very natural and reasonable demand in the case of certain regions of the Arab world. Jordan, for example, is a part of southern Syria that was carved out for well-known purposes, under well-known circumstances. Jordan does not possess the constituent elements either of a state or of a region, in the strict geographical sense. No sensible person can dispute this fact. Indeed, many Western writers have confirmed it. Similarly, Aden and the other protectorates form, undoubtedly, a natural complement to the Yemen. Other principalities of the Arabian Gulf are parts of bordering Arab states, and it would be perfectly natural and reasonable if such regions were to unite.

However, some Arab regions differ very much from others. The Yemen is different from the Najd, while al-Sha'm (Greater Syria) differs from Arab North Africa, even though all these regions are parts of the great Arab homeland, complementing each other and constituting through their conjuction a "complete entity" from the geographical, historical, economic-mercantile, and political points of view.

Furthermore, social or political circumstances may, at a certain period, necessitate the creation of ties between two Arab regions that are stronger than those of a federation. Such a case would be considered an exception to the general rule itself.

5. Our federal system must be a mixture of "idealism" and "realism." Idealism is valuable insofar as it helps us to frame higher principles, which emanate from our existence as a single nation, and to support our view concerning the sublime goals of life. But when idealism is either neglected or overemphasized, it can blind us to reality, turning the good that we desired into an evil, whose consequences are felt, without exception, by everyone.

It may be advantageous to explain these ideas further. When we stress the unifying forces in the Arab nation and their antecedents, we must also not forget the forces making for disunity and their antecedents. To attempt, at the present time, with all the factors making for disunity, to attain complete union, a total merger, would be a rash undertaking. It would be tantamount to denying certain palpable facts, which no reasonable person can possible do.

6. It is futile to tackle our problems emotionally. A certain measure of rationality is necessary, but our rationality must not be so predominant as to render us overcautious and, perhaps, cowardly. We must remember that for many centuries we have lived in subjection to several foreign powers: the Turks, the Persians, the British, the French, the Italians, the Spanish, and the Portuguese. These nations have, at different times, occupied various parts of our homeland. They have handed down to us, willy-nilly, particular conditions and have created among us dissensions and differences.

We have living among us today ethnic and religious minorities, with some of whom no merger is possible, while with others we are linked by national or religious ties. Some time must elapse before we can succeed in proving our good faith to them and consolidating our own power. Evolution is the *sine qua non* of politics.

Therefore, despite the fact that federation seems to be the final and ultimate answer for some of us, according to others, it is only a reasonable step forward in our progress.

33.   A View of Arab Unity*

Nabih Amin Faris

Nabih Amin Faris (1906–72), a former curator of Arabic manuscripts at Princeton University (1937–42) and head of the Arab Desk, U.S. Office of War Information (1942–45), returned to Lebanon to become professor of Arab history in the American University of Beirut. He has written more than a dozen books on various aspects of Arab culture and history, including al-'Arab al-ahya [The Living Arabs] *(Beirut: Dar al-'ilm lil-malayin, 1947) and Min al-zawiya al-'arabiyya* [From the Arab Viewpoint] *(Beirut: Dar Bairut lil-tab', 1953). His careful examination in these works of the historical, political, and cultural foundations of Arab nationalism has gained for him a leading position in the movement for Arab unity.*

In the following extract, Faris presents the background of the Arab nationalist movement and, on the basis of its history, proposes a federation as the best way to secure Arab unity.

*Extract from Nabih Amin Faris, *Dirasat 'arabiyya* [Arab Studies] (Beirut: Dar al-'ilm lil-malayin, 1957), pp. 104–11.

Arab unity is a dream long pursued by the Arab elite, which has striven with enthusiasm and conviction to achieve it. But the pursuit has met with many obstacles, some of which were the work of imperialists, while others are believed to be the responsibility of the Arabs themselves, with their social, economic, and political circumstances. Still others were caused by a combination of all these factors.

The origins of Arab nationalism have deep historical roots. Nationalism itself appeared as an effective force during the caliphate of 'Umar and, to a certain extent, during the Umayyad caliphate, especially in the period preceding what are called the "reforms of 'Umar ibn 'Abd al-Aziz," which attempted to reconcile the Arab and Islamic ideas. As a result of these "reforms," the emphasis shifted to Islam, and the Arab element no longer had the upper hand in running the affairs of state. Islamic and non-Arab elements began to affect administration. Thereafter, the Islamic idea dominated the affairs of the caliphate and was exploited by princes and sultans for purposes of domination in the name of religion. Were it not for this religious element, the Arabs would not have acquiesced, as they did in most cases, in the rule of the Buwayhids, the Seljuqs, the Mamluks, and, finally, in four centuries of Ottoman hegemony.

In fact, despite its ancient origins and its appearance in various social, political, and ideological forms at various periods, Arab nationalism did not crystallize until after the proclamation of the Ottoman constitution of 1908 and the emergence and activities of the Eurasian movement, represented in the Society for Union and Progress [*Jam 'iyyat al-ittihad wal-taraqi*]. To a great extent, therefore, the Arab idea was a reaction against Turanianism, which attempted to "Turkify" all national groups within the Ottoman Empire. To a lesser extent, the Arab idea attempted to underline nationalistic elements and to withhold its support of the Islamic idea as expounded by the advocates of the Islamic League [*al-Jam 'iyya al-islamiyya*]. The various secret societies fostered an Arab spirit and called for a renaissance that would restore Arab glory and the right of the Arabs to the caliphate, which was usurped by the Ottomans. Nevertheless, certain secret societies and quite a number of those working for the Arab cause were, even at that time, toying with the idea of a dualistic Ottoman state, including both Arabs and Turks.

World War I broke out, and the great Arab revolt began. This revolt did not possess the necessary prerequisites for success and did not win the support and adherence of a strong and conscious Arab public opinion. It was weak and soon became even weaker as a result of the rivalries of Arab families, the plots of imperialists, and the weakness of its popular base. But in recent Arab nationalist history, it remains the great Arab revolt not because of the success it achieved, but because it was a symbol: It was the first revolt against the caliph that aimed at Arab unity and in which the sharif of Mecca, the descendant of the Arab Prophet, rose up in arms against a foreign caliph for the sake of Arab nationalistm.

Before this Arab movement had time to achieve liberation and unity, or even to grow stronger and organize the countries of the Fertile Crescent, it was stricken with the loss of a number of its ablest supporters, who were executed by the Turks. Later on, it was faced with a rival created by the imperialist powers in the settlements that followed the war, by which the countries supporting the Arab movement were divided into artificial states and principalities. This fragmentation led, as a matter of course, to the emergence of regional movements directed against liberation from imperialism. The Pan-Arab movement was thus reduced to narrow regional ideologies, and the sentiment for unity was shattered. The imperialists had totally isolated the Arab countries from each other, creating artificial frontiers, entities, and governments. Each Arab region was thereafter politically isolated, and economic and cultural life was diversified. In each area, a ruling class arose whose interest it was to preserve this regionalism and independence in order to continue its authority and influence. Consciously or otherwise, these ruling classes fostered regional consciousness. This tendency was strengthened and supported by elements that were concerned with keeping the Arab countries fragmented and by others that sincerely believed that such regionalism was in fact realistic and truly reflected the historical nature of each region and its inhabitants. Thus, the process of "Balkanizing" the Arab world was completed and consummated in the Charter of the Arab League.

But the ideal of Arab unity still enjoys the allegiance of an elite, which sees it not solely as the realization of a dream but as the best means for coping with the turbulent Arab scene, for making the Arabs freely contribute to history, and for securing them a place in the progress of civilization. And this, in spite of the fact that the obstacles in the path of unity are far more formidable at present than they were at the turn of the century. At that time, the ideal of unity was at least comprehensive, despite its opacity. Today, it is no longer comprehensive and must, in addition to facing the imperialists and Israel, meet opposition from the interested parties entrenched in every Arab political entity: kingdoms, republics, shaykhdoms, and so on. These obstacles render the realization of Pan-Arab unity a remote prospect. There can be no way out except by violence or by federation. An Arab country may be able to play a role similar to the one played by Prussia in forging German unity, if international circumstances are favorable. But a unity forged by violence can also be dissolved by violence, and this may lead to consequences that can turn the Arab problem back to where it was a hundred years ago.

The only avenue open to the Arabs now, if they wish to overcome most of the practical difficulties in the way in unity, is a federal union. Federation may, in the end, prove to be the best means for unity.

In order to secure as successful a federation as possible, we must take into account the present Arab scene with all its drawbacks and must bear in mind and work to strengthen the very important underlying cultural and economic influences upon unity or federation.

The Arab world is made up of two groups of lands, in Asia and in Africa. The Asian Arab lands are divided into three main regions: the valley of the Tigris and Euphrates, natural Syria, and the Arabian Peninsula. The African Arab lands are divided into two main regions: the Nile Valley and the countries of the Maghrib. All these regions constitute natural geographical and economic units, and the social conditions prevalent in these regions are very similar. Their historical legacy is, to a great extent, a common one. It is not, therefore, unreasonable if we advocate a political union of the regions of each of these lands to complement their geographical, economic, and historical unity. A federal union can thereafter be created from among these smaller units, and a United Arab States could emerge.

As regards these smaller political unities, I would suggest the following:

1. The Fertile Crescent. This would include the first and second regions, that is, the Tigris and Euphrates valleys (including Kuwait) plus natural Syria. The geographical, economic, and historical links binding them, together with their almost identical social and cultural levels, necessitate such a division. This unit would include Iraq, Syria, Jordan, and Palestine, after the last has been liberated. It is advisable that Lebanon should be excluded for reasons that I shall later expound.

2. The Arabian Peninsula. This would include Sa'udi Arabia, the Yemen, and those forgotton shaykhdoms, like Bahrain, Qatar, the Trucial Coast shaykhdoms [today United Arab emirates], the sultanates of Muscat and Oman, the Aden Protectorate, and the Crown Colony of Aden [South Yemen].

3. The Nile Valley. This would include Egypt, Sudan, and Libya, which is only an extension of the western Egyptian Desert on the one side and of Tunisia on the other. But the requirements of the present situation oblige us to treat this area on the basis of the present political setup.

4. The Maghrib. This would include Morocco, Algeria, and Tunisia.

The Arab world stands at the threshold of events of momentous importance. The centuries-old imperialist sway has begun to wane while the responsibilities engendered by independence are many in number and of grave importance. The Arabs will not be able to meet the challenge of the modern world of progress unless they stand united politically and economically. Reason dictates solidarity and unity.

Before I bring my arguments to a close, I would like to turn to Lebanon and to my reasons for wishing to exclude it at present from unity. I do this not because Lebanon has been tardy in working for the Arab cause; indeed, since the dawn of the modern Arab awakening, Lebanon has worked in the forefront of those who struggled for Arabism. Its contribution to the revival of Arabic poetry, literature, science, and the Arab spirit has been of major importance. Lebanon is of the very core of Arabism geographically, economically, and culturally. When national consciousness is firmly established among the Arabs, we shall find Lebanon to be the cornerstone of the Arab structure. Therefore, one must not impose upon Lebanon any solution that it does not wish to accept of its own free will.

On July 9, 1946, I openly advocated the creation of a United Arab States. Today, ten years later, I believe that the setbacks suffered by the Arab world would not have taken place if it had been united. Calamities will cease only with federation. A United Arab States is the ideal means toward achieving Arab unity, which has been and still is the Arabs' ultimate hope.

34.   Ideological Problems in the Arab World as Seen by Its Leaders*

All Arab leaders have issued ideological declarations at one time or another. Some were intended for domestic consumption, some were designed to stress or reject a particular viewpoint. Seldom were ideological positions stated frankly and confronted with the views held by others. A unique opportunity to look into the actual beliefs of Arab leaders was provided by the unity talks held in Cairo in March 1963. The discussions continued in April, after the Iraqi delegation joined the talks. The result was a tripartite declaration issued on April 17, 1963.

The participants in the discussion included some of the leaders and chief ideologists of the Arab world, such as Egyptian President Nasser; Michel 'Aflaq and Salah al-Din Bitar, the founders and philosophers of the Ba'th; Luai Atasi, a general and chairman of the Revolutionary Council of Syria; Hani Hindi, then minister of planning and later leader of the pro-Nasser Syrian Arab Nationalist Movement; 'Abd al-Rahman al-Bazzaz, then

*Extracts from Walid Khalidi and Yusuf Ibish, eds., *Arab Political Documents, 1963* (Beirut: Slim Press, 1964), pp. 120–23, 136–38, 143–45, 147–56. The spelling of names in the original text has been adapted. Reproduced by permission.

the Iraqi ambassador in Cairo and later premier, well-known writer on Arab nationalism; several members of the Egyptian Presidential Council, notably Premier 'Ali Sabri, Marshal 'Amir, and Col. Kamal Rifa'at; and other political personalities. Membership in the discussion committee alternated considerably.

The discussions were held in secret, but when the Ba'thists repressed the Nasserites in Syria and Iraq several months later, the Egyptian government published the minutes first in al-Ahram and then in a special volume, Mahadir jalsat mubahathat al-wahda [*Minutes of Discussions on Unity*] *(Cairo: Dar al-qawmiyya lil-tab'a wal-nashr, 1963). A selected English translation of the minutes appears in* Arab Political Documents, 1963 *(Beirut: Slim Press, 1964). For the Ba'th view on the talks, see Riad Taha,* Mahadir muhadathat al-wahda [*Records of Unity Talks*] *(Beirut: Dar al-kifah, 1963). For a lengthy analysis of Arab foreign policy, based on unity talk records, see Malcolm H. Kerr,* The Arab Cold War, 1958–1964: A Study of Ideology in Politics *(London: Oxford University Press, 1965).*

'AFLAQ: . . . By freedom, do you mean democracy or liberation?

NASSER: As we understand it and as it is found in the [National] Charter [of Egypt], freedom means a free country and a free citizen. The Charter explains this in great detail and perfectly clearly. Socialism, again, implies sufficiency and justice and the Charter also defines these two terms very fully. Unity is a popular, historical, and actual will, and the Charter devotes a whole chapter to constitutional unity in all its forms. The socialist path is defined, beginning with internal trade and ending with the popular control over the means of production, passing through agriculture, the private sector, and the public sector. All national activity is fully defined in the Charter.

'AFLAQ: The slogan of the Arab Nationalist Movement is Unity, Liberation, and Socialism. There, freedom means liberation.

NASSER: Naturally, for we have to liberate ourselves from the domination of feudalism and capital.

'AFLAQ: Not quite. Liberation there implies liberation from imperialism.

NASSER: When the revolution broke out in 1952, we had our six well-known principles: the destruction of feudalism, and of exploitation and the domination of capital, and the creation of a strong army, social justice, and a proper democratic life. We began to implement these principles from the very first day. Last year, we promulgated our Charter, in which is contained a detailed exposé of all these principles. What is implied there by the freedom of the individual? We maintained that this freedom entails total freedom for the people and its denial to enemies of the people. In order to buttress this freedom, we spoke of self-criticism, of the freedom of the press, and of all popular organizations. We linked the election ticket to the loaf of bread; in other words, socialism is a prerequisite of freedom. We also advocated that democracy, socialism, and freedom are interdependent. Now then, how does the Ba'th define democracy?

'AFLAQ: In fact, I believe that you do not lack a definition of democracy and socialism but I have observed that, sometimes, socialism has taken the place of democracy.

NASSER: Have you read the Charter?

'AFLAQ: Yes.

NASSER: Then it appears that you were reading one line and skipping the next. It is not at all what you imagine. Our revolution was the first to call for social democracy, meaning that political [democracy] was inconceivable without social democracy. This fact led us to socialism and to the inevitability of socialism as a prerequisite for true democracy. Otherwise, democracy would have become the dictatorship of capitalism and feudalism. This is what is generally termed bourgeois democracy. But there was never any mention of socialism taking the place of democracy. What I said was that socialism was necessary for democracy, in order to avoid exploitation. . . .

We got rid of feudalism and capitalism and all foreign concerns were nationalized. In this, we acted as the vanguard of the working people, who now rule in Egypt. We do not govern in the interest of a class but of the coalition of workers, peasants, and intellectuals and, indeed, of the whole working people. In this way, our policy is other than what you imagine. France, for example, which is a capitalist country, might institute nationalization but this would only be in the interests of the capitalist government. Here, however, it is the working people who rule the land and its task is to abolish class differences. In the public sector, we have implemented democracy by specifying that a certain ratio of workers should be present on the boards of management of the companies. Now, the ratio is two workers out of seven board members and we plan to increase this proportion until only one member will be an appointment.

Then, we come to face the eternal problem of all socialist countries: bureaucracy. This goes hand in hand with socialism. We have already proffered a solution: association of the workers in the board of management and a share of the profits. For example, when the workers are getting 25 per cent of the profits, their representative on the board may, let us say, object to the unnecessary purchase of a car for the board since this might directly affect the profits. This has actually happened in some companies.

Then again, we have organized trade unions and the Socialist Union°

°The U.A.R. government-supported political organization.

within a factory. If any flaw is detected, the union in question will inform the General Union of Labor whose duty it will be to inform the minister of labor. The Committee of the Socialist Union will similarly inform the Higher Council and in this manner the people's wealth will not be squandered. This procedure is entirely democratic and, as a result, there has been a rise in production and the worker now feels that he is his own master and that he owns the factory.

SABRI: Workers nowadays are more careful about their factory's machines than was the owner in the old days.

NASSER: The next point, which complements the socialist setup, is the fixing of wages. Our law states that £5,000 is the maximum wage—not, by the way, the maximum income. Hence, the rest is all profit. We also fixed a minimum wage for workers. In the past, this was 15 piasters a day. Now it is 25. We also fixed the wages for overtime and the social relations within the factory. Now, certain workers are receiving very substantial wages. We also specified bonuses. What all this adds up to is that all the people now share in production. Our experiment is not really the same as the Yugoslav one. We have studied this latter, together with the Russian, the Chinese, and the Indian practice. We also invite certain experts in socialist economy and discuss matters with them. The last one was here two weeks, Professor Petelheim, professor of planning at the Sorbonne. He is regularly consulted by the Russians, the Yugoslavs, the Indians, and the Algerians. Baghdadi, Sabri, and I met him and he told us about what he saw here and there. Petelheim's view, for example, was that our own experiment was unique and very advanced.

It seems that your [i.e., 'Aflaq's] impression of our experiment is very sketchy. One of you said yesterday that our experiment "could be termed" socialist. It is not that at all. It is in fact socialist and built upon a revolution which has destroyed the alliance of feudalism and capitalism and has given all power to the working people. It has also radically altered social relationships and has ended all foreign exploitation by nationalization. We were not content simply to drive the British out and "Arabize" our economy; we also obtained complete control of it. For your information, Mr. 'Aflaq, the consensus of opinion among world economists was that such a process of socialist transformation was inconceivable within ten years, especially as we had begun this only in 1956. In 1952, we were simply army officers, who knew nothing more than military strategy. Our meetings then with traditional economists only made things more complicated, since they could not discover a solution. But after that we launched into this process, having honestly and conscientiously attempted to learn. Please don't forget that your present slogan, "No Socialism without Socialists," was the one we launched in 1961, prior to the July, 1961, socialist decrees.

BITAR: Socialism is to be protected by socialists. What we want to arrive at is government by the people.

NASSER: Fine. We are prepared to have immediate elections and let the people govern. But we should like to know what you mean by "the people."

'AFLAQ: The workers, of course.

NASSER: Who else?

'AFLAQ: The working people, i.e., the peasants and workers, who are in the [Ba'th] Party.

NASSER: But do you fancy that government by the people, even though you have elections, is merely a few people sitting in a room and deciding affairs? You are mistaken, for then you would have isolated the whole people and ruled as a tiny minority. . . . Political stability can never come about in Syria unless all banks and insurance companies are nationalized. Otherwise, capitalism will be ruling Syria and your government will be a façade.

'AMIR: We believe that Syria is ruled by big business.

NASSER: If we ask ourselves how we can achieve political stability, we soon realize that this can only be through making the banks run the country, especially in Syria. They can give loans to, say, Khalid al-'Azm and deny them to a small merchant in the market [*suq al-hamidiyya*]. The banks, being the wealth of the country, must not be controlled by Reaction—otherwise your socialism will be meaningless. Banks, and thus the nation's wealth, must pass into the hands of the people. . . .

What I am trying to say is that there are no ideological or methodological differences between us. I do not remember any such ideological conflict during the Union except that, during the Union, you asked that all newspapers should be suppressed in Syria and I refused. However, our sole conflict arose over one issue, which you then called partnership. You asked that a committee be formed of three Syrians and three Egyptians which would run the Union. These three Syrians were to be Bitar, 'Aflaq, and [Akram] Hawrani. But what about all the other nationalist groups in Syria? This, I maintain, was our main difference by reason of which you all tendered your resignation—a resignation which, I repeat, amounted to not merely a withdrawal from the government but to a conscious blow against the Union. I have already stated that this step helped the cause of secession. No genuine unionist could have tendered a collective resignation and engaged in such party maneuvers. Now, then, on what basis are we going to cooperate in the future? If party tactics are to be the order of the day, then, I regretfully deline!

BITAR: But I have told Your Excellency that we only resigned a year after you yourself had, to all intents and purposes, dismissed us.

NASSER: That is a matter of opinion. . . .

[The following excerpt from the meeting that took place on the afternoon of April 7, 1963—a meeting at which only the Egyptian and Syrian delegations were present—relates to the basic point of disagreement between Nasser and the Ba'thists—a disagreement about the structure of the proposed union and the role of political organizations—and to Nasser's criticism of Ba'thist philosophy, expressed in the slogan Unity, Freedom, and Socialism.]

NASSER: . . . I fully agree with Mr. Atasi that genuine national unity in each country must precede the creation of a federal union. Otherwise, we should be leaving ourselves to deal with endless problems and headaches within a union. Furthermore, I believe that political unity must subsist concurrently with or precede a constitutional union. Otherwise, we should have, in each country, various antagonistic political groups. These groups would not be able to meet together without such a political unity. The business of government would then become one of coalition. In such circumstances, it would be better to have contractual government or confederation. Such a contractual government is of course a simple and clear state of affairs. But if we create a federation, with one organization here, two or more in Syria, two or more in Iraq, we should all add up to a collection of six or seven diametrically opposed groups. Each one would then plan its own programs and we should therefore meet with two obstacles: The first would be regionalism. We simply must take this into account in our union, for one of our mistakes in 1958 was our attempt to do away with regionalism. We repeated the slogan of "No Regionalism" which we had, in fact, taken over from you without pondering it too long. In point of fact, this regionalism exists and will make itself felt when we come to create the union. If we take it into account, we can then proceed to solve the problems it creates, but this takes some degree of patient work.

The second obstacle or danger in the union would be the conflict or the clash and competition between parties or groups. Each would attempt to win over the maximum numbers of people to its side and this might make party officials oblivious of the interests of the union as a whole. They might consider that their aim would be to win support for their party to assume office. The solution of this problem lies, to my mind, in the national unity of the regions and then in the union itself. This implies the unity of political action on two levels. How, then, are we to achieve this national unity? For this to come about, there must be a unity of aims, and this, I think, generally speaking, exists. On broad matters of principle I see no differences but there will be in matters of implementation. It follows that there must be something, call it a charter or program, that will embody our common notions concerning the principles upon which we are agreed. For instance, what do we mean by freedom? Or socialism? If these are empty slogans, they will lead to opportunism. The worst fault of political parties is slogans. Their implementation is often left vague. This *laissez-faire* attitude could lead to the assumption of power by a small minority, usually those with financial interests. Thus, before we sign the constitution of the union, we must draft a charter in which we lay down the broad outlines of our joint political endeavor. This is a safeguard to the union. . . . What do we mean when we say "Unity, Freedom, and Socialism"? How does unity relate to the Arab world, for instance? President al-Sallal [of the Yemen] sent me a telegram proposing to come last Friday and I replied by saying that his arrival would embarrass me a great deal since we still had problems to solve and his arrival might therefore be interpreted as an attempt to create a sort of Cairo-San'a' axis within the union to face a Baghdad-Damascus axis. Had he come last Friday, this possibility would obviously have occurred to some of you. Thus, I asked him to delay his arrival until after an agreement on union had been reached. He could then act freely in any manner he pleased. What, then, do we mean by unity? Perhaps our answer to this question will be the simplest of all. What do we mean by socialism and freedom? In a future union, I could not possibly claim that our own eleven-year-old socialism should be put into effect in Syria in so many hours. However, it is well known that socialism aims to do such and such and must therefore progress along certain lines.

Then again, what do we mean by freedom? Are we simply to be satisfied with current definitions throughout the world or should we not rather specify in a written charter what this implies, how it is to be practiced, and who is entitled to it?

Having done this, the rest—and I mean here the constitution—will be easy. This latter we can then agree upon, provided, of course, that mutual trust exists. Do you agree to all this? . . .

ZUHUR: There are, in fact, two stages. The first will be to create a Unionist Front in Syria and the second the merger of popular organizations within one charter and one internal organization. But, meanwhile, where do we stand? In other words, how are we, as separate states, to coordinate our efforts?

NASSER: I believe that, as states, we must also begin to create a front. In other words, one common front will then link our front here, yours in Syria, and also the one in Iraq. . . .

BITAR: Your Excellency, we seem to agree that drafting the political framework of the union is our simplest task, seeing that we have interpreted the unity of these three states to mean a federal union. Your Excellency's recognition of regionalism, not necessarily as an anti-Arab sentiment, but as the legacy of long historical separation, is a valid one. Federal union, in my opinion, is to be based on the fact that we are one nation and that one day we shall all constitute one state. But within this single state, we must not refuse to recognize the existence of various regions, a situation which, I repeat, is not antithetical to Arab nationalism. Other federal unions throughout the world have clearly shown that such a setup is both constructive and useful. The most important difference between our union and others, such as the Indian or West German or Italian, is that ours is revolutionary, not evolutionary. If left to themselves, Egypt and Syria would remain separate. But circumstances have bred national revolutions which seem to render their merger inevitable. The proof of the revolutionary spirit of any Arab revolution lies in its unfolding, day by day, the genuine Arab character of each country. . . . Constructive criticism cannot destroy unionist forces within each of the three countries; any political union between them would be a mere formality. I can therefore say that when we departed, on March 21, our intentions were of the best. The article "More Royalist than the King" in no way justifies such a campaign against our party. *Al-Ahram* claims that our intent was malicious. Very well, then, let us talk about this. Good and bad intentions are very personal and psychological concerns. How, then, can we objectively plan away such subjective legacies of the past? Our newspaper may perhaps tomorrow publish an article which we may or may not have scanned beforehand and which produces an adverse reaction here. Let us also suppose that this article is erroneous. The reaction to it should be in the form of constructive criticism. In any case, such errors can never be said to be the result of malice or of good intentions unless we constantly meet together and form some kind of body to deal with such problems. As far as the [Ba'th] Party is concerned, *al-Ahram's* interpretation of the incident has been false and illusory. The fact that *Le Figaro*, for example, prints someone's statement does not make that statement true. We all know what journalists are like. It is said that our article was never disaffirmed, but I say that we have never seen it in the first place. . . .

35. The Saudi Era

Muhammad Hasanayn Haykal

The spectacular rise to power of Abd al-Aziz Abd al-Rahman, or ibn Saud, in Arabia at the beginning of the twentieth century was barely noticed except by some few specialists. Ibn Saud was born in Riyadh in 1880; in 1902 he took back his town from the Rashidis, who had driven his family away. He soon won the loyalty of tribes in Central Arabia. In 1924 and 1926 he defeated Sherif Hussein and took the Hijaz, together with Mecca and Medina, the two holy Muslim cities. By 1932, Saudi Arabia had become a kingdom, and the ruler, content with his conquests, made peace with his neighbors, including Yemen, whose Zayidi Shiite population opposed the fundamentalist Hanbali doctrine of the Saudis. By 1936 the Saudis had concluded an oil exploration agreement with the United States; in 1938 oil was struck at Dahran. The oil royalties at the time amounted to an annual rent of $25,000, plus $5 for every five long tons (2,240 pounds) and some small loans. The need for oil during World War II brought increased Saudi oil output; this reached 1.3 million barrels per day in 1960 and 3.8 million barrels by 1970. Master of more than one-fourth of the world's proven oil reserves, the Saudis saw their oil revenues skyrocket in 1973 after oil prices registered a sharp rise. By late 1980 the Saudis were producing over 9 million barrels of oil a day, with an annual value of more than $100 billion. The per capita income of the Saudi population—consisting of 5 to 7 million people both settled and nomadic—reached incredible heights and caused a sharp change not only in living standards but also in the values and attitudes of a people accustomed to austere living. The reaction to this change was evidenced by the capture of the central mosque in Mecca by a group protesting in the name of Islamic fundamentalism the customs and mores of the urban dwellers.

Saudi Arabia became overnight an influential member of the world financial community and a powerful new force in Arab and Muslim affairs. The custody of the holy Muslim sites gave the Saudis a commanding position symbolically in the eyes of the average Muslim, while the oil income enabled them to back their policies with money. The government philosophy of the Saudis is based on an ideology that draws its essence from fundamentalist Hanbali doctrines and the late eighteenth-century Wahhabi revivalist-fundamentalist movement of Muhammad 'Abd al-Wahhab. This has been discussed by Ahmad Muhammad Gamal (a professor of Muslim culture at the King Abdul Aziz University in Jedda) in Ala ma'idah al-Qur'an, din wa dawla [On the Relation of the Koran, Religion and State] (Beirut: Dar al-kitab al-lubnaniyyah, 1973).

The fact that Saudi Arabia is a huge country with a sparse population and a relatively small army makes her vulnerable to attack and covetous ambition of her neighbors and the big powers. Consequently, the Saudis have to bolster their defense by seeking the military protection of the United States, to which they export a large amount of oil at a special price, while at the same time using their money to dampen rivalries in the Middle East and to placate their ideological enemies, such as the Syrians and the PLO. Saudi relations with Libya were severed recently due to the latter's attack on Saudi Islamic doctrine and practices.

Saudi Arabia expects oil revenues in 1981 to reach $123.5 billion, while assets abroad should come to $145 billion, most of these tied to the dollar. The government has launched a five-year development plan calling for $250 billion in investments, plus an expenditure of $105 billion for the armed *forces. Lack of population and skills has forced the Saudis to employ about 2 million foreign laborers and technicians from Yemen, Egypt, Sudan, South Korea, the Philippines, Palestine, and other countries. These workers are predominantly Muslims and perform a variety of functions, thus creating a two-tier society of rich native employers and dependent working outsiders. Alarmed by the growth in the number of outsiders, the Saudis have initiated a training program so as to employ as many natives as possible and to induce some 500,000 Bedouins to settle in cities. Yet the sparse settlement patterns and the low literacy rate (15 percent in 1980) make inevitable the employment of additional foreigners. Saudi society has been changed by the influx of money more rapidly and deeply than the leaders have wished. To counteract the effects of change, the Saudis have striven to maintain the Islamic identity of the country by consulting frequently with religious leaders and have attempted to distribute the oil wealth beyond the 11,000 princes and princesses and other leading families. The Saudi policies, despite their claim to conform to Islamic precepts, raise serious questions. Muslims are strictly forbidden to naturalize, except a few people with special skills, although immigration in Islam is free and the idea of "citizenship"—a secular innovation—is alien. The accumulation of Saudi money in foreign banks and the huge investments in a variety of projects of secondary import while the rest of the Muslim world is poverty stricken has aroused a variety of criticisms. Yet the stability of Saudi Arabia is now considered a necessary condition for the stability of the entire Middle East and Gulf area. Thus the Saudi government faces the difficult task of maintaining a peaceful course of interior change—including industrialization and settlement of Bedouins— while at the same time preserving stability in the region.*

Saudi Arabia's rise as a financial and political power as well as the complex problems she has encountered have been duly noticed. The following extract from an article by Muhammad Hasanayn Haykal, a former close associate of Nasser and one of the best-known journalists in the Arab world, represents an Arab view of Saudi involvement in world politics. The excerpts of Haykal's article, which appeared originally in al-Anwar *(Beirut) on May 23, 1977, are taken from the* Journal of Palestine Studies *6, no. 2 (Summer 1977): 158–63 passim. It was written just prior to Amir Fahd's trip to Washington in 1976 to meet President Carter and to the fall of Iran's shah. For background, see David Howarth.* The Desert King *(New York: McGraw Hill, 1964); David Finnie,* Desert Enterprise *(Cambridge, Mass.: Harvard University Press, 1958); Sheik Rustum Ali,* Saudi Arabia and Oil Diplomacy *(New York: Praeger, 1976); and* Area Handbook for Saudi Arabia *(published by the American University, 1978). A good discussion of Saudi Islamic ideology is to be found in Vincenzo Strika, "Ideologia e madih politico in Arabia Saudiana,"* Annali *339, n.s. 29 (1979): 197–218, published by the Oriental Institute in Naples.*

The heart of the matter is that Saudi Arabia with its immense revenues and the major role it performs at the present stage—the Saudi era in contemporary Arab history—and with the values it represents and advocates, is not an ordinary state. Therefore its political self-expression is bound at times to be involved and very complex . . . .

I shall try to explain some of this in the following points, so as to make what I want to say clearer. Let me start by explaining what I mean when I say "simple" and "complex" political expressions. If we try to express Saudi policy in simple terms, we can say the following:

Saudi Arabia wants to reach a solution—any solution—of the Middle East crisis, because this will save her innumerable problems and intolerable burdens.

As regards the problems, continued armed conflict, which is the alternative to a solution of the Middle East conflict, would help to reinforce political and social interactions which would give the forces of the left in the Arab world greater opportunities. Moreover, armed conflict would impose the need for armaments capable of confronting Israeli armaments. This means the possibility of returning to the USSR as a source of arms. And Saudi Arabia wants none of these things, for political and social reasons. As for the burdens, continued armed conflict—which is the alternative to a solution—in the Middle East crisis would require Saudi Arabia to respond to innumerable demands. Saudi Arabia could neither reject them or scale them down; if it did it would get itself into a situation that is morally—and politically—intolerable. Therefore the policy of reaching a solution—any solution—of the Middle East crisis can be an expression in simple terms of Saudi Arabia's strategy for the avoidance of problems and burdens. But the fact is that simple expressions give a superficial view of things. For Saudi Arabia cannot accept a solution—any solution—of the Middle East crisis. What I mean is that Saudi Arabia can only accept a peaceful solution of the crisis. But it can probably accept only solutions which are the most inflexible in their support of Arab rights. This is enjoined not by any political choice in Saudi Arabia, but by the legitimacy of the Saudi regime.

Why is this? I propose to deal in detail with the various kinds of legitimacy to be found in the world today so that, to the extent that they are applicable to Saudi Arabia, we may understand what options are open to it, or rather imposed on it.

In the world today there are three kinds of legitimacy. First, there is traditional legitimacy, based on tribal or religious chieftainship. This is the oldest kind of legitimacy in the history of human evolution. Then there is the legitimacy of the one man. This is the legitimacy of periods of transition, when the role of the chief, commander or leader is the basis of legitimacy. It generally depends on what practical achievements the chief, commander or leader is able to bring about for his people, which persuade them to follow him on the basis of his ability to embody and realize their aspirations. Finally, there is constitutional legitimacy, affirmed and established in a society which has passed through the stages of traditional legitimacy and the legitimacy of the one man and developed to the stage where the authority of the state can be based on genuine institutions depending on economic and social forces capable of exerting free, independent and balanced political influence.

The legitimacy of Saudi Arabia, for example, has always been of the first kind—traditional legitimacy. Gamal Abdul-Nasser's legitimacy was of the second kind—the legitimacy of the one man. Many different examples of the third kind of legitimacy—constitutional legitimacy—are to be found in the advanced industrial world, both in the West and the East—in Britain, for example.

However, as I am concerned with Saudi Arabia in this article, I intend to go into traditional legitimacy in greater detail. As I said, traditional legitimacy is based on the tribal or religious chieftainships. These are symbols of sets of values and relationships; they are concerned with heritage, traditions and things sacred, and it is from this concern that they derive their power and their right to rule as the highest authority in society. This truth has always been perceptible in the policy of Saudi Arabia as the result of an appreciation, if only instinctive, that the basis of power is this concern for heritage, traditions and things sacred.

King Abdul-Aziz ibn Saud, the founder of the kingdom, was a man of extraordinary innate intelligence, and it was this intelligence that enabled him to see clearly that the legitimacy of his regime lay in its ability to protect the Islamic holy places, not only in Mecca and Medina, but also in Palestine. The records of the meeting of the King with the American President Franklin Roosevelt on board an American warship in Lake Timsah in 1945 are to be found in a series of documents published by the U.S. State Department. It is not going too far to claim that this record shows that Abdul-Aziz was the first Arab politician to adopt an unshakable attitude on the Palestine problem. This attitude was not merely a matter of sympathy with the Palestinian people—it went further than that. It showed clearly that the King realized that the legitimacy of his whole regime was linked to the situation in the Islamic world and its holy places.

This was also King Faisal's attitude. His insistence on the Arab character of Jerusalem found expression in his famous words to Henry Kissinger and other world political figures he met. I want to pray in Jerusalem before I die. The future of Jerusalem was central to all King Faisal's thinking, and I think that he too realized that the legitimacy of the Saudi regime was inseparable from the Islamic holy places. In this connection let me recall two incidents: I recall a three hour talk between

King Faisal and myself in the Palestine Hotel in Alexandria in 1970, during which the King said:

"Resolution No. 242 on the solution of the Middle East crisis may be enough for others. But as far as Saudi Arabia is concerned, what are we in the sight of the Muslims, and before them in the sight of God, without the liberation of Palestine and the restoration of the Arab character of Jerusalem?"

I also recall a recent talk between myself and Mr. Yasser Arafat, the head of the PLO. Yasser Arafat was telling me that he believed that the assassination of King Faisal was the result of a successful conspiracy. He said: "King Faisal, especially towards the end of his life, saw very clearly the importance of Jerusalem and the absolute necessity of its recovery. This is why they got rid of him. The King was a martyr to his insistence on the recovery of Jerusalem."

Regardless of what actually happened and of conspiracies, if any, the above provide clear indications that the Saudi regime is well aware of the facts as regards the basis of its legitimacy. . . .

In practical terms, this awareness means that Saudi Arabia cannot accept just any solution of the Middle East crisis, and that a solution it can accept must maintain the Arab character of Jerusalem. Thus the political expression of Saudi Arabian strategy becomes complex, rather than simple. According to the simple expression, Saudi Arabia may want a solution—any solution. According to the complex expression, Saudi Arabia can only accept a solution that comes into collision with the most complicated point in the Arab-Israeli conflict—Jerusalem. The simple expression may save Saudi Arabia certain problems and burdens.

But only the complex expression can be in keeping and in harmony with the legitimacy of the Saudi regime. It may be argued that Saudi Arabia does not need to make this difficult choice, as it will not be a party to any negotiations in Geneva or elsewhere, and if another party accepts less than the required minimum, that party, and not Saudi Arabia, will be responsible. But the facts of the Arab situation tell another story: Saudi Arabia may not be one of the Arab negotiators, but it is the main guarantor of most of the Arab negotiators, so that it will sustain part of the losses, if there are any.

I now come to another illustration of the fact that Saudi Arabia cannot express itself politically in simple terms, but is sometimes obliged to use complex and extremely complicated ones. If, for example, Saudi Arabia chooses to express its policy in simple terms, it can assume that the United States' pressing need for Saudi Arabia's revenue and wealth and the roles it can play mean that the negotiations between it and the U.S. will be just a picnic—all it has to do is to ask and all the U.S. has to do is to respond. But this is not true, for something bigger and more serious than this is involved.

The dangers to which any country is exposed are in exact proportion to the extent of the vested interests of others in it, especially if the balance of power is in favour of those who have such interests. Let us pause for a moment and consider the details of the overall picture more carefully.

There is a small country—Saudi Arabia; and a big country—the U.S. To live, the big country needs the resources of the small country. What course are the relations between these two countries going to follow? Every effort will certainly be made to create an atmosphere of mutual satisfaction, even of friendship, between the two. But there is a certain limit after which danger may show its teeth—at a certain moment the smile may become a ravening mouth. This is not mere fantasy. We all remember that when Saudi Arabia imposed an embargo on the export of its oil to America during the 1973 war, American plans for the occupation of the oilfields in the Arabian Peninsula were openly discussed. Thus there is a desire for mutual satisfaction, but there is also a readiness to pounce. Between the two there lies a single parting of the ways at which we may all find ourselves at the first shock of attempts to solve the Middle East crisis. Here I suggest that we take a look at some of the more important features of President Carter's line on the energy crisis and the discussion they have given rise to in the U.S.

Let us, for example, consider the following points:

1. *Carter's statement:* "Energy resources have become a question that lies at the very heart of the problem of the national security of the American people and all the peoples of the West."

2. *Carter's statement:* "At present the U.S. imports half of its oil requirements, and one quarter of the oil imports at present come from Saudi Arabia alone. But in 1980 we shall be importing from Saudi Arabia alone half our oil requirements."

3. *The CIA report on which President Carter based his plan for the confrontation of the oil crisis, which gives the following figures:*
   In 1970 America's oil imports cost 3.7 billion dollars.
   In 1976 America's oil imports cost 36 billion dollars.
   In 1977 America's oil imports will cost 45 billion dollars.
   In 1985, if things stay as they are America's oil imports will cost 550 billion.
   The CIA report adds:
   In no circumstances can the U.S. afford to pay this bill! . . .
   If we reflect on all this we can well imagine that Amir Fahd, when he meets President Carter in Washington, will find a smiling mouth. But the smiling mouth can always turn into a ravening one. . . .

Thus Saudi Arabia's policy cannot be expressed in simple terms based on America's need for Saudi Arabia. It must be expressed in complicated terms that allow for the fact that America needs Saudi oil, but that Saudi oil is a question connected with the national security of America. A third and last illustration of the fact that Saudi Arabia cannot express itself politically in simple terms, but is sometimes obliged to used complex and very complicated ones: In simple terms Saudi Arabia can fancy that in the East it has reached the stage of being the "greatest small or regional power" and that, this being the case, it is safe, as no challenge from any local quarter confronts it.

But the facts tell another story. Leaving aside the Israeli threat in the Red Sea and the plans of the Israeli military establishment, which believes that by a single swift strike it can reach the oil wells in the Arabian Peñinsula, obtain full control of them and protect them on behalf of the U.S. if necessary—leaving this aside, I want to turn eastward. On the other side of the Gulf there is a challenge from Iran that cannot be ignored. Like others, I believe that there is a Saudi-Iranian conflict which has politico-geographical causes. And although I, like others, am always in favour of this conflict being kept under control so as to prevent its turning from a contradiction without hostility into a hostile contradiction, the danger is there, especially if we ask ourselves a question which events have made unavoidable:

Why is Iran building up this armed military strength? This huge force cannot be directed against Iran's neighbour to the north, the USSR; however huge this Iranian force, it can never face Soviet strength. Iran's real hope of self-defence against its northern neighbour lies not in its own strength, but that of the U.S. Therefore this force is intended for possible developments in the south which are still not clear. In the light of her special concentration on naval stength, it seems clear that Iran is seeking to ensure that she has the last word in the affairs of the Gulf, and this is a situation Saudi Arabia may find itself face to face with at any moment. The problem is that in the case of any challenge from Israel, Saudi Arabia will have Egypt and Syria, at least, at its side. But in the case of a challenge from Iran, Saudi Arabia will find itself far away from Egypt and Syria, especially as the challenge, if it arises—which God forbid—will rely on naval strength in the Gulf, and as far as I know there is so far no significant Arab naval force in the Gulf. Thus the simple expressions of Saudi strategy are not sufficient; there must be complex and complicated expressions. All this makes Amir Fahd's visit to Washington, more important, and perhaps more serious. . . . To support its regime's claims to legitimacy Saudi Arabia has to adopt a hard-line attitude as regards the protection of the Islamic and Arab holy places. . . . The immense interests of others in the country, along with this hard-line attitude, may herald great dangers. . . . There are regional contradictions in addition to the major problems such as the energy crisis and the pressures of the era of naval strategies.

We can thus see that in confronting Washington with demands for Arab rights, Saudi Arabia is at the same time obliged to draw up a complex balance sheet required by security considerations. May I suggest that Saudi Arabia's security cannot be ensured unless it is based on extensive Arab support? Here too, simple expressions are not enough for Saudi Arabia: it is obliged by force of circumstances to resort to complex ones. If it chooses simple expressions it can content itself with combating communism, in the name of religion, and with the loyalty of certain elements in the government in a number of Arab capitals, in the name of the world. But this is not enough to safeguard Saudi Arabia's national security, which depends on the acceptance and agreement of the masses who can, if necessary, give their support, and can fight if necessary. That is to say, Saudi Arabia needs the acceptance and consent of masses who may not be in agreement socially, but who, at the national level, are capable of giving a strong new impetus which will support Saudi Arabia against Washington, strengthen it in the area and provide it in all circumstances with the safety margin required for the performance of its role in its complicated political terms.

The heart of the matter is that, through force of circumstances, Saudi Arabia bears a huge historic responsibility. It is, as I said, the Saudi era. Thus the responsibility for the consequences of the present stage is Saudi Arabia's, however hard it tries to keep out of the limelight and to withdraw humbly to the rear ranks.

XI. THE PALESTINIANS

36. Introduction

The Palestinians constitute the central problem in the recent history of Arab-Israeli relations. They are also an important factor in the internal politics as well as in the international relations of the Arab countries.

The establishment of Israel in 1948 created simultaneously the conditions for the rise of an Arab Palestinian nation, mostly in Diaspora. The beginning of the problem lies in the displacement of 700,000 to 800,000 Arabs, natives of Palestine, during the spring of 1948. The circumstances of the displacement are well known. The Arabs claim that the Israelis used massacres and pressure to force the Palestinians out of their ancestral villages and towns so that incoming Jewish migrants would have a place to settle and create a pure Jewish state. The Israelis contend that the Arabs left the territory at the urging of their leaders. Neutral observers state that in any event the displacement of persons during wars and civil strife is a common occurrence but that at the end of the hostilities refugees are usually allowed to return to their homes, or at least to dispose of their properties.

The Palestinian problem emerged initially as a refugee issue, as indicated by numerous writings on the subject in the period from 1950 to 1965. It was expected that after a certain time the refugees, camped originally in the neighboring Arab countries, would gradually settle there and become absorbed in the population of the host countries, with which they share a common language, culture, and religion. The opposite has happened. Instead of being absorbed and assimilated, the Palestinians have developed into a nation in exile, with their sense of identity, personality, memories, and attachment revolving not around the host country but around Palestine, most of which is now under Israeli control. For almost two decades after 1948 the Palestinian refugees were a pawn in the internal and international politics of Egypt, Iraq, Syria, Lebanon, and Jordan, where most of them lived. Gradually after 1967 they emerged as a distinct political and cultural entity, bent on deciding their own destiny and affairs.

The failure of most countries to absorb the refugees may be attributed both to the refusal of the Palestinians to forget their origin or their native land and to the lack of sufficient arable land or large industry to provide an adequate living in the host countries and also to the fact that the Palestinian refugees were a source of cheap labor and could be manipulated by various local political factions. The separation of the "guests" from the "hosts" became clearer after the Palestinians in 1968 began to reject their former status as "refugees" and to opt for an independent political identity as Palestinians. By this they remained united on cultural and historical grounds with other Arabs, while acquiring a distinct new political personality.

The term "Palestinian" encompasses all the Arabs whose origin is in Palestine, including all those living in various Arab and other countries, those living in the Israeli-occupied territory west of the Jordan River, and the Arab population left in Israel; the latter are officially designated as "Israeli Arabs" or "the Arab minority." The total number of Palestinians in 1981 was estimated to be roughly 4.1 million. Of these, about 1.8 million still are registered as refugees (some became refugees a second time in the war of 1967) by the United Nations Refugee and Works Agency

(UNRWA), the organization which has cared for the refugees since 1948, although, according to the latest figures, only 650,000 now live in 61 refugee camps located mainly in Lebanon and Jordan. The location of the Palestinians in 1981 was as follows: 1.1 million in Jordan; 400,000 in Lebanon; 1.2 million in the West Bank and Gaza under Israeli occupation; about 500,000 in Kuwait (where they make up 20 percent of the population), as well as Egypt, Syria, and other Arab countries; and 200,000 elsewhere—including about 70,000 in the United States, and the rest in Israel. The latest study by Elias H. Tuma, "The Palestinians in America," *The Link*, vol. 14, no. 3 (1981), gives the number of Palestinians in 1981 as follows:

West Bank	818,300
Israel	530,600
Gaza	476,700
Jordan	1,160,800
Lebanon	347,000
Kuwait	278,800
Syria	215,500
Saudi Arabia	127,000
United States	110,200
Elsewhere	325,000
Total	4,389,900

This last figure represents an essential increase over the figure of 3,255,000 given for 1975. The figure for 1975 was issued by the Arab Information Center while the one for 1981 was released by the *al-Fajr* and Palestine Institute of Statistics.

The Palestinians show certain unusual characteristics. The literacy rate is very high among them, with a ratio of two university graduates for every 1,000 people. Currently at least 80,000 Palestinians are estimated to be enrolled in universities. They also hold important administrative and professional positions in various Arab countries, making them an elite group in the Arab world. Palestinian grievances are manifold: first, they say that they have been uprooted from their soil by outsiders under the banner of Zionism; second, they consider that the West has made them the scapegoats for centuries of Christian European antisemitism, being unconcerned with the fact that the new Zionist "home" was being established at the expense of an innocent group; and third, they have found the Arab countries, because of incompetence and weakness, unable to restore the Palestinians' rights despite promises and some mismanaged attempts. Thus the Palestinians have a deep feeling of injustice, compounded by anger at the perceived Western indifference to their plight.

The essence of the Palestinian demand is that they be permitted to return to the country of their origin, that is Palestine, to take possession of their lands, and to develop their own culture and way of life in a secular Palestinian national state. But the land of the Palestinian aspiration is today under Israeli sovereignty, and the majority of its inhabitants are Jews, many of whom were actually born there. There are therefore two peoples who claim the same piece of land. Cognizant of the substantial Jewish presence there, the leaders of the Palestinians have advocated the establishment of a democratic secular state in which Muslims, Jews, and Christians have equal rights. Palestinian society, inside or outside of Israel, has its own conflicts and contradictions, but all of these are obscured by and subordinated to the single aim: return to the homeland. The Palestinian struggle against Israel is handicapped by lack of a territory of their own to serve as a secure base of operation. They have to depend on the goodwill, passing interest, or weakness, as the case may be, of a host Arab country in order to have a base from which to fight.

The pecularities of the Palestinians' status and situation and the nature of their aspirations has led them to develop their methods and organization accordingly. The chief organization of the Palestinians is the Palestine Liberation Organization (PLO). The PLO is governed by a National Council elected by a Congress which meets periodically and gives direction to the movement. The PLO is actually formed of a number of political groups—al-Fatah (the largest), the Popular Front for the Liberation of Palestine (PFLP), the Popular Democratic Front for the Liberaton of Palestine (PDFLP), the Popular Organization for the Liberation of Palestine, the Palestine Liberation Front, to cite just a few of the militant political and commando groups. In addition, the PLO includes a variety of professional organizations. The military arm of the PLO is formed by the Palestine Liberation Army with about 47,000 soldiers, while other commando groups have about 35,000 fighters. Originally the PLO was established in Egypt in 1964 by some old-guard Palestinians and was recognized by the Arab League as the representative of the Palestinian people. But the war of 1967 discredited the PLO along with Nasser, who controlled it. Consequently, the Harakat al-Tahrir al-Filastini (Palestine Liberation Movement—al-Fatah is the inversed acronym), organized in the 1950s by a small group in Gaza, took over the PLO in 1969. The al-Fatah, organized by Yasser Arafat, defended the idea that the liberation of Palestine was first of all a Palestinian affair and that armed struggle was necessary to create both consciousness and unity. Al-Fatah consolidated its position against the opposition of the PFLP and the Arab Liberation Front, which were more radical but advocated the idea of first building an organization before engaging in action. The PLO achieved a relative success against an Israeli military unit at Karameh in Jordan in 1968 and then, under the pressure of its radical wings, became embroiled in an armed struggle with King Hussein's forces. It suffered heavy casualities and left the country in 1970. The clash with the Jordanian forces was precipitated by the PFLP and PDFLP under George Habash and Nayif Hawatmeh, respectively, the two Marxist leaders about whom there will be further discussion. After the debacle of 1970, the PLO worked actively to achieve international recognition and support. It established relations with radical leftist organizations throughout the world and increasingly received material and moral support from the USSR. The Palestinian movement was on its way toward achieving international stature.

The turning point in the history of the PLO came in 1974 when it was accorded "observer" status by the United Nations and had a representative stationed in New York, and when Yasser Arafat addressed the UN General Assembly (see speech). Finally at Rabat, in Morocco, all the Arab states, including Jordan, recognized the PLO as the sole representative and spokesman for the Palestinians. The Jordanian recognition was important because it amounted to a formal relinquishment of the king's right to speak on behalf of the Palestinians on the West Bank of Jordan, who had been his subjects until the Israeli occupation in 1967.

After 1970 the PLO base of operation was shifted from Jordan to Lebanon. By 1975 or 1976, Lebanese political tensions had degenerated into a civil war between the leftists—that is, the underprivileged and dissatisfied elements consisting in the majority, but not exclusively, of Muslims—and the rightists, composed mostly of the established groups dominated by the Maronite Christians. The Palestinians, left without options, were forced to side with the leftists and eventually faced the Syrian army, which at the time supported the rightists, once more suffering heavy losses. Since then the Palestinians have made peace with Syria but remain in a rather precarious position in Lebanon because of Israeli attacks on Palestinian positions in the southern part of the country and demands by right-wing groups, notably the Maronites, that they be disarmed and forced to retire to their camps.

The Camp David agreements and the peace treaty between Egypt and Israel in 1978 and 1979 dealt another heavy blow to the PLO, depriving it of vital Egyptian support and breaking the unity of the Arab front in the confrontation with Israel.

The position of the PLO toward Israel remains formally unchanged. The PLO covenant, if applied as it stands now, would necessitate the dissolution of Israel as a Jewish state and its replacement by a new secular state in which Jews, Muslims, and Christians would have equal rights. In practice the PLO has given some signals that it may accept a Palestinian state established on the West Bank of the Jordan and in Gaza. However, it has refused adamantly to declare openly that it recognizes the "right" of existence of Israel, for Israeli borders are not defined and Israel has not yet recognized any Palestinian "rights." This refusal has led the United States and other countries to withold recognition of the PLO. Israel has refused to have anything to do with PLO, a position maintained both by the government and the opposition. However, the efforts of Israel and the United States to create an alternative Palestinian representation among the inhabitants of the West Bank have produced no result. There are those who believe that the PLO holds, and has held since the Covenant of 1969, the view that only those born in Palestine should be recognized as citizens of the country. However, the expulsion of Jews not born in Israel is not emphasized any longer by the PLO. Actually the various organizations within the PLO have differed from each other on this issue. The PDFLP regarded the Israeli Jews as a national community rather than a religious community and wanted to recognize them accordingly, while other groups did not make such differentiation.

Israel has refused both to recognize the PLO as the spokesman for the Palestinians and to negotiate outstanding problems with them. Premier Begin has referred to the PLO as "murderers," "terrorists," and other unflattering epithets. (The Palestinians in turn have reminded Begin of his own terrorist activities as head of the IRGUN in the 1940s.) Yet, in the face of these mutual accusations and despite denials, the PLO and the Israeli government have had a variety of dealings that are akin to mutual recognition. The last such occurrence, one of exceptional importance, happened in July, 1981. For about two weeks Israel shelled the Palestinian positions in southern Lebanon and attacked PLO headquarters in Beirut, killing hundreds of innocent Lebanese civilians without being able to destroy the headquarters. The Palestinians in turn shelled the Israeli towns in the northern part of the country, killing a few Israeli civilians. Eventually a cease-fire was negotiated, ostensibly by the United Nations but actually through the United States' intermediary in the area, namely Philip Habib, President Reagan's special envoy to the Middle East. The essential fact in this cease-fire is that it took place between the two parties involved in the shooting, although negotiations did not take place directly but through intermediaries. One intermediary was Saudi Arabia, which, while it still does not recognize Israel, nonetheless played a basic behind the scenes role in securing the cease-fire. (Incidentally, a unit of the Popular Front for the Liberation of Palestine objected to the cease-fire and continued the shelling.)

It is probably not too early to say that the negotiation process, with its implicit political and legal significance, may open the way to direct Israeli-PLO contacts and negotiations, which are in fact the precondition to settlement of the Arab-Israeli conflict. All this, it must be remembered, took place just about one month before Premier Begin and President Sadat were due to meet with President Reagan in Washington to seek ways to reactivate the stalled Israeli-Egyptian talks. The talks were stalled because of Israel's refusal to deal with the Palestinian question as stipulated in the peace treaty signed by the two countries.

The PLO, despite its outward unity and its successes in the international field, is beset by ideological conflicts. The largest organization, al-Fatah, has essentially a middle-of-the-road philosophy, whereas its two main ideological opponents, PFLP and PDFLP, are Marxist and regard al-Fatah as representing essentially the reformist viewpoint of the conservative Arab regimes rather than the revolutionary aspirations of the masses. They demand that the future regime of Palestine be based on a Marxist-Leninist philosophy, while al-Fatah remains committed to a mild form of nationalism and socialism. During the past three years there has been some shift toward Marxism among intellectuals affiliated with the PLO, largely as a reaction to the passiveness of the Arab regimes and out of sympathy for the successful revolutionary movements in Algeria and elsewhere in Africa.

The philosophy, tactics, and strategy of the PLO are continuously evolving, depending on world political circumstances and the attitude and policies of the Arab states. There is no question that each Arab state has viewed the Palestinian question within the framework of its own interests and ideology and, when suitable, has tried to influence and dominate the movement by creating its own Palestinian group; in 1968, for example, Syria established a Palestinian commando group, SAIGHA (the Thunderbolt), and Iraq had her own Arab Liberation Front. On the other hand, the Palestinians have their own following. They enjoy great popularity among the masses in every Arab country and, in case of need, are capable of mobilizing some groups against the regime. Moreover, many Arab intellectuals tend to consider the Palestinians the only truly revolutionary and unifying force in the Arab world and support them as such. So far Palestinians are the only Arab group to have successfully overcome religious and tribal differences (about 15 percent of the Palestinians are Christians), fostered national unity, and projected their movement to the entire world, despite difficult conditions. All this has increased their prestige in the eyes of Arab youth and radicals in the Muslim countries throughout the world.

The methods used by the Palestinians, from plane high-jacking to attacks inside and outside Israel, have attracted widespread criticism from a variety of sources, despite the fact that many attacks on individuals were carried out by extremist factions such as the Black September group. Lately there has been less emphasis on violence and more reliance on political approaches. Practically all issues related to the Palestinians affect

Israel in a variety of ways, and vice versa. Consequently this section must be read together with the one on Israel.

The literature on the Palestinians is rich. The *Journal of Palestine Studies*, a quarterly published since 1971, has excellent information. A list of publications on various issues was issued by the Palestinian commando organizations in the *Journal of Palestine Studies* 1 (1972): 136–51. The Institute for Palestine Studies in Beirut, Lebanon, issues a biweekly *Arabic Bulletin* and a series of monographs. The PLO Research Center, also located in Beirut, published the monthly *Shu'un Filastiniya*. For further reading reflecting both the Palestinian and Israeli attitude on the issues, see Ibrahim Abu-Lughod, *The Transformation of Palestine: Essays on the Origin and Development of the Arab-Israeli Conflict* (Evanston: Northwestern University Press, 1971); Elia T. Zureik, *The Palestinians in Israel* (London: Routledge & Kegan Paul, 1979); Rosemary Sayigh, *Palestinians: From Peasants to Revolutionaries* (London: Zed Press, 1980); Ann M. Lesch, *Arab Politics in Palestine 1917–1939* (Ithaca, N.Y.: Cornell University Press, 1979); Walid W. Kazziha, *Revolutionary Transformation in the Arab World, Habash and His Comrades from Nationalism to Marxism* (London: Charles Knight, 1975); William B. Quandt, F. Jabber, and Ann M. Lesch, *The Politics of Palestinian Nationalism* (Berkeley: University of California Press, 1973); Y. Porath, *The Emergence of the Palestinian Arab National Movement 1918–1929* (London: Frank Cass, 1979); Jacques Berque, M. Rodinson et al., *Les Palestiniens la crise Israélo-Arabe* (Paris: Editions sociales, 1974); Mario Offenberg, *Kommunismus in Palästina, Nation, und Klasse in der antikolonialen Revolution* (Meisenheim: Anton Hain, 1975); Gabriel Ben-Dor, ed., *The Palestinians and the Middle East Conflict* (London: Turtledove Publishing, 1979); S Avineri, ed., *Israel and the Palestinians* (New York: St. Martin's Press, 1971); Fred J. Khouri, *The Arab-Israeli Dilemma* (Syracuse, N.Y.: Syracuse University Press, 1976); Zeev Schiff and Raphael Rothstein, *Fedayeen-Guerilla Against Israel* (New York: David McKay, 1972); Edgar O'Ballance, *Arab Guerilla Power 1967–1972* (London: Faber and Faber, 1973); Michael Curtis et al., *The Palestinians: People, History, Politics* (New Brunswick: Transaction Books, 1975); Thomas Kiernan, *Arafat, The Man and the Myth* (New York: W.W. Norton, 1976); Olivier Carré, *L'ideologie palestinienne de résistance, Analyse de textes (1964–1970)* (Paris: Armand Colin, 1972); Michael C. Hudson, "The Palestinians: Retrospect and Prospects," *Current History* (January 1980): 22–48; Nissim Rejwan, "Palestinians Under Israeli Occupation," *Midstream* 2 (February 1971): 43–52; Noam Chomsky, "Nationalism and Conflict in Palestine," *Liberation* 14, (November 8, 1969): 7–20; Mark A. Tessler, "Secularism in the Middle East—Reflections on Recent Palestinian Proposals," *Ethnicity* 2 (1975): 178–203. MERIP Reports, published in Washington, D.C., Nos. 53, 60, and 83, and *Race and Class*, a quarterly published in London, provide additional information and interpretative views on Palestinians.

37.   Basic Documents of the PLO

The three documents reproduced here are the Palestinian National Covenant, which is the constitution of the movement; the political communique of the Second Conference of the Central Union of Palestinian Women; and the Palestine Resolution of the Seventh Arab Summit Conference held in Rabat, October 29, 1974. The Covenant appeared in Leila S. Kadi, ed., Basic Political Documents of the Armed Palestinian Resistance Movement *(Beirut: PLO Research Center, 1969), pp. 137–44. The conference papers are from the* Journal of Palestine Studies *4, no. 1 (Autumn 1974): 204–5 and no. 2 (Winter 1975): 177–78.*

Palestinian National Covenant

ARTICLE 1:   Palestine is the homeland of the Arab Palestinian people; it is an indivisible part of the Arab homeland, and the Palestinian people are an integral part of the Arab nation.

ARTICLE 2:   Palestine, with the boundaries it had during the British Mandate, is an indivisible territorial unit.

ARTICLE 3:   The Palestinian people possess the legal right to their homeland and have the right to determine their destiny after achieving the liberation of their country in accordance with their wishes and entirely of their own accord and will.

ARTICLE 4:   The Palestinian identity is a genuine, essential and inherent characteristic; it is transmitted from parents to children. The Zionist occupation and the dispersal of the Palestinian Arab people, through the disasters which befell them, do not make them lose their Palestinian identity and their membership of the Palestinian community, nor do they negate them.

ARTICLE 5:   The Palestinians are those Arab nationals who, until 1947, normally resided in Palestine regardless of whether they were evicted from it or have stayed there. Anyone born, after that date, of a Palestinian father—whether inside Palestine or outside it—is also a Palestinian.

ARTICLE 6:   The Jews who had normally resided in Palestine until the beginning of the Zionist invasion will be considered Palestinians.

ARTICLE 7:   That there is a Palestinian community and that it has material, spiritual and historical connections with Palestine are indisputable facts. It is a national duty to bring up individual Palestinians in an Arab revolutionary manner. All means of information and education must be adopted in order to acquaint the Palestinian with his country in the most profound manner, both spiritual and material, that is possible. He must be prepared for the armed struggle and ready to sacrifice his wealth and his life in order to win back his homeland and bring its liberation.

ARTICLE 8:   The phase in their history, through which the Palestinian people are now living, is that of national (watani) struggle for the liberation of Palestine. Thus the conflicts among the Palestinian national forces are secondary, and should be ended for the sake of the basic conflict that exists between the forces of Zionism and of imperialism on the one hand, and the Palestinian Arab people on the other. On this basis the Palestinian masses, regardless of whether they are residing in the national homeland or in diaspora (mahajir) constitute—both their organization and the individuals—one national front working for the retrieval of Palestine and its liberation through armed struggle.

ARTICLE 9:   Armed struggle is the only way to liberate Palestine. Thus it is the overall strategy, not merely a tactical phase. The Palestinian Arab people assert their absolute determination and firm resolution to continue their armed struggle and to work for an armed popular revolution for the liberation of their country and their return to it. They also assert their right to normal life in Palestine and to exercise their right to self-determination and sovereignty over it.

ARTICLE 10:   Commando action constitutes the nucleus of the Palestinian popular liberation war. This requires its escalation, comprehensiveness and mobilization of all the Palestinian popular and educational efforts and their organization and involvement in the armed Palestinian revolution. It also requires the achieving of unity for the national (watani) struggle among the different groupings of the Palestinian people, and between the Palestinian people and the Arab masses so as to secure the continuation of the revolution, its escalation and victory.

ARTICLE 11:   The Palestinians will have three mottoes: national (wataniyya) unity, national (qawmiyya) mobilization and liberation.

ARTICLE 12:   The Palestinian people believe in Arab unity. In order to contribute their share towards the attainment of that objective, however, they must, at the present stage of their struggle, safeguard their Palestinian identity and develop their consciousness of that identity, and oppose any plan that may dissolve or impair it.

ARTICLE 13:   Arab unity and the liberation of Palestine are two complementary objectives, the attainment of either of which facilitates the attainment of the other. Thus, Arab unity leads to the liberation of Palestine; the liberation of Palestine leads to Arab unity; and work toward the realization of one objective proceeds side by side with work towards the realization of the other.

ARTICLE 14:   The destiny of the Arab nation, and indeed Arab existence itself, depends upon the destiny of the Palestinian cause. From this interdependence springs the Arab nation's pursuit of, and striving for, the liberation of Palestine. The people of Palestine play the role of the vanguard in the realization of this sacred national (qawmi) goal.

ARTICLE 15:   The liberation of Palestine, from an Arab viewpoint, is a national (qawmi) duty and it attempts to repel the Zionist and imperialist aggression against the Arab homeland, and aims at the elimination of Zionism in Palestine. Absolute responsibility for this falls upon the Arab nation—peoples and governments—with the Arab people of Palestine in the vanguard.

Accordingly the Arab nation must mobilize all its military, human and moral and spiritual capabilities to participate actively with the Palestinian people in the liberation of Palestine. It must, particularly in the phase of the armed Palestinian revolution, offer and furnish the Palestinian people with all possible help, and material and human support, and make available to them the means and opportunities that will enable them to continue to carry out their leading role in the armed revolution, until they liberate their homeland.

ARTICLE 16:   The liberation of Palestine, from a spiritual point of view, will provide the Holy Land with an atmosphere of safety and tranquility, which in turn will safeguard the country's religious sanctuaries and guarantee freedom of worship and of visit to all, without discrimination of race, colour, language, or religion. Accordingly, the people of Palestine look to all spiritual forces in the world for support.

ARTICLE 17:   The liberation of Palestine, from a human point of view, will restore to the Palestinian individual his dignity, pride and freedom. Accordingly the Palestinian Arab people look forward to the support of all those who believe in the dignity of man and his freedom in the world.

ARTICLE 18:   The liberation of Palestine, from an international point of view, is a defensive action necessitated by the demands of self-defence. Accordingly, the Palestinian people, desirous as they are of the friendship of all people, look to freedom-loving, justice-loving and peace-loving states for support in order to restore their legitimate rights in Palestine, to reestablish peace and security in the country, and to enable its people to exercise national sovereignty and freedom.

ARTICLE 19:   The partition of Palestine in 1947 and the establishment of the State of Israel are entirely illegal, regardless of the passage of time, because they were contrary to the will of the Palestinian people and to their natural right in their homeland, and inconsistent with the principles embodied in the Charter of the United Nations, particularly the right to self-determination.

ARTICLE 20:   The Balfour Declaration, the Mandate for Palestine and everything that has been based upon them, are deemed null and void. Claims of historical or religious ties of Jews with Palestine are incompatible with the facts of history and the true conception of what constitutes statehood. Judaism, being a religion, is not an independent nationality. Nor do Jews constitute a single nation with an identity of its own; they are citizens of the states to which they belong.

ARTICLE 21: The Arab Palestinian people, expressing themselves by the armed Palestinian revolution, reject all solutions which are substitutes for the total liberation of Palestine and reject all proposals aiming at the liquidation of the Palestinian problem, or its internationalization.

ARTICLE 22:   Zionism is a political movement organically associated with international imperialism and antagonistic to all action for liberation and to progressive movements in the world. It is racist and fanatic in its nature, aggressive, expansionist and colonial in its aims, and fascist in its methods. Israel is the instrument of the Zionist movement, and a geographical base for world imperialism placed strategically in the midst of the Arab homeland to combat the hopes of the Arab nation for liberation, unity and progress. Israel is a constant source of threat vis-à-vis peace in the Middle East and the whole world. Since the liberation of Palestine will destroy the

Zionist and imperialist presence and will contribute to the establishment of peace in the Middle East, the Palestinian people look for the support of all the progressive and peaceful forces and urge them all, irrespective of their affiliations and beliefs, to offer the Palestinian people all aid and support in their just struggle for the liberation of their homeland.

ARTICLE 23: The demands of security and peace, as well as the demands of right and justice, require all states to consider Zionism an illegitimate movement, to outlaw its existence, and to ban its operations, in order that friendly relations among peoples may be preserved, and the loyalty of citizens to their respective homelands safeguarded.

ARTICLE 24: The Palestinian people believe in the principles of justice, freedom, sovereignty, self-determination, human dignity, and in the right of all peoples to exercise them.

ARTICLE 25: For the realization of the goals of this Charter and its principles, the Palestinian Liberation Organization will perform its role in the liberation of Palestine in accordance with the Constitution of this Organization.

ARTICLE 26: The Palestine Liberation Organization, representative of the Palestinian revolutionary forces, is responsible for the Palestinian Arab people's movement in its struggle—to retrieve its homeland, liberate and return to it and exercise the right to self-determination in it—in all military, political and financial fields and also for whatever may be required by the Palestinian cause on the inter-Arab and international levels.

ARTICLE 27: The Palestinian Liberation Organization shall cooperate with all Arab states, each according to its potentialities; and will adopt a neutral policy among them in the light of the requirements of the war of liberation; and on this basis it shall not interfere in the internal affairs of any Arab State.

ARTICLE 28: The Palestinian Arab people assert the genuineness and independence of their national (wataniyya) revolution and reject all forms of intervention, trusteeship and subordination.

ARTICLE 29: The Palestinian people possess the fundamental and gen- uine legal right to liberate and retrieve their homeland. The Palestinian people determine their attitude towards all states and forces on the basis of the stands they adopt vis-à-vis the Palestinian case and the extent of the support they offer to the Palestinian revolution to fulfill the aims of the Palestinian people.

ARTICLE 30:   Fighters and carriers of arms in the war of liberation are the nucleus of the popular army which will be the protective force for the gains of the Palestinian Arab people.

ARTICLE 31.   The Organization shall have a flag, an oath of allegiance and an anthem. All this shall be decided upon in accordance with a special regulation.

ARTICLE 32:   Regulations, which shall be known as the Constitution of the Palestine Liberation Organization, shall be annexed to this Charter. It shall lay down the manner in which the Organization, and its organs and institutions, shall be constituted; the respective competence of each; and the requirements of its obligations under the Charter.

ARTICLE 33:   This Charter shall not be amended save by (vote of) a majority of two-thirds of the total membership of the National Congress of the Palestine Liberation Organization (taken) at a special session convened for that purpose.

Communique of the Second Conference of the General Union of Palestinian Women

The General Union of Palestinian Women, as an important base of the Palestinian revolution, struggles for the sake of defeating all liquidation settlements and emphasizes the revolutionary line which rejects reconciliation, recognition and negotiation with the enemy. The Union also reaffirms its condemnation and rejection of the Egyptian-Jordanian Communique which:

1. Represents a reversal from the resolutions of the Algiers Summit Conference which stated that the Palestine Liberation Organization is the sole legitimate representative of the Palestinian people wherever they exist.
2. Calls for the division of the Palestinian people, the killing of its character and the obliteration of its national identity, which is the guarantee of its revolutionary march and armed struggle against Zionism, imperialism and reactionary forces.

3. Accepts the proposal for liquidation based on a United Arab Kingdom which was condemned and refused by the Arab masses, and the Arab national forces.

The continuity of the revolution, until the destruction of the Zionist enemy and liberation of all occupied Palestinian soil, requires the struggle for the establishment of a revolutionary base on all liberated land that will guarantee the continuity of the revolution and offer more conditions for its success.

The achievement of the revolutionary fighting power of the people over the land liberated by armed struggle cannot occur except by a change in the balance of power between the revolution and its enemies—which is something that cannot be achieved except by armed struggle.

The revolutionary power must in the first place guarantee the continuity of the revolution. Therefore we must refuse, as a price for its acceptance or continuity, negotiations with the enemy, recognition of the legitimacy of the Zionist occupation over any part of Palestine, acceptance of the authority of the Jordanian conspirators over any part of the nation, succumbing to the international and Arab official acceptance of the division of the Palestinian people, or silencing the revolutionary shotgun.

The dangerous situation which the Palestinian cause and Palestinian existence are facing, emerges from the fact that this imperialist reality has found its way to existence. The Alexandria Communique was not the result of a miscalculation and that is why we must face the real event and not its symptoms. This requires from us the following:

1. We must depend basically on our own potentials, for it is necessary to develop and solidify our national unity. The unity of the revolution is the practical answer to the efforts which take place, and will take place for the sake of liquidating the revolution, and destroying the gains of our Palestinian people, including the right of representation.

2. The unity of the revolution will strengthen the cohesion with the Arab masses, the international liberation movement and the socialist countries, namely the Soviet Union and China. Such forces are capable of destroying all Zionist and imperialist plans.

3. The formation of the national Jordanian-Palestinian front in Jordan, and the exercising of armed struggle against the institutions and symbols of the conspiratorial regime for the sake of overthrowing it and replacing it by the national democratic

rule is the practical answer to its conspiracies, and is capable of changing Jordan into a secure base of the revolution and a starting point for liberation.

4. It is imperative to continue escalating the political, military and popular struggle in the occupied land.

5. We must intensify the work with the Arab liberation movement groups for the sake of strengthening the cohesion of the revolution, in order to defeat the conspiracy against the Arab liberation movement, namely the Palestinian revolution.

6. We must move widely on the international level, especially with the socialist countries, non-aligned countries, and liberation movements in order to gain support for the point of view of the revolution.

Palestine Resolution of the
Seventh Arab Summit Conference,
Rabat, October 1974

The Seventh Arab Summit Conference after exhaustive and detailed discussions conducted by their Majesties, Excellencies and Highnesses the Kings, Presidents and Amirs on the Arab situation in general and the Palestine problem in particular, within their national and international frameworks; and after hearing the statements submitted by His Majesty King Hussein, King of the Hashemite Kingdom of Jordan and His Excellency Brother Yasser Arafat, Chairman of the Palestine Liberation Organization, and after the statements of their Majesties and Excellencies the Kings and the Presidents, in an atmosphere of candour and sincerity and full responsibility; and in view of the Arab leaders' appreciation of the joint national responsibility required of them at present for confronting aggression and performing duties of liberation, enjoined by the unity of the Arab cause and the unity of its struggle; and in view of the fact that all are aware of Zionist schemes still being made to eliminate the Palestinian existence and to obliterate the Palestinian national entity; and in view of the Arab leaders' belief in the necessity to frustrate these attempts and schemes and to counteract them by supporting and strengthening this Palestinian national entity, by providing all requirements to develop and increase its ability to ensure that the Palestinian people recover their rights in full; and by meeting responsibilities of close cooperation with its brothers within the framework of collective Arab commitment.

And in light of the victories achieved by [the] Palestinian struggle in the confrontation with the Zionist enemy, [and] at the Arab and international [meetings] . . . at the United Nations, and of the obligation imposed thereby to continue joint Arab action to develop and increase the scope of these victories; and having received the views of all on all the above, and having succeeded in cooling the differences between brethren within the framework of consolidating Arab solidarity, the Seventh Arab Summit Conference resolves the following:

1. To affirm the right of the Palestinian people to self-determination and to return to their homeland;
2. To affirm the right of the Palestinian people to establish an independent national authority under the command of the Palestine Liberation Organization, the sole legitimate representative of the Palestinian people in any Palestinian territory that is liberated. This authority, once it is established, shall enjoy the support of the Arab states in all fields and at all levels;
3. To support the Palestine Liberation Organization in the exercise of its responsibility at the national and international levels within the framework of Arab commitment;
4. To call on the Hashemite Kingdom of Jordan, the Syrian Arab Republic, the Arab Republic of Egypt and the Palestine Liberation Organization to devise a formula for the regulation of relations between them in the light of these decisions so as to ensure their implementation;
5. That all the Arab states undertake to defend Palestinian national unity and not to interfere in the internal affairs of Palestinian action.

38.   The Palestinian Problem: Causes and Solutions

Yasser Arafat

Yasser Arafat (Abu Ammar) was born of Sunni Muslim parents, probably in Jerusalem in 1924. He was among the refugees who in 1948 went to Gaza. In 1951 Arafat moved to Cairo where he attended the Engineering School and established contact with the Muslim Brethren. In Cairo he founded al-Fatah with Khalil al-Wazir (Abu Jihad) and Salah Khalaf (Abu Ayad). In 1956 he was elected chairman of the Palestinian Student Union of Cairo and acquired some military training. In that same year he went to Kuwait, where al-Fatah was expanded with the addition of Faruq al-Qaddumi (Abu Lutuf), Muhammad Yusif an-Najjar (Abu Yusif), Kamal Adwan, and others who have remained in the leadership of al-Fatah. After 1968 al-Fatah took control of the PLO and changed the direction and scope of the

Palestinian movement (see Introduction). There is no question that the close relationship between the leaders of al-Fatah, and their ability to devise a consistent strategy and tactics—namely, to engage directly in struggle, to avoid becoming involved in the internal affairs and politics of the host Arab countries, and to maintain the distinct, separate identity of the Palestinians—has secured them considerable success. Al-Fatah's policy of not becoming involved in the politics of the host countries has been challenged by the Marxists within the movement, who have regarded the Palestinian struggle as part of the world anticolonialist and antiimperialist revolution and consequently have sought allies among the lower classes and revolutionary parties in the Arab countries and throughout the world. Arafat has had to play a very delicate diplomatic game both to hold the PLO together and to achieve agreement and understanding with the host governments, as in Jordan in 1970 and Lebanon in 1975–76. The Jordanian attack on the Palestinians in 1970 actually wiped out many small extremist groups, allowing al-Fatah to consolidate its power in the PLO. Arafat's organizational and diplomatic skills have won the admiration of his enemies as well as his supporters. A considerable amount of myth and legend has grown up around Arafat, and this gives the Palestinian movement a certain drive and élan.

The excerpts below are from a speech in Arabic delivered by Arafat to the United Nations on November 13, 1974. It attacks Zionism and demands the restoration of Palestinian rights. The official UN text was compared with the Arabic and printed in al-Nahar *in Beirut on November 14, 1974: the excerpts are from a corrected version published by the* Journal of Palestine Studies 4, no. 2 (Winter 1975); 181–92 passim. *After relating the Palestinian movement to anticolonialist struggles in the third world, Arafat dealt specifically with his own cause. A number of sections have not been reproduced due to space limitation.*

Even as today we address this General Assembly from an international rostrum we are also expressing our faith in political and diplomatic struggle as complements, as enhancements of armed struggle. Furthermore we express our appreciation of the role the United Nations is capable of playing in settling problems of international scope. But this capability, I said a moment ago, became real only once the United Nations had accommodated itself to the living actuality of aspiring peoples, towards which this international organization owes unique obligations.

In addressing the General Assembly today our people proclaims its faith in the future, unencumbered either by past tragedies or present limitations. . . . If we return now to the historical roots of our cause we do so because present at this very moment in our midst are those who, as they occupy our homes, as their cattle graze in our pastures, and as their hands pluck the fruit of our trees, claim at the same time that we are ghosts without an existence, without traditions or future. We speak of our roots also because until recently some people have regarded—and continue to regard—our problem as merely a problem of refugees. They have portrayed the Middle East question as little more than a border dispute between the Arab states and the Zionist entity. They have imagined that our people claim rights not rightfully their own and fight neither with logic nor legitimate motive, with a simple wish only to disturb the peace and to terrorize others. For there are amongst you—and here I refer to the United States of America and others like it—those who supply our enemy freely with planes and bombs and with every variety of murderous weapon. They take hostile positions against us, deliberately distorting the true essence of the problem. All this is done not only at our expense, but at the expense of the American people and its well-being, and of the friendship we continue to hope can be cemented between us and this great people, whose history of struggle for the sake of freedom and the unity of its territories we honor and salute...

In any event, in focusing our discussion of the question of Palestine upon historical roots, we do so because we believe that any question now exercising the world's concern must be viewed radically, in the true sense of that word, if a real solution is ever to be grasped. We propose this radical approach as an antidote to an approach to international issues that obscures historical origins behind ignorance, denial and a slavish obedience to the fait accompli.

The roots of the Palestinian question reach back into the closing years of the nineteenth century, in other words, to that period which we call the era of colonialism and settlement and the transition to the eve of imperialism. This was when the Zionist imperialist plan was born: its aim was the conquest of Palestine by European immigration, just as settlers colonized, and indeed raided, most of Africa. This is the period during which, pouring forth out of the West, colonialism spread into the furthest reaches of Africa, Asia, and Latin America, building colonies everywhere, cruelly exploiting, oppressing, plundering the peoples of those three continents. This period persists into the present. Marked evidence of its totally reprehensible presence can be readily perceived in the racism practised both in South Africa and in Palestine....

So the Zionist movement allied itself directly with world colonialism in a common raid on our land. Alow me now to present a selection of historical facts about this alliance.

[After giving a summary of Jewish migration and Arab-Israeli relations Arafat continued as follows.]

a) We distinguish between Judaism and Zionism. While we maintain our opposition to the colonialist Zionist movement, we respect the Jewish faith. Today, almost one century after the rise of the Zionist movement, we wish to warn of its increasing danger to the Jews of the world, to our Arab peoples and to world peace and security. For Zionism encourages the Jew to emigrate from his homeland and grants him an artifically-made nationality. The Zionists proceed with their destructive activities even though these have proved ineffective. The phenomenon of constant emigration from Israel, which is bound to grow as the bastions of colonialism and racism in the world fall, is an example of the inevitability of the failure of such activities.

b) We urge the people and governments of the world to stand firm against Zionist attempts at encouraging world Jewry to emigrate from their countries and to usurp our land. We urge them as well firmly to oppose any discrimination against any human being, as to religion, race, or colour.

c) Why should our people and our homeland be responsible for the problems of Jewish immigration, if such problems exist in the minds of some people? Why do the supporters of these problems not open their own countries, which are much bigger, to absorb and help these immigrants?

Those who call us terrorists wish to prevent world public opinion from discovering the truth about us and from seeing the justice on our faces. They seek to hide the terrorism and tyranny of their acts, and our own posture of self-defence.

The difference between the revolutionary and the terrorist lies in the reason for which each fights. For whoever stands by a just case and fights for the freedom and liberation of his land from invaders, settlers and colonialists would have been incorrectly called terrorists; the American people in their stuggle for liberation from the British colonialists would have been terrorists, the European resistance against the Nazis would be terrorism, the struggle of the Asian, African and Latin American peoples would also be terrorism. It is actually a just and proper struggle of the Asian, African and Latin American peoples, consecrated by the United Nations Charter and by the Declaration of Human Rights. As to those who fight against just causes, those who wage war to occupy the homelands of others, and to plunder, exploit and colonize their peoples—those are the people whose actions should be condemned, who should be called war criminals: for the just cause determines the right to struggle. . . .

The small number of Palestinian Arabs whom the Zionists did not succeed in uprooting in 1948 are at present refugees in their own country.

Israeli law treats them as second-class citizens—even as third-class citizens since Oriental Jews are second-class citizens—and they have been subject to all forms of racial discrimination and terror after the confiscation of their land and property. They have been victims of bloody massacres such as that of Kafr Qassim; they have been expelled from their villages and denied the right to return, as in the case of the inhabitants of Iqrit and Kafr Bir-im. For 26 years, our population has been living under martial law and has been denied freedom of movement without prior permission from the Israeli military governor—this at a time when an Israeli law was promulgated granting citizenship to any Jew anywhere who wanted to emigrate to our homeland. Moreover, another Israeli law stipulated that Palestinians who were not present in their villages or towns at the time they were occupied are not entitled to Israeli citizenship. . . .

The Palestinian people have produced thousands of engineers, physicians, teachers and scientists who actively participated in the development of the Arab countries bordering on their usurped homeland. They have utilized their income to assist the young and aged amongst their people who could not leave the refugee camps. They have educated their younger brothers and sisters, have supported their parents and cared for their children. All along the Palestinian dreamt of return. Neither the Palestinian's allegiance to Palestine nor his determination to return waned; nothing could persuade him to relinquish his Palestinian identity or to forsake his homeland. The passage of time did not make him forget, as some hoped he would. When our people lost faith in the international community which persisted in ignoring its rights and when it became obvious that the Palestinians would not recoup one inch of Palestine through exclusively political means, our people had no choice but to resort to armed struggle. Into that struggle it poured its material and human resources and the flower of its youth. We bravely faced the most vicious acts of Israeli terrorism which were aimed at diverting our struggle and arresting it. . . .

It is through the armed revolution of our people that our political leadership and our national institutions finally crystallized and a national liberation movement, comprising all Palestinian factions, organizations and capabilities, materialized in the Palestine Liberation Organization.

Through our militant Palestine national liberation movement, our people's struggle has matured and grown enough to accommodate political and social struggle in addition to armed struggle. The Palestine Liberation Organization has been a major factor in creating a new Palestinian individual, qualified to shape the future of our Palestine, not merely content with mobilizing the Palestinians for the challenges of the present. . . .

The Palestine Liberation Organization has earned its legitimacy because of the sacrifice inherent in its pioneering role, and also because of its dedicated leadership of the struggle. It has also been granted this legitimacy by the Palestinian masses, which in harmony with it have chosen it to lead the struggle according to its directives. The Palestine Liberation Organization has also gained its legitimacy by representing every faction, union or group as well as every Palestinian talent, either in the National Council or in people's institutions. This legitimacy was further strengthened by the support of the entire Arab nation which supports it, and further consecrated during the last Arab Summit Conference, which affirmed the right of the Palestine Liberation Organization, in its capacity as the sole representative of the Palestinian people, to establish an independent national authority on all liberated Palestinian territory.

Moreover, the Palestine Liberation Organization's legitimacy has been intensified as a result of fraternal support given by other liberation movements and by friendly, like-minded nations that stood by our side, encouraging and aiding us in our struggle to secure our national rights. . . .

The Palestine Liberation Organization represents the Palestinian people. Because of this, the Palestine Liberation Organization expresses the wishes and hopes of its people. Because of this, too, it brings these very wishes and hopes before you, urging you not to shirk a momentous historic responsibility towards our just cause. . . .

I am a rebel and freedom is my cause. I know well that many of you present here today once stood in exactly the same position of resistance as I now occupy and from which I must fight. You once had to convert dreams into reality by your struggle. Therefore, you must now share my dream. I think this is exactly why I can ask you now to help, as together we bring out our dream into a bright reality, our common dream for a peaceful future in Palestine's sacred land. . . .

In my capacity as Chairman of the Palestine Liberation Organization and commander of the Palestinian revolution I proclaim before you that when we speak of our common hopes for the Palestine of tomorrow we include in our perspective all Jews now living in Palestine who choose to live with us there in peace and without discrimination.

In my capacity as commander of the forces of the Palestine Liberation Organization I call upon Jews to turn away one by one from the illusory promises made to them by Zionist ideology and Israeli leadership. They are offering Jews perpetual bloodshed, endless war and continuous thraldom.

We invite them to emerge into a more open realm of free choice, far from their present leadership's efforts to implant in them a Masada complex and make it their destiny.

We offer them the most generous solution—that we should live together in a framework of just peace in our democratic Palestine.

In my formal capacity as Chairman of the Palestine Liberation Organization I announce here that we do not wish one drop of either Jewish or Arab blood to be shed; neither do we delight in the continuation of killings for a single moment, once a just peace, based on our people's rights, hopes, and aspirations, has been finally established.

In my capacity as Chairman of the Palestine Liberation Organization and commander of the Palestinian revolution I appeal to you to accompany our people in its struggle to attain its right to self-determination. This right is consecrated in the United Nations Charter and has been repeatedly confirmed in resolutions adopted by this august body since the drafting of the Charter. I appeal to you, further, to aid our people's return to its homeland from an involuntary exile imposed upon it by force of arms, by tyranny, by oppression, so that we may regain our property, our land, and thereafter live in our national homeland, free and sovereign, enjoying all the privileges of nationhood.

I appeal to you to enable our people to set up their national authority and establish their national entity in their own land. . . .

39. The Views of the Popular Front for the Liberation of Palestine (PFLP) and the Popular Democratic Front for the Liberation of Palestine (PDFLP)

George Habash and Nayef Hawatmeh

George Habash was born in 1926 in Lydda of Greek Orthodox parents and was trained in the Medical School of the American University in Beirut. He was one of the original founders of the Arab National Movement (ANM), a group seeking Arab unity and opposed to al-Fatah. He gradually tilted toward Nasser's view of Arab unity and had to leave Jordan, where he was working, going to Syria in 1957. An ideological rift eventually developed in the ANM, and by 1967 it had turned toward Marxism-Leninism. A younger group under Nayef Hawatmeh, a Jordanian Christian who adopted a Marxist philosophy, split and formed the Vengeance Group, *while another faction under Ahmad Jibril founded the Palestine Liberation Front and conducted several raids in Israel. In 1968 these two groups and another small*

*one combined to form the PFLP and came under Habash's command.
Habash was arrested in Syria and kept in jail for eight months. During this
period Hawatmeh tried to take over the organization, but was unsuccessful
because of disputes over the place and role of the middle classes in the
Palestinian state. Habash eventually escaped from jail and assumed the
leadership of the PFLP; Hawatmeh went on to establish in 1969 the PDFLP,
which received help from Syria and was recognized by the PLO as a
separate commando group. Habash, like most of the leaders of the ANM,
abandoned nationalism and socialism as proposed by Nasser and the Ba'th
as being ideologically too weak to mobilize the masses and spark the
recovery of Palestine. He adopted Marxism and has been its main proponent
and defender in the PLO. He claims that a social and political revolution in
the Arab world, based on Marxism, will speed up the liberation of Palestine.
As tactics, he sees unity and armed struggle as going hand in hand. Habash
has been very critical of the moderate or conservative Arab regimes and has
accused them of being ready to sign a peace with Israel for the sake of good
relations with the United States. The moderates in turn have shown
considerable hostility toward Habash and his group. He has also frequently
clashed with his PLO colleagues because of disagreement with their
moderate tactics. Despite his radicalism, Habash has achieved considerable
stature in the PLO and abroad, especially among Marxist regimes, and is
usually ranked second to Arafat.*

*The excerpts below, the first by George Habash and the second by
Nayef Hawatmeh, are from statements given out during press conferences
convened for the purpose of discussing the October War of 1973 and de-
nouncing various peace plans floated in 1974 by Henry Kissinger. (One of
these plans involved a Palestinian state under joint Jordanian-Israeli
sovereignty.) The statements appeared originally in newspapers in Beirut (al-
Hadaf) on November 2, 1974; and the excerpts are from translations
published by the* Journal of Palestine Studies 4, *no. 2 (Winter 1974): 175–
77 and 3, no. 3 (Spring 1974): 198–202 passim.*

Statement by George Habash

The Palestinian revolution's slogan of a democratic society in Palestine is the only way to the freedom and progress of all the inhabitants of
the area, including the Jews themselves. It is the only way to a just and
permanent peace. The proposal for a "just and permanent peace" discussed by Kissinger, the emissary of imperialism, is a proposal to ensure
the survival of the "cockpit of tension" in the area.

This is what the Popular Front for the Liberation of Palestine wanted
to say on the occasion of the Rabat Summit Conference. . . . The interests

of certain Arab regimes are completely opposed to the policy of the people's war of national liberation. The palace-dwellers who are linked to imperialism, and those who join with imperialism in exploiting the wealth of peoples and the toil of workers—these regimes and social forces, immersed as they are in a life of luxury, can never follow this course of the revolutionary political line. They want stability and tranquility so that they may continue to wallow in their life of corruption, ease and luxury at the expense of the millions. These reactionary and subservient regimes and forces execrate such a policy and revile those who advocate it.

But this policy is the only one that serves the interests of the millions of the masses of our Arab nation and its overwhelming majority.

It is our afflicted and deprived working class who live in shanty towns around the Arab capitals and cities, and our poor peasants who eke out a wretched existence in the countryside of Egypt, Sudan, Tunisia, Morocco, Jordan, Lebanon and the Arabian Peninsula—it is these who daily experience the harshness of life, it is these who every moment realize how heavy is the yoke of national and class oppression they are living under. It is they who want change. It is they who realize that the rifle and the people's national war are the way of settling their contradiction with their national and class enemies, starting with Israel and imperialism and ending with the reactionary and subservient forces.

The national policy proposed by the Popular Front for the Liberation of Palestine as an alternative to the policy of settlement and surrender, is the policy of the nationalist forces and regimes, the policy of the revolutionary classes of the masses of our nation.

Our object in presenting this policy on the occasion of the Rabat conference is: first, to disclose the inability of the reactionary, subservient and surrenderist regimes to embrace this nationalist line; secondly, to establish the political line which our Palestinian and Arab masses want the nationalist, progressive and anti-imperialist regimes, as represented by Iraq, Algeria, Democratic Yemen and Libya, to make the basis of their struggle; thirdly, our object is also to help the masses to distinguish between Arab solidarity in support of a nationalist political line, and "Arab solidarity" in support of the line of settlement and surrender.

Our Palestinian people, in particular, have had bitter experience of so-called "Arab solidarity"—the solidarity of the Arab regimes—on more than one occasion in the history of their national struggle. It was in the name of Arab solidarity that the great strike in Palestine in 1936 and our people's armed revolt were defeated. It was in the name of Arab solidarity, too, that the armies of the Arab states came in in 1948, under the command of King Abdullah and Glubb Pasha, to anaesthetize the Palestinian and Arab masses and to carry out the conspiracy of the foundation of Israel.

Today we are entitled to declare in a loud voice that under the banner of the summit conference and Arab solidarity an attempt is being made to bring about a political settlement that will give Israel a stronger foothold and restore imperialist domination of the area. At the summit conference the subservient forces will submit Kissinger's proposal for a declaration of the termination of the state of war with Israel in return for promises—mere promises—of withdrawal from certain Arab territories. Our masses resolutely declare that the termination of the state of war with the usurping Zionist enemy is flagrant treachery to the history of our struggle. It is the duty of the nationalist regimes to thwart this conspiracy.

Our Palestinian and Arab masses call on the representatives of Iraq, Algeria, Democratic Yemen and Libya to resist this surrenderist attitude and to struggle for Arab solidarity based on the people's national war ... and not on the secret diplomatic manoeuvres at which Kissinger is so expert and which the Arab rulers who admire Kissinger are so fond of praising. We warn against all manoeuvres aimed at bringing in the nationalist forces and regimes to provide cover for surrender and imperialist settlements.

By settling the Arab-Israeli conflict American policy hopes to implement a comprehensive plan covering the whole of the Arab area. The object of this plan is: firstly, to consolidate the reactionary regimes; secondly, to encircle or destroy the progressive regimes; thirdly, to silence Arab guns in Palestine, Amman and Eritrea. After that American imperialism will be assured of obtaining full control of Arab oil wealth—production, prices and profits—thereby depriving our masses of the possession of this important basic resource and preventing their use of it to combat the poverty, misery, disease, distress and hunger from which they suffer.

These are the outlines of the proposed American plan for the area which imperialism hopes to implement through the "settlement" of the Arab-Israeli conflict. Therefore all forces must unequivocally face up to their responsibilities before the masses during this fateful period in the history of Arab struggle.... The October war (of 1973) generated new convictions in the ranks of our Palestinian and Arab masses. It also focused attention on the way in which Palestinian and Arab national unity becomes very strong, very strong indeed, when an armed confrontation with the usurping enemy is at its height. In addition there is the level of preparedness of our masses from the Maghreb to the east of the Arab Peninsula, their very high state of preparedness for all sorts of sacrifice on behalf of the goal of the liberation of a part of Arab territory, the goal of the liberation of Palestine. It is essential that we keep these things in mind, regardless of how difficult we find the new political situation since October. If we are convinced of this, then I believe that it is the duty of all of us to give prominence to these facts. Naturally we must not go too far in the other direction and adopt a delusory concept which makes light of the enemy and the capacities of the hostile alliance of Israelis, Zionists, imperialists and reactionaries. But in my estimate, if the thinkers, writers and Arab revolutionary organizations make every effort to present their case to the Arab masses, the October war can ensure that the revolutionary, scientific view will prevail so that the Arab masses will be able to form their standards and define sound attitudes to them.

Internationally, I think the most important change that has taken place is that imperialism as a whole, and American imperialism in particular, has shifted its position regarding the Arab-Israeli conflict—within limits, of course. American imperialism wants to contain the results of the war as rapidly as possible, to prevent their reaching their logical conclusion. It has therefore developed a great eagerness for achieving containment of the problem through a settlement in the face of the post-war balance of forces.

Statement by Nayef Hawatmeh

We state unequivocally that all settlements [of the conflict] based on the [proposed] American-Zionist-Hashemite solution will lead to surrender and the liquidation of the Palestine problem. Our attitude to all other interested parties who do not precisely define their concept of Palestinian rights will be clearly determined by the support they provide for the principles implied by the concept of the national rights of the Palestinian people. These national rights are derived from all the contemporary and historical rights and achievements of the Palestinian people, and we shall oppose anything that leads to their infringement.... The clear implication of this, from our viewpoint as Palestinians, is that our struggle is towards the liquidation of the Zionist occupation and its dislodgement from the Arab and Palestinian territories occupied in 1967. This approach derives from the general strategy of total liberation of the soil of the homeland; this national achievement will be employed in the service of the general strategy, at the same time enabling our Palestinian people, in all the territories which have been liberated and from which the enemy has withdrawn, to decide their own destiny there and establish their own independent Palestinian jurisdiction. This requires the mobilization of the masses of our people, both internally and externally, for this clearly expressed purpose, because the struggle for this achievement serves the general strategy of pursuing total liberation of the soil of the homeland in subsequent stages.

Regarding the Arab nation, this approach also implies a demand for an unambiguous commitment by the nationalist Arab regimes and the forces of the Arab revolutionary movement to follow this policy alongside us. Such a commitment will necessarily lead to the sabotage of bipartite solutions, partial solutions and the American-Zionist-Hashemite solution. We are immediately responsible for struggling against these solutions which lead eventually to a plan for the liquidation of the Palestine problem at this stage, for the obliteration of Palestinian national identity and personality, and the reannexation of these Palestinian territories, either within the framework of the process of Israeli expansion, or to the United Arab Kingdom [proposed by Jordan]. The adoption of such a solution would by necessity mean the creation in the area of a situation based on the concept of dual security maintained by Israel and the Arab states who would conclude the settlement. The Palestinian problem and all our national gains would thus be threatened with liquidation. Not only would the state of war with Israel be terminated and the confrontation frozen, but the whole Arab-Israeli conflict would be stabilized and the situation that existed from 1948 to 1967 would be restored....The essence of the conflict is how we can, in the light of the facts established by the October war, work out a concrete programme which will make it possible to frustrate action involving surrender and liquidation and to frustrate the annexationist and expansionist plan—whether expansion on the part of Israel or annexation on the part of King Hussein. This programme will in effect make it possible to stiffen national positions on the fighting fronts, so as to promote greater inflexiblity in the face of reactionary and imperialist pressures and of bipartite solutions—which all tend towards surrender and liquidation.

40.   The PLO and the Palestinian State

Sabri Jiryis

Originally the PLO rejected any proposal to establish a Palestinian state on a part only of the original area of Palestine. After 1973, there was some change in this attitude, as indicated in a new political program of the PLO. There was also some discussion about the recognition of Israel by the PLO. The comments of Sabri Jiryis on this issue appeared in Shu'un Filastiniya *(May 1975); the excerpts are drawn from the translation published in* Journal of Palestine Studies *6, no.2 (Summer 1977); 150–51 and 4, no. 4 (Summer 1975): 139–40.*

The proposal to establish a Palestinian state in the West Bank and the Gaza Strip after the withdrawal of Israeli forces from them, along with all the other Arab territories occupied in 1967, as part of an overall settlement of the Middle East crisis, was put forward at the beginning of the seventies.... At the time this proposal aroused violent reactions among Palestinians, whatever organization they belonged to and whatever their point of view, and it was described in the most unflattering terms. What is more, certain people who had set themselves up as custodians of what they called Palestinian "patriotism," took it on themselves to exercise surveillance over people and to take note of everything they did, lest someone should get out of control and start talking about the "pygmy state" or indulge in even worse forms of "capitulationism"....

However, this attitude changed considerably after the October 1973 War, as a result of the new situation that had arisen. The Twelfth Session of the [Palestine] National Council (Cairo, 1974) endorsed the Ten Point Programme, which approves the establishment of "the independent combatant national authority for the Palestinian people over every part of Palestinian territory that is liberated." But it would be wrong to think that this programme involves any major change in previous attitudes for, according to its preamble, "It is impossible for a permanent and just peace to be established in the area unless our Palestinian people recover all their national rights and, first and foremost, their rights to return and self-determination in the whole of the soil of their homeland, " where "whole" is the operative word. Similarly, Point Four of the Programme says: "Any step taken towards liberation is a step towards the realization of the Liberation Organization's strategy of establishing the democratic Palestinian state specified in the resolutions of previous Palestinian National Councils." The "democratic state," according to the resolutions of previous National Councils, is that which must be established in Palestine "after the comprehensive and total liberation of Palestinian soil from occupation by Zionism and its base Israel."

A comparison between the expression quoted above and those used in the new Political Programme shows that a tangible and fundamental change has taken place in the Palestinian attitude. The new program does not use the expressions "democratic state," "national authority" or "Palestinian mini-state," but talks of an "independent national state" that is, in short, an independent state on part of the territory of Palestine.

What has happened in the last seven years to turn the objectionable "mini-state" into a "national state" although the geographical frontiers and the size of the population on which the "mini-state" was to be based are not so very different from those which may form the basis of the "state"? Of course, many things have happened at several levels and there have been changes and developments that have, firstly, led to greater realism and reasonableness in the Palestinian arena in general, and left their mark on Palestinian collective political thinking. Other things, too, have happened, things that are extremely limited, but also extremely important, in that the Palestinians have been made to understand by a number of states, large, medium-sized and small, which support them or sympathize with them, that the ceiling of Palestinian struggle in this stage—and let us not deceive ourselves, this stage may well last at least to the end of the century—is an independent Palestinian state in part of the territory of Palestine, and that there is not a single state of any importance that is prepared to go further than that with them. Moreover, many quarters have made it clear to the Palestinians that if they want to go their own way they will have to bear the responsibility for their actions and confront their destiny alone. This advice has obviously had its effect, especially in the light of the ordeal of Lebanon in 1976, and the new political programme is as clear, realistic and reasonable as it could be.

The new Political Programme is not made less clear or realistic, in its call for the establishment of an independent Palestinian state on part of the territory of Palestine, by the request to the Palestinian National Council "to realize our inalienable rights as endorsed by the General Assembly of the United Nations since 1974, and in particular in resolution 3236" or by the attempts by certain quarters to interpret this as meaning the establishment of the Palestinian state in the whole of Palestine, although there is nothing in the United Nations resolutions to support this interpretation. . . .

An unconditional recognition of Israel in our present situation would mean both abandoning the rights of the Palestinians and legitimizing an entity that is hostile to the aspirations and interests of the Arab nation. Despite the current powerful trends, both international and regional, that talk of "ending the state of belligerency" between the Arabs and Israel or call for the establishment of "permanent peace in the Middle East," it is still, of course, not easy to talk of recognizing Israel. This is because, for many at least, it is still "nationally impermissible to recognize Israel," especially as to do so involves "national treason requiring punishment for its perpetrators." However a more profound examination of this aspect shows that the "bugbear" of recognition of Israel does not exist and that the controversy about recognition or non-recognition is a storm in a teacup.

[Jiryis pointed out that although Israeli leaders constantly repeat that they cannot possibly deal with the Palestinians so long as they refuse to recognize the existence of the Israeli state, such attempts are, he maintained, a cover-up for Israel's own refusal to recognize the Palestinians' existence. The Israelis have always insisted that the Palestinians are just refugees who should be repatriated to other Arab countries.]

There is nothing strange in this Zionist-Israeli attitude to the Palestinians because a different attitude indicating Israel's recognition of them would automatically raise the question of their national rights. This question is a contradiction of the concepts of Zionism and would lead to the Palestinians being regarded as at least an auxiliary factor in deciding the future of Palestine, which is of course rejected by Zionism and Israel. There is nothing, therefore, to support any of the interpretations to the effect that Israel is seeking recognition by the Palestinians as part of the attempts to reach a political settlement in the area. Such recognition, which would certainly entail Israeli recognition in return, would raise the question of all the rights of the Palestinians, supported by United Nations resolutions, including their rights in the territories occupied in 1948, with all that this would involve. It might also lead to the Arab minority in Israel, which constitutes nearly a tenth of the population, being granted national rights. All these are problems Israel can do without. . . .

It is therefore clear that there are no grounds for the current quarrels between Palestinians about the "bugbear" of recognizing Israel because if the question does not exist there is no reason why it should paralyze their thinking and involve them in side battles. However, the problem is not as simple as that, nor can it be solved so easily. All the forces, both international and regional, that are seeking a political settlement in the area assume that there must be a "just" and "permanent" peace between the states of the area, whereas Israel demands prior recognition of her by the Palestinians. At the same time there seems to be no possibility of an Israeli withdrawal from the occupied areas without "termination of the state of belligerency" against Israel by the countries concerned or at least an undertaking "not to use force" in settling disputes with her. Obviously such an attitude puts the Palestinians in a difficult situation. But the difficulty of the situation is due, to some extent, to the tendency to ignore the aspect [we have presented] and to the failure to present things in their true light. Both these trends are caused by the dismay that prevails in many Palestinian circles when there is talk of recognizing Israel which leads them, in turn, to relinquish the strong cards supporting the Palestinian attitude, both at Arab and international levels. It does not weaken the Palestinian position to talk of recognition of them or by them: the Palestinians need to be recognized before they recognize others. Israel, which is in control of their territory and denies their rights must first recognize them and their rights—a recognition which would have "disastrous consequences" for the Zionist entity—and then "study" the question of being recognized herself. Meanwhile the Arab states should shelve the question of a "just and lasting" peace until that stage has been reached. Failure to present things strongly and clearly enough can only do harm to the Palestinians and the Arabs when the question is raised, especially in international circles.

41.   The USSR and the Palestinians

The Soviet regime has been a steady supporter of the PLO, regarding it as the revolutionary organization best able to replace the existing regimes in the Middle East with Marxist ones, despite the fact that the PLO's majority has so far rejected Marxist doctrine. On July 31, 1974, the first day of the visit to Moscow of Yasser Arafat, the official Soviet government newspaper Izvestia *published one of the most important articles on the Palestinians to have appeared in the Soviet press for years. Written by editor-in-chief Lev Tolkunov, the article focused on "the painful destiny of the Palestinians and their struggle for their rights." It appeared in excerpts in the* Journal of Palestine Studies *4, no. 1 (Autumn, 1974): 164–75.*

The Israeli aggression and the violence of the occupiers in the occupied territories led to a new wave of Palestinian refugees. The sum total of refugees became 1.8 million; there are now more than two million Palestinian Arab refugees if we take into consideration the fact of their population increase at the rate of 55,000 per year. These refugees suffer under very difficult conditions.

When we talk about the Palestinian resistance we cannot but discuss the class structure of this movement. We saw in Beirut luxurious houses and buildings, especially in the area overlooking the sea and in the mountains, which are owned by wealthy people from the Arabian Gulf. They are also Arabs but they own millions and hire hundreds of thousands of Palestinians to work in the construction business. They pay them very low wages, fire them without indemnity, and withhold their social rights. On the other side, a certain number of Palestinians have started somewhat prosperous businesses in the Arab countries; they are also refugees from Palestine but they own stores and barber shops or work in trading companies. . . .

There is also an elite Palestinian bourgeoisie, as well as Palestinian millionaires in Lebanon itself. This "elite" owns, for example, hotels and restaurants in the expensive Raouche area. Abdul-Muhsin Kattan, who is well known in Lebanon, is considered one of the richest Beiruti personalities. The Palestinian millionaires also own the Starco Centre, which includes a hotel, restaurant, cinema and other businesses. The Palestinian bourgeoisie usually meet with the local bourgeoisie. They can obtain, or rather buy, Lebanese citizenship and thus become excluded from restrictions put on other Palestinians. But these [elite] Palestinians, the bosses, if we can say so, usually support and fund the Palestinian organizations. For some of them this support arises from patriotic feelings, for others, from a desire to gain a political capital based on calculations for the future. . . .

The difficult and even hopeless conditions in the camps, and the terrorism of the Israeli military gang, led a group of Palestinian organizations—and their number is not large—to the road of irresponsible acts which greatly harmed the resistance movement. These acts were, primarily, hijacking civilian planes, mailing bomb packages, or doing things which were generally condemned such as the kidnapping and killing of the Israeli athletes at the Olympic games in Munich. . . .

Most of these operations were carried out by the "Black September" group, named after the bloody massacre of the Palestinians in Jordan in September 1970. Members of this group consider terrorism as their basic tactic. Progressive Arab public opinion condemns such actions, which spoil the reputation of the Palestinian resistance movement, and which are seriously harmful to the common struggle of the Arab people. In addition, terrorist activities become a winning card in the hands of the reactionary conglomerates. This happened in Jordan in 1970, and in Lebanon in 1973 when serious armed fighting erupted between the Lebanese Army and the Palestinian fighters. Quite a number of victims fell on both sides. Although these fights were stopped later, they only served the interests of the enemies of the Arab world. . . .

The Arab Palestinians and the resistance movement have had many hard experiences, but no hardships or sacrifices can stop the struggle of the Palestinian fedayeen. In spite of the Israeli aggression and the conspiracies of the Arab reactionaires, specific actions are being taken now to unite the various organizations, and to prepare a political programme. In the course of discussing the position of the Palestinian people with respect to Israel, all Palestinian organizations, more or less, are now taking more realistic positions. Many of them think that in case the West Bank and Gaza are liberated, it is possible to establish on this land a Palestinian state. . . .

At the same time, it should be well known that the Palestinian movement is not harmonious in its class structure. Besides the forces which are oriented towards progressive evolution, and which represent the nucleus of the movement, there are some reactionaries, some extremists, and some who do not understand the realistic balance of power. They do not take into consideration the characteristics of the struggle, nor do they choose the right tactics. At the same time, the Arab reactionary forces are doing their best in order to prevent this movement from becoming firmly rooted. It is a top priority to establish close relations with the progressive forces in the Arab world, as well as to increase cooperation with the socialist countries....

During my numerous visits with the Palestinian leaders and the ordinary Palestinians, I had the chance to hear the USSR highly praised for its position concerning the settlement in the Middle East. The Palestinian leaders emphasize that the decisive power which helped the Arabs achieve specific success during the October War was the support of the USSR....

Yasser Arafat, George Habash and Nayef Hawatmeh talk about the USSR as an indispensable power for the Palestinian resistance movement. They knowingly appreciate our position, which is derived from the general direction of Soviet foreign policy, its principle and our pro-grammes for peace....

Some people in the Middle East are now planning to "put their hands" on the Palestinian state if it materializes. Such a state in Gaza and the West Bank will establish the Palestinian entity within the framework of the Jordanian Hashemite kingdom. Heated efforts are being made to switch off the revolutionary spirit of the Palestinians, and to separate them on the basis of class, in order to place at the head of the Palestinian state, when it is established, a bourgeoisie that is closely connected with Arab reaction, international imperialism, and proimperialist governments in the Middle East. These plans take into consideration, of course, that the Palestinian movement, although it has become a very important political element, still suffers from a difficult condition. There are also plans to create dissensions and divide the movement, for the sake of making some benefits in the end.

PART TWO

Political and Social Thought in Israel

XII. INTRODUCTION TO
POLITICAL AND SOCIAL THOUGHT
IN ISRAEL

Even the idea of setting forth in a few pages a picture of the extremely complex, varied, and continuously evolving patterns of thought in Israel is an act of intellectual temerity if not sheer folly. The problem arises from both the nature of this volume and from the ever changing Israeli intellectual sense. This anthology, it should be repeated, aims at giving the student a direct view of the main currents of thought and problems in various countries of the Middle East. Consequently, emphasis is placed on ideas that have an immediate relevance to current developments. But space limitations prevent providing indepth historical background or an extensive survey of all the relevant ideas in the region. The difficulty with the presentation of Israeli thought lies in the sheer impossibility of giving proper coverage to views of all the established parties as well as to those of the numerous formal and informal associations and of the prominent individuals all busy formulating, expressing, defending, or tearing apart, as the case may be, each other's doctrines. For example, in the Knesset in 1977 the parties represented included: the Likud Union (consisting of Herut, Liberals, La-Am, and so forth), the Alignment (Labor and MAPAM), the Democratic Movement for Change of Y. Yadin and H. Rubinstein, the National Religious Party, the Agudat Israel, the Poulei Agudat Israel, the Democratic Front for Peace and Equality (Rakah, Black Panthers), the Shelli and various other parties holding just one seat each. The ideologies of these parties would require dozens of pages to define—and even then the differences are not likely to become sufficiently clear: e.g., MAPAI, MAPAM, the Left, and Rakah are basically leftist parties but their styles of socialism show great variation. In addition to the official parties—23 by one count—there are political groups far to the right, such as Gush-Emunim (which is supporting the Likud position), Rabbi Meir Kahana's group, and other extraparliamentary political groups. Finally there are scores of informal and spontaneous movements—as the excerpts will show—which do not have representation in the Knesset but exert considerable influence, such as the trade unions, the Histadrut, the Kibbutzim, and the Moshavim, which are active and politically influential organizations.

A comparison of the Knesset of 1977 with the one in 1969 will show considerable change of leadership and ideological position among these parties. However, the changes have not been chaotic ones but have followed from well-founded reasons and goals. For example, the section of this volume dedicated to those who advocate some accommodation with the Palestinians covers four different organizations and individuals belonging to the mainstream of Israeli life. These groups have little in common with the Communist Party (Rakah) or the Matzpen or other radical socialist groups. These political parties reflect a variety of social, economic, cultural, and political facets of everday life in Israel. We do not deal with the socioeconomic problems that have sponsored the new parties but concentrate rather on some basic issues that involve the regime and ideology of the Jewish state as a whole. By necessity the choice of excerpts for this anthology has been arbitrary, but I believe that they provide a fairly accurate picture of current ideological mood in Israel.

Israeli thought is shaped essentially by three basic factors that at times are contradictory and conflicting. The first and most powerful factor is the Jewishness of the majority of the Israelis that stems from two historical and ideological sources: Judaism and Zionism. These two are not one and the same as there are Jews who are not Zionists and there are pro-Zionists who are not Jews. On the other hand it is impossible to think of Zionism without Judaism and of Israel without both of these ideologies—at least as the state stands today. This intertwined relationship between religion, state, political identity, and statehood is a source of controversy and also of intellectual energy and creativity.

The second factor is the identification of most Israelis—at varying levels and degrees, to be sure—with Western culture and civilization. Some Israelis claim that this identification undermines their Jewishness while others maintain that it reinforces it. The view depends on the individual's interpretation of Judaism and Zionism, democracy and individual freedom. There is no question that the controversies between those who regard the religion as the way of life and those who regard it just as a source of culture and values are continuing in Israel. The arguments are particularly complex and difficult not only because these issues are debated in the framework of the discussion of national statehood and all it entails, but also because the Israeli Jews who form a majority in Israel have to deal with non-Jewish groups whose economic and political demands cannot be satisfied by Judaism alone.

The third factor influencing Israeli thought derives from a variety of matters associated with the establishment of the state of Israel and her relations with the neighboring Arab countries and the myriad of political and moral issues raised by the Palestinian question. The Palestinian question, viewed in the past as part of the issue of relations with the Arab states, has acquired its own place as an issue of vital importance.

I shall review briefly some of the elements mentioned above. The history and tenets of the religion of Judaism are too well known to need comment here. Judaism acquired its contemporary political significance within the framework of Zionism, and there was an immediate divergence of opinion with those who regarded it as purely a religious way of life. There are a number of Orthodox Jews such as the Satmar Hasidic who reject Zionism and oppose the very government of Israel. Some object even to the use of the name Israel, considering it a break with the Jewish past and a violation of the tenets of Judaism, as only the Messiah can reestablish Israel. However, the overwhelming majority of Israelis and of Jews in general associate Zionism with Judaism and the two with the state of Israel.

Zionism inevitably, therefore, is the fountainhead of thought in Israel. Practically all other currents of thought eddy about it—appearing as elaborations, exceptions, or negations of Zionism. Views on the history of Zionism are diverse and conflicting. Some have claimed that Zionism began when the Lord said to Abraham, "Unto thy seed will I give this land" (Genesis XII, 7) and that Moses was the first great Zionist when he led his people out of Egypt. Others find the beginnings of Zionism in the nineteenth century in the writings of Theodor Herzl and in the First Zionist Congress held in Basel in 1897. The truth is that, like all other ideologies that have come to be accepted as the basis of a national state, the ideal of Zionism has been embellished and related to all historical, spiritual, and cultural manifestations and achievements of the Jewish people. In the Zionist view, the history of the Jewish people consists essentially of the history of the Jews in Western Europe. The brilliant achievements of the Sephardic Jewry in the Ottoman Empire are not given equal weight, despite the existence of serious studies of the history of Ottoman and Eastern Jews. In any event, however, the organization of the community life, on the basis of the Jewish law among the Eastern Jews is a part of the history of the Jews in the Middle East, in particular, and of history in general. National ideologies, it must be remembered, have their own specific vision of national future and consequently appraise history subjectively and formulate their goals accordingly. Zionism is not an exception to this rule. Like other such ideologies, it has selected from the history of the Jewish people those passages suitable to its own purposes, while conveniently ignoring others.

The impartial scholar can distinguish three periods in the history of Zionism. The first period was roughly that before the beginning of the nineteenth century, during which Zionism, if it can be said to have existed at all, manifested itself chiefly in religious forms. The second period begins with the age of liberalism, with the opening up of possibilities for Jews to become part of the new egalitarian, rationalist European society and the deep crisis created by reformism, which raised the idea of giving up some Jewish traditions and habits of thought. Until the age of reformism and liberalism, Jews as a whole were apolitical, their indentity and way of life derived from a common faith expressed in the Torah. The nineteenth century was also the age of capitalism, nationalism, and anti-Semitism. These ideas converged to begin the process that converted religious Zionism to a political ideal. The writings of Moses Hess, Peretz Smolenskin, Leo Pinsker, the gentile Laurence Oliphant, Judah Alkalai, and so forth, notwithstanding their differences in approach and emphasis on political, oral, or religious factors in defining Jewishness, prepared the intellectual foundations that nurtured Zionism later. That the views of these writers were little known, rejected, or even derided at the time by the majority of the Jews is irrelevant to the study of Zionism as an ideology. A new ideology is traditionally formulated by a minority and then is gradually adapted to fit the more pedestrian views and wishes of the majority at the same time as the larger group is being brought to accept the basic tenets of the ideology.

Throughout history there were Jews who desired to return, and many religious Jews did return, to Jerusalem to die and be buried there. In the nineteenth century this desire for return acquired greater impetus as religious fervor assumed political overtones. The Ottoman government, in need of population, in 1857 issued a proclamation, publicized by its embassies in Europe, inviting people to settle in the Ottoman lands. Among the many inquiries received came some from Russian Jews asking for permission to settle in Palestine. In 1840 Jerusalem already had a substantial Jewish population, overwhelmingly Sephardic, living in dire economic conditions.

The Basel Congress of 1897 marked the acceptance of Zionism as a political ideology, as defined by T. Herzl in his *The Jewish State—An Attempt at a Modern Solution of the Jewish Problem*. Piecemeal Jewish immigration, the Balfour Declaration of 1917, which promised a national home in Palestine to the Jews (but provided also that the rights of the established population should not be prejudiced), the establishment of the British mandate in 1920, and subsequent developments were the concrete factors through which Zionism gradually transformed itself from utopian dream—all ideologies are utopian at their inception—into a political reality. Some Zionists in this period considered the relations between Jews and Arabs, but these discussions did not go beyond the theory.

The third and probably the most decisive phase in the history of Zionism began on May 14, 1948, when Ben-Gurion announced formal establishment of Israel and received immediate diplomatic recognition from the United States, the USSR, and a number of other smaller states. Until 1948 the Jews in Palestine, despite the existence of Jewish administrative, military, and labor organizations that later became the institutions of the new Israeli state, lived under the British mandate. Zionism, although an ever-present goal, was not the basis of their official political life. The establishment of the state rendered the old-style Zionism obsolete, because the relations between the Jews and the state, as well as the relations between Israelis as nationals of an internationally recognized political entity and the outside world, had to be conditioned by a new set of factors, most of which had little in common with the old Zionism or its historical and religious foundations. In the old days Zionism, although regarded sympathetically by some Western states, was not a recognized international entity. The situation changed the very day the state of Israel was proclaimed. The need to review and revise Zionism in the light of the reality it had engendered was obscured and overshadowed by the uncertainty that surrounded the existence of Israel. The successful war of 1948 against Arab neighbors and the Sinai campaign of 1956 against Egypt did not dispel the uncertainty. The victory in the war of 1967 was decisive proof of Israel's military prowess and ability to survive. The addition of conquered territories—Sinai, Gaza, the Golan Heights, and the West Bank of the Jordan—and the rule of over a million Arabs living in those territories reinforced the Israeli feelings of self-confidence but also hastened the day of reckoning with the principles and mode of life preached by old Zionism. In its formative years Zionism could isolate itself and nurture an image of its future society without any challenge or impediment from the outside world; but once Israel was established as a state, it had to follow the path of other nations, amending its original ideology in order to coexist with the other states. The question was not one of abandoning Zionism but of reconciling it not only with the ideas and expectations of a new generation of Israelis but also with international realities, the norms and the values of other national states. A series of events can be seen as precipitating the adjustment of Zionism to the new internal and international conditions.

The Yom Kippur or Ramadan War of 1973, and especially the Egyptians' successful crossing of the Suez and their demonstration of ability to repulse Israeli counterattacks and cause considerable losses in men and material, had a sobering effect on Israel, despite the advance westward toward Cairo registered by Israeli troops during the last phase of the war. The effects of the war increased the influence of those Israelis who had regarded an honorable peace with the Arabs, rather then their outright surrender and forced acceptance of Israeli terms, as the best guarantee for Israel's survival and prosperity. The peace movement thus acquired a new momentum and changed overnight the entire spectrum of Arab-Israeli relations, especially after President Anwar Sadat of Egypt visited Jerusalem in December 1977 and addressed the Knesset. The visit was followed by the "Framework for Peace in the Middle East Agreed at Camp David," or the Camp David Agreements as they are known popularly, signed on September 17, 1978, and, finally, by the Egyptian-

Israeli Peace Treaty of March 26, 1979. The peace treaty produced a polarization of views and a political realignment in Israel, as some conservative moderates moved to the Right and some liberals moved to the Left in favor of peace, while others joined the conservatives.

The adjustment problems faced by Zionism are seen in at least three major areas. The first is in the issues surrounding the defining of the place and function of Judaism as a culture and as a religion. There is no question but that the Israeli culture, identity, and personality are intimately bound to Judaism. However, living in a strict observance of the Torah and accepting it as a sole normative source is hardly acceptable to all the Israelis, despite the fact that much of the legislation in the country is rooted in religious policy. The situation changed after 1977 during the Likud government of Menahem Begin, who favored and promoted the religious approach—although to a far lesser extent than the Orthodox Jews demanded. The second issue of vital importance to Israel to which the ideology of Zionism has been forced to come to grips is the issue of relations with the Jews living abroad or in Diaspora. Linked to this is the problem of immigration/emigration, which can play a decisive role in the existence of Israel. The third area in which Zionism was faced with adjustment problems is the area of Israel's relations with its Arab neighbors and, especially, the Palestinians. The Palestinian question that appeared as a refugee problem ten years ago has acquired today worldwide dimensions and has created in Israel political crises and divisions hardly conceivable a few years ago.

These then are the three problems that seem to permeate Israeli political and social thinking at the present time. Discussions engendered by these problems revolve around Zionism—in support or in opposition, or as a demand for reinterpretation in new form or according to its original tenets. This is natural, as Zionism and Israel until the present time have been regarded, at least by the governing elites, as being synonymous, and any attempt to separate them has been fiercely resisted.

The excerpts presented in the next sections are taken largely from the Israeli press and illustrate the points raised in this general outline. For the history of Zionism and the establishment of Israel see a collection of 41 volumes printed under the title *The Rise of Jewish Nationalism and the Middle East* (Westport, Conn.: Hyperion Press, 1975); Theodor Herzl, *A Biography* (London: East and West Library, 1957); David Ben-Gurion, *Israel: Years of Challenge*, (New York: Hold, Rinehart, 1963); Martin Buber, *Israel and Palestine, History of an Idea*, (London: Hogarth Press, 1952); Israel Cohen, *A Short History of Zionism* (London: Frederick Muller, 1951); Abba Eban, *My People: The Story of the Jews* (Newport: Random House, 1968); Samuel Halpern, *The Political World of American Zionism* (Detroit, 1961); Paul Goodman, *Zionism in England 1899-1949*

(London: Zionist Federation of Great Britain and Ireland, 1949); Ben Halpern, *The Idea of the Jewish State* (Cambridge; Harvard University Press, 1961); Abraham S. Haldin, ed., *Zion in Jewish Literature* (New York: Herzel Press, 1961); Arthur Hertzberg, *The Zionist Idea* (New York: Doubleday, 1959); Joseph Heller, *The Zionist Idea* (New York: Schocken Books, 1949); James W. Parkes, *A History of Palestine from 135 A.D. to Modern Times* (New York: Oxford University Press, 1949; rev. ed., London: Pelican Books, 1970); Y. Beck and D. Zohar, eds., *A Zionist Anthology* (Tel Aviv: Schenkman, 1971); Walter Laquer, *A History of Zionism* (New York: Holt, Rinehard & Winston, 1972); Nahum Sokolow, *History of Zionism 1600–1918*, 2 vols. (London: Longmans, 1919; reprint, New York: KTOV, 1970); Chaim Weizmann, *Trial and Error: The Autobiography of Chaim Weizmann* (New York: Harper, 1949).

On the redefinition, reinterpretation, criticism, and defense of Zionism, see Ehud Ben Ezer, *Unease in Zion* (New York: NYT Book, 1974); Moshe Davis, *Zionism in Transition* (New York: Arm Press, 1980); V.D. Serge, *Israel, A Society in Transition* (London: Oxford University Press, 1971); Irene L. Gendzier, *A Middle East Reader* (New York: Pegasus, 1969); Jacob Hen-Tov, *Communism and Zionism in Palestine* (Tel Aviv: Schenkman, 1974); Jacob Tsur, *Zionism-National Liberation Movement* (Tel Aviv: Schenkman, 1976); A. M. Elmessiri *The Land of Promise— A Critique of Political Zionism* (New Jersey: North American, 1977); Saul Friedlander and Mahmoud Hussein, *Arabs and Israelis: A Dialogue* (New York: Holmes and Meier, 1975); Mordecai S. Chertoff, *The New Left and the Jews* (New York: Pitman, 1971). A useful book of readings with bibliographical reference is N. Gordon Leven, Jr., ed., *The Zionist Movement in Palestine and World Politics, 1880–1918* (Lexington, Mass.: D.C. Heath, 1974). Another excellent bibliographical source is Frank J. Shulman, *American and British Doctoral Dissertations on Israel and Palestine in Modern Times* (Ann Arbor, Mich.: Xerox Microfilm, 1973). For other references see The Institute for Zionist Research, Tel Aviv, founded in memory of Chaim Weizmann, which publishes a series of studies on the history of the movement and Palestine; and *Zionism*, 4 vols. (Tel Aviv: Massad, 1970–75). (The last volume is in English.) A succinct bibliography on all aspects of Israel was compiled by Bernard Reich in *Israel in Paperback* (New York: Middle East Studies Assn., 1971). The U.S Department of State publishes, through University Publications of America, the O.S.S. State Department and Intelligence and Research Reports, which contain a variety of firsthand information on Middle East and Israeli affairs. *The Socialist Review* occasionally publishes articles critical of Zionism; see the issues of June 1975; September–October 1979; and May-June 1980. A variety of views on Israel and Zionism are published in *Commentary, Issues, Jewish Week*, and *Midstream*.

XIII. FACETS AND INTERPRETATIONS OF CURRENT ZIONISM

42. Zionism and Diaspora Jews

Abba Eban

Abba Eban, the former foreign minister of Israel, one of the leading Jewish intellectuals of our time, and a prolific writer, is a moderate Zionist. In the piece reproduced below, he deals with Zionism and the relations between Israel and the Diaspora Jews; it appeared in the Jerusalem Post *(weekly edition), December 5, 1975.*

Since Zionism is the immediate theme of our encounter, let us have some idea of what it is about. There is a confused notion that equates Zionism with everything that is virtuous and free of sin. Pay your taxes, patrol your neighborhood at night, work harder, strike a little less often, dig some public gardens, behave better in buses—and you will receive a municipal or even a ministerial accolade for Zionist virtue. The truth is that good citizenship is admirable in itself, but it is not the same as Zionism. If Zionism means everything in general it will mean nothing in particular.

Zionism is a very concrete idea focused on a unique concept of solidarity. A Zionist is one whose passionate conviction proclaims: "All the past generations of Jews are my fathers. The communities of Jews everywhere are my brethren. The land of Israel is my people's home." To the outer world Zionism speaks with equal simplicity: If there is an international tapestry there has got to be a Jewish thread. It is only as a sovereign people in its land that the Jewish people can say what it has to say, do what it has to do. Twenty-seven years ago we tore down the "No Jews Admitted" sign from the family of nations. It is never going to be put up again.

History works by contradiction rather than in logic; and the paradox is that our greatest predicament arises from a victory, not from a defeat. Since 1967 our neighbours' aggression compelled a transformation of the particular "Israel" which nearly all the non-Arab world had known and recognized for two decades. There was a vast inflation in size—and, more important, a dramatic change in the human spectacle.

Israel is a Jewish State by destiny and vocation, but through decisions taken by others there are a million non-Jews and non-citizens added to its rule. This generates a complex series of repercussions in terms of nationhood, identity, democracy, self-determination, independence, equality. All these concepts in which the Israeli condition was clear, simple, lucid and straightforward eight years ago are now intricate, ambivalent and confused. The contradictions can only be resolved by peace with secure boundaries so conceived as to ensure Israel's Jewish preponderance and our liberation from an unwanted tutelage over a million extra Arabs. But peace—alas—requires Arab cooperation. The anomalous result is that for Israel to be truly itself in the deepest human and democratic sense, it needs the assistance of its adversaries.

Just because Israel, by harsh necessity, is not what it desired to be in its human composition it is vital that we, at least, present a vision of what we aspire to be. A clarification of Israel's vision of peace is essential for our Jewish dialogue, quite apart from the regional and international necessities. Nearly forty years ago Chaim Weizmann said: "The choice lies between a Jewish minority in the whole of Palestine or a compact Jewish State in a part." The inexorable truth is that this reality has not substantially changed. By the pathos of numbers there is still a mark of interrogation hovering over the crucial issue of Jewish identity. When the Jewish Unity Conference disperses our problems will endure; and we may even have a graver picture of them at the end than at the beginning. But we shall have served good purposes if we banish two illusions: the illusion that our task is salesmanship rather than creation. And the illusion of unequal pride between Israel and Diaspora Jews.

One of the Conference's preparatory documents speaks of "a sophisticated (!) world wide information programme to explain the Zionist enterprise." Sophistication is not the right note. It all sounds very much like a carbonated beverage having trouble in some markets through lack of promotional skills. The hard truth is that our real tasks are concerned not with images but with realities. We insult world Jewry if we ask it only to improve the label and not to join with us in improving the product as well. The Hebrew revival, the Kibbutz, the Moshav, chalutziut, religious Zionism, the elective democracy, the formative academic and scientific institutions of Israel—all that is original and distinctive in our society was created by voluntary Zionism in the pre-State period. The State has given protection and stability to all of these. Its own creative originality lies in the future.

The problem is not for world Jewry to display what Israel builds. The challenge is for Israel and world Jewry to build new realities together in equal parternership and involvement. Let American Jews build a whole city in Galilee, contributing the resources, materials, plans, and the population. Let other communities take total responsibility for similar enterprises in due proportion.

From Jewish scientists and technologists we want not "expert advice" but the direct integration of their talents in the enlargement of our productivity and research. From Jewish businessmen we need not only cheques and bonds, but the transfer to us of the immense productive and managerial skills by which they have enriched free societies.

Jews abroad acknowledge that Israelis exceed them in the inner harmony of their existence and in the totality of their involvement in the Jewish fate. Let us Israelis confess that the Jewish communities of the world command a greater scope and quality of intellectual resources that we have yet managed to concentrate or generate here. There is no room for any condescension or recrimination or for anything except an entire equality of partnerships between those who build great deeds together.

Concrete issues exist around us in abundance. What is needed is a vision to unite them—and to endow them with broader meaning. Only thus can we reverse the downward curve of confidence and give the Jewish leadership a mission sense of motion, leadership and hope.

43. Gush Emunim's View of Zionism

Yosef Hermoni

Gush Emunim is the exponent of Zionism in its most radical and militant form. It holds a mystical view of Israel and its lands and condones no compromise with or acceptance of the Arabs. Many of the settlements on the West Bank of the Jordan were built by the followers of Gush Emunim. The writer of the following piece, Yosef Hermoni, is a member of Kibbutz Ayelet Hashahar, and the article appeared in Iggeret, *the weekly organ of* Ihud Hakevutzot Vehakibbutzim. *It was translated and appeared in the* Jerusalem Post *(International Edition) weekly, June 22, 1976.*

It is not my purpose here to defend any particular action of Gush Emunim. All I wish to do is discuss the hatred some people have for the movement.

The tendency to despise the devotion of Gush Emunim to some particular piece of Eretz Yisrael, the facile way some of our sober people use the term "holy madness" to describe those screechy, pesky Levingers, the frothing hatred that is bent on annihilating this "barrier to peace"—all these are reactions and forms of discourse whose significance goes far beyond Gush Emunim per se. They go to the very heart of the meaning of our presence here between the Jordan and the Mediterranean.

The attempt to present the irrational aspect of our affinity to Eretz Yisrael (call it religious, spiritual, mystical, or whatever you like) as devoid of significance or even dangerous is one that knows no green lines. Those who jeer at sentiments roused by rockhills in Samaria are jeering at the act of Jews kissing the ground upon landing at Lod Airport. No intellectual acrobatics can stop Zionism from withering away once it has been cut off from its mystical, Messianic dimension, the very root of its existence. The profound affinity to Eretz Yisrael, this holy madness with which the Jewish People has been sick these 20-odd centuries, is something the only logic of which is illogic. Any attempt to understand the Zionist phenomenon without taking into account the "holy madness" of it is a sterile one.

Zionism is mysticism. It is a secular expression of Judaism and the religion of the secularists among us. To be sure, it has additional, mundane meanings (a safe haven for a persecuted people, etc.), but it has no meaning when it is cut off from the sanctity of rocky hills in Samaria, sandy dunes in the Coastal Plain, and other things beyond the chemical composition of polluted Kinneret waters.

Mysticism is not the wellspring from which the roots of Zionism draw their nourishment. It is more: Zionism *is* mysticism. I think that even our sensible people will agree that "the State of Israel is a *vision* fulfilled." And what is a vision? Not a historical forecast, the sum of a calculation of social, economic and climatic factors. Not an assessment of the prospects, trends and probabilities of measurable developments. "Vision" is a concept from the world of the very-inexact sciences. The same goes for Zionism. The vision of the Jewish People returning to its land never knew any green or any other lines. The vision of the Jews returning to the Samarian rockhills and the Judean mountains is of the very stuff of the Zionist vision. Whoever derides and mocks this vision is mocking the entire Zionist vision and deriding the Jewish People's undertaking in Eretz Yisrael.

A Jew for whom the Western Wall is no more than a heap of large stones possesses a castrated Jewishness. A Jew whose skin did not tingle when Jerusalem was liberated either has no skin or no Jewishness. Jewish history and its young offspring, Zionism, are a history of sanctified symbols without which they have no future. Stripping Zionism of its ability to experience mystical emotions means the strangulation of Zionism.

And here lies the importance of Gush Emunim: in guarding and fanning the embers of the pure, abstract vision and putting fashionable sobriety in its place. (Sane realism is a vital commodity which should be kept within reach. But it is meaningless unless somewhere above it flies the flag of vision.) Gush Emunim, described as the standard-bearer of "insane Zionism" is indeed carrying that standard. A good thing too, for there is no such thing as "sane Zionism."

"Come on now, be realistic!" say the sane ones in our midst when you try to tell them that one day there will be five, six, seven, eight million Jews living here. And they add: "Who's going to come here? They're happy in the affluent countries, and those in the Soviet Union aren't being permitted to come. That's the way things are."

This sober realism is umbilically linked to the almost physical revulsion that the sober ones feel towards Judea and Samaria. The demographic bookkeeping and the scorn felt towards the people clinging to the Samarian rocks somewhere at Kaddum are Siamese twins. It is no oversight that the population calculators do not take the factor of *aliya* [immigration—also "going up," in a physical and symbolic sense] into consideration. It is an expression of their view of Zionism as an instrument whose job is done.

Those who declare categorically that the slender trickle of *aliya* cannot reshape a statistical reality and shows no prospect of turning into a stream, are passing the death sentence on Zionism. The demographic-bookkeeping theories are positive proof that "realistic Zionism" is a dewinged, sane, impossible Zionism.

What is this near physical disgust that our sober ones feel towards the passionate yearning and mysticism of Zionism? It seems to me that this is a natural, human expression of fatigue. Hikers climbing a mountain sometimes start grumbling about the long way remaining till they reach top. Breath comes short, feet turn heavy and long for level ground. Zionism, too, is getting tired of climbing—and the level meadows are a long way off. We all know this. But too many of us are wont to sink into a Nirvana of pipedreams of peach and lush plains. The razor-edged, cliff-like truth is eagerly and consistently being pushed behind curtains of Western affluence and of the lifestyles of satiated societies.

There is no explaining the shock of the Yom Kippur War and the cult of weeping that followed, the truama caused by the death of several thousand youngsters—about one third of Auschwitz's daily toll—except against the background of this sinking into a national Nirvana, this national pipedream of comfort-just-around-the-corner, this frightening "sobriety." And the hatred of Gush Emunim is nothing less than hatred of the need to look behind the curtain of sensible euphoria.

Gush Emunim with its demands on us is not *the* centre of Zionism today or its only standard-bearer. It would be more accurate to describe it as a shaft of light shattering our Nirvana-befuddlement. Gush Emunim— that band of people dancing like a band of savages—how easy it is to sic the satire-hounds on them. With satire and scorn we try to stop the tears, the dreams, the longings of dynamic, constructive Zionism that have infiltrated into our oh-so-measured lives, for—it is said—they are endangering democracy. Is this a real concern about any real threat to democracy? Or can this nail-biting about democracy be no more than a cover for our fear lest someone comes along and explode our pipedreams?

44. What is Zionism Today?

The following two brief statements on Zionism, emanating from two people in Israel's academic establishment, best express the current view on the issue; Shlomo Avineri is a professor of political science at Hebrew University of Jerusalem, and Shalmi Bar-Mor is affiliated with the Education Department. The writings appeared in a special supplement of the Jerusalem Post *sponsored by the World Zionist Organization, February 14, 1978.*

Shlomo Avineri on
the Revolution in Zionism

Zionism is basically a revolution, not only in the territorial aspect, aiming at the establishment of a Jewish state in the Land of Israel. It is also a revolution in the sense that it has created a new focus of identification and self-identity for the modern Jew in the post-Emancipation era.

Historically speaking, one can say that in pre-Emancipation times, the focus of Jewish self-identity was centered around religious symbolism, and institutionally, around the Jewish community, which was an all-encompassing institution. With the advent of Emancipation and secularization, what was left of the community became nothing more than a religious institution—which means a partial rather than a total experience.

Zionism, by trying to redetermine Jewish identity in terms of a relationship to a body politic, has created a new dimension of Jewish life. In this sense, one can say today that we certainly do not have a uniform definition of being Jewish. We have numerous definitions. Some of them are ethnic. Some of them are religious. Some of them are cultural. Some of them are purely political.

But certainly there's one thing which, due to Zionism, is very much a universal Jewish experience. Among people who consider themselves Jews, there is a sensitivity to and identification with Israel which transcends the mere identification with things Jewish.

If people are concerned about Israel, as they were most acutely in 1967 or 1973, what they are concerned about is not just the individual lives of 3 million Jews. Perhaps under some extreme conditions, the individual lives of 3 million Jews can be preserved somewhere else, if there is a danger to the existence of Israel. What they are concerned with is the corporate identity of the State of Israel. The collective existence of Israel transcends the sum total of the individual lives of the individual Jews living in Israel.

This is the revolution in Zionism. It has created a common denominator which does not determine Jewish identity, but is the only common denominator which Jews of various branches and various belief systems have.

Shalmi Bar-Mor on Extending Jewish Identity

I believe in Israel as the solution to the Jewish problem. The Holocaust is the· most extreme expression of this problem, and Israel becomes the answer to it.

The way I see it, the Holocaust is the result of the combination of several factors. Some of these factors are unique to the period between 1933 and 1945. Others are more profound historical factors. All these combine, and the result is that 6 million Jews died. After this period, some of these factors disappeared and some did not. The Jewish People were left with the immediate need of how to confront this problem.

One of the obvious conclusions is a framework where Jews attempt to control their own destiny, a framework where Jews are not powerless objects, as they were during the Holocaust. They become an active factor in determining their own destiny. That is the essence of the Jewish State.

The other side of the dilemma is the Jewish People. I have a certain knowledge of Jewish communities and I do know that the actual coming to Israel, as far as many Jews are concerned, is a very far-fetched idea. However, the problem of assimilation is acute. But I also see that the idea of Israel has become a central theme that gives Jews a Jewish identity.

Therefore, I believe in Zionism the same way that American Jews see it—as being pro-Zionist. This means being in favour of the idea of Israel, in favour of the idea of the centrality of Israel in their Jewish identity. We who understand Zionism in its most simple form, realize that for most Jews this notion is totally unrealistic. But on the other hand, Israel really has become a central theme of their identity.

A classical Zionist would say "either-or." As a matter of fact, the last Zionist Congress made such a decision. And leaders from the Diaspora said, "Reality is more powerful than all your decisions." And I believe that. Therefore, I would do everything in my power to have Jews abroad extend their Jewish identity through an awareness of Jewish history, an awareness of the Holocaust—anything that might deepen their identity as Jews, and the centrality of Israel in their lives—even if it isn't translated into actually coming to Israel to live.

45.   Zionism and Peace

The first excerpt below was written by Eli Eyal, the head of the Information Department of the World Zionist Movement and appeared in the Jerusalem Post, *November 21, 1978; the second was written by Yosef Nedava of the Haifa University. The two excerpts represent the Zionist concepts of peace with the Arabs.*

Eli Eyal on the Zionist Concepts
of Peace with the Arabs

But a true peace with Egypt is only a partial peace; we are still in a state of belligerency with our other immediate neighbours. Even assuming that peace spreads to other Arab states, there will always be a faction within the "Palestinian movement" which will clamour that they have been wronged. The essence of this supplement is to show the conflicting characteristics between the Jewish liberation movement and the Palestinian movement.

In contrast with Zionist compromise there has invariably been Palestinian rejectionism. Against Zionist conciliation, there has always been Palestinian absolutism. Zionism today does not face the alternative *peace versus war* but peace versus the nullification of Zionism.

Despite the spectacular peace agreement between Israel and Egypt, Zionism continues to be a political outcast in the eyes of 72 members of the U.N. The irony of it all is that a national liberation movement such as Zionism is equated with a form of racism by the Arab-Soviet front, which champions another national movement, the Palestine movement which has usurped much of the Zionist movement's wisdom.

Copying our call for *Shivat Zion* (Return to Zion), they have made the call for *Auda* (the Return) and in every refugee camp you will find at least one school bearing the name Auda. And here, without going into the questions of rights—and they have rights—for us Eretz Yisrael is the homeland of our people. For them it is the homeland of inhabitants. We have been a nation *ab initio.* They form a nation *post factum.* There is no doubt that they have rights and that the Palestine problem has to be solved, whatever the political outcome may be.

Zionism's ironic victory stands out all the more in that the Palestinians have taken from Herzl his *bon mot* that a people is one that has a common foe. They have adopted from Zionism the symbolism of refugees, of homeless people. They imitate Zionism's tenacity of purpose.

Being an adherent of the Zionist liberation movement, why should I not show understanding for the Palestine Liberation Organization? How can I be expected to appreciate a liberation movement whose *raison d'être* is absolutist? Both the substance and the form of its Covenant is worded in totally absolute terminology designed to destroy the Jewish State. In the present era of aspiration to international detente and reconciliation, this is anachronistic lingo.

Furthermore, why should I appreciate a national movement which is itself not independent. Today PLO matters are settled by the Syrian Defence Ministry in Damascus. Contrary to this I can imagine a Zionist who shows understanding for Egyptian nationalism which freed Egypt from the yoke of imperialism.

It is interesting to stress common features between the Zionist Revolution [and the American Revolution] such as their striving to solve their national problem without detriment to others.

The American Revolution gave Americans their national conscience; the Zionist revolution gave Jews statehood. Both movements base themselves on social and political ideals. And the fulfilment of the national dream of both—the American and Zionist—rests upon the norm that the welfare of their society is not at the expense of others.

In contrast with Palestinian absolutism, Zionism in its strivings has always used understatement. When we aspired to a National Home we yearned for a spiritual centre. When we aspired to a Jewish State we yearned for a national home. Even Ben-Gurion was so realistic that when drafting our Declaration of Independence he did not lay down the final aims of Zionism.

The Arabs played the game in the opposite manner. They constantly aspired to the absolute and therefore always missed their bus by one station. They rejected the Peel Plan, then wanted it when the U.N. voted for Partition. They rejected the Partition borders, then wanted them after the War of Independence in 1948. They rejected the 1948 borders, then wanted them after the Six Day War of 1967.

Despite the uncertainty of a true peace, this supplement is imbued with a positive outlook for the future. This is because Zionism has always been a movement based on idealism tempered by realism, and vice versa.

Yosef Nedava on
Zionism's Conception of Peace

Zionism is but another facet of Judaism and can be epitomized as a movement of national liberation seeking to bring about the return to Zion by peaceful means always stressing the *spiritual* aspect of the Jewish destiny. The precariousness of Jewish existence throughout the ages, in a state of permanent minority, placed through some quirk of Providence at the crossroads of bustling humanity, surrounded more often than not by hostile neighbors, is enough to account for the Jewish people's sincere quest for peace. Indeed, historical experience has proved that small nations can hardly hold their own in face of relentless onslaughts.

However, from time immemorial the Jewish people has held firm to yet another conviction: in order to survive, even against tremendous odds, a people should fight instead of taking the line of least resistance.

It seems that into this sequence of events, one can fit the five Arab-Israeli wars, which despite transient euphoria do not seem to end all bloodshed.

It has often been argued that Zionism's misfortune lies in the failure of its leaders to foresee the extent of unyielding Arab opposition to its very nature. It is claimed that the Zionist leadership, in the formative period of the movement, overlooked the existence of the considerable native population in Palestine, not realizing that it was bound to resist all attempts at its eviction. . . .

This argument is completely baseless. Ever since the inauguration of new Zionist settlement in 1882, avenues to finding ways and means for Jewish-Arab coexistence were explored. In 1891, the philosopher Ahad Ha'am warned the Zionist leadership not to disregard the Arab problem: he felt that the dormant local population was biding its time, and was tolerant so long as Zionist settlement was of benefit to it.

Yitzhak Epstein, a well-known educator urged the Jewish Yishuv in Palestine in 1905 to watch its step, lest it awaken "the sleeping lion."

Herzl was also aware of the existence of the Arab inhabitants. He was no naive statesman who supposedly laboured under an illusion that the "Land of Israel was a land without a people, waiting for a people without a land."

It was because of this awareness that he proposed *political* Zionism. Zionist authority would merely inherit the legal authority of the Turkish Sultan.

On the contrary, danger lay in the proposed policy of Zionist "infiltration." In his *Jewish State*, Herzl admitted openly that "the

(Turkish) government would put an end to the entry of Jews into Palestine at the insistence of the local population, which would consider itself in danger."

In the wake of the Balfour Declaration, and more particularly after 1919, the Arab national movement greatly intensified mainly in reaction to the positive steps taken to implement Zionism. Dr. Chaim Weizmann was on the alert and did his best to arrive at a *modus vivendi* with Emir Feisal, the representative of the awakening Arab world, and their agreement might have taken effect, except that extraneous factors intervened.

Missed Opportunities

Over the years, as the Zionists missed the historic opportunities to build the Jewish National Home quickly, and as the Arab opposition assumed threatening dimensions, Dr. Weizmann was ready to go a long way towards appeasing the Arabs in order to persuade them to keep peace. He spoke of political parity, a kind of *condominium* in Palestine under which no party would dominate the other. In 1931 he suggested giving up the prospect of establishing a Jewish State, and even envisaged a possibility of setting up a binational state for the sake of peace.

Dr. Judah Magnes and leaders of the Brit-Shalom movement were persistently and most assiduously exploring prospects for an Arab-Jewish peace, and were ready to pay an exorbitant price for it: acceptance of minority status for the Jews in Palestine (40 percent of the population).

However, all their efforts were of no avail. Arab nationalist leaders would not concede the existence of *moderate* Zionists. In one of the numerous conversations Haim Margalit-Kalvarisky had with Arab extremists, Avni Abdul Hadi told him frankly that he would rather negotiate with Jabotinsky, the reputed Zionist extremist, than with the so-called moderate Zionists, who were nothing but "hypocrites," trying to disguise their real intentions.

Ben-Gurion tried for many years to reach an agreement with the Arabs on the basis of Marxist premises. He believed the Zionist and Arab workers could join forces for their mutual betterment. After strenuous efforts in this direction he was completely frustrated, for there was no Arab proletariat to speak of. In the final analysis, the Arab, any Arab, would always subordinate his inchoate class consciousness to his inbred religious nationalistic loyalty.

When considering the Arab problem and the preservation of peace in Palestine, Vladimir Ze'ev Jabotinsky may have been the greatest realist of all. He came into close contact with the Arabs since 1918. He had numerous conversations with them and became acquainted with their nature and ideology. He understood the importance of the Arab national movement and felt that their antagonism could be appeased by neither bribery nor inducement. They did not care for Zionist benefits.

Native Opposition

Historically, a movement such as Zionism always meets with opposition from the native population. This is inevitable, and it is immaterial that there is room in the country for both the local population and the newcomers.

Jabotinsky was convinced of the moral and historical claims of Zionism, and sincerely believed that the Jewish argument was incontrovertible. His proposal for solving the Arab problem, which he made in 1921, was based on the idea that once a Jewish majority was constituted in Palestine and was strong enough to ward off any attacks, the Arabs would reconcile themselves to the Zionist presence. Equity would dictate that the Jews should have at least a small state of their own.

Ahad Ha'am feared that such a far-reaching solution would never be accomplished without violence, and in principle he was not prepared to sanction the establishment of a state if even a single Arab child were killed in the process. However, ever since the Arab riots in Jerusalem in 1920, the situation in Palestine began deteriorating.

The cause of the Arab-Israel conflict is rooted in the effectiveness of the *moderate* Arab camp. To be sure, over the years of strife and bloodshed there arose various moderate Arab factions who were willing to reconcile with Zionism and work out a formula for Jewish-Arab coexistence. But their voice was always drowned in internecine strife. During the Mandatory period (1922–1948) thousands of moderates were assassinated by their extremist brothers. It was almost a foregone conclusion from the beginning that in this internal war, the extremist followers of the Mufti of Jerusalem, Haj Amin al-Husseini, would have the upper hand. Western observers often fail to grasp the difference between traditional warfare, and the *jihad*, or Moslem holy war. The jihad precludes compromise, and peace with the "infidel" cannot be considered. No "alien" sovereignty was admissable.

"No Recognition"

This same view is at the root of the present Arab-Israel conflict; it was demonstrated very clearly at the Khartoum Summit Conference of 1967 which presented the ultimate programme of the three noes—"no recognition, no peace, and no negotiations with Israel."

This by no means implies that peace will never come to the Middle East. Things are bound to change. But one should not lose sight of the underlying prerequisites of change. Peace is a concomitant of democracy. One cannot cherish principles of peace unless one is inbued with democratic ideals. Education for peace is a long process. It may take generations but belligerency cannot end without the inculcation of these human elements.

46.   THUS (*Kakh*) the Greatness of Israel Will Be Achieved

Rabbi Meir Kahana

Rabbi Meir Kahana, born in the United States, was the founder of the League of Jewish Defense before he emigrated to Israel, where he established the Kakh (THUS) movement. He has been a strong defender of the rights, including freedom to emigrate, of Jews in the USSR. His movement is opposed to withdrawal fom any of the territories occupied by Israel in 1967, and to any compromise with the Arabs. It uses radical, and at times violent, means to oppose the government and to intimidate the Arabs. It advocates the expulsion of the Arabs from the West Bank. The leader has a romantic vision of Israel and its place in the world. The excerpts below are translated from a brochure published in 1980 by Rabbi Kahana.

[Our goal is] to restore Judaism to pristine splendor, namely to restore to the oriental and East European Jews the pride and splendor of which they have been deprived by the Israeli governments and to eradicate the spiritual povery in which the young Jewish Israelis are living [today].

Arabs to Arabland [It is necessary, in order to] implement the plan, to transfer the Arabs living in Eretz Yisrael to the Arab countries. The danger of their becoming a majority in Yisrael as a result of their high birth rate is already evident. It is imperative to prevent the conversion of Israel into a "Falastin" [Palestine] in a "democratic" way. There is no chance for co-existence between Jews and Arabs except by separating them: Arabs to [go] to the Arab lands and Jews to Zion.

Closing the Gap [It is necessary] to deal with the activities which aim at closing the social gap between Jews in Israel. [These activities should become] a real offensive to reorganize the suburbs and convert them into a force which would play an important role in political decisions. [It is necessary] to cancel the financial benefits given to the Arabs and to use these financial resources to solve the problems of the Jews, such as: [helping] the young couples, improving slums in the suburbs, creating educational facilities, rehabilitating the marginal youth, the older people, the prisoners, and the like.

Sovereignty and Authority [It is necessary] to exercise Israeli sovereignty over all the liberated parts of the State, by annexing immediately Judea, Samaria, the Gaza strip and the Golan Heights. Every Jew must be allowed to use his right to settle in any place in Eretz Yisrael. Not one step in retreat [must be taken].

Abrogation of the Capitulation Agreements. The "Camp David" Agreement must be invalidated by rejecting these agreements or any other plan for "autonomy," which would include any suggestion for any kind of autonomy for the Arabs in Eretz Yisrael. Any negotiation with the Arabs should be based on the latter's recognition of the Jewish people's sovereignty over all parts of Eretz Yisrael. It is necessary to lead a strong struggle against any further retreat, and to continue the pressure to return to the lines which existed prior to the agreements in order to regain control of the oil fields.

Terror Against Terror. [It is necessary] to evacuate the foreigners from the Temple Mount, and to put an end to a disgraceful situation, namely, to the small Palestinian state in Jerusalem which the Arabs had established on the most sacred place of the Jewish people—the Temple Mount . . .

Extermination of the [Christian] Mission[s]. [It is necessary] to exterminate by every means the missionary plague spots in the country by confiscating the Missionaries' property and by placing it at the disposal of the needy.

Limited Government [It is necessary] to free the economy, [so that] private enterprise, released from the heavy government control, would increase production, and to coordinate wages with productivity. Heavy tax fines must be imposed in order to avoid tax evasion. The Jewish economy must rely on Jewish manpower.

The Protection of the Entire Nation. Supreme effort must be concentrated to release our brothers from Russia, Syria, and all other "distress" states. Israel is the protector of all the Jews wherever they live. The responsibility for their defense is hers and only hers. [It is necessary] to call for an emergency immigration to Israel of all the Jews in Diaspora and especially in the U.S. before they face a holocaust, God forbid.

A.B.C. [It is necessary] to develop deterrent weapons, and allocate all resources needed for this purpose.

Removing of Traitors. [It is necessary] to call upon each Jew wherever he lives to return to Israel and follow the way of life acording to the Torah and the Commandments, the way of life that preserved the existence of the nation in the Diaspora and will preserve its existence in our future.[We advocate] the establishment of an integral Jewish State; the observation of Shabbat as prescribed by law; conversion as prescribed by law; the prevention of abortions; the denial of civil marriages; the denial of recognition to the Reformists and Conservativists and their institutions. [We must have] confidence and trust in God, the Rock of Israel and its Redeemer. "THUS" and only "THUS" we shall be nearer the coming of the complete redemption, speedily and in our time.

47.   Portrait of a Zionist: Menahem Begin

Begin, Prime Minister of Israel 1977–81 (he was charged again to form the government after his party won 48 seats in the national elections held on June 30, 1981), co-founder of the Herut Party, then leader of the Likud, was born in Poland (then part of Russia), in 1913 and came to Palestine in 1942. He soon became involved in the uprising against the British as the leader of Irgun, which carried out many acts of violence against the British and the Arabs, e.g., the blowing up of the King David Hotel. Yet, he signed peace with Egypt in 1979, renouncing Israeli claims to the Sinai and opening the way to radical changes in Israeli-Arab relations as well as in Israel itself. He can probably be said to have only admirers and enemies, for his views and policies are not such as to be approached neutrally. His two books, White Heights, *on the labor camps in the USSR, and* The Revolt, *on the underground in Palestine, provide excellent insights into the personality of this controversial leader. The excerpt below is somewhat critical of Begin; it is taken from an article by Meir Merhav which relies partly on* The Revolt *to give a good picture of Begin's personality. The article appeared in the* Jerusalem Post, *August 23, 1977.*

No more than a tenth of today's three million Israelis were 14 to 45 years old in 1944–48, when Menahem Begin led the Irgun's revolt against the British. Even then, only a few were aware of its significance; fewer still knew the beliefs and principles, the basic values and the political concepts which guided it. No more than a handful of close associates knew Menahem Begin himself.

Time has dimmed the memory of those who knew and understood. For the rest, Begin was first the leader of the dissident undergound which, at best, had a secondary role in Israel's renascence, and secondly, the leader of a futile opposition whose fiery oratory merited little more than a small-type reporting.

As a leader, no less than as a person, he has remained an enigma for most people. No wonder, therefore that they measure him by the yard-sticks they applied to the kind of leader which they knew—the politician, whose principles yield to expediency, or even the statesman who ulti-mately bends to reality in the recognition that compromise may be the only way to pursue his long term purpose.

No surprise, then, that each new statement of Mr. Begin's is taken as an adroit tactical move rather than as a declaration of principle, each political act as a clever feint rather than as a purposeful thrust.

Many of those who disagree with Mr. Begin's declared aims mute their opposition either because they believe that, if nothing else, the sheer weight of responsibility will make him accept that which he has no power to change, or that his colleagues in the cabinet and his partners in the coalition will moderate his positions. No harm will therefore come—so they believe—from Mr. Begin's probing for the limits of his power.

Nothing could be more erroneous; nothing could be more indicative of ignorance of the unswerving constancy with which Mr. Begin has held the same position, in practically the same words, and for nearly the same reasons, on almost the same public issues, over a period of 30 years; and nothing could show more clearly how little the sources and quality of Mr. Begin's leadership are understood.

The leadership is genuine. However, it derives not from intellectual stature or profundity of thought, but from constancy of purpose, single-minded determination, a sense of mission and an absolute inner certitude of being right and in the right, which have characterized him throughout. This is why it is Begin and no one else who makes foreign policy in the present Government.

Mr. Begin's steadfastness can be illustrated even with respect to secondary issues. Thus, he spoke recently of the need to give the president more real authority. In the Knesset debate of February 16, 1949, he opposed the government's bill that defined the President's authority and proposed to give him a limited power of legislative veto.

In the same debate, Mr. Begin argued in favour of a functional government composed of eight ministries. The number of ministries should not be subject to considerations of party politics, he said. He also demanded that it be established by law that the seat of Government would be in Jerusalem, irrespective of the practical constraints that existed at the time. For, as he said on June 15, 1949, "not every political declaration is a declamation. There are statements which are political acts."

But these are minor matters. When it comes to the central issue of our time, Mr. Begin made his most important statements in Knesset debate on the Rhoades armistice agreements in April, 1949.

To put those statements into perspective, here is a paragraph from Mr. Begin's foreword to the 1972 edition of his book, *The Revolt*, in which he quotes his radio broadcast of May 15, 1948: "The homeland is historically and geographically an entity. Whoever fails to recognize our right to the entire homeland, does not recognize our right to any of its territories. We shall never yield our natural and eternal right . . . When the day arrives, we shall materialize it . . . ."

On April 4, 1949, Mr. Begin called for a vote of no confidence in Ben Gurion's government, for having signed an armistice with, and thereby recognizing, the Hashemite Kingdom of Jordan, and thus giving up to its king, "the slave of the British," "a vast area in the western part of the homeland." Referring to the mutual defence treaty between Britain and Abdullah, and heaping scorn on the government, Mr. Begin said:

"We have achieved nothing through peaceful ways. You, who sit on the green chairs, have deluded yourselves into believing that if you agree to the partition of Eretz Israel, you will get the State of Israel peacefully . . . Is it also written there [in the UN partition plan] that the British will have their guns positioned at the same distance where they will be according to this agreement?" And turning to the Religious Front members in the House, he said:

"Gentlemen, I want to ask you on your conscience . . . how did your hand not tremble . . . to the enemy . . . [and giving] official recognition to the rule of Abdullah over the Old City in Jerusalem?"

But not only Mr. Begin has remained constant. In the generation that has gone by since he said these things, there have been vast changes in Israel's reality, within and without. Yet the basic dilemmas have remained the same, and so have the conflicting answers to the problems. Note, for example, Ben-Gurion's reply in that debate to his opponents, who then also included Mapam:

"A Jewish state in existing reality, even only in western Eretz Israel [that is, without Transjordan] is impossible if it is to be democratic, for the Arabs in western Eretz Israel outnumber the Jews . . . Do you want to have, in 1949 . . . a Jewish state in the whole of Eretz Israel and . . . [should] we drive out the Arabs [to accomplish this], or do you want to have democracy in that state? We want a Jewish state, even if it is not in the whole of the country . . . ."

The minor changes that have to be made to restate this argument in terms of our own times are obvious. Of course Mr. Begin never accepted, and does not accept today, the premises, the analysis and the policy conclusions of his opponents. In *The Revolt* he encapsulates his attitude towards the Arabs:

"Partition will not ensure peace in our country. From the Arab's point of view there are two possibilities only: either they will want, and be able, to rise in arms against Jewish rule, or they will not. In the first case they will fight even against a partition state. In the second case they would not fight against Jewish rule even in the whole country."

And in the foreign policy debate of June 15, 1949, Begin said: "... Peace does not depend on signing peace treaties. Peace between us and the Arab States depends mainly; and perhaps only, on the military, economic, territorial and strategic power relations which will be set up between us and them."

He scorns Ben-Gurion's choice between democracy and Jewishness, and simply denies the relevance of the demographic facts: "We—a minority in Eretz Yisrael? If we accept that assumption, then there are many parts of Eretz Yisrael which should not have been included in her boundaries ... Such an argument cuts the ground from under everything on which we based ... our link with the homeland."

For Mr. Begin, nationhood, sovereignty, the very existence of a nation are not a matter of mere empirical fact. They are the reflection of ideas, of the "supremacy of moral forces," of historical rights, of sacred faith, of legal claim and, above all, of the proof of fire and steel. A nation exists insofar as it is willing and able to fight for its existence. "We fight, therefore we are."

That lesson is the result of the forces which shaped Begin's world view and, in particular, his conception of Zionism.

Mr. Begin's outlook is that of the Polish Jew whom anti-Semitism, powerful enough to hurt and too weak to crush his pride, goaded into Zionist rebellion. It is that of the generation which saw the lofty ideals of a Woodrow Wilson and a Tomas Masaryk go up in the flames of World War II. The collapse of that world left him with a Treblinka complex. The world is against us, at best indifferent. Our very existence is constantly in danger.

Many Israelis share this catastrophistic conception of Zionism, but Mr. Begin is its epitome. In *The Revolt* he says: "Just as 'the world' does not pity the thousands of cattle led to the slaughter-pens in the Chicago abbattoirs, equally it did not pity ... the tens of thousands of human beings taken like sheep in Treblinka. The world does not pity the slaughtered. It only respects those who fight."

Nothing has changed in that attitude, which also explains how he views the Palestinians. They—indeed the Arabs in general and the PLO in particular are out to destroy Israel. They are Hitler in a new guise. The PLO's Covenant is a new *Mein Kampf.* Nothing they say or do can persuade Begin that they want peace. And nothing that we can offer them will do away with that eternal enmity. The only answer to anyone out to exterminate the Jewish people is resistance. Only those who fight can expect to establish and maintain their rights.

And the right of the Jewish people to Eretz Yisrael is not only an absolute moral and historical right, it is also grounded in international law—and it is exclusive. Today, it also includes the right of possession which, to the jurist, is nine-tenths of the law.

48.   The Three Eras of Zionism

Yigal Elam

In this essay Yigal Elam, a lecturer at Tel-Aviv University and author of Introduction to a Different Zionism, *presents a succinct history of Zionism, relations with the Arabs, and the current situation created by peace with Egypt. This excerpt appeared in the* Jerusalem Post, *November 21, 1978, and was presented by the Information Department, World Zionist Organization.*

History never pampered Zionism, which has known two great tragedies—the Holocaust in Europe and the conflict with the Arabs. One might almost think that these tragedies were part of the Zionism fate; like the tragedies, where it becomes clear that the cruelty of fate is not as coincidental as it appears, as if it were predetermined by capricious, vindictive, and uncompromising gods. In reality it is brought about by the flaws of the heroes themselves, and by their original sins.

Thus it is not difficult, ostensibly, to prove that Zionism not only knew in advance that the Holocaust would take place, but even that it built itself because of its awareness of the Holocuast and its results.

However, when the Holocaust occurred, Zionism found itself completely unprepared. And when the ashes settled in Europe, at the conclusion of World War II, it became clear that the Jewish Holocaust was also the Zionist Holocaust. Millions who were the reservoir of the Zionist venture had perished. In the reckoning of history, the Holocaust was not a Zionist "asset." It was a holocaust, pure and simple. Zionism was not prepared to confront it because it did not anticipate it at all, and because in reality the Holocaust was not a foundation stone of the Zionist idea.

That is, the Zionist idea did not grow out of knowledge of the anti-Semitic world, but from knowledge of the national existence of the Jewish people.

The Zionist demand was first and foremost the demand of justice for the Jewish people, a demand for the realization of the sovereignty of the Jewish people, "as all the other nations." This phrase, "as all the other nations," served as the key for the Zionist programme, which was formulated by the first Zionist Congress, led by Herzl, in Basel, in 1897.

The Zionist formulation proposed to guarantee the status and integration of the Jewish people among the family of nations. The Zionist solution was under no conditions directed toward the removal and the renewed ghettoization of the Jews in the face of the modern world, once the gates of the ghettos were destroyed.

And what about the Arabs in Eretz Yisrael? It is true that as far as the perceptions of Zionism were concerned, the relationship of Arabs to Eretz Yisrael was not the same as the Jews to the land. The centre of Arab nationalism, to which the Arabs of Eretz Israel also related, was elsewhere. There was talk of a unified Arab kingdom based on the triangle of Baghdad-Damascus-Mecca.

The Zionists and the British in their naivete, believed that the Arab nationalism realized there would allow the Jewish nationalism to develop simultaneously, in the limited area of Eretz Yisrael west of the Jordan river. The Arabs were not willing to forego the "Arabism" of Eretz Yisrael, and so the dispute erupted in all its intensity.

In terms of history, this was a superfluous and unavoidable conflict. Both sides paid a heavy price.

The Palestinian Arabs certainly did not come out ahead. Not only did they bring about destruction and create refugees, but they also let the possibility of sovereignty slip through their fingers, when they could have had a state side-by-side with the Jewish one.

Had the Palestinians shown a readiness for Arab-Jewish coexistence in Eretz Yisrael, it would have been conceivable that a binational state would have arisen in the full territory of Eretz Yisrael, to the benefit of all . . . .

The anti-Zionist stereotypes which gained popularity not only in the Arab world, but also in the Third World and the New Left in the late 1960's sounded more and more similar to ancient anti-Semitic stereotypes. The apex was reached when Zionism was proclaimed as "racism" [an allusion to the UN resoultion of November 11, 1975, condemning Zionism as racism] . . . .

Originally, when Zionism confronted the oppression of the Jewish people, it occupied itself with self-rehabilitating the oppressed, not denigrating the anti-Semites.

Instead, Zionists asked what part Jews played in the development of anti-Semitism, not to purify the anti-Semites, and not to indulge in self-mortification. Rather, early Zionists felt that by dealing with this issue, they could free themselves from their seemingly hopeless position. What they realized was that the victim had to cease being the victim. Self-redemption was the key, and was not an impossible task. It entailed a radical internal reform, a shift in values, and a change in personal principles. The Jew became independent once again.

It must be stressed that independent national Jewish consciousness did not begin because of confrontations with anti-Semitism, but there is no doubt that this traumatic experience presented Zionism with its challenges and its main goals. World anti-Semitism helped the Zionist consciousness become a revolution aimed a producing a new Jew and a new society.

The return to the homeland was not seen as a return to the Jewish past, nor as only a refuge from the persecutions of the anti-Semitic world. The move to Eretz Yisrael was accompanied by a decision to build a Jewish society which would be a paragon; the national revolution was also meant to be a cultural and social revolution: The new Jewish society in the future Jewish state would be an exemplary model of a society and a nation in the modern era. This was the Zionist decision, based on self-criticism aimed at proving what Jews were capable of doing. Jewish sovereignty was seen by Zionism not as an act of conquest and opposition, but rather as an act of creation.

Therefore the conflict with the Arabs was unforeseen and completely unnecessary as far as pure Zionism was concerned. Not only was it not in keeping with the idealistic views of the Zionist revolution, it also drove the Zionist endeavor off its main track, robbed it of valuable resources, and forced the Jewish settlement and the Jewish state in Eretz Yisrael to arm itself and to adopt a siege mentality.

In Europe the trap was sprung around the Jews, and in Eretz Yisrael Zionism had to contend with mountains of obstacles that the Arab opposition created.

The tragedy of the Holocaust and the tragedy of the conflict with the Arabs were interwoven. The experiences of the Holocaust created an indelible impression on the soul of Zionism. The long conflict with the Arabs and the war for existence shifted the trauma to a new setting. The possibility of a Holocaust in Eretz Yisrael in the period immediately following the Jewish Holocaust in Europe had to be considered. As a result, Israeli society became attuned to the reality of the siege, and developed a siege mentality....

But Zionism arrived to breach the walls of the ghetto. Zionism certainly did not come to change the European ghetto for a Middle

Eastern one. From the day that the state was proclaimed its highest governmental interest was to arrive at a peace settelement with the Arab nations, a peace including physical security, and the promise of free creativity and free and fruitful trade with the outside world. In the early years, this interest was expressed by Israel's leaders. But this voice kept getting weaker with the solidifications and continuation of the conflict. It appeared that Israel was becoming reconciled to the state of constant belligerency.

The instant that it became possible to place Zionism as the antithesis of peace was a sad moment in the movement's history. The same was true when an attempt was made to equate Zionism with racism . . . .

With a speed that is unbelievable, the militant consensus that dominated Israel for the past 10 years was converted to a consensus for peace. Swift changes such as these do not happen easily in a democratic society. However, because the desire for peace is so deeply embedded in the philosophy of Zionism and in the foreign policy of the State, when Sadat arrived in Jerusalem, it appears that he gambled correctly on the basic questions: Is Israel able to reject a peace proposal and still survive? Can Israel deny this goal and not collapse?

Zionism is now standing before the third and most decisive era in its history—the era of the creation of the conditions of peace. In the first era, Zionism fought for Jewish sovereignty. This era ended in 1948. In the second era Zionism struggled to achieve peace. This period is quickly drawing to a close. We are now standing at the door of the third era. The era of peace . . . .

Only now is the opportunity being presented to Zionism to realize its original vision of a model society. This means a society in which the maximal creative capacity and human cooperation will be reached, as a model for all of mankind.

49. An Arab View of the Current Zionism

Adnan Abu-Odeh

The peace treaty between Egypt and Israel, as well as the peace movements in Israel, have produced strong repercussions in the Arab world. Diplomatic relations were severed; and Egypt was ousted from Islamic organizations, in which the Arab view prevails. Even the "moderate" regimes of Jordan and Saudi Arabia condemned Egypt for having broken the Arab solidarity and recognized Israel without there having occurred in advance Israeli recognition of the Palestinians and their rights. Yet the peace treaty and the

changed atmosphere in Israel produced certain other repercussions in the
rest of the Arab world. The excerpt below indicates a certain willingness, in
Jordan at least, to adopt a more positive attitude toward negotiations with
Israel if she abandons "expansionist-Zionism" and is willing to deal with
Arabs on the basis of mutual acceptance of territorial rights and obligations.
The author, Adnan Abu-Odeh, is the former Minister of Information in
Jordan, and the excerpt was delivered as a lecture in Amman in January
1980. It appeared in the Middle East Monthly New Outlook *(August 1980):*
6–9.

Israel was not created by a people who had lived in their land for
hundreds or thousands of years during which they spoke a single language.
Nor was it established by the majority of the people in the country of its
creation, for these were, in 1948, Palestinian Arabs. Israel was conceived
by European Jews and established in Palestine, in Asia, to be a homeland
for individuals or groups coming from many countries and with diverse
cultural backgrounds. All that united them was their common religion.
Most Israelis, in their accounts of Zionist history, attempt to obscure this
background. Israeli writers promote the idea that the 1948 war was against
the Arabs as a war of liberation, in which Israel had won the right to self-
determination. Strong efforts are made by Zionist historians to present the
Jewish minority that lived in Palestine at the beginning of this century as
having constituted the nucleus of a people who then simply expanded
under the British Mandate to the point where they could establish a state.

Zionist settlement, as we know it, was dictated in fact by constant
efforts to achieve three objectives: First, the psychological mobilization of
Jews, wherever they lived, and especially in Europe, in support of the
projected nation-state, by the use of religion and fear of persecution as
basic themes. Jews were made to feel that they were aliens in the
countries they lived in, so that they would take the decision to uproot
themselves from their cultural environment and their homelands and go to
Israel as immigrants. Second, the securing of land and work for these
immigrants through collective efforts; this was the reason for the establishment of the World Zionist Organization, the Jewish Agency, the Jewish
National Fund, and other political and financial institutions. Third, the
uprooting of the original population, and Palestinian Arabs, from their
land.

The Arab World rejected the State of Israel, established in 1948, and
war was fought. The State of Israel, however, became a member of the
United Nations, with the same rights and obligations as the other member
states. In Israel itself, state institutions were set up and the military
terrorist organizations were dissolved and replaced by the army. The first

Knesset was elected and the first parliamentary government formed. But behind the familiar facade of statehood, Israel retained a number of institutions that had been established by the Zionist movement in the period before the building of the state, e.g., the Jewish Agency, the Settlement Department and the Jewish National Fund, which had close links with the earlier settler movement.

Thus, Israel had two sets of institutions, those of the state, and parallel with them, those of the Zionist movement. Even the political parties in Israel made a point of retaining their own settlement departments. In other words, the establishment of the State of Israel did not put an end to the Zionist movement's institutions. On the contrary, the government allotted a ministerial portfolio to absorption, thereby proving that the state was still operating in conformity with the principles of the Zionist movement. It was understood, however, that these settlement institutions would operate within the boundaries established in the 1948 war. The Israeli government called for permanent peace with its Arab neighbors, who persisted in rejecting her. Nasserism was anathema to Israel. There started to grow in the consciousness of the Israeli people the seeds of Israeli nationalism, as a natural and viable alternative to the Zionist idea with its expansionist tendencies and its emotional content. The question was, basically, whether Israel was to be the expression of grand national ambitions, i.e., a country whose destiny was subordinated to the original plans of Zionism, or whether it should regard itself as a state in the Middle East, whose principal purpose was to seek accommodation with other states and achieve a normal existence.

Then came the 1967 war in which Israel won a rapid military victory that astonished her as much as it astonished her enemies. The war likewise served to win her the admiration of her friends and sympathizers. But the outcome of the war was not the only surprise. The Arabs accepted U.N. Resolution 242, implicitly recognizing Israel, and the world wished for peace between the Arabs and Israel, in this area which is strategically and economically important because of its oil reserves. All were surprised to find that, instead of exploiting its military victory to obtain the peace it claimed to have been seeking for two decades, Israel was now dragging its feet, procrastinating and impeding the peace efforts being made under the auspices of the United Nations. The international community was also surprised to see the dormant aspirations of settler Zionism breaking out afresh, and Israel transformed into a broad base from which settlers fan out in all directions, northward to the Golan, eastward into the West Bank, and southward into the Gaza Strip and Sinai. The seeds of Israeli nationalism, which had started to germinate and flourish on the eve of the June War, went into hibernation in the sands of Sinai, the soil of the Jordan Valley and the summits of the Golan. This was revealed in statements like the one made by Yehuda Harel, one of the settler leaders in the Golan Heights, when he was interviewed by the *New York Times* correspondent in August 1975: "Israel is a country without frontiers. Our frontiers will be where we settle."

One manifestation of the change that has taken place in Israeli thinking was the renewal of the settlement movement in the occupied territories. Instead of setting peace with her neighbors in the forefront of its priorities, Israel chose territorial expansion. If we recall that Israel's seizure of land had, from the start, been one of the principal causes of its conflict with the Arabs, we realized that in taking this step it had decided once more to risk provoking the hostility of its neighbors through expansion. It had chosen to follow the course of the Zionist movement, rather than acting in accordance with the requirements and interests of the state on the basis of international law and the rules governing international relations. This situation remained unchanged until the outbreak of the 1973 war. Regardless of its military results, which Arabs and Israelis appraise differently, this war had one important and unexpected result: it made the Israeli people aware of the yet unexploited Arab capacities. Today there are two tendencies in Israel: the Zionist idea of Israel as an organic body with expanding frontiers; and the second, that sees Israel as a national home which does not need expanded frontiers so much as recognition, as a prelude to co-existence with the wider environment. These conflicting trends can be found in most Israelis, even those who come down on the side of the Zionist idea.

In its unmitigated form, the Zionist trend is characterized by emotionalism, impulsiveness and aggressiveness. It denies the existence of the people of Palestine, and believes that the population of the occupied territories must be dispersed and absorbed in the other Arab countries. It maneuvers to gain time to create a fait accompli, and to exploit the land and natural resources of which it has already taken possession. It believes in force and in the effectiveness of military superiority to prevent any increase in Arab strength. It favors preemptive war. It also exerts every kind of economic and psychological pressure on the Palestinian Arabs under its rule, with a view to fragmenting their national cohesion. The advocates of this trend believe that Israel's policy of force and her military superiority will one day oblige the Arabs to accept her on her own terms, and that in the meantime Israel should expand over as large an area as possible.

The second trend, on the other hand, acknowledges the existence of the Palestinian people and their right to establish an independent state or national entity. It sees the settlements in the West Bank and the Gaza Strip as a curse rather than a blessing, because they impede efforts to achieve peace and render it more difficult to attain. It argues that these make Israel a garrison constantly in danger of attack, with doubtful prospects of being able to hold out, because in the long run time is on the side of the Arabs. It believes that Israel can survive only if she can do away with her image as an alien body in the area—an image that is intensified the more Israel provokes her neighbors and makes them feel that it endangers their very existence. It insists that Israel must withdraw from the territories it occupied in the June War, and allow the Palestinian people to decide their own future in their homeland. This alone will assure Israel's survival as a national state for the Jews. The people who follow this trend of thought maintain that Israel must accomplish these aims soon, before bitterness and hostility reach such a pitch that rapprochement becomes no longer possible, and that failure to do so would be a betrayal of the original objective of Zionism, namely, the establishment of a national home, not a fortress under perpetual siege.

As we have seen, these two trends reflect a division in the consciousness of the Israeli people that transcends the limits of political parties and blocs. They are differing concepts of how survival is to be ensured, not of a political or economic program. The Zionists are not the first settlers in history, nor is Palestine the first land to be subjected to colonial settlement. Nor, indeed, is this the first time that Palestine has been subjected to such settlement. The Phoenicians settled North Africa in ancient times, the Crusaders settled the coast of Syria and Palestine, as well as part of Egypt and Jordan in the Middle Ages, and the Europeans settled North America, Australia and many parts of Africa. A study of these patterns of settlement and their results shows that some of them met with success, others with disappointment and failure. For example, the Crusader pattern of settlement failed, while the European pattern succeeded in North America and Australia, though it failed in Africa. It may well be that the peace agreement recently concluded in London, under the auspices of the British government, to solve the problem of Rhodesia, marks the beginning of the end of another chapter in the history of European settlement in Africa. Before that, the French had had to give up Algeria, and the Portuguese left Angola and Mozambique. Why does one settlement succeed and another fail? An analysis of the patterns of success and failure enables us to distinguish a number of factors that govern the destiny of settlement movements. The numerical ratio between the settlers and the indigenous population is one constant factor; there is also a series of variable factors, such as military or technological superiority, political relations, links with world powers, or common interests with such powers.

Before trying to apply these criteria to successful and unsuccessful settlements, I want to make clear that by "constant factor" I mean the one that continues to operate against one party, without being liable to change, and by "variable factors" those that are not necessarily restricted to one party to the exclusion of the other. If, for example, settlers enjoy military, technological or economic superiority over their opponents, that does not mean that this superiority is necessarily permanent; for the other party may progress in one of these fields and turn the variable factor to its side of the conflict. Settlement, in its profoundest sense, is the uprooting of the indigeneous population and its replacement by foreign settlers. Such an operation, by its very nature, cannot be achieved without severe tensions culminating in a bloody conflict, and the more firmly rooted the culture of the natives, and the stronger their sense of identity, the longer will the conflict last and the more elusive its resolution. If we take the American case as a successful pattern of European settlement, we find that the Europeans had no difficulty in building a bridgehead in North America, thanks to the variable factor of their technological superiority over the Indians. As a result, Europeans poured into America, until in a relatively short time they achieved numerical superiority over their opponents. An example of an unsuccessful European settlement is that of the Crusaders in Syria and Egypt. The reason for the preliminary success achieved by the Crusaders was the variable factor of their military superiority over the local Moslem population. Once the region was united under the leadership of Saladin, it was certain that the Moslems would win the final victory, because the constant factor was turned in favor of the original population, with its distinctive civilization and superior numbers.

But which of these patterns applies to the present situation in Isreal? Can Israel last and survive, in conformity with the European pattern in America, or is she doomed to failure, as happened to the Crusader kingdom in the same area which Israel is trying to claim in the twentieth century? Israel has succeeded so far, thanks to the variable factors of military, scientific, and technological superiority and its close links with a world power, the United States. On the other hand, Ben-Gurion himself pointed out the constant factor, namely the overwhelming demographic superiority of the Arabs. Should Israel's policy of annexation and the denial of Palestinian rights continued, a Crusader, rather than an American, outcome seems more likely.

As I see it, the peace agreement with Egypt was an expression of the trend in Israel placing the preservation of the state in the Middle East above ideological considerations, especially as it involved the dismantling of the settlements in Sinai. On the other hand, insistence on a unified Israeli Jerusalem and on Begin's so-called "autonomy" plan for the Palestinians is a clear expression of the persistence of the Zionist trend. In basing its proposed solution of the Palestine problem on a partial withdrawal from the West Bank and the Gaza Strip, and the restoration of the Palestinian people's links with Jordan, the Israeli Labor Party is trying to achieve a compromise between the rationale of the state, which is prepared to recognize that the Palestinian people exist and have their own land, and the Zionist ideology, which cannot accept the Palestinian people's full right to self-determination, and seeks to establish new settlements on the West Bank and Gaza.

At present, the emotional trend of the Zionist movement still prevails over the more rational attachment to the survival of the state. Is there any hope of the rational trend growing and expanding? Could it become the basis for a program of a broad-based Israeli political party? And if this happens, what will be the attitude of the Palestinians, and of other Arabs, who have on more then one occasion hinted that they are prepared to have dealings with the state, but not with the movement? Until this interplay is settled in favor of the state, the Israeli people will continue to suffer from this dualism between expansionist settler ideology and the desire for normal existence and peace.

XIV. ISRAELI-ARAB RELATIONS AND PEACE

50. Peace Now—Shalom Akhshav

The Peace Now movement exemplifies best the attitude of some Israelis toward peace with the Arabs and Palestinians and provides excellent insights into the nature of the Israeli society and the opinion-making processes.

Peace Now emerged spontaneously in March 1978 when 348 reserve soldiers, including many officers who fought in wars and held reserve commissions in combat units, sent a letter to Prime Minister Begin urging him to seek peace with Egypt. An open letter in the Israel press was followed by a demonstration in Tel Aviv, attended by 100,000 people, prior to Premier Begin's departure for talks at Camp David in 1978. Apparently the demonstration had some effect on Begin's attitude toward Egyptian demands in the negotiations that culminated in the peace treaty, as indicated by the premier's correspondence.

The movement has no formal leaders, no paid officials—except a treasurer—and relies entirely on voluntarly contributions. It is governed by a national council, composed of representatives from its city forums and the kibbutz, that meets once or twice a week. The original membership consisted predominantly of persons 25 to 35 years of age—middle-class professionals, students, and teachers at the University or high schools, most with university educations—who had served in Israeli armed forces and had relatively secure incomes. Its members, politically speaking, sympathize with labor and centrist politics. Some of the Sephardim, that is, the Oriental Jews, showed a certain reluctance at the beginning to join the movement, as it conflicted with their traditional submission to the authority of the established government. Eventually the Chief Rabbi of the Sephardic Jews indicated in an interview that withdrawal from the West Bank was religiously acceptable if it saved Jewish lives. Peace Now has consistently refused to identify with or convert itself into a political party, despite the rather impressive number of its domestic (about 300,000) and foreign supporters.

The movement has precise and limited goals: namely, to reach agreement and conclude peace with the Arabs by finding a compromise solution that would reconcile the rights of Jews and of the Arabs in the occupied areas, especially the West Bank and Gaza. It hopes to create a humane Zionism which will offer true prospects of peace to the Arabs and, subsequently, attract the finest Jews from all over the world to Israel. Peace Now has opposed the establishment of settlements on the West Bank and found itself pitted against the policies of the Gush Emunim, which it considers a messianic group marginal to most Diaspora, as well as Israeli, Jews. It advocates demilitarization of the West Bank and the granting of autonomy to Arabs living there, including the right to decide their political destiny as they see fit. It believes also that the incorporation of the Arabs into Israel, or continuous Israeli rule over them, will harm the Jewish character of the state.

Peace Now began to appeal to Jews in Diaspora by sending delegations to France, the U.K., and the United States. The Israeli government and some hard core Gush Emmunim sympathizers attempted to discredit the movement by claiming that leaders of Breira had infiltrated it. (Breira— Alternatives—was born abroad in 1974 to advocate peace and understanding with the Arabs. It had about 200 members and was rather active in the United States. Breira was accused of being a front organization for the PLO, of attracting the "enemies" of Israel, and so forth. Eventually it disbanded, largely because of disputes between Zionists and non-Zionists about the meaning and function of Zionism among Jews.) The Israeli government's negative attitude toward Peace Now stemmed from the fear that the movement would induce the Jews in Diaspora to think that the government and the state were two separate entities and thus undermine the key concept on which the state was established. (This concept rejects the secular European idea of state, government, and authority.) Peace Now rejected the accusations, stressing the fact that it was essentially a Zionist movement in complete agreement with the tenets of fundamental Zionism. It claimed that the early Zionist platforms did not seek to remove the Arabs and described the policies of the government as being contrary to the long-range goals of Zionism. It stated that because the movement was an open one, it could not prohibit the members of the Breira, whose ideology it rejected, from joining it. It claimed that Americans for a Progressive Israel, like other organizations of Diaspora Jews who opposed Breira, lent support to Peace Now.

Although Peace Now is an open, nonpolitical movement—at least for the time being—and may disappear as soon as its chief objective—peace—is attained, it has found support among individuals long associated with particular political groups. Some members of the socialist MAPAM, e.g., Simha Flapan, have supported Peace Now but have not been able to dominate it. MAPAM, it should be remembered was formed originally in 1927 and grew through its union with the Ahdut Avoda (Labor Unity) and Paole Zion Smol (Zion Workers of the Left) in 1947. MAPAM claims to represent the views of many Marxists and radical Socialists and also of intellectuals such as the philosopher Martin Buber, Judah Magnes, the first President of the Hebrew University, and some former members of the League for Arab-Jewish Rapprochement and Cooperation. All these accept in varying degree the idea of a binational state. MAPAM places emphasis on socialist solidarity but has been beset by sharp internal dissension due to the condemnation of Zionism by the USSR and other socialist countries in Eastern Europe. A small group—the Ahdut Avoda—left MAPAM in 1953 and joined the MAPAI, while a smaller group went to the Communist party. Other leading Israelis, e.g., General M. Peled and A. L. Eliav, not associated with MAPAM, also have defended an accommodation with the Arabs inside and outside Israel and have supported the Peace Now movement but without being able to politicize it or assimilate it.

This group has joined with S. Flapan to publish an English monthly, the New Outlook, and up to 1980 had organized six symposia. One was held in Washington, D.C., on October 27–29, 1979, with Peace Now participation; this was followed by other similar meetings in the United States and Canada. The meetings were described by the Likud government as a "knife in the back," although 16 members of the Knesset participated and the event received endorsement from the Alignment (MAPAI-MAPAM-Ahdut Avoda). The last was scheduled to be held in Israel but was cancelled, and a site in Europe was being sought. The initiative was called Shalom and received the support of various groups in the United States and Canada identified with social and democratic issues. The basic purposes of the Peace Symposia are to establish a dialogue with the Palestinians, to engage the Jewish people in the United States in the discussion, and to achieve international visibility for the movement. Speakers from Peace Now asked during the symposia that

Palestinians and Arabs in general respond by initiating similar movements among themselves.

For further views on Peace Now, see the Jerusalem Post *International Edition, July 29–August 1979, December 30, 1979, and January 5, 1980. For views in favor of a binational state (this is not the view of Peace Now), see Simha Flapan,* Zionism and the Palestinians *(London: Croom Helm, 179); David Vital,* The Origins of Zionism *(New York: Oxford University Press, 1975); and Allon Gal,* Socialist Zionism, Theory and Issues in Contemporary Jewish Nationalism *(Tel Aviv: Schenkman, 1973). The excerpts below are from a recent declaration (December 1980) issued in Israel by Peace Now and translated from the Hebrew.*

Peace Now—Statement

The movement—Peace Now—was established and still exists because of deep concern for the peace and security of the State of Israel. The movement is active because it [holds] the conviction that peace is the [only] basis for implementing the goals of the State of Israel. The movement has a broad and comprehensive viewpoint concerning security, which is not limited to territorial matters but embraces additional components [such as] the strength of the Israeli Defence Force and the faith of the soldiers in their right destiny; the quantity of weapons obtained by Israel; relations concerning aid and other matters between Israel and the U.S. and other states; security arrangements to be determined through negotiations; the preparedness of the other [Arab] side to reach peace; the demilitarization of the evacuated areas; the time element in the peace agreements, the establishment of mutual confidence between the parties ready to accept peace; the success of the peace processes and the moral, social and economic strength of the State of Israel. All of these, and not just one element, are the components of security. . . .

Peace Now will oppose in democratic ways an Israeli government which will not take into consideration all these elements of security and peace, and will ignore options likely to lead toward a negotiated settlement [of the dispute]. The Movement does not deny the existence of [powerful] historical and religious reasons . . . but believes that Israel's peace and security have priority over them.

The Movement demands that every government in Israel consider the broader aspects of security with all its components and be ready to engage in any negotiation which does not threaten this broad aspect of security. The Movement will oppose any kind of extremist stand that will reject negotiation.

The Movement demands from each government in Israel to maintain the traditional goals of the Zionist Movement to establish a [genuine] Jewish state and not a bi-national [state]; a democratic [state] that does not deny the rights of part of its inhabitants; that does not rule another nation, exactly as itself will not agree to be ruled; earns its living from its work; encourages a genuine settlement of the dispute and does not expand at the expense of the others.

Continuing to rule over one and a half million Arabs, living in the West Bank and the Gaza Strip, will change the democratic character of the State of Israel and will create de facto a bi-national state.

The annexation of the West Bank will cause in the near future to have an Arab majority in Eretz Yisrael, a situation most dangerous to . . . Israel. The continuation of the [Israeli] rule, without granting [full] rights to all the Arabs living in the areas to be annexed, will turn Israel into an undemocratic and immoral state, harboring two kinds of inhabitants: citizens and subcitizens. On the other hand the granting of equal rights to the Arabs in the annexed areas will inflict severe damage to the Jewish character of the State of Israel. This is the basic idea of Zionism, the national liberation movement of the Jewish nation to establish a Jewish state, a sister to other states in the world, in which equal rights will be granted to Arab minority and other minorities.

The autonomy plan should be only an interim plan to be carried out with the view that Israel maintains no basic claim of sovereignty over the West Bank and the Gaza Strip.

Israel must express its readiness to withdraw to defendable borders, which will be agreed upon in comprehensive negotiations, and only after paying due attention to security considerations. . . .

Israel should end the efforts to establish settlements on the West Bank and the Gaza Strip and to enact legislation aimed at changing the status quo . . .

The establishment of settlements aimed at creating *faits accomplis* in the area do not guarantee a better bargaining point; on the contrary are compelling the other side to adopt more extremist stands.

The settlements damage the peace process and the stability of peace with Egypt, and are regarded as indications of the intention of the government to establish an Israeli sovereignty over the West Bank and to continue to rule over one and a half million Arabs. The settlements cause agitation among the inhabitants of the West Bank and the Gaza Strip and are stirring enmity [among Arabs]. The investment in settlements cost billions [of pounds] and cause harm to Israel's security and image . . . A state with a shaky economy can not maintain a modern army, and a state with an embittered society will face disintegration in the army too. The settlements lead to corruption, arrogance and immoral deeds. The settlements alienate the World Jewery from Israel, harm Israel's relations with other states and divide the nation.

The State of Israel has paid a substantial price in order to reach the peace agreement with Egypt. The Palestinians are the next step in the peace process, a step in which slow progress may undermine the stability of the peace agreement with Egypt.

Israel should consider the Palestinian issue as the problem of a group of people with their national distinctiveness, and not only as a refugee problem.

Jerusalem is the Capital of Israel. It should not be divided. Each suggestion for a settlement will be discussed in detail within the framework of the general negotiations.

The status of the existing settlements. It will be discussed within the framework of the negotiations for the future status of the West Bank and Gaza Strip.

Our Zionism

We are Zionists. We are Zionists in a state which stopped functioning as a Zionist State. Our Zionism derives directly from the declared aims of the Zionist Movement from its very beginning: to establish a framework of a Jewish state for the Jewish nation in Eretz Israel, which will secure the existence of the Jew. We have never exchanged this vision for any extremist messianism whose main object is to worship sacred sites in false excitement and by ignoring new circumstances. We have never given priority to a stone, tree, and [old] grave over the independence and safety of the life of men, women and children, within the [secure] borders where it is possible to guarantee their independence and security. . . . According to our judgment, as the second generation of Israel, we do not doubt that the state framework has already been achieved; our aim now is to concentrate on the harmony, strength and integrity of the society.

In our opinion, peace is a precondition for the implementation of Zionism. We have never wanted to rule another nation, exactly as we do not want that others rule us. We think that the lives of the sons are more important than the graves of the ancestors. . . .

Our Zionism is the same Zionism that took the Jews out of their Ghetto in the Diaspora and out of their status as [guardians] of graves and led the Jews to agriculture to produce and to establish a [new] society, law, a [genuine Jewish] culture. . . .

We are Zionists, who believe that as many Jews as possible from the state and Diaspora should participate in every discussion that will decide the fate and the future of the State of Israel, by taking into consideration the big difference between the responsibility of the Israeli citizens and that of the Jews in the Diaspora. We think that the State of Israel is also the state of the Jews living abroad, if they or their children want it, and identify themselves with the state, and consider it as their home now or in the future.

We are Zionists who fought and will fight for the independence of the state, its security, and for [making it]law-abiding, democratic and an accepted members in the family of nations. We are Zionists who wish to mend as soon as possible the corruption caused by the occupation and the rule established over another nation, for our own sake no less than for the sake of the others. We want to return as soon as possible to a balanced order of priorities, a balance that places the quality of the human being over the size of the land. . . .

[*After mentioning various options—UN Resolution 242, Camp David Agreements, involvement of Jordan—for initiating peace talks, the declaration of Peace Now continues as follows.*]

The Israeli Government should maintain negotiations with [those] Palestinians, who will agree that negotiations are the only way to solve the Middle East conflict. These negotiations should be based on the following principles:

(a) The Palestinians should recognize the right of the State of Israel to exist as a Jewish State within secured borders, and abandon terrorist activities. Israel on her side should recognize the right of the Palestinians to national existence, as long as it is compatible with the security of Israel.

(b) Both sides should maintain negotiations by adhering to the principle that peace in the area will be achieved through the mutual renunciation of the two sides to part of their political claims, based on the historical rights.

(c) Israel should waive its claim of sovereignty over the West Bank and the Gaza Strip, and should base or her claims solely on security considerations....

The autonomy mentioned in the Camp David Agreements is a transitional phase leading to a comprehensive general solution of the Arab-Israeli conflict. The autonomy is [part of the peace agreement] with Egypt and should be granted to the West Bank and the Gaza Strip. The negotiations among all the parties in the peace talks will be based on Camp David Agreements and the Security Council Resolution 242.

51.   Another View of on Peace Now[*]

Orly Lubin

In the first two years public opinion in Israel has undergone enormous changes. Sadat's visit to Jerusalem profoundly altered certain assumptions that the Israeli public held for thirty years. There can be no doubt that this reaction of the Israeli public has an important impact upon subsequent developments.... "Peace Now" had undertaken to continue this momentum in Israeli thinking, to push public opinion further in the direction of accepting certain fundamental principles and political actions on the Palestinian question. So far we have done this effectively. And we have undertaken to do this because we are convinced that negotiations between Israelis and Palestinians will not take place until the political climate on both sides has been changed. The man or woman in the street is as important in this respect as his or her representative in government. Our aim in this work is two-fold: to pressure our own government by providing that hundreds of thousands of Israelis oppose its Palestinian policy; to develop sensitivity and understanding among the Israeli public of our Palestinian neighbors so that genuine exchanges of ideas and feelings between the two peoples will be possible.

This is not the only work to be done, but it is essential and constructive. As it comes at a time when so much misunderstanding and suspicion exist, it may be the most important task to be done.

"Peace Now" is committed to the peace process because we paid heavily for the war process, and because there must be a just solution of the Palestinian problem. But there is a third and no less important reason for our commitment, and that is that the peace process is necessary for the

---

[*]This description of the Peace Now movement by Orly Lubin appeared in the Middle East monthly *New Outlook* (November–December 1979): 33–34.

moral and social sanity of our country. The occupation is a corrupting influence on our society. It is a disgrace to Zionism. We cannot feel free while we rule another people, especially because we are Jews. There are tendencies in the Israeli political system whose values and goals are dangerous. At the present time, the major obstacle to the success of these influences is "Peace Now." We are Gush Emunim's more powerful enemy. We stand in the way of their settlements by publicizing them and by mobilizing mass support against them. We have shown the Israeli public that Gush Emunim and its supporters, in and out of the government, have no monopoly on concern for Israeli security. "Peace Now," in other words, stands for sane Zionism, for the Zionism that bases itself on the ethical right of every people to national self-expression. "Peace Now" believes that the peace process is not just for peace, but also necessary for the maintenance of the democratic character of Israeli society. This concern we share with many other Israelis. We will continue to work with them and to develop our own strategies in the struggle to reach the hearts and minds of Israelis.

52.   Israeli-Arab Relations

Arie Eliav

Arie (Lova) Eliav is a maverick politician, a wartime hero, and the author of New Targets for Israel *(1968),* Between Hammer and Sickle *(1965),* No Time for History *(1970), and other works. This excerpt expressing Eliav's views was taken from a speech he delivered while receiving, together with Issam Sartawi, a PLO official, the peace award of the Kreisky foundation of Austria. It appeared in the* New Outlook *(November–December, 1979): 41–42.*

I will speak simply, because the conflict in the Middle East is so complicated, so fraught with danger, that we must speak simply and return to first principles if we are to understand it. This conflict is now a century old. It has poisoned our region, and infected social and political bodies very far away. It is time to cure ouselves of this costly ailment. But the statesman, like the physician, must first make his examination and produce his diagnosis before he may begin his treatment. That is what I propose to do today.

We must clearly establish that the conflict in the Middle East consists of the confrontation of two national movements which claim the same plot of land—Eretz Yisrael, or Falastin, or Palestine, as the British Mandate called it—for their national home. One of these movements is Zionism, the movement of national liberation of the Jewish people. This is my movement, into which I was born, and of which I am proud. The other is the movement of national liberation of the Palestinian people.

Zionism asserts the national, historical, and religious right to all of the Land of Israel. The Palestinian movement asserts the national, historical, and religious right to all of Falastin. And Eretz Yisrael and Falastin are one and the same, and this precious territory is today two polities, the State of Israel, and the West Bank and Gaza.

What we have proclaimed before, and have struggled for all these years, I repeat today: This land, from the sea to the Jordan, is the land of our fathers. In this land the Jewish people was born and grew. In this land the Bible was written, and the prophets had their visions. From this land our fathers were exiled, and to it they began to return as a modern, national movement in the last century. We have dreamed of it always.

But in the same breath we proclaim that this land is also the land of the Palestinians, that on this land the Palestinian people grew, and that this is the land they worked. We have full rights to this land. And so do they.

These are the simple words—"and so do they"—that have made us doves, and made us for many years voices in the wilderness. From the diagnosis comes the cure; and for us the cure is compromise. Compromise is even worthier than justice; this we earn from an ancient Jewish tradition, and it is in the spirit of this tradition that we speak. The rabbis in the Talmud once ruled that a disputed cloak should be divided. So too should a territory, when the rival claims are just and peace is the goal.

Nor is this territory like the baby brought before Solomon: The land may be divided; it will not die. And the peoples who share it will live and flourish.

We have said before, and I say again, that Israel must declare before the Palestinians, the Arab world, the Jewish world, and the entire world, that we recognize the right of the Paelstinian national movement to self-determination and that for a full peace, and nothing less than a full peace, and for the satisfaction of mutual security requirements that include demilitarization and verification, Israel agrees that the West Bank and Gaza will comprise the territory upon which the Palestinians will decide their own political destiny. There they will live alongside us in peace. There they will determine the manner of their own government, and their relations—federative, confederational, or otherwise—with Jordan and Israel.

The peace that we have concluded with the mightiest of our neighbors, Egypt, is great and important. But the peace is not complete. Peace in our region will not be complete until it is concluded, through compromise, with the Palestinians. . . .

There will be no peace until we recognize the national movement of the Palestinians: That is my challenge to Zionism. And there will be no peace until they recognize the national movement of the Jews: That is my challenge to Palestinians.

There are many, of course, who mock these ideals, The Palestinians, so they say, are only refugees; they still dream, some of them, of the destruction of the Jewish state; they are, so it is said, the instruments of intrigues by Arab governments and foreign powers. How to give them a state?

How to imagine a day when a Palestinian state joins our own in the social, economic, and cultural development of this region and others? Much easier to say, as many in Israel do even after Sadat has been in Jerusalem, that between us and the Palestinians there can never be peace, that for us the better part of wisdom is only to create facts on the ground and gain time.

But I reject this arid, fruitless pessimism. This conflict is not our fate, it is only our problem. And it is a problem which has a solution. There have been such problems before, there have been still greater wars, and they have ended. Only yesterday we were bitter enemies with Egypt. Today we are at peace, and we have begun to understand and respect each other. It has been done. There is no reason to believe that it cannot be done with the Palestinians. We must never dispair of reconciliation.

We must stop creating facts which are not facts, but only obstacles on the long road to a settlement. And we must begin to talk not least among ourselves, to remind ourselves as Israelis, as Zionists, as Jews, as men, that we do not wish to rule over another people, that we wish to live in peace with equals, with a people as free and proud as our own.

There have been many false starts and many bitter disappointments. We may not finish the work, but neither may we desist from it. We may choose war, or we may choose peace. But if we choose peace, we will have chosen life.

XV. THE VIEWS OF THE ANTI-ZIONIST AND THE NON-ZIONIST JEWS AND ARABS IN ISRAEL

Among Israeli Jews opposed to Zionism—but not necessarily to the state—are the Orthodox Jews, the political Left (including Arab parties and individuals), and a variety of other groups and individuals whose opposition stems from a variety of humanist and legal reasons. The total number of such persons probably varies between 5 and 10 percent of the total population.

Most of the Orthodox groups that originally opposed Zionism, such as Agudat Yisrael, have accepted it; but the Neturei Karta (Guardians of the Walls), a Hasidic group, has maintained its opposition. Neturei Karta have refused to become citizens, pay no taxes, do not serve in the army, and are devoted entirely to prayer, governing every aspect of their lives by the Law, consisting of 613 commandments. They find political Zionism contrary to Judaism and consequently have suppored any initiative to dismantle Zionism. Neturei Karta's influence in public life is limited.

The extreme Marxist Left is also opposed to Zionism, while other leftist parties accept it in varying degrees. The history of Zionism and of Israel is closely related to various currents and individuals that can be called leftist: many early Zionist settlers in Palestine were leftist members of the Bund or were Bolsheviks. However, political and economic realities have compelled many leftist groups (such as MAPAM), although Zionist, to make consider-able concession to the idea of a binational (Arab-Jewish) state. (See the section on Peace Now in Chapter XIV.) The ideas of Ber Borochov (d. 1917 in Kiev), who attempted to link Zionism to Marxism, were preserved in the Poale Zion Smol (Workers of the Zion Left) party, which merged with two other parties to form the MAPAM in 1948. Borochov was opposed to capitalism but regarded Zionism as solution to the problems of the Jewish proletariat; he expected to see the "natives" of Palestine assimilate into the group that brought them progress and order. Hence Marxist anti-Zionists now reject Borochovism, while some other leftist Zionists cling to it because of its attempt to reconcile Marxism with Zionism; in other words, Borochov was in a way the precursor of national socialism and communism.

The anti-Zionist Left of Marxist origin includes Matzpen (Israeli Socialist Organization), which split in 1962 from Maki (the then Communist Party). Maki in turn split into two groups, and of these Rakah (Reshima Communist Hadasha) has survived as the Communist Party of Israel. In the 9th Knesset, Rakah headed the Democratic Front for Peace and Equality, which included the Israeli Black Panthers and independent Arab groups. Rakah held altogether 5 seats out of 120 in the entire Knesset.

The individual anti-Zionists in Israel vary greatly in background, reasons for their beliefs, and degree of their rejection of Zionism. They include some people who were originally closely identified with Zionism, such as Uri Avnery, Jews disenchanted with their social and economic status, and Arabs who object to their inferior position in Israeli society. A good article citing considerable literature on this topic is Charles Glass, "Jews Against Zion, Israeli Jewish Anti-Zionism," Journal of Palestinian Studies 5 (1975): 56–81. Other writings include Alan R. Taylor, The Zionist Mind (Beirut: Institute for Palestinian Studies, 1974); David J. Schnell, "Native Anti-Zionism Ideologies and Radical Dissent," Middle East Journal 31 (Spring 1977); Arie Bober, ed., The Other Israel, The Radical Case Against Zionism, (New York: Doubleday, 1972); and Noam Chomsky, Peace in the Middle East (New York: Random House, 1974). There have been vigorous Zionist attacks on the anti-Zionist Left, notably from outside Israel. See Commentary in the United States. See also the illuminating analyses by Walter Laqueur in "Zionism, the Marxist Critique and the Left," Dissent (December 1971): 560–74, and Who is Left, Zionism Answers Back (Jerusalem: Zionist Lib, 1971). The excerpt below is intended to provide an example of the anti-Zionist views and also an insight into the conditions that led some individuals to use anti-Zionism as a channel of protest against the establishment.

53. Israel Without Zionists[*]

Uri Avnery

Avnery was born in Germany in 1923 and migrated to Palestine in 1933. He is a journalist, a past Member of the Knesset (MK), and the editor of Haolam Hazeh. He took part in the War of 1948 and was wounded in combat while in the much celebrated commando unit, the Desert Foxes. Among Avnery's many books, the best known is Israel Without Zionists; A Plea for Peace in the Middle East (New York: Macmillan, 1968). Avnery, who adopted the ideas of the Canaanite Movement—a sort of counterpart of the Phoenician Movement in Lebanon—claims that he is a secular Hebrew nationalist for whom Zionism became obsolete after its creation of the nation because it

---

[*]*Israel Without Zionists: A Plea for Peace in the Middle East.* New York: Macmillan, 1968. (A new edition appears as *Israel Without Zionism.* New York: Macmillan, 1971.)

*does not fit the realities of Israel. He claims that Israel is a new Hebrew
nation that has its homeland in Palestine and appears in a political form as
the state of Israel. Avnery, believes that historically Zionism did not pay
attention to religion until the Holocaust, that it ignored the possibility of
peace with the Arabs, and that some of its basic tenets, such as the
immigration of all Jews in the world to Israel, have failed to materialize. He
holds that abandonment of Zionism is a precondition to establishing
mutual confidence and acceptance between Jews and Arabs for a peaceful
life in Israel, which would become the kernel of the Semitic Union. The
excerpt is taken from* Israel Without Zionists, *pp. 4–5, 208–13.*

My name is biblical, Uri, meaning light. Avner, or Abner, was the field
marshal of King David, a figure I always liked. I was not born with this
name. I gave it to myself. Like most of my age group in what was then
Palestine, I changed my name immediately on reaching age eighteen.
With this one act we declared our independence from our past; we broke
with it irrevocably. The Jewish Diaspora, the world of our parents, their
culture and their background—we wanted nothing to do with. We were a
new race, a new people, born the day we set foot on the soil of Palestine.
We were Hebrews, rather than Jews; our new Hebrew names proclaimed
this. . . . My father was also a Zionist. When he married my mother, in
1913, some of his friends gave him as a wedding gift a document stating
that a tree had been planted in his name in Palestine. But Zionism, in pre-
Hitler Germany, did not mean immigration to Palestine; I don't believe
this idea ever entered my father's head. It meant, first of all, to be
nonconformist (and I strongly suspect my father amused himself by
upsetting the assimilationists aound him, who hated Zionism). It also
meant an awareness of the suffering of the Jews elsewhere, and a
sympathy for the striving of the few pioneers who were trying to build a
new country in the Near East—a place too far away to be quite real. . . .

Throughout the Middle East there persists the naive notion that the
conflict was created in some devious way by British imperialism and
American intervention, and that we otherwise would all have lived happily
ever after. This is a superficial view; as we have seen, the vicious circle was
created by the clash of two authentic historical movements. Foreign
influences acted on this stuation but did not create it. If these influences
were removed tomorrow—by some Divine intervention—the confrontation between the two movements would still go on. The solution, then, has
to be found between the two sides themselves [Arabs and Jews].

The first part of the solution I propose is the setting up of a federation
between Israel and a new Arab-Palestinian republic. . . . This, together
with the settlement of the refugees, can be done by Israel in cooperation

with the Palestinian Arabs, independent of any official contact between Israel and the Arab states. The second part of the solution is Semitic Union, a great confederacy of all the states in the Region.

The two parts are not contradictory. I do not view the Palestinian federation as a replacement for a general Israeli-Arab peace. On the contrary, such a peace will be much easier to achieve once the Palestinian problem is solved by common consent. The Palestinian problem is both the reason and the pretext for the belligerent attitude of the other Arab nations toward Israel. In all their statements, Arab leaders maintain that the only reason for their war against Israel is either to "liberate Palestine" or to "restore the rights of the Palestinian-Arab people." Once the Arabs of Palestine declare themselves liberated and agree that their rights have been restored, the main obstacle to peace will have been removed. Or to put it another way, those Arab leaders who wish, deep in their hearts, to reach some settlement with Israel will be able to say so and act accordingly once the Palestinian problem has been solved. Before this, any such statement or action would be considered treason against the Palestinian Arabs. Thus, a solution in Palestine is almost a prerequisite to a general Semitic peace settlement, and at the same time, a Semitic peace is necessary to make the Palestinian solution meaningful and enduring.

I would like to explain here why I use the term *Semitic*. The reason has nothing to do with race; indeed, in the Middle East race is as uncertain as anywhere in the world. Both to Hebrews and to Arabs, race, today, means little. The term *Semitic* should, rather, be viewed as emphasizing an historical heritage, common to all peoples speaking languages of the Semitic family—Arabic, Hebrew, Amharic, and so forth. It also emphasizes the common cultural and spiritual background of all the peoples of our Region, so much influenced by their past. In this respect, the Semitic family of culture includes even the Turks, the Kurds, and the Persians, who are descended from different races and speak non-Semitic languages, but whose history is bound up with the culture of the Semitic world and the great religions of the Semites. Yet the main reason for the indispensability of this term is that it automatically includes Arabs and Hebrews, explains itself readily in the Region and throughout the world, and has the same meaning in all languages.

It is my deepest belief—and perhaps the point at which my friends and I differ from other people who aspire to peace in the Region—that such a peace cannot and must not contradict the national aspirations of both Hebrews and Arabs. Nationalism will reign supreme in our generation in all the countries of the Region, and nothing will stop it. Any idea, inspiring as it may be, which runs counter to the national feelings of the people concerned, will be by-passed by history.

I am a Hebrew nationalist, and I want to deal with Arab nationalists. I want to tell them: The last fifty years have shown that neither you nor we can achieve our national aspirations as long as we fight each other. Our two great national movements can neutralize each other, or they can be combined in one great regional movement of liberation and progress. This is what the Semitic idea means—an ideal combining the two nationalisms, an ideal with which nationalists on both sides can identify.

Joining a great Semitic confederacy would mean, for Israel, putting an end to the Zionist chapter in its history and starting a new one—the chapter of Israel as a state integrated in its Region, playing a part in the Region's struggle for progress and unity.

For the Arabs it would mean recognition of a post-Zionist Israel as a part of the Region, a part which could and should not be abolished because, in its new form, it is a factor in the struggle for the common good.

Let me be quite clear about this. A lot of nonsense has been written about solutions which do not recognize the existence of Israel as a sovereign state. Not one single Israeli, and certainly not I, would ever agree to any such solution. The existence of Israel as a sovereign state is the point of departure for any solution, as much as the rights and the aspirations of the Palestinian nation and any other Arab people. Semitic Union not only provides a framework for mutual acceptance, but has many other advantages. . . .

All this sounds very optimistic. Indeed, it is.

I am an optimist. I believe that nothing in history is pre-determined. History in the making is composed of acts of human beings, their emotions and aspirations.

The depth of bitterness and hatred throughout our Semitic Region seems bottomless. Yet it is a comparatively new phenomenon, the outcome of the recent clash of our peoples. Nothing like European anti-Semitism ever existed in the Arab world prior to the events which created the vicious circle.

We have seen, in our times, Germans and Frenchmen cooperating, if not loving each other, after a war which lasted for many hundreds of years and whose bitter fruits are deeply embedded in both German and French culture. We are witnessing today the beginnings of an American-Soviet alliance which would have been unthinkable only a dozen years ago.

We are not dealing, therefore, with mystical phenomena, but with matters which can be changed by policy decisions, by new ideas, new leaders and new political forces—in short, by a new generation all over the Middle East disgusted with the mess their fathers have made and by the conventional lies of propaganda.

The first step has to be made by Israel. Throughout the last three generations, since the appearance of the first Zionist settlers in Palestine, it has been our side which has held the initiative, the Arabs reacting to our actions. It is up to us to change, by deliberate steps, the climate of hatred and suspicion in the Middle East.

We can start this by helping the Palestinian Arabs to set up their state and by settling the refugees. We can assume a completely new stance in the Region by supporting Arab nationalist aims in spirit and action, with a hundred small gestures, each insignificant by itself but contributing, in sum, to a gradual change in the atmosphere. By truly integrating the Israeli Arabs into the framework of our state and turning it into a pluralistic society, we can show the Arab world a new face—Israeli Arabs representing Israel, side by side with Hebrew Israelis, in all fields of endeavor, from the General Assembly of the United Nations to the playground of international soccer.

Nothing will change overnight. Each of our acts will be suspect in the beginning. Each will be denounced as a new Zionist plot. But slowly, by concerted action, suspicion will be dispelled and confidence gained, providing the psychological framework for new Arab policies.

54. The Arabs in Israel and Rakah, the Communist Party

Yosef Goell

Yosef Goell, a political scientist at the Hebrew University, spent a month in an Arab village and studied Arab views on Israeli government and politics. His visit came shortly after the occurrence of a rather startling event with profound political significance, in Nazareth: Tawfik Zayyad, a longtime member of the Communist Party who spent two years (1962–64) in the USSR studying political economy, was elected mayor of Nazarath. He was also a member of the Knesset elected on the Rakah ticket. Goell's article provides an excellent insight into the material situation of the Arabs in Israel and their change of attitudes—that is, the shift toward the anti-Zionist Left.

In another article on the Arabs in Israel (not reproduced here) Goell described an organization that seems to take root in Arab villages. The Abna'al-Balad or Sons of the Village (some of these groups have adopted slightly different names) began to be established in a number of villages by Palestinian Arabs within Israel in about 1970 in order to encourage local unity and to replace the old traditional structures based on the family or regional allegiances with associations that promoted national identity. Among the leaders of the movement to establish these organizations is Muhammad Kivan. The organizations have been active in opposing the confiscation of Arab land and in supporting mayoral candidates through alliances with the political parties. Sometimes they organized strikes, usually for achievement of practical purposes such as electricity, water, and so forth. Politically they generally support the PLO.

On the Communist Party in Israel, see Dunia H. Nahas, The Israeli Communist Party *(London: Croom Helm, 1976), and Robert Wistrich, ed.,* Communism, Israel and the Middle East. *The literature of Arabs in Israel is fairly rich. See Jacob Landau,* The Arabs in Israel *(1969); Fouzi El-Asmar,* To Be An Arab in Israel *(1975); Elia Zureik,* The Palestinians in Israel *(1979); Ian Lustick,* Arabs in the Jewish State *(Austin: University of Texas Press, 1980); and Sabri Jiriys [Jurays],* The Arabs in Israel *(translated from the Arabic by Inea Bushnaq) (New York: Monthly Review Press, 1976).*

The excerpts reproduced below appeared in the Jerusalem Post, *weekly and international editions respectively, January 13, 1976, and March–April 4–10, 1979.*

The 85 per cent of Israelis who are Jews have frequently ignored the fact of the other 15 per cent: Israel's Arabs. "Professional" leftists, liberals or humanitarians were intermittently agitated over the excesses of the Military Government in the 1950s and early 1960s (in the Arab areas of Israel-proper—the administered territories did not yet exist). Following the abolition of the Military Government by the Eshkol Government in 1966 and the calm atmosphere in Israel's Arab areas during three subsequent wars, even this interest waned.

Understandably so, perhaps. Are we not sufficiently embroiled with the *real* Arabs, the ones who have been whetting and swishing their scimitars from across our borders? Is not the problems of "our" more than one million Arabs in the territories sufficiently troubling?

And after all, Israel's 420,000 Arabs have never been better off. Why stir up trouble where none exists?

But last month two developments brought home to a wider public the potential for trouble on this issue: the Arab Communist party scored a stunning victory in the Nazareth municipal elections and Arab university students rejected their share of guard duty at campus dormitories.

What follows is a report of a personal attempt to understand the attitude of Israel's Arabs towards the Jewish majority. It is based on a four-week stay at a large Israel Arab village.... The discussion turned to Nazareth when I arrived. Taking part were a teacher, a student, the enterprising owner of a fleet of trucks and an engaging young man who identified himself as an entrepreneur and businessman: later I was told he worked as a professional thief in Tel Aviv a day or two a week, spending the rest of the time as an "entrepreneuer" in the village.

"Why are the Jews so upset over the Nazareth results?" asked one of them. "The Arabs who voted for Zayyad (as mayor of Nazareth) are neither Communists nor Fatah supporters. They simply oppose Seif-ed-Din and his corrupt Old Guard. (Seif-ed-Din Zuabi, Deputy Speaker of the Knesset and former Mayor of Nazareth, was not a candidate in these elections, but is viewed as the dominant figure in the "establishment" of that Galilee town.)

"You Jews have not kept up with the emergence of a new generation of Israeli Arabs and especially of educated Arabs, who will no longer go along with the Seif-ed-Dins and their masters in the Jewish establishment."

"In that case," I asked, "why the vote for Fatah rather then for a non-Communist, non-establishment alternative? Sensitivity was a two-way street: Jews could interpret the vote for Rakah only as a collective slap in the face." Replied the "entrepreneur":

"No alternative exists. You're either for the Seif-ed-Dins—and there's no difference in the establishment between Mapai, Mapam and the National Religious Party—or you're against them—and then there's only Rakah." The teacher added:

"Attempts by reform-minded young Arabs to try a third way have been slapped down by the Jewish establishment which really runs Arab politics. They ran up against vetoed budgets and job blacklisting. Besides it gave us a moment of brief but deep satisfaction to hit out at the Jewish establishment after years of insults and discrimination."

It was a compliment to Israel, I suggested, that the Arabs felt free to protest in this way at a time of intense external Arab-Israel conflict. But such momentary pleasures came dear in the long run. To redress legitimate Arab grievances required independent Arab action and Jewish understanding. But *Jews would* feel no strong urge to promote Arab education, housing and job opportunities if they felt Israel's Arabs supported Fatah.

The others replied that they were loyal citizens and had done nothing to make that loyalty suspect. It had, it was true, been satisfying to hit out that once and perhaps it was even worth the cost. "That's the trouble with us Arabs—we think of the moment and not of the long run."

The gist of this conversation was repeated in a number of talks in subsequent weeks, with the two points figuring prominently again and again: a need to give expression to a deep sense of resentment and hurt; and the lack of a reasonable political alternative for a younger generation of Israeli Arabs possessed of new self-confidence, itself a product of 10 years of Israeli prosperity and 20 years of Israeli schooling.

Why should Israeli Arabs have any resentment to express? Are they not continuing to enjoy unprecedented prosperity? Certainly. A walk through this village and others in the Little Triangle and in Galilee is an eye-opener.

The traditional all-purpose, one-room stone, adobe, or unplastered concrete hovels of former years are today liberally interspersed with villas and two-story homes which would not be out of place in Savyon or Herzilya Pituah. Living space is anywhere up to 150 to 200 square meters, though one should remember that most of them house families of 10 to 15 persons.

The gap between rich and poor seems to be much wider than in Jewish Israel, but many families have most of the electrical appliances of Jewish Israel. One housewife, explaining her two washing machines, said: "I couldn't bear the thought of my machine breaking down on washday. The second one is insurance."

Standards of home construction and furnishings, especially of the ubiquitous guest rooms, have long since passed beyond mere considerations of need and comfort to showy keeping-up-with-the-Mahmouds.

In truth, Israel's Arabs have never had it so good, materially. But at a certain point Israel's Arabs stopped comparing their situation and achievements to their former condition, or even to that of Arabs outside Israel, and turned their gaze on the surrounding kibbutzim, moshavim and Jewish towns and cities where they work. Given this new frame of reference, Israel's Arabs are aware they have quite a way to go to catch up.

This gap between Jewish and Arab standards of living is exacerbated by another gap—an even more serious one because it exists entirely within the Arab society—the gap between private comfort and even affluence, and public poverty and neglect.

A hard-working, enterprising Israeli Arab can today provide his family with a roomy, well-furnished home equipped with electrical appliances, and he may aspire to a good education for his children. But the home will be in a village where sewage meanders down muddy, unpaved alleys: current will be too weak for the operation of more than one appliance at a time and the village school will be woefully under-equipped.

It would perhaps be natural to blame poverty and neglect of the public domain in Arab villages on Israeli discrimination, and many Arabs do so. Part of the truth does lie in this direction, especially in the small per capita grants in aid which the Ministry of Interior allots Arab local councils, as compared with Jewish settlements.

But this is only part of the truth and, it would seem, a small part. The major problem lies in the direction of the seeming inability of Arab communities to organize effectively at the local level to insist on a minimally acceptable balance between private well-being and public poverty.

There are few, if any, local governments in Jewish settlements which could compare for fecklessness and outright corruption with what passes as the norm in Arab towns and villages. Local taxes are either non-existent, uncollected, or collected with a vengeance only from the *hamulla* (clan) that is out of power. There are few attempts at independent parental action to improve schools and kindergartens or to provide youth club-houses, playing fields or parks.

It may sound basically unfair for an outside Jewish observer to complain bluntly of these matters. But a growing number of Arab villagers, especially young parents, are the ones who are complaining. Nevertheless, they seem to be unable to bring themselves to act in unison to correct some of the more glaring defects which are not due to external discriminatory policies. Two conversations might serve to illustrate.

A well-to-do father complained that his little daughter had to urinate in the street because her kindergarten lacked a toilet. His solution was to send his older children to school in Nazareth and to East Jerusalem, and to plan the same for his daughter.

"Why don't you get together with the other parents to demand a proper toilet, or perhaps even pay for it?"

"I wouldn't think of it. That's not my responsibility."

A group of teachers and young intellectuals was asked whether they would vote for reform-minded candidates in local elections regardless of *hamulla*. One replied with remarkable candor:

"No, I don't think I could bring myself to vote for a man from another *hamulla*. Perhaps my children will be able to." This from men in their late twenties and early thirties.

The educated young men—and women—who could provide an alternative Arab leadership are available. They were not there in the 1950s and were perhaps before their time in the 1960s. The selection of such a new leadership for Israel's Arabs cannot be done by Israel's Jewish establishment, not if it is to be effective and trusted by the Arab population.

It is not for the Jewish establishment to encourage the growth of such an alternative leadership through direct support—budgetary and political. It must also withdraw the blind support for the increasingly bankrupt old guard of village notables, on the one hand, and clearly indicate that the Rakah alternative will not be unthinkingly rewarded, on the other.

Encouraging an alternative leadership for Israel's Arabs would require today a clear policy of relative deprivation aimed at Rakah-administered Nazareth. Relative here means not punishing Nazareth but rewarding and encouraging Arab villages and townships which show ability and willingness to organize under such an alternative leadership for the forthcoming local elections.

What leads me to assume that there are young Arabs prepared to put themselves forward as an alternative? My answer is I believe I have met some of them. They are young people who care deeply about the fate of Israel's Arabs and who recognize that the first and major losers of a worsening in Arab-Jewish relations would be the Israel Arabs themselves.

Most have never dared speak out for such a third alternative, for the few who have been disappointed by the failure to gain the support of the Jewish establishment. This was a failure of the last seven or eight years, due primarily to Jewish inattention to the changes occurring in Arab society. I believe there is still time for both Jews and Arabs to strike out in such a new direction, even and perhaps especially in a time of heightened external troubles.

"AHAVA YEHUDIT-ARAVIT! Ahava Yehudit-Aravit!" (Jewish-Arab amity) [brotherhood].

The wild-eyed demonstrators orchestrated by an arm-waving conductor were not members of a Jewish leftist group on one of the country's campuses. They were a Communist Party (Rakah) claque shouting down challengers from the nationalist extremist Ibn al-balad (Sons of the Village). The scene was a recent tumultuous mass meeting in Nazareth of the head of Arab local authorities and the National Committee for the Defence of the Lands.

The joint meeting was a complete Rakah triumph. The party leaders wisely did not insist on excluding the young firebrands of the competing Ibn al-balad from the hall. But all attempts to demur from the Rakah slogans and resolutions adopted at the end of the meeting were instantaneously shouted down by the claque. At times, slogan-chanting turned into shoving and physical threats. But these were kept in check by discreet hand signs from party boss Tewfiq Toubi, a Knesset member, sitting on the dais in silence.

One of the ironies of the politics of the Israeli Arab community in 1979 is that Rakah, the same Rakah which was always considered the spearhead of Arab nationalist radicalism in Israel, is today viewed by most Arabs and by many knowledgeable Jews as a moderating force.

What is radical and what is moderate in today's Arab politics is of course relative. What is clear, however, is that in 1979 the Arab "street" in Israel has been totally "Palestinized." It would be extremely rare to find any Israeli Arab who would not subscribe to the claim that Israel's Arabs are part of the Arab-Palestinian nation.

Rakah firmly insists that it adheres to its standing policy of calling for the establishment of an independent Palestine in the areas occupied by Israel since 1967 "alongside" Israel and for allowing Israel's Arabs their "national rights."

Interviewed in the Knesset last month, Rakah leader Tewfiq Toubi explained what was meant by the demand for national rights. In addition to the fight for according Israeli Arabs equal rights with the Jewish majority, as citizens, the party also insists that Israeli Arabs must be assured communal and regional rights as a distinct cultural and national entity.

This means assuring Arabs control over their own education and cultural development; equal rights for the use of Arabic, and large-scale official assistance to solve such burning problems as housing and community development in the Arab areas of Galilee, the "Triangle" and for the Negev Beduin.

Toubi also spoke of the need to foster the development of Arab intervillage regional projects, including the establishment of Arab regional councils like the ones kibbutzim have throughout the country.

What makes the fulfilment of such demands a question of "national" as opposed to individual or communal-ethnic rights? Toubi simply ignores the question, as do other Rakah leaders. The party leadership is careful to a fault to avoid crossing the fine line that divides such demands from anything smacking of eventual irredentism aimed at severing the concentrated areas of Arab population in Central Galilee and the Triangle from Israel and their inclusion in an independent Palestine.

Lower-echelon Rakah activists, however, at times speak in terms which can ony be interpreted in such irredentist fashion.

All, however, heatedly dissociate themselves from the Ibn al-balad demands for the establishment of a Palestine that would supplant Israel as a Jewish state.

The Ibn al-balad had been forming over the past three years. They make no bones about their identification with the Rejectionist Front in the PLO and in the surrounding Arab states.

By-and-large the Ibna-l-balad are made up of younger elements compared with the middle-aged leaders who control Rakah, with most of the activists in their early and late 20s, with a smattering of lawyers and teachers in their early 30s.

The generational aspect of the clash between the two groups is reflected in charges that Rakah has sold out to the Zionists, and that Rakah has persistently diluted its Arab-Palestinian nationalism in two ways: it has always included Jews in the party and thus diminished its Arab ethos; it has also "tainted" its Arabism with Moscow-lined communism, which leaves most of the younger Palestinian nationalist firebrands cold.

Generally unmentioned is another sociological difference between the two groups. The leadership core of Rakah has always been heavily Christian while 80 per cent of Israel's Arabs are Sunni Moslems. In recent years Rakah has tried to overcome this imbalance by operating through a broader Democratic Front which includes many Moslems and other non-Communists, but it no secret that the "Greek-Orthodox mafia" which is reputed to run Rakah is resented by many Moslem voters and especially by young Moslem radicals. An important factor in the emergence of the new anti-Israel radical nationalism is the crystallization of a Palestinian national identity, and its organizational expression in the PLO, two factors which were nearly non-existent, or at best embryonic in the mid-1960s.

To this has been added the success of the PLO in winning international recognition for the cause of Palestinian nationalism, and the hope for the eventual defeat of Israel and its supplanting by a Palestinian "democratic-secular" state engendered by the Yom Kippur War and the serious political troubles Israel has encountered since.

It is not possible to assess the electoral strength of the "Sons of the Village" because the moment called for a boycott of the last Knesset elections. At the local level, however, they have succeeded in winning a number of seats on the councils of Makr and Umm el Fahm and in winning the chairmanship and the majority of the council in the small village of Kabul in Western Galilee.

Judging by electoral results, Rakah has made impressive progress. Starting from a situation in which it controlled the council chairmanship only in one Arab village, it (or its Democratic Front) has since won the mayoralty of Nazareth in1975 and retained it in 1978, and the chairmanships of 19 of the 31 contested councils in Galilee and one of those in the Triangle.

And what of the many reputed Labour Alignment supporters among local Arab politicians who are neither Rakah and certainly not Ibn al-balad?

They have either faded away or are lying low waiting for this radical paroxysm to pass over. There is reason, however, to believe that erstwhile claims that the mass of traditional politicians were supporters of the Labour Alignment or of other Jewish parties, were always a case of wistful thinking.

Many traditional Arab politicians did indeed identify themselves in such fashion as long as the Labour Alignment was the ruling party. Since its electoral debacle in May 1977 all such identification has vanished. To be sure, pragmatic bread and butter politics which seeks to circumvent the need for political identification along nationalist and ideological lines, is still dominant. But none of the traditional hunters, who have a good ear to the ground in their communities, would be so foolhardy today as to identify themselves as Alignment.

55. The Black Panthers:
A Portrait of an Oriental Jew

Susan Bellos

The Oriental Jews or Sephardim, that is, Jews from the former Ottoman domains in the Middle East, North Africa, and the Balkans, whose rich history and achievements have hardly been studied in the West, have always been indentified with the Middle East. They are the authentic inhabitants of the Middle East as much as the Arabs, Persians, and Turks— the major groups in the area. In Israel they are a majority, and some leaders, such as Eliezer Shmuell of the Ministry of Education, have supported the idea of replacing the stereotypes and prejudices against the Oriental Jew with an understanding of his history and folkways. Oriental Jews—among whom those from Morocco occupy a special place—are strongly pro-Israel and committed Zionists. In the elections of 1981 they have supported the right-wing Likud bloc. However, it was from their ranks that there arose the Black Panthers, a sort of radical protest group. The portrait of Charles Biton, a Black Panther who eventually joined the Rakah (an exceptional act), provides insight into the situation of the Oriental Jews' social mobility in Israel. The following article by Susan Bellos appeared in the international edition of the Jerusalem Post, *August 2, 1977*

Charles Biton, the 28-year-old Knesset Member from Jerusalem's Musrara slum district, looks really disadvantaged, which makes him something of an oddity in the marble corridors of power. He is tiny and looks as if he never had enough to eat as a child.

His shirt is unbuttoned, his jeans neat.

He is either laughing or agitated or running, and he seems a natural target for either mothering or bullying. Though he might easily be confused with the extra help hired to do the washing-up after a big do, he has made an impression on the public after only two months as a parliamentarian.

During his first weeks, Biton exposed the sale of matriculation papers on the streets and rocked the Education Ministry out of its tacit policy of turning a blind eye to the wholesale cheating that accompanies the present examination system.

He has also forced the public to take note of conditions in prisons in general and of charges of mistreatment of inmates of the Beersheba jail.

This was partially achieved by storming a session of the Knesset Internal Affairs Committee with a group of furious wives and mothers of Beersheba prisoners.

Attempts to trace the origins of his confrontationist style lead one to his father, who immigrated to Israel from Morocco in 1949, when Charlie was just a baby. Unlike many of the immigrants who spent the winter of 1949–50 huddled in tents in a camp at Pardess Hanna, Charlie's father had the gumption to go to Jerusalem by himself to look for a place to live.

The only place he found was among the abandoned houses in the deserted former Arab quarter of Musrara, which bordered on no-man's land. A group of families including the parents of future Black Panther leaders Reuven Abergil, Sa'adia Marciano and Haim Turgeman, picked themselves up and became the founders of today's Musrara.

This may partially answer the question why the protest movement started there and not say in Katamon, where the population was the same and the physical conditions were just as squalid. Charlie and the other Panther leaders inherited from their parents two vital qualities: intelligence and initiative.

However, back in Musrara in the 1950's nobody—not even Charlie's perspicacious mother—ever imagined his future achievements. The family lived in an abandoned hovel, and the children went to the only local school, Beit Ya'akov, which was part of the Agudat Yisrael network and therefore not supervised by the Education Ministry.

Charlie stayed at school until the age of 13. He and the brighter Panther leaders learned to read and write, and also to loathe their often harsh schoolmasters.

Charlie was involved in a series of minor delinquencies, like stealing scrap-iron from no-man's land and fruit from nearby markets. For some petty thefts he was sent to Tel Mond reformatory for a year, where he was taught to be a locksmith—a trade he has worked at, on and off, for about 10 years. Because of his record, Charlie was not taken into the army.

In 1969, Charlie and a number of other Musrara youths, with the assistance and encouragement of some Jerusalem Municipality street workers, decided to try to change their lives by forming a political movement—the Black Panthers. The Black Panthers started as a protest of disadvantaged Oriental youth, and Charlie's political techniques are those of the street-direct action, sit-ins, demonstations and confrontations with the police.

Charlie Biton was the only Black Panther who was smart enough to get into the Knesset by joining the one party prepared to offer him a safe seat—Rakah, in its Democratic Front for Peace and Equality. The irony is that although Charlie was actually elected by the Arabs of Israel (only a few thousands Jews voted for the DFPE), he sees himself, and to quite a large extent is seen by others, as the spokesman for some of Israel's most disadvantaged Jews. And many of them, like Charlie of Moroccan origin voted at the other end of Israel's political spectrum. Charlie, who says quite firmly, "We are an independent action inside Rakah," is well aware of this and seems intent on using Rakah just as much as it is using him.

"Well, why shouldn't we have joined Rakah?" he asked. His group of Panthers were always committed to the "left" and they had no objections to the six points Rakah made a condition of the joining: peace; a return to the 1967 borders; recognition of the "right" of the Palestinians to a state of their own; a pledge to fight against ethnic discrimination and to struggle for the working class and women's liberation.

He added, I don't see why Lyova Eliav (Sheli MK, active in Council for Israel-Palestinian Peace) couldn't have agreed to this."

Rakah includes men who are either old Communists or veteran Arab nationalists. Its MKs are very much part of the Knesset and they know and respect its rules. Apparently, they enjoy neither Charlie's pranks, nor his talent for publicity.

Whom does he get on with then?

"Well, not politically you understand, but David Levi (Likud Absorption Minister) was very nice to me. And Aharon Abuhatzeira—the Minister for Religious Affairs—came over to me on the first day and said it was good to see another Moroccan in the House."

Ezer Weizman has also been friendly; but Amnon Lin (Likud La'am has already told him to button up his shirt and mind his manners. ("Who does he think I am, his son?")

Charlie is powerfully and healthily aware that his world has nothing to do with politicking in luxurious surroundings. Both his parents are cleaning workers and they still live in Musrara. Charlie himself lives with his wife Levana and their two small daughters in a 70 sq. m. flat in Ramot.

He has no car. Two of his sisters are gainfully employed—one as a nurse and the other as a clerk at the National Insurance Institute; his brother Avi, keeping other political channels of communication open, is MK Samuel Flatto-Sharon's chauffeur.

Charlie's real world is still that of marginal youth, tens of thousands of young people who neither work nor study and live in a semi-delinquent subculture.

So far Charlie is a freak in the Knesset. He doesn't fit in because his system of values is still partly that of the streets and the poor neighborhoods. This is a section of the population that has as yet been entirely unrepresented in the Knesset. Charlie represents what might be called the non-respectable poor.

He has already been severely reprimanded by the Knesset House Committee for an "assault on the dignity of the Knesset." But this, in addition to snubs by more conventional MKs and functionaries, will only spur him in his running battles.

For the past seven years, Charlie Biton has channelled all his energies into political action. He gets up early in the morning, keeps appointments, reads educational reports, and takes his job very seriously. It will remain to be seen whether he will be the Knesset's prize naughty boy, or whether he will develop into a genuine leader.

XVI.   IMMIGRATION/EMIGRATION AND DIASPORA

Aside from war and peace, there is hardly any other issue so vital to Israel as immigration (aliya) and emigration (yodim—to "go down," physically and symbolically). A substantial part of Israel's population was born abroad, either in Europe or in the Arab countries. But the sabra, that is, those who were born in Palestine and Israel, are changing now the balance in favor of a "native Israeli" population. Israel's leaders estimate that a Jewish population of about 5 to 6 million is essential to ensure long-range security and economic strength; the neighboring Arab countries, on the other hand, fear that such a large population cannot be accommodated within Israel's present boundaries but that she will have to expand further. The population influx that followed the establishment of Israel and the war of 1967 has slackened considerably, especially since 1973. Statistics suggest that in 1979 and 1980 emigration from Israel has for the first time exceeded immigration. The increase in emigration is attributed chiefly to inflation and a variety of other economic factors. The emigration has been directed chiefly to the United States; There are over 50,00 Israelis living in New York alone. The overwhelming majority of the expatriates have maintained their Israel citizenship and say that they plan eventually to return. The problem of low immigration and high emigration has focused attention anew on the Jews in the Diaspora and their relations in Israel.

Another question of immense political importance is the extent to which Diaspora Jews can participate in Israeli affairs without either hurting the sensibilities of those in Israel, who are resentful of the patronizing attitude of the outsiders, or antagonizing their own governments. The American Jewish Committee and the American Jewish Congress, which are providing considerable material and moral support to Israel, have advocated greater participation of Diaspora Jews in Israeli affairs.

On the topic of the Jews who leave Israel and their reasons for emigrating, former Colonel Ya'acov Hasdai has published an interesting book, Emet Betzel Hamilhama [Truth in the Shadow of War]. Those interested in these issues will find relevant material in demographic studies of Israel; see M. Curtis and M. Chertoff, eds., Israel, Social Structure and Change (New Brunswick, N.J.: Transaction Books, 1971), and Amos Elon, The Israelis, Founders and Sons (London: Sphere, 1971).

Migration is a topic that arouses deep interest among Israeli and Diaspora Jews. This anthology devotes a minimum of space to this important topic, as it is somewhat outside the purpose of dealing with currents of thought in the Middle East. But see, for example, the discussion of the relation of Israel to Diaspora Jews in Link (July–August 1980)—Link is a publication of the Americans for Middle East Understanding—in which concessions to the Arabs are defended.

56. Diaspora and Zionism[*]

I. Navon

The third question, that of immigration and absorption, is more complex and difficult than most of our problems, but it is also the most vital. Aliya is the meaning of our existence and the condition for our development. The solution, however, is not entirely in our hands. The days of mass immigration have passed. Aliya is now the fruit of a personal decision by the Jew who lives in the Diaspora. At Passover he says "Next year in Jerusalem" but he goes on living where he is. This is a painful situation, but it has not been proved to be inevitable. It is difficult to agree—we must not agree—that only three million Jews will live in their homeland, and eleven million will continue to live in exile. The "prisoners of Zion" who reached us this week can perhaps show the Jews of the world the meaning of yearnings for the homeland and the struggle for Aliyah. On another occasion I tried to describe the conflicting processes that are taking place among these Jews. On the one hand, Jewish organizations with memberships in the millions join the Zionist movement, but, on the other hand, entire branches of our people wither away as a consequence of growing assimilation. A significant proportion of those who are lost consist of idealistic youth seeking a sublime idea, a great challenge, to which they can dedicate their spiritual powers and thus express their creative impulses.

---

[*]This speech by I. Navon, the President of Israel, was broadcast on Independence Day, May 1, 1979 and was released by the Government Press Office.

I am not sure that we are familiar with the spiritual world of these young people, their ideals and yearnings. But it seems obvious to me that we should not try to attract them with material inducements. We must confront them on the spiritual level. We must find a way to reveal to them the eternal values of Judaism and its great heritage, to awaken within them a sense of a common historic destiny, to confront them with challenges that will win their hearts and enable them to realize both personal and national goals: The development of the desert, bold pioneering in all fields of activity, participation in the creation of a society of quality, living on the fruits of its labours, the unification of the nation and the enhancement of its cultural, scientific and technological standards, as well as other subjects that will fit in with their inner needs. The Jewish people is undergoing an accelerated sociological process that is transforming it more and more into a university-trained population. We must exert our minds to find new roads to this people. The old methods have lost direction and will not do any longer.

The Zionist movement alone cannot grapple with the task. The government and the Zionist organization must establish a special head-quarters, which will be at work every day and every hour. What can be more vital than this?

57.   Stemming the Flow*

Chaim Herzog

When a human body bleeds, by the very nature of things, all efforts are concentrated on stopping the bleeding. What seems to be so natural in the human body does not appear to be natural in a body politic, a state. I am referring to the very dangerous development whereby *yerida* (emigration) has reached an annual total of about 20,000.

It is superfluous to dwell on the very serious significance of such a development, which involves a high percentage of Israel-born sabras, ex-army personnel, graduates of institutes of higher learning, men and women who grew up, were nurtured in this country, fought for it and, for one reason or another, decided to leave.

For years, this dangerous process has been developing, our national body has been bleeding, and nothing has been done to deal with the problem.

---

*The following excerpt appeared in the weekly edition of the *Jerusalem Post*, August 17, 1976.

We are a free society, and by its very nature people will fall by the wayside and people will join it. But it is inconceivable that our society, with all the problems that face it, having regard to the basis on which it is structured—religious, ideological, national—should not raise a finger in the light of such a menacing development.

I would like to be proved wrong, but I do not remember that a government in Israel—the present one or those which preceded it—ever conducted an in-depth analysis and discussion on this vital subject. For years we have been concentrating to an obsessive degree on the subject of our borders, but we have rarely applied ourselves to the no less important issue of the society within those borders.

Every Israeli who becomes established in the U.S. receives permission to work and thereafter acquires American citizenship, becomes a focal point which draws additional members of the family. A very dangerous process is then set in motion. In my view, the scope of the problem has reached proportions which call for urgent steps to be taken to reduce it. Of late, this subject has also come in for comment on a number of occasions in the press and in the electronic media of the U.S.—a coverage which has hardly been flattering to Israel.

It is wrong to look upon *yordim* as lost cases. In the past few years, a steady stream of Israelis returning to Israel has developed, and the Ministry of Labour has been active in helping to find jobs for thousands of Israeli university graduates who were interested in returning.

An investment in this vital and valuable potential, similar to that invested in aliya, could contribute considerably to bringing back to Israel part of this very large Jewish community.

One must remember that many of the emigrants have not succeeded in the U.S., although there are a few success stories. After a few years, the dream of becoming rich over-night evaporates and gives way to frustration and disappointment.

In many cases, they do not achieve the standard of living to which they were accustomed in Israel. But they have burned their bridges; they are loath to admit failure, and they are fearful of embarking on a fresh start. So they decide to stay a year, and then another year. In the hope that they will soon turn the corner. This is the period in which advantage could be taken of their attitude, given the correct organization and motivation.

For this purpose, a special authority should be created, with full powers. Such an organization is necessary, even if only to check those bizarre instructions issued by government or public institutions which tend to encourage emigration, or at least create conditions for it.

For example, when a boy concludes his studies at a technical school, as a *handasa'i* (practical engineer) he will have studied two post-secondary school years. If he wants to continue his studies towards the degree of engineer, the higher education authorities in Israel do not recognize his two post-secondary school years. They insist that he start the course—in other words, five years of studies.

He therefore chooses to go to the U.S. where his two years of post-secondary education in Israel are recognized. Thus, after a period of two to three years, he concludes his studies as an engineer—instead of five years in Israel. If he tries Grenoble in France, he could become an engineer within one year.

In the U.S., I found that eight out of eleven boys who had concluded a course for practical engineers in a certain subject at an ORT school in Israel were obliged, because of the reasons I have mentioned, to go to America. Most will be snapped up by an American market eager for such technicians, and a very high percentage of them will thus certainly stay abroad.

Over the years it has been impossible to get the institutions of higher learning to change their regulations, although they cause emigration in such large numbers.

The government of Israel forbids the employment of *yordim* in government offices abroad, even of a woman who left Israel because she married a foreign citizen. As opposed to this, one may employ for up to five years an Israeli who has come to study. This instruction creates a situation whereby the government in many cases (not all) makes emigration easier, because a very distrubing percentage of those whom the Government of Israel has enabled to be absorbed in the U.S. remains after they receive a much sought-after green card, namely the license to work.

During my three years at the U.N. I witnesses about 15 such cases within the limited framework of the small delegation to the U.N. and the consulate-general. Multiplication of these figures by the number of government offices in the U.S. would produce a very alarming figure.

58. Diaspora "Lobby" Needed*

Representatives of at least two major national Jewish organizations in the Diaspora—the American Jewish Committee and the American Jewish Congress—have in recent months publicly advocated greater participation of Diaspora Jewry in Israeli affairs. Leaders of the "non-Zionist" wing of the Jewish Agency voiced similar sentiments at its recent sessions.

---

*The following excerpt appeared in the weekly edition of the *Jerusalem Post*, July 17, 1979.

A few years ago such expressions would have been roundly condemned in Israeli establishment circles. The response would have been: only if you settle in Israel, pay taxes, and serve in the army are you entitled to express yourself with respect to Israel's internal concerns. Your role is limited to giving generously to Israeli fund-raising efforts, and to exert pressure on your respective governments when Israeli interests are involved. And Disapora Jewry would have mouthed a meek "Amen."

This pattern of relations was inaugurated by the dominant Jewish figure since Israel's rebirth, David Ben-Gurion, and it prevailed until recently without serious challenge. Much of the Jewish establishment abroad owed its existence, privileges, and status to the recognition afforded it by the sovereign government of Israel, and it behaved according to Israeli wishes.

But a new generation of Diaspora leadership that did not experience the European catastrophe, has no ambivalence concerning the immediate Jewish future in the deomcratic Diaspora, did not know Ben-Gurion, and views Israeli leaders more critically than did its predecessors is emerging. Although members of the younger Jewishly-committed generation are more concerned than their elders with the quality of Israel's national life, a growing indifference if not alienation towards Israel is apparent on the part of large numbers of thoughtful Jews abroad.

Unless they begin to feel an involvement in Israeli affairs that is deeper than giving charity or applying political pressure, they may end up ignoring Israel altogether. A one-way relationship between givers and takers cannot last indefinitely; only an *organic* inter-relationship based upon mutuality of concern and influence can endure.

Israeli spokesmen tend to interpret demands for such greater involvement as an attack on Israel's sovereignty. But in their parochial manning of the political-party bulwarks of Israel, they ignore the reality that world Jewry does, in fact, influence Israel all the time—without however having any *systematic* voice in the crucial issues affecting its society.

The money raised by world Jewry influences Israel's budgets and governmental services. The extraordinary efforts of the Diaspora on behalf of Israel Bonds contribute powerfully to investment in Israel. The Jewish lobby abroad affects Israel's political policies, military strength, and the receipt of grants-in-aid. The encouragement of tourism and of investment in Israel has no small effect on the country's morale ana economy.

Through the Jewish world, Israel's normal information services are only as good as their back-up by local Jewry. Malben, Hadassah, WIZO, Ort, friends-of-Isreali universities and cultural foundations directly affect the quantity and quality of essential social services in the country. The reception accorded Israeli representatives who visit the Western Diaspora for political, military, economic, or educational purposes can make all the difference between the mission's success and failure. The pressure exerted by Orthodox Jewish circles abroad with respect to religion in Israel is felt in the country all the time. Allocations made to Israeli political parties and the Histadrut from tax-exempt funds raised by Jews abroad help these bodies function as they do.

The relationship between Israel and world Jewry is *sui generis*, and the meaning of "sovereignty," when viewed against this relationship, differs substantially from the generally accepted legal definition. Influencing Israeli society does not mean threatening to withhold support from it, or making decisions for it. It means seeking to influence its decision-makers *before* they reach their decisions, with the State of Israel retaining the sovereign right to decide as it wishes.

Nevertheless, the bulk of Diaspora influence in Israel should not bear directly upon "sovereign" issues. At stake is the *ethos* of Israel's national life, rather than issues which must be resolved by government decision. Through qualified and dedicated "lobbyists" in Israel, representing major Jewish organizations abroad, Diaspora Jewry should seek to influence the general climate of the Israel society, with respect to two major areas: Israel's *civic* quality of life, and Israel's *Jewish* quality of life . . . .

Diaspora organizational offices in Israel should also provide political education to their affiliated groups and key individuals visiting Israel, a regular newsletter to the organization's membership incorporating a precis of significant veiwpoints on current Israeli issues, and periodic visits of the Israeli representative to the organization's chapters abroad. In turn, the organization's headquarters in the Diaspora must help coordinate the "political" dimension of influencing Israel by meeting Israeli leaders who visit their countries and giving them the benefit of their knowledge of selected issues.

Such a vibrant pattern of relationships between Israel and the Diaspora will motivate Jewish organizations in the Diaspora to be far more concerned with Israel's day-to-day life than they now are. It will impel them to study Israeli issues with greater profundity and commitment. It will tend to democratize them and arouse the interest and participation of large numbers of Jews hitherto indifferent or inactive. It will force them to face up to, and deal more effectively and responsibly with, Jewish education and aliya—two foremost subjects of concern to Israel. It will give Israel the moral sanction to intervene more forcefully in the issues of Jewish survival in the Diaspora.

Indeed, such a relationship will strengthen the concept of one Jewish People.

XVII. VIEWS OF
VARIOUS POLITICAL GROUPS

59. The Centrist View: Shinui (Change)

*Shinui or Mifleget Merkaz (Change-Centrist Party) movement was founded
after the October War of 1973 by a group, mainly of intellectuals and
professionals, wishing to bring change in the political structure of Israel. The
movement wanted to establish itself as a major party and to replace the
traditional parties, especially the Labor Party (MAPAI). In addition to its
criticism of the government and of the MAPAI, Shinui called attention to the
need to resolve socioeconomic problems through liberal-socialist ideas. In
December 1976, it merged with the Democratic Movement headed by
Yigael Yadin to form the Democratic Movement for Change (DMC). In
1977 the party won 15 seats in the Knesset, and despite severe opposition
from former Shinui members it joined the Likud coalition government. In
September 1978, the Shinui faction left the coalition government and the
DMC because of disagreement on internal and foreign policies—the peace
with Egypt, the establishment of new settlements in the West Bank and
Gaza, and the abandonment of socioeconomic goals. It reorganized itself as
a liberal centrist party with six members. Its future is uncertain. Its
membership includes some well known individuals, such as Professor
Amnon Rubinstein (MK), Samuel Toledano (MK), Mordekhai Virshuvski
(MK), Ze'ev Vertheimer (MK), Joseph Tamir (MK), and Zeidan Atshi (MK),
and so forth. The excerpt below was translated from a pamphlet in Hebrew
put out by the party in 1980.*

Shinui combines a moderate, responsible foreign policy . . . with a
national and progressive approach toward economic and social affairs—an
approach that realizes the need to end the inflation, while gradually
eliminating governmental deficit financing. These internal and foreign
affairs are combined, and we do not believe that it is possible to separate
them.

Shinui believes that without a political leadership which maintains
examplary conduct, no change will take place to improve Israeli society.

Consequently, our Knesset members are fully participating in the debates and in its committees; our KMs have waived their immunity for traffic offenses. We propose to reduce the financing of political parties by the state . . . .

We emphasize the need for a fundamental change in the present Israeli political system: such change includes the adoption of a constitution and the guarantee of civil rights. [We advocate] changes in the election system; in the structure of the political parties and of the local and municipal governments; in the powers of the Knesset and the government: . . . to grant the PM power to discharge ministers . . . .

Shinui-Centrist Party stands for the right of each citizen to be free of any ideological or religious coercion. Our faction in the Knesset has opposed any legislative initiative stemming from pressures exerted by extreme religious circles, initiatives that led to legislation which harmed the citizen's liberties . . . . Contrary to the Alignment [MAPAI and MAPAM] we consolidated and presented a clear and wholesome autonomy program, based on a realistic and moderate political approach. Contrary to the Alignment, we opposed the Jerusalem Law, whose approval causes such a political catastrophe [allusion to strong negative reaction to the annexation of Jerusalem].

The economic and social views of the Alignment [the party deemed likely at that time to win the elections of 1981]—social demagogy, nepotism, and the anti-productive approach toward economic problems—are outdated and harmful. The Alignment promises to all: renewal of the economic growth, maintenance of real wages, reduction of the gap in the balance of payments, full employment, subsidies for basic products. Contrary to the alignment, we think that it is forbidden to delude the public. The process necessary to strengthen the Israeli economy will not be so easy, and the Israeli public will be asked to spend much effort in order to rehabilitate it.

Contrary to the Alignment, the Shinui suggests that the huge staff in the public services—which has become enormous under the Alignment government, and in part of which there is broad invisible unemployment—be cut. In contrast [to the Alignment], Shinui suggests that a productive economy be encouraged. The social initiatives of Shinui aim at directing aid to those who need it instead of dividing benefits, as practiced under the Alignment rule.

Shinui fights religious coercion and opposes "deals" with the religious parties. The Alignment continues to cooperate as in the past with the religious parties, hoping to renew the "coalition." Shinui takes a stand against the Alignment, which supports the Law of the Chief Rabbinate—a law that discriminates against various Judaic groups. We submitted instead the draft of a fundamental law to grant equal rights to all the movements in

Judaism . . . Shinui supports the de-politicization of various economic and social segments of the society, such as the economic enterprises, the welfare services, culture and education, the trade unions, the Zionist organization, sports and youth groups . . . .

[The aim of the Shinui in the coming elections] is to provide an alternative to the National Religious Party and the other religious parties . . . . Shinui presents an alternative to the failure of the past [of the Alignment and the National Religious Party] and the present failure [of Likud and the National Religious Party] so as to prevent a future failure [by Alignment and the National Religious Party]. Only Shinui can break this despairing, vicious circle . . . .

Since the Liberal Party has become a satellite of the Herut, and since . . . social democracy became dominant in the Alignment, there is no longer a centrist party in Israel. There is now an urgent need for such a centrist power, and Shinui will go to the election of the tenth Knesset as a centrist party.

60. The Fifth of Iyar' Movement (Heh Be-Iyar)

This movement is an outgrowth of the concern expressed by many secular-minded Israelis about the religious policies of the government. It was formed on April 28, 1979, as a reaction to "laws to be passed in the Knesset and any measure which entails religious coercion and infringements against civil liberties, women's rights, or freedom of speech." Many intellectuals, such as the writer Yoram Kaniuk, poet Haim Hefer, Menahem Peri, Shulamit Aloni (MK), Yehoshua Porat, Yoela Marshefi, Moshe Dor, and others, supported the movement. Its principles were published in the New Outlook *(July-August 1979): 65–67.*

"The Fifth of Iyar Movement" was established in order to realize the following principles of the Proclamation of the Independence of the State of Israel.

The State of Israel will . . . maintain complete equality of social and political rights for its citizens, without distinction of creed, race, or sex. It will guarantee freedom of religion and conscience, of language, education, and culture. It will safeguard the Holy Places of all religions and will be loyal to the principles of the United Nations Charter . . . .

Thirty-one years after these words were proclaimed as the "credo" of the State of Israel, the *reality* in which we live is one where:

THERE IS NO complete equality of social and political rights;

THERE IS rising discrimination based on race, religion, sex and country of origin;

THERE IS NO freedom of religion and conscience;

THERE IS coercion of religion and conscience affecting the individual, women, and minorities not considered Jewish according to Orthodox Halakha;

THERE IS NO freedom of education and culture;

THERE ARE nationalistic and religious dictates which prevent the granting of a broadminded, humanistic, liberal education;

THERE IS NO extending of our hand in good neighbourliness;

THERE IS the domination of a neighboring nation and the systematic expropriation of its freedom and land.

THE STATE OF ISRAEL was created by the force of the moral claim of the return of the People of Israel to their Homeland to build a dynamic, creative, open, and just society. We have now turned into a closed, arrogant, nationalistic, violent and expropriatory society whose moral character is continually being undermined.

Amidst a feeling of deep distress we have risen to struggle for the application of the following principles in our everyday lives, laws, education, and human rights:

- Equal rights and opportunities in all areas of life, in theory and in practice, for every man and woman residing in this country, equality before the law without distinction of religion, race, nationality, or political affiliation.
- Every man is entitled to freedom of thought and expression, including the freedom to maintain his beliefs undisturbed, to request information and views and to receive and provide them through all means and without restrictions.
- Every man is entitled to freedom of assembly, organization, and peaceful demonstration.
- The state-media must allow suitable expression for every opinion and view without discriminating against anyone because of his ideas or beliefs.
- Every man has the right to lead a secular or religious life according to his choice without any coercion or limitations of any kind.
- Equal status and protection will be provided for every religious community, belief, and movement.
- Every adult man and woman is entitled to marry and have a

family without any limitation or disqualification because of race, citizenship, nationality, or religion, in either a religious or civilian framework, according to his or her own free choice. It is every woman's fright to plan her family and determine the number of her children and the time of their births without any legal limitations prohibiting the cessation of an unwanted pregnancy.

- It is every man's right to choose the kind of education for his children as he sees fit. Education must be based on the principles of the freedom of thought, creativity, and criticism, the right to knowledge through open inquiry in the spirit of science and scientific achievement, the foundations of humanism, tolerance, and equality, and through the appreciation of the achievements and culture of our fellow man.

- The State of Israel must strive for peace with all of its neighbors, a peace which will guarantee the physical security and sovereignty of the State of Israel as the state of the people of Israel.

The continued domination of another nation in the West Bank and Gaza corrupts and endangers the very existence of the State of Israel.

As long as Israeli rule exists in the Occupied Territories the rights of the inhabitants thereof will be preserved according to the principles of International Law and the Geneva Convention.

The Fifth of Iyar, Israel Independence Day, 5729

61.   The New Right:
Tehiya, Brit Ne'emanei Eretz Yisrael

Renaiscence, the Covenant of Eretz Israel Faithful, was founded in October 1979, by various people belonging to Gush Emunim, the Land of Israel Movement, Ein Vered Circle, and other rightist groups. Two Gush Emunim leaders, Hanan Porat and Gershon Shafat, were part of the movement. Later Geulah Cohen lent her support to the movement. Begin's Herut party was very concerned with these developments. The group gained power because of the consternation caused by the policies of Premier Menahem Begin, who was considered the prophet of the true believers in Israel, prior to his signing of the peace with Egypt, which it opposed. The interview below with Yuval Ne'eman, the well known nuclear scientist acting as secretary of the organization, indicates the reasons that led to the estab-

lishment of the Tehiya. In the elections of 1981 Tehiya won three seats—not twenty as it predicted—in the Knesset. One must note that the organization's chief purpose is to find a remedy to the growing schism between the secular and religious Israelis. The question, needless to say, is not seen as a matter of individual freedoms and choice but as one that goes directly to the very foundation on which Israel was established. The interview appeared in the international edition of the Jerusalem Post, *October 14–20, 1979.*

QUESTION: Why a separate party? Given your great influence on the Begin government—witness the history of Gush Emunim settlement over the past two years—wouldn't it be preferable for you to continue working from within the existing parties?

ANSWER: Nearly everyone associated with our new party has tried, each in his own way, to work from within ever since the '67 war. I, for example, tried to get many of my ideas across while serving as chief scientist to the defence establishment under Defence Minister Shimon Peres. [Ne'eman resigned that position in protest against the 1975 Interim Agreement on Sinai.]

When Herut was in the opposition, they certainly talked the right way. But they've changed. Even today, for example, I agree with every word of Prof. (Moshe) Arens [chairman of the Knesset Foreign Affairs and Defence Committee], but he's been completely neutralized. We believe we have no alternatives but to set up a new framework and appeal for popular support with a clear line on the major issues confronting Israel today.

As for me, the last straw was the signing of the Camp David accords. I was shocked that under Begin's leadership, the majority of the Zionist parties in the Knesset voted to abolish an entire settlement bloc at Yamit.

QUESTION: How do you explain the change in Begin and in Herut? Is it simply a matter of human frailty and "selling out," or have the responsibilities of the premiership convinced him that hard realities would simply not permit the realization of his lifelong ideals?

ANSWER: I have no intention of engaging in mud-slinging against Begin, but I simply don't buy the latter explanation. The give-away that he had no intention of practicing what he had always preached was his appointment of Dayan as his foreign minister. That was his first act in office, carried out from the hospital bed where he was recovering from his heart attack, and before he even had a chance to come into contact with the hard realities you speak of.

How do I explain the change in Begin? I would guess that perhaps the closest we can get to the truth is that he sees everything in extremely personal terms. He was clearly shocked by his worldwide portrayal immediately after his election, as Israel's arch-terrorist and warmonger. Apparently he determined that he would go down in history as the man who brought "peace" to Israel. . . .

QUESTION: Some Tehiya founding fathers and mothers have been speaking of winning 20 mandates in the next elections. Is that bluff and wild imagination too?

ANSWER: It's very far from bluff. If you look at the polls and see the sharp decline in support for the Likud and the increase in the uncommitted floating vote, it's obvious that those votes will have to go somewhere. It all depends on the success we have in projecting our image as a party of true renascence. If we are seen as a simple one issue party, it's reasonable to look forward to seven or eight seats. But if we are successful in projecting ourselves as a party that stands for much broader principles, we may get as many as 20.

QUESTION: But aren't you in fact a one-issue party?

ANSWER: No. Far from it. Our jumping-off point is the idea of devotion to the original Zionist concept of Eretz Yisrael. But applying that concept to real life requires a reversal of the moral decline and loss of confidence that has sapped Israel's energy right across the board.

Making it possible for Israel to stand up to the political pressures being exerted against her, and to the continuing Arab military threat to our existence, requires a revolutionary change in the economy, in our attitudes to work and productivity, to the idea of "Hebrew Labour." It also requires a return to our cultural heritage by healing the tragic schism that has developed between so-called secular and religious Israelis.

If you call that one-issue politics, so be it. But that one issue encompasses every facet of our national life, and we intend to address ourselves to them all.

It's no secret that we are made up of people of widely differing religious and secular backgrounds, at a time when the tensions around this schism seem to be heating up more than ever before.

But I and my colleagues believe that our vision of Eretz Yisrael will be strong enough to bridge those differences. Besides which, the concepts of people and religion are totally inter-meshed in the Jewish people.

I myself am not religious. But I am persuaded that what many of our so-called secular elements are lacking is the clear vision of the Jewish nation as the embodiment of a millenia-old cultural heritage that has emerged so impressively among our religious members.

I believe that we will succeed in making the synthesis by stressing the need to return to that heritage and to our religious and cultural roots without the coercion that has made the concept of religion so hateful to so many young secular Israelis.

QUESTION: Let's return to some of the "unconverted" who, while they may sympathize with your ideal of a Zionist renaissance and may even feel very strongly that Eretz Yisrael should be incorporated in the modern State of Israel, have never managed to get over the intellectual, moral and political hurdle of the existence of 1.7 million Palestinian Arabs in those areas. What do you tell them about how you propose to deal with that embarrassing reality?

ANSWER: All these territories must be annexed to Israel: the Golan, Judea and Samaria and Gaza, and Sinai must not be relinquished. The arguments against annexation are largely spurious, and the demo-graphic demon is used largely as a pretext.

Look at the Golan. There are no Arabs there, and the Druse for the most part want to be part of Israel. And yet both the Labour and the Likud governments have twisted and turned and refused to annex the Golan.

As to the Arab population where it does exist: between 400,000 and 450,000 are refugees whom the Egyptians and the Jordanians consciously and consistently perpetuated in that status. Their humanitarian problem will not be resolved in a hypothetical Palestinian state, because they are not natives of those areas. They must be resettled, as part of a real peace settlement in Kuwait, Saudi Arabia and the other Arab oil coun-tries which have the wherewithal to resettle them.

In regard to the real Arab attitudes to the refugees, one should not overlook the fact that even the few hundred refugees Israel resettled in the el-Arish area were forcibly expelled and returned to Gaza at Egypt's insistence as part of the "peace" treaty.

As for the remaining Arabs, they should be given three choices:

1. Those completely opposed to living in a Jewish state could choose the option taken by Algeria's Jews, who left Algeria when it became independent, although their forebears settled in the area long before the Arabs;

2. Those wanting to remain in their native towns and villages but not to participate in Israel's national life could remain as resident aliens, a status not unknown in Western democracies;

3. Those who, like Israel's Druse minority, want to remain and become fully integrated in Israel, would be given every opportunity to do so.

PART THREE

Political and Social Thought in Turkey

XVIII. INTRODUCTION TO POLITICAL AND SOCIAL THOUGHT IN TURKEY

The first two and one-half decades after the establishment of the republic in Turkey (1923) were chiefly a period of political and cultural consolidation. The Turkish national state had been established in opposition to the universalist doctrines of Islam and of Ottoman tradition, both of which had rejected the idea of a national state. In an effort to instill in the Turkish people a sense of national identity, the ruling elite—that is, the modernist, secularist group—adopted radical nationalist views. It relied heavily on Turkey's past, and at times it even created theories to bolster the Turkish national ego—as, for example, the sun-language theory, according to which all languages were said to have originated in Turkish and that Turks were among the original creators of world civilization.

Two social forces—the bureaucratic elite and the rural elite—combined to create the unity and stability that were essential to root the idea of belonging to a nation and to a national state. The former—intellectuals, military and civilian bureaucracy, and segments of the urban population—controlled the main urban centers and enjoyed relatively free access to political power if it conformed to the nationalist, secularist principles of the republic. The latter—notables, landowners, and the newly rising commercial class—dominated mainly the rural areas. The first group was oriented toward cultural and political modernism; the second was motivated chiefly by economic and social considerations. Both groups enjoyed relatively high social status. The urban intelligentsia controlled the government but had limited economic means at its disposal. The rural elite had limited political power but owned land, shops, and other forms of wealth. This sharing of power by two sections of public life had profound social and economic drawbacks, but it also created an atmosphere of political quiet, in which the Turkish national state could be firmly established and a sense of national unity could be fostered.[1]

A Turkish national identity came into being after 1920. The new nation's internal cohesion was built around the idea of the territorial integrity of a modern state that rose above religious differences and a vague promise of future welfare and prosperity. Traditional influences certainly went into the new concept of nation and nationhood, but they seemed to be, in the main, the cement rather than the foundation blocks of the new nation. Minority nationalism and regional allegiances gradually lost their dynamic appeal. The Kurdish elites and the elites of other Muslim groups were accepted by the ruling Turkish political and social circles and, in fact, were assimilated into the Turkish nation. Islam was "removed" from politics and the importance of religious differences was minimized. The modern concept of nation was in fact superimposed on religious allegiances and created new loyalties to the national state.

Nationalism became the ideology of the new Turkish Republic. Republicanism, populism, secularism, statism, and reformism—officially proclaimed as additional principles in 1931 and incorporated in the constitution of 1937—were merely corollaries of nationalism.[2] Nationalism aimed at creating an integrated Turkish national state or a modern political system that superseded all religious, regional, and group identities and loyalties. In fact, the reforms undertaken in 1923–35 were practical measures designed to consolidate the modern national state and to create a political community sharing its ideals, a feeling of identity that was purely Turkish. In other words, the republican state tried to assure its own survival by creating a self-confident Turkish nation proud of its past and its achievements. In the latter context, history was reinterpreted and rewritten, often arbitrarily.[3] The Ottoman failures were attributed to men who were alien to the national spirit, while its achievements were hailed as the result of Turkish genius. The lack of clearly defined concepts of modern statehood and nationhood, and especially the tendency to regard the latter in the light of communal feelings inherited from the *umma* (the Muslim community), led to contradictions. These were solved, however, by political decisions that asserted the supremacy of the state and its sustainng social order, the ruling bureaucracy-intelligentsia.[4]

Atatürk, although less of a believer in the absolute power of ideology, did not hesitate to use ideological appeals in order to enhance the feeling of Turkish national identity and solidarity. Atatürkism[5]—that is to say, the six principles of the Turkish Republic—became in fact an ideology attributed to Atatürk. Much of this ideology, born from the demands of a rising national state, has become outdated by economic and social pressures that I shall discuss later. Yet Atatürkism still survives as the chief foundation of Turkish national statehood and appears as a predominantly political ideology.

Economic development, a preoccupation of the contemporary emerging states, did not become a major issue in Turkey until the late 1920s. The civil code of 1926, adopted almost intact from Switzerland, regulated in detail the acquisition, transfer, and inheritance of every kind of property, including land; the Obligations Code regulated all forms of transactions. The enforcement of these codes depended on sound, modern administrative and judicial systems, which, in turn, more than ever needed a rational economic basis.

As in the past, the economy had a capitalist orientation in the sense that it permitted a degree of freedom of enterprise and accumulation of private capital, diversification of occupations, and social stratification. The integrated political system and the relatively rational, uniform economic relations had a generalizing impact on the social structure, unifying various social groups with similar interest into larger classes that gradually acquired, under the impact of expanding education and political liberalization, a rational understanding of their respective group positions and interests.

In the context of economic development and the reconciliation of social conflicts, the government backed *Kadro* (1932–34), a review that attempted to formulate an ideology of economic development by borrowing ideas from Marxism, Italian corporatism, and socialism, but without accepting any one as its main source. *Kadro* claimed that Turkey's problem was not class conflict but the need for capital, increased production, and economic self-sufficiency." It was shut down in 1934 primarily because of its increasing reference to social classes and their conflicts and its efforts to give a new economic orientation to the program of the ruling Republican Party. These attitudes threatened a small group in that party, which claimed to represent the ideas of an integrated modern state, but which had become, in fact, the spokesman for the new ruling elite.

The social balance in Turkey was upset by the introduction of a multiparty system in 1945. This political experiment offered the rural groups an opportunity to acquire political initiative and to gain office influence in government and it enabled the masses, hitherto deprived of a political role, to participate in public life through direct vote.

The main concern of Turkish leaders at the beginning of the experiment (see Inönü's speech in Chapter XIX) was that the reforms were not sufficiently rooted to permit the evolution of politics within the generally accepted principles of a modern republic. The question defined in general as "acceptance of Atatürk's reforms" referred actually to a more basic question—whether or not the republican regime and the national state, together with all the loyalties they entailed, were firmly rooted. The first year of the multiparty system proved that the modern national state and the republican regime were generally accepted and could provide the basic framework in which politics could follow their natural course.

The ideologies that emerged in the 1940s reflected to a large extent the conflicts created by social restratification. Liberalism was the first major ideology to emerge after the political liberalization and the replacement of one-party rule with a multiparty system in 1945–46. Though disjointedly formulated, the liberal ideology represented the grievances of the agrarian, commercial, and working classes against the ruling bureaucracy and its statist philosophy. The bureaucracy was supported and relied upon by the Republican Party, which had incorporated in its organization most of the upper intellectual groups. It was obvious that the elites, after achieving their main purpose—the establishment of a national state—had little justification for their political supremacy, especially since the republican regime was hardly challenged by any group, however conservative.

The drive against the ruling order was eventually organized and led by the Democratic Party with the support of many intellectuals, including military men from the lower urban classes. This broad base of support brought the Democratic Party to power through elections in 1950.

During the multiparty period, and especially after 1950, the approach to economic development followed a rather different course. The state continued to play a major part in establishing cement and sugar factories and other major industries, but it also provided extensive credits to agriculture, which was almost entirely privately owned, and to private industry. Moreover, departing from past practices, the government refrained from entering into direct competition with private enterprises, at least in some fields. In other cases, often guided by political motives, it provided tax exemptions, crop subsidies, and other economic inducements and opportunities to landowners, contractors, and commercial groups, to enable them to accumulate capital and participate in economic development on their own initiative. As a consequence of the additional activity in the private sector, a new entrepreneurial and managerial group developed rapidly in a relatively competitive atmosphere. This group also acquired politial power in the ruling Democratic Party. Members of this group, using government power for their own advantage, made up much of the membership of the Vatan Cephesi (Fatherland Front), which was created by the Democrats in 1958 to crush the opposition.

Under the guise of economic liberalism, however, the Democrats soon espoused the demands of the major agrarian and commercial groups and threatened to convert their rule into an oligarchy of wealth and power, without the participation of the old intellectual bureaucratic elites. Nationalism became a conservative ideology incorporating a body of ideas based on the Ottoman-Islamic cultural heritage, which the Democrats used to muzzle social criticism. Many pressing social and economic problems could not be aired, lest they be considered subversive. Thus, a new ruling group used nationalism to prevent other groups from expressing their demands. Liberal intellectuals demanded the establishment of parties divided on ideological lines to clarify the political position of each social group.

The rise of this new type of middle class oriented toward economic activity occurred without compensatory developments elsewhere in society. The inflationary policies the government used as a means of development caused a sharp decline in the living standards and social status of the salaried class, which had already lost political power to the agrarian and commercial groups. Meanwhile, the peasantry and the workers, who benefited initially from the abolition of political restrictions and economic measures designed to win them over to the ruling Democratic Party, began to voice new demands. These demands could no longer be satisfied by the give-away policy the government had practiced in 1950–57.

Thus, in 1955–59, the social structure of Turkey had become further differentiated and diversified into a variety of social groups, each conscious of and interested in its own economic and political destiny. These were the new social foundations on which a new ideology could develop. The intelligentsia and the military and civilian bureaucracies, which were apathetic to true social reform and to the economic plight of the lower classes in 1920–45, gradually emerged in the late 1950s as the champions of social justice, economic development, and general welfare for the masses. They attacked the faulty tax system, the government's unplanned policy, and especially the groups that benefited from economic liberalism in 1950–58. The entrepreneurial groups answered by pointing to the increase (more than twofold) in national income, and to the participation in economic and political life of the lower classes, not as exploited groups, as the statists and socialists claimed, but as dignified, free citizens. They claimed the citizens realized that the existing democratic political and social regime had enabled them to liberate themselves from bureaucratic rule and that they would not accept the domination of the new "socialist" elites.

All these discussions took place in 1955–60, in newspapers and reviews such as *Forum, Pazar Postası (Sunday Mail), Varlık (Existence), Dost (Friend),* and a variety of smaller publications, especially those published by schoolteachers. Among these reviews, *Forum* deserves special mention. It began to publish in 1954 and gradually assembled in its list of contributors Turkey's leading intellectuals, and especially those who were social-minded. *Forum* adopted an evolutionary democratic viewpoint and provided an objective, balanced analysis of Turkey's major problems. It was, indeed, the main source of learning for democratic-minded Turkish intellectuals.

In 1958–59, Turkey seemed ripe for a basic social and political change from within, since the Democratic Party government proved dangerously blind to the new forces developing in society. The government's repressive measures against opposition in 1959–60—that is, against the Republican Party, which included all dissatisfied groups—were desperate efforts to stem the rising tide of demands for change. The Democrats had already had a warning in the elections of 1957, when, contrary to their expectations, they failed to win an absolute majority vote but stayed in power because the opposition votes were split among three parties. What Turkey needed was a government that would recognize the various social groups, accept as legitimate their claims for sharing economic and political power, and establish the constitutional system accordingly. The basic task was to harmonize the political regime and the social structure by establishing a new balance among the existing social groups on the basis of their power in society.

This situation provided the social and political bases for the ideological reorientation of the intelligentsia, chiefly the secularist, modernist, and nationalist groups. Deeply attached to their authoritarian, statist, and elitist philosophy, this group began gradually to embrace social justice and economic development. Soon socialism became their new ideology. The revolution of 1960 destroyed the ideological shields of the upper economic groups and permitted free discussion. As a consequence, social-ism—ranging from Marxism to Fabianism, and justifying itself primarily on economic and social grounds—became a major ideological current. Nationalism, in turn, notwithstanding its various subdivisions, espoused economic liberalism, traditionalism, and religion, and became the ideology of the economic and social *status quo*.[7]

Turkey thus entered the age of modern ideology at the level the West had attained in the nineteenth and early twentieth centuries. All this was possible thanks to a modern political structure—the national state—which generated a new pattern of ideological development.

The revolution of May 27, 1960, removed the social and political barriers to reform that had beem embodied in the Democratic Party government. The revolution began as a *coup d'état* directed against the oppressive policy initiated by the Menderes government; it soon became a social and political movement in which all groups participated.

The military could hardly anticipate the ideological struggle that followed their coup. The old regime was accused of having destroyed the bases of Kemalism through its reactionary, regressive policies. But the return to Kemalism (*Atatürkçülük*) urged by the intelligentsia had little in common with the meaning attached to the concept in 1923–45. National-ism had been the dominant feature of Kemalism in the past; now, social and economic questions acquired priority. In fact, Kemalism was de-scribed as a progressive social and economic ideology that had been perverted by privileged groups into a narrow political dogma. Conse-quently, it was necessary to engage Turkey on the right path of moderniza-tion by achieving rapid economic development and social justice. This modernization was often referred to as Westernization, but no longer in the same context as in 1930–60. This was to be an economic and social Westernization to create material advance and comforts, but not by the methods used in the West. The apologists for rapid economic and social development rejected the democratic political means of the West as totally inadequate and proposed a system of executive supremacy to carry out their plans most efficiently.

The key ideological problem in Turkey after 1960, therefore, concerned the method of achieving economic and social development. There was unanimous agreement about the need for development and the fact that the state had to have some role in it. There was disagreement about the extent and nature of the authority the government should be granted. In other words, the question was whether economic development and social justice should be imposed by a group from the top or should be carried out by terms of a consensus of all social groups capable of contributing to but also sharing in economic development. Development presented as an economic problem was in reality a political and ideological question that could determine the very characteristics of Turkish democracy.

The ideas about executive supremacy or statism and socialism were expressed in newspaper and magazine articles throughout 1960–61. Toward the end of 1961, a group of intellectuals, many of whom had been associated with *Forum* (and some with the Republican Party),decided to publish a new periodical, *Yön (Direction)*, to express more cohesively their ideas about socialism, statism, and social justice. Many of these intellectuals had been associated with the State Planning Organization (SPO) established in 1960, and their plans for economic development were based on a rather extensive statism. Political parties were banned from activity during the SPO's initial activities. and therefore could not express their viewpoints. After the elections of October 1961, however, a popularly elected parliament convened. The Justice Party, the main opposition group representing free enterprise, was associated with the Republicans in a coalition government. It began to object violently to the expanded statism proposed by the SPO. Clearly, the statism proposed by intellectuals and accepted initially by the Republican Party had to be modified if the coalition was to survive at all. The Republicans seemed willing to compromise. They thus dashed the hopes of the new elite group, which sought to consolidate itself in power as the agent of social justice and economic development. The publication of *Yön* on December 20, 1961, therefore, must be viewed as the intellectuals' reaction to the abandonment of their brand of statism. They described the rejection of statism as a direct blow to social justice, democracy, and modernization, and blamed the political parties and parliamentary democracy for its rejection.[8]

The socialist intellectuals' strong attacks on parliamentary democracy were coupled with even stronger condemnation of private enterprise. The new middle classes in entrepreneurial positions, whose number and power increased considerably after 1950, reacted to these attacks by defending private enterprise as being capable of achieving economic development and as providing the foundations necessary for political democracy. Economic and social issues thus became the main forces determining Turkey's ideological orientation. Political institutions were

considered determined by the economic and social structure. The socialists regarded the elimination of the last vestiges of the traditional social
organization as an essential condition of Turkey's rapid modernization.
They proposed the virtual elimination of landowners, capitalists, and all
major enterprises forming the upper layer of the existing system based on
private property. The apologists for free enterprise advocated the imposition of restrictions on state enterprises, full parliamentary control of the
civilian and military bureaucracies, and subordination of government
functions to the needs and traditions of society. The policies of all the
coalition governments in 1961–65 reflected, to a very great extent, the
thoughts prevailing among various social groups, indicating the emergence of a process of mutual social interaction that could lead to a natural
relationship between politics and social structure.

The new ideological outlook in Turkey drastically changed the
orientation of nationalism and Islamism, the two other major currents of
thought. Nationalism was officially accepted as the regime's ideology,
although it included a great variety of other tendencies, and it was
incorporated in the constitution in 1937. But this nationalism was devised
and implemented chiefly with an eye to political purposes intimately
connected with the establishment and consolidation of the national state.
By 1960, a sense of national identity and allegiance to the national state
prevailed among all major social groups. Having achieved its major
political mission, therefore, nationalism was bound to acquire a new form
and to conform to the new social and economic currents. Representatives
of conservative nationalism—racists, Turanists, Islamists, and Ottoman-
ists—appeared as apologists for free enterprise, parliamentary democracy,
and liberalism, not because they held firm convictions but because they
hoped that these concepts offered the best means of maintaining the
status quo. As usual, all the nationalists presented their views as out-
growths of Atatürk's ideas. But taking courage from the developing social
consciousness, the moderate social-minded groups and the leftists offered
their own interpretation of nationalism.

The struggle over nationalism was concluded with the adoption of the
constitution of 1961. After intensive debate, the drafters agreed to
mention nationalism in the preamble only. Article 2 of the constitution
defined the Turkish state as a *national*, secular, social republic. The old
brand of nationalism, however, maintained its vigor among the small-town
intelligentsia and middle-school students and teachers. But as the following translations indicate, even they were influenced, to some extent, by
the current thinking about human rights, economic development, social
organization, and modernization.

The ideological and political developments in Turkey took a new
course, notably after 1975, as the result of three interrelated forces: the

economic development, stimulated by a more rational and systematic investment policy; intensive social change, caused by urbanization and relative industrialization; and by the almost unlimited freedom of assembly and speech brought about by the new constitution of 1961. The freedom of speech permitted all the resentment and reaction, hope and expectation generated by continuous change occurring since 1920 to be openly expressed. The increase in the literacy rate (from roughly 40 percent in 1960 to about 80 percent in 1980) and the more than doubling of the national income enabled many lower urban and rural groups to articulate their demands and aspirations through more active participation in ideological debates and politics. A variety of debate clubs known as *Fikir kulupleri* (Ideas Clubs) became the forums for discussion. Until roughly 1965, these discussions were confined to the pages of a few reviews and the gatherings of associations of limited consequence, and there was no clear evidence of developing polarization. Yet, the new political climate as well as the continuous preoccupation with the need for rapid economic development inevitably brought under discussion the existing social and economic underdevelopment, unbalanced income distribution, and a variety of similar shortcomings. The underdevelopment was attributed eventually either to the historical factors, such as colonialism, imperialism, and feudalism, or to the inadequacy of the capitalist system or parliamentary democracy to rid the country of the obstacles to rapid development. Marxism appeared to the impatient as the ideal ideology for explaining and overcoming Turkey's economic stagnation. Turkish social thought gradually moved toward a more leftist extreme, due partly to the growing disillusionment with the West resulting from the U.S. negative attitude toward the Turkish position on Cyprus. The ideological catalyst of all these developments from 1962 to 1965 was the Marxist Labor lparty, which was able to assemble around itself all the major leftists groups, including important segments of the press and the academics; it secured 3 percent of the total vote case in the elections of 1965 and over a dozen deputies in the House of Deputies. The percentage, though small, was significant because the Labor Party included in 1965 many of the aggressive and dynamic social-minded young persons who had left the Republican People's Party (RPP) because of its social conservatism. The Republican Party therefore moved to the Left, espousing a policy known as *Ortanın solu* (left of center—see the section dealing with Bülent Ecevit). The promoters of the new ideology in the RPP borrowed the terminology of the radical Left, attacking their political adversaries as feudal-minded, regressive capitalists, although the basic structure and philosophy of their own party differed little from their opponents'. Ideologically, the shift of the Republicans to the Left represented the deep-seated resentment of a large segment of the bureaucratic-intelligentsia toward the new bourgeois rather any real loyalty or attachment to the workers or peasants whose cause they claimed to espouse. For lack of any true ideology, or even of a tenable philosophical or historical foundation, they dipped into the rhetoric of humanism, egalitarianism, and liberalism. The Republicans under Ecevit were able to secure the loyalty of many uncommitted leftists and to act as a protective political shield for the entire Left, although these often criticized and belittled the Republicans, calling them pseudoleftists. Through the turn to the Left the Republican Party gained a new life tenure however short that may prove to be—but it undercut two constitutional pillars that had assured Turkey a certain political stability and consensus. The Republican Party was established by Atatürk, and in more than one way it represented his political legacy. By rejecting nationalism as defined by Atatürk—that is, the idea of a unitary national state with Turkish cultural and historical characteristics—the Republicans disassociated themselves from, if not rejected, the 50 years of the Republic whose reforms were, incidentally, their own creation. The demands to change the regime, so well expressed in Ecevit's slogan *bu düzen değişmelidir* (this order must be changed), destroyed the implicit alliance that had existed between the dominant political elites on the issue of the structure and functioning of Turkey's democracy. These elites had quarreled before about government power but not about the regime or its brand of democracy. (See excerpts expressing Suleyman Demirel's desire to reestablish the alliance around a common understanding of democracy.)

The ideological development within the Republican party tilted the political balance to the Left and forced elements on the other side of the center, ranging from moderate conservatives to radical nationalists and Islamists, to regroup their forces and oppose the Left on behalf of democracy, freedom, national culture, and so forth. The leftists in the RPP also demanded extensive rights and freedoms ostensibly on behalf of democracy, freedom, and human rights but more in the spirit of the change favored by Marxists and Leninists. A variety of nationalist groups, diffuse and without central directing bodies, began to organize after 1967–68 under a variety of names, such as *Ülkü Ocakları* (Idealists hearths), *Milliyetçiler Derneği* (Nationalists' Association), and so forth. Eventually the leadership of the secular nationalists was undertaken by Alparslan Türkeş and his party (studied in some detail in another section). Some of the religious groups in turn, bent on reviving the historical and cultural attachments, congregated around the National Salvation Party (NSP). Thus, by 1975 the ideological debates in Turkey centered in the fully organized political parties seeking to implement their respective program and seeking government power through elections. After the TIP or Labor Party split into several groups in 1968, due to differing views on Soviet intervention in Czechoslovakia, the left lost its power. The vote gained by the radical Left was insignificant; by the 1970s six leftist parties received only about 3 percent of the total vote cast while the extreme rightist vote hovered around 15 percent. Consequently, the leftist radical parties relied on a variety of supporting groups and violent means to disseminate their ideas. Meanwhile proportional representation allowed the minor parties to take away votes from the majority parties—the RPP and the Justice Party (JP)—and thus to force the latter to combine forces with them in a variety of weak coalitions. Once in the government the minor parties sought to promote their own interests, in utter disregard for the country's long-range welfare. The subterfuge used to undermine the regime reached incredible proportions. Many of the leftist radicals, who had no interest in or even respect for Atatürk, found it suitable to falsify his views and use them for their own purposes. The "speech of Bursa" is one example. At a dinner gathering in the 1930s Atatürk reportedly called the Turkish youth the guardian of the reforms and of the state and urged them to defy the police and the courts in order to defend the Republic and its reforms. Actually there is no written evidence that such a declaration ever emanated from Atatürk. Oral statements issued in informal gatherings such as dinners and drinking parties were not recorded and, according to Atatürk's own pronouncement, had no policy value. (See Mahmut Gologlu, *Atatürk Ilkeleri ve Bursa Nutku* [Atatürk's Principles and the Speech at Bursa] [Ankara: Kalite, 1973]).

Eventually government authority weakened. Without a strong executive to enforce law and order, political instability, violence and terrorism increased. Thus, between January 1961 and January 1980, Turkey had 19 governments, while about 5,000 people were assassinated for political reasons. The military intervention in 1971 occurred, as one would expect, as the inevitable consequence of the ideological strife and slow economic development. Whereas the military intervention of 1960 aimed at settling the political quarrels between the political elites contending for the control of government power, the intervention of March 12, 1971, proposed to protect the regime against the leftist upsurge and to expedite the enforcement of social reforms, such as land and agricultural reform, that supposedly could stem the unrest. The military ruled in 1971–73 through a civilian government and the existing Parliament dominated by political parties. At the end, civilian rule was restored and thousands of jailed leftists, religious zealots, and terrorists were pardoned through an amnesty law sponsored by the RPP and NSP. However, the political balance could not be restored. On the contrary the political center, or middle of the road, declined considerably as the RPP, after defying the wishes of its perennial leader Inönü, who resigned over the issue, brought Ecevit to the chairmanship of the party. The JP on the other hand moved further to the right and joined forces whenever necessary with the rightist

NSP and NAP (Nationalist Action Party). Thus the political strife intensified further, and meanwhile inflation and terrorism went rampant. Consequently, the military had to intervene once more on September 12, 1980,
to save not merely the democratic regime but the country and to assure
the citizens the security of life and property. Politics and ideology, born
out of the desire to establish a Western-type democracy in Turkey, ended
by destroying it. (See General Kenan Evren's speech.) The military suspended all political activity, dissolved the Parliament, and began a massive
hunt for the members of all the radical leftist and rightist parties and
organizations suspected of having engaged in terroristic activities. The
military pledged to reinstitute democracy and to turn power to a civilian
government once a new constitution with proper safeguards to protect the
regime was enacted. One of the goals of the forthcoming regime is to
prevent small radical groups or parties from exerting disproportionately
widespread influence as in the past and to liberate the big parties from
domination by one leader or by small groups. A Constituent Assembly is
due to be chosen in 1981 to draft a new constitution. It is clear that
Turkey is about to enter a new phase of political and ideological development.

The introductions and the excerpts in the section dedicated to
Turkey cover the main political and ideological developments occurring
since the 1950s and present a general account of the personalities who
have guided—or rather, misguided—Turkey through these past turbulent
years. The English bibliography below cites material on the sociopolitical
life of Turkey; there is also a very rich bibliography in Turkish, occasionally
mentioned in this anthology, for those interested in further reading.

C. H. Dodd, *Politics and Government in Turkey* (Berkely and Los
Angeles: University of California Press, 1969) and *Democracy and Devel-
opment in Turkey* (Hull: Eathen Press, 1979); Frederick Frey, *The Turkish
Political Elite* (Cambridge, Mass.: M.I.T. Press, 1965); W. M. Hale, ed.,
Aspects of Modern Turkey. Kemal H. Karpat, *Turkey's Politics*, (Princeton,
Princeton University Press, 1959), *Social Change and Politics in Turkey*
(Leiden: E.J. Brill, 1973), and *The Gecekondu, Rural Migration and
Urbanization* (New York and London: Cambridge University Press, 1976);
Ergun Özbudun, *Social Change and Political Participation in Turkey*
(Princeton: Princeton University Press, 1976). The most comprehensive
study of radicalism in Turkey is by Jacob M. Landau, *Radical Politics in
Modern Turkey* (Leiden: E.J. Brill,1974). A more detailed analysis of
events in Turkey since 1970 is found in Kemal H. Karpat, "Turkish
Democrocacy at Impasse: Ideology, Party Politics and the Third Military
Intervention," *International Journal of Turkish Studies* 2, no. 1 (1981), pp.
1–43.

Notes

1. See Kemal H. Karpat, "Society, Economics, and Politics in Contemporary Turkey," *World Politics* 17 (October 1964): 50–74.
2. Note the fact that Egypt also had six principles but of a different kind. See Chapter VII.
3. Bernard Lewis, "History-writing and National Revival in Turkey," *Middle Eastern Affairs* 4 (June–July 1953): 218–27.
4. These issues have been treated at great length in Kemal H. Karpat, *Turkey's Politics* (Princeton, N.J.: Princeton University Press, 1959), and in various articles in which I have tried to point out that nationalism, although serving initially the integrative purposes of the national state, expressed also a variety of thoughts and values inherited from the past and was also a means of easing the effects of rapid social change. See, for example, "Recent Political Developments in Turkey and Their Social Background," *International Affairs* 38 (July 1962): 304–23, and "Society, Economics, and Politics in Contemporary Turkey," *World Politics* 17 (October 1964): 50–74.
5. Also referred to as Kemalism.
6. See Karpat, *Turkey's Politics*, pp. 70–73.
7. Discussed in Kemal H. Karpat, "Ideological Developments in Turkey Since the Revolution of 1960," in *Turkish Yearbook of International Relations 1966* (Ankara: The School of Political Science).
8. See Kemal H. Karpat, "The Turkish Left," *Journal of Contemporary History*, no. 2 (1966): 169–86.

XIX.   FOR A NEW DEMOCRATIC ORDER

62.   The Causes of the Revolution of May 27, 1960, and the New Constitutional Regime*

The social motives of the Turkish revolution of 1960, the emerging political struggle between political parties and the military, and, finally, the features of the new Turkish constitutional regime may be discerned in the following documents. The first extract, a military communique, was issued following the take-over and was printed in all Turkish newpapers on May 28, 1960. It

---

*The first extract appeared, in an English translation, as "Communique Issued by the Turkish Armed Forces," in *Middle Eastern Affairs* 11 (June–July 1960): 189. The second and third extracts appeared in *News from Turkey*, May 30, 1960. I have altered and condensed these English texts after comparing them with the original Turkish texts. The Turkish texts of all three extracts appear in Sabahat Erdemir, ed., *Milli Birliğe Doğru* [Toward National Unity] (Istanbul: Bakanoğlu Matbaasi, 1961), 1:293, 318–21, 317–18.

stressed national unity and claimed that the takeover was not directed against any particular group, although in reality it was aimed at the Democratic Party. The second extract, the report of the constitutional committee, which was composed of university professors, provides an insight into the intellectuals' views of the revolution. The third extract is a message from Ismet Inönü to his party in which he stressed the need for a return to civilian rule.

ANKARA COMMUNICATION OF
THE COMMITTEE OF NATIONAL UNITY [1960]

Owing to the crisis into which our democracy has fallen and to the recent, sad incidents and in order to prevent fratricide, the Turkish armed forces have taken over the administration of the country.

Our armed forces have taken this initiative for the purpose of extricating the [political] parties from the irreconcilable situation into which they have fallen and for the purpose of having just and free elections, to be held as soon as possible under the supervision and arbitration of an above-party and impartial administration, and for the purpose of handing over the administration to whichever party wins the elections.

The action is not directed against any person or class. Our administration will not resort to any aggressive act against personalities, nor will it allow others to do so.

All fellow-countrymen, irrespective of the parties to which they may belong, will be treated in accordance with the laws and all the principles of law.

For the elimination of all our hardships and for the safety of our national existence, it is imperative that we remember that all our fellow-countrymen belong to the same nation and race, above all party considerations, and that, therefore, they should treat one another with respect and understanding, without bearing any grudge.

All personalities of the [Democratic Party] cabinet are requested to take refuge with [i.e., surrender to] the Turkish armed forces. Their personal safety is guaranteed by the law.

We are addressing ourselves to our allies, friends, neighbors, and the entire world. Our aim is to remain completely loyal to the United Nations Charter and to the principles of human rights; the principles of peace at home and in the world set by the great Atatürk are our flag.

We are loyal to all our alliances and undertakings. We believe in NATO and CENTO, and we are faithful to them.

We repeat: Our ideal is peace at home, peace in the world.

Preliminary Report of the Professors' Committee
Charged with Preparing the Draft
of the New Constitution [1960]

It would be wrong to view the situation [i.e., the military takeover] in which we find ourselves today as an ordinary political coup.

It is regrettable that, for many months and even years now, the political power that should have been the guardian of civil rights and that symbolized the principles of state, law, justice, ethics, public interest, and public service has lost this quality; it has become instead a materialistic force representative of personal influence and ambition and class privilege.

Whereas the power wielded by the state should represent a social capacity that derives its vigor from the law to which it is attached, this power was transformed into the means of achieving personal influence and ambition. That is why political power ended up by losing all spiritual bonds with the true sources of state power, which reside in its army, its courts of justice and bar associations, its civil servants desirous of demonstrating attachment to their duties, and in its universities; it descended into a position of virtual enmity toward the basic and essential institutions of a true state and also toward Atatürk's reforms, which are of vital importance and value in making it possible for Turkey to retain the position that she merits in the world community of civilized states.

The pressure and oppression that the state brought to bear on citizens in general and on the political opposition, then on civil servants and the press, was extended also to the youth in our universities and even to their experienced instructors with thirty and forty years of service to their credit, then to the many other educators and their aides and students who demonstrated or indicated great promise for the future. This was done to such an extent, in fact, that the state let loose against the universities a mob of persons in authority and their underlings on the police force [or unknown persons dressed up to impersonate the police], each so blinded by the desire to further his own interests as to forget all about professional integrity and its sacred prerequisites; it caused these persons to use firearms and kill or cripple innocent students in surroundings that no rule of law or regime with the slightest attachment to such concepts would have dared to defile. . . .

No clique that caused acts so totally devoid of any connection with the true concepts of right, law, and state could continue to be looked upon as a social institution; this group, in the guise of a government, had lost every semblance of a social or national institution. This particular deed stripped every semblance of a social or national institution from the government and showed it up for what it had become, namely, a means and a tool for the realization of personal power and ambitions.

The situation was the same from the viewpoint of legitimacy. The legitimacy of a government is not derived solely from the manner of [its] acquisition of power, but also from the manner in which it respects, while in office, the constitution that brought it to that elevated position; by the manner in which it cooperates with public opinion and the army, with the legislature and the judiciary and with institutions of learning; and by its ability to continue to exist as a rule of law.

Instead, the government and political power kept formulating new laws totally contrary to the constitution, and then proceeded to utilize these laws to violate the constitution. It also engaged in activities without the benefit of any law.

Then, again, it behooves the government to be a factor of peace and tranquility, but this one forfeited any claim to legitimacy by the manner in which it set political and state institutions and their staffs at each other's throats, by the manner in which it vilified each of them at home and abroad and transformed each into a factor of anarchy.

The political power also caused the Grand National Assembly (whose function is to represent the nation) to lose its attributes as a legislative organ; by transforming the Assembly into a partisan group serving personal and group interests, it brought it to a state of actual and effective disintegration.

These are the reasons why we are faced today with the necessity to reorganize and re-establish our state and social institutions, political power, and a legitimate government.

We look upon the action of the Committee of National Unity [i.e., the military government] in arranging for the administration to be taken over by state forces and institutions as a measure dictated by the imperative need to re-establish a legitimate rule so as to redress a situation in which social institutions had been rendered virtually inoperative, in which the people were led to anarchy by being set at each other's throats, and in which there was being exerted a conscious effort to destroy all the ethical and moral foundations required to support such institutions.

Two initial measures are required to remedy such a situation:

(1) to set up a functioning and provisional government to provide at the outset the type of democratic adminstration desired by the nation, to safeguard human rights and liberties, and to look after public interests;

(2) to draw up a new constitution, since the present constitution has been violated and rendered inoperative, to ensure the establishment of a state based on the rule of law, to reorganize state bodies, and to provide for all social institutions firm support based on the principles of democratic rights and justice.

Furthermore, there is the need to formulate a new electoral law calculated to ensure the manifestation of the people's true will to prevent oppression by a political majority, and thereby to forestall the degeneration of political power.

Once these preparatory measures are completed, in a short time elections will be held, institutions will be created, and a state truly based on the rule of law will have been re-created. . . .   It is essential that the proposed constitution should contain every necessary provision to realize the true ideology of a state based on the rule of law. It must safeguard human honor and dignity, and personal rights and freedoms no less than all social rights. It must be in the nature of a factor of equilibrium for the establishment and preservation of social institutions; it must make provision for institutions to ensure that an incumbent parliamentary majority shall not be able to paralyze political activity, that is, the mainstay of democracy by exceeding its legitimate rights in order to crush and oppress a parliamentary minority that may develop and become tomorrow's administration in power.

Not only are the members of this commission in complete agreement on these principles, but they are in complete accord also with the chairman of the Committee of National Unity and the esteemed commander [Cemal Gürsel] of Turkey's armed forces.

THE MESSAGE SENT BY THE CHAIRMAN OF THE PEOPLE'S REPUBLICAN PARTY ISMET INÖNÜ TO THE PEOPLE'S REPUBLICAN BRANCHES [1960]

The glorious Turkish Army has taken the destiny of the nation into its hands and put an end to the manifestly anticonstitutional regime of oppression that was leading the country to material and spiritual collapse.

In an address to our beloved nation, General Cemal Gürsel, chairman of the Committee of National Unity and commander-in-chief of Turkey's armed forces, declared that the Committee of National Unity was determined to establish a decent, fair, honest, and democratic rule and quickly turn over the administration of the state to the national will.

In the interim, it is of paramount importance that you should preserve peace and tranquillity among citizens. The PRP [People's Republican Party] organizations must be seriously on guard against sentiments of revenge and the venting of personal grudges that tend to become contagious at such critical moments; they must also endeavor to protect citizens from such sentiments and tendencies.

The firm decision of the Committee of National Unity to establish a rule of fair and honest democracy constitutes the best guarantee of present and future confidence and tranquillity in our country. It behooves our citizens to await the fair, free, and honest elections with calmness, and with full confidence in the unsullied traditions of the Turkish Army.

I salute you one and all with affection and esteem, and extend all best wishes for success in the realm of service to the nation.

63.   The Meaning of May 27*

Kemal Uygur

Kemal Uygur was a major or kurmay, *a staff officer representing the elite of the military who is charged with planning and assumes the highest responsibilities in the Turkish armed forces. He was one of many partici-pants in an annual essay competition initiated by the newspaper* Cum-huriyet *[Republic] in honor of its founder, Yunus Nadi. The article expressed simply but emotionally the general view of the causes of the revolution and the army's role in it. The competition title for 1960 was 27* Mayısın manasını anlatın *[Explain the Meaning of May 27].*

Revolutions are born of needs. But they are legitimate only if they manifest the needs of an entire nation, not the needs only of an individual or specific group. A revolution that is not supported by the masses without a doubt assumes the character of an opportunist movement undertaken for the promotion of selfish interests. In such a situation, there is no unity of thought in the society. Consequently, revolution occurring in such condi-tions manifests itself as a bloody clash between groups mutually opposed in interest and conviction. The result is that such a country is dragged into a dark chasm, from which it is able to extricate itself only with difficulty. The best example of this is the series of *coups d'état* that have recently occurred in Syria.

After this simple introduction, let me focus on the following point:

The needs that the Turkish nation accumulated over the past ten years were manifested in the form of the "great revolution and national reform movement of May 27, 1960." This movement drew all its strength from the entire nation. As a result it was bloodless and achieved success within a few hours, thus stirring the admiration of the world and earning the title "Model Revolution."

The Atatürk reforms were suppressed in favor of the special interests of the reactionary regime of recent years, and the natural rights of the nation were violated. The national reform movement was a reaction against this. The result of the restoration of these violated values in the

---

*Extract from Kemal Uygur, "27 Mayis" ["May 27"], *Cumhuriyet* [Republic], Istanbul, November 18, 1969, essay no. 19.

name of the nation may be stated briefly: It may be described as the *beginning* of the process of resuscitating in every field a *Turkey* that had been moving backward, of bringing it to a point from which it may move to achieve the level of modern nations.

Now, what are the causes and factors that drove the nation to such a revolution? Let us list them in order.

Economic causes. The inflationary policy that they followed was like a nightmare for the country and left it no room to breathe. Investments were sacrificed to an unjust, unplanned, and partisan policy and resulted in an extremely burdensome public debt. The treasury was completely drained. In order to meet its internal needs, the government ceaselessly printed paper money. This printing operation, undertaken without any basis in value, caused a decline in the value of the currency, both internally and externally. Commerce degenerated. There was no hesitation is using influential persons, not only to secure personal interests, but even to undertake various illegal actions.

Governmental and political causes. Within the public service, corruption, bribery, and intrigue were spreading. Members of the ruling party had assumed complete dominance of the machinery of the state. Foreign policy was unproductive and humiliating. As a result, the external prestige of the state had fallen sharply. Moreover, there was no such thing as stability in policy. Only a face-saving policy was attempted, and the maintenance of such a system was accepted as the only solution. Is not the Cyprus policy the best example of this? Its form changed from annexation to partition and finally to independence, whereby the Greeks gained the main influence.

Social causes. The ties of mutual love, tenderness, and affection among citizens were shattered as a result of degenerate partisanship. In place of sincerity, there was a feeling of doubt and suspicion. The people were divided into two opposing groups that regarded one another as enemies. Prosperity and happiness gave way to uneasiness.

Poverty was resurrected and was not slow to undermine the morals of the innocent children of the country. Particularly deplorable was the fact that state officials operated houses of prostitution as private sources of income.[1]

Exploitation of religion. Religion became a fearsome weapon in the hands of men of state. Fanaticism was fanned. As a result, the bigots who had been lying in wait stepped fearlessly onto the scene. Nor was it long before the bigots' tongues, like the tongue of the snake, poured poison into pure, clean spirits.

Violation of right and freedom. There was no room for freedom of thought and expression in the country. The press had been silenced. There was an attempt to cover improprieties by means of press censorship. Rights and the rule of law were denied to those who belonged to any party other than that in power.

Abandonment of knowledge and learning. In everything he did, Atatürk always relied on the teachings of science, saying "the truest guide in life is science." And this is also one of the most important elements influencing others. But the fallen regime was so blind that it could not see this well-lighted way. With every step, it sank deeper into a pit. Such important national causes as education were being abandoned as a result.

Oppression and violence. All the measures and arrangements that were made served no purpose other than to drag the country ever closer to the precipice. Leadership sold out in the face of increasing blunders and abuses. These opportunist manipulators had lost confidence in the bureaucracy, the judiciary, and the military, because they themselves had undermined the procedures for maintaining confidence in these fundamental elements of the state machinery. But what had happened was irrevocable. In order to make the regime permanent, they even took the path of oppression and violence. They wanted to employ murder against those who resisted their designs. For this purpose, they were actively trying to use the security organization and a number of innocent and deceived people whom they were actively trying to arm.

Arbitrary government. The country was lost in confusion because of legal disorder and a haphazard form of administration. Laws and regulations followed no standard but were adapted to suit personal circumstances. There was no room for planning in [government] action. The basic controlling factor in all types of activity was the eagerness to secure votes.

Terrible ambitions. But even all this was not enough for them. The aroused personal interests and ambitions, which had now assumed a fearful form, with everything that had come to pass, had become insatiable. They said to themselves: "Let us arrange matters in such a way that the people's eyes will not see, their ears will not hear, their minds will cease funtioning, and we can assume complete supremacy in all our actions. Thus, we can easily perpetrate our crimes, fill our personal coffers, control the havens of debauchery, and ultimately secure the permanent endurance of our regime." And what else could one expect from Celal Bey [Bayar], the Balkan guerrila [*komitacl*] and unlucky clerk of the Young

Turks, or of Adnan Bey [Menderes], who administered the government as though it were a farm, since he had no other experience.

Suppression of the constitutions. The fearful effort was soon transformed from intention into action. Those who established the "Investigation Commission" did not hear the cries of their own consciences, weak as they were. Personal greed had blinded their eyes, darkened their hearts, and deadened their minds to feelings of virtue and conscience. The law that established the Investigation Commission [with absolute powers to investigate the opposition] and determined its activities was passed by the Grand National Assembly, which manifests the national will. But the commission was given absolute powers superior to those of the Assembly. This law was the death warrant of the fallen regime. It violated the constitution and transformed the parliament into a party caucus, thus depriving it of its legitimacy. Social conscience and national will were completely crushed. The rights and freedoms of the citizen could no longer be discussed. The Investigation Commission had assumed a position superior to the national will and had the power to perpetrate all sorts of evils. Let us pause here and consider for a moment.

The eternal leader Kemal Atatürk says:

> To make matters in the country even more deplorable and critical, those in power are not above negligence, corruption, and even treason. They are even capable of tying their personal interests to the political goals of the invaders. The nation might suffer ruin and exhaustion in its utter poverty.
>
> Oh, son of the Turkish future! Even under these circumstances it is your duty to preserve the independence of the Turkish Republic.[2]

Yes, it was past time to save Turkish independence and the republic from this oppressive enemy. The spirit of the Father [Atatürk] again addressed the youth and reminded them of their duty. The enlightened youth [i.e., the student demonstrations] on April 28 [1960] placed the first black seal on the accursed government. Its mouth frothing with hatred and rage, fearing for its very existence, the government struck out and shot down the country's youths with the bullets of the police. These noble martyrs painted crescents [i.e., the national emblem] on the golden pages of history with their blood. The full terror of the tragedy that reigned fell over the country like a black cloud. The presses had been brought to a stop. Censorship stretched like a black veil over the truth.

Love of duty and patriotism. The time had finally come to break the evil and oppressive hold of this ten-year-old government, which had become tyrannical and illegitimate. Where was the power that would break this hold? It was [to be found in] an organization that was nothing but the personification of the youth: the army.

Was it not the most natural and legitimate duty of the army? Did not the law order it so? Of course it did. All the citizens, with tearful eyes, said to the army, "Do your duty."

It was May 27. The army undertook its duty and, within a few hours, without bloodshed, completed the job and broke the back and arm of the tyrant. The sun, when it rose that day, shone more brightly. With golden hair and a sweet smile, it spread across the fatherland, spreading the good news of the birth of right, justice, and freedom.

Long live the dear and sacred Turkish fatherland! Long live the Turkish nation, to eternity, with its army, its rights, justice, and freedom. . . .

Notes

1. This was not proven.
2. The call to youth charging them with the defense of the regime was the concluding paragraph of Atatürk's six-day speech. See *A Speech Delivered by Ghazi Mustapha Kemal, President of the Turkish Republic, October, 1927*, trans. Hans Kohn (Leipzig: K. F. Koehler, 1929), pp. 723–24. An earlier version was delivered by Atatürk at the war memorial of Dumlupinar, near the Dardanelles, on August 30, 1924.

64.   Democracy and Revolution in Turkey*

Ismet Inönü

Ismet Inönü (1884–1973) has been belittled by his enemies and described as a great statesman by his supporters. He commanded the armies that defeated the invading Greek forces in 1921, became prime minister in 1923, and was Atatürk's chief collaborator. After Atatürk's death in 1938, Inönü became president of Turkey and assumed dictatorial powers as head of state and permanent chairman of the only political group, the People's Republi-

*Extract from Ismet Inönü, *Ulus* [Nation], Ankara, September 9, 1960. The speech also appeared in *Cumhuriyet* [Republic], Istanbul, on September 9, 1960, and it is reproduced in S. Toktamış, ed., *Ihtilalden Sonra Ismet Inönü* [Ismet Inönü after the Revolution] (Istanbul, 1962), pp. 22–27.

can Party. In 1945, at the peak of his power and prestige, Inönü decided that the time was ripe to initiate Turkey's transition to a democratic, multiparty system. He silenced opposition in his own party and gradually created the legal and political conditions necessary for a multiparty system. See Kemal H. Karpat, Turkey's Politics (Princeton, N.J.: Princeton University Press, 1959).

Inönü's party lost power to the Democratic Party in the first truly democratic national elections, held in 1950. For the following ten years, he was in the opposition and fought staunchly to preserve democracy. In 1959–60, the ruling Democratic Party tried to silence all opposition, but its efforts met violent resistance from the press, the intellectuals, and, especially, the Republican Party. The Democrats finally attempted to use the army against Inönü's party. At this point, the army intervened (May 27, 1960), ousted the Democrats, and installed inself in power.

Three months after the revolution, a group among the junta, backed by some intellectuals and newspapers, began a campaign against political parties and democracy. They described the party system as the cause of regression and internal dissension and advocated a strong government headed by an elite. The attacks on democracy brought forth a strong statement from Inönü, who had retired temporarily from public life after the coup. Inönü asserted that the ultimate purpose of Turkish reforms was to create and consolidate democracy based on a multiparty system. On balance, he felt, the free political system had resulted in more good than evil since its inception in 1945. He rejected the view that military intervention was necessary to resolve the struggle among the parties, and he emphatically reminded the army that it should relinquish power to a civilian government elected by the people. This speech, clearly defining Turkey's major political issues, had profound signifiance in mobilizing the forces of democracy and paving the way for the return to a multiparty system.

Inönü's speech is also essential for an understanding of the philosophy of and the approach to democracy in Turkey. The speech, slightly shortened in translation, was addressed to Turkish youth on the fortieth anniversary of Izmir's liberation from the Greek occupation. Inönü, who had supported his party's switch to the left eventually came to oppose his secretary general but without success. He retired from the chairmanship in 1972, and died in 1973. (See also excerpt 78 in Chapter XXIII.)

During Atatürk's time (1920–38) there were serious attempts to establish a multi-party system. The Progressive Republican Party was established on its own and included the members of the Second Group [of the First National Assembly, 1920–22]. This party did not last because of reactionary uprisings in the East [i.e., the Kurdish revolt] and the newness of the reforms [republic, secularism]. The establishment of the Free Party [by Fethi Okyar] in 1930 was due to Atatürk's initiative and desire. The leaders of this party decided to end their activity, since the party could not continue to work during a period in which the reforms were barely striking roots. Thus, the two parties could not survive. Their closure, regardless of the importance of the causes and motives that necessitated it, was a regrettable experience, and [can be described] as a reason for the delay in our democratic evolution. The multi-party life began afterward in 1945.

I [Inönü] had a position [president] during that period. I must stress the fact that my role was markedly different from Atatürk's. I opened the way to democracy but did not choose the people [who engaged in politics]. I gave everybody an equal chance. The multi-party experiment was met with hesitation not only by those accustomed to rule under a one-party system but also by honest patriots who feared, on the basis of past experience, that the reactionary forces would prevent the country's progress. I, the spokesman for those supporting the new experiment, was encouraged to initiate the democratic experiment, which was the purpose of [Atatürk's] reforms, by the following consideration: the belief that our nation had achieved an inner [structural] strength based on the [lessons] drawn from the democratic experiments in the past twenty-five years.

In my estimation, the time was ripe for trusting the safeguarding of the republican regime and the reforms to the nation through a free political life. This new [democratic] way of life would strengthen the Turkish nation internally and gain it the respect of the outside world for being a civilized [*medeni*] society.° New generations were brought up in twenty-five years. The majority of the nation consisted of men of twenty-five years of age who could not give up the use of the Latin alphabet. This generation was going to defend the reforms for the sake of its own life and its own interests. The forward-looking group among women, who formed half of the nation, was used to the new way of life to such a degree as to find it impossible to bear the return to the old life. The other reforms also had been tried through long experience in the past years. In short, a mass of people, powerful enough to resist the reactionary forces, had come into being. If the methods of civilization [i.e., democracy] could resist the old attitudes long enough, they were bound to create useful influences in the national structure. Finally, in comparison with the time of the first attempt to introduce a regime of freedom and democracy, we were [in 1945], as a nation, in a more consolidated and mature state. Difficulties were bound to arise any time we entered the democratic regime. The importance attached to difficulties is bound to be forgotten soon after the

---

°Inönü equates civilization and democracy.

initial experiments. The national life, thereafter similar to the life of advanced nations, would assume a natural course.

We entered the experiment of democracy when we [Inönü] had extensive power and wide reputation. Now, fifteen years afterward, we can consider our gains, that is, the foresight in our decision [to adopt democracy], as well as our losses, or the evil resulting therefrom, and balance one against the other. We have registered more gains than losses during the last fifteen years. True, certain reactionary forces evolved more rapidly than our estimations in 1945. . . . The reactionary currents left no impact on the national structure. The youth, the idealists, the political parties, and the politicians upholding the republic and the reforms were supported by the people as a whole. This protection turned into victory. The fear, thanks to the nation's backing, did not materialize that the reactionary forces . . . , through evil-minded politicians, would become masters of the country, would destroy the bases of the Turkish Republic, and return to the Middle Ages. . . .

[*After condemning the Democratic Party rule in 1950–60, Inönü continues:*]

I am not at all apprehensive of the final result. It means that certain forces in human nature will resist [all efforts] until the regime of freedom and civilization is assimilated by the nation. It is a law of nature that such a regime will be established at a high price and through sacrifices. If one views past events with such an attitude, then these events must be considered as constituting the natural phases of an evolution. The future, therefore, must be viewed with the enthusiasm felt for an ideal cause, which shall be victorious. . . . The nation's firm intervention [i.e., the military revolution] occurred as the reform of May 27. It ended the unfortunate, lost period [1950–60] and opened a new, progressive, and enlightened era.

Three months after the revolution, we seem not to recall the social and political life that prevailed in the period before it. . . . It is a very wrong and dangerous diagnosis to view the revolution of May 27 as a military intervention caused by the struggle among political parties and as aiming at ending such struggle. Such a diagnosis views as equals the minority [i.e., the Democrats] who wanted to enslave the nation by force . . . and the majority [i.e., the opposition] who fought . . . to safeguard the nation's rights. The old government was a minority that had lost its legitimacy. It was forced out not by one or two political parties, but by a front of national resistance and opposition composed of the nation's majority. This struggle forced the ruling [Democrats] to resort to the last means, that is, to use this great, honest, and enlightened army, established to defend this country, as an oppressive tool against the people. The army . . . refused to become a tool for oppressing the people. . . .

It is, therefore, wrong to look upon the revolution of May 27 as an intervention aimed at ending the inter-party struggle, instead of seeing it as an action directed against men who tried to install oppression despite the nation's resistance. A correct diagnosis is the first step in the cure of an illness or the repair of a wrong. Actions based on wrong diagnosis are either effectless or harmful to the main goal. This point must be properly instilled into the nation's conscience. What is the future? One wrong aspect of the diagnosis is the belief that the People's Republican Party is anxious and impatient to assume power as soon as possible, and the main role is attributed to my own power ambition. I have achieved in the past all the political positions that a man may aspire to in his lifetime. The impact of such positions on me are less important than the events of daily life. The only important problem for all of us is to convince the citizen that the main safe way for the country is to see that the work undertaken by the revolutionary regime is finished in success and honor. The revolutionary period will end in October, 1961, when responsibilities are to be transferred to the Grand National Assembly. Who will come to power? This has no importance for me. There is going to be a free, honest election, and the nation will establish its own rule. The PRP certainly will strive to perform its duties . . . in opposition or in power, it will fulfill its duties with dignity and enthusiasm. The forthcoming government may for formed by one of the existing parties or by those to be established anew. I am not concerned or apprehensive about these alternatives. Regardless of who assumes power, a progressive era will begin for the nation. The power [i.e., government] thus established will continue to rule until the nation decides the opposite. . . . I am viewing the future with peace and faith in bright, progressive achievements.

65.   The Military Takeover in 1980 and the Third Phase

Address by General Kenan Evren

The unrest in Turkey caused by the small civil war between the rightists and leftists and aggravated by a mounting inflation of over 100 percent annually had reached an extreme level. Governments proved unable or unwilling to curb the violence. For months the population had waited and had hoped for the military, the only organization with its cadres intact and not beset by political strife, to take over and establish order. The military finally and very reluctantly obliged on September 12, 1980, but assured the population that they would return power to a civilian government as soon as conditions would permit it. A Constitutional Assembly is to be selected in 1981 to draft a new Constitution. The proclamation was read by General Kenan Evren (b. 1918 in Alashehir, he was the commander of the Land Forces), who became head of state and of the National Security Council, the governing body. It provides a good description of Turkey's internal situation that necessitated the takeover. The statement below was released by the Turkish Embassy in Washington, D.C. and is being published with only insignificant editorial changes.

On the occasion of the victory day on August 30, I had the opportunity to address you over the radio and television and in the limited time made available, I tried to explain very briefly the political and economic situation of our country, the anarchic and separatist activities that exist and the measures needed to be taken. As you will also recall, in the course of the last two years in all my declarations and in my speeches which I made over the radio and television on various occasions I had articulated these issues of vital importance. . . .

As you also know and observe, anarchy, terrorism and separatism have been taking the lives of more than 20 of our compatriots every day. The Turkish citizens who share the same religion and identical national values, for reasons of political opportunism have been divided into various camps through the creation of artificial divisions and have been practically turned into enemies who lost all their senses to the extent to shed each other's blood unscrupulously.

Ten years ago, it would not have been possible even to imagine that our Republic founded on the principles of Atatürk would find itself in this present situation.

In spite of the promises of the various governments which came to power until now to take with top priority the measures necessary for the establishment of internal security against the infiltration and subversion activities employed by special warfare which is spreading every year at an increasing scale in the world for which there are numerous examples in world history, the initiatives taken by them promising to produce results were lost in the turmoil of clashing political interests and simple partisan considerations, whims, illusions, unrealistic exigencies and of overt and covert designs running counter to the fundamentals of the Turkish State. While the nature of the goals and the methods of the enemy and the level which the anarchy, terrorism and separatism reached necessitated the taking of special legal measures, administrative rearrangements, the improvement of social conditions, the reorganization of national education and labor conditions, the deputies and senators who carry the mandate of the nation have for months, without any sense of responsibility remained observers to this situation being motivated solely by partisan interests and by party discipline. Every measure taken by the Administration with the hope of success was undermined by the opposition parties even though they were in the interest of the country.

Even at those times when national unity and solidarity were utterly needed, political divisions and polarizations were almost encouraged for the sake of political interest and gaining political power; oil was poured onto the fire instead of a joint effort to put it out.

Certain constitutional bodies interpreted and applied the concept of the rule of law, which they never ceased to pretend to cherish, only in the defence of individual interests, at times at the risk of the disintegration of the state, totally disregarding the defence of the interest of the state and the nation, the principle in the constitution regarding the separation of powers which carries with it the concept of collective responsibility was in practice turned into a conflict of powers.

It is indeed sad that while divisive and subversive activities originating from within and without were being deployed with all intensity, exploiting our religion and any other subject of national interest, certain people, as if unaware of the fact that they themselves would perish under the rubble of the collapsing state, defended an autonomy completely divorced from realities, and some narrow-minded so-called scientific concepts which only they themselves believed in and some abstract legal notions in total disregard of the conditions prevailing in the country.

The cries of those, who being aware of this bitter truth, looked for a solution and called for national unity have fallen on deaf ears. Here I would like to acknowledge with gratitude the fact that some Turkish press have issued from time to time warnings in this respect.

The political parties, instead of taking the measures so eagerly expected by the nation in this critical period have opted to try to enhance their chances for elections by continuously increasing internal tension, by provoking subversive and divisive centers and by competing with each other in issuing declarations and engaging in activities which were bound to further encourage such centers.

The political parties coming to power, by filling all the government departments with their partisans have forced public servants and citizens to fall into different camps. With these policies they paved the way for the emergence of some centers supporting anarchy and separatism. Furthemore, they have not abandoned their partisan policies and actions which led the public servants, police and teachers to organize themselves into hostile camps. Consequently, the people who were impartial were forced to knock at the party doors in order to obtain what they should normally get from the state. Thus, the authority of the state doomed to vanish and instead of the state safeguarding the rights and liberties of the citizens and providing impartially services for them the responsibility of the state eroded gradually, hence creating a vacuum of authority.

Some misguided individuals with perverted ideologies and deep fanaticism have openly displayed disrespect for our national anthem which represents the independence and unity of the Turkish Nation, by remaining seated or chanting the International instead, so as to demonstrate their protest. What is more, the responsibles [parties] tried to cover these actions and defended them by finding some pretexts.

As you may recall, the Turkish Armed Forces which have followed these extremely regrettable events for a long time have fulfilled their responsibilities vis-à-vis the great Turkish Nation by warning through the President of the Republic all the constitutional bodies which have failed to exercise the authority conferred upon them by the Turkish Nation . . . .

In spite of the several warnings made by the Turkish Armed Forces within the last eight months, no satisfactory response in respect of any of these measures has been received or no constructive effort has been witnessed from the legislative and executive organs or from other constitutional bodies. The National Assembly which enacted some legislation, devoid of substance, following our letter of warning, of 22nd of March, concerning the election of the President of the Republic which has been led into an impasse because of partisan considerations, wasted so much time which was so precious for solving the crisis that we were in. In no country the high office of the President and its election have been taken so lightly and so much time have been spent in vain.

Our constitutional bodies which were supposed to bring solutions to the problems of law and order as well as economic problems and enact legislation, have remained indifferent vis-à-vis the nightmare looming over the country. In spite of the fact that our constitutions have stipulated clearly that no Turkish citizen could be discriminated against on account of his religious conviction, our political parties, running after even a single vote and seeing some advantages in provoking sectarian divisions which were forgotten in the Atatürk era of our Republic, caused our citizens to kill each other for the sake of their political interest in the provinces of Erzincan, Sivas, Kahraman Maraş, Tunceli and Çorum.

In the course of the last two years, terrorism has caused 5.241 losses of life, 14.152 wounded or disabled, whereas, during the War of Independence, in the Battle of Sakarya, the total casualties were 5.713 deaths and 18.480 wounded. Even this simple comparison reveals clearly that a hidden war is being waged in Turkey in utter disregard of any human consideration.

It is because of these and other similar reasons which are well-known by all of us that the Turkish Armed Forces have been obliged to take over the rule of the country in order to protect the unity of the nation and the country, to safeguard the fundamental rights of the people, to free the people from fear by ensuring the safety of life and property, to secure the prosperity and happiness of the people, to reinstitute and maintain in an impartial manner the rule of law, in other words, the authority of the state. As of today, until a new government and a legislative body are created, legislative and executive powers will be exercised for a temporary period by the National Security Council under my Presidency and composed of the commanders of the land, air and naval forces and the commander General of the Gendarmerie.

We believe in the necessity of realizing in the shortest possible period a rapid economic and social development oriented towards, to quote Atatürk, elevating our national culture to the level of contemporary civilization and providing our fatherland with the most advanced means and resources of the world. For the realization of this objective, we have no doubt that our great nation will have faith in the administration of the Turkish Armed Forces which stem from the nation herself and which, marching only in the direction of the principles laid by Atatürk, have not taken sides in the political polarization in our country. In order to get out of this crisis, we expect the Turkish Nation to enter an era of solidarity and a new life style, the characteristics of which would be self-discipline and self-sacrifice, which we believe is aspired by the nation. We also expect an intensification of efforts to demonstrate the strength of our nation. And for this, we believe in the Turkish Nation . . . .

The Republic of Turkey, remaining faithful to all its alliances and treaties including NATO, is determined to further develop its economic, social and cultural relations with all the countries, in particular with her neighbors, under equal conditions and on the basis of mutual respect to sovereignty and noninterference in internal affairs.

We will continue to pursue a foreign policy aiming at the solution of international disputes by peaceful means.

The Turkish Armed Forces which have repeatedly proven their loyalty to parliamentary democracy by various actions will constitute in the shortest possible time, a council of ministers and will hand over the executive power to it. And after having prepared a constitution, an electoral law and a law for political parties which will have all the safeguards against the degeneration and the blocking of the parliamentary system as has been the case, and would be worthy of the Turkish Nation and also, after having made the necessary arrangements, will transfer the ruling of the country to an administration which will have full respect for human rights and freedoms, and will recognize priority to national solidarity and will realize social justice and will attach prime importance to the peace, security and prosperity of the individual and the society. It will be based upon a free democracy, secularism and social justice. Until such time that these preparations are completed all the political activities at all levels in our country are suspended. Political parties whose activities are hereby suspended, will be allowed to resume their functions prior to the elections, the date of which will be announced according to the new constitution and the new electoral and political party laws . . . .

[After speaking of the necessity of taking certain administrative and economic measures, the General continued.]

I repeat once again that the Armed Forces had to take over the administration of the country in order to secure for the Turkish Nation the prosperity and happiness which she rightfully deserves, to give a new strength and impetus to Atatürk principles that are being eroded, to ensure the unity of the motherland and the nation, to restore democracy which failed to control itself on sounder foundations and to reinstate the vanishing authority of the state. As the privates, non-commissioned officers, officers and commanders, we all are ready to sacrifice everything, including our lives for the sake of the prosperity and happiness of our motherland and our nation. Ill-willed persons and organizations whose numbers have been greatly increasing may fabricate lies in order to contradict this and may resort to disruptive propaganda. Do not believe such persons or organizations. All our actions will take place before the eyes of the public . . . .

I expect the patriotic and noble Turkish Nation to respect each other's rights, to bury their differences in a spirit of affection and understanding and to assist the new administration with the awareness that we are all equal citizens on this sacred land.

I wish you all a very happy and bright future.

General Kenan Evren
Chief of General Staff and President
of the National Security Council

66. For a Great Turkey: Economic Development and Democracy

Suleyman Demirel

Suleyman Demirel, born in 1924 in the village of Islamköy and raised in difficult circumstances, typifies the generation that arose in the countryside in the 1950s and eventually came to place its stamp on Turkey's political destiny. Practical minded and fully aware of the economic and technological forces of this century, Demirel remained attached also to the traditional Turkish culture and its values. In speech and manner he is not different from the usual urbanized intelligentsia, although he managed to preserve the informality and openness—as well as shrewdness—of the country folk. After graduating from the School of Engineering in Istanbul, he directed in a creative manner the Water Works Directorate. He entered politics in 1961 and in 1964 was elected chairman of the Justice Party, the successor to the Democratic Party. Demirel has espoused liberal views on economics and a traditionalist view on culture and religion. He was ousted from power twice by military interventions in 1971 and 1980, although these coups were not directed specifically against him or his party. As chairman of the Justice Party, and as prime minister for most of the time since 1965, Demirel played a major role in reshaping Turkey's economic and social life through his practical policies. A believer in parliamentary democracy, and in economic development achieved more through private enterprise than through state intervention or socialism, he became in the eyes of his implacable enemies—that is, the Republican Party and the extreme Left—the symbol of capitalism and friendship with the West. Demirel's views are probably closer to a moderate form of social democracy than genuine capitalism. His major shortcoming is a product of his main quality. Concerned with practical matters and the day-to-day administration of the government and his party, he has failed to develop the necessary political finesse to handle the complex problems created by rapid socioeconomic change and by the intelligentsia's continuous struggle for recognition and power. His goodwill and tolerance towards his ideological enemies has been met with derision, condescension, and vicious attacks which have forced him to seek support among the radical rightist parties, to the detriment of the middle-of-the-road ideology of his own party. Unfortunately, neither Demirel nor his party have been studied objectively by either Turkish or Western scholars, chiefly because of their relatively liberal economic stand in favor of religious freedom, respect for traditional culture, and the acceptance of a dose of nationalist thought. A serious, objective, and detached study of the ideology of the Justice Party and of Demirel should contribute greatly to the understanding of the true dimensions of Turkish politics and thought.

Demirel's views have been published in a variety of publications: See Muhtelif Konuşmalar [Various Talks] (Ankara: *Justice Party General Center, 1969; and Uğur Gümüştekin, ed.,* Demirel'in Büyük Hedefi, Yeni Bir Sosyal Mukaveleye Doğru *[Demirel's Great Goal: Towards a New Social Contract] (Istanbul: Birlik, 1974). The excerpts below are taken from* Süleyman Demirel's Büyük Türkiye *[Great Turkey] (Istanbul: Dergah, 1977), pp. 11–12, 15–30 passim.*

On Development

Today Turkey ranks as the 25th country in the world [in living standards]. Ten years hence we shall be the tenth. In the year 2000 the situation will be much better because Turkey will reach the standard of today's federal Germany.... We do not like these figures, that is, the figures related to economy. Our entire energy is devoted to increasing these figures through plans and [state] budgets and to placing Turkey ahead of others. Turkish development is an active one. It is a successful development with a clear future .... Today the national income of Turkey is 40 billion dollars; in the year 2000 it will be 400 billion, and the income per capita will rise from the current 900 to 5,000 dollars.

On Democracy

Personal views and emotional attitudes rather than impersonal principles and objectives are dominating the political life of our country. This derives from the fact that certain concepts are not clear. We believe, therefore, that the fate of our democracy today and in the future demands that we arrive at a common understanding concerning some fundamental concepts and consider the country's problems in accordance with the requirements of the regime and the general interest of the country rather than the personality [conflicts] and personal views .... We are trying to develop a government structure which will not create a constitutional crisis. We are striving to make election by the people a powerful principle that cannot be replaced by anything else. [We need] the balance necessary to restore tranquility and order and to do away with fear, regardless of the peoples' political ideas and beliefs. Nobody, including the opposition, should be apprehensive [when another] party acquires [government] power. And, naturally, when the opposition assumes the power the old government should not fear it either. Consequently, the political parties which constitute the essential elements of our regime must strive to search for at least a few ideas to build a common ground between them and to maintain a dialogue between the government and the opposition . . . . The real factor which enables democracy to survive is the state of law that grants rights and obligations, and—probably more—it is a mode of thinking and philosophy based on mutual tolerance and civilized acceptance. Societies without this tolerance and acceptance to create a balance are bound to end in formal democracy consisting of sterile legal forms. As citizens with different ideas we are obliged to tolerate each other . . . .

[After stating that political freedoms and obligations cannot be separated from social and economic rights and that Turkey's problems should be solved in accordance with their specific nature by individual and state action or the combination of both, Demirel dealt with freedoms.]

We must learn how to live with freedoms; we must not be afraid of their implementation and, to a lesser extent, of their abuse. The essence of freedom lies in its usage, while the abuse is punishable . . . . [But] we cannot abolish freedom in order to fight abuses of freedom, except when the abuses of freedom threaten the security of the state and the regime . . . . The legal, political, economic, and social regime of the country have been defined in the Constitution. Those people who have accepted the regime of the country as defined by the Constitution as secular, democratic, social minded, and as a state of law and the laws issued accordingly . . . have no reason to demand the change of the existing order [as does Bülent Ecevit].

Turkey cannot adopt a closed economy. Consequently, she should be able to compete, that is, to adapt herself to the requirements of foreign markets. The industrialization of Turkey should not be pushed in such a direction as to ignore comparison [with other economies]. Turkey must enlarge her internal markets and protect her producers and consumers according to the rules of a market economy . . . . Our belief in free enterprise is at the foundation of our development philosophy. Free enterprise is being debated by some ideologies but our idea [of free enterprise] is gaining strength every day and is being appreciated by citizens with common sense . . . . There are people who want to create a class struggle in our country. They want to abolish free enterprise and to divide the population into two classes: one a ruling group, master of everything, and the other an immense mass of citizens without the right to complain.

[*After devoting several pages to the virtues of the social welfare state,
Demirel concludes by appealing to nationalists, republicans, and con-
stituionalists to defend and perpetuate democracy for the achievement of an
ideal Turkey.*]

We say, let us create a Great Turkey; Turkey living in security,
tranquility, prosperity and order; Turkey which corresponds to the nation's wishes, brilliant, powerful and whose word is respected.... We
have defined clearly our position and believe that we shall reach our goal.

XX. ATATÜRKISM

67. Atatürkism is Secularism*

Yaşar Nabi Nayir

*Yaşar Nabi Nayir (1908–81) was born in the old Turkish town of Üsküp-
Skoplje in Macedonia (now Yugoslavia) and emigrated to Turkey when he
was quite young. Even as a youth he was identified with Atatürk's
nationalist, secularist, modernist, republican policies. He purposely avoided
involvement in practical politics, but through his writing he fought vigorously to uphold the principles of the modernist regime, and his interest in
literature was a consequence of and complementary to his political views.
For about 40 years, Nayir published the weekly review Varlık [Existence].
Through it, and through his books, he succeeded in generating a modern
way of thinking in Turkey. Several literary schools have been formed around
Varlık, some that have imitated the West and some that have been genuinely
Turkish. The thousands of books published by the Varlık publishing house
under Nayir's direction provide a splendid source for studying the develop-
ment of Turkish thought and literature.*

*After the revolution of 1960, both rightists and leftists newly in-
terpreted Atatürk's ideas, and some of them perverted his original meaning.
Consequently, Nayir assembled a collection of 35 articles on Atatürk and his
ideas by some of Turkey's best-known intellectuals. The following extract*

*Extract from Yaşar Nabi Nayir, *Aratürkçülük Nedir?* [What Is Atatürkism?] (Istanbul:
Varlık Basımevi, 1963). pp. 283–92.

summarizes some of these articles, but stresses secularism as the foundation of Atatürk's thought and presents a general picture of the modernization reforms. It should be noted that Nayir's views on secularism have remained rather dogmatic and that he regarded the society at large as still unaffected by modernization. His secularist views are shared now by only a small minority.

The new system of thought and the new path [of life] brought about by Atatürk's words and reforms constitute Atatürkism. If the great leader's words and deeds were studied as a whole, on would come to the conclusion that this system of thought was founded on secularism and on orientation toward the West. Let's consider the main reforms. The foundation stone of Atatürk's reforms was the abolition of the sultanate [1922], followed shortly by the abolition of the caliphate [1924]. There are kings in the West, and there are also internationally accepted religious offices. But the concepts and attributes of those cannot be compared in any way with the divine authority of the Ottoman rulers. The Ottoman sultans were for centuries the representatives of a rigid tradition, whereby the ruler was considered the sole master of the country and God's representative and shadow on earth.... Despite the constitution that deprived them of authority and power, the sultans could still nurture the hopes of those who had an interest in the maintenance of the old order. The annihilation of scholarship, which was the main fortress of opposition to secularism, could not be accomplished as long as the foundations [of the sultanate–caliphate] remained intact.

The weekly holiday law seems insignificant among other reforms. Actually, it had a profound meaning because ... it tested in a masterful way the resistance potential of conservatism. The weekly holiday was changed from Friday to Sunday, that is to say, to the holiday of the West. Thus, it removed one of the main obstacles to orientation toward the West and assimilation into it ....

The educational reform law that closed the old traditional school [*medrese*] was the chief blow directed at scholasticism and backwardness [traditionalism]. The secular education directed by the state was the only type permitted, and this forestalled reactionary attacks. The *medreses* had prevented all associations with the West as well as every step forward and had been the standard-bearers of opposition to modernization. The subsequent closing of religious courts [*şeriat*] proved that logically there could not be two different court systems in a country.... This was a natural consequence of the first reform and completed the total, categorical liberation of state affairs from theocratic pressure. The law concerning dress reform, besides changing the primitive oriental look of our people, ended the domination of those who used [the traditional head-dress] as a symbol to achieve authority over the ignorant people. The law closing the convents and mausoleums abolished the last nests of back-wardness and inertia. The civil code [introduced in 1926] abolished the provisions that derived from Islam and were not compatible with modern legal understanding. It was one of the most decisive steps taken toward adapting the way of life to Western rules.

The script reform broke the last ties to Islamic Eastern civilization and culture. Indeed, in order to establish our national culture within Western civilization and in order to evolve from the *umma* system into national statehood, it was essential to liberate ourselves from the influence of Arab religious philosophy. We could not achieve this liberation as long as we used Arabic writing and reading. We could not achieve language reform with this writing and could not liberate our language from the stringent rules of Arabic and Persian grammar. The fundamental change in language occurred only after new generations, unaware of Arabic, graduated from our universities . . . . Today, the new generations find it easy to understand the West in various branches of science and fine arts and equally difficult to understand and assimilate the East. This difference opened a gap in understanding between the new and old generations, but this gap will disappear by itself as the old generations grow smaller and the new ones increase in size. Then the Western way of thinking and understanding will be greatly accelerated . . . .

[After mentioning the university reform, the emancipation of women, the introduction of surnames, and the abolition of titles, Nayir concludes by stating that these were steps in the transition from theocracy to secular democracy.]

The foundation of Atatürk's reforms is secularism. Consequently, it is more appropriate to talk not about *reforms* but about *one reform* by Atatürk. What was the justification for this great reform achieved by Atatürk in the short span of fifteen years between the proclamation of the republic [1923] and his death [1938]? Atatürk diagnosed the sickness of the Ottoman Empire while he was still a student at the war college . . . . In order to save the state, there was no other solution but to destroy everything ranging from the government apparatus to the citizen's men-tality and to build them anew. Nobody had the immense power necessary for such an undertaking, and there were only a handful of people who believed in the necessity of total change . . . .

[After mentioning variuos reform attempts that had, in the past, been opposed and eventually destroyed by religious reactionaries, Nayir continues:]

What did the continuous regression and decadence in the Islamic world mean while the Christian, Western world living in welfare and happiness advanced at an incredible speed? Did it indicate that one of the religions was stimulating progress, while the other was its enemy? One cannot accept this hurried [superficial] view. History shows that Christianity, which is 600 years older [than Islam], kept the Western world under heavy oppression in the Middle Ages and opposed all innovation. Islamic countries, on the other hand, achieved brilliant progress, were opened to science, and for long kept Europe in fright. This means that religions are what men interpret them to be. Consequently, the fault lies not with religion but with the so-called men of religious learning [ulema], who changed religion as they pleased and, taking gifts from the bigots, permitted them to exploit the people as they wished. Traditions, as we call them, are a centuries-old, superstratified accumulation of these opinions and superstitions . . . imbedded in the people's minds.

Atatürk was very fond of democracy. He admired the French Revolution. He had such a belief while preparing the War of Liberation [1919–22] and made reliance on the people a habit from the very beginning . . . .

[Atatürk, according to Nayir, met with opposition of a conservative majority in the First National Assembly (1920–22) and fought desperately to persuade the majority and to prevent it from crushing the enlightened minority.]

He [Atatürk] realized that a Western type of democracy could benefit only the reaction . . . as long as people were not enlightened and not delivered from ignorance and bigotry. This man [Atatürk], who was so fond of democracy, realized that real democracy could not be established before delivering the nation from the oppressive influences of the theocratic order . . . Atatürk never interfered with the faith and worship of people, but stood fast with unyielding will before the clergy [hojas] and men who had gone to Mecca on pilgrimage [hajis], when they tried, on behalf of religion, to interfere in worldly affairs. Expressing his views on religion, Atatürk stated: "A natural religion must be compatible with reason, technology, science, and logic." He differed from false men of religion on this point. These men wanted reason and logic, science and technology to follow unconditionally religious commands and opinions expressed on behalf of religion. They defended the view that the worldly order should be directed by men who spoke on behalf of God. Atatürk said the following in order to warn the people about the empty words of these ignoramuses:

> There is a yardstick for our religion available to everybody. If you use this yardstick, you will realize immediately what conforms and what does not conform to religion. If something satisfies reason, logic, the interest of the nation, the interest of Islam, do not ask anyone and accept it, for that thing is religion. If our religion [Islam] was not compatible with reason and logic it could not have been perfect and the last of religions . . . .

It is for these reasons that Atatürk was firm against all reactionary movements, regardless of how unimportant these might have been . . . . Atatürk's declarations on religious bigotry have the value of a testament for the Turkish nation. Atatürk said:

> You must know that the evil men who guided us along wrong paths covered themselves often in religious garb. They deceived our pure and innocent people with the words of the *şeriat.*° Read our history and see that all the evils that destroyed and enslaved our nation came out of the curse and evils that acted in the guise of religion . . . . The reactionaries believed that they could be backed by a certain class. This is definitely a misconception. We shall smash all the opponents and march on our way toward progress. We shall not hesitate on the path of progress. The world is progressing at a tremendous speed. Can we remain outside this stream?

Atatürk, who loved democracy and placed great value on national will, never permitted the reactionaries to enjoy the tolerance necessitated by national will [respect for elected reactionaries]. He knew that the slightest weakness in this field would lead to the destruction of democracy and open the way to the re-establishment of the sultanate and the caliphate and to their natural intellectual consequence, which is the darkness of the Middle Ages. Democracy was acceptable, but in order to establish the real democracy based on the people . . . it was essential to remain alert so as not to be defeated by the admirers of the autocratic ages and be sabotaged by those who were accustomed to seek personal interest by deceiving the people . . . . It was necessary to enlighten the nation and enable it to differentiate the good from the evil . . . .

Atatürk's basic ideal was a great, emancipated Turkey, even more developed than contemporary civilization; it was to be a country that lived according to the Western yardstick and was an inseparable part of the West. But Atatürk knew that this ideal could be reached only by secularization in every field. His understanding of history and his own

---

°Islamic religious law (the equivalent of the Arab *shari'a*), which became a general type of common law under the Ottoman Empire. It was abolished in 1923–26.

observations indicated clearly that the West reached this high level of living only after the entire social order was secularized. The period between the Renaissance and the French Revolution in the West was a struggle between theocracy and secularism. Almost two hundred years later, we are still waging the same battle. We have incessantly lost time with occasional advances and regressions. Consequently, twenty-five years after Atatürk's death, we are far from having achieved his dream of Westernization . . . . This is the reason for which I regard secularization, and insist upon it, as the foundation stone of Atatürk's reforms.

68.   Atatürkism is Economic Liberation and Anticolonialism[*]

Şevket Süreyya Aydemir

The publishers of Kadro *[Cadre], a review published in 1932–34 and initially with Turkish government suport, tried to develop a socialist, statist, nationalist philosophy for republican Turkey. They took their direction from Marxist and corporatist views. The late Şevket Süreyya Aydemir (b. 1897) was the leading ideologist among the five intellectuals who published* Kadro. *Around 1960, he again became prominent in Turkish affairs, and he associated himself with the socialist groups that emerged in 1960–65. His economic outlook is authoritarian but not extremely leftist. His publications include an autobiography,* Suyu Arayan Adam *[Man in Search of Water] (Istanbul: Remzi Kitapevi, 1959), a three volume biography of Atatürk,* Tek Adam *[Unique Man] (Istanbul: Remzi Kitapevi, 1963–65), and a biography of* Ismet Inönü, Ikinci Adam *[Second Man], 3 vols. (Istanbul: Remzi Kitapevi, 1968).*

What is Atatürk's ideology? This is a topic whose thesis, antithesis, and synthesis were not developed systematically by Mustafa Kemal, who was above all a realistic man of action. Nevertheless, there is a movement [of national liberation] led by Mustafa Kemal, and this movement has an axis made up of ideas and principles. These ideas, when put together, form one of our era's currents of thought. This current opened and determined the fate of an epoch, not only for us, but for all countries resembling our own.

---

[*]Extract from a speech at Robert College [now Bogaziçi University] in Istanbul, "Atatürk ve Atatürk Ideolojisi" ["Atatürk and the Atatürk Ideology"], in Nusret Kurosman, ed., *Çeşitli Cepheleriyle Atatürk* [Atatürk in His Various Aspects] (Istanbul: Istanbul Matbaasi, 1964), pp. 26–40.

The name of this current is Atatürkism and its pioneer is Atatürk . . . .

The movement of national liberation is not an event limited only to Turkey. It left its mark on the course of contemporary events . . . . The struggle for liberation and for national freedom was the pioneering and leading movement aimed at the liquidation of colonialism. It also provided the principles of thought and action for an underdeveloped country seeking, through free, civilized, and peaceful means, a place among the nations of the progressive world . . . .

The Turkish movement of national liberation, which began in 1919 and developed under Mustafa Kemal's leadership, was the consequence [of economic colonialism] and had the following basic characteristics: unconditional national independence, unconditional popular sovereignty, unconditional economic and financial freedom . . . . Mustafa Kemal's principles . . . embodied the following ideas:

1. Anti-imperialism [means] national independence.
2. Anti-capitalism [means] a free national economy and opposition to foreign capital and privileges.
3. Unconditional popular soveriegnty [means] the return of everything to the true masters of the country.

These three principles are the concrete expressions of Atatürk's ideology, and we must be ready to struggle for them today . . . .

69. Atatürk and His Economic Policy*

Kenan Bulutoğlu

Kenan Bulutoğlu is a member of the Faculty of Economics, Bogaziçi University. He belongs to a group of Turkish economists who advocated in the 1960s for land reform and increased government intervention in the economy and who define their program as socialism. This article stresses that a certain legacy in the economic field—namely statism—has been inherited from Atatürk and that, consequently, contemporary Turkish governments must take into consideration Atatürk's economic policies as well as his cultural and social legacy. There is an obvious ideological bias in the article, and the quotations are chosen accordingly. Bulutoğlu was a

---

*Extract from Kenan Bulutölu, "Atatürk ve Iktisadi Siyaseti" ["Atatürk and His Economic Policy"], *Cumhuriyet*, Istanbul, November 13, 1963.

minister in Ecevit's cabinet, which implemented some of these statist policies.

It is difficult to reach precise conclusions regarding the nature of Atatürk's economic policy and its swings to the left or right throughout his lifetime. First of all, since Atatürk was not an economist, it would be irrelevant to attempt to find a set of coherent decisions derived from a clear, well-defined economic doctrine. But as a statesman, as the founder of a modern state, he followed an original, noteworthy economic policy. It would be even more diffucult to distinguish these policies, which can be ascribed directly to his own ideological inclination, from those that stemmed from the advice of politicians who participated directly in the exercise of power. Moreover, the fact that economic concepts were often applied by changing somewhat their original Western meaning also helped somewhat to render uncertain his economic policy.

Economic subjects virtually were not dealt with in the Great Speech.[1] This indicates that, during the War of Independence and the first years of the republic, problems of economic policy were not a major preoccupation of the government. In any case, for Mustafa Kemal, economic problems were secondary to political independence and, therefore, could be solved after the latter was achieved. In an interview with the tradesmen and artisans of Konya in 1923, he candidly declared that, apart from economic independence, he did not have a well-defined program of action in the field of economics:

> I can formulate my ideas in two categories: those concerning the present and those concerning the future. For the time being, the only things I am preoccupied with are the capitulations [i.e., the special privileges granted to the Western Powers]. With regard to what must be done in the future, especially in order to make Turkish trade competitive with world trade, I am confident that you know better than I what measures are necessary.

Even at that time, however, Atatürk had realized the importance of economic issues:

> The new Turkish state will lay its foundations not on the bayonet but on economic power, upon which the bayonet also is based. The new Turkish state will be an economic state.[2]

Not until after World War II was the term "economic state" introduced into books of political science or used commonly together with the term "economic democracy." Atatürk, who grasped very well the importance of economics, influenced also by the pressure of subsequent events, initiated a constructive economic policy. I shall try to outline the features of this economic policy in the three special fields where it was most noticeable: economic independence and anticolonialism, industrialization and statism, and feudal conditions and agrarian reform.

Economic Independence and Anticolonialism

As I pointed out above, the most clear economic credo of the participants in the War of National Liberation, and of Mustafa Kemal himself, was their uncompromising, hostile attitude toward the exploitation of the economy by foreign capital under the privileges and protection accorded by the capitulations. The speeches of Mustafa Kemal on this subject are unreserved, violent, and bitter:

> We are men decidely devoted to the doctrine that teaches us to fight, nationally united, the imperialism that wants to ruin us and the capitalism that wants to swallow us. (Speech in the Grand National Assembly, January 1, 1920.)

Capitalism here means exploitative foreign capitalism, i.e., colonialism with all its political aspects.

After the abolition of the capitulations, the foreign companies and utility monopolies established in key sectors of the economy—such as mines, railways, utilities, and so on—under the privilege of concessions were nationalized. Atatürk's suspicious attitude toward foreign private capital was only too clear. Nevertheless, he pointed out that he would welcome the kind of foreign capital that would work for the interests of the country:

> It would be erroneous to think that we are against foreign capital. We are always ready to grant necessary guarantees to foreign capital and it is desirable for foreign capital to add to our labor and to our wealth, and to bring about good results—but not as before. (Inaugural speech at the Congress of Economy, Izmir, 1923.)

The kind of foreign capital he was most cautious about consisted mainly of private companies that aimed to use the Turkish economy as a reservoir of raw materials and, hence, as an open market. He admitted, however, that the capital borrowed from foreign powers could be helpful in economic development, provided that it was used for good purposes. During Atatürk's lifetime, in fact, Turkey received credit from various foreign powers, but the amount did not exceed that of the old debts, which were being repaid at the same time. It must also be noted that Atatürk thought that foreign capital could not be the main force behind economic development and that the main support had to come from internal resources:

> In order to preserve the structure of the state, it is necessary and possible to govern with the revenues and resources of this country and without having recourse to foreign countries.

This cautious attitude of the young republic toward foreign debt is understandable. Public finance was still under the heavy burden of Ottoman debts, contracted during the period of [the empire's] decline.

During the period of the Ottoman Empire, the Turkish economy had all the characteristics of a dependent, semicolonial economy. The capitulations prevented the adoption of a protective tariff and thus hindered the development of a national industry. Modern capitalist technology was introduced in the country to produce only those goods that could not be imported from abroad and had to be produced in Turkey. This was a dichotomic type of economy, which still prevails in many underdeveloped countries; an enclave sector made up mainly of foreign companies confined to the port cities or a series of companies scattered throughout the country exploiting natural resources [such as] mines or plantations. It is noteworthy that the impact of this sector on national development decreased even more because of the fact that the foreign companies used to take out of the country a large part of their production in the form of profits. Except for this small modern sector, the entire economy was feudal. A large majority of the Turkish statesmen in the years of decline were aware of the fact that the development of a national manufacturing industry was dependent on the abolition of the capitulations and the introduction of a protective tariff system.

According to the Treaty of Lausanne [1923], a full protective tariff policy could be adopted only by 1927. Republican Turkey had long looked forward to the day when it could enact a protective tariff as the date for completing its economic independence. Flags were hoisted on the anniversary of the Treaty of Lausanne partly to hail this event. Today, forty years later, the flags are again hoisted. But now the purpose is to greet the admission of Turkey into the Common Market, the abandonment of the freedom to impose tariffs, which was secured in the past as the yardstick of sovereignty. This participation could have been hailed as a success if, during the past forty years, Turkey had established an industrial capacity capable of competing fully with the industries of the Common Market countries. Would these countries then accept Turkey in the Common Market?[3] The answer can perhaps be found in their refusal to admit the United Kingdom into the Market.

Desire for Rapid Industrialization and Statism

During the first years of the republic—starting with the Economic Congess of Izmir in 1923—the policy followed was to place trust in private entrepreneurship and in its ability to achieve economic development. In spite of these encouraging measures, the actual result cannot be considered satisfactory. Furthermore, the outbreak of the Great Depression, the increasing foreign trade deficit, and, consequently, the pressure on the value of the Turkish lira contributed to the government's turning to a new and more interventionist policy. After Inönü's speech in Sivas, statism was enforced [beginning in 1930–31] as the government's official economic policy.

Atatürk defined statism as follows:

> The statism that we are implementing is a system peculiar to Turkey, engendered by its own needs. It means that while recognizing private entrepreneurship as the main basis, but realizing that many activities are not undertaken, the state must be given the control of the economy to face all the needs of a large country and of a great nation. . . . The state wanted to perform certain economic activities that had not been undertaken by private enterprise in the shortest possible time and it succeeded in doing so. . . . The way we have chosen to follow is a system different from economic liberalism. (Inaugural speech at the Izmir Fair, 1935.)

He also pointed out that statism was not in any way the same as collectivism or Communism, which aimed at removing all instruments of production and distribution from the ownership and control of private enterprise. This definition—doubtless like many other similar definitions proposed by official and nonofficial interpreters of statism—is not clear. Furthermore, since statism was the government's official economic policy, no one dared speak against it. Instead, everyone tried to interpret it according to his own tendencies and interests.[4]

The economic functions of the state, beginning with limited intervention and going toward fuller intervention, can be ranked as follows: (1) to provide public services; to undertake activities that by their nature can be undertaken only by a central body using public finance [i.e., taxes], such as defense, justice, police protection, and so on; (2) the construction of a basic infrastructural network, such as highways, railways, harbors, dams, and so on; (3) utility and resource monopolies, i.e., those activities that by their nature can be operated efficiently only in monopoly conditions: utilities, mines, etc.; (4) production for market demand.

Those with conservative tendencies would define statism in such a way as to cover only the first two groups of activities. Those with leftist leanings would include in this concept all natural resources and those activities that were not undertaken by private entrepreneurs, either because of high degrees of risk or simply for lack of capital. The group supporting the view that large sectors of the economy should be left to private business were headed by Celal Bayar, then minister of economy. Those advocating bold government initiative in erecting new plants and accelerated industrialization were seeking support from Ismet Inönü, then prime minister.

Atatürk himself favored the doctrine defending accelerated industrialization according to which the government would set up new public enterprises to meet the market demand. Furthermore, Atatürk pointed out that statism was a policy that conformed basically to the wishes of the Turkish people:

> The policy that our party follows is on the one hand entirely democratic and popular, and on the other hand it is, from the economic standpoint, statist. By their temperament, our people are genuinely statist, for they feel that they have the right to ask the state for all that they absolutely need. Consequently, there is a fundamental similarity between the program of our party and the aspirations of our people. (Speech at Izmir, January, 1931.)

Significantly, the policy makers who implemented statism tried to present it as an economic system above and beyond the controversy concerning capitalism versus socialism. Doubtless, as an economic system, statism represented a movement toward collectivism rather than toward capitalism and was, therefore, a kind of leftist radicalism. But the political philosophy supporting this view on economics was not clearly determined. The government claimed that its policy was neither socialistic nor capitalistic. The collectivist structure in industry did not stem from a prior labor movement; it was generated by the governing elite's desire for rapid industrialization. The intellectual movement led by *Kadro*[5] tried to define the philosophy of this shift toward collectivism. Statism, *Kadro* explained, was a movement to achieve the synthesis between the need for industrialization and the goal of a classless society.

As in every mixed economy that lacked strong ties with the masses, statism ran the risk of becoming state capitalism. This, indeed, became a reality and, due to a series of developments, gained momentum. After 1946, strong tendencies toward Trujilloism transformed state economic enterprises into an outright [economic] instrument in the hands of the private interest groups that controlled the government. The fact remains, however, that Turkey, as an underdeveloped country, was the first to use statism as a means for industrialization.

In our time, many underdeveloped countries (India, Egypt, Algeria) have adopted more or less the same policy and are openly declaring that socialism as a political philosophy underlies their policy of industrialization.

Policy Against Feudal Institutions

Atatürk tried to eliminate the feudal institutions through some more or less formal legal reforms. But the emancipation of landless peasants from serfdom by way of radical land reforms was one of his most cherished goals. He frequently declared that agrarian reforms were necessary and that it would be advisable to limit the size of private land ownership in order to achieve them:

> First of all, it is necessary that no peasant be left landless in our country. More important than that is to provide for a statute to prevent the parcelling of land and keep it large enough to provide a living for the peasant's family. It is necessary to limit the size of land ownership according to the fertility of land and the density of population in the region. (Inaugural speech in the Grand National Assembly, November, 1937.)

Despite Atatürk's statement about the necessity of an agrarian reform in almost every one of his inaugural speeches in the Grand National Assembly,[6] the government failed to implement an extensive agrarian reform in his lifetime or thereafter. Even during Atatürk's lifetime, in fact, the big landowners exercised an important influence in the People's Republican Party, then the party in power and the only one legally in existence. Pretexts such as the lack of regular land surveys and the priority of settling first the immigrants [exchanged populations] led to the repeated postponement of land reform. Finally, even when reform was voted in 1945, its enforcement was effectively blocked and it was considerably watered down with later amendments.

The agrarian reform was the only one of Atatürk's economic programs that was not implemented. After his time, the increasing number of landless peasants came to look upon land reform as a matter of life or death. Today, many countries recently liberated from colonial rule are trying to undertake the first steps in an economic policy that was pioneered by Atatürk. With his remarkable reforms, which broke the vicious circle of traditionalism in Turkey, Atatürk—this magnificent radical from a semicolonial feudal society—is still leading his own country, and countries in similar situations, toward progress.

Notes

1. Atatürk's six-day speech, *A Speech Delivered by Ghazi Mustapha Kemal, President of the Turkish Republic, October, 1927*, trans. Hans Kohn (Leipzig: K. F. Koehler, 1929).
2. Most of the quotations in this article are taken from Korkut Boratav, *Türkiye' de Devletçilik, 1923–1950* [Statism in Turkey, 1923–1950]; Bilsay Kuruç, *Iiktisat Politikasının Resmi Belgeleri, Türk Iktisad Gelişmesi Araştırma Projesi serisi nos. 16, 17* [Official Documents of the Economic Policy. Project series 16, 17 of Turkish Economic Development] (Ankara: School of Political Science, 1962). The references are given by the author and have been preserved intact.
3. Turkey was accepted as an associate member.
4. Serbest Fırka (the Liberal or, more correctly, Laissez-Faire Party of 1930) opposed statism from its very inception, but it directed its criticism more against state capitalism than against popular statism, arguing that statism enriched a few with the taxpayers' money. After the party was disbanded (in the latter part of 1930) at the government's request, no one dared speak openly against statism. When the principle of statism was inserted into the constitution in 1937, a member of the Grand National Assembly asked the government: "If a citizen speaks and advocates laissez-faire, will he be brought before the criminal court and charged with attempting to change the state regime?" A member representing the views of the government answered: "An action against the principles of statism, like any action against the constitution, will be prosecuted as a crime." Another member answered: "No activity in favor of laissez-faire which contradicts the doctrine of statism will be allowed." Fortunately, this narrow-mindedness has never been enforced. To the best of our knowledge, no one was taken before the court on the charge of advocating laissez-faire, even in the period when statism was at its peak, but many were imprisoned on charges of socialism or Marxism.
5. See Section XVIII.
6. Especially the inaugural speeches of 1929, 1936, and 1937.

XXI. SOCIALISM AND STATISM

70. For Social Justice and Development[*]

In its first issue, the review Yön *[Direction] published an ideological statement proposing statism as a means of providing social justice and stimulating economic development. The statement brought together ideas that had been more or less floating around and proposed them as guideposts for concerted action. It was framed to appeal mainly to intellectuals and, despite its claims to democratic order, it lacked that populist democratic spirit so dear to the Turkish masses. At first, the declaration was signed by more than 160 people—more than half of whom were junior academicians, journalists, or writers—and later by about 500. The publication of the statement had a brief impact:* Yön's *circulation went up to 30,000, but soon dropped back to about half that number. Some of the original signatories eventually came to disagree with the revolutionary, antiparliamentary views subsequently adopted by* Yön. *Others, dissatisfied with* Yön's *"bourgeois statism," supported more radical leftist reviews such as* Sosyal Adalet *[Social Justice] and* Eylem *[Planned Action]; the latter expressed the viewpoint of a Marxist group that was associated with the* Türkiye İşçi Partisi *[Labor Party of Turkey]. Some of* Yön's *contributors—Doğan Avcıoğlu, Mumtaz Soysal, and Sadun Aren, for example—eventually deviated to the left, but the review continued to publish many articles on social problems. The manner of* Yön's *thought, and the implicit totalitarianism and rejection of parliamentary democracy in his writings, have left a profound mark on Turkish social thinking.*

The undersigned, holding responsible positions in various segments of Turkish society, consider it appropriate to publish this statement embodying their common views at this time, when the Turkish people, in the midst of very grave economic, political, and social problems, is searching for a course that will lead to the realization of all its aspirations. We believe that such a statement will open the way for significant debates that will prove helpful in the solution of our problems.

---

[*]Extract from "Bildiri" ["Declaration"], Yön [Direction], Istanbul, no. 1 (December 20, 1961); 12–13. This English version has been adapted from Frank Tachau's translation, which appeared in *Middle Eastern Affairs* (March 1963): 75–78.

1. We believe that the aims assumed by the Atatürk reforms, such as attainment of the level of modern civilization, the final solution of the problem of education, the enlivening of Turkish democracy, the realization of social justice, and the establishment of a democratic regime on firm foundations, depend upon the success we will achieve in rapid economic development, that is, in the rapid increase in the level of national productivity.

(a) In the broadest sense, Westernization—the aim of the Atatürk reforms—can be realized by approaching the level of productivity of the West. As the level of productivity in Turkey rises, the country's social structure will change, the dichotomy between city and village will disappear, opportunities will increase, and rationalism, the basis of Western civilization, will spread among the masses.

(b) Given a low level of productivity, the hope for a basic rise in the cultural level of the masses is a sheer delusion, no matter how much effort is put forth. Unemployment, starvation, nakedness, cold, and misery will impede the orientation of the masses toward education; the struggle for existence will assume greater importance than the urge to learn.

(c) Democracy is, above all, a regime based on human dignity and the supreme value of the individual. A government that cannot eliminate hunger, unemployment, and homelessness, no matter how much we may favor it, will inevitably cease to be democratic and ultimately will collapse. . . .

(d) A policy of social justice that fails to emphasize the rapid increase in national income will be unable to do more than share the poverty. On the other hand, a development policy that does not recognize social justice is doomed to failure. Consequently, one of the chief means of [achieving] a policy of social justice must be an increase in the level of productivity.

2. We consider it essential that such persons as teachers, writers, politicians, labor leaders, businessmen, and administrators, who are in a position to give direction to Turkish society, reach agreement on the main tenets of a clear philosophy of development.

(a) In the twentieth century, as the result of developments in the means of communication, the masses have learned of the high standard of living prevailing in other countries or among other social classes; more important, they realize that the achievement of this standard is possible for them. As a result, our poverty is even more painfully obvious. The situation is further aggravated by the rapid population increase and the failure to deal with our problems in a manner consonant with this increase.

Turkey is today in a serious economic and social crisis. The social crisis has emerged as a natural consequence of the economic crisis. A backward agriculture, quite apart from failing to secure the resources needed to match our increasing imports, is not even capable of meeting the basic needs of the increasing population. Landlessness, which pushes increasing numbers into the cities, results in difficulties in the way of employment and housing for this flood of new urbanites. If basic measures are not taken, then the problems of shanty towns and unemployment will become dangerous sores in the national life and may [even] prepare the way for social and political upheaval.

Because of the rapid increase in population, half of the Turkish population consists of children under the age of eighteen. As recent events have clearly shown, a large segment of this avalanche of children will be deprived of education and a secure future.

(b) The most deplorable fact is that, among those who have control over Turkey's future, there is as yet no realization of the serious problems that confront us. They have not as yet adopted an applicable philosophy of development. The concept of development has not yet been understood in all its ramifications. What is overlooked is that development cannot succeed without basic reforms and, by the same token, that one of the results of development will be changes in the social order and in individual behavior. Consequently, it is idle to wish for development, while at the same time opposing fundamental reforms and new methods. The upshot of this situation is that many of those in positions of authority in the society sincerely believe that the solution to the development problem lies in a slight increase in foreign aid, the development of tourism, and increased exports of agricultural products.

(c) The task of directing the development of Turkey toward a clearly defined goal is beyond the competence of the State Planning Organization, which is responsible to the political authorities. It is true that the State Planning Organization, which has brought the country's leading experts together, has drawn up a strategy of development and indicated the first steps to be taken in this direction. But this cannot be considered adequate. The prospective plan will merit consideration and attain success only when those who are in a position to give direction to Turkish society arrive at some agreement on a clear philosophy of development.

3. As starting points for our philosophy of development, we consider it essential to utilize all our capabilities, rapidly to increase investments, to plan the entire economy, to bring about social justice for the masses, to put an end to exploitation, and to make the masses masters of democracy.

We believe these goals are attainable through a new concept of statism.

(a) The Turkish economy will continue as a mixture of private and state enterprise. However, we do not believe that an economic system based primarily on private enterprise can bring Turkey, given its present social structure, to the level of contemporary civilization quickly and with social justice. In the light of history and economics, we believe that development based on private enterprise is slow, painful, wasteful, and impossible for an underdeveloped country dedicated to the principle of social justice. Such a development process, moreover, is not democratic, because, in a broad sense, political power depends upon economic power.

(b) Private enterprise depends on profits. If the motive power of an economic system consists of the profit incentive, the inevitable result will be a very slow rate of development, increasing inequities in the distribution of income, the adoption of a philosophy of a "millionaire in every district," the wasteful diversion of national wealth from the most useful to the most profitable projects, and the frequent occurrence of stagnation and unemployment. Nowadays, no underdeveloped country can afford these features.

The process of development in the Western countries, in spite of colonization and [other] favorable conditions, took place slowly, wastefully, and with difficulty, and was realized under liberal regimes that were not subject to popular vote. It is only in the twentieth century, with the basic rise in the level of productivity, that the economic systems of the Western countries have been brought to a satisfactory level of operation. In spite of this, the socialist parties, thinkers, and even liberal politicians of the West are pointing out that the economic systems of their own countries are wasteful, that they neglect basic necessities, and that they are inadequate from the point of view of rapid development and estalishment of social justice.

(c) This is why we consider it necessary for Turkey to adopt a new concept of statism adequate to the needs of our day. Furthermore, we think it important to point out that the popular notion that private enterprise is inevitably profitable and state enterprise inevitably unprofitable has been fostered by extensive propaganda and is not based on sound arguments. We wish to recall that, in places like England and France, some industries have been nationalized for the purpose of greater productive potential.

We believe the reasons why some state enterprises remain unprofitable are not to be sought in the policy of statism itself; on the contrary, the causes lie in our failure to apply a systematic and sufficiently extensive policy of statism.

4. We realize that the new statism, in order to attain the goals we have outlined above, must necessarily assume the form of judicious state intervention.

(a) In order to speed up development, it is necessay to increase national savings and to direct a significant portion of increased national income into savings; this can be accomplished only through broad and skillful state intervention.

Through statism, it is possible to increase the yield of taxation, one of the chief sources of savings. In our day, equity in taxation is a necessity. But the most important objection nowadays to taxation of high incomes, with the object of securing justice in taxation, is that this will result in a decline in investment by these funds. Statism, because it directs national savings into investment, counters this objection. Furthermore, statism brings about an equilibrium between the blessings and the pains of development and facilitates the adoption of the concept of saving by the masses. Additionally, the profits of state enterprises may, without deviations from the policy of taxation, become an important source of savings.

The goal of increasing savings potential by rechanneling unproductive forces into productive uses should become attainable by means of democratic but planned organization by the state.

(b) We believe that, with our present capabilities, it is possible, through better organization and administration, to create much greater and more productive savings than at present. Accordingly, total planning of economic life is necessary. Planning must bring with it the authority and the means to direct economic activity toward the desired goals in due time and in their entirety. One of the main conditions for securing this is that the key industries dominating various sectors of the economy be placed unconditionally under state control. We consider statism an indispensable element in any serious planning.

(c) Planning requires a transition to large economic units. The Turkish economy, however, is based upon very small enterprises in the fields of agriculture, industry, and commerce. Accordingly, it is necessary to develop productive cooperatives in order to organize farming, to spread cooperativism among small crafts, and to establish large units insofar as possible in agriculture and commerce, just as in industry, by reducing the number of retail sales outlets and shortening the process of transferring commodities from producer to consumer.

The foundations of the Turkish economic system must be built upon the organization of a broad cooperative sector side by side with the state sector.

(d) Statism is also the most suitable system for avoiding inequities in the distribution of income, realizing social security, countering the pressure of a class of middlemen on producers and consumers, and eliminating the imbalances among various districts.

The basic goals of statism are to bring the working class to a high level of merit and to raise wages derived from labor to a high level. A system that permits the oppression of those who must live from the sale of their mental and physical capabilities, a system that closes its eyes to the unjust profits earned by the land speculators and the middlemen who exploit the field of commerce, a system that fails to protest the fact that such as these enjoy incomes in excess of those earned by higher civil servants, intellectuals, professionals, and scientists—such a system cannot continue to operate in the twentieth century.

(e) Statism is a weapon in the struggle to resist the monopolization of the democratic regime by one element alone; it serves to secure control of democracy by the masses. The inauguration of a planned educational mobilization, widening the road opened by the village institutes, enabling millions of the peasants' and laborers' children to achieve equality in the field of education and in the national administration, preparation of the masses for improvement by means of adult eduction—all this can be accomplished only by means of a sensible policy of statism.

It is the function of statism to strengthen the labor unions and to achieve a fundamental land reform that will replace the rural landlords with farmers' organizations and cooperatives. Moreover, these measures can be accomplished only by means of state intervention.

The goals we wish to achieve may be subject to debate on this or that individual point. It is the purpose of this statement to open the way for such debates.

We believe that the first necessity for the resolution of the crisis in which we find ourselves today is for those who represent the various segments of Turkish society, as well as those who have attained positions of responsibility for the nation's future, to proclaim openly their ideas and to agree on a fundamental philosophy of development.

71.   For Freedom and Private Enterprise*

Ahmet Hamdi Başar

Yön's statement calling for socialism aimed clearly at limiting the freedom of private enterprise and eventually restricting party activities. The coalition government, composed of the Republican Party, which supported statism, and the Justice Party, which supported private enterprise, was deadlocked in passivity. It failed to back officially any specific ideology. The ideological discussions, therefore, were carried on freely by individuals and private organizations.

A statement opposing Yön's statism-socialism appeared in Barış Dünyası [World of Peace], a review edited by the late Ahmet Hamdi Başar (b. 1897). An advocate of rational economic development based on private

---

*Extract from Ahmet Hamdi Başar, "Kalkınma Prensiplerimiz" ["Our Principles of Development"], Barış Dünyası [World of Peace], Istanbul, April 1962, pp. 18–22.

enterprise, Başar considered classicial socialism and capitalism obsolete and recommended first national consolidation and then economic methods suitable to conditions in developing countries. Başar, who had written a dozen books on various Turkish economic and political problems, believed that both socialists and liberals had a wrong conception of the material world and its relation to social values. The statement of the Barış Dünyası *was submitted to, and received the endorsement of the trade and industrial chambers, which, in all Turkish cities and towns, represent entrepreneurs, trade and craft organizations, and other sections of the middle classes engaged in economic occupations.*

The main solution to our problems is work. Article 1. Our main problem is the need to increase our working capacity to the maximum, to use our resources in the most rational fashion, to raise our production well above the present level, and to achieve national development in the shortest possible time. We believe that large investments will increase work capacity and productivity, and we shall thus solve all our problems.

Statism is a commonly acceptable regime. Article 2. Our development depends on our consolidation as a modern nation and on acquisition of technology. We are faced with endless needs in the social, economic, political, and cultural fields. This could be solved through the regulatory, protectionist, constructive intervention and assistance of the state. We consider such statism as a doctrine and a regime acceptable to all.

It is dangerous for the state to become capitalist and investor. Article 3. The national development duties of the state must rely on a philosophy accepted by the majority. The political regime in charge of the administration must also conform to this view. The underdeveloped countries are deprived of the benefits of freedom and individualism under which the West developed. The development philosophy of a new country is faced by two problems totally different from each other; namely, whether the state should intervene in economic life as investor and administrator or should help establish a regime based on private property and initiative.

We believe that the state should assume the responsibility of establishing a regime of private property and private initiative and of assuring economic freedom for citizens. If the state assumed the role of a capitalist and employer and made the citizen a hired hand, this would create great dangers in underdeveloped societies. Those societies did not mature through a historical process and did not develop a middle class with enough consciousness to assume power over the administration. The political power [group] representing the state could deprive the citizen not only of his economic freedom but also of his political rights by expanding its authority in the economic field, regardless of whether it came to power through elections or other means.

The natural form to be taken eventually by such a regime would be an open or disguised dictatorship. One may think that a free political life will prevent the establishment of such a dictatorship. In reality, political parties in underdeveloped countries are not mature and are not based on classes with social consciousness as in the West. These parties are unable to play a peacemaking role among social classes, and consequently society is surrendered to a partisan class. We, as a nation, ought to realize today from experience what it means to have the power in the hands of such a class, and that dictatorship can be established through partisanship even in a multi-party system. . . . State capitalism cannot be defended under any conditions in societies in which the ruling class consists of partisans [members of a party]. Consequently, we must face the state development policy in our country . . . with the demand that it achieve economic freedom for the citizen through a regime of private property and initiative and bring about social justice.

Our regime is a statism that should develop private enterprise and achieve social justice. Article 4. We believe that private initiative and acquisitive ambitions derive from natural human instincts that should not be detroyed but stimulated. The purpose is not to use these instincts as means for selfish, materialistic, unlawful, and immoral purposes. This can be prevented by giving proper form and spirit to the moral and legal regulatory order of society.

The liberal ideas of the eighteenth and nineteenth centuries cannot be accepted in any society today. The contemporary principle is social security and justice. The great differences in wealth and living standards can cause the destruction of both the poor and the rich. But the rights of capital, initiative, and labor should not be ignored, and a certain degree of social differentiation must be accepted. The modern, progressive societies can avoid disintegration if they accept the spirit of mutual understanding and assistance among social classes and consider events not from the viewpoint of class interests but from that of national interest. . . . A nonpartisan state can become an institution that would guarantee social peace and mutual assistance among classes. The state would lose its impartiality if it became a capitalist and employer . . . and the representative of a social class. The worker would naturally be deprived of his rights, chiefly the right to strike, in a system of state enterprise. Strikes would appear as rebellions against the state. . . .

Our middle class must be improved. Article 5. We cannot accept the idea that state capitalism is necessary in our country, because we do not yet possess a strong middle class... In the republic, many people belonging to the middle class were trained ... in trade, industry, banking, and other fields of activity. Private enterprise dominates in totality our trade and more than half of our industry, ... and the overwhelming majority of agriculture is privately owned and managed. But the qualitative and quantitative development of our middle class was not accompanied by a similar evolution in the field of social responsibility, and this is most upsetting. Our middle class did not fight for economic freedom, as in the West. On the contrary, it was attached to the state to a very large extent, and consequently, despite its growth in strength, it avoided, to a shameful degree, becoming involved in or working for the solution of national problems and thus left itself open to dangers. We hope these people realize that they would not be able to go along forever with all those who would hold power. . . .

It is possible to achieve rapid economic development and social justice based on private enterprise. Article 6. We believe that, in view of the present conditions, Turkey could neither reach rapidly the level of contemporary civilization nor achieve social justice without an economic system based on private enterprise. We believe, in the light of history and economic sciences, that economic development not based on private enterprise is faulty, costly ... and unable to prevent in developing countries the annihilation of opposition by those who hold state power in their hands. . . . Private enterprise is based on profit, which is the driving power of the economic system. The state can take measures to enlarge profit opportunities and thus strengthen the enterprises and increase the speed of development. . . . In our country, the state enterprises operate in many fields in a manner far costlier than private enterprises. The state enterprises, despite long term credits given at 1.5 per cent interest, foreign loans, and many privileges, ... cannot compete with private enterprises, ... which operate with great difficulty and still make profits. . . . We want to point out that the claim that state enterprises could be profitable and productive is deprived of sound foundations and rests on propaganda. The fact that the state and its enterprises are transferring some of their operations to [private] contractors in order to become more effective proves this point. . . . We find it possible and useful that the state should retire in a planned and programed manner from the operation of economic enterprises. It can encourage the establishment of cooperatives and joint companies by entrepreneurs and capitalists, ... producers, managers, and workers, and urge the people to invest in them.

We are totally opposed to state capitalism. Article 7. We find dangerous the state investment of funds secured through taxation and the subjection of high incomes to heavy taxes. Such a policy would destroy the sources of income. . . .

Our greatest problem is the establishment of a modern state. Article 8. The state structure, organization, and mentality . . . are, to a large degree, incapable of achieving the nation's material and moral development and consolidation and [its] democratic administration. . . . Despite many successful reforms, we have not been able to engage in building a modern, populist state because of our inability to reform [economic] statism. The modern state [should be] in the hands of capable people, experts and elites with morality and integrity. . . . In addition, there is a need for planning bodies to regulate the society's life as a whole by cooperating in a democratic fashion with professional and popular organizations and by defining state responsibilities and authority in conformity with popular sovereignty. . . .

It is possible to solve all problems in peace and mutual understanding. Article 9. We are firmly against all movements that create animosity among classes, groups, and nations. We want to work for embodying in our life a moral mentality nourished by love, a feeling of mutual assistance, sacrifice, and tolerance, . . . which we find in the noble character of our nation. . . . National solidarity based on brotherly feelings, mutual sacrifice, assistance, and tolerance is the only road to development.

72.   On Yön and Statism[*]

Kemal H. Karpat

Yön's proposal for adopting statism was criticized on social, political, and historical grounds by Kemal H. Karpat, a political scientist who has taught at Montana State University and at New York University and who is now Professor of Middle East Studies at the University of Wisconsin. The article appeared in Forum, *a liberal social-oriented review published in Ankara. The review resumed publication as* Yeni Forum *in 1979.*

I have carefully read the declaration and the articles published in *Yön.* To express concisely the scattered ideas floating around is to render a

---

[*]Extract from Kemal H. Karpat, "Yön ve Devletçilik Üzerine" ["On Yön and Statism"], *Forum*, Ankara, December 1, 1962, pp. 8–9; December 15, 1962, pp. 13–15; January 1, 1963, pp. 11–13.

service to the intellectual life of the country. I appreciate this and hope that these ideas will be given additional elaboration. It is impossible not to agree with the general purposes expressed at the beginning of Yön's declaration. However, the idea of total statism, through which these aims are to be attained, does not correspond either to Turkey's realities or to her economic and social history.

The main struggle in Turkey today is, to put it generally, a struggle between the state bureaucracy and productive groups. This bureaucracy and the intellectual groups formed within it have hitherto decided their role in society and their relations with the people according to their interests and views and by having control of power. Thus, from a position above the people, they have made modernization and progress a cultural problem and have refused to recognize the economic and social problems that are to give depth, significance, and form to modernization. In reality, theirs was an elitist attitude; the intelligentsia was an aristocratic group that lived above society, it was supported by the state, and derived its power justification from diplomas. . . .

It is unnecessary to dwell further upon these background matters. The main point is this: The intelligentsia, in which the bureaucracy is included, has emerged as a distinct social group. It has its own philosophy, point of view, interests, means of communications, schools, etc. It has regarded each event and every other social group and its activities from its own point of view and has determined its interest position accordingly by using the state power, which it has held in its own hands.

The separation of the intellectual from society and the assumption of a materially and spiritually superior position for himself will prevent him from being a true leader. People believe only in those men who have come from their own ranks, in those who understand and respect them and who secure their material and cultural development. But people will believe in the intellectual who secures the free development of all people through their own participation. No one will submit to being taken by the hand and led like a child. Everyone would prefer to develop freely his own personality. The main problem is to provide everyone with equal opportunity for development in every sense, and this is something that has never been achieved in our history.

In Turkish social history, the intellectuals and the people have been separated. The power of the state has passed in absolute fashion into the hands of the intellectual. This situation has tragically resulted in breeding suspicion and distrust between the two sides. In order to bridge this gap, Ziya Gökalp and Atatürk (through the principle of populism) exerted certain efforts, but these efforts have been perverted by the intelligentsia, which has applied populism in an erroneous and incomplete fashion. If the history of the War of Independence [1919–22] is objectively studied, it will show that, besides resistance to the invading forces [the Allies and Greeks], the masses followed Atatürk, hoping to be rid of the oppression of the intellectual bureaucratic group. The popular program prepared by the government in September, 1920, and the discussions around it are enough to give an outline of the basic ideas of the Turkish Republic concerning the wishes of the lower groups. The people will recognize the intellectual's value, not according to his diploma, but according to his practical social, economic, and cultural contribution to their own betterment. In order to understand the relations of a person with other people, it is necessary to look first at that person's place in society and to consider whether he enjoys in fact more political, social, and cultural privileges than the others. My opinion is that many of the intellectuals who defend the idea of statism are merely revealing their negative reaction against the multi-party system and democracy. Under the present circumstances in Turkey, the creation of a statist system is only an effort to restore to the intellectual the privileged social position he had lost. There is no doubt that economic and social problems have, in our era, come into the foreground and exercised a profound impact on political life. But such a situation does not necessitate the intrusion of the state in every economic activity and its regulation of all social life. One cannot decide in advance that various voluntary, private organizations are unable to cope with and solve at least part of the economic and social problems. Such a thought is dangerous and directly opposed to human nature. If one believes that free individuals in a society cannot solve, through free discussion, the problems of that society, then it is difficult to believe that the intelligentsia of that society, which is principally to blame for social backwardness, should be able to solve such problems. How can one say that the intelligentsia, which for fifteen years has not produced any noteworthy economic, political, or social work (a small group of capable men excepted), should, after taking over state power, become capable of solving all the society's problem? Instead of advancing total solutions, would it not be more practical to take specific problems one by one and give to every individual the opportunity of participating in the discussion and eventual solution of such problems? . . .

I don't believe that a group (intelligentsia) that defends social justice in an abstract fashion and styles itself as its representative and enforcer will achieve success. I have never seen, in any part of the world, true happiness created by a group that adopted abstract principles and acted arbitrarily in enforcing them to create happiness for others. Social justice can be achieved only by objectively looking at the reality of human life and by considering its problems one by one in the light of free thought. We cannot separate social justice from social responsibility. If we try to give each individual and organized body a sense of responsibility toward other individuals and toward society as a whole, we can then achieve social justice.

The spread of social responsibility can and is being undertaken by organizations, schools, the press, and literature. The intellectual can assume a creative function in society by inbuing himself with a sense of social responsibility. The first and most important reform must take place in the field of education, for our education is still immersed in vagueness, in cultural scholasticism with tinges of feudal romantism. Our present educational system is turning out men trained in the concepts of the sixteenth century. The state can accomplish a reform in education and should help to educate men with a sense of social responsibility.

Yön defends statism as the only solution to economic problems. But if the state gains absolute authority in the economic field, it is bound to spread its power into other fields of activity. In a country such as ours, there the state is used to regulate all the material and spiritual aspects of the individual's life (only in the multi-party era did we begin to free ourselves from this), it is obvious that the state will eventually control all activity.

Yön points to the widening scope of state activity in the West and uses it as another reason for expanding statism. There are great differences, however, between the meaning attached to the state in the West and *Yön's* conception of the state. In the West, the state is a body performing public duties under the control and administration of the people. If some private enterprises have in time been taken over by the state, this is because the services performed by them have become public. Besides, these organizations passed under state control as a result of mutual agreement (and with compensation), without giving rise to any crises. Western man regards the state as a body born within society, not above it, and as working to meet the people's needs . . . .

Yön on the other hand elevates the state once more to a supreme position and proposes to introduce the masses to democracy chiefly through statism. Today in Turkey, the masses are on the way to attaining democracy by themselves through political parties. The state could abolish the obstacles that prevent the people from achieving full political education. With this aim in view, it can help the social groups to reach mutual understanding while learning to remain neutral. *Yön* recognizes no place for political parties.

It is difficult to understand the kind of democracy *Yön* and its new statism would bring about. A real democracy today does not reject political parties. Consequently, *Yön's* "democracy" is not the usual kind of democracy, *Yön* deals also with the problems of materializing "democracy." Since political parties are rejected, this "democracy" would use forced short cuts or revolutions. Consequently, the statism proposed by *Yön* is nothing but the coming to power without elections of a small intellectual group and the establishment of an authoritarian system. Such a system is not different from a fascist or semifascist regime.

Let me sum up my thoughts. It is impossible not to agree with some of the factual views and objectives proposed by *Yön*. But the totalitarian, statist methods recommended in order to reach these objectives are dangerous and may lead Turkey to disaster. Though an authoritarian regime appears to be a short cut, still I believe that in reality it is long, hard, and full of dangers. The alternative is to widen the base of the present political system and strengthen it by taking into account public opinion, facts, and history. Thus, we may succeed in becoming a really progressive society. Today, a new social order is being created. Certain social groups that formerly wielded power and had special privileges are now forced to abandon their places to others. Meanwhile, the intellectuals must establish working relations with other groups and harmonize with the needs of society. Instead of giving orders from above, they must learn how to take their place in society according to their abilities and practical potentialities. It is natural that they will not easily abandon their old superior social status. They will defend their privileged positons in various ways by advancing all kinds of ideas. Viewed within the framework of the general social change occurring in Turkey, *Yön*'s ideas are in reality a defense of the old privileged position of the intellectuals.

XXII.   NATIONALISM AND ISLAM

73.   Nationalist Action for the Fatherland

Alparslan Türkeş

Alparslan Türkeş, born in 1917 in Cyprus into the family of a small businessman, has emerged in the 1970s as the leader of the secular nationalists and activists. A military officer by career, he was associated very early in his life with nationalist causes and took a leading part in organizing a secret officer group that overthrew the Democratic Party government of Adnan Menderes in 1960. He was second in command of the National Union Committee, which ruled Turkey after 1960, until he and his supporters, known as the "fourteen," were ousted from the junta for advocating the establishment of a strong nationalist government to carry out social, educational, and economic reforms. Assigned to a diplomatic post in India, Türkeş returned to Turkey in 1963. With several of his friends from the "fourteen," he joined the Republican Peasant National Party, a small regional party, becoming its chairman in 1965. The party program and activities evolved under Türkeş's strong leadership toward a militant national-social ideology. The party changed its name to Milliyetçi Hareket Partisi—Nationalist Action Party (NAP)—in 1969, and gradually it began to play an important part in Turkish politics. The party's electoral showing was rather modest in 1969 and 1973, when it received about 3 percent of the votes cast; but the total was nevertheless equal to that received by all the leftist-Marxist parties combined. In 1977, however, Türkeş's party got 6.4 percent of the vote and increased its seats in the Assembly from three to sixteen. Türkeş joined, as deputy prime minister, two coalition governments under Demirel's premiership. The party's success in 1977 can be attributed to Türkeş's effort to deemphasize secularism and to stress instead the affinity between nationality, religion, and history, as well as to the fear caused by the emergence of a strong Left, which secured him considerable support among conservative and business groups. The NAP also trained commando groups known as Bozkurtlar (Gray Wolves) and maintained close relations with various rightist organizations. It published reviews, such as Milli Hareket [National Action], Devlet [State], and some dailies. The party was suspected of having played a major part in organizing armed attacks against leftist groups and their sympathizers. Eventually, after the military takeover on September 12, 1980, the party was, like all other political organizations, suspended, and Türkeş was arraigned and brought to stand trial for a variety of violations of common law. It was rumored that a group within the army that was sympathetic to Türkeş was planning a coup, but the rumor has not been verified as yet.

The ideology of Türkeş which was enshrined in the program of the NAP was expressed first in a booklet entitled Dokuz Işik *[Nine Lights] issued in 1965, and then elaborated in a larger book,* Türkiye'nin Medeleleri *[Problems], published in 1969. The "nine lights" which are cardinal to Türkeş's ideology are the following:* Türkçülük *(nationalism-Turkism), defined as a deep sense of identity rooted in the consciousness of the historical greatness and contemporary situation of Turkey;* Ülkücülük *(idealism), which is the quality necessary to achieve happiness, prosperity, independence, and liberty;* Ahlakçılık *(morality), the expression of the Turkish spirit in accordance with the laws of nature;* Toplumculuk *(social mindedness), which refers to the establishment of social harmony and support for economic enterprise, social security, welfare, and education;* Ilimcilik *(scientism), the adoption of scientific mentality;* Hürriyetçilik *(freedom), denoting respect for freedom of speech, writing, research, and so forth, in conformity with the UN Charter;* Köycülük *(peasantism), or support for the development of the villagers in every possible way;* Gelişmecilik ve Halkçilik *(development and populism); and* Endüstricilik ve Teknikçilik *(industrialization and technology). These last eight principles are regarded as the practical means to materialize the aspirations embodied in* Türkçülük. *In foreign affairs,* Türkeş *defended membership in the NATO but demanded active promotion of Turkey's interests abroad, including support for Turks living under foreign rule.* Türkeş's *views have been elaborated and propagated in a variety of publications, books, periodicals, and newspapers too numerous to be cited in a general study such as this. A rich bibliography, as well as ample information on* Türkeş *and his party until 1974, can be found in J. Landau,* Radical Politics in Turkey, *pp. 205–42, 273–79 and C.H. Dodd,* Democracy and Development in Turkey, *pp. 118–21. For a more detailed view of the party, see 50 Yıla Doğru [Towards the 50th Year] (Istanbul: Ergenekon Yayınları, 1973) and* Milliyetçi Hareket' in El Katabı *[Handbook of the Nationalist Movement] (Ankara: Emel, 1973); see also Alparslan Türkeş,* Temel Görüşler *[Basic Views] (Istanbul, 1975).*

The excerpt below is taken from Türkeş's *book* Türkiyenin Meseleleri *[Problems of Turkey] (Istanbul: Milli Hareket Yayınevi, 1965), pp. 5–14 passim.*

Our cause as Turkish nationalists is to glorify the existence of the Turkish nation and to assure its existence forever. There is no other idea and no other cause above this idea. No action and attitude can be legitimate which does not strive to preserve the national existence of the Turks and to enhance and perpetuate it .... Every nation strives and fights to assure itself a superior position, a better living, more happiness, and a higher level of civilization and progress. Nations which do not possess national consciousness, feelings, and sacred ambition are doomed to perish .... This is a struggle which can be traced to the oldest periods of history. The Turkish nation, which is in the middle of this struggle, must rid itself of neglect, poverty, backwardness, and weakness, as well as of the need to beg help from others, and must become a nation advanced in civilization and living standards and be able to stand by its own strength and to secure respect and honor everywhere. The primary condition for making the Turkish nation the most powerful, civilized, and comfortable living nation is to have the ideal and ambition for the realization of these goals. This is the meaning as well as the goal of this movement that is unfolding under the standard of the Nationalist Action Party .... The difference between Turkey and the advanced and modern nations of the world is widening and lengthening instead of diminishing ... the development plans applied in our country are mere propaganda for development and are just deceiving and lulling the people.... According to the research of scientists belonging to OECD, Turkey will reach the level of today's European countries ... after 249 years. As conscientious Turkish nationalists we consider it a sacred duty to rebel and to reject such a slow development which condemns the Turkish nation to misery....

Among the fundamental problems of Turkey, the moral crisis occupies the first place. No nation can exist without moral strength. History records the establishment and the rise of many states and civilizations. All this was possible not on the basis of the power of money or of the mob but on the basis only of the pure faith, spirituality, and an ideal living in the hearts of the people. States and civilizations perished not because of poverty or lack of money but for want of spirituality and morality and faith.... Moral crisis [derives] from the crisis of faith.... This means that the religious beliefs are undergoing a crisis. This means that moral rules and values which are fed by religious and national beliefs are undergoing a crisis... Islam is not the cause for the backwardness of the Turkish nation. Islam is a religion of high virtue and morality, which in the course of history disseminated light and opened the way to civilization wherever it went.... Another important problem faced by Turkey is the crisis of authority, the lack of seriousness and decision in administration. If order and, above everything else, the state authority is not supreme, subversive activities aiming at destroying the country will find free hand. The subversive activities we see in our country are the consequences of the lack of determination in the administration and of the authority crisis....

The advance in science and technology assures power and superiority to nations which are able to achieve it. In order to escape as soon as possible from the pitiful situation in which Turkey finds herself today, she is obliged to achieve a massive and rapid development in science and technology. In order to reach this goal, scientists and technologists of high quality and of world stature must be trained. This means that the national educational system implemented blindly in this country must be changed so as to produce men of the quality [described above] ....

Another problem faced by Turkey is social injustice and social disorganization. The Turkish nation possesses a high civilization. In our old civilization we had establishments which organized society and achieved social justice and social assistance, such as *vakıfs* [pious foundations], *imarets* [establishments to assist the poor], *loncas* [guilds] ... These are no longer in existence and have not been replaced by an organization capable of meeting today's needs. Another problem faced by our country is low productivity and high consumption. Today, our production system is based on old methods, while in consumption we are imitating the Western countries ... the reforms and revolutions carried out in this country and described by high sounding names . . . have been confined to imitating the consumption patterns of the West. This is a grave mistake because . . . all these attempts increased consumption in the Western manner . . . and did not spur production activities. . . . Another problem is the failure to train our intellectuals in a proper way. The Turkish intellectuals have been educated for many years in such a manner as to alienate them from the Turkish people. . . . The children of this country who study in the high school . . . or in more superior schools do not return anymore among the people and share their life but seek to find a comfortable position in a few cities, like Istanbul and Ankara, and live in ivory towers in the polluted air of those cities, looking down upon the people. . . . Another problem faced by our country is the lack of a well trained elite cadre of administrators. . . .

[*After pointing to the failure of the educational system to produce national-ist patriotic youth, to the lack of industrialization, and to the spending of taxes for purposes of secondary importance, Türkeş attacked communism. He also called for national unity and rejected foreign models of development and nation-building.*]

The Turkish nation possesses its own true characteristics, its own history, national traditions, and national spirit. The Turkish nation cannot develop and liberate itself [from underdevelopment] by copying the systems of foreign nations which were developed in accordance with their own specific conditions. The salvation and development of the Turkish nation can be achieved only with a system which is one hundred percent national and local and is loyal to the national realities, the national spirit, national historical traditions, and the morality of the Turkish nation and its faith and adopts these as guides to modern science and technology. . . . This is what we are trying to do, and we define the movement as the system of Nine Lights, the view of Nine Lights.

74.   The Question of "Outside" Turks*

Necdet Sancar

Necdet Sancar is an exponent of nationalism and Pan-Turkism in its new form. In the past, Pan-Turkism was a theory of territorial expansion known as Pan-Turanism. Unity of race and language was its basis, and its purpose

---

*Extract from Necdet Sancar, "Dış Türkler Meselesi" ["The Question of 'Outside' Turks"], *Son Havadis* [Last News], Istanbul, October 11, 1961.

was to unite all Turkic groups in one country, the Turan. Most Turkic groups outside Turkey (totaling some 50–60 million people) live in the Central Asian republics of the Soviet Union and in China's northwestern provinces. Pan-Turanism and Pan-Turkism (there are some differences of emphasis between the two) were, therefore, movements that threatened the internal security and unity of the Soviet Union.

After World War II, following the emergence of new concepts of human rights and freedoms, Pan-Turkism changed its content considerably. The apologists for Pan-Turkism advocated the liberation of Turkic groups from Soviet rule (some even discussed the fate of Turks under Chinese rule) as a consequence of the right of self-determination and independence as granted to the former Western colonies in Asia and Africa. The idea of uniting all these Turkic groups in one single state, Greater Turkey, was abandoned. Governments in Turkey have rejected the idea of dealing with the Turkic groups in the USSR. The following article presents the arguments of Pan-Turkists concerning the Turkic groups living in the Soviet Union.

Turkey is the only independent area of the [Turkic] lands stretching from the Aegean Sea to beyond the Altai Mountains. Turks inhabit these lands in a scattered fashion. A small group of Turks who do not possess their freedom live in the Balkans, some on the [Mediterranean] islands, and some in the Arab countries, our southern neighbors. But the great mass live in Asian lands, which begin east of Turkey and extend to the Sea of Japan. We call these enslaved men, who have the same origin [*soydaş*] as us, the "outside" Turks. This is one of the most important problems of Turkey and of the Turks of Turkey. This problem is important for several reasons.

The outside Turks present a problem of national honor. We must think of a nation whose members are enslaved and held prisoner by others, although they are perhaps twice as many as its sons who enjoy liberty. Does not this painful situation hurt and wound, in fact trample under foot, national honor? This is the reality faced by Turks today. Only about 25 million people have their freedom on these lands created by God as the Turk's own domain, whereas twice as many are slaves and prisoners. No other nation in the world faces such a tragic situation. . . .

This painful reality is not encountered by any other modern nation in the world and cannot be borne by the high feeling of human honor. . . .

The outside Turks constitute for Turkey a question of state security. States with a population of 25 or 30 million people surrounded by enemy nations cannot regard their future with confidence. Turkey is one of these states. Consequently, the independence gained by outside Turks, in addition to [satisfying] our national honor, will constitute a guarantee for

Turkey. . . . If the Eastern Turks can establish their independent states on their own fatherland, then Turkey will have on its side a trustworthy brother power and, in case of war, will receive great help from it. . . .

Finally, the outside Turks constitute for the Turks of Turkey a humanitarian problem: Is not the principle of self-determination a humanitarian principle of our age? Those who do not accept this principle are the inhumane regimes and states. In this era of freedom, how can one forget millions of Turks living on their own lands as the slaves of others? Are the descendants of the Turks who lived for 1800 years as the most advanced and superior nation on earth inferior to the Negroes of Africa so as to leave the [outside Turks] under the yoke of tyranny? The civilized world is obliged to think about these unfortunate enslaved people. Indeed, lately, America [the United States] has begun to deal with the question of Turks enslaved by Moscow. . . .

It is indeed painful that the Turks of Turkey are apparently unaware of this problem, which is so important for them. . . . For years, these national problems, vital to Turkey's future, have been covered with a veil. Governments deprived of a national policy have not included in their program the problem of outside Turks. The people who are considered intellectuals . . . prefer to remain silent when faced with the policy of their governments and of high politicians, who avoid the problem of outside Turks. Common people, on the other hand, deprived of the enlightened guidance of intellectuals, are unaware of this national and human problem. . . . Propaganda has made the question of outside Turks appear not as the problem of the freedom of enslaved millions but as a dangerous adventure likely to push Turkey into tragedy. The heroes promoting this negative propaganda based on lies and calumnies are the enemies of Turkey's national problems. The local reds are the leaders and the most fierce exponents of this viewpoint.

It would be a great blow to Russia if the Turks living in their homeland in Asia were to gain their freedom. This is the reason why the native reds are the greatest enemies of the outside Turks. If the Turks living in the eastern Turkic lands were to win their independence, Russia, which is the real fatherland of our own reds, would be shattered, the best lands it exploits would be taken away, and the Kremlin's plans for world domination would go bankrupt. . . . But neither the thick veil thrown upon national problems, nor the sneaky foreign propaganda . . . can obscure the great importance that outside Turks have for the life of Turkey. Those Turkish intellectuals who understand the significance of national problems . . . have defended the cause of freedom for the outside Turks despite everything.

Patriotic Turkish intellectuals, whose number is increasing everyday, will continue to defend this problem as a national cause. This problem will come to an end when the entire Turkic world is independent. . . . The liberation of outside Turks is not a question of armed intervention, as foreign propaganda tries to insinuate. . . . It is a national problem and, therefore, must rest upon ideas, national consciousness, and nationalism. National consciousness and nationalist ideas can never accept any action that may endanger the national life or existence of Turkey. Still, there are a considerable number of things to be done without endangering Turkey. First of all, the Turks of Turkey must be made aware of the importance of the problem of outside Turks. . . . The second question is to make the outside world aware of this problem.

75.   Nationalism-Racism-Turanism in Turkey (A Criticism)

A. N. Kırmacı

The extremely ethnocentric, isolationist wing of the nationalist movement, advocating a conservative, antisocial, elitist nationalism, prevailed in Turkey until the end of World War II. (The moderate and liberal groups remained a minority and, despite their better intellectual preparation, their views had limited impact.) This extreme, antisocial nationalism, which had strong traces of racism, survived well into the 1950s. The Democratic Party government (1950–60) modified considerably the anti-Ottoman, anti-Islamic, and materialist features of the old nationalist ideas, emphasizing instead Turkey's historic spiritual heritage, including Islam. Consequently, racism lost its primacy. The racists, nevertheless, were free to spread their ideas by adjusting them to the new spirit. Türk Yurdu [Turkish Homeland] expressed a highly refined and sophisticated view concerning Turkey's Ottoman Islamic heritage, while reviews such as Hür Adam [Free Man] and Serdengeçti [Volunteer] represented the lowbrow aspect of racist, extremist nationalism. Critics advanced the view that the old type of nationalism, open to racist and Turanist interpretations, was obsolete and utterly unsuited to the spirit and needs of the century. They ridiculed the concepts, myths, and beliefs of the extreme nationalists, and attempted to replace the old type of nationalism with patriotism. Many of the ideological bases of the

---

°Extract from A.N. Kırmacı, "Tükiyede Aşırı Cereyanlar: Milliyetçilik-Irkçılık-Turancılık" ["Radical Currents in Turkey: Nationalism-Racism-Turanism"], Vatan [Fatherland], Istanbul, November 24–27, 1960.

old nationalism, including Ziya Gökalp's ideas, were consequently reinter-preted in the light of new concepts.

On nationalism in Turkey and on Ziya Gökalp, see Niyazi Berkes, Turkish Nationalism and Western Civilization *(New York: Columbia University Press, 1959), and Uriel Heyd,* Foundations of Turkish Nationalism *(London: Luzac-Harvill, 1950).*

The following article appeared in four installments in the daily Vatan *[Fatherland]. Although it is a rather balanced piece of writing, occasional phrases and ideas can be construed as damaging to the nationalists' reputation.* Vatan, *originally a liberal daily, began to support leftist causes after Ahmet Emin Yalman was ousted as its editor in 1960. A. N. Kırmacı is apparently a pen name for one of* Vatan's *writers.*

Before considering the history and nature of nationalism in Turkey and the world, we must stress emphatically the differences between nationalism and patriotism and the need for keeping the two well separated. Patriotism, or love for one's country, is a natural feeling. It is instinctive, inborn in man. This feeling has been present everywhere since the beginnings of social life. It has not been created by history, indoctrination, propaganda, and has not been forcefully and artificially imposed on human societies. This inner and ever-present feeling is rooted in nature, in the land on which one lives, in the air one breathes, in the water one drinks. There are no abstract or ideological aspects of this feeling. . . .

Nationalism, and especially extreme nationalism as applied after World War I, is a confused, abstract, and vague feeling that originated in the not-too remote history of feudalism and the age of empires. Nationalism, when moderate, has some good and constructive aspects, such as defense of national interest, solidarity, and the recognition of the right of self-determination. But it can have extremes and abnormal aspects, such as the refusal to recognize the right of existence to other nations, the desire to revive the glories of the past, to expand everywhere, and to create new forms of empires. The nationalism of the Kemalist regime—that is to say, nationalism in its moderate form—is a normal principle worthy of respect both for us and for others. Nationalism in its extreme, exaggerated, abnormal form is a dangerous and harmful feeling.

The dangers and harm created by [extreme nationalism] are external and internal. Externally, one can no longer [expand] wherever and whenever one wants to.[1] . . . In such a case, God forbid, one may be deprived [of his own territory]. . . . Internally, the danger is also worth considering. The danger lies first in the fact that the sympathizers and promoters of extremism are everywhere—weak and pitiful men who lack ideas, understanding, and integrity. They are enemies of true patriots, of men of thought, and of free intellectuals. . . . They display the darkest form of bigotry toward freedom of thought by branding those who do not hold similar thoughts as leftist, Communist traiter, atheist, Masonic, Zionist, and at least [foreign] agents. But [these extreme nationalists] are the first to fall victim to the trap of real leftists, Communists, and atheists. These nationalists, advancing exaggerated ideas, have not produced one great man, an internationally known thinker, philosopher, artist, sociologist, etc. . . . They ignore the true patriots and free intellectuals. Although they are unaware of the ethics of science, religion, civilization, individual, and society, they propose to give lessons to others in national ethics, values, and education. Still worse, these people often do not believe in their own contentions . . . but strive to build for themselves the reputation of heroes, of models of integrity and morality . . . through soapbox oratory, demagogy, and exploitation of citizens' noble and pure feelings. . . .

[*After giving examples of the damage caused by extreme nationalism to Turkey and the world in general, the author continues his discussion.*]

The nationalism in today's republic—that is to say, Kemalist nationalism—is based above all on liberal, free, and democratic foundations. It recognizes equality in the rights of the individual and society and holds them as sacred and inalienable. It respects the rights and interests of other nations as equal to its own. This is the human and modern understanding of nationalism. Nationalism is different from national bigotry. . . . Kemalist nationalism . . . is an effort to take an honorable place in the family of nations, it strives to work for the ideals of humanity on the path of culture, civilization, and progress as a country and as a nation having the full mastery of its rights and interests within the boundaries of the National Pact.[2] This nationalism has nothing in common with mysticism and chauvinism. In other words, Kemalist nationalism means a free, independent, healthy, and indivisible country and a nation [that strives] in every field of culture and civilization—political, social, economic, financial, and legal. It is the reality of freedom and independence and the ideal of culture and civilization.

Kemalist nationalism is not aristocratic, either. It rejects categorically, in every sense of the word, the supremacy of a class or a group. It does not accept the rule of ideology [*fikir*] and terminology. It is populist. It is, therefore, opposed to the aristocracy of sultanate, caliphate, religion, and even of capital. . . . Kemalist nationalism relies on the sound foundations of reality and national interest and works on the path of right and truth. . . . It is warm love and sincerity, an honest wish and aspiration. In order to be a Turk, it suffices to want to be a Turk and cherish the idea of being one.[3]

Thus, this nationalism is not aggressive, belligerent, and adventurous. It is peace loving and humanist and has the motto: "Peace at home, peace abroad."

[*The author analyzes and rejects racialism as being deprived of sound foundations and concludes that it can lead only to dictatorship and eventually prepare the ground for leftism. He then analyzes the historical causes that gave birth to racialism in Turkey and finds that racialism, Turanism, and the mystical concept of "red apple" [kizil elma] were related and were born basically from the fact that the Turks were deprived of a true concept of national identity. The concept of kızıl elma,[4] found in early Turkish writings, was often referred to by Ziya Gökalp. Kırmacı, apparently quoting Gökalp's ideas about kızıl elma agrees that the concept expressed the yearning for a country with a true Turkish national culture.*]*

> Son, this is our desire on earth: a country with a pure Turkish culture. For centuries, Turks have covered themselves with the glory of heroic deeds. . . . They have invaded India, China, Egypt, Byzantium, the East, and the West . . . but never fulfilled the *kızıl elma*, their wish on earth. Many times, Turks conquered continents. But in reality, they were the ones who were invaded, because their spirit and soul were subject to the environment they conquered. They became Hindus, Arabs, Persians, or Europeans according to the country conquered. A Turkish law and philosophy were not born. . . . We have produced hundreds of famous poets, scientists, philosophers, but they produced their works in Arabic, Persian, Russian, and Chinese. . . . These [thinkers] gave to each of these nations a glorious history. The Turk always sacrificed himself for the others, and his own being remains incomplete. . . . Thus, son, you will find the *kızıl elma* in national unity, national existence, and there the culture and social conscience of the Turkish community will develop. . . .

Ziya Gökalp has insisted upon *hars*, or national culture, as having the basic meaning of that indestructible quality of national identity [i.e., national personality]. It was not a culture that rested exclusively on unity of flesh, blood, bones, form, color, or origin. That culture was to be the product of nature, of the place and time, and, if one may say also, in part of the land on which one lives, of the fatherland, and the climate . . . The source of culture is in the people [*halk*]—indeed, the large masses of people. Consequently, the nationalism of Ziya Gökalp is democratic in the truest sense of the term. Extreme nationalism and racialism, as they are understood today, have no relationship whatsoever to this democratic attitude. . . . The utterly dangerous psychology created by extreme nationalism and racialism in men, and especially in the leaders of this movement, is the same everywhere. This psychology manifests itself in megalomania;

... once in power, such men begin to think that mankind did not produce and will never produce men similar to themselves. ...

[*After bitterly criticizing Hitler and Mussolini and the great harm they caused to mankind, the author concludes.*]

One cannot ignore the fact that the sympathizers of these extreme movements still exist in Turkey as they do elsewhere in the world and that, at times, they try furtively, behind the scenes, to play effective roles. But we cannot and will never accept these men as the masters of our destiny. Those days ... are past for Turkey. After the struggle for national liberation and the movements for establishing a republic and reforms, Turkey has become a country that looks forward not backward. Blessed and many times [blessed] be Atatürk.

Notes

1. An allusion to Turanism.
2. The pact of 1919, which laid the political and territorial foundations of modern Turkey.
3. İnönü's expression.
4. According to Osman Turan, the *kızıl elma* was a myth that "symbolized the ideal of world domination." The idea derived from a brilliant metal ball on Justinian's monument in the church of St. Sophia. The Turks believed that possession of that ball would help them achieve world domination. Osman Turan, "The Ideal of World Domination Among the Medieval Turks," *Studia Islamica* 4 (1955): 77–90.

76. Science, Nationality, and Westernism; Women in Islam

Necmettin Erbakan

Necmettin Erbakan, born in Sinop in 1926, belongs to the Kozanoğlu family, which had established de facto rule in southeastern Anatolia until defeated by the central government army in 1865. One of the six children of a judge, Erbakan completed his religious education in Trabzon and Istanbul, along with his lay studies. He graduated from the Engineering University in Istanbul in 1948 and continued his postdoctoral studies in mechanical engineering in Germany, working in a tank plant. Upon his return to Turkey he eventually (1965) became professor at his alma mater. He showed his interest in business by establishing a motor plant and by becoming the head of the Union of Chambers, a position from which he was ousted by Suleyman Demirel, the chairman of the Justice Party, his schoolmate and political adversary. Erbakan tried to join the Justice Party but was refused admission, as he was suspected of ambitious political designs. He entered the Parliament in 1969 as an independent deputy from Konya, the religious center which became the stronghold of his party, the Milli Nizam Partisi (Party of National Order). Closed down in 1971 for violating secularism by the military regime then in power, the party reemerged two years later as the Milli Selamet Partisi—National Salvation Party (NSP). In 1972, while still a member of the National Assembly, Erbakan introduced unsuccessfully a resolution to amend the constitution to permit full religious freedom, as a "democratic regime cannot exist without the rights and freedoms of thought and belief." He advocated recognition of history, nationality, traditions, and religion as part of Turkey's national identity and heritage, and he won an impressive victory in the elections of 1973, when his party, though newly formed, gained over 11 percent of the total votes cast and secured 48 seats in the National Assembly. In 1974 Erbakan became deputy prime minister in a coalition government in association with the Republican People's Party (RPP), the father of secularism. Eight months later the coalition with RPP ended due to Premier Ecevit's refusal to share power with his partner, and Erbakan joined other coalitions headed by Suleyman Demirel. As deputy premier he introduced ambitious plans for massive industrialization and advocated better distribution of income. Nevertheless, his party lost considerable popularity in the elections of 1977. He attempted a comeback in 1979, embracing a more orthodox Islamist view. He supported the Islamic revolution in Iran and sided with other Muslim countries, while growing increasingly hostile to Western culture and capitalism. In 1980 his party organized a series of rallies to assert the Islamic character of Turkish society and to advocate closer identification with Muslim causes throughout the world. These meetings played an important part in undermining the authority of Demirel's government and in precipitating the military intervention of September 12, 1980, which led to the arrest of Erbakan and the banishment of his party.

The actual views of Erbakan on Islam cannot be called truly fundamentalist; he does not even appeal for return to traditional religion. He is basically a religious-nationalist who sees the need to recognize and reconcile the Turks' historical identity with the science and technology of contemporary society but rejects the Western arts, literature, social mores, and culture that were the backbone of Turkey's early cultural reformism. Erbakan rejected the view that the West should be regarded as superior because it was the source of science; he claimed that Muslim mathematicians and astronomers had dealt with physical laws centuries before the West. He continuously attacked the tendency of the Muslims, especially the Turks, to feel inferior toward the West because of its science and technology, and he spoke out against their preference for Western literature, music, and arts to the detriment of their own. He saw "culture" as the ensemble of all the values which give the nation its personality and religion and as a unique, basic system of thought and belief. Despite his Islamist views, Erbakan was at first regarded with considerable suspicion by Muslim fundamentalists in the Middle East. Even the Saudis treated him rather coldly in the early 1970s, although recently he seemed to have become more popular due to his new and strong pro-Islamic views on international policy. His compromises, made for the sake of government position and power, enabled the Justice Party successfully to attract into its ranks many of the followers of the NSP, *and deprived Erbakan of much following and indirectly forced him, for lack of suitable issues, to embrace a more extremist Islamic view. There is no evidence that Erbakan or his party were connected with the Muslim Brethren; in fact, the opposite may be true, as many religious groups suspected of having relations with the Brethren acted independently of, and even hostilely toward, Erbakan. The* Nurcular, *that is, the followers of Said Nursi (discussed below), who represent one of the main Muslim fundamentalist groups in Turkey, maintained their independence. Erbakan's views on Islam are not expressed in a cohesive organized fashion, but in a variety of fragmented, simple statements accompanied by concrete examples designed to support his contentions.*

The views of Erbakan and of the NSP were disseminated in a variety of publications, especially the Milli Gazete, *the party newspaper. One of the most comprehensive studies is Tufan Çorumlu,* Büyük Türkiyeye Doğru, Erbakan Olayı *[Towards Great Turkey, the Event of Erbakan] (Istanbul: Selamet Publications, 1974); a critical book is Necdet Onur's* Erbakan Dosyası *[Erbakan's File] (Istanbul: n.p., n.d.). Erbakan's own publications include* Milli Görüş ve Anayasa Değişikliği *[National View and Constitutional Amendment] (Ankara: Seler Offset, 1972);* Islam ve Ilim *[Islam and Science] (Ankara: Aga'-Iş, 1972);* Üç Konferans *[Three Talks] (Istanbul: Fetih, 1974). The excerpts below are from* Üç Konferans, *pp. 23–26, 49–73 passim.*

Islam and Science

[The first point to be made is that] the history of science indicates that mankind's knowledge began to increase at a point in the happy

century—*asr-ı saadet*—or the seventh [A.D.].... This first point represents the date at which Muslims took science from other human beings
[from all over the world] and began to develop it. The next point to be
made concerns Renaissance, that is, the period after the Crusades when
the Europeans began to implement the science they took from the
Muslims. There is therefore a period of seven centuries between the
"happy century" and the Renaissance when the Muslims developed the
entire science of mankind. Research shows that 60 to 70 percent of today's
positive sciences were developed by Muslims. What is the meaning of all
this? It means that more than half of the science with which these
[Western] people try to impress and make the Muslims feel inferior
belongs actually to the Muslims....

These [Western] people are not content to tell us that we [Muslims]
are unaware of the existence of Western sciences, but they also disseminate and repeat the false ideas of the anti-Muslim orientalists [who claim]
that Muslims have not contributed to science as much as I have tried to
describe. They claim that Muslims adopted and assimilated the sciences of
ancient Greece, India, and Egypt and advanced them just a little, and then
surendered them to the Europeans. This is completely wrong. It is true
that Muslims studied and adopted the sciences of ancient Egyptians and
Greeks and Indians but they did so following three distinct characteristics.

1. They indicated the source book from which they took the
    information. They said, we read the book of Ptolomey, of Euclid,
    and indicated the content. They said, we read the book of
    Pythagoras, and indicated what they took from these books;
2. The Muslim scientists, in adopting the information supplied by
    the ancients, did not take it uncritically. They did not accept that
    information immediately either. They accepted the information
    after correcting and [supplementing it];
3. The Muslim scientists were in a more developed position than the
    Greeks, Egyptians, and Hindus from whom they took the science.
    This was a reception of science from the bottom upward....

The Europeans, on the other hand, often [deviated from the] three
characteristics [indicated above] after establishing contacts with the
Muslims through the Crusades and after beginning to take the Muslims'
science.

1. Europeans never mentioned the source of [their] science. They
    read books written by Muslims but never mentioned the informa-
    tion or its source. Other Europeans who read their books believed
    that the [book] was the writer's original creation....

2. Europeans adopted these sciences without understanding their [true] meaning. . . .

3. The Europeans' level of [intellectual] development was inadequate at the time of the acceptance [of this science] to allow them an [authentic] understanding. Europeans adopted the Muslims' science from the top downwards. The Europeans' command of language was not sufficient for the reception. The Europeans could not comprehend the terms in the Muslim books. They began to understand the terms adopted in the 14th century only in the 18th. . . .

[Erbakan goes on to describe how Muslims were superior in science by giving examples from astronomy, mathematics—trigonometry was their creation, and they first used sine, cosine, and so forth—physics, chemistry, geography, and so on.]

Islamic Economics and Women in the West and East

The view of the Western world is dominated by Christian thought. There is in this thought an after life idea, but it is not clear as is the case with the Muslims. The idea of Trinity dominates the Western thought. There is no unity about the Oneness of God, a clear belief that He is the only divine Being. . . . As far as women are concerned, at first sight the Western woman appears to be far ahead and in a happier position [than women in the East]. But she is not fully satisfied and at peace with herself because equality with men demands that she be employed in the heaviest jobs as men. Women [in the West] are expected to earn money. If the woman does not contribute [financially to the household], then this materialistic way of [looking at things] is likely to look upon her as an inferior [member of the family]. A man earning money would feel that he brings a greater contribution to the family. This undermines true happiness. . . . When compared with the Eastern woman the Western woman appears to enjoy better living conditions and humane treatment. Now, one may ask . . . what is the real happiness and where is the woman's place? The woman's real place is in Islam. . . . Today, there is not yet a truly Islamic world with its own world view, economic, and social systems. But the fact that such a system does not exist does not deny the truth that Islam has the most ideal system. Consequently, we shall define the value attached to women by Islam and the means devised to lead women to happiness only after viewing briefly the [ideal] economic and social systems of Islam and its world view.

Islam has its own unique economic system which is neither Eastern [communist] or Western [capitalist]. Islam has two dimensions, material and spiritual, and has managed to maintain both of them in a balanced fashion.... The Islamic economic system takes materialism into full account. Everyone has a right to possess property for himself. It is immune, and nobody has the right to question or envy [the property right].... Islam attaches also importance to profit and to earning as indicated by the saying "the giving hand is superior to the receiving hand." The meaning of this saying is that every Muslim is obliged to work for a living and to help others... The hard worker is loved by Allah and is Allah's beloved. Such a view [on the work ethic] appears to resemble the Western concept. But the Islamic system is not similar to the Western capitalism. The big difference is the following: The Muslim must earn, but not to squander ... the Muslim is obliged to spend his earnings in a beneficial manner. The Western man does not have such a principle; he can spend his earned money as he wishes.... In this manner the Islamic system corrects the harmful aspects of the Western economic regimes, and thus it is capable, through its own measures, of reaching lofty ideals in a way unattainable by capitalism.... Thus in this [Islamic] economic system the materialistic and spiritual aspects [of life] cannot be separated from each other....

In the social life of Islam the family is the basis of society. It is a concept of family which includes not only all the members of the family but also their rights and their obligations of [mutual] respect and love. It places high priority on neighborliness. Even the 40th house in a row is considered a neighbor.... A Muslim in meeting another one should not think about what he could get, but about what he could give and how he could benefit the other....

Now let us take a look at the place of the woman in the Muslim world [which has developed] such a social system. The Muslim woman has a place in the economic life of society and can work. In fact women are encouraged to take work in certain services.... In one Muslim country, for instance, women were preferred, in fact encouraged, to work as nurses in hospitals. It is also preferable that the doctors taking care of women be women. In a Muslim structure women work in other professions too.... In Islam women can work and can become a factor of economic life. Islam has placed an equal obligation on women as on men to engage in science as much as in praying. The Almighty does not differentiate people as man, woman, black, or white. The best person is the one with the greatest fear of God. In God's view there cannot be a question of man's or woman's superiority over one another.

Islam has assigned duties to women in accordance with their nature. Islam never imposed working obligations on women as in the [communist]

East or West. . . . In a Muslim family the woman is not obliged to perform any work. She is not obliged even to take care of [provide a living for] the child. It is the duty of the male to take care of the house and to supply all its needs. In Islam women are advised to perform duties compatible with their nature; but if she works more than [required], this is something which she accomplishes voluntarily and must be considered a favor for which she will be rewarded in the next world.

[After quoting a number of verses from the Koran to support his views on women, Erbakan continued.]

Woman in the Islamic world is a respected being. She is the foundation of society and is the model of cleanliness and good upbringing. . . . She is a candidate for Paradise. In the Islamic framework, the Paradise is at the service of mothers. The Paradise is under her feet.

77. Nationalism in Islam

Said Nursi

Said Nursi was born in 1873 in the village of Nurs in Bitlis, Eastern Turkey, and died in 1960. He is known by various names—al-Ustad Bediuzzaman to his followers, and Said Kurdi to his enemies, notably the secularists who denounced him. Nursi defended the orthodox principles of Islam, stressing their spiritual and universalist dimensions; socially he was a conservative, defending the status quo. He played a major role in the ideological discussions during the Young Turks era (1908–18) and, thereafter, in modern Turkey. His defense of a spiritualism rooted in religion contrasted sharply with the materialism and the alienation perceived by some to lie in secularism. Nursi still has a large number of followers in Turkey, despite a legal ban on his teachings, as well as abroad, including several groups in the United States and Canada. Literature on Nursi and his views includes Çetin Özek, Türkiyede Gerici Akımlar ve Nurculuğun İçyüzü [Regressive Movements in Turkey and the Inside of Nurculuk] (Istanbul: Varlik, 1964); Faruk Güventürk, Din Işığı Altında Nurculuğun İçyüzü [The Inside of Nurculuk in the Light of Religion] (Ankara: Okat, 1964). The excerpt below on Islam's view of nationalism, although published originally in 1931, retains its contemporary value. It appeared as the third subject of the twenty-sixth letter of his book Mektubat [Writings] (Istanbul: Sinan, 1958). It was translated and published by his followers (Talabat-an-Nur) in the United States (El Cerrito, Calif., 1975).

> O mankind! We created you from a single [pair] of a male and a female, and made you into nations and tribes, that ye may know each other. (*Qur'an* 49:13)

In other words, to know each other in order to establish social relations and to help each other, and not to hate each other and quarrel with each other.

This topic has the following seven points under consideration:

1. I would like to write, not with the language of the "New Said" who would like to withdraw from the present social life, but perhaps with the language of the "Old Said" who was connected to the then social life of Islam.

    This I would like to do for the purpose of rendering a service to [the message of] the Glorious Qur'an and establishing ramparts against the attacks on it.

2. To explain the principle of *ta'aruf* and *ta'awun* (mutual acquaintance and assistance) which the above verse clearly points to, we say that:

    > An army is divided into divisions, regiments, battalions, squadrons and squads in order that the various relations of each soldier and his duties are specific and well understood, and that all the individuals within the army should perform their duties according to the rules of mutual cooperation and be guarded against the attack of the enemy. Thus these divisions and partitions are not for the purpose of rivalries and hostilities among the soldiers. Similarly, the whole Muslim society is a vast united army which is divided into tribes and nationalities, yet this society has a multitude of ones in its pious foundation. Its Creator is one; its Provider of needs is one; its Book is one; its nation is one . . . one, one, and thousands of ones.

    Thus, this multitude of ones requires and forms the foundation of brotherhood, sincerity and unity in the Islamic *Ummah*. Therefore, as the above verse stresses, divisions into tribes and nationalities are for the purpose of mutual acquaintance and assistance, not for antipathy nor for dispute and enmity.

3. Within this twentieth century the idea of nationalism has surely flourished. In particular, the intriguing Europeans have viciously implanted this idea among Muslims in order to arouse in them antagonism toward each other so that they could become fragmented, exploited and an easy prey, or even be annihilated. And yet the idea of nationalism has an emotional appeal. It has a flavor which leads to heedlessness, and it has a strength which breeds

inauspiciousness. It is therefore quite difficult at present to advise those who are preoccupied with social order to detach themselves from this doctrine of nationalism.

However, there are two types of nationalism. The first is a source of antagonism; it is ill-omened and dangerous. It survives by exploiting and exterminating other ideologies: it perpetuates hostility and suspicion toward other systems. This type of nationalism is a source of hostility and a catalyst for confusion and disorder. Furthermore, a *hadith* clearly discourages it: "Islam cuts off the partisanship of the Days of Ignorance." Also the Glorious Qur'an states that:

> When those who disbelieve had set up in their hearts zealotry, the zealotry of the Age of Ignorance, then Allah sent down His peace of reassurance upon His Messenger and upon the believers and imposed on them the word of self-restraint, for they were worthy of it and meet for it. And Allah is Aware of all things. (*Qur'an* 48:26)

Thus the above *hadith* and *ayat* categorically forbid nationalistic rivalry because the rational and sacred Islamic Ideology does not need this philosophy. Indeed, is there any other ideology which has three hundred and fifty million followers?° Is there any other ideology besides Islam which can provide a sincere and eternal brotherhood to its followers? Certainly the dangers of racist nationalism have been seen time and again throughout history. For example the Umayyad Dynasty had included an element of nationalistic rivalry into their political administration. As a result, not only did the Muslim world become resentful toward them, but the dynasty itself had numerous disasters. Similarly, the European nations of this century have again delved deeply into their racist philosophy, and this has caused, for example, a permanent hostility between the French and the Germans. Furthermore, the horrible events of World War I proved how nationalistic rivalry was a source of a tremendous loss for mankind.

As in our case [the Ottomans], during the "Freedom Movement" (1908–18)—similar to the time of the destruction of the Tower of Babylon when the confusion of languages led to divisions of people and to an eventual disintegration—inspired by nationalistic rivalry with the Greeks and Armenians heading the

---

°The population of Muslims throughout the world was approximately 350 million when this article was written.

list, numerous separatists formed various nationalistic organizations under the title of "clubs" or refugee organizations. This eventually caused great division and dispersion and the unavoidable exploitation of Muslims by foreign powers has proven the ills of this philosophy.

Now more than ever, Muslim peoples are desperately in need of one another. They are being wronged and not prospering, and are being exploited by foreign powers. With the state of affairs as it is, for Muslim peoples, inspired by racist nationalism, to treat each other with indifference or hostility is nothing but to invite indescribable disasters. This is similar to the foolishness of someone who turns his back on poisonous snakes to avoid a fly. . . .

4. The second type of nationalism is a positive one. It is necessary to social existence. It is a source of mutual assistance, understanding and solidarity. It assures a beneficial strength and becomes a means of increasing collaboration for Islamic brotherhood. This positive established concept must be used to serve Islam. It must be the armor and castle of Islam, for there are a thousand bonds of brotherhood in the Islamic ideology. The Islamic brotherhood continues in this world and in the Hereafter, so it is eternal. No matter how strong the brotherhood of nationalism is, it can only be a small fraction compared to the brotherhood of Islam. It would be a serious mistake to substitute the Islamic brotherhood with a nationalistic one. It would be like replacing precious diamonds in the treasury of a castle with the stones of the castle walls. . . .

It should be noted that the Turkish peoples, who are in great numbers in the Muslim world no matter in which part of the world they live, are all Muslims. Unlike other peoples, they are not divided as are Muslims and non-Muslims. All Turkish tribes in the past have been Muslims. Those Turks who left Islam, as well as those who did not embrace Islam, also abandoned their Turkish identity [as in the case of the Hungarians].

O Turkish brothers, you must be extremely careful. Your nationality has blended with Islam; they are inseparable. If separated, you will be utterly destroyed. All your past glories have been recorded as Islamic history. Since no force will be able to erase this sense of pride from the face of the earth, why should you, then, because of the evil suggestions and deceitful role of Satan, erase that sense from your hearts?

5. The awakening peoples of Asia have begun to follow nationalism and they are imitating the European ways in every aspect, so

much so that in the process they are sacrificing a great part of their spiritual and cultural values. Still, each nation's value structure needs a different cloth; even if it uses the same material, it needs a different design. . . . The Asian nations' awakening, progress and proper administration ought to be through faith, through religious conviction. Thus, philosophy and science should be auxiliaries of the faith, but not a substitute for it.

Second, it is a great error to compare Islam to Christianity and to become indifferent toward Islam on the premise of European ideas. Moreover, Europeans are protective of their religion. Very many Westerners, including a number of political leaders such as Woodrow Wilson, Lloyd George and Venizelos, were very fond of their religion. Obviously, Europeans guard their religion. Probably in some aspects they are very zealous and fanatical.

Third, one cannot compare Islam to Christianity, because when Europeans were following religion strictly, they were uncivilized; they became civilized by abandoning their fanaticism and bigotry. Moreover, religious controversies have caused three hundred years of internal conflicts and wars among the European nations. [Islamic societies reached high civilization and unity through Islam.]

6. Finally, we say to those extremists who are involved in nationalistic rivalry and racism that the world, especially our country [Turkey], has historically been the place of many migrations and constant changes. However, after the establishment of the Islamic government [Ottoman Empire] in this country, people from other races and ethnic groups have settled, mixed and become citizens. Under these conditions, the real origins of people can be distinguished only when the tablets of God's decrees, which are to be preserved to the end of time, are uncovered. Therefore, to establish one's conduct and benevolence on sheer racialism is both meaningless and very harmful.

7. We remind those people who attempt to demonstrate superfluous patriotism through this negative nationalism that if you possess true love and respect for this nation, and if you truly have affection, then you must follow such a patriotism that concerns the majority of the people; otherwise, a service which operates in a merciless manner against the majority while it enhances the temporal, mundane lives of a heedless minority, who do not need such compassion, is not patriotism. . . . *Alas! Where is the respect for the nation and where is the sacrifice for its sake?*

We cannot cease our hope for Allah's mercy and compassion. For Allah,

Who designated the great army of this land and this esteemed people for one thousand years for the cause of Islam and appointed them as a standard bearer for this duty, Insha-Allah will not scatter them because of temporary failures. Allah again will kindle that light and will make them continue to carry out their obligations.

XXIII. LEFT OF CENTER: SOCIALISM AND MARXISM

78.   Left of Center: What Is It?

Bülent Ecevit

Bülent Ecevit (b. 1925) began his career as a journalist and a deputy from Ankara in the Grand National Assembly. As a member of the People's Republican party, he was minister of labor in the coalition governments in 1961–65. It was largely because of his efforts that labor legislation was enacted and workers as a group were incorporated into the social and constitutional system that emerged after the revolution of 1960.

Ecevit's political career, which began under Inönü's protective wing, showed a spectacular development in the 1970s. He and a group within the Republican Party claimed that the party's leaders at the national and provincial level, although faithful to Atatürk's basic principles of republicanism, secularism, and modernism, were socially conservative and unwilling to acknowledge the demands of the youth, the workers, and the lower income groups in the cities for a social democratic program. Moreover, Ecevit and his group contended that because the party appeared identified with the old bureaucratic military groups bent on maintaining the political status quo, it lost considerable popularity, as shown by the results of the elections of 1961 and 1965. Consequently, they proposed the drastic ideological reorientation of the party toward a form of social democracy that came to be known as the ortanın solu (left of center). The new ideology rejected Marxism and communism, as well as the old form a nationalism, formulated by Atatürk, that had been basis of the party until the 1960s. Instead, it preached social justice, populism, and economic development based on massive state support, without rejecting private enterprise or individual ownership of property. The new ideology called for a liberal political democracy and proposed grandiose social programs well beyond the country's economic capacity. The fundamental weakness of the left of center ideology was its lack of profound philosophical roots or of organic connection with the cultural, historical, political, and traditional forces within Turkish society. It was, in fact, the result of sentimental political impulse stemming from a humanitarian sympathy for the underdog which could, when expressed with Ecevit's eloquence, captivate certain audiences and attract them to the party. The new ideology had a temporary appeal for the fast expanding group of the educated, the bureaucracy, and certain segments of the urban population. For the rest of the population, despite the efforts of Ecevit's group to build their ideology into a true dynamic force, the left of center remained essentially a rootless, ephemeral current of thought that appeared no different from any of the other eclectic and impractical ideas developed by Turkish intellectuals in the past by collating selected bits from various European ideologies that were hardly suitable to Turkey's conditions. Ecevit rejected Marxism, but the nature of much of what he proposed, coupled with his expression of the intention to "change the existing order," led his opponents to accuse him of crypto-Marxism and communism. Finally, the provocative, ruthless tactics he used to defeat his opponents, as well as his continuous support for all radical leftist groups, led many to believe that Ecevit strove to make up through activist ferment what his ideology lacked in depth and scope.

The "left of center" ideology, disseminated by the periodical Özgür Insan [Free Human Being] nevertheless profoundly affected developments within the party. A dissenting group under Turhan Feyzioğlu broke off to form the Republican Reliance Party. Ecevit's denunciation of the military intervention of 1971 led to a conflict with Inönü and eventually to the latter's resignation as chairman of the party in 1972, whereupon Ecevit was elevated to that position and a political era came to an end. Ecevit was only the third man after Atatürk and Inönü to hold the position of chairman of the Republican Party, but he abandoned most of the old ideology of the party, despite the fact that it was also the ideological foundation of the Republic. Meanwhile, the massive influx into the cities of new immigrants who leaned temporarily toward social democracy increased the Republicans' vote. Ecevit regarded the electoral success as an endorsement of his "ideology" and, consequently, he shifted even further to the Left, replacing the "left of center" watchword with words such as "democratic Left" and "socialism." He rejected many of his former ideas; for example, he originally favored nonpolitical trade unionism, as the excerpts in this work indicate, but he shifted later to a position in favor of worker's direct participation in party politics. He was briefly a prime minister in a government established in coalition with the religious National Salvation Party in 1974, and at that time he had a chance to enhance his popularity by ordering the Turkish army into Cyprus in accordance with existing treaties. He occupied the position of prime minister again in 1978–79, until the by-election of October 1979 dealt the RPP a crushing defeat; its vote dropped to 27 percent and it lost to the Justice Party all five assembly seats contested. He resigned as premier in 1979, and shortly after the military takeover on September 12, 1980, he relinquished his seat as party chairman.

There is no question but that Ecevit played a major ideological and political role in Turkey in the period from 1965 to 1980. It is still too early to pass final judgment on him. It may be stated that, by gathering the bulk of the Left around his party, he inhibited the growth of the five or six ultraradical leftist parties. During the ten years from 1970 to 1980, Turkey achieved a social, economic, and political transformation of major proportions both in depth and scope, one that reached the remotest villages, and altered much of the country's traditional, as well as "conservative" outlook. Ecevit committed many errors. He lacked true understanding of Turkey's cultural and historical problems. Although basically ignorant of authentic Turkish-Islamic traditions of the people whom he proposed to lead (his speeches, full of unintelligible words and expressions completely outside the village vernacular, show his ignorance in this regard), he sought nevertheless to express the views of the downtrodden as nobody had ever done before. He did help articulate many of Turkey's problems and, inadvertently, probably speeded up Turkey's inevitable transformation into a more modern society, and probably also prepared the ground for the emergence of a real leader.

Ecevit's writings, usually delivered as speeches, have appeared under various headings. There is also a fairly rich literature about him, written by both his enemies and his admirers. From his own words one may cite Ortanin Solu *(Left of Center), which was printed first in 1966 and had gone through six editions by 1974;* Bu Düzen Değişmelidir *[This Regime Must Change] (Ankara: Tekin Yayınevi, 1968; 3d ed., 1974),* Kurultaylar ve Sonrası *[Conventions and After] (Ankara: Ileri, 1972), and* Atatürk ve Devrimcilik *[Revolution and Atatürk] (Ankara: Tekin, 1970; 3d ed., 1974). For information about Ecevit, see Ali Topuzoğlu,* Halk Adamı, Ecevit, *[Ecevit, People's Man] (Istanbul: Özdemir, 1975).*

The first excerpt below appeared in Ecevit's Ortanın Solu, *6th ed. (Ankara: Tekin, 1974), pp. 1–6 passim; the latter two are from* What Is Left of Center? *(Ankara: Turkish Press Directorate, 1979), pp. 13–14, 25–46.*

This is not a scientific work. This is the definition and justification of an understanding of humanity and a political attitude based on that understanding. The book strives to evaluate the political and social conditions in Turkey from the view point of a [humanitarian] understanding and behavior and proposes to solve the problems of the Turkish society and to indicate reliable ways to solve these problems according to that [humanitarian viewpoint]. If a human being's thinking is liberated from pressure and his personality is allowed to develop freely, and if he receives education in accordance with his ability and aptitude, he will reach a certain level of development. A social order and a government which does not permit everybody to reach their due level [of development] is against humanity. A social order and a government which allows some beings to reach their due level and prevents others from doing so is against both humanity and justice. . . . If you rebel on behalf of society and humanity as well as of those who did not find the means [to develop], and if you see this [failure] as a blemish and as an injustice against humanity, and if you can feel inwardly the instinct and the desire to correct this injustice and deprivation in society, then you are a person [ideologically] left of center. . . .

The Republican Peoples Party's View of Turkey's Reform and Foreign Relations

In countries that are in the process of development, capitalist regimes face difficulties in following independent policies of defense and foreign relations, and in being sufficiently libertarian and democratic. For, international capitalism by which such regimes involuntarily become influenced, is disturbed by libertarian democracy in developing countries and by labor rights and public opinion pressures that come with libertarian democracy. International capitalism carries the notion that a regime which curtails democracy, civil liberties and labor rights can provide greater profit, leave a larger share of added value, and permit greater freedom in steering the economy of the country.

Since the democratic leftist concept of progress and development as advocated by the Republican Peoples Party postulates a system different from capitalism wherein the people and the state shall mutually supervise national economy. The Republican Peoples Party is in a good position to follow nationalistic courses in economic, foreign and defense policies as well as in international relations in general. In this respect, nationalism and populism complement each other. Thus, authenticated by the democratic leftist stance through the concentration of economic power in the hands of the people, through the extension among working people of the liberties to organize and of their rights to participate in administration, libertarian democracy shall constitute a strong guarantee for independence and national sovereignty. In the democratic leftist system which the Republican Peoples Party intends to institute, populism shall be the source of nationalism, and freedom shall be the foundation of independence. In such a system together with accelerating development, extensive social justice, and strong democratic tradition, national independence shall also be reinforced and based on sound foundation. The Republican Peoples Party adheres to principles of honesty and consistency, essentials of morality as well as of an open regime, as unequivocal rules of foreign policy and international relations. In this age of extensive communication, the Republican Peoples Party believes that the tactics of showing different faces to different groups of states have lost its currency, and that in order to establish sound relations with other states, and to obtain the support of world public opinion, honesty, consistency, and reliability are necessary qualities. The Republican Peoples Party considers it a duty to ensure the interest and contribution of every section of society to matters of foreign policy and international relations, and to establish extensive international relations as a political party. While establishing solidarity and intellectual cooperation with political parties close to the democratic leftist stance for national interests as well as the interests of mankind, the Republican Peoples Party shall attempt to cultivate and develop close relations with other political establishments in friendly and neighbouring countries for the sake of mutual interest and regional as well as global peace. The Republican Peoples Party considers it important to accelerate Turkey's opening to the world, and to further her international relations by means of cultural, scientific and sports exchanges and with the help of youth groups, labor unions, cooperatives, professional associations and people in business.

Ideological Approach to Foreign Politics

We should also avoid any ideological approach to issues of foreign politics. Examples abound in our day and age, illustrating that it is impossible to relate foreign politics to ideology beyond a certain measure.

States which claim to take up issues of foreign politics from an ideological angle have been forced to accept the weight of different extra-ideological factors even if they may be able to behave ideologically—consistent up to a point.

Not only can we observe that certain super-powers who claim to be missionaries of democracy in the world establish close friendship and alliances with countries living under dictatorial regimes of the most repressive kind, but we can also observe that certain communist states who claim to look at all issues, including those of foreign politics, ideologically are able to behave with deadly animosity towards each other. The relations between USSR and China and their approaches to USA illustrates clearly that point.

The Significance of Small States in Our Age

Our age is one in which great States are becoming even more powerful yet in which smaller States are also growing in significance and influence. These smaller countries will be successful in their foreign politics to the degree that they utilize this particularity of the age.

One of the basic conditions for this success lies in being attentive and sensitive not only towards the animosity of super powers but also towards their friendship. This attentiveness and sensitivity is accomplished by avoiding the emotional as well as the ideological approach to foreign politics.

It is one thing to be a great and powerful State, it is another to be a great nation. No one can take away the greatness of the Turkish Nation. It is quality of greatness molded by history. Indeed, the Turkish Nation has been able to preserve her greatness even when she had lost all her material resources. However, Turkey is no more a super State. Neither is the Turkish State one of the most powerful States of the world—not anymore. We must come to terms with this reality. But when facing this reality we must also not be caught in an inferiority complex and feel that we must follow other great and powerful States in whatever they do.

Even if their country may be small and their State powerless, nations have the possibility to cope with even the most powerful of States. The Turkish nation has given the first and the most successful example of this in this age. In a period when it had lost all her material stength, when its State had collapsed out, when its land was being divided it was able to subdue the greatest and the most powerful States of the World.

These possibilities have increased in the present day world. For great powers are being crushed under their own greatness in small wars. Their greatness has even become obstacles for them in certain cases.

A Turkey which is attentive towards the particularities and possibilities of the time, which assigns as much importance to her economic interests and development as to her national security and independence and which conducts a type of foreign politics developed within the framework of free and democratic exchange of ideas, can not only further her alliance with powerful States without being tricked, crushed or without compromising her independence but it can also strengthen its security with new friendships and be of benefit to peace, regionally as well as globally.

79. The Philosophy and Purpose of the Labor Party of Turkey*

The Labor Party of Turkey was established by a small group of trade unionists in 1961. One year later, its leadership was assumed by Mehmet Ali Aybar (b. 1910), a Turk who was educated in France, where he became a Marxist. Despite its efforts, the Labor Party has failed to attract many workers, and its membership is composed mainly by the urban intelligentsia. Yet the party's propagandists, although hindered by an internal struggle between "dogmatists" and "revisionists," have fought energetically to spread their views in towns and even villages. For tactical reasons, the party has accepted outwardly the idea of free parliamentary elections. An extensive party program was adopted at the party convention on February 11, 1964. The party split into several groups due to dissension over the attitude toward the USSR after the invasion of Czechoslovakia in 1968. It lost power and influence because of internecine fights. Eventually Behice Boran, representing the pro-Soviet wing became chairwoman without being able to resuscitate it. Numerically, as one of the six leftist-marxist parties, its power is insignificant. It retains a certain historical importance for having brought Marxism to public attention and for having established the first and largest leftist political party. These excerpts are taken from a pamphlet expressing the party's basic viewpoint, which was preserved in the new program. (See also Kemal H. Karpat, "Socialism and the Labor Party of Turkey," Middle East Journal 21 [Spring 1967]: 157–72.

In Articles 2 and 3 of its bylaws, the Labor Party of Turkey [Türkiye Işçi Partisi—TIP] has indicated the people to whom it belongs, the people whose rights, freedom, and interests it defends, and the means to be used in attaining these goals. The Labor Party of Turkey is the party of our poor people, who depend on their labor for their livelihood. The two articles describing the characteristics and purposes of the party are as follows:

Article 2: The characteristics of the party. TIP is the political organization of the Turkish labor class and of the working classes and groups (farm hands, small farmers, salary and wage earners, craftsmen, artisans, low-income professionals, progressive youth, and socialist intellectuals) gathered around it and following its [labor class] democratic leadership for attaining power through legal means. TIP evaluates events at home and

---

°Extract from *Türkiye Işçi Partisi Kimlerin Partisidir?* [To Whom Does the Labor Party Belong?] Istanbul: Sıralar Matbaası, 1962), pp. 1–4.

abroad from the viewpoint of the labor class and of the toiling popular masses; it defends their rights and struggles to materialize their rights and freedoms.

The toiling masses of people constitute the majority of the nation and are the real source of all riches and values and the only driving force for social progress. They bear the heavy burden of this progress. Consequently, the struggle for the rights, freedoms, and interests of the masses of people is a struggle for the rights, freedoms, and high interests of the Turkish nation as a whole.

TIP ranks are open to all citizens who accept the party program and bylaws and side with labor, regardless of their race, faith, sect, color of skin, sex, and class [social] origin.

Article 3: The purpose of the party. The purpose of TIP is to materialize the principles indicated in its program through the rights and freedoms recognized by the constitution and the laws. The question of making Turkey an advanced society and the question of placing the toiling masses of people in a position to decide about the affairs of the country (and of enabling them to live in human conditions) are two interrelated aspects of the same problem. One cannot be achieved without the other. If the toiling masses of people cannot be made to display enthusiasm and confidence for work through the achievement of [decent] human living conditions, Turkey cannot develop herself and cannot reach the level of contemporary civilization. TIP has understood this truth and made it a goal in its program as is presented below in résumé:

To educate and enlighten the working class and all the toiling masses and to transform them into the driving, enlightened force behind the nation's development and progress; to make the labor class and the toiling masses of people the deciding force in the country's affairs, through the full use of the rights and freedoms guaranteed by the constitution; to suppress the dangerous influence and domination of big landowners and big capitalists in cities, who jeopardize the democratic regime, delay economic development and cultural progress, and oppose social justice and security; and to give priority to industrialization and make a planned statism working for labor and though the participation of the toiling masses of people the basic force organizing and directing the national economy and social and cultural life.

The private sector shall be made a useful section of the national economy to be tied to a plan and thus provide the political democracy with an economic and social core and prepare the conditions for transition to a more advanced social order through democratic means. For this purpose, (*a*) all means of production and exchange shall be nationalized, beginning with those in key positions in the national economy and following these with [the nationalization of other enterprises] necessary for economic development and social progress; (*b*) the branches of basic [heavy] industry shall be established and operated by the state as state property. . . .

[*The program states further the party's goal of distributing land to landless peasants, of training personnel needed for development, of achieving economic and cultural progress simultaneously, of finding employment opportunities and distributing income according to one's effort, all through a general plan. It concludes on the following high note.*]

The purpose is to end the system of exploitation of man by man and to make Turkey a country where people rely on each other as brothers, cooperate in freedom and equality, and live in an advanced civilization and culture, in full independence in the service of humanity, peace, and democracy.

80. Radical Marxist and Communist Thought

The radical leftist-Marxist groups in Turkey consisted, until the military takeover in 1980, of at least six political parties and dozens of ultraradical groups involved in a variety of violent actions. The numerical strength of these parties has been insignificant, as shown by their consistently poor showing in the elections, in which they garnered less than 3 percent of the total votes cast. However, the political activities of these parties and groups, and especially their ideological output—books, reviews, journals, and films—was so rich and varied as to demand lengthy and critical analysis. None of the legally established leftist parties, such as the pro-Chinese Workers and Peasants Party of Turkey, the Socialist Revolutionary Party, the Labor Party of Turkey, the Union Party of Turkey, and so forth, used the term "communist," despite the fact that their programs were clearly inspired by Marxism and Leninism. The Turkish Penal Code forbids the establishment of communist parties. The real Communist Party is therefore outlawed, but it operates through a variety of front organizations directed by its Central Committee and a radio station located in East Germany. The Marxists and Leninists freely established a variety of political parties, simply avoiding the term "communist" and complying with some formalities of the law. The Republican People's Party on the other hand, which shifted considerably to the Left (see the section on Bülent Ecevit), claimed that it was not Marxist and Leninist and accepted parliamentary democracy; it

distinguished itself from the Marxists by calling its own brand of leftism
"democratic Left," although in practice the differences seemed to be
rather minimal. See, for RPP's type of leftism, Demokratik Sol Düşünce
Forumu *[Forum for the Ideas of the Democratic Left] (Ankara: Kalite,*
1974). The views of the radical Marxist left appeared in a variety of
publications such as Aydınlık, Proleter, Kurtuluş, Eylem, Ilke, Party
Bayrağı, *and so forth, which varied in revolutionary zeal and vituperative-*
ness, and alternated in backing Soviet, Chinese, and other Marxist regimes.
   The first excerpt, part of one of the party's campaign speeches read over
the state radio, is from the rather serious periodical that disseminated the
views of the Worker's Socialist Party of Turkey, Ilke *[Principle] 12, nos. 70–*
72 (October–December 1979):41–44 passim.

We are living through great changes . . . the fundamental event is the
transition from capitalism to socialism. The great change in our time finds
its concrete expression in the revolutionary phase of the global [transfor-
mation]. The World Socialist System, which is gaining additional influence
and respect in the balance of forces, is registering new successes in every
field. The international workers' movement is challenging the supremacy
of the bourgeois class. . . .

The oppressed people's struggle for national liberation from imperialism, colonialism, neo-colonialism, and from the oppression of the dominating nations [meaning dominating ethnic majority] is gaining new
dimensions. The general crisis of capitalism is deepening. The growing
inflation, the energy crisis, the drop in production, an army of hundreds of
millions of unemployed, the moral and ideological disintegration are the
concrete evidence of the doom of imperialism. The contradictions and
conflicts among imperialistic powers are deepening. The economy of
these countries is being militarized in the hands of the armament
monopolies which are pushing the arms race to incredible dimensions. . . .
Turkey is located in one of the areas subject to very intensive attacks by
imperialism and regression. There are various plots engineered against the
independence of the peoples of the Middle East, against democracy,
peace, and socialist struggle. The imperialists who are rejecting the right
of the Palestinians to have their own free state and decide their own
destiny are cooperating with the zionists against the Palestinian people
and all the nations of the Middle East. . . . Turkey's foreign policy is
conditioned by her international relations and her place within the
imperialistic and capitalistic system. Turkey looks upon war, disarmament,
and the issues related to national-social liberation with the imperialists'
glasses. Turkey boasts about her place and importance within the aggressive NATO pact. She is instigating chauvinism in order to divert away

the attention of the working classes [from] the high cost of life derived from the country's economic and political structure, economic crisis, unemployment and political pressures. . . .

[*The speech ended with a call for unity to create a world without exploitations and war, to stop nuclear arms, to respect the independence and integrity of other countries, to secure Turkey's withdrawal from NATO, to create a demilitarized Cyprus, and to cut all relations with imperialists.*]

81. The Ideological Basis of Revolutionary Proletariat

The extreme radical leftist groups, like other Marxists, offer an historical explanation of the situation and the evolution of Turkey's current economic and political regime. The explanation is based not on a thorough and critical study of the historical reality but on selected clichés that provide them with the necessary arguments to fight the regime. The revolutionary proletarians claim that the Turkish working class began to develop as a consequence of European capitalist investments and of increased exports, which led to a monopolistic capitalism supported by an alliance of feudal lords and compradors (agents controlling imports and exports). The alliance of imperialism, monopolistic capitalism based on compradors, and feudalism produced a reaction and a by-product, which was the national capitalism. It became subsequently the dominant system and maintained its monopolistic-imperialistic-feudalistic basis. This regime was based not on real accumulated capital or industry but on a network of commercial enterprises that served the system. The feudal structure of agriculture permitted the exploitation of agricultural workers and prevented them from gaining a true proletarian consciousness. Turkey consequently possessed a formidable army of future revolutionaries that needed only to be organized and mobilized. The following excerpt represents the views of the Revolutionary Proletariat Party, which took Albania as a model, and is taken from the ultraradical Party Bayrağı *[Party Flag] (March 1978): 5–9, 11–13.*

In conclusion, the workers' class in this country of ours which is half colony and half feudal [fiefdom] consists of proletarians and half-proletarians whose number cannot be minimized. This class constitutes an enormous revolutionary force with boundless energy in our society. This society [in turn] is oppressed, undermined and degenerated by the pressure of imperialism, comprador-monopolistic-capitalism, and feudalism. The proletariat today is capable of leading all the progressive, revolutionary, and development-oriented elements and of fulfilling to the end the revolutionary phase. [The method for achieving revolution was through the organization of the workers around a political party and through uncompromising action, as indicated.]

The revolutionary proletariat in our country, as in the entire world, is growing and becoming stronger. This development cannot be resisted. Neither the imperialists and their servants nor the opportunists and revisionists can stop it. Marxist-leninist parties in all countries are being consolidated or new ones created. These parties are becoming stronger by purging from their ranks all the opportunists and revisionists, while various marxist-leninist groups and movements are closing ranks against opportunism and revisionism and are moving towards the creation of [political] parties.... The revolutionary proletarians in our country have fought resolutely after 1974 for the unity of the revolutionary proletarians and for the establishment of revolutionary proletarian party and for marxism and leninism. The hearts of the revolutionaries in our country were and are filled with the desire to create marxist-leninist unity and to establish a party which would fight for the interests of the workers' class, poor peasants, and other working people. This struggle was deprived until today of a program and ... of policies capable of achieving unity and of becoming the foundation for a [political] party.... the great struggle within the workers class which began with the report of comrade Enver Hoja submitted to the 7th Congress of the Albanian Labor Party ... found its echo in our country too.

PART FOUR

Political and Social Thought
in Iran

XXIV. INTRODUCTION TO POLITICAL AND SOCIAL THOUGHT IN IRAN

This anthology has consistently linked contemporary Middle Eastern thought to the social structure and the ideological and cultural underpinnings prevailing in the country under discussion. Following this, one can say that the direction of Iranian thought during the past 20 years and previously was determined by the struggle of Shiism with the monarchy, the rapidly changing social structure brought about by the late shah's so-called White Revolution (land reform), the influx of oil money, and the foreign interference in the affairs of the country. Each one of these elements shall be briefly studied.

Iran is the only Muslim country where the *Ithna ʿashari*, or the Twelfth Imam, Shiism, is a state religion. The population, with the exception of the Kurds, Turkmen, some Arabs and the Baluchis (roughly only one-sixth of the total of 38 million people), is Shiite. Iranian Shiism is different from that of Turkey, Syria, Yemen, and other Arab countries, though in Iraq and Lebanon it is similar. The difference arises from doctrine and also from an evolutionary pattern that gave Iranian Shiism certain unique features. The doctrine holds that the Twelfth Imam, Muhammad al-Mahdi, disappeared from the world in 874 A.D. As he was the unique head of the community, he could not legitimately be replaced; but he will return in the future, bringing redemption and freedom for the oppressed and the destitute. Until manifestation, that is, the Imam's return, the religious leaders have the duty and the responsibility to guide the community. This guidance or *taqlid* is performed by the *mujtahid*, the religious leader, who becomes *marjaʿ-i taqlid* (the highest position) when chosen by the believers. The political implications of this doctrine are far reaching. The authority of the Imam, and by implication of the *mujtahid*, derives from a semidivine source and, consequently, cannot be superseded by worldly authority. Thus the *marjaʿ* can use his authority to direct the believer against the wishes of the state or the monarch. The logical implication of this view is that the monarch must obey the authority of the *mujtahid*. Shiism, besides rejecting tyranny, places special value on social justice, and on sacrifice and matyrdom as the means by which to fight tyranny and achieve justice. The Imam Huseyin, who died in the seventh century in a rebellion against Yazid, is a potent symbol for Shiite opposition to tyranny and martyrdom in the cause of justice. The story of this event is enacted annually in passion plays during the month of Muharram.

The evolution of the Iranian monarchy followed a special path of its own too. Until the sixteenth century most of the population of Iran was

Sunni. With the rise of the Safavid dynasty, which relied on the Turkmen (Turkish) tribes to combat the Ottoman Sunnis in the West, Shah Ismail Safavi was led by political reasons, that is, to separate himself religiously from the Ottomans, to adopt and spread Shiism, making it in effect the state religion of Persia. Religion and state were thus brought together for strictly political reasons. The alliance between religion and monarchy was, however, uneasy, and it took a turn for the worse during the reign of Shah Muhammad (1834–48). A number of scholars have attributed the flourishing of Shiism and, indirectly, its opposition to the shahs, to the desire of the Persians to maintain their cultural identity against the Arabs. A few pieces of evidence can be cited to support his view: Imam Huseyin married the daughter of the last Sassanian emperor (who was Persian and was defeated by the Muslim Arab armies) and the later Imams descended from this union; the Iranian monarchs, beginning with the Safavids, arose mostly from the Turkish-speaking groups; the ancestors of the Qajar dynasty (preceding the Pahlavis) were accused of fighting in the Umayyad army against Imam Huseyin; and so forth. Such arguments, stemming mostly from the European scholars who seem to accept the idea that the sense of race and ethnicity is all powerful, do not accord with the history of Iran.

The majority of the Iranian population—probably still 55 percent, despite frantic efforts at Persianization during the last decades—has always been non-Persian. The Turkish-speaking Azeris are the largest non-Persian group and these, like the Kashgais, Baluchis, Kurds, Turkmen, and others, have played an active part in leading and holding the Iranian commonwealth together. The most powerful argument against the racist theory is the rebellion against and the ousting of the last shah, the only Iranian monarch of Persian stock in centuries. There is no question but that there are Persian nationalists in Iran who have strongly advocated a policy of Persianization. The late shah in fact introduced a program of assimilation, closing the schools and publications of the various ethnic groups, notably the Azeris. (It is reported that at a reception the empress, who is of Azeri stock, spoke Turkish to a diplomat but that the shah intervened and prohibited it and that thereafter she did not speak her maternal tongue in the presence of others.)

The most powerful force holding together the Iranian multiethnic and multireligious society was the Shiite Islamic faith shared by Persians and other non-Persian ethnic groups, such as the Azeris and the Arabs. In addition, a high degree of ethnic and linguistic tolerance existed, coupled with a great deal of local autonomy granted to all the major groups. Throughout the centuries the non-Persians enjoyed linguistic freedom, for Islam, be it Shiite or Sunni, does not accept ethnicity as a basis for social and political organization but instead lays emphasis on an Islamic identity and sense of solidarity above ethnic loyalties. It was in fact the late shah who violated this traditional ethnic-religious balance through his policy of forced Persianization, a policy that turned religious Persians as well as non-Persians against the throne.

The simmering doctrinal dispute between the Shiite religious establishment and the throne came into the open during the Qajar rule in the second half of the nineteenth century. The development of capitalism and a market economy enabled Russia and, especially, England to secure in Iran a variety of economic privileges that were protected by special legal safeguards. These privileges were formally granted by the Qajar monarchs who, addicted to luxury, appeared to deviate from Islamic traditions of piety and model behavior. In these circumstances the *mujtahids* rose against the shah and the foreigners to defend the faith and, indirectly, Iranian national interests. Moreover, some rulers, notably Nasiruddin Shah (1848–96), became involved in some governmental reforms that eventually affected the *waqfs* (pious foundations) and the courts, all of which were the preserve of the *ulema*. The deepening conflict between the religious establishment and the monarchy was the expression not only of the historical-doctrinal opposition between them but also of the conflicts within the Iranian society, now subject to foreign domination and capitalist penetration. The conflicts burst into the open in a revolt against a very lucrative tobacco concession monopoly granted by the shah to the British in 1891. The *ulema*, assisted by the bazaar merchants, led the revolt, and eventually Nasiruddin Shah was forced to withdraw the concession, although he had to assume a heavy debt to pay indemnity to the British. Interestingly enough, the view of the British of the "enlightened" Shah Nasiruddin and the "fanatical clergy" in 1892 were in many ways similar to the American view of Shah Muhammad Pahlavi in 1978. The revolt of 1891–92 was followed by the rise of anticolonialist sentiment, spread throughout the Middle East through the efforts of Jamaleddin Afghani, by the assassination of the shah in 1896, and, finally, by the acceptance of the constitution of 1906. Modeled, in part at least, on the Ottoman constitution of 1876, the Iranian constitution of 1906 codified and limited the powers of the shah and recognized the *mujtahids* as a group upholding the religion and law. The religious establishment, despite its political activities, was content to restore what they considered to be the integrity of Islam and to maintain their own privileges. Meanwhile Iran remained underdeveloped.

Until the end of the First World War, Iran remained a poor and powerless country dominated by the Russians and the British, despite agitations seeking to rid the country of foreign influence. It was the rising nationalism that enabled Reza Shah to achieve his spectacular journey from the village of Alasht, where he was born in 1878, to the throne of

Iran. Illiterate but extremely intelligent, he taught himself how to read and joined the Cossack brigade set up to defend the shah. The brigade was commanded by Russian officers. Reza took over the command of the brigade, then became minister of war. He ousted Premier Seyyid Ziya Tabatabai, and rose to the premiership in 1923. In 1925 he ousted the last Qajar ruler and then crowned himself as Reza Shah Pahlavi. Already in 1923, following the establishment of the Republic of Turkey, many Iranians had demanded a similar regime in their country. Reza Shah attempted to follow the reforms of Atatürk in Turkey, notably his secularist measures, with the clear intention of curbing the power of the *mujtahids.* However, his efforts ran into the stiff opposition of the religious establishment, and he was forced to rescind his anticlerical measures. He humbled himself at Qum, asking forgiveness from the *mujtahids* and promising noninterference in religious matters; but later, after having consolidated his power, he reneged on most of his promises. Reza Shah did manage to introduce a series of reforms, and the process created a small group of privileged modernists who became the supporters of the monarchy and its reformist endeavors. These endeavors remained limited in scope and depth, but the shah managed in the process to become the largest landowner in Iran.

Reza Shah was a nationalist in his own way. In order to rid the country of British influence, he pursued a pro-German policy, which led to his ouster in 1941 and his replacement by his son, Muhammad Pahlavi. The country was occupied eventually by British, Soviet, and American troops in order to secure the supply route for the Soviets fighting the Germans in Russia. The last foreign troops were withdrawn from Iran in 1946, in accordance with an agreement signed between allies in 1942; but the withdrawal was only accomplished by means of an American ultimatum after the Soviets had set up Kurdish and Azeri "republics under trusted leaders."

In the late 1940s Iran appeared to have developed a sizable native middle class, and a fairly large intelligentsia that fought to assert Iran's economic and political independence. For example, a bill establishing a joint Soviet-Iranian oil company was defeated in the Parliament in 1947, and demands were voiced that the concession accorded to the British-controlled Anglo-Iranian Oil Company set up at the turn of the century be revised. It was on the strength of the Iranians' anti-British sentiment that the National Front under Muhammad Mossadeq, who had been jailed by Reza Shah for his outspoken opposition, gained power, succeeded in nationalizing the oil company in March 1951, and refused to compromise despite strong pressure from the West. Taking advantage of the deteriorating conditions in the country, the shah tried to dismiss Mossadeq, only to face popular resistance and revolt. The shah fled the country in 1953 but after one week was restored to his throne by a military countercoup engineered by the CIA. The old scenario was enacted once more: the shah appeared to owe his throne to foreign powers. The nationalist movement of Mossadeq, which enjoyed the wide support of the clergy, the intelligentsia (some abandomed him in 1953), and the population, had the potential to achieve a democratic political regime but was undermined and destroyed by the shah. He put Mossadeq under house arrest, where he died in 1967, and gradually managed to silence all opposition. By 1962 he began his reforms, notably the land reform that consisted largely of the distribution of the royal lands accumulated by Reza Shah to the villagers. The effect of these reforms is highly debatable. The apologists portrayed the reforms as a "white revolution" that brought Iran into the modern age, while critics dismissed them as mere superficial whitewash. The truth is that the reforms, such as the literacy campaign, land distribution, rural and urban reconstruction and development, industrialization, and a variety of social programs (workers' profit sharing, social security), although overdue and inevitable, accelerated the social change of Iran. The reforms received an enormous boost in 1973, after the sudden rise in oil prices (the shah was part of the group that engineered the price hike). Iran's oil revenues rose to over $17 billion in 1978. The money was poured into industrial-commercial schemes, but also into a variety of sophisticated weapons designed to make Iran the guardian of the Gulf, and even of the Indian Ocean. The shah was portrayed in the Western media as a truly enlightened ruler and some writers did not hesitate to describe the monarchy (following the shah's own wish) as the natural regime for Iran.

The widespread effects of the social and economic changes initiated by the shah were felt both in the countryside and in the cities, especially after 1973. Large numbers of villagers left their villages, either because their products became noncompetitive with the imported commodities or because of higher wages in the cities. The population of the big cities swelled. The newcomers, cut off from their traditional village life, became destitute and alienated in the cities. The agricultural production fell drastically, and Iran, which was self-sufficient in food before 1960, by 1978 had to import more than 70 percent of her food.

Meanwhile the commercial and industrialist classes, as well as the working classes, especially those in the oil industry, grew rapidly in size; so also did the intelligentsia class being educated in the newly established universities.

The effect of the change in occupation and living habits, the increase in urbanization, communication, and literacy produced social unrest and cultural alienation and a desire for a solution to these ills. The shah responded to the variety of demands and criticisms by instituting a series of repressive measures, jail, and torture.

The disintegration of the traditional values, the threat to family life, and the rise of vulgar materialism turned the population once more to the fountainhead of its spiritual life—that is, to Islam. The *mujtahids* who spoke against the oppressive regime of the shah were now fundamentally different in philosophy and outlook from their predecessors. Whatever their personal grievances (loss of lands, dwindling of rural following, and so forth), the members of the religious establishment associated themselves with the intelligentsia and the workers, and with their demands for freedom and social justice. The reaction to the oppressive policies of the shah, who had become the symbol of corruption, oppression, and cultural degradation as well as the channel for foreign influences, manifested itself in an uprising that began at Qum in June 1963. Known as the events of 15 Khordad, the uprising resulted partly from the preaching of the Ayatollah Khomeini and his disciples, and partly from the armed struggle of various radical Islamist and leftist groups. The shah arrested Khomeini and sent him into exile in 1967, but he could not stop the growth of opposition not only to his personal rule but to his policies and to the monarchy as a whole (see the next chapter). The ideological and philosophical bases of this movement stemmed from a new and dynamic interpretation of Islam that sought the rejuvenation of society through reliance on the Koran and on the people as a whole. Khomeini and Ali Shariati were the spiritual and intellectual leaders of the new movement, as explained in detail further on.

The shah tried to fight the rising tide of the opposition with draconian measures that resulted in thousands of deaths; the Shiite ideas of martyrdom for a just cause and opposition to tyranny seemed to give the population endless strength and determination. The army, although armed with ultramodern weapons, seemed powerless and unwilling to fight the resurgence. Although in exile in Iraq, the Ayatollah Khomeini became the spiritual leader of the revolt. Late in 1978 the uprising escalated when government employees, customs officials, and industrial workers employed especially in oil, textile, and construction industries struck and brought the whole economy to a halt. The strikers were protesting not only the spiraling inflation, rising unemployment, and cancellation of annual bonuses, but also the refusal of the regime to permit Khomeini's return, to lift martial law, to implement the constitutional laws, to allow employees to participate in the running of factories and government offices, and to punish those responsible for the massacre of peaceful demonstrators during the previous months.

Early in 1979, the United States decided not to support the shah or an army takeover, giving its backing to Shapur Bakhtiar, appointed premier by the shah. By January 16, 1979, the shah had left Teheran, and on

February 1, 1979, Khomeini returned to Iran. Mehdi Bazargan was appointed as prime minister and charged with beginning the preparations for the establishment of an Islamic Republic. On March 31, 1979, the voting for such a republic began. The monarchy thus came to an end. In a special election Bani-Sadr was elected president of Iran.

Soon, however, a split began to develop between the modern-minded liberal Islamists and the conservative clergy. Eventually, the modern liberal Islamists, headed by Mehdi Bazargan, an Azeri Turk, and Bani-Sadr, another non-Persian belonging to a small Turkic group, were ousted from power. Bazargan was dismissed as premier and replaced by a man of limited ability but enjoying the confidence of the clergy. Finally in 1981 Bani-Sadr was first deprived, by Khomeini, of his position as commander of the armed forces, and then dismissed as president by a Parliament tightly controlled by the Islamic Republican Party (the latter was headed by Ayatollah Muhammad Beheshti, who was also the head of the Supreme Court). Bani-Sadr eventually found refuge in France.

Meanwhile Muhammad Ali Rajai, the premier picked by the leadership of the IRP, was elected as president of Iran in a special election held on July 24, 1981. It should be remembered that one of the principal reasons for the dispute between former President Abolhasan Bani-Sadr, and the IRP concerned the appointment of Rajai as premier. Bani-Sadr found Rajai unqualified to fill the premiership, although in reality he wanted his own man as premier. Meanwhile, in response to the shah's admission to the United States for medical treatment, despite cautions by the embassy, the Iranian militants—mostly Fedayi—took hostage the American personnel working at the American embassy in Teheran. This unlawful act, despite the temporary unity it created among diverse and conflicting groups, had disastrous effects on the economic situation of Iran and placed the Islamic revolution in an unfavorable light before world opinion.

In 1981 the strife in Iran between the ruling clergy and its one-time ally the radical Mujahedin intensified. Beheshti and President Rajai, along with many other leaders, were killed by bombs allegedly planted by the Mujahedin. In turn, thousands of the Mujahedin were tried and executed summarily.

The revolution was the work of the social forces rather than political ones. However, since 1979 a series of political organizations have emerged. Consequently, the division in Iran is no longer a simple dichotomy of the monarchy versus the people but consists of many separate and often rival political forces, each with its own ideology, its own social base, and its own vision of the future. The following are some the major groups.

The Dominant Religious Group. This group is represented by the Islamic Republican Party (IRP), headed by Ayatollah Muhammad Beheshti, who was killed in the summer of 1981 along with many officials by a bomb placed at the headquarters of the IRP, the ruling organization. Drawn predominantly from the members of the clergy who organized the bazaar demonstrations of 1978, the religious elements control the Parliament and many of the key positions in the government. Convinced that most of the ills of the contemporary society—especially alcoholism, the breakdown of families, unemployment, and the lack of discipline among youth—are all caused by the failure of the government to implement Koranic regulations, they urge a return to the basic tenets of Islam.

Religious Conservatives. Although this group fully participated in the political revolution against the shah, it does not advocate a fundamental revolution against either the social structure or the established institutions. Its main spokesman is Ayatollah Shariatmadari, a native of Azerbaijan. Shariatmadari favors the enforcement of some Koranic regulations, but he opposes the establishment of a theocracy and argues that all groups, including the Left, should have the right to participate in a constitutional democracy. His group, called the Party of the People's Islamic Republic, has been banned.

Religious Reformers. Organized into the "Movement for the Liberation of Iran," this group demands gradual social change as well as the elimination of the theocracy in favor of a democratic government.

Religious Radicals. Led by the Mujahedin-i Khalq (which can be translated as Holy Fighters of the People, known generally as Mujahedin), this groups seeks a fundamental social revolution based on Islam. Anticapitalist, antiimperialist, antitraditionalist, and at times even anticlerical, they aspire to create a new independent nation that would borrow technology from the West but, on the other hand, would remain faithful to the revolutionary spirit of early Islam.

Secular Reformers. Led by the National Front, this group favors the establishment of a modern democratic constitution. Complaining that the leadership of the National Front was too identified with Khomeini's entourage, Matin Daftari, a leading human rights lawyer and grandson of Mossadeq, left that party and formed the Democratic National Front. His program is tailored to bring together the other groups, from the religious conservatives on the Right to the secular radicals on the Left. The two National Fronts find much of their support among the professional and salaried middle class, among such newly formed organizations as the

Writers Association, Lawyers Association, Engineers Association, Professors Association, Teachers Union, and Government Employees Union.

The Secular Radicals. These are divided into the Fedayi, the Tudeh Party, and the Unity Conference. The latter takes in several Marxist-Leninist organizations, including Peykar (a group that split from the Mujahedin in 1975) as well as several smaller groups, some opposed and others friendly to the USSR. The Left as a whole has little following. Its support is limited to university students, white-collar workers, and some trade unionists, especially oil workers. Although the Left fully supported the revolution against the shah, many Marxists realize that the establishment of a Islamic state would endanger their own existence. The Marxist Left has been hurt in the last ten years by the fact that the Soviet Union and the People's Republic of China have openly supported the shah.

For further readings on Iranian thought and politics, in addition to the bibliography mentioned in relevant sections further on, see Shahrokh Akhavi, *Religion and Politics in Contemporary Iran: Clergy-State Relations in the Pahlavi Period* (Albany: SUNY Press, 1980); Hamid Algar, *Religion and State in Iran, 1785–1906* (Berkeley: University of California Press, 1969); James Bill, *The Politics of Iran: Groups, Classes and Modernization* (Columbus, Ohio: Charles A. Merill, 1972); and Nikki R. Keddie, ed., *Scholars, Saints, and Sufis, Muslim Religious Institutions since 1500* (Berkeley: University of California Press, 1972). For further reference, see Iraj Afshar, *Index Iranicus*, vol. 1 (1919–58) (Tehran: University of Tehran), 1961; this work is a bibliography containing some 6,000 titles compiled by the editor of *Rahnama-ye-Kitab* [Guide to Books], a periodical review of Iranian publications. See also Richard W. Cottam, *Nationalism in Iran* (New York: Frederick A. Praeger, 1963); Amin Banani, *The Modernization of Iran, 1921–1941* (Stanford: Stanford University Press, 1961): Leonard Binder, *Iran: Political Development in a Changing Society* (Berkeley: University of California Press, 1962); and Sepehr Zabth, *The Communist Movement in Iran* (Berkeley: University of California Press, 1966).

The following articles are very useful: F. Kazemzadeh, "Ideological Crisis in Iran," in *The Middle East in Transition: Studies in Contemporary History,* ed. Walter Z. Laqueur (London: Routledge & Kegan Paul; New York: Frederick A. Praeger, 1958), pp. 196–203; James A. Bill, "The Social and Economic Foundations of Power in Contemporary Iran," *Middle East Journal* 17 (Autumn 1963);400–13; Richard N. Frye, "Iran and the Unity of the Muslim World," in *Islam and the West,* ed. Richard N. Frye (The Hague: Mouton, 1957), pp. 179–93; A.K.S. Lambton, "A Reconsideration of the Position of the Marja' al-Taqlid and the Religious Institution,"

Studia Islamica 20 (1964): 114–35; M. A. Salem Khan, "Religion and State in Iran: A Unique Muslim Country," *Islam and the Modern Age* 2 (1971): 67–88; and Ervand Abrahamian, "Kasravi: The Integrative Nationalist of Iran," *Middle East Studies* 9 (1973): 271–95.

XXV.   THE MONARCHY: FRIENDS AND FOES

82.   The Shah of Iran: Proclamation on Reform and Statement of the National Front

Muhammad Pahlavi (1919–80) ruled Iran from 1941 to 1979 and died in exile in Egypt in 1980. His father, Reza Shah Pahlavi, also died in exile in South Africa. Throughout his life the late shah was a controversial figure. Educated in Switzerland, he remained aloof, if not alienated, from his people. He spent much effort and money to bolster the idea of "Persian mystique" as a continuous cultural tradition built around the "kingly glory" that found its expression in the Shahinshah, the King of Kings. The sumptuous festivities at Persepolis that marked the twenty-five hundredth anniversary of "continuous kingly rule" in Iran were intended to promote the mystique of the monarchy and help to perpetuate the shah's own rule. The shah became involved in a series of modernist reforms in the 1960s. These stirred negative reactions among the shah's opponents and won praise from his supporters. Finally, faced with mounting criticism against his oppressive rule from practically all segments of the population, he left the country in 1979. The extracts in this chapter provide an overall view of the shah's own opinion on the reforms as well as those of his followers and his adversaries, now and in the past. The literature on the monarchy in Iran is rich indeed. See Robert Graham, Iran: The Illusion of Power *(New York: St. Martin's Press, 1979); Fred Halliday,* Iran: Dictatorship and Development *(New York: Penguin Books, 1979); George Lenczowski, ed.,* Iran Under the Pahlavis *(Stanford: Hoover Institution Press, 1978); Amin Saikal,* The Rise and Fall of the Shah *(Princeton: Princeton University Press, 1980); Fereydoun Hoveyda,* The Fall of the Shah, *trans. Roger Liddell (New York: Simon and Schuster, Wyndham Books, 1980); Sepehr Zabih,* Iran's Revolutionary Upheaval: An Interpretive Essay *(San Francisco: Alchemy Books,*

1979); William H. Forbis, Fall of the Peacock Throne: The Story of Iran *(New York: Harper and Row, 1980); Ashraf Pahlavi,* Memoirs From Exile *(Englewood Cliffs, N.J.: Prentice Hall, 1980). The following extracts are from* Ettela'at *[Air Mail Edition], Tehran, November 15, 1961. These English versions have been adapted from Peter W. Avery's translation, which appeared in* Middle East Journal *16 (Winter 1962):86–90. Reproduced by permission.*

THE SHAH'S PROCLAMATION ON REFORM

[To] His Excellency Doctor 'Ali Amini, Prime Minister:

The statement of His Majesty the Shah at the meeting of the Council of Ministers on 20th Aban in the year 1340 [November 11, 1961] in the Marble Palace is forwarded herewith:

"Our concern for this country and its people has made us determine that steps in preparing the ground for achieving the social, material, and intellectual advancement of the realm should be taken without delay, for the attainment of the basis of a developing society in a rapidly progressing world. These steps include the possibility of achieving sound government of the people by the people, which is at the root of democratic principles. Every minute we lose in seizing this valuable opportunity is tantamount to a grave crime on our, the government's, and the nation's part. We have always put the lofty interests of nation and country above all else. Thus, for the comfort and well-being of the people, for the establishment of social justice, and for the progressive development of individual members of the community toward a life in keeping with the standards of the modern world, we decree that the necessary steps be taken. No difficulty or hindrance can be admitted in this process as an obstacle to the implementation of the required measures. Accordingly, acting on the right given us by the Fundamental Law, we being recognized as one of the originators of law, we commission the government, until the convening of a parliament (based, we hope, on valid elections without the need again ensuing for annulment of elections due to their improper conduct), to put into execution the laws required for convening village councils and, in respect of the laws governing city, provincial, and district councils also, to bring about the necessary modifications in the existing laws, after careful scrutiny with regard to the circumstances and the needs of the day. These may be put temporarily into execution with our Royal Assent so that, with a period of practical experiment and removal of obvious defects, they may be submitted to the legislature to gain legal validity and affirmation after the opening of both houses of parliament.

The meaning of democratic government is this, that the people's affairs be assigned to the people themselves as they gradually obtain the right degree of maturity; that they possess authority to act in the administration of all local matters; that they participate and take action with respect to price regulation of foodstuffs, public health, education, municipal affairs, local road construction, with the joining of branch roads to main trunk routes, without tampering with or damaging the bases of the country's central domestic and foreign policy.

For essential reforms the government must:

1. In the administration and recruitment of civil servants, expediting the drafting of a new civil service law with attention to essential minutiae, put into effect rules of service in a uniform manner equally applicable to every ministry, taking the special duties of each ministry into consideration, but obviating all forms of discrimination. . . . In laying the foundations of each ministry's organization on the basis of present and future needs, the conditions of permanence and promotion in the state service will be merit, honesty, and personal ability. Above the level of director general, the Council of Ministers will carry out the necessary investigations.

2. Guaranteeing civil servants' livelihood to cover their own and their dependent's welfare and to free them from apprehension about their future is an aim whose achievement must, of course, begin with giving employees living accommodations under a special scheme. Then, gradually, provision must be made for other amenities, such as cooperative societies, etc., to meet the officials' needs. Accomplishment of this duty on the government's part will begin with rigorous application of the principle of first things first. The most important categories of civil servants must be given priority, and these include army, police and gendarmerie employees, schoolteachers, and Ministry of Justice officials, all of whom have a specially important standing. Houses assigned to these categories must, as far as possible, be close to their place of work to economize in transport and obviate waste of time in travel.

3. The government must not relax vigilance in the sphere of agriculture and its mechanization. The law for land reform and limitation of proprietorship should be put into effect; if the land reform law proves impracticable, the government must, with utmost dispatch, embark on its revision in whatever way is deemed necessary to assure its proper and complete execution; and meanwhile, regulations must be instituted to guarantee the welfare and well-being of those cultivators left under landowners. For the benefit of the cultivators, advantage must be taken of the results accruing from the attraction of experts and commissioning of various cooperative establishments.

The government must especially strive to achieve an extraordinary increase in production. For local road construction between villages and joining branch feeder roads to main trunk routes and other development projects, development and construction battalions of young people must be set up and the means of mechanizing agriculture furnished, including familiarization with cultivators, the use of chemical fertilizers, and modern agricultural methods, the digging of irrigation channels, construction of rural houses, and exploitation of the land.

The development and construction battalions, losing no time joining forces with municipal authorities in towns, will assist in building factories and workers' housing.

4. Under the present law, the condition of labor is relatively satisfactory. However, employers must be persuaded to build houses for workers; and this can be arranged so that it is reckoned as a portion of the insurance employers are legally bound to pay.

The government must give special attention to the protection of home industries and promotion of the country's own factory products. This must be done in such a way that, when local products have as far as possible matched the same products abroad, improvements will continue and consumers' desire for home goods be increased, which will be in their best economic interests.

The government must guide and aid factory owners in renewal of plants and also training of technical personnel and management for the proper maintenance of industrial installations. It will protect every type of production unit and domestic industry against foreign markets. In the factories, after assessments have been made, workers, should they be willing, may have 25 per cent of the stock sold to them on a suitable installment basis. Thus, the workers themselves may be participants in the factory's profits and, becoming concerned in the proper running of the business and quality of the products, not spare their best efforts.

5. In the matter of taxes, which are still not received in a proper or equitable manner from the wealthy, the minister of finance has the duty, after close study and anticipation of sound and just collection of revenues, to make proposals that will ensure that the wealthy pay dues relative to their capacity. Illegal impositions on the impecunious will be avoided, while dealings between payer and revenue collector will be based on a feeling of mutual confidence and understanding. Thus, gradually, the routine of rendering taxes due will become general, with an ethical relationship established between taxpayers and collectors.

Special attention should be paid to the stabilization of a revenue system so that the people's and investors' confidence will be attracted.

6. As regards education, which is essentially important, our future being to a large extend dependent upon it, there must be a revision of educational programs. This will ensure that our education system possesses the practical and useful aspect that is consonant with the state of a society and country in the process of maturing and developing. You must leave no stone unturned to extend and broaden free elementary education

and intermediate vocational training, while taking steps for general secondary education at the intermediate and higher levels according to what obtains all over the world. So that no talent may be deprived on the grounds of lack of means, the Ministry of Education must watch pupils from the very first day they enter primary school, keeping records of all those with outstanding ability. Thus, at the right time, either directly or through city, provincial, or district councils, study scholarships will be made available to these youngsters of ability. The utmost care must also be exercised in sending students to foreign countries, so that, while the country's finances are not wasted, intelligent individuals, of value for their country's needs, may be trained for service under the supervision of conscientious people.

In conclusion, as we have said, all regulations are secondary to the survival of the country and its people. If we wanted merely to follow anachronistic and outmoded rules, neglecting the present world situation and taking advantage of existing opportunities, we would be guilty of a major crime toward our people. The country's advancement and its people's welfare will take precedence over the observance of regulation-bound views and personal predilections. Without loss of time, the government must, trusting in our special support and gracious favor, devote itself to eradicating the roots of corruption with complete sincerity and the utmost speed. In achieving this great task, it must fear no obstacle or hindrance. We are convinced that every individual of the noble and sensible Iranian nation will take part in this process, based as it is on social justice, with one mind and one voice with all their strength, and so increase the glory of this historic land."

> Hirad,
> Head of the Imperial Bureau

STATEMENT OF THE NATIONAL FRONT

The establishment of legal government is the aim of the Iranian National Front [so as to avoid] the return to despotism fifty-five years after the constitution was inaugurated.

Fellow-countrymen: The Fundamental Law clearly lays down the rights and spheres of responsibility of the nation, the constitutional monarchy, and responsible government. On the strength of this Fundamental Law, the Iranian nation was not and is not in a position to infringe upon the real rights of the constitutional monarchy. Therefore, justice and expediency decree that the Throne should, on its part, preserve the rights of the nation—particularly as, in accordance with Article 39 of the

Supplement to the Fundamental Law, the Throne is bound by oath to do this and because, whenever the Fundamental Law, which defines the relationship between the nation and the Throne, is not respected, irreparable harm to the state results.

With these facts in mind, the National Front, on the basis of the Fundamental Law and of constitutional conventions, strongly protests against the statements Dr. Amini made as prime minister to the Association of Press Correspondents. Warning is given that the instructions issued from His Imperial Majesty's bureau concerning the enactment and modification of laws without parliamentary approval cannot be considered in the best interests of the Throne and must be deemed contrary to the clear purport of the Fundamental Law because:

In the instruction issued from the Throne to Dr. Amini, in spite of the fine words in the preamble about the desire for securing social justice and reform, the following statement occurs: "According to the right given us by the Fundamental Law, we being recognized as one of those with the right to initiate law, we charge the government, until the convening of parliament, with putting into execution laws required for forming village councils; and in respect of the laws governing city, provincial, and district councils also, with bringing about necessary modifications in existing laws, after careful scrutiny with regard to circumstances and the needs of the day. These may be put temporarily into execution upon receipt of our Royal Assent so that, with a period of practical experiment and removal of obvious difficulties, they may be submitted to the legislature to gain legal validity and authorization after the opening of both houses of parliament." After this, the Throne confers on the government the right of lawmaking, which is parliament's prerogative, in respect of enacting, modifying, revising, and abrogating civil service, land reform, tax, and education laws, although this is contrary to the Fundamental Law in both letter and spirit, as will be shown below. Abrogating the rights of parliament, which are in fact the rights of the nation, is in no way consonant with the essential substance of the Fundamental Law, the guarantee of the country's stability, independence, and constitutional sovereignty.

The Throne's statements given above are expressly contrary to the Fundamental Law and against the interests of the realm and the people because:

In the above instruction, it has been asserted that the Throne is one of the initiators of law; apparently, Article 27 of the Supplement to the Fundamental Law, defining the separation of powers, is the basis of this interpretation. But the primary purpose of drawing this article was to separate the duties of the three powers so that one power should not interfere in the functioning of the other. The above interpretation, however, whereby the government is deemed to have the right to enact laws, one of the special rights of parliament, goes contrary to what is intended by the word "lawmaking" in the drawing of the above-mentioned article.

Initiation of law means the preparation of bills and the drafting of a law. What lawmaking is intended to mean, with mention of the fact that each of these two houses of parliament and His Imperial Majesty have the right to initiate law, is that both houses or His Majesty through the government have the right of preparing drafts or bills. Confirmation of this opinion lies in the fact that, in this article and others, the promulgators of the Fundamental Law upheld a difference between the *initiation* and the *enactment* of law. In the Fundamental Law, it has been made clear that laws are valid and can be executed only after parliament has passed them and they have received the Royal Assent. . . .

For the reasons given, the Throne and the executive power do not have the right of enacting laws, and the enactment of law is among the special rights of parliament. If the case were other than this, certainly reference or indication would have been given on this matter. Lack of reference to the right of enacting law, in the section dealing with the rights of the Throne, confirms that the matter of *initiating* is not the right of *enacting*.

The Supreme Court, in giving a guiding opinion, has clearly stated that enactment, modification, and recision of laws is one of the special duties of parliament, and no other body has the right of enacting law.

Now you, Dr. Amini, and your respected colleagues should realize that, according to the clear purport of Article 64 in the Supplement to the Fundamental Law, where it is laid down that "ministers cannot, by using verbal or written orders from the sovereign, relieve themselves of responsibility," you do not have the right to take steps to modify or abrogate laws.

The National Front gives notification to the leaders of Iran, who have attained their high places through the blessings of this same Fundamental Law and constitution, that it will concentrate its efforts on reviving the constitution and, by preventing infringement of the Fundamental Law, [will] seek to insure the safety of the country.

The National Front cannot tolerate any infringement on the rights of parliament, which is the representative of the whole nation; neither can it tolerate violation of the Fundamental Law, because it considers embarking on such a dangerous course injurious to the state, nation, and constitution, and, in this connection, it proclaims to all classes of the people, whose Fundamental Law was obtained by the sacrifice of the lives of their gallant forebears, that, for the preservation of the Fundamental Law and the nation's rights and for the protection of the constitution, the utmost vigilance will be shown and the followers of individual rule [will] not [be] permitted to deprive the people of the rights. November 15, 1961 (24 Aban 1340). Executive Committee of the National Front.

83.   The Tudeh Party View on the Shah's Reforms

The Tudeh (Masses) Party, established in Iran in 1941 by German-educated intellectuals, was a leftist-Marxist radical organization with a pro-Soviet attitude. It became increasingly active in Iran's internal politics, adopting at first a liberal facade and thus receiving support from leading intellectuals and from the trade unions. Although the party was outlawed in 1949, its members continued to be active. Some of its militants went abroad to engage in the systematic dissemination of leftist propaganda directed chiefly at the many Iranian students in Europe and the United States. Donya [World], a periodical published somewhere in Europe, and pamphlets and books also published abroad were smuggled into Iran and distributed among Iranian intellectuals. The late shah's policy was particularly effective in liquidating the party's cells in Iran. During the 1960s and 1970s Tudeh had a limited impact on developments in the country, despite its efforts to infiltrate the opposition youth groups. It was successful to some extent in establishing relations with the Mujahedin and Fedayi without achieving any lasting results. In fact, both those groups criticized Tudeh at various times, accusing it of serving primarily the interests of the USSR in Iran. After the return of Khomeini and the establishment of the Islamic Republic, Tudeh supported the new regime with the obvious goal of strengthening its weakened organization and possibly acquiring control of the youth groups. A branch of the Fedayi and a few of the Mujahedin reportedly are in contact with Tudeh and following its lead, although the main bodies refused to enter elections together.

Nuraldin Kianuri, the current (1980) Tudeh leader, is the son of an Islamic leader, Ayatollah Fazollah Nuri, martyred in 1907; he replaced the veteran Iraj Eskandari as soon as Khomeini appeared to be gaining the upper hand in 1979. Tudeh publishes a daily, Mardom, which sells about 20,000 copies, as well as weeklies. Tudeh supports the present regime because it believes it will create a popular antiimperialist front that will destroy the socioeconomic foundations of the colonial system. Kianuri was openly antagonistic to Bani-Sadr, for he feared his nationalistic-Islamic views more than Khomeini's purely religious concepts. The party is today weak, but its chances for gaining power and influence will increase greatly after the Imam's death and the expected internal strife.

Ehsan Tabari on Reaction or Revolutionary Change in Iran°

The Persian administration, headed by the Shah, is scrambling to confirm and perpetuate the existing social and economic conditions in order to preserve its power. After the successful *coup d'état* of August 19, 1953, the Shah and the reactionary administration turned all their attention to revenge. The regaining of power enabled them to crush savagely those vast social forces that had been fighting the people's enemies, the imperialists, the courtiers, etc. The American and English imperialists helped the Shah to create a regime of terror and oppression. He concentrated despotic powers in his hands, committed unprecedented treasons openly and daringly, gave the nationalized oil back to the colonialists, violated neutrality, and opened the country's doors to the imperialists' goods and capital. And to carry out these aims, he chose violence and terror as the only effective method. The security organization[1] was thus created along with military courts, secret trials, terror on the streets, physical tortures, destruction of home and properties belonging to liberals and true patriots.... The blackest strata of the ruling class put at the Shah's disposal the most bloodthirsty individuals, such as Azmudeh and Bakhtiar, in order to have their revenge on the revolutionary elements.

With the passing of time, however, the ruling class realized that shooting alone could not guarantee power perpetually in a land where people were stirred to defend their national interests.

Consequently, while not abandoning terror, another method came to be used along with it, beginning with the premiership of Manuchehr Eqbal [Manichir Iqbal]. This second method consisted of political maneuvering designed to deceive public opinion. At the order of the Shah, two political parties—*Melliyun* and *Mardum*—were set up.[2] The Shah promised "100 per cent free elections." In his monthly press conference, he claimed that, in the course of the following ten years, the living standard of every Persian would be raised to "ten times" the current level. This machinery of deceit became even more colorful under 'Ali Amini, who declared himself the champion of "revolution from the top."... It took Amini only a year, however, to flee from the arena he had entered so

---

°Ehsan Tabari was for a long time the head of Tudeh. The following extract is from his article "Tasbit-e ertija'i ya tahavvul-e enqelabi" [Confirmation of Reaction or Revolutionary Change], *Donya Organ-e Te'orik va Siyasi-ye Komite-ye Markazi-ye Hezb-e Tude-ye Iran (The World: The Theoretical and Political Organ of the Central Committee of the Iranian Tudeh Party)*, Second Series, III (Summer 1341 [1962]):3–9.

noisily.[3] Once more, the initiative rested with the Shah, with little change in the tactics used for the past ten years in manipulating public opinion.

Why did the Shah and his imperialist masters find this so-called gradual change advisable? Here are the reasons:

The method of terror and intimidation did not work because:

1. Intelligent public opinion, created by the vast propaganda activity of the Tudeh Party and other patriotic and progressive groups, proved to be very different from the public opinion of Reza Shah's time. Surely, the Shah aspires to the absolute rule of his father and would like very much to lean on a throne on the backs of a silent and obedient mass. He recently said to the reporter of *Le Monde*, the French newspaper, "My father's dictatorship was a necessity, so is my power." He also declared to a reporter of the *Deutsche Zeitung*, "The prime ministers are responsible to my person; whoever is not able to carry out his duties must go."

The expectations of the father and son may be identical, but the social milieu is radically different. Muhammad Reza Shah rules an Iran where social and national consciousness have reached proportions that were unimaginable during his father's time. The people's legitimate demands can be heard, muffled but steady as the roar of an approaching storm. Thus, he is trying to postpone the fatal hour by reconciliation, retreat, [and] maneuvering. . . .

2. Another reason must be sought in the daily change of balance of power in favor of the forces of peace, democracy, and socialism and against those of war, reaction, and imperialism. The period prior to World War II, when British imperialism imposed dictatorships on the world's nations, is past history. Even the postwar period, when this role was transferred to the new leader of capitalism [the United States], has run its course. In today's world, progressive forces have gained enough strength to be able to influence the people's destinies.

Furthermore, the internal conflict within the imperialist camp has become stronger. John Foster Dulles' power structure is threatened by frightening splits; this is, indeed, different from those times in which the *coup d'état* of 1953 was carried out under the leadership of [U.S.] General Norman H. Schwarzkopf and [U.S Ambassador] Loy Henderson. In many Asian, African, and Latin American countries, basic changes are taking place. The Iranian people, who were among the first to rise against imperialism after World War II, hear of popular uprisings in Cuba, Algeria, other Middle Eastern countries, Indonesia, India, etc. To prop up the crumbling structure of feudalism is impossible in an Iran where both the forces of production and the capitalist system of production have grown [to be contradictory]. The Shah is trying to find new bases of social support by shifting [the emphasis] from the feudalists to the capitalists.

What Is the Content of the Shah's Reformist Claims?

These reforms do not aim at basic changes in the structure and order of the society, i.e., they do not aim at transferring political leadership from the procolonialists to the anticolonialists and at eradicating feudalism and introducing a dynamic and progressive economic system. On the contrary, these claims are designed to perpetuate the privileges of the court, landowners, and capitalists, and to continue an antinational foreign and domestic policy. In other words, these insignificant pseudo-reforms are affected in order to leave intact what is basic and essential [in the old system]. Under the pretext of land reform, for instance, the Shah is trying to sell out the undesirable villages to the peasants, while leaving whole villages of superior quality in the hands of the landowners. He hopes to create by this an antirevolutionary stratum and thus save the large estates from the pending blows of revolution. He further hopes to transform landowners into capitalists by encouraging the former to buy state-owned factories and guaranteeing them 6 per cent profit. Again, the Shah wants to "improve the situation of the worker" by having him share in the profits of the industries. This scheme, which is a mechanical imitation of the [methods of] some Western capitalist countries, is designed to dull the workers' class-consciousness by creating in them a fanciful image of participation in ownership. The insincerity of such a promise is all too obvious in a country where labor laws and workers' insurance are not enforced, where working hours sometimes reach 10-12 hours; where medieval methods of labor hiring, especially in rug weaving, are prevalent; where the workers do not belong to labor unions and have no right to strike. . . .

The *coup d'etat* regime claims to decentralize the administration, allegedly so that the different provinces may develop their own economies more efficiently. But, in practice, the Shah is trying to revive the ancient satrapy system, by giving vast powers to governors who are chosen by him in the first place and who are obedient to him in every way. The purpose of a truly sincere, genuine decentralization, however, should be to give the essential rights to different peoples [i.e., ethnic groups] of the land, within the framework of an undivided and independent Iran. The *coup d'etat* regime claims that it is fighting corruption and bribery, but the "great trials" of Amini's rule were designed primarily to settle political accounts among the rival groups in the ruling class. Our courts of justice, moreover, acted as legal bathhouses, out of which the dirtiest thieves of public funds emerged forever cleansed. The Shah is talking about strengthening democracy by introducing city and village councils, while at the same time he deems it within his own right to set up or dissolve not only cabinets but the two [legislative] chambers, to direct legislation, to invest powers, to command the army, to represent the government. The claims to create a modern industry and technology by means of long-term economic plans are also insincere. His five-year or seven-year plans serve the strategic goals of the imperialists by providing them with markets. These plans are not concerned with the orderly development of our own economy. Even as such, these plans are either never carried out or carried out very badly. As an example, one may indicate the dams that were built at exorbitant cost; becuse of major technical defects, they proved useless.[4]

These pseudo-reforms are intended to deceive the backward and gullible elements by offering them a mirage of reforms and to create hope among those people who are favorably disposed toward "quiet, gradual, and peaceful progress" without the need for an organized, active, and revolutionary struggle.

The Shah's Reformist Promises
Will Not Satisfy True National Aspirations

1. The people want the government to follow a positive neutral policy by leaving CENTO, by annulling the mutual agreement with the United States, and by expelling the American advisors. The people want a radical land reform: Crown lands, state lands, and privately owned lands should be distributed among the peasants without compensation and in the shortest possible time.

The people want to industrialize the country and to introduce metallurgy but, since the colonial allies do not want this, everything ranging from needles to tractors is imported. The people want protection of customs and the domestic market, promotion of domestic products and of exports. They are acting for economizing in the export of currency, for the nationalization of oil industries, the ousting of the international oil consortium, and the establishment of chemical and petrochemical industries. The people want free activity for various political parties, truly free elections, and a chance for activity for those who have been forced by the present regime to exile themselves. . . .

2. The present administration lacks both sincerity and ability, even for the realization of these superficial reforms. The planned reforms are often superficial, erroneous, and amateurish. The present administration is not capable even of coping effectively and speedily with such small matters as

earthquake and flood damages, let alone the daily increase in the cost of living, inflation, the bankruptcy of domestic industries, chronic deficits in the budget, and lack of balance between exports and imports.

3. The governmental machinery is corrupt and fully engaged in the embezzlement of public funds. It is unable to enforce laws, it discriminates in the allocation of funds to privileged individuals, and it falsifies reports and statistics. Even if the ruling class wanted, it would not be able to control this labyrinth of useless bureaucracy through the thick walls of its palaces.

4. For speedy and profound reforms, a coordinated, continuing, and useful activity is needed. And for this, the participation and productivity of the whole nation are necessary. City-dwellers and villagers alike must be inspired by enthusiasm for work and with respect and confidence in their leaders. The Shah and his administration are not forces capable of stimulating physically and psychologically the people who, in the last analysis, constitute the gold backing of any reform.

5. The ruling class and its imperialist masters are torn between their internal conflicts and intergroup rivalries, thus paralyzing each other's activities. In spite of repeated attempts by the Shah to reconcile them, intergroup provocations explode at times so intensely that they threaten the very existence of the regime itself.

6. The administration lacks the necessary financial resources. There is no doubt that Iran is potentially very rich, but actually it has grown very poor because of the age-old colonialist exploitation and social and economic retardation. In order to remedy this situation, the present regime knows only two ways: to give the oil riches to the colonialists and to contract heavy loans. The country is so poor that the government has had to spend the funds earmarked for the five-year plan to meet its budgetary deficit. Furthermore, the government has had to resort to auctioning the state factories in order to pay the compensation due to the rich land-owners.

7. The speedy progress of the socialistic nations and the increasing weakness of the capitalistic ones will not allow these painfully slow changes to bear fruit.... The Shah said on his last trip to America, "This kingship business is only a headache for me." One must say that this "kingship business" will generate more dangerous headaches, because it is an outdated and condemned insitution.

However, the present regime will not collapse by itself. The two above-mentioned methods, i.e., terror and reform, promise to help it live longer than one might expect. The only sure way of attaining our national aspirations is to overthrow the regime by a persistent and definite revolutionary struggle. The Tudeh Party of Iran and other progressive elements in the country offer "revolutionary change" as the only alternative to the Shah's "reactionary perpetuation." The urgency of our alternative becomes more evident when we realize that our country is lamentably underdeveloped due to centuries of social and technical stagnation. We are at least 100 years behind the developed societies. This situation places before the present generation of Iran a weighty and grave historical duty: to achieve the historical greatness of Iran in the shortest possible time through organized, untiring activity based on scientific and exact planning. Some of the representatives of the ruling class offer alternatives to our proposal. Mr. Matin Daftary, the leader of *Ettefaq-e-Melli* [the National Union Association], suggested that the way to reform was to bring "retiring [literally, secluded or withdrawn], competent men" to hold responsible positions. Mr. Kaviani expressed the same idea in different words in one of the recent issues of [the weekly] *Khandaniha*. Mr. Amirani [then editor of *Khandaniha*] maintained that affairs would fall into their proper courses if they were entrusted to onlookers with insight, who had gained perspective owing to their distance. The present leaders cannot see, because they are too close to the source of affairs. Some of the right-wing members of the National Front maintain that reform must be sought in an overt manner through militancy, while remaining within the limits of law, and through individuals who are not affiliated with Communism.

We believe that all these schemes for leadership are misleading and that they originate in the politically satisfied minds of those who are in no hurry and who, furthermore, do not concern themselves with the thousands of hungry, sick, and homeless people of Iran, who want the most expedient and definite change. There is only one way to basic reform in our society: concentrated fighting by the genuine aspirants for change who dare to use any means of struggle to oust imperialism, to secure political and economic independence and democracy, to defend neutralism and peace, to eradicate feudalism, and to adopt noncapitalist means of development. Our party knows both the direction and the method for such reforms. It has been appealing for a long time to the progressive elements in the country to consolidate their forces in a united front. Nevertheless, we realize that our duty extends well beyond the attempts to recruit followers for action from the existing progressive groups. Our ultimate aim is the mobilization of the absolute majority of people in cities [especially the workers] and in villages by taking utmost advantage of the revolutionary atmosphere prevailing in the society. Our party can fulfill its crucial historical tasks only by attaining the level necessary to become ideologically and structurally a "workers' party," in the fullest sense of the expression.

Notes

1. The Iranian secret police and intelligence service.
2. The Melliyun (National) Party, generally the majority party in Iran, was established in 1958. The Mardum (People's) Party, established in 1957, has advocated a program of social welfare and land reform.
3. Amini resigned in 1962, when his proposal to cut government expenditures by 15 percent was rejected.
4. The first two plans favored large projects that needed considerable foreign currency. The third plan, introduced in 1963, tried to avoid the errors of the first two. It paid closer attention to the private sector, and its investment quota was raised almost to the level of that of the state sector.

84.   Masculine History:
The Background of the Monarchy in Iran

Reza Baraheni

Reza Baraheni, born in Tabriz in 1935 of Turkish-speaking Azeri parents, is one of the most distinguished poets, novelists, and critics of Iran, with a doctorate in English literature and more than 20 books to his credit. He has a rather unique historical and sociological grasp of Iran's society and the place of the monarchy in it. He fought, with the intellectuals of the country, first against the censorship imposed by the shah and later against the shah's growing dictatorship. Eventually he was jailed for over three months and tortured. He was released in 1973, through the efforts of European and American writers, and settled in the United States. Baraheni, like many progressivist and liberal Iranians, advocated the preservation and the development of the native Islamic-Iranian culture and civilization together with the Western ideals of liberty and progress in an atmosphere of mutual respect and acceptance rather than through colonial and imperialistic pressure. The three excerpts below, rearranged to complement each other, provide a description of Iran's ethnic composition and the historical place of the shah in Iran's history, as seen by Baraheni, and provide a glimpse at the alienation and estrangement of the late shah from his people and country. Baraheni is profoundly versed in Iranian history and mythology and he discusses the rule of the shahs as conforming to a pattern that he calls masculine history, *that is, the accumulation of wealth in the hands of the ruling fathers. Baraheni's sociocultural and economic views on the history of the Iranian monarchy have a certain intellectual value beyond their overt, narrow scope—that is, the expression of harsh criticism of the shah. Baraheni makes references to the Oriental mode of production, which was mentioned by Marx and Engels but was eliminated from Marxist discussion by Stalin. This much-discussed concept, supported by some empirical research such as K.A. Wittfogel's theory on Oriental despotism, claims that the scarcity of rain and, consequently, the low productivity of land in Asia necessitated irrigation, leading to the creation of a corresponding infrastructure and to a pattern of social and political organization different from that of the West.*

The following excerpts give an excellent picture of the antishah feelings on the eve of the monarchy's fall. The excerpts are taken from Reza Baraheni, The Crowned Cannibals, Writings on Repression in Iran *(New York: Vintage Books, 1977); footnotes and explanations in the original are not reproduced.*

The Historical and Economic Foundations of
Monarchy in Iran

The Shah considers monarchy to be the "natural regime" of Iran. In the summer of 1961 he told France's Press Club: "Only those regimes are in danger which are not natural. The Iranian regime is a natural regime which has stayed with us for the last 2,500 years. This regime was not imposed on us by foreigners; monarchy is not the creation of the colonialist powers." In other speeches and books he considers monarchy to be the pillar of Iran's natural identity, the irreplaceable structure of its existence.

What is the truth behind this claim? It must be traced back to the accumulation of wealth in the hands of the ruling fathers at the origins of what has been termed "Oriental Despotism." How did the accumulation of wealth take place in the early phases of Iranian history? What were its immediate effects?

Until the lower stage of barbarism, fixed wealth consisted almost entirely of the house, clothing, crude ornaments and the implements for procuring and preserving food: boats, weapons and household utensils of the simplest kind. Food had to be won anew day by day. Now, with herds of horses, camels, donkeys, oxen, sheep, goats and pigs, the advancing pastoral peoples—the Aryans in the Indian land of the five rivers and the Ganges area, as well as in the then much more richly watered steppes of the Oxus and the Jaxartes, and the Semites on the Euphrates and the Tigris—acquired possessions demanding merely supervision and most elementary care in order to propagate in ever-increasing numbers and to yield the richest nutriment in milk and meat. All previous means of procuring food now sank into the background. Hunting, once a necessity, now became a luxury.

This increase of wealth was connected with the downfall of matriarchy and the rise of patriarchy. . . . This theory of the downfall of matriarchy and the rise of patriarchy, outlined first by Morgan, reinforced by Engels and molded into a convincing documents on the rise of various classes in the dawn of civilization, was augmented by later research on the part of many anthropologists and mythologists in the West. None of these studies, however, provides specific examples from the culture and history or prehistory of Iran. Let me clarify a few points.

All Iranian myth, legendary history, religion and religious cults start with the supremacy of men over women. Kayoomarth, the first king and the first great father, was a man who had tamed the animals of the earth. Later, Zoroaster, whose religion is one of men and with whom we enter the era of patriarchy, sought temporal aid in the form of Vishtaspa, a man. This does not mean that there was no matriarchy in Iranian prehistory: At present archaeology has discovered the existence of indigenous (non-Aryan) matriarchal cults in Iran and Central Asia. All the archaeological researchers of the Soviet Union speak of the existence of these cults before the arrival of the Indo-Iranians in these regions. And certainly there are significant reminiscences of these cults and rituals in the literary works, sculptures and objects dug out of the archaeological sites. Moreover there are undeniable examples of matriarchal culture in the folklore of the various nationalities and tribes living in Iran today. . . . Matriarchal societies of the Iranian plateau and Western Asia had given their place, because of the increase in production, to patriarchal societies, and the rule of women had given its place to the reign of men, and it was no longer possible to sacrifice men for the fertility of the land.

The increase in level of production, the accumulation of wealth, the soaring power of men in both family and society, and the concentration of all productive forces in the male domain led also to the concentration of all art, literature and culture in the hands of men. This, one may say, happened elsewhere in the evolution of society from savagery to barbarism to civilization, and therefore my definition of Masculine History is in no way different from the Western modification of historical patriarchy. . . .

The Economic Structure of
Masculine History in Iran

The lands, the waters, the gold, the mines, the beasts, the men, women and children, the seasons and months—in sum, all things that are on the earth or that fall from the sky—belong to the Shah of Shahs of Iran.

He is the absolute possessor of everything both objective and subjective. He is God himself walking on earth.

The great poet Saadi (1215?–1292) said in the first chapter of his *Rosegarden*, dedicated to "The Nature of Kings," that: "To want anything contrary to the wish of the Shah, would be equal to playing with your life. If he calls day, night, you should simply say, Behold the moon and the Pleiades." The epic poet Ferdowsi (935–1020) said that the Shah was one who "drove wolves and sheep together to the watering area...."

The concept of Zillullah, or the Shah as God's Shadow, which was used by most of the shahs of Iran to give their rule a certain religious legitimacy during the Islamic era, should be studied in the light of the mythological definition of the word *farreh*. As soon as the man gains supremacy of the woman and matriarchy is over-thrown, and as soon as he gains control of the productive powers of both society and the family, he turns his objective economic power into an abstract divine halo, thus claiming to be the sole representative of God on earth. This halo acts as the moral, religious and divine justification of his economic power....

The Ethnic and Economic Situation of
Iran under the Shah

The present population of Iran is thirty-four million. There are only fourteen to sixteen million Persians in the country. Of the rest, ten million are Azarbaijanis, four million are Kurds, two million are Arabs and two million are Baluchis. There are other ethnic minorities too, such as Christians, Jews and Zoroastrians. But only one language is the official language of the country. The Shah considers all Iranians to be Aryans, thus overlooking the ethnic diversity which exists in the country. Everyone has to learn one language, Persian. This is a great injustice to the other nationalities.

I belong to the Turkish-speaking Azarbaijani nationality. The men and women of my generation were told by the Shah to forget about their language and to read and write everything in Persian. We did so under duress and learned Persian. When I write a poem or a story about my parents, my mother, who is alive and doesn't know how to read or write or speak Persian, cannot understand it. I have to translate it for her so that she can understand.

The Shah's efforts to Persianize the Azarbaijanis and the Kurds and the Arabs and the Baluchis have failed. But his cultural discrimination still prevails. For instance, the 3,000 American children brought to Iran by their parents working for Grumman can go to an English-speaking school.

Yet millions of native Iranian children born to Azarbaijani, Kurdish and Arab parents do not have even one school in which they can study everything in their native languages. This is only one aspect of the Shah's racism.

Another aspect lies in the fact that the Shah is purging the Persian language of all that is Arabic and Turkish. This makes learning Persian even more difficult for those whose native language is Arabic or Turkish. In doing so, the Shah is also purging the present Persian language of 40 percent of its vocabulary. Arabic, though a Semetic language, stands in relation to Persian, an Indo-European language, as Greek and Latin do to English, from the standpoint of vocabulary. Imagine eliminating all Latin and Greek words from English because the two ancient languages are alien in spirit to English. In passing, let me note the ironic fact that the Shah himself speaks Persian very badly; he is more at home with French and English.

The Shah is destroying not only the cultures and languages of the Iranian Azarbaijanis, Kurds and Arabs, but he is also mangling the linguistic and cultural identity of the Persians themselves. He is destroying the traditions of a whole civilization. Of this whole tradition and civilization he wants to preserve only the worst part, that is, the crown placed upon his head by the CIA. . . .

Every schoolteacher with experience will tell you that in some villages schoolchildren are taken out to graze the grass for their lunch. In many villages people still exchange their daughters for a cow because they can milk a cow and till the land with it but they can hardly do that with their daughters. A half-skilled laborer in Tabriz, the second or third biggest city in the country, gets even less than twenty-five cents an hour, while a pound of meat costs more than two dollars, onions—if found at all—are priced at fifty cents a pound, and potatoes are not to be had at any price.

In Quri-Chai, the northern slums of Tabriz, there is only one school for 100,000 schoolchildren. In most of the cities of Baluchestan, there is only one bath for the entire population (in the city of Bampour, for instance), but since people are so poor that they cannot afford to pay the nickel required to go the the bath, it has fallen in ruins. People have actually frozen to death in winter in this great oil-producing country.

Yet the Shah and the Iranian government claim that Iran wil have reached the standard of living of the industrially advanced nations in a matter of a few years!

We need schools, jobs, food, health facilities, democracy, freedom of the press, a revolution in our legal system. We are one of the richest countries of the world. We should be able to do wonders with our wealth.

But the Shah has grabbed that wealth, is arming us to the teeth and helping the whole Middle East arm itself to the teeth....

Thus we live on the precipice of a gargantuan doomsday. Those Iranians who have refused to believe it are tormented and shot. The infernal hours of this mad doomsday have become part and parcel of every Iranian's daily life. There are a million cars in Teheran, a city originally built for people using camels, mules and horses. Now nearly everyone spends hours every day sitting and sweating in cars or buses on the small crossroads of the city, hooting and swearing at countrymen in other means of transportation. All the payments for these cars are pocketed by members of the Royal Family and those close to the inner court. The whole circus of Iranian monarchy operates on the basis of profiteering and exploitation.

The Shah and the Queen are flown in helicopters to the sites of the multiple companies they own or to the airport, from which they fly to St. Moritz and to their summer and winter resorts on the shores of the Caspian Sea and the Persian Gulf. Very rarely do they ride in cars through the streets of Teheran. Separate from everything, they are alienated as well from the pattern of city life in Iran. They peer at their distant mist-covered city from behind shuttered windows, meditating on hundreds of young men and women who await the day when they will have the chance to tighten the noose around the self-declared "Father and Mother" of the nation. The marble and mirrors of their numerous palaces reflect everything in the guise of their future killers. These tyrants are also prisoners, the prisoners of their own blind arrogance and ambitious tyranny.

To witness the collective dispossession of the nurtured tradition and way of life in an entire nation, travel to Iran. The people of the country are being alienated from their cultural and ethnic roots and thus from their identity. They have been denied all that is of merit in the West while their own values are corroded. The cultural denuding thus involves a double alienation which gnaws at our vitals like a cancer.

85. The Monarchist Antirevolutionary View

The friends of the old regime now in Diaspora, or keeping silent in Iran while blaming Khomeini in every possible way, continue to regard the shah as a great modernizer and as a revolutionary. Some, curiously enough, blame his downfall on the West, especially on the United States, which supposedly did not want a strong and well-armed Iran capable of defying its wishes. Others blame the human rights policy of the United States, which supposedly compelled the shah to liberalize the regime and enabled the opposition to organize and recruit its large following. This view does not reflect the real situation, for the revolution had been in the making since 1963. The excerpts below are taken from Abdul Rahman, The Betrayal of Iran (n.p., 1979), pp. 3–36 passim.

The Revolution of the Shah of Iran

The deep attention paid by the Shah to the spiritual forces within the people of Iran, the need of society for social reform, and the tendency towards socialist economies in the world of private enterprise placed the Shah in the position of taking a firm and categorical decision. The Shah needed a mutation and fundamental transformation to establish a new system. Only a revolution and social movement could replace the old and worn-out system prevailing in Iran with a progressive one. The Shah praised the revolutionary path and began to lead the revolutionary movement in society himself.

The first revolutionary movement which was taking place in the direction of creating new and fundamental changes was land reform, the dividing of the land of major landowners among farmers who actually cultivated the lands belonging to the major landowners.

The carrying out of the land reform which is usually mentioned today simply in passing or, to put it more plainly, as merely of historical interest, had in reality an unbelievable effect from the point of view of its social impact and the fruits that it bore. It is not in fact possible to enumerate all of them in this brief treatise. It must be mentioned, however, that in many regions of the country the "feudal" powers ruled in a harsh manner over the farmers who were regarded in fact as peasants or even serfs. As a result of the respect for the principle of ownership based on centuries of national tradition and heritage and also the respect held for ownership in Islam as well as the relation of many of the landowners in the region with foreign powers, the landowners wielded a great deal of power. It did not seem possible to break into the enclosure under their control.

The Shah of Iran who had the complete backing of the Iranian nation and also the total obedience of the powerful Iranian army, which was an extraordinary force under his command, announced the program for land reform rapidly and made the big landowners feel the sharp edge of the revolution. In a very short time, which was hard to imagine, those who tilled the land and who had a harsh and difficult life resembling that of slaves came to possess land and water.

Parallel with this development, the big landowners who were a small minority were thrown into a corner in the new social order and the land reform was carried out throughout the country with complete order and in peace. Land reform which was the basis for major transformations in Iran from both the productive and social points of view made possible the replacing of the old and worn-out system of landlord and peasant with a new system for which the nation paid a very low price. The rapid and natural motion of the land reform throughout Iran which, thanks to the power of the Shah and the army, had made any kind of opposition on behalf of the land owners impossible, caused the revolution and the major transformation within Iranian society to be carried out without any bloodshed which usually accompanies revolutions. . . .

The first important obstacle to land reform was the power of some of the clergy and religious authorities. At that time a group among them considered giving the land of the big landowners to the peasants as being against Islamic Law, basing their views upon the principle that "People have jurisdiction over their property." This group therefore began to oppose the land reform movement and its activities led to the events of June 1963 and the exiling of Khomeini from Iran.

It must, however, be said that the opposition of some of the clergy in Qom was due more to political reasons than religious ones. It was related to the concern of superpowers which feared the termination of the rule of the big landlords who were a means of extending foreign influence in the region.

The second form of resistance to land reform came from the landlords of Fars. The incidence in this province was parallel with that of Qom and related to the same superpowers which wanted to protect their vassals in Iran in every possible manner. . . .

The West, USA, and
the Shah of Iran

After the end of the Second World War and the victory of the Allies over Germany, America entered into the arena of the Middle East. America considered Western Europe and especially Great Britain and France to be in its debt. To maintain its economic and military power, it began a series of activities to legitimize its presence in the Middle East oil-producing countries including Iran. Among these efforts one may include economic activities in the form of assistance in the fields of technical matters, hygiene and food, putting an end to the monopoly of Great Britain over Iranian oil, the forming of the oil consortium with the partnership of the United States, the signing of a treaty with Iran, and the sharing of the United States in 55% of the oil income of the consortium.

The partnership of America in Iranian oil, a partnership which did not exist before the events of the 28th of Mordad (the return of the Shah in 1953) created at the same time certain responsibilities among which the following may be counted:

1. Guarding the oil resources and the oil-producing countries before the Soviet Union and the danger of international Communism.
2. Keeping the oil flowing to the West.
3. Providing for the oil needs of the industrial countries of the West and America at a reasonable price....

The Great Escape

The Shah of Iran was fully aware of the power and role of the West in controlling the economic enclosure of Iran and other oil-producing countries in the Middle East. He therefore awaited the appropriate opportunity to have Iran escape from this economic and social trap. Not only for the Shah but for the leader of any country who feels responsible for his nation, development and the economic self-sufficiency of his country is his ideal and final goal. The economic self-sufficiency of Iran which was the final goal of the Shah was not only one thought or decision among others which would be realized over the years along with other projects in the country. Rather, it was a great battle with the industrialized West which without doubt would face severe and general resistance on the part of the West led by America....

The Leadership of the Revolt against the Shah

Ruhollah Musavi Mostafavi who is known as Khomeini and who is originally Indian possessed and still possesses certain characteristics and qualifications which made him more than anyone else suitable to lead the "religious" revolt against the Shah and the system of monarchy in Iran. The most important of these characteristics are:

1. He is angry, vengeful, and obstinate. He only thinks of Pan-Shi'ism. The national identity, independence, and the freedom of the people of Iran mean nothing to him except as a means of serving Pan-Shi'ism.
2. Fifteen years of being away from Iran in exile has increased the harshness and evil which had existed in him since childhood to an

inconceivable degree and he is totally devoid of his compassion and chivalry which is found more than usually among the religious scholars and clergy of Iran.

3. As a result of his fanatical adherence to Shi'ism, being away from his followers and fighting against the Shah of Iran from outside the country, he had gained great influence among fanatical followers.

4. Since he possessed the degree of *ijtihad* (that is, being able to give views on the Sacred Law) and the title of *marja'i taqlid* (one who can be emulated by the Shi'ite faithful), he was followed blindly by those religious fanatics who consider following his orders a religious obligation.

5. He is a person who is uncompromising and unbending, opposed to foreign influence and a believer in a fanatical religious system with its economic and social norms.

6. He possesses piercing and evil eyes, a fact which is necessary for one who wants to lead a "religious" rebellion. This is in fact one of its results.

7. The love for gaining power and becoming a leader, something which is in his blood.

8. Profound enmity toward the person of the Shah and the deep desire to take revenge upon him and to destroy his system in Iran. In fact he views everything that has been built and created in Iran during the last fifty years with enmity, considering it to be illegal and unnecessary (exactly what the West wanted to achieve). . . .

For experts concerned with Iran it was certain that Khomeini being away from the country for fifteen years was a very valuable factor because different political groups and in fact the people of Iran as a whole could not gain enough knowledge of his personality, thought, and future programs. In others, each person in Iran made of him someone who reflected that person's own thoughts and goals, and each person saw in his being the embodiment of the goals that person was struggling for and the ideals of his life. That is why without Khomeini revealing his political doctrine, liberals considered him the symbol of liberalism, those who favored democracy saw him as the flagbearer of freedom, and the ordinary people saw him as the creator of a developed Iran with a blooming economy and better life for everyone. Those same experts concerning the problems of Iran and the Middle East all agree that if, like others members of the clergy, Khomeini had remained among the people of Iran, his personal moral characteristics would have prevented him from even becoming a leader of the clergy in purely religious matters.

XXVI. THE NEW ISLAMIC FUNDAMENTALISM AND SOCIAL REVOLUTION IN IRAN

86. Introduction

In its simplest definition, Islamic fundamentalism means first of all a return to the Koran and Sunna for the organization and regulation of the individual and collective life of Muslims. The implication of this view is that any belief, attitude, institution, or activity not conforming to the religious law must be abandoned or altered. This is, more or less, the core of the doctrine of many Muslim fundamentalist movements throughout history. In more modern times, fundamentalist Islamic movements have included the Wahhabis, the modernist reformist group of Abduh, and others as well as the Muslim Brethren (discussed in Section IV).

The common feature of the early fundamentalist movements was their desire to return to the basic sources of Islamic faith and law. It was in essence a movement aimed at restoring a pattern to the life that had lost, ignored, or violated its original purity and purpose. The sought-for return to the fountainheads of Islam would revitalize and modernize society, it was thought by Afghani, Abduh, and other reformers. These fundamentalist movements, whatever their merits and contributions, adopted a passive view of the world and, especially, of their society; for them the dynamics of the Islamic society consisted merely of opposition to, and defense of the Muslims against, alien influences and encroachments. It appeared that the Islamic society simply reacted to outside stimuli, without being able to generate from within the necessary spiritual and intellectual energy required for the creation of a continuous, self-perpetuating, innovative social motion. Indeed, the early fundamentalism did not seek within Islam itself for the ethical and social forces that would enable it to develop its own original pattern of social and political interaction that conformed to the Islamic ethos but also met contemporary needs of life. Consequently, the early fundamentalist movements lost vitality in a short time and degenerated into passiveness or retreated from the world into the shelter of intellectual abstraction.

The chief characteristic of the recent fundamentalist movement originating in Iran has been, on the other hand, its preoccupation with the actual problems of the society and its dynamic search for solutions, including the removal of obstacles to the attainment of goals defined in accordance with the teaching of Islam. The forces opposing and undermining Islam are seen as consisting both of the bad influences from the West and also of concrete local factors, such as oppressive regimes and a faulty social order established in violation of Islamic rules—that is, the native adaptations of colonialism, imperialism, and so forth. The fundamentalists pin the blame for Islam's wanting situation directly on Muslims who accepted or submitted to a social order in total contradiction of Islamic precepts. They focus their attention first on man, as a being with many psychological, social, and political dimensions, and propose a policy based on Islam's teachings and action in accordance with the policy. Religion for them is not merely a faith but actually the source of social and political ideology. The new fundamentalism based on the Koran places the responsibility for man's fate directly and squarely on the individual man. In its view, God appointed the Prophet as a messenger only and did not hold him responsible for man's decline or advancement. People (*al-nas*) themselves are responsible for their own progress or decline through their decision to be properly guided or to be misguided. They are also responsible for all that happens in society and in history and cannot shift the blame to others.

The new Iranian Islamic fundamentalism owes much to the Ayatollah Khomeini's social and political teachings and to Ali Shariati's interpretations of Islam, the Koran, and the Prophet's message. The following sections are devoted to a brief survey of the life and main ideas of Khomeini and of Shariati and the Mojahedin—who represent the new fundamentalism. For sources on Islamic fundamentalism, see the publications of the Mizan Press of Berkeley, Calif.; *Mojahet* (the review of the People's Mojahedin Organization of Iran); *Islamic Revolution*, a monthly published in Falls Church, Va.; and the various publications of the Institute of Policy Studies, Washington, D.C. See also the bibliographical references in the other sections dealing with Iran.

87. Islamic Government and Society

Ayatollah Khomeini

Ayatollah Ruhullah al-Musavi al-Khomeini (Ayat-u-Allah al-Khumaini) was born in 1902 in Khomein, a small town 60 miles south of Teheran. His grandfather, Sayyid Ahmad, known as al-Hindi—that is, the Indian (some claim he was from India, others say he only resided there)—and his father were religious scholars. Khomeini studied in Qum, the city of learning and piety, with the Ayatollah Hairi, who had a dynamic and contemporary view of education, and other renowned scholars. From the start Khomeini combined religious learning with political and revolutionary views, as evidenced in his book, Kashf-e Asrar [Unveiling of Secrets], published in 1941, in which he denounced the monarchy and all its laws as violating the Koran. At the same time Khomeini defended traditional religion against secularist attacks, as indicated by his strong reply in 1946 to Ahmad Kasravi, an Azeri writer with modernist-nationalist-Westernist views who had criticized the ulema. He became a member of the group of Ayatollah Burujirdi, the leading scholar of the time in Qum. Upon the death of the leader in 1961, Khomeini acquired the position of marja'-i taqlid (an individual Office whose sayings are to be followed). Under his direction the mosque and the Office became centers of social and political activity directed against the monarchy. In March of 1963, the Faydiya madrasa (school) in Qum where Khomeini delivered his sermons was attacked by the shah's troops; a number of people were killed and Khomeini was arrested and then released. He was rearrested after the revolt of June 1963, known as "events of 15 Khordad," a turning point in Iran's internal politics. Khomeini was exiled to Bursa in Turkey; after several months he went to Najaf, the center of Shiite learning in Iraq. Throughout his stay in Iraq, Khomeini maintained relations with the revolutionary groups and denounced the acts of the monarchy.

It must be mentioned that Khomeini was not the first religious leader to rise against the monarchy. Practically all revolutionary movements in the recent history of Iran had a religious basis or were led by religious leaders, as mentioned in the introduction. The predecessor of Khomeini was the Ayatollah Kashani, who mustered a following and opposed Reza Shah to the point of forcing him to rescind his "modernist" reforms. (These were a pale imitation of Atatürk's reforms in Turkey.) However, Kashani, like other leaders, did not question the existence of the monarchy, which he regarded as part of the Iranian life; he, like other ulema (the Iranians prefer the term mujtahid), was ready to accept and live with the monarchy as long as it respected their traditional place in society and their privileges, and the constitutional setup. Khomeini not only rejected entirely the monarchy but also called upon the religious leaders to take an active part, that is, to join the liberals, leftists, and Marxist and Islamists, that is, the fedayi and mujahedin, in the struggle against the shah. It should be pointed out that the individual attitudes of the leading Iranian ulema toward revolution, the monarchy, and the shah were not the same. Khomeini, Talegani, and Montazeri represented the group dedicated to struggle and the overthrow of the monarchy. A large group, whose head could be considered to be the Ayatollah Shariatmadari (in one interview he said he accepted the shah), *although opposed to some acts of the regime and taking issue with it on some matters, preferred to dedicate itself to the study of religion and not become involved in politics; hence they were considered harmless by the shah. They were sensitive to the criticism that they were ignoring* nadhir, *that is, the religious duty of the* ulema *to warn people of the danger to the faith. A third* ulema *group of limited consequence worked with the regime. The first and second groups represented the leading cadres of the* ulema *and, if united, could move the entire religious establishment and the masses of the people— as ultimately they did. (This alignment also decided more or less the hierarchy of power that emerged after the shah's overthrow).*

The struggling young ulema, *known as* ruhaniyun-i *Mubariz, fol- lowed also Khomeini's teachings; and the youth from the rapidly expanding middle classes, in universities offering no possibility of free discussion, developed a keen interest in religion as the sole avenue left through which to combat the evil and injustice that was assumed to stem chiefly from the government. At the same time a new interest developed in* jihad—*holy war—as an active means for changing the situation, thus turning religion into a social movement. The Koranic commandment to "consult people in affairs" gave a democratic dimension to the movement. Consequently, many intellectuals who until then had remained outside the religious movement made peace with and joined the fundamentalist Islam that had become a social movement of political liberation. The teachings of Ali Shariati and of Bazirgan (known as Muhandis-engineer) were vital in bringing the intellectuals into the mainstream of this Islamic revolutionary social movement that Khomeini came to lead. These developments, besides reemphasizing the value of the native culture and identity, undermined the influence of the modernist, Westernist intellectuals who had been the shah's chief supporters. This was in fact the "return to self," which resulted from the rejection of Westernism in its liberal and doctrinaire (Marxist) form. The failure of the Marxists to dominate and subvert the Sazmani Muja- hedin-i Khalq, despite infiltrations and pressures, may be due to this "return to self" movement. (There were Marxist elements in the early Mujahedin groups—hence their name Islamic Marxists—but these eventually opted for Islam.) Khomeini rejected vehemently the label Islamic Marxist as having been invented by the shah to discredit the movement, for, he said, the "Muslim people must remain homogeneous is their struggle and forbid any systematic collaboration with communist elements" (reported in* Le Monde *of May 10, 1978). Eventually, after 1978, the Sazmani Mujahedin entered the mainstream of the Islamist revolutionary struggle and played a decisive part in achieving its final victory.*

The events leading ultimately to the ousting of the shah began in Qum on January 8, 1978, and spread to the entire country. Throughout this period Khomeini was active in issuing statements and encouraging the

Iranians to persist in their struggle. The shah meanwhile brought pressure on Iraq to expel Khomeini, who eventually found refuge in France in October 1978. Now he became, thanks to the Western press, a world figure, and he was able to increase further his influence inside and outside Iran among both Muslim and non-Muslim revolutionaries. On Feburary 1, 1979, after the shah left Iran, Khomeini returned in triumph and proceeded immediately to establish the Islamic Republic. A public referendum in March 1979 approved the Islamic Constitution, which had been drafted largely under the direction of the Ayatollah Beheshti and created in Iran the type of government demanded by Khomeini. Since his return, Khomeini has been the rallying point as well as the symbol of the Iranian revolution. Addressed now as "Imam," the highest title in Shiite Islam, he found himself in the middle of the conflict between leftist and rightist groups—especially the conflict between the clergy-dominated, conservative Islamic Republican Party (IRP) and President Bani-Sadr's smaller group composed of the modernists and revolutionaries. A heart ailment in 1980 reduced greatly Khomeini's activities and indirectly aided the IRP to assume greater political power, a development apparently contradictory to Khomeini's views. (See also the Introduction to Political and Social Thought in Iran.)

The taking of the American hostages, a lawless act to which he was compelled to acquiesce, made Khomeini the target for attacks and ridicule in the Western press and obscured greatly his efforts and achievements in the Iranian revolution and the Republic. It is still too early to pass final judgment on Khomeini. However, one can say that he was instrumental in transforming Islamic fundamentalism from a passive theological idea into a dynamic movement with great potential to achieve political and cultural regeneration in Islam. This was, in fact, a development that directed Islamic societies throughout the world into the stream of contemporary life and, at the same time, increased their sense of Islamic identity. The question is whether the revolution will survive after Khomeini's death, and whether the Islamic Republic can accommodate all the conflicting demands of the groups that made its victory possible. Already the increasing violent strife between the government and the Mujahedin, and the summary executions among the latter group, have harmed Khomeini's image as a religious leader above mundane politics.

Publications in English about Khomeini must be used with considerable care. Islamic Government (Joint Publication Research Service, Arlington, Va., 1979), a translation by the U.S. government of Khomeini's Velayat-i Faqih [Government of Jurists], appeared in an edition published by Manor Books (New York, 1979). The book entitled Ayatollah Khomeini's Mein Kampf includes a variety of other writings full of factual errors and ugly derogatory remarks against Khomeini, Iran, and Islam. A shorter book, Sayings of the Ayatollah Khomeini (Bantam Books) includes material from *several of Khomeini's writings.* Al-Bayan Bulletin, *appearing sporadically in 1977–79, has valuable information on Khomeini's teachings and life. For background on Islam in Iran and on Qum's religious life, see Michael M.J. Fischer,* Iran: From Religous Dispute to Revolution *(Cambridge: Harvard University Press, 1980). See also Louise Rinser,* Khomeini und der islamische Gottesstaat *(Percha: R.S. Schultz, 1979);* Principes politiques, philosophiques, sociaux et religieux d'Ayatollah Khomeiny *(Paris: Editions Libres, 1979);* Islam and Revolution: Writings and Declarations of Imam Khomeini *(Berkeley: Mizan Press, 1981); Ali-Reza Nobari, ed.,* Iran Erupts *(Stanford: Iran-American Documentation Group, 1978); and Shaul Bakhash, "The Iranian Revolution,"* New York Review *(June 26, 1980):22–26, 31–34. For further bibliographical information on Iran's revolution in English, French, and German, see Fred Halliday, "Testimonies of Revolution,"* MERIV *Report (May 1980): 27–29, and* MERIV *Report no. 75/6.*

The following excerpts provide a general picture of some of Khomeini's views on Islam and government, as well as the embodiment of these views in the Iranian Constitution. The first two excerpts are from Islamic Government, *pp. 6–35 passim (see above). The constitutional articles in the third extract are taken from* The Constitution of the Islamic Republic of Iran, *trans. Hamid Algar (Berkeley: Mizan Press, 1980), pp. 26–33.*

A. The Nature of Islam, Monarchy, and Colonialism°

Islam is the religion of the strugglers who want right and justice, the religion of those demanding freedom and independence and those who do not want to allow the infidels to dominate the believers.

But the enemies have portrayed Islam in a different light. They have drawn from the minds of the ordinary people a distorted picture of Islam and implanted this picture even in the religious academies. The enemies' aim behind this was to extinguish the flame of Islam and to cause its vital revolutionary character to be lost, so that the Moslems would not think of seeking to liberate themselves and to implement all the rules of their religion through the creation of a government that guarantees their happiness under the canopy of an honorable human life.

They have said that Islam has no relationship whatsoever with organizing life and society or with creating a government of any kind and

---

°These sections by Khomeini are reproduced in this anthology as they appeared in the English translation. We have adhered to the original as a matter of principle. However, one must stress the point that the translator used terms and concepts derived from Christianity and Western experience that invariably distort much of Khomeini's thinking and Islam's stand.—K.H.K.

that it only concerns itself with the rules of menstruation and childbirth. It may contain some ethics. But beyond this, it has no bearing on issues of life and of organizing society. It is regrettable that all this has had its bad effect not only on the ordinary people but also among college people and the students of theology. They misunderstand Islam and are ignorant of it. Islam has become as strange to them as alien people. It has become difficult for the missionary to familiarize people with Islam. On the other hand, there stands a line of the agents of colonialism to drown Islam with clamor and noise.

So that we may distinguish the reality of Islam from what people have come to know about it, I would like to draw your attention to the disparity between the Koran and the Hadith books on the one hand and the (theological) theses on the other hand. The Koran and the Hadith books, which are the most important sources of legislation, are clearly superior to the theses written by religious interpreters and legists because the Koran and the Hadith books are comprehensive and cover all aspects of life. The Koran phrases concerned with society's affairs are many times the phrases concerned with private worship. In any of the detailed Hadith books, you can hardly find more than three or four chapters concerned with regulating man's private worship and man's relationship with God and few chapters dealing with ethics. The rest is strongly connected with social and economic affairs, with human rights, with administration and with the policy of societies.

You, the youths who are the soldiers of Islam, must examine more thoroughly the brief statements I am making to you and must familiarize people throughout your life with the laws and rules of Islam, and must do so with every possible means: in writing, in speeches and in actions. Teach the people about the catastrophes, tragedies and enemies that have engulfed Islam since its inception. Do not hide what you know from the people and do not let people imagine that Islam is like present-day Christianity, that there is no difference between the mosque and the church and that Islam can do no more than regulate man's relationship with his God.

At a time when darkness prevailed over the Western countries, when American Indians were inhabiting America, when absolute regimes exercising domination and racial discrimination and resorting to the excessive use of force with total disregard for the public opinion and for the laws were in existence in the Roman and Persian empires—at that time, God made laws which he revealed to the greatest prophet, Muhammad, may God's peace and prayers be upon him, so that man may be born under their canopy. Everything has its ethics and its laws. Before man's birth and until the time he is lowered into his grave, laws have been drawn up to govern him. Social relationships have been drawn up and government has been organized, in addition to determining the duties of worship. Rights in Islam are high-level, complete and comprehensive rights. Jurists have often quoted the Islamic rules, laws and regulations on dealings, permissibles, punishment, jurisdiction; on regulating relations between states and peoples, on war and peace and on human rights.

Islam has thus dealt with every aspect of life and has given its judgment on it. But the foreigners have whispered to the hearts of people, especially the educated among them: "Islam possesses nothing. Islam is nothing but a bunch of rules on menstruation and childbirth. Theology students never go beyond these issues in their specialization." It is true that some students pay greater attention to this, and they are wrong in doing so. This (excessive attention) at times helps the enemies to achieve their goals. This makes the enemies, who have been working for hundreds of years to plant the seeds of negligence in our scientific academies so as to attain their goals against us and their goals in our wealth and in the resources of our country, rejoice.

At times, the foreigners whisper to the people: "Islam is deficient. Its judiciary laws are not what they should be." To further deceive and mislead the people, the agents of the British tried, on the instructions of their masters, to import foreign positional laws in the wake of the well-known revolution and of the establishment of a constitutional regime in Iran. When they wanted to draw up the country's basic law—meaning the constitution—those agents resorted to Belgian laws which they borrowed from the Belgian Embassy. A number of those agents, whom I do not wish to name, copied those laws and corrected their defects from the group of French and British laws, adding to them some Islamic laws for the purpose of camouflage and deception. The provisions in the constitution that define the system of government and that set up the monarchy and the hereditary rule as a system of government for the country are imported from England and Belgium and copied from the constitutions of the European countries. These provisions are alien to Islam and are in conflict with it.

Is there monarchy, hereditary rule or succession to the throne in Islam? How can this happen in Islam when we know that the monarchic rule is in conflict with the Islamic rule and with the Islamic political system? Islam abolished monarchy and succession to the throne. When it first appeared, Islam considered the sultanic systems of rule in Iran. ... God's prophet, may God's prayers be upon him, sent messages to the king of the Romans (Hercules) and the king of Persia urging them to set the people free to worship God alone because only God is the sultan. Monarchy and succession to the throne are the ominous and null system of government against which al-Husayn, the master of martyrs, rose and fought. Rejecting injustice and refusing to submit to Yazid's succession and rule, al-Husayn staged his historic revolution and urged all the

Moslems to follow suit. There is no hereditary monarchic system in Islam. If they consider this a defect in Islam, then let them say: Islam is defective. . . .

What we are suffering from currently is the consequence of that misleading propaganda whose perpetrators got what they wanted and which has required us to exert a large effort to prove that Islam contains principles and rules for the formation of government.

This is our situation. The enemies have implanted these falsehoods in the minds of people in cooperation with their agents, have ousted Islam's judiciary and political laws from the sphere of application and have replaced them by European laws in contempt of Islam for the purpose of driving it away from society. They have exploited every available opportunity for this end.

These are the destructive plans of colonialism. If we add to them the internal elements of weakness among some of our people, we find that the result is that people begin to grow smaller and to despise themselves in the face of the material progress of the enemies. When some states advance industrially and scientifically, some of us grow smaller and begin to think that our failure to do the same is due to our religion and that the only means to achieve such progress is to abandon religion and its laws and to violate the Islamic teachings and beliefs. When the enemies went to the moon, these people imagined that religion was the obstacle preventing them from doing the same! I would like to tell these people: The laws of the Eastern or the Western camps are not what led them to this magnificent advance in invading outer space. The laws of these two camps are totally different. Let them go to Mars or anywhere they wish; they are still backward in the sphere of securing happiness to man, backward in spreading moral virtues and backward in creating a psychological and spiritual progress similar to the material progress. They are still unable to solve their social problems because solving these problems and eliminating hardship requires an ideological and moral spirit. The material gains in the sphere of overcoming nature and invading space cannot accomplish this task. Wealth, capabilities and resources require the Islamic faith, creed and ethics to become complete and balanced, to serve man and to avert from him injustice and poverty. We alone possess such morals and laws. Therefore, we should not cast aside our religion and our laws, which are directly connected with man's life and which harbor the nucleus of reforming people and securing their happiness in this world and in the hereafter, as soon as we see somebody go to the moon or make something.

The ideas disseminated by the colonialists among us include their statement: "There is no government in the Islamic legislation and there are no government organizations in Islam. Assuming that here are important Shari'a laws, these laws lack the elements to guarantee their implementation. Consequently, Islam is a legislator and nothing more." It is evident that such statements are an indivisible part of the colonialist plans that seek to divert the Moslems away from thinking of politics, government and administration. These statements are in conflict with our primary beliefs. We believe in government and we believe in the need for the prophet to appoint a caliph (successor) after him and he did. . . .

You must show Islam as it should be shown. Define governance to the people as it is. Tell them: We believe in governance; that the prophet, God's prayers be upon him, appointed a successor on the orders of God; we believe in the need for forming government; and we seek to implement God's order and rule to manage people, run their affairs and care for them. The struggle for forming government is a twin to the faith in governance. Write and disseminate the laws of Islam and do not conceal them. Pledge to apply an Islamic rule, rely on yourselves and be confident of victory.

The colonialists prepared themselves more than three centuries ago and started from the zero point. They have gotten what they wanted. Let us now start from scratch. Do not allow the Westerners and their followers to dominate you. Familiarize the people with the truth of Islam so that the young generation may not think that the men of religion in the mosques of Qum and al-Najaf believe in the separation of church from state, that they study nothing other than menstruation and childbirth and that they have nothing to do with politics. The colonialists have spread in school curricula the need to separate church° from the state and have deluded people into believing that the ulema of Islam are not qualified to interfere in the political and social affairs. The lackeys and followers of the colonialists have reiterated these words. In the prophet's time, was the church separated from the state? Were there at the time theologians and politicians? At the time of the caliphs and the time of 'Ali, the amir of the faithful, was the state separated from the church? Was there an agency for the church and another for the state?

The colonialists and their lackeys have made these statements to isolate religion from the affairs of life and society and to tacitly keep the ulema of Islam away from the people and drive people away from the ulema because the ulema struggle for the liberation and independence of the Moslems. . . .

°The term "church" should be "religion," or, better, "pulpit."

B. Proof of Need for Forming Government and Revolution

Need for Executive Agencies

A collection of laws is not enough to reform society. For a law to be an element for reforming and making people happy, it requires an executive authority. This is why God,may He be praised,created on earth, in addition to the laws, a government and an executive and administrative agency. The great prophet, may God's prayers be upon him, headed all the executive agencies running the Moslem society. In addition to the tasks of conveying, explaining and detailing the laws and the regulations, he took care of implementing them until he brought the State of Islam into existence. In his time, the prophet was not content with legislating the penal code, for example, but also sought to implement it. He cut off hands, whipped and stoned. After the prophet, the tasks of the caliph were no less than those of the prophet. The appointment of a caliph was not the sole purpose of explaining the laws but also for implementing them. This is the goal that endowed the caliphate with importance and significance. The prophet, had he not appointed a caliph to succeed him, would have been considered to have failed to convey his message. . . .

Need for Continued Implementation of Laws

It is obvious that the need for implementing the laws was not exclusive to the prophet's age and that this need continues because Islam is not limited by time or place. Because Islam is immortal, it must be implemented and observed forever. If what was permissible by Muhammad is permissible until the day of resurrection and what was forbidden by Muhammed is forbidden to the day of resurrection, then Muhammad's restrictions must not be suspended, his teachings must not be neglected, punishment must not be abandoned, tax collection must not be stopped and defense of the nation of the Moslems and of their lands must not be abandoned. The beliefs that Islam came for a limited period and for a certain place violates the essentials of the Islamic beliefs. Considering that the implementation forever of laws after the venerable prophet, may God's prayers be upon him, is one of the essentials of life, then it is necessary for government to exist and for this government to have the qualities of an executive and administrative authority. Without this, social chaos, corruption and ideological and moral deviation would prevail. This can be prevented only through the creation of a just government that runs all aspects of life.

"Horses you can muster so that you may scare away the enemies of God and your enemies." Had the Moslems adhered to the meaning of this

Koranic phrase and had they been ready to fight under all circumstances, it would not have been possible for a handful of Jews to occupy our land and to damage and burn our al-Aqsa Mosque without being faced with any resistance. All this came about as an inevitable result of the failure to form an upright and faithful government. Had the current Moslem rulers tried to implement the laws of Islam, abandoning all their differences, putting aside their disputes and their division and uniting in one hand in the face of the others, the bands of Jews and the puppets of America and Britain would not have been able to reach what they have reached, regardless of how much America and Britain help them. The reason for this is, of course, the fact that the Moslem rulers are unfit and unqualified.

The phrase "prepare for them all the force you can muster . . . " orders that we be fully prepared and alert so that the enemies may not subject us to the worst forms of torture. But we did not unite, we split into factions, our hearts were disunited and we did not get ready and so the unjust went beyond all limits in tyrannizing us and inflicting injustice upon us. . . .

Need for Political Revolution

At the early stage of Islam, the Ommiads° and those supporting them tried to obstruct the stability of the government of Imam 'Ali ibn Abu Talib, even though it was a government that pleased God and the prophet. With their hateful efforts, the method and system of government changed and deviated from Islam because the programs of the Ommiads were in complete conflict with the teachings of Islam. The Abbasides came after the Ommiads and followed the same path. The caliphate changed and turned into a sultanate and a hereditary monarchy. The rule became similar to that of the emperors of Persia and Rome and the pharaohs of Egypt. This situation has continued until our present day.

The Shari'a and reason require us not to let governments have a free hand. The proof of this is evident. The persistence of these governments in their transgressions means obstructing the system and laws of Islam whereas there are numerous provisions that describe every non-Islamic system as a form of idolatry and a ruler or an authority in such a system as a false god. We are responsible for eliminating the traces of idolatry from our Moslem society and for keeping it away from our life. At the same time, we are responsible for preparing the right atmosphere for bringing up a faithful generation that destroys the thrones of false gods and destroys their illegal powers because corruption and deviation grow on their hands. This corruption must be wiped out and erased and the severest punish-

---

°The proper usage is *Ummayyad.*

ment must be inflicted upon those who cause it. In His venerable book, God describes Pharaoh as "a corrupter." Under the canopy of a pharaonic rule that dominates and corrupts society rather than reform it, no faithful and pious person can live abiding by and preserving his faith and piety. Such a person has before him two paths, and no third to them: either be forced to commit sinful acts or rebel against and fight the rule of false gods, try to wipe out at least reduce the impact of such a rule. We only have the second path open to us. We have no alternative but to work for destroying the corrupt and corrupting systems and to destroy the symbol of treason and the unjust among the rulers of peoples.

This is a duty that all Moslems wherever they may be are entrusted—a duty to create a victorious and triumphant Islamic political revolution.

Need for Islamic Unity

On the other hand, colonialism has partitioned our homeland and has turned the Moslems into peoples. When the Ottoman State appeared as a united state, the colonialists sought to fragment it. The Russians, the British and their allies united and fought the Ottomans and then shared the loot, as you all know. We do not deny that most rulers of the Ottoman State lacked ability, competence and qualifications and many of them ruled the people in a despotic monarchic manner. However, the colonialists were afraid that some pious and qualified person would, with the help of the people, assume leadership of the Ottoman State and (would safeguard) its unity, ability, strength and resources, thus dispersing the hopes and aspirations of the colonialists. This is why as soon as World War I ended, the colonialists partitioned the country into mini-states and made each of these mini-states their agent. Despite this, a number of these mini-states later escaped the grip of colonialism and its agents.

The only means that we possess to unite the Moslem nation, to liberate its lands from the grip of the colonialists and to topple the agent governments of colonialism, is to seek to establish our Islamic government. The efforts of this government will be crowned with success when we become able to destroy the heads of treason, the idols, the human images and the false gods who disseminate injustice and corruption on earth.

The formation of a government is then for the purpose of preserving the unity of the Moslems after it is achieved. This was mentioned in the speech of Fatimah al-Zahra', may peace be upon her, when she said: ". . . In obeying us lies the nation's order, and our imamhood is a guarantee against division."

Need for Rescuing Wronged and Deprived

To achieve their unjust economic goals, the colonialists employed the help of their agents in our countries. As a result of this, there are hundreds of millions of starving people who lack the simplest health and education means. On the other side, there are individuals with excessive wealth and broad corruption. The starving people are in a constant struggle to improve their conditions and to free themselves from the tyranny of the aggressive rulers. But the ruling minorities and their government agencies are also seeking to extinguish this struggle. On our part, we are entrusted to rescue the deprived and the wronged. We are instructed to help the wronged and to fight the oppressors, as the amir of the faithful ('Ali) instructed his two sons in his will: "Fight the tyrant and aid the wronged. . . . " [This is in effect the Shiite political philosophy.]

If we want to immortalize the rules of the Shari'a in practice, to prevent violation of the rights of weak people, to prevent corruptions on earth, to apply the Shari'a laws justly, to fight the heresies and the deviations decided upon by the rigged up—parliamentary—councils and to prevent the influence and intervention of the enemies in the affairs of the Moslems we must form the government, because all this is carried out by a government led by a trustworthy and pious ruler who commits no injustice, deviation or corruption.

Previously, we did not work and did not rise together to form a government to destroy all the traitors and corrupters. Some of us have displayed lukewarmness even in the theoretical sphere and have failed to call for Islam and for spreading its laws. Perhaps some of us have been preoccupied with imploring God for these things. As a result, all these conditions have come into existence: the influence of the Islamic law in the Moslem society has diminished; the nation has been afflicted with division, weakness, and degeneration; the rules of Islam have been obstructed; and the situation has changed. The colonialists have used all this as an easy opportunity, brought foreign laws to which God has given no power, spread their poisoned cultures and thoughts and disseminated them among the Moslems, and we have lost the formations of the proper government. All this is obvious.

Islamic System of Government:
Distinction from Other Political Systems

The Islamic government is not similar to the well-known systems of government. It is not a despotic government in which the head of state dictates his opinion and tampers with the lives and property of the people. The prophet, may God's prayers be upon him, and 'Ali, the amir of the faithful, and the other imams had no power to tamper with people's property or with their lives. The Islamic government is not despotic but constitutional. However, it is not constitutional in the well-known sense of the word, which is represented in the parliamentary system or in the people's councils. It is constitutional in the sense that those in charge of affairs observe a number of conditions and rules underlined in the Koran and in the Sunna and represented in the necessity of observing the system and of applying the dictates and laws of Islam. This is why the Islamic government is the government of the divine law. The difference between the Islamic government and the constitutional governments, both monarchic and republican, lies in the fact that the people's representatives or the king's representatives are the ones who codify and legislate, whereas the power of legislation is confined to God, may He be praised, and nobody else has the right to legislate and nobody may rule by that which has not been given power by God. This is why Islam replaces the legislative council° by a planning council that works to run the affairs and work of the ministries so that they may offer their services in all spheres.

All that is mentioned in the book (Koran) and in the Sunna is acceptable and obeyed in the view of the Moslems. This obedience facilitates the state's responsibilities, however, when the majorities in the constitutional monarchic or republican governments legislate something, the government has to later exert efforts to compel people to obey, even if such obedience requires the use of force.

The Islamic government is the government of the law and God alone is the ruler and the legislator. God's rule is effective among all the people and in the state itself. All individuals—the prophet, his successors and other people—follow what Islam, which descended through revelation and which God has explained through the Koran and through the words of His prophet, has legislated for them. . . .

Yes, government in Islam means obeying the law and making it the judge. The powers given to the prophet, may God's peace and prayers be upon him, and to the legitimate rulers after him are powers derived from God. God ordered that the prophet and the rulers after him be obeyed: "Obey the prophet and those in charge among you." There is no place for opinions and whims in the government of Islam. The prophet, the imams and the people obey God's will and Shari'a.

The government of Islam is not monarchic, not a shahin-shahdom and not an empire, because Islam is above squandering and unjustly undermining the lives and property of people. This is why the government of Islam does not have the many big palaces, the servants, the royal courts, the crown prince courts and other trivial requirements that consume half or most of the country's resources and that the sultans and the emperors have. The life of the great prophet was a life of utter simplicity, even though the prophet was the head of the state, who ran and ruled it by

---

°The legislative council is one of three powers in all states in modern ages. These are the legislative power, the judiciary power, and the executive power (cabinet).

himself. . . . You know that most of the corrupt aspects of our society are due to the corruption of the ruling dynasty and the royal family. What is the legitimacy of these rulers who build houses of entertainment, corruption, fornication and abomination and who destroy houses which God ordered to be raised and in which His name is mentioned? Were it not for what the court wastes and what it embezzles, the country's budget would not experience any deficit that forces the state to borrow from America and England, with all the humiliation and insult that accompany such borrowing. Has our oil decreased or have our minerals that are stored under this good earth run out? We possess everything and we would not need the help of America or of others if it were not for the costs of the court and for its wasteful use of the people's money. This is on the one hand. On the other hand, there are state agencies that are not needed and that consume money, resources, paper and equipment. This is a waste banned by our religion because such waste escalates the people's problems, wastes their time and effort and consumers' monies of which they are in the direct need. In Islam, when Islam was the ruler, justice was dispensed, restriction established and disputes settled with utter simplicity. The qadi (judge) saw to it that all this was done by a handful of persons with some pencils and a little ink and paper. Behind all this, the qadi directed people to work for an honorable and virtuous life. But now, only God knows the number of the justice departments, bureaus and employees—all of which are futile and do the people no good, not to mention the hardship, difficulties, waste of time and monies, and, consequently, the loss of justice and rights that they cause the people.

Qualifications of ruler. The qualifications that must be available to the ruler emanate from the nature of the Islamic government. Regardless of the general qualifications, such as intelligence, maturity and a good sense of management, there are two important qualifications:

1. Knowledge of Islamic Law
2. Justice

In view of the fact that the Islamic government is a government of law, it is a must that the ruler of the Moslems be knowledgeable in the Law, as the Hadith says. Whoever occupies a (public) post or carries out a certain task must know as much as he needs within the limits of his jurisdiction and the ruler must know more than everybody else. Our imams proved their worthiness of the people's trust by their early search for knowledge. What the Shiite ulema fault others for revolves mostly around the level of knowledge attained by our ulema—a standard that the others failed to rise to.

Knowledge of the law and of justice are among the most important mainstays of the imamate. If a person knows a lot about nature and its secrets and masters many arts but is ignorant of the Law, then his knowledge does not qualify him for the caliphate and does not put him ahead of those who know the law and deal with justice. It is an acknowledged fact among the Moslems since the first days and until our present day that the ruler or the caliph must know the Law and possess the faculty of justice with a sound faith and good ethics. This is what sound reason requires, especially since we know that the Islamic government is an actual embodiment of the Law and not a matter of whims. . . .

C. The Islamic Constitution of Iran

Chapter I: General Principles

Article 1. The form of government of Iran is that of an Islamic Republic, which received an affirmative vote from the Iranian people on the basis of their longstanding belief in the Qur'anic government of truth and justice, after their victorious Islamic Revolution led by the eminent marja-i taqlid, Ayatullah al-Uzma Imam Knomeini, in the referendum of Farvardin 9 and 10 in the year 1358 of the solar Islamic calendar, corresponding to Jummadi al-Ula 1 and 2 in the year 1399 of the lunar Islamic calendar [March 29 and 30, 1979].

Article 2. The Islamic Republic is a system of government based on belief in:
a. The One God (as stated in the Islamic creed "There is no god but God"), His exclusive possession of sovereignty and the right to legislate, and the necessity of submission to His commands;
b. divine revelation and its fundamental role in the expounding of laws;
c. the return of God in the hereafter, and the constructive role of this belief in man's ascending progress toward God;
d. the justice of God in creation and legislation;
e. continuous leadership and guidance, and its fundamental role in assuring the continuity of the revolution of Islam;
f. the exalted dignity and value of man, and his freedom, joined to responsibilities, before God;

Which secures equity, justice, political, economic, social, and cultural independence, and national solidarity by recourse to:
a. continuous *ijtihad* of the *fuqaha* possessing the necessary qualifica-

tions, exercised on the basis of the Book of God and the Sunna of the Ma'sumin, upon all of whom be peace;

b. recourse to arts and sciences and the most advanced results of human experience, together with the effort to carry them still farther forward;

c. rejection of all forms of oppression, both the infliction and the endurance of it, and of dominance, both its imposition and its acceptance.

Article 3. In order to attain the objectives specified in Article 2, the government of the Islamic Republic of Iran has the duty of directing all its resources to the following goals:

a. the creation of a favorable environment for the growth of spiritual virtues based upon faith and piety and the struggle against all forms of vice and corruption;

b. raising the level of public awareness in all areas, through the correct use of the press, the mass media, and other means;

c. free education and physical training for everyone at all levels, and the facilitation and expansion of higher education;

d. strengthening the spirit of inquiry, investigation, and initiative in all areas of science, technology, and culture, as well as Islamic studies, by establishing research centers and encouraging researchers;

e. the complete expulsion of imperialism and the prevention of foreign influence;

f. the elimination of all forms of tyranny and autocracy and all attempts to monopolize power;

g. the securing of political and social freedoms within the limits of the law;

h. ensuring the participation of the entire people in the determination of their political, economic, social and cultural destiny;

i. the abolition of all forms of impermissible discrimination and the provision of just opportunities for all, in both material and nonmaterial matters;

j. the creation of a proper administrative system and the elimination of unnecessary government organizations;

k. strengthening the defense of the nation to the utmost degree by means of universal military training for the sake of preserving the independence, territorial integrity, and Islamic order of the country;

l. the planning of a correct and just economic system, in accordance with Islamic criteria, in order to create prosperity, remove poverty, and abolish all forms of deprivation with respect to food, housing, work, and health care, and the provision of universal insurance;

m. the attainment of self-sufficiency in industrial, agricultural, and military science, and technology, and all related matters;

n. securing the comprehensive rights of all citizens, both women and men, and the establishment of judicial security for all, as well as the equality of all before the law;

o. the expansion and strengthening of Islamic brotherhood and public cooperation among all the people;

p. the formulation of the foreign policy of the country on the basis of Islamic criteria, brotherly commitment to all Muslims, and the unstinting support of all oppressed and deprived people throughout the world.

Article 4. All civil, penal, financial, economic, administrative, cultural, military, political, and other laws and regulations must be based on Islamic criteria. This principle applies absolutely and generally to all articles of the Constitution as well as to all laws and regulations, and the *fuqaha* on the Council of Guardians have the duty of supervising its implementation.

Article 5. During the Occulation of the Lord of the Age (may God hasten his renewed manifestation!), the governance and leadership of the nation devolve upon the just and pious *faqih* who is acquainted with the circumstances of his age; courageous, resourceful, and possessed of administrative ability; and recognized and accepted as leader by the majority of the people. In the event that no *faqih* should be so recognized by the majority, the leader, or the Leadership Council, composed of *fuqaha* possessing the aforementioned qualifications, will assume these responsibilities in accordance with Article 107.

Article 6. In the Islamic Republic of Iran, the affairs of the country must be administered on the basis of public opinion expressed by means of elections, including the election of the President of the Republic, the representatives of the National Consultative Assembly, and the members of councils, or by means of referenda in matters specified in other articles of this Constitution.

Article 7. In accordance with the command of the Qur'an contained in the verses "Their affairs are by consultation among them" (42:38) and "Consult them on affairs" (3:159), councils and consultative bodies—such as the National Consultative Assembly, the Provincial Councils, the Municipal Councils, and the City, Neighborhood, Division, and Village Councils—belong to the decision-making and administrative organs of the country.

The nature of these councils, together with the manner of their formation and the limits of their powers and functions, is determined by the Constitution and laws arising from it.

Article 8. In the Islamic Republic of Iran, summoning men to good by enjoining good and forbidding evil is a universal and mutual duty that must be fulfilled by the people with respect to each other, by the government with respect to the people, and by the people with respect to the government. The conditions, limits, and nature of this duty will be specified by law. This is in accordance with the Qur'anic verse "The believers, men and women, are the protectors of each other; they enjoin the good and forbid the evil" (9:71).

Article 9. In the Islamic Republic of Iran, the freedom, independence, unity, and territorial integrity of the country are inseparable from each other, and their preservation is the duty of the government and of all individual citizens. No individual, group, or authority has the right to infringe in the slightest way upon the political, cultural, economic, and military independence or the territorial integrity of Iran under the pretext of exercising freedom. Similarly, no authority has the right to withdraw legitimate freedoms, even by establishing laws and regulations for that purpose, under the pretext of preserving the independence and territorial integrity of the country.

Article 10. In accordance with the verse "This your nation is a single nation, and I am your Lord, so worship Me," all Muslims form a single nation, and the government of the Islamic Republic of Iran has the duty of formulating its general policies with a view to the merging and union of all Muslim peoples, and it must constantly strive to bring about the political, economic, and cultural unity of the Islamic world.

Article 11. Since the family is the fundamental unit of Islamic society, all pertinent laws, regulations, and programs must tend to facilitate the foundation of a family and to protect the sanctity and stability of family relations on the basis of the law and the ethics of Islam.

Article 12. The official religion of Iran is Islam and the Twelver Ja'fari school of thought, and this principle shall remain eternally immutable. Other Islamic schools of thought including the Hanafi, Shafi'i, Maliki, Hanbali, and Zaydi schools, are to be accorded full respect, and their followers are free to act in accordance with their own jurisprudence in performing their religious devotions. These schools enjoy official status for the purposes of religious education and matters of personal status (marriage, divorce, inheritance, and bequests), being accepted in the course for cases relating to such matters. In areas of the country where Muslims following one of these schools of thought constitute the majority, local regulations, within the bounds of the jurisdiction of local councils, are to be in accordance with the respective school of thought, without infringing upon the rights of the followers of other schools.

Article 13. Zoroastrian, Jewish and Christian Iranians are the only recognized religious minorities, with the right freely to perform their religious ceremonies within the limits of the law and to act according to their own customs in matters of personal status and religious education.

Article 14. In accordance with the verse "God does not forbid you to deal kindly and justly with those who have not fought against you because of your religion and who have not expelled you from your homes" (60:8), the government of the Islamic Republic of Iran and all Muslims are duty-bound to treat non-Muslims in an ethical fashion and in accordance with Islamic justice and equity and to respect their human rights. This principle applies to all who refrain from engaging in conspiracy or activity against Islam and the Islamic Republic of Iran.

88.   A New Understanding of Islam and Man

Ali Shariati

Ali Shariati was born in Mashhad, Iran, in 1933 and attended school there. After graduating from the Teacher's Training College, he went to France in 1960, earning a doctorate in sociology in 1964. He returned to Iran and began teaching at Mashhad University, attempting to interpret the society's problems in the light of Islamic principles. He was a good Muslim and had made the Hajj three times. He was transferred to Teheran, where he lectured at the Husayniya Irshad, a religious meeting place, and attracted thousands of students to his classes. Originally the shah's government let him lecture freely—he did not criticize the regime—in the hope that some of his criticisms of certain features in contemporary Iranian Islam, such as the clergy, would divide the opposition. The authorities arrested and kept him in jail for 18 months after realizing—too late—the true significance of his teachings. He was released from jail in 1975 and then left for England, where he died under mysterious circumstances in June 1977, three weeks after his arrival.

Shariati believed that Islam was essentially dedicated to human beings' social progress, that it was realistic and natural, fostered a sense of justice and responsibility, and was oriented toward civilization and the community. He thought that at the present time Islam had deteriorated and deviated sharply from the original prophesy. The central pillars of Islamic doctrine and the source of the dynamism in Shariati's views were Tawheed *(the oneness of God corollary of which was unity-integration),* Jihad *(an eternal struggle for people to do good deeds and avoid wrong deeds), and* Hajj *(the evolution of man toward God). The Koran had to be studied not as a piece belonging to history but as a living guide to everyday life.*

Shariati viewed Tawheed *(or* Tauhid*), that is, the perpetual social action in Islamic society toward unity-integration, as the basic foundation of Islam. The idea developed by Shariati of* shahadat, *or* martyrdom, *as an inner attitude and commitment to social action had a deep impact upon the young revolutionaries of Iran. Presently Shariati's speeches (some still on tape), articles, and books written in Persian are rapidly being translated in various Muslim countries. One can safely state that Shariati has established a genuine Muslim sociological school centered on the human being and on his interaction with his faith and society for the new, Islamic fundamentalism. For Shariati's biography and basic teachings and a bibliography, see* On the Sociology of Islam: Lectures by Ali Shariati, *trans. Hamid Algar (Berkeley: Mizan Press, 1977);* Marxism and Other Western Fallacies, An Islamic Critique, *trans. R. Campbell (Berkeley: Mizan Press, 1980):* Hajj, *trans. Ali A. Behzadnia and Najla Denny (Houston, Texas: Free Islamic Literatures, 1980) (a first translation of this work by Somayyah and Yaser apparently appeared in 1977); David H. Albert, ed.,* Tell the American People *(Baltimore: Movement for a New Society, 1980). The excerpts below, somewhat rearranged, were taken, with the permission of the Mizan Press, from* On the Sociology of Islam, *pp. 41–55, 70–75, 82–85 passim and* Marxism and Other Western Fallacies, *pp. 24–27.*

A. The World View of Tauhid

My world-view consists of *tauhid. Tauhid* in the sense of oneness of God is of course accepted by all monotheists. But *tauhid* as a world-view in the sense I intend in my theory means regarding the whole universe as a unity, instead of dividing it into this world and the hereafter, the natural, and the supernatural, substance and meaning, spirit and body. It means, regarding the whole of existence as a single form, a single living and conscious organism, possessing will, intelligence, feeling and purpose. There are many people who believe in *tauhid,* but only as a religious-philosophical theory, meaning nothing but "God is one, not more than one." But I take *tauhid* in the sense of a world-view, and I am convinced that Islam also intends it in this sense. I regard *shirk* in a similar fashion; it is a world-view that regards the universe as a discordant assemblage full of disunity, contradiction, and heterogeneity, possessing a variety of independent and clashing poles, conflicting tendencies, variegated and unconnected desires, reckonings, customs, purposes and wills. *Tauhid* sees the world as an empire; *shirk* as a feudal system.

The difference between my world-view and that of materialism or naturalism lies in this, that I regard the world as a living being, endowed with will and self-awareness, and having an ideal and a purpose. Existence is therefore a living being, possessing a single and harmonious order that is endowed with life, will, sensation and purpose, just like a vast and absolute man (man likewise resembles the world, but a small, relative and defective world). To put it differently, if we take a man endowed with awareness, creativity and purpose, exemplary to the utmost degree in all of his aspects, and then enlarge him to the utmost degree, we will have before us the world.

The relationship of man with God, of nature with metanature, of nature with God (all of these are terms I use reluctantly), is the same as that of light with the lamp that emits it. It is also the same as the relationship between an individual's awareness of his limb and the limb itself: his perception is not separate from his limb, nor is it alien to it; but neither is it part of the limb, and still less, the limb itself. At the same time, the limb itself, without his consciousness of it, is a meaningless corpse.[1] So it is that I do not believe in pantheism, polytheism, trinitarianism, or dualism, but only in *tauhid*—monotheism. *Tauhid* represents a particular view of the world that demonstrates a universal unity in existence, a unity between three separate hypostases—God, nature, and man—because the origin of all three is the same.[2] All have the same direction, the same will, the same spirit, the same motion, and the same life. . . .

This manner of regarding the "signs" or phenomena of the world is closer to the approach of modern science than to that of ancient mysticism. It is not a question of the *wahdat al-wujud* of the Sufis, but a *tauhid-i wujud*, scientific and analytical. According to *tauhid*, multiplicity, plurality and contradiction are unacceptable, whether in history, society or even in man.

Tauhid, then, is to be interpreted in the sense of the unity of nature with metanature, of man with nature, of man with man, of God with the world and with man. It depicts all of these as constituting a total, harmonious, living and self-aware system.[3]

Notes

1. How profound, beautiful and clear are the words of Hazrat Ali: "God is outside of things, but not in the sense of being alien to them; and He is inside things, but not in the sense of being identical with them."
2. It hardly needs stating that I do not intend here a substantial unity in essence

and quiddity. Do not permit these philosophical and theological terms to tire your brain; simply expel them from your mind. For I am convinced that this is the only thing to do with this kind of apparently insoluble philosophical-literary problem. My meaning in saying that God, nature and man have the same origin is that they are not remote from each other, not alien to each other, not opposed to each other, and that no boundary exists among them. They do not have each a separate and independent direction. Other religions believe that God exists in a special, metaphysical world of the gods, a higher world contrasting with the lower world of nature and matter. They also teach that the God of man is separate and distinct from the God of nature. Thus God, the world and man are all separate from each other! We do not accept this separation.

3. The Light Verse (Qur'an, 24:35) illustrates this concept of being, since it demonstrates the special relationship between God and the world according to the world-view of *tauhid*. The whole of existence is like a burning lamp; this is neither "unity of being" (*wahdat al-wujud*) nor multiplicity of being, but *tauhid* of being.

B. How to Understand Islam

It is for this reason that I am convinced that the greatest, most urgent and most vital task confronting us today is to speak—to speak correctly, to speak out of a sense of suffering, yet at the same time precisely and scientifically, and thus to analyze what afflicts us. For all those who have set to work in our country and elsewhere in the Islamic world in the hope of accomplishing something have seen very little result for their efforts or no result at all. The reason is that when they set to work, they did not know what needed to be done, and it is certain that as long as we do not know what we want, we will also not know what to do.

Our first task is, then, the knowledge of our religion and our school of thought. Yes, centuries after our historical adhesion to this great religion, we must still begin, unfortunately, with an attempt at knowing our religion.

As I said in our previous session, there are various ways of knowledge of Islam. One is the knowledge of Allah, and comparing Him with the objects of worship in other religions. Another is the knowledge of our book, the Qur'an, and comparing it with other heavenly books (or books that are said to be heavenly). Yet another is the knowledge of the personality of the Prophet of Islam and comparing him with the great reforming personalities that have existed throughout history. Finally one more is the knowledge of the outstanding personalities of Islam and comparing them with the prominent figures of other religions and schools of thought.

The duty of today's intellectual is to recognize and know Islam as a school of thought that gives life to man, individual and society, and that is entrusted with the mission of the future guidance of mankind. He should regard this duty as an individual and personal one, and whatever be his field of study, he should cast a fresh glance at the religion of Islam and its great personages from the viewpoint of whatever may be his field of study. For Islam has so many different dimensions and varying aspects that everyone can discover a fresh and exact vantage point for viewing it within his field of study.

Since my field of study is the sociology of religion and the project is connected with my work, I have tried to codify a kind of sociology of religion based on Islam and drawing on the terminology of the Qur'an and Islamic literature. In the course of my work and research, I came to realize that there are many wholly untouched topics that we have not even imagined existed. One of the facts I encountered in my study of Islam and the Qur'an was the existance of scientific theories of history and sociology peculiar to the custom and method of work of the Prophet. What is implied here is something different from using the Qur'an, certain verses of the Qur'an, the philosophy and certain methods used by the Prophet, or the political, psychological and ethical system of life of the Prophet, and then analyzing them by means of contemporary science. We might, for example, try to understand the cosmological verses of the Qur'an with the help of physics, or to deduce the meaning of the historical and sociological verses of the Qur'an in the light of sociology. What I mean is something quite different: namely, that I extracted from the Qur'an a whole series of new topics and themes relating to history, sociology and the human sciences. The Qur'an itself, or Islam itself, was the source of the ideas. A philosophical theory and scheme of sociology and history opened themselves up before me, and when I later checked them against history and sociology, I found them to be fully correct.

[*After pointing out the importance of migration, which Shariati discovered through the Koran, and after dealing with various philosophies of sociology in the West he continues.*]

In Islam and the Qur'an, none of the foregoing theories is to be found. Now from the point of view of Islam, the prophet is the greatest of all personalities; and if Islam were to believe the role of the prophet as the fundamental factor in social change and development, it would have to recognize all the prophets, and especially the Prophet Muhammed, as constituting that fundamental factor. We see, however, that this is not the case. The mission and the characteristics of the Prophet are clearly set forth in the Qur'an, and they consist of the conveying of a message. He is responsible for conveying a message: he is a warner and a bearer of glad tidings. And when the Prophet is disturbed by the fact that the people do not respond and he cannot guide them as he would wish, God repeatedly explains to him that his mission consists only of conveying the message of inspiring fear in men and giving them glad tidings, of showing them the path; he is not in any way responsible for their decline or advancement for it is the people themselves who are responsible.

In the Qur'an, the Prophet is not recognized as the active cause of fundamental change and development in human history. He is depicted rather as the bearer of a message whose duty it is to show men the school and path of the truth. His mission is then completed, and men are free either to choose the truth or to reject it, either to be guided or to be misguided.

"Accident" also has no decisive role to play in Islam, for all things are in the hand of God, so that accident, in the sense of an event coming into being without any cause or ultimate purpose, is inconceivable, whether in nature or in human society. . . .

The conclusion we deduce from the text of the Qur'an is, then, that Islam does not consider the fundamental factor in social change and development to be personality, or accident, or overwhelming and immutable laws.

In general, those addressed by every school of thought, every religion, every prophet, also constitute the fundamental and effective factor of social change within that school. It is for this reason that we see throughout the Qur'an an address being made to *al-nas*, i.e., the people. The prophet is sent to *al-nas*; he addresses himself to *al-nas*; it is *al-nas* who are accountable for their deeds; *al-nas* are the basic factor in decline—in short, the whole responsibility for society and history is borne by *al-nas*.

The word *al-nas* is an extremely valuable one, for which there exist a number of equivalents and synonyms. But the only word that resembles it, structurally and phonetically, is the word "mass."

In sociology, the masses comprise the whole people taken together as an entity without concern for class distinctions that exist among them or distinguishing properties that set one group apart from another. "Mass" means, therefore, the people as such, without any particular class or social form.

Al-nas has exactly the same meaning, i.e., the masses of the people; it has no additional meaning. The words *insan* and *bashar* also refer to man, but they refer to ethical and animal properties respectively.

From this we deduce the following conclusion: Islam is the first school of social thought that recognizes the masses as the basis, the fundamental and conscious factor in determining history and society—not the elect as Nietzsche thought, not the aristocracy and nobility as Plato claimed, not great personalities as Carlyle and Emerson believed, not those of pure blood as Alexis Carrel imagined, not the priests or the intellectuals, but the masses. . . .

The following can also be deduced from the Qur'an: while the people are those to whom the Qur'an addresses itself and they constitute the axis and fundamental factor in social development and change, and while they are responsible before God, at the same time personality, change and tradition also have been recognized as capable of affecting the destiny of society. According to Islam, there are then four fundamental factors of social development and change—personality, tradition, accident and *al-nas*, "the people."

Tradition, in the form derived from Islam and the Qur'an, has the sense that each society has a fixed basis, or in the words of the Qur'an, it has a road, a path, a particular character. All societies contain definite and immutable laws within themselves. A society is like a living being; like all organisms, it has scientifically demonstrable and immutable laws. From a certain point of view, then, all developments and changes that take place in a society take place on the basis of a fixed tradition and immutable laws that are the very fundament of social life.

Islam thus appears to approach the theory of determinism in history and society; but it has something further to say on the subject, modifying the law it has established. In Islam, we have both human society (*al-nas*) being responsible for its fate, and also the individuals that compose society being responsible for their destinies. The Qur'anic verses, "For them shall be what they have earned, and for you shall be what you have earned" (2:134), and "Verily God does not change the state of a people until they change the state of their own selves" (13:11) bear the meaning of social responsibility. By contrast, the verse, "Every soul is accountable for what it has earned" (74:38) sets forth the responsibility of the individual. Both society and the individual are therefore answerable for their deeds before the Creator, and each constructs his own destiny with his own hands.

In sociology, these two principles are apparently contradictory—on one side, the responsibility and freedom of man in changing and developing his society; on the other side, the notion of a determining, fixed, scientifically established law, one inaccessible to human intervention, and providing the immutable basis for the movement of society. But the Qur'an looks upon these two poles—the existence in society of determining, fixed and immutable laws, and the collective and individual responsibility of man for social chance and development—in such a way that not only are they not contradictory, they even complement each other. . . .

Islam, as a scientific school of sociology, believes that social change and development cannot be based on accident, for society is a living organism, possessed of immutable and scientifically demonstrable norms. Further, man possesses liberty and free will, so that by intervening in the operation of the norms of society, once he has learned of them, and by manipulating them, he may plan and lay the foundations for a better future for both the individual and society. Thus on the one hand there exists the responsibility of man; and on the other hand, the belief that society, like a living organism, is founded on immutable and scientifically demonstrable laws. . . .

"Personality" is not in itself a creative factor in Islam. Even the prophets are not regarded as persons who have created new norms in the existing society. From the point of view of sociology, the superiority of the prophets to other teachers—apart from the rank of prophethood itself—is that they have recognized the divine norms that exist in nature and the world better than mere reformers, and on this basis they have been better able to make use of their freedom as men to advance their aims in society. It is a truth fully attested by history that the prophets have always been more successful than reformers who were not prophets. . . .

Personalities in Islam are those who understand well the divine norms; who have discovered these norms by means of a scripture (in the particular sense accorded to scripture by Islam, that of wisdom and guidance), and make of this the secret of their success.

The proportional influence of each of these four factors on a given society depends on the circumstances of that society. In societies where *al-nas*, the mass of the people, are advanced and stand at a high level of education and culture, the role of personalities is reduced; but in societies that have not reached that level of civilization, for example a tribe or a clan, the personality or the leader may be influential. At each different stage of society, with respect to progress or backwardness, one of the four factors mentioned will have more effect than the other three.

In general there are five major factors that build a man. First, his mother makes the structure and dimensions of his spiritual form. The Jesuits say, "Give me your child until he is seven years old, and he will remain a Jesuit until the end of his life, wherever he goes." The mother rears the spirit of man as something tender and sensitive, full of emotion, and gives each child its first instruction with her own gestures while suckling it.

The second factor in the making of man is his father, who makes the other dimensions of the spirit of the child after the mother.

The third factor that builds the outer and apparent dimensions of man is school.

The fourth is society and environment. The stronger and more powerful the environment, the greater will be its educative effect upon man. For example, if somebody lives in a village, the formative effect upon him of his environment will be less than in the case of one who lives in an extremely large city.

The fifth educative factor in the building of personality consists of the general culture of society or that of the world as a whole.

There are thus five dimensions which taken together form a mold into which the spirit of man is poured and from which it is extracted once shaped. . . .

C. Man in Islam

The question of man is the most important of all questions. The civilization of today is based upon humanism, the nobility of man and the worship of man. It is believed that the religions of the past crushed the personality of man and compelled him to sacrifice himself to the gods. They forced him to regard his own will as totally powerless when confronted by the will of God. They compelled him always to be seeking something from God by way of prayer, supplication and entreaty. The philosophy of humanism is, then, a philosophy that, since the Renaissance, has opposed religious philosophies—philosophies founded on belief in the unseen and supranatural realm—and its aim has allegedly been to restore nobility to man. The roots of humanism lie in Athens, but as a universal philosophy, it has become the basis of the modern civilization of the West. In reality, it arose as a reaction to scholastic philosophy and medieval Christianity.

My purpose tonight is to examine—within the limits of my capability and the present occasion—the question of man from the viewpoint of our religion, Islam, and to seek an answer to the question: what kind of a phenomenon does Islam see in man? Does it see in man a powerless creature whose ultimate aim and ideal is to stand helpless before God? Does Islam deny man all notion of nobility? Or, on the contrary, does belief in Islam itself impart a form of nobility to man, and make an acknowledgement of his virtues? This is the topic I wish to discuss.

In order to understand the place of "humanism" in different religions, and the concept of man that each of them holds, it is best to study the philosophy of the creation of man that each has set forth . . . .

How is the creation of man explained in Islam or the Abrahamic scriptures, of which Islam is the culmination and perfection? Can we deduce the status and nature of man from the manner in which the creation of man is described in the Qur'an, the Word of God, or in the words of the Prophet of Islam? From examining the story of Adam—the symbol of man—in the Qur'an, we can understand what kind of a creature man is in the view of God and therefore in the view of our religion. By way of introduction, let me point out that the language of religion, and particularly the language of the Semitic religions, in whose prophets we believe, is a symbolical language. By this we mean a language that expresses meaning through images and symbols—the most excellent and exalted of all the languages that men have ever evolved. Its value is more profound and eternal than that of expository language, i.e., the clear and explicit language that expresses meaning directly. A simple and straightforward language, one deprived of all symbol and image, may be easier for purposes of instruction, but it has no permanence.... The audience of a religion is, moreover, not a single generation or age, but different and successive generations which follow upon each other throughout history. They inevitably differ with each other with respect to way of thought, level of thought, and angle of vision. The language that a religion chooses in order to convey its concepts must, then, be a versatile and multifaceted language, each aspect and facet of which addresses itself to a particular generation and class of men....

How was man created, in the view of Islam?

First God addresses the angels, saying, "I wish to create a viceregent for Myself upon earth." See how great is the value of man according to Islam! Even the post-Renaissance humanism of Europe has never been able to conceive of such exalted sanctity for man. God, Who in the view of Islam and all believers, is the greatest and most exalted of all entities, the creator of Adam and the master of the cosmos, addresses the angels and presents man to them as His viceregent. The whole mission of man according to Islam becomes evident from this divine address. The same mission that God has in the cosmos, man must perform on earth as God's viceregent. The first excellence that man possesses is, then, being God's representative on earth.

The angels cry out saying, "You wish to create one who will engage in bloodshed, crime, hatred and vengeance." (Since before Adam, there had been other men who, like the man of today, busied themselves in bloodshed, crime, corruption and sin, and the angels wished to remind God that if He were to create man again and grant him a second opportunity on earth, man would again engage in bloodshed and sin.) But God replies, "I know something that you do not know," and then sets about the task of creating man.

It is at this point that the symbolic aspect of the narrative begins. See what profound truths concerning man are hidden beneath these symbols! God desires to create a viceregent for Himself out of earth, the face of the globe. One might expect that the most sacred and valuable of materials would have been selected, but God chose, on the contrary, the lowest of substances. The Qur'an mentions on three occasions the substance from which man was fashioned. First it uses the expression "like potter's clay" (55:14); that is, dry, sedimentary clay. Then the Qur'an says, "I created man from putrid clay"(15:26), foul and evil-smelling earth; and finally it uses the term *tin*, also meaning clay (6:2, 23:12). So God set to work, and willed to create a viceregent for Himself; this precious vice-regent He created out of dry clay, and then He inhaled some of his own spirit into the clay, and man was created.

In human language, the lowest symbol of wretchedness and baseness is mud. No creature exists in nature lowlier than mud. Again in human language, the most exalted and sacred of beings is God, and the most exalted, sacred and noble part of every being is its spirit. Man, the representative of God, was created from mud, from sedimentary clay, from the lowliest substance in the world, and then God inhaled into him not His blood of His body—so to speak—but His spirit, the most exalted entity for which human languages possess a name. God is the most exalted of beings, and His spirit is the most exalted entity conceivable, the most exalted concept that could ever arise in the human mind.

Thus man is a compound of mud and divine spirit, a bidimensional being, a creature with a dual nature, as opposed to all other beings which are one-dimensional. One dimension inclines to mud and lowliness, to stagnation and immobility. When a river overflows, it leaves behind a certain muddy sediment that lacks all motion and life, and the nature of man, in one of its dimensions, aspires to precisely this state of sedimentary tranquility. But the other dimension, that of the divine spirit, as it is called in the Qur'an, aspires to ascend and to mount up to the highest summit conceivable—to God and the spirit of God.

Man is composed, then, of two contradictory elements, mud and the spirit of God; and his splendor and importance derive precisely from the fact that he is a two-dimensional creature. The distance between his two dimensions is the distance between clay and the spirit of God. Every man is endowed with these two dimensions, and it is his will that enables him to decide either to descend toward the pole of sedimentary mud that exists in his being, or to ascend toward the pole of exaltation, of God and the spirit of God. This constant striving and struggle takes place in man's inner being, until finally he chooses one of the poles as the determinant for his destiny....

This is true humanism. See how great is the dignity and stature of man; so great, indeed, that all the angels, despite their inherent superiority to man and the fact that they are created of light while he is created of mud and clay, are commanded to fall down before him. God tests them because of their protest, and asks the angels, concerning the names; they do not know the names, but Adam does know them. The angels are defeated in this test, and the excellence of Adam—which lies in his knowledge of the names—becomes apparent. This prostration of the angels before Adam serves to clarify the Islamic concept of man. Man knows certain things that the angels do not know, and this knowledge endows man with superiority to the angels despite the superiority of the angels to man with respect to race and origin. In other words, the nobility and dignity of man derive from knowledge and not from lineage. . . .

[In criticizing Marx for taking back from man "with the hand of dialectical materialism" what he gave him in the context of society, Shariati defines the Islamic concept of man.]

In Islam, although the interval stretching from man to God extends to infinity, that from God to man is altogether eliminated. Man is presented as the sole being within creation having the divine spirit, bearing the responsibility of the divine trust, and finding incumbent upon it the assumption of divine qualities.

The most basic of the specifically human qualities, by the general consent of humanists, may now be delineated:

1. Man is a primary being. That is, among all natural and supernatural beings, man has an independent self and a noble essence.

2. Man is an independent volition. This is his most extraordinary and inexplicable power: volition in the sense that humanity has entered into that chain of causation upon which the world of nature, history, and society are completely dependent as a primary and independent cause, and continues to intervene in and act upon this deterministic series.

Freedom and choice, his two existential determinations, have imparted to him a godlike quality.

3. Man is an aware being. This is his most outstanding quality: awareness in the sense that, through the wonderful and miraculous power of reflection, he comprehends the actualities of the external world, discovers the secret hidden to these senses, and is able to analyze each reality and each event. He does not remain on the surface of sensibles and effects, but discerns what is beyond the sensible, and induces the cause from the effect. In this way, he both transcends the limits of his senses and exends his temporal ties into the past and the future, into times in which he has no objective presence; he acquires a correct, broad, and profound grasp of his own environment. . . .

4. Man is a self-conscious being. This means he is the only living being possessing knowledge of his own presence. He is able to study himself and thus to analyze, know, evaluate, and consequently change himself—as a being independent of himself. . . .

5. Man is a creative being. This creative aspect of his behavior sets him altogether apart from nature, and places him beside God: it puts him in possession of a quasi-miraculous power that enables him to transcend the natural parameters of his own existence, grants him a limitless existential expansion and breadth, and places him in a position to enjoy what nature has not given him. . . .

6.　Man is an idealistic being, a worshipper of the ideal. By this is meant that he is never content with what is but strives to transform it into what ought to be. That is why he is constantly engaged in re-creating and why he demonstrates that he is the only being not the product of but rather the producer of his environment, or to put it simply, why he is constantly engaged in making reality conform to his idea. . . .

7.　Man is a moral being. It is here that the very significant question of value arises. Value consists of the link that exists between man and any phenomenon, behavior, act, or condition where a motive higher than that of utility is at issue; it might be called a sacred tie, as it is bound up with reverence and worship to the extent that people feel it justifiable to devote or sacrifice their very lives to this tie. Moreover, this is likewise worth considering: there is no question of a natural, rational, or scientific justification here; and also, this sentiment, as the most sublime existential manifestation of the human species, is acknowledged in all religions and cultures throughout history as constituting the greatest of resources, the grandest of glories, the most precious of emotions, the most miraculous of events. . . .

89.　Revolutionary Fundamentalism in Action: The People's Mojahedin Organization of Iran

The People's Mojahedin (or Mujahedin) Organization of Iran (PMOI), known as Mujahedin-i Khalq or simply as Mujahedin or Islamic Marxists (a name used by the shah's regime but rejected by PMOI), is the activist manifestation of Islamic fundamentalism as expressed by Ali Shariati and Ayatollah Khomeini. It was instrumental in mobilizing the masses and leading them against the shah's regime and eventually overthrowing it. It brought together various segments of the intelligentsia, the liberals, the Fedayi, and the masses and provided them with a plan of action and a corresponding strategy based on an Islamic interpretation of social conditions. The PMOI provided both an ideological interpretation of the Koran and a kinetic view of social interaction corresponding to a modern concept of political action. Both were rooted in the Islamic ethos and in the Iranian history and culture. Thus, while the Marxist views of the Fedayi were culturally alien to the masses, the symbols, values, beliefs, and aspirations of the Mujahedin were shared by the overwhelming majority of the Iranians. Whereas the Fedayi exploited ethnic and linguistic differences, the Mujahedin appealed to common ties of culture and solidarity among Iran's diverse ethnic groups.

The beginning of the PMOI goes back to various freedom movements of the 1950s. The present organization emerged from the debacle of 15 Khordad (June 5, 1963) when the shah's forces dealt a crushing blow to an uprising organized by the group. The leaders of the time—Mohammad Hanif Nezhaad, a Tabrizi who studied at the Karaj Institute of Agronomy, Said Mohsen Mahmud Asqarzadeh, and Abdulrasool (sentenced to death in 1972)—assessed the errors of the early uprisings and, undaunted by the defeat, proceeded to reorganize the movement. (One source claims that they took power from the Koranic commandment that "Verily, falsehood must disappear" and Caliph Ali's statement that the experience of the predecessors will prevent one from doubt and uncertainty.) They came to the conclusion that the failures in the past were caused by leadership shortcomings, not by lack of readiness on the part of the people, and, as well, by the failure to approach the struggle as a science with its own body of knowledge, methods, and ideology, and by the lack of an appropriate revolutionary organization. Armed struggle occupied a basic place in the strategy of the movement. Lack of space prevents a detailed treatment of the PMOI. Suffice it to say that the reorganization paid off in the overthrow of the monarchy.

Since the advent of the Islamic regime in Iran, the Mujahedin have been beset by internal dissension and changing fortunes in their relations with the ruling party. The Islamic Republican Party (IRP) headed by the late Ayatollah Beheshti (killed by a bomb planted in the IRP headquarters, supposedly by a PMOI sympathizer) has been suspicious of the revolutionary doctrines of the PMOI, including its concepts of social justice and struggle against imperialism. To put it in the simplest terms, the IRP has stressed the religious and theological dimensions of Islam, while the PMOI has emphasized the social and political goals in accordance with its own dynamic concept of the world and the Iranian revolution. The issue has produced a split in the PMOI: a majority of the leadership sided with the government, while a minority supported President Bani-Sadr; a few have joined the leftist Fedayi. The group supporting Bani-Sadr, although maintaining its Islamic ideology, is sympathetic to socialist movements in the world. It continues mobilization campaigns among the shanty town dwellers, the poor and landless peasants, and the workers. Its stronghold is the University of Teheran. The current government has used repressive measures, including jailing, murder, repression, and forceful breaking up of meetings convened by the radical wing of the PMOI. After the ousting of Bani-Sadr from the presidency in 1981, the radical wing of the PMOI continued its struggle against the clergy and has been subject to harsh punishment.

The radicals, headed by Massoud Rajavi, are active in Iran and abroad. They published a review, Mojahed, *in Persian and several Euro-*

pean languages. (*The genesis of the movement is discussed at some length by Halliday,* Iran, Dictatorship and Development *pp. 235–48). The first extract is the Mujahedin's interpretation of the Koran, entitled "How to Study the Qoran." It is taken from* Mojahed *1, no. 4 (April 1980): 40–42 passim. Footnotes and a number of sections of the original are omitted. The second extract describes the impact of Ali Shariati on the philosophy of the PMOI. It was written by Soroosh Irfani, a psychologist at the University of Shiraz, and appeared in* Iran Week, September 14, 1979. *The third extract, a new interpretation of populism, is from* Mojahed *1, no. 6 (June 1980): 50– 52 passim. Spelling in the original has been preserved.*

A. How to Study the Koran:
A Revolutionary Fundamentalist View

In the previous section, in explaining the function of the Qoran, we pointed out that this treatment involves the presentation of a picture of the world as the point of departure for a universal overview, whereby one is provided with a set of guidelines to shape the life of a human being. This worldview and ideological approach, this path and way of life, is part and parcel with the issues which a human individual encounters, from the moment of first attaining self-consciousness, up to the point where, reaching that unity of which one had no idea before, unless one possesses a sense of the realization of that unity on the social plane, a conflict will continue to exist.

As we indicated previously, this issue has a philosophical dimension, because of its aspects that cover the whole range of what we understand as science, being fundamentally empirical and capable of being established experientially, as well as being intolerant of conflict.

From another angle, every value system and every ideological con- struct, by its own nature involves the projection of a world-view, elaborated within the framework of an all-embracing philosophy founded on a particular comprehension of the universe. The Qur'an is precisely this: namely, a set of guidelines to praxis based on the ideological values which it presents in terms of the background of the Towhidi world outlook, from which the particular practical principles are inferred—with this distinction, that the absolute and transcendent aspect comes into play within the context of the given emperical factors.

If there exist schools of ideology concerned with human progress which should possess an inherent contradiction between its philosophical [a priori] fundamentals in presentation of his mode of comprehending the world and its guidelines for action, the Qoran is not one of these, for it is completely free of any such duality or contradiction. All its ramifications and specifications are directed towards one principal foundational source, logically, explicitly and harmoniously presented, and this principle is Towhid (the Divine Unity). This is to say that the fundamental and harmonic answer to any given existential question is *Laa elaaha ellaa'llah* ("There is no god but God," or "There is no being but Being").

However, given this basic fundamental, one must understand that the entire content of the Qoran and the matter of every one of its verses is the refraction of this ground of unity into the myriads of cases of practical problems which arise in society, interpretable in philosophical terms which can be expressed in the practical light of dealing with human issues. For the Qoran contains the very realities which arise in practical situations, the most tangible realities which can be discussed, which bear not the slightest possibility of refutation or denial.

If any contradictory views should come out of the Qoran, they come only through putting into practice the irrefutable philosophical principles induced from the Qoran. The multiplicity and variety which the Qoran presents is so vast that it might be said without exaggeration that every single phenomenon in the world has been covered. But it must be emphasized that this point should not allow for misinterpretation of expressions like this section of Surah al-Nahl, 89: ("*We reveal this Book to you as an exposition of all things*"). One might read this as saying that everything is explained in its precise form in the Qoran, so that there is no need of any other text for scientific study. This is an erroneous assumption. As our earlier discussion on the basic application of the Qoran indicated, none of the branches of science and technology are the subject of the Qoran as such, while it can be said that the verse we have quoted means that the Qoran may provide the *philosophical exposition* of anything in question.

We can say, then, that in the light of the overall philosophical expositions of the Qoran, such expressions are framed within the plan, the schema, of the universe as reflected by the Qoran. The Towhidi position is founded on this conceptualization. . . .

We have stated that the Qoran is a guide to action, whereby an important part is devoted to the outline and explication of issues in the social kinesis (the whole process of social change and development). The relevant verses indicate how change in the human community is brought about, how the movement and positional changes of the various social groupings takes place, with the elaboration of contradictions, antagonisms and social struggles and the provision of guidelines for the human individual to aid in determining what position should be taken. The

Qoranic view is harmonious with values and traditions involved in the evolution of being....

If we emphasized the Qoran's role as a guide to action in the social context, it is equally so in the area of providing guidance for the individual in shaping the kinesis of his life within the framework of society. We realize that there is a conventional view that religion is purely a matter of individual conscience and does not relate to social concerns, in fact, standing apart from social issues. We, on the other hand, take a very different view, namely, that religion is inextricably involved with the social plane of existence. It is not our concern here to refute the foregoing unscientific point of view, one which places the individual squarely counter to society. We only comment that such a perspective distinguishes the individual as an entity apart from the community, setting him off from society and ascribing a different content to him from that of the social group as a whole.

By no means should it be assumed that we regard religion or the Qoran as merely an accessory to the society or just an indirect influence on the Human community. Quite the contrary. We want to make it very clear that the Qoran is fundamentally and foundationally involved with the structuring and activation of society, in a very particular way....

The fact of the matter is that the Qoran places as much stress on the society as it does on the individual, especially when one takes into account the point that a great deal of what is explained about the individual concentrates on the human being's interrelationship with his fellows in the community. The study of man, or anthropology, holds a noble place in the congeries of social sciences, for it explains how man enters the process of action and undertakes the responsibility of taking stands in the society, reflecting on an individual's precise role in and existential dynamics with the experiential world around him, embodied in the community....

In the light of this discussion revolving around the importance of the question of the nature of man, it is clear that this subject has paramount importance in the Qoran. Many verses expound the question of man, *ensaan*, both as a social animal and with attention to the particulars of his individuality. Man is viewed both as an individual unit with an interdependent relationship in the social collective and as a microcosmic phenomenon in his own right, without parallel and existentially responsible for his actions. The Qoran, as with other scriptural expressions, in the very act of providing *guidance*, also stresses man's inherent direction towards development of a sense of responsibility for his actions (as part and parcel with his growth of consciousness). This is the basis for the Qoranic perspective of Towhidi (Divinely integrated) anthropology....

B. Soroosh Irfani on Shariati and the Philosophy of the PMOI

In accepting *Shahadat* (martyrdom, a central point in Shariati's thought) as the acme of their quest for furthering the Creator's design for the evolutionary growth of man and society, the Mujahedeen Khalq were among the forerunners of Iran's Islamic Revolution. Following their mentor [Shariati], the Mujahedeen believe that *Islam*, by virtue of having fallen into the hands of capitalism and imperialism, has lost its dynamic impetus, distorting the meaning and implications of liberating concepts like *Tawakul* (reliance and trust in God), *Sabr* (patient detachment) and *Taqua* (an attitude of revolutionary renunciation and self restraint). *Tawakul*, in essence, is the liberating experience of self assurance, daring, and competence, where "The limit of your experience is the limit of your belief," as the Eastern esoteric disciplines tell us. Also, the Humanistic psychologists have been referring to this human ability of transcending fear and vacillation and committing oneself in the face of the unknown as the "Chutzpah" factor—the indispensable factor for movement toward expansive dimensions of consciousness.

The Mujahedeen regard *Infaq*, the readiness to part with one's material possession, as a practical expression of devotion and worship. Whereas *Namaz*, the ritual Muslim prayer, is an expression of the relationship of the individual to the Creator (*Khaleq*), *Infaq* expresses the relationship of the individual with the masses (*Khalq*) thereby facilitating the unfolding of that higher human potential of *Taqua*: "You will not attain unto *Taqua* until you spend that which you love" (Al-Imran, 92).

Since *Touhid* is the very foundation of Islam, anyone lacking the Touhidi worldview is not a Moslem. "Anyone who does not comprehend the message in the verse 'the earth belongs to God' is not a Moslem," Iqbal reminds us. For actualizing *Touhid* in the world, the individual must participate in the evolutionary movement directed toward integration, leading ultimately to a State characterized by classless harmony. Since personal growth is inseparable from social struggle, by choosing to struggle for integration of social classes in the society, the individual accelerates the process of his inner integration of personality development. And according to Shariati, there is an interplay and continuity between personality and will. And Personality, as Shariati would have us believe, is the individual's will vis-à-vis the will of the society, nature, or history. Personality, as dynamic will, is the effect which the individual has on his environment or the effect he leaves upon it. It is the power by means of which the individual creates or changes the environment, with his own decision and initiative.

Subscribing to this view, the Mujahedeen maintain that in the battle of evolutionary and counter-evolutionary forces, the basic condition for victory stemming from the eternal law of evolutionary movement, is man's Will. God helps those who choose to follow His path, His design in creative evolution directed toward integration and harmony (*Touhid*).

It is because of the Mujahedeen's conviction of the correspondence between the individual's struggle for evolution of the society and his endeavor for the flowering of personality, that they wage a battle on two fronts: the inner battle for spiritual and psychological integration (psycho-spiritual Touhid, *Jihad-e-Akbar*), and the external battle for integration of society (Social Touhid, *Jihad-e-Asghar*). Any attempts for spiritual and psychological Touhid would remain only neutral without the corresponding endeavors for effecting Touhid in the human society. With such a worldview, as one advances on the battlefield of life, one is consciously dispensing the human responsibility for actualizing the spirit of Divine Unity in human organization for achieving the "Touhidi classless society."

C. On Populism

If we look upon populism as the reliance on the power of the people and the struggle for the realization of the people's will and of popular demands (popular ideals), we observe that there have always been revolutionaries and those who sought to correct the ills in a given system throughout history, those who have struggled for popular ideals, with boundless love, sacrificing themselves for the masses.

From time immemorial, the Towhidi Prophets have been in the forefront of the most authentic and selfless revolutionary populists of history. When in the blackest days of ignorance and slavery today's pioneering, revolutionary leaders were unthought of, the Towhidi Prophets were the heralds of the rule of the people, their accession to the inheritance of the earth, and most particularly, of the most deprived and rising forces of the society—the *moxtaz afin,* the based ones—those who hoisted the banner of continuing struggle for liberation from the yoke of the slaveholders and exploiters and who, by presenting explicit reasons and clear explanations, called the people to rise up and activate the concepts embodied in a system based on equity. The Qoran expresses their mission in these terms: "We sent the Prophets with clear proofs, accompanied by the Book and the Balance, so that the people would rise up to bring about equity" (*Al-Hadid* [Iron], 25).

Those who have placed obstacles in the path of evolution, the enemies of God and the people, are the ones who have sought to block the growth of these movements. When they witnessed the wide base which the Prophets had amongst the masses, they would become confused and frightened, resorting to trickery and the inflicting of harm, with a view to making the people dubious of the Prophets, to isolating them among the people. The fear which befell these enemies often took such a hold on them that they would kill or enslave the supporters and sympathizers of the Prophets, in order to eliminate the popular base which they enjoyed. (See the verse *Al-Qesas*, 4.) These conflicts and struggles were the natural result of the revelations which came to the Prophets and the revolt which they induced. . . .

As great anti-imperialist struggles take shape with an anti-exploitive content, the true meanings of populism and democracy have become revived and these concepts have their content once again restored with an explicitly popular sense. This content has been termed the "new democracy," an objective which may be attained by bringing the anti-imperialist, liberation struggle to victory with the toppling of the puppet regimes. Such a content has irrefutably clear demarcations, in contrast with the false bourgeois brands of "populism" and "democracy."

The new democratic revolutions, which in the present historical period involve a broad section of the peoples under domination, aim in the first stage at establishing the rule of the whole people [in a given country] under the leadership of the anti-exploitation forces. . . .

For a revolutionary system, there is no capital, no potential higher and more deserving than the support and confidence of the people. Indeed, when the revolutionary movement and the individual revolutionary do not possess the supportive power of the masses, what can they hope to achieve? Without this support, one cannot aspire to achieve the mobilization of the people, which is a necessary condition for victory in the battle against imperialism. Without this, the survival, the very existence, of the revolutionary is cut off—like that of a fish out of water.

XXVII.   THE LEFTIST VIEW OF IRANIAN HISTORY AND SOCIETY: THE FEDAYI

90.   Introduction

The Organization of Iranian People's Fedayi Guerillas (OIPFG), known generally as People's Fedayi, was formed by the merger of two Marxist-Leninist groups led by Bijan Jazani and Massud Ahmadzadeh. It began its activities in the country with an attack on a gendarme post in Siahkal in February 1971. It afterward played an important role in the struggle against the shah. Despite its many activities, it remained a relatively small group confined to universities and a few working groups. The Marxist teachings of the Fedayi have made little inroad into the thought of the Iranian masses, who have so far remained cold toward that materialistic view of the world with its threat of cultural and social alienation. In order to gain a social basis, the Marxist groups have been active among the non-Persians, notably the Kurds. The Kurdistan Democratic Party, whose early leader, Qazi Mohammed, who presided over a Free Kurdistan in 1945, was executed by the old regime, has maintained some contact with the Fedayi. The present leader of the KDP, Abdul Rahman Qassemlu, shares some of the Marxist views of the Fedayi but sees them largely in the context of his armed drive to secure recognition of the Kurdish national rights and autonomy. (The allegiance of many Iranian Kurds belongs to their religious leader Sheikh Ezzeden Husseini, who is loyal to Khomeini but favors recognition of the Kurdish rights. Ideologically he differs from the secular-leftist Qassemlu.)

The OIPFG met with considerable animosity after the IRP established itself in power because of both its philosophical tenets (materialism vs. religion) and its political stand (favoring minorities, democratic rights, and so forth). Differences of opinion with regard to the OIPFG's attitude developed within the organization too. A majority of the leadership, in the past critical of the idea of armed struggle, held the view that the revolution in Iran had produced a government free of imperialism, independent and national even though capitalistic. A minority claimed that Iran was still a "dependent capitalist state within the imperial system" and that the main struggle remained the one between oppressed people and imperialism. The majority regarded the United States as being

536

the only source of imperialism and, consequently, supported the USSR as well as the Khomeini regime. Its position is close to that of the Tudeh party, although the leaders seek to maintain their independence. The minority group of the OIFPG found itself opposed to Tudeh, to its own majority, and to the regime; some of its members were arrested and killed. The split, which was aired in the organization's publication *Kar* [Labor], took its final form when the minority split again into two groups, but then seemingly came together again. The dissident minority calls itself Fedayi "Guerillas" and the majority is referred to as People's Feday or just as "Fedayi."

The Fedayi Guerillas, although Marxist-Leninist in ideological orientation, are in large measure dedicated to the supremacy of Iranian national interests. Consequently, they have been continuously at odds with the Tudeh, whom they regard as placing Soviet interests above those of Iran. It should be noted, incidentally, that those of the Fedayi who are the allies of Tudeh were the major force in capturing the U.S. embassy. On leftism in Iran, see MERIV Report, No. 86 (Washington, D.C., 1980).

91. The Social History of Iran: A Leftist Interpretation

Bijan Jazani

The extracts below, providing a picture of the Fedayi's recent view of Iranian history and society and the Tudeh, were written by Bijan Jazani, who was born in Teheran in 1937 and killed in 1975 in jail. A painter as well as a writer, he had been condemned to 15 years in prison after being arrested in 1967. The extracts are from B. Jazani, An Introduction to the Contemporary History of Iran *(London: Iran Committee, n.d.), pp. 8–15, 41–47, 61–63 passim, and* Socio-Economic Analysis of a Dependent Capitalist State *(London: Iran Committee, n.d.), pp. 17–22 passim.*

At the start of the 19th century, the feudal-monarchic state of Iran found itself next to two exploitative European empires, namely, Czarist Russia in the North and the British Empire in the South and East. The British had already swallowed up the Indian sub-continent and were busy strengthening their position. Czarist Russia, which combined the features of a feudalist empire with that of capitalist expansionism, attacked the Iranian feudalists, who had combined to create the Qajar dynasty. During its history, the feudal monarchy of Iran had engaged in wars to capture farming lands and enslave the peasants of such lands; to acquire more income, either through plundering the public treasury and levying tributes or by exploiting the peasants and captured farming lands. However, when faced with the aggression of the Czarist army, the feudal system resisted; the result was that the feudal army engaged in two series of wars with the Russian aggressors. The Iranian army was decisively defeated in 1828 and the Treaty of Turkomanchei was signed. As a result of this treaty the feudalists ended up losing enormous amounts of valuable lands and the peasants working on them, as well as accepting Russian domination, over their own (i.e., the feudalists') economic and political life. The Czar was given the right to interfere in Iranian court matters under the pretext of protecting the Crown Prince and the reigning Sultan; at the same time, Russian businessmen acquired considerable commercial concessions. The commercial protocol of the Turkomanchei treaty formed the basis for the concessions imposed by the Russians after these wars.

Having surreptitiously expanded their commercial and political influence in Iran over a few decades (it did not, incidentally, meet any resistance from the feudalist monarchy), the British eventually began to adopt an aggressive stand when faced with Iran's persistence in retaining its power over an important portion of Afghanistan. The result of this prolonged dispute, during which Russia supported Iran, thereby trying to get closer to the position of her rival (i.e., Britain), was that, by renouncing her sovereignty over Herat (in Afghanistan) and accepting the capitulations (as was the case in the Treaty of Turkomanchei), Iran signed the Treaty of Paris in 1857....

The expansion of foreign capitalist activities in Iran, which was the means by which foreign influence spread, speeded up the growth of the Iranian bourgeoisie and greatly affected its development as well as its social and economic characteristics. At the beginning or even before the bourgeoisie assumed a definitive class character, some elements in the feudal aristocracy were beginning to get acquainted with the system of capitalism in the West. They were influenced by it and this encouraged reformist tendencies in them.

During the two decades prior to the Constitutional Iranian Revolution (1906–09), Russian imperialism had the upper hand in Iran. The Russian Bank in Iran undertook to pay off all outstanding Iranian debts to the British Bank in return for control of the most profitable customs duties. Russian businessmen expanded their activities greatly and the level of business transactions between Iran and Russia far exceeded that between Iran and Britain. Russian investment in roads, rail and telegraph lines increased, thus putting Russian influence in Iran on a par with that of Britain....

The Iranian commercial bourgeoisie achieved unprecendented

growth at the beginning of this century. On the whole this bourgeoisie had a nationalist character with comprador elements in it. A financial bourgeoisie was emerging from this bourgeoisie and showed tendencies towards investment. At the same time the absence of security for capital, which was an effect of the political domination of feudalism, as well as the influence of, and competition by, foreign capital, had blocked the bourgeoisie's advance towards industry, thus inevitably pushing the commercial bourgeoisie towards the ownership of land. The comprador feature of the bourgeoisie derived from the fact that with the import and sale of industrial goods it had amassed huge profits and this provided it with the greater part of its capital. On the other hand with the export of Iranian goods, this bourgeoisie played an important role either independently or as an agent of foreign companies. Up until the end of the nineteenth century, shawls were one of the most important items for export. At the start of the present century this product faced stiff competition from Britain and her Indian colony and lost its foreign market. Inside the country the shawl industry was capable of developing and becoming machine intensive, thus playing an important role in the development of the bourgeoisie. However, carpet weaving was condemned to remain labour intensive. This type of dual relationship between the bourgeoisie and foreign capital was bound to open the bourgeoisie to comprador influence. A tendency towards the ownership of land and the failure to invest in industry was a powerful objective factor for the growth of such a comprador feature.

The Constitutional Revolution of 1906 succeeded in destroying the dictatorial rule of the Qajars and securing a share for the bourgeoisie in the Government. The feudal aristocracy no longer had total domination over the bourgeoisie; capital received some sort of guarantee and tax collection began to be based on a proper system; the bourgeoisie acquired a lever by which to secure its rights. Once it secured these advantages for itself, the bourgeoisie turned its back on the revolution. In conditions where the revolution should have been continued for the safeguard of its victories and should have carried on the struggle against imperialism, particularly the Russian imperialists, the bourgeoisie, framed by its fundamental weaknesses, settled for compromise. Here one can safely claim that the bourgeoisie achieved its "constitution." The compromise, which resulted in a feudal-comprador Government, divided the bourgeoisie right down the middle; that section of it that was in favor of continuing the revolution remained within the ranks of the people, assumed their leadership and preserved its nationalist character, but the comprador section of the bourgeoisie (this consisted mainly of comparatively larger bourgeois elements) created the nucleus of a comprador bourgeoisie cooperating with the foreign capitalists and and the feudalists, having first ensured a firm guarantee for its capital and having managed to rob the aristocratic feudalists of some of their lands. This division occurred after the Revolution and during its decline. However, some changes had to take place before an open rift and before the appearance of contradictions between them became apparent. . . .

Iran in 1941–53 and the Tudeh Party

The dictatorial regime that had shown great capabilities in suppressing the people and in silencing the opposition turned out to be a complete coward in the face of foreign invasions. An army, gendarmerie and police that had been reorganized, modernized and re-equipped at the cost of mass poverty and had, under the direct command of Reza Khan and his cronies, been very efficient in stamping out internal dissent revealed themselves to be weaker and far less capable than the worst kind of army in the era of Fath-Ali Shah in 1828.

The higher ranking officers of Reza Khan's army are said to have deserted their military posts in veils in the face of the allied invasion of the country. The Russian army occupied the whole of the north [Khorasan, Gilan, Azerbaijan, and the northern part of Kurdistan] and the south was taken over by the British colonial army; they were subsequently joined by the U.S. army. The Iranian army in the Russian sector was disarmed, although the gendarmerie and the constabularies were allowed later on to undertake normal police duties. The administrative and military headquarters of the Russian army was in charge of practically the whole of the occupied areas and throughout the duration of the occupation the Government was unable to take any effective public measures without first consulting the occupying forces. The areas occupied by the British and the Americans were more or less governed by similar rules. Tehran, being the seat of the Government, was not occupied although all three powers had garrisons stationed in the vicinity of the capital. Thus the Central Government was devoid of the necessary power to effect its rule and the people were confronted with two other political factors, namely, the direct role of the colonialists and the power of internal reaction. The arrival of the imperialist armies increased the input of direct colonial rule, while at the same time the demise of the dictatorship facilitated the return of the Khans and feudalists to their respective seats of power where they found the opportunity to reopen relations with the colonialists. On the other hand, in this situation, the progressive forces were also able to grow at an unprecedented pace. . . .

Only a few weeks after the collapse of the dictatorship [Reza Shah was forced to abdicate in 1941] Tudeh Party declared its existence. The constituent members of the Party included some of the group of fifty-three detained in 1937, activists of the old Communist Party, and a number of liberal democrats who were under surveillance in the time of the old regime. From the very beginning, the Government and Communist Party of Russia kept an eye on the organization and programme of the Tudeh Party; and given the lack of experience of the founding members and Russia's extraordinary position in Iran, the recommendations and advice of the Soviet Communist Party played a decisive role in shaping the Tudeh Party.

a. [As a consequence of all this] The Party had not come into being as a result of a period of sustained struggle by the working-classes against the people's enemy. The activities of the old Communist Party had fizzled out during the second decade of Reza Khan's rule; during the political recession no fighting group existed that could have accumulated experience and revolutionary character in a struggle against the dictatorship. In other words not only the people but also the vanguard left the scene of struggle and, that the conditions were not ripe for the masses to be mobilized in a short space of time, the movement lacked a revolutionary vanguard. The important fact that the regime's downfall was due not to the people's struggle but due to an outside factor, clearly demonstrated the ineffectiveness of the leading forces and their organisations. Those who had founded the Party and those who joined it during its first months were neither conscious revolutionary workers nor intellectuals who had been trained in a revolutionary working-class ideology and tested in the fire of real struggle. Therefore, whereas sections of the petit-bourgeoisie were rapidly becoming mobilized, the Tudeh Party was undergoing a growth that was more quantitative than qualitative.

b. During this period the relations linking the Russian Government and Party to other communist parties was one-sided; world communist parties and their leadership regarded Russia as an infallible source of advice and the latter's approval of any party was a guarantee of that party's genuineness. In the case of our country, due to the old position of the Russian Government and Party, as well as the present dominant position of the Russian army, it was doubly so, and the experience and unoriginality of the leadership of the working-class movement in Iran made the effects of such a one-sided relation far worse. In fact the relations were crystallised in the form of Tudeh Party's blind following of the policy of the Russian Communist Party and Government.

c. Considering the experience of the old Communist Party in Iran, whose former members regarded the re-establishment of such a party as an ultra-leftist act, and also because of the importance of the relations between the Russians and other allied powers in 1941–42, the founding members decided against the choice of the name "Communist Party";

they did not reveal their long-term programme. Instead they settled for
establishing a "democratic party." The existence of the 1931 law prohibiting communist tendencies was no longer regarded as a serious impediment, so much so that no attempt was made by the Party to repeal it. Given
the country's deplorable economy, the slogans adopted by the Tudeh
Party attracted the mass of the proletariat; intellectuals were also rapidly
attracted to the Party. In a matter of two years, the Tudeh Party and the
unions affiliated to it represented a colossal force and played an important
part in areas occupied by the Red Army.

Despite this great advantage, the Party failed to embark on a serious
struggle against colonialism and internal reaction during the period 1941–
44; it neither demanded land reform nor began a struggle against British
colonialism. The political slogans of the Party in these years were directed
against dictatorship, whereas with the downfall of the old regime and the
occupation of the country, the return of the dictatorship was not considered to be a serious possibility. It also expended some energy propa-
gating against fascism, although despite some pro-German groups in Iran
this too had not been a major problem. The plain fact is that the Party felt
obliged to accept the existing *international* contradictions as a guide to
action *in Iran*; hence its refusal to initiate a serious fight against Britain and
her support in Iranian society and instead waited for the outcome of the
war. . . .

The Features of Dependent Capitalism in Iran

Dependent capitalism has been established in Iran in the past
decade. This system determines the socio-economic infrastructure and
political and cultural superstructure of our society. Compared with other
historical socio-economic formations (from the very first commune to
communism) this one may be regarded as a semi-formation, or an unstable
and transitory formation. The feature of dependency, which is an inseparable part of this system, is a guarantee of foreign exploitation and
imperialist domination in the country. The comprador bourgeoisie acts as
the ruling class through which imperialism operates. As we have said
before, this semi-formation is one of many systems which, as a result of
colonial relationships on a world scale, have appeared in exploited
countries in the space between the historical formation of feudalism and
the establishment of socialism. In this part we shall attempt to illustrate
dependent capitalism and its main characteristics in Iran by dealing with
the social, political and economic processes of our society.

The main features of dependent capitalism in Iran are as follows:

(I) The growth of the comprador-bourgeoisie and the consequent rule of this class; this has come about as a result of the channelling of the national bourgeoisie towards comprador capitalism, the dissolution of feudalism, the fragmentation of the small bourgeoisie, and the polarization of the petit-bourgeoisie. The comprador bourgeoisie has achieved qualitative and quantitative growth in five sectors (financial, commercial, industrial, agricultural and bureaucratic); ultimately by the amalgamation of monetary, industrial and bureaucratic bourgeoisies it will become a dependent financial oligarchy.

(II) With the end of feudalism, capitalist relationships are established in the villages and in the agricultural sector in general. This fragments the peasantry into various sections and forces them to join the reserve army of labour.

(III) Foreign capital investment in various sectors will expand in an unprecedented fashion and foreign exploitation will assume immense dimensions under neo-colonialist relations. The system of production will become directly or indirectly dependent on the economic and production system of the imperialist monopolies.

(IV) The formation of a minority consumer class, consisting of the bourgeoisie and the better-off section of the petit-bourgeoisie as a complementary element of the new economic system and as a base for the neo-colonialist culture.

(V) The organisational consolidation of dictatorship as the most fundamental feature of the ruling apparatus and of the anti-popular regime, leaning heavily on imperialism. . . . The final stage of [the growth of comprador bourgeoisie] culminated in the channelling of the national bourgeoisie and the feudalists in the direction of comprador bourgeoisie. Today, what is left of the national bourgeoisie is engaged in small undertakings and the remnants of feudalism are rapidly disappearing from the rural areas. The comprador bourgeoisie is growing rapidly in the fields of industry, finance and agriculture, largely managing to offset its historical failure sustained because of the one-sided growth of bureaucratic and commercial comprador bourgeoisies. Therefore, today, there are five sections to the comprador bourgeoisie. . . .

The following factors highlight the comprador character of the commercial bourgeoisie:

(a) it imports foreign consumer goods and is the sole agent for their sale and distribution;

(b) in commerce, it is an inseparable part of the comprador system by virtue of possessing the right to sell and distribute goods produced by the dependent industries;

(c) it has an undeniable role in the formation of the consumer class in service industries;

(d) its reciprocal relation with the monetary comprador bourgeoisie, the banks and insurance companies, and ultimately with Government, turns it into one of the most essential pillars of the dependent capitalist system.

92.   The OIPFG View of the Current Sociopolitical Situation in Iran (1980)

The following excerpts are taken in part from a pamphlet setting forth the OIPFG view of the political attitude of the Iranian middle classes and the workers in their struggle against the shah in 1978.

We will now survey the present situation of the movement. What exists in the democratic movement of our people today is the struggle of the urban masses, made up mainly of the radical petit bourgeoisie. The Iranian petit bourgeoisie, because of its class position vis-à-vis imperialism and its client status and because of its historical tradition of struggle. possesses a high degree of class consciousness. By altering its religious framework it can approach the other toiling masses, including the working class, and be its ally in the united anti-imperialist front. However, because of its radicalization and broad base, the petit bourgeoisie is a potential rival of the working class movement and can claim leadership of the whole of the revolutionary movement. To the extent that the radical petit bourgeoisie understands its class interests and has considerable political power, any dealings with this group must be done in a serious and highly conscious manner.

On the one hand, the petit bourgeoisie in our society manifests itself as a force struggling against imperialism in a resolute and militant manner. On the other hand, the petit bourgeoisie, unlike the proletariat, does not form a homogeneous class, i.e., in the sense of an historical cohesiveness in the struggle against dictatorship and imperialism. Depending upon which of its factions dominate, the petit bourgeoisie will leave different and significant impacts upon the liberation movement. If the ideological representatives of affluent groups within the petit bourgeoisie with conservative and anti–working class views take on the leadership of the national struggles, they can create obstacles for the unity of the popular forces. At the present time, it is this group that is playing a major role in the activities of the petit bourgeoisie. The anti-communist propaganda of recent months has intensified the contradictions between the petit-bourgeoisie and the working class. Undue emphasis of this contradiction and its intensification at the present stage does not benefit the popular forces and in fact weakens both the petit-bourgeoisie and the working class before the enemy in varying degrees. We support the struggle of the radical and militant factions of the petit-bourgeoisie that express the interests of the broadest national and anti-imperialist forces in our society, and we consider this support to be of benefit to the working class and the liberation movement. Dispersion and distortion of the national forces weakens the unity of the popular forces in the united front, and also weakens the strength of the working class in the realization of the popular democratic revolution.

We now turn to the proletariat. It is our view that the proletariat cannot play its destined role in the people's struggles without a militant vanguard organization. Without a proletarian organization to promote and protect the interests of the working class at the fore of the popular struggle, the working class cannot participate in the united front and cannot realize hegemony. In the present situation the working class movement lags behind the struggle of the other anti-imperialist sectors, for the years following the coup d'etat of 28 Mordad (August 1953) saw a stagnation in the working class movement. Contributing to the stagnation of the working class was the absence of the proletarian vanguard, the severe suppression of workers' demands by the Shah's dictatorial apparatus, and the peasant origins of much of the proletariat. . . . Revolutionary Marxist-Leninists who consider themselves to be the ideological representatives of the proletariat and who are seeking to promote themselves to the level of the vanguard of this class must address themselves to the relative backwardness of the working class movement, for a lack of attention to this reality can be catastrophic. Without a thorough understanding of this point Marxist organizations will only tail the petit bourgeoisie, and the working class movement in the factories will simply remain in the stage of trade union activity and/or tail petit-bourgeois ideology. . . .

The gap between the working class movement and the liberation movement in the present stage presents the greatest responsibilities to genuine Marxist-Leninists. Taking socialist consciousness to the working class and linking with the demands and struggles of this class constitutes the most important task for Marxist-Leninists.

The Tudeh Party is compelled to use the reputation of some other forces. To achieve this they hunt down those forces in which they can see such practical tendencies. We would want to see now whether the Tudeh Party's recognition of those whose activities are under the name of "People's Fedaiis" is correct or not!

93. The Tudeh Party as Seen by the Fedayi Halq (1980)

The excerpts herein are from the pamphlets The Principal Tasks of Marxist-Leninists at the Present Stage of Development of the Communist Movement in Iran *(n.p., October 1978), pp. 8–10, and* Those Addressed by Traitorous Tudeh Party's Central Committee Are Not People's Fedaii Guerillas *(n.p., March 1980), pp. 5–6, 11–13.*

The Tudeh Party is one of the most adamant organizations subjectively and objectively. Adamant in its decadence, adamant in pursuing anti-proletarian goals, while assuming the role of being pro-proletarian. The Party's policy is in accordance with the Party's method, the Party's method is in accordance with its practical tendencies, and its practical tendencies are in conformity with the Party's class interest. One can truly say that the Tudeh Party has never abandoned their political line. In every step they take they follow exactly the same goals, the same policies, and the same interest. If today the Tudeh Party initiates the preachers of "Valayet Faqheh" [OIPFG members rejecting armed struggle] if they vote yes on the new constitution and add fuel to the fire of the reactionary rulers' power, that is, in fact, the continuation of the same policy that approved Mohamad Reza Shah's reforms; called the 15th of Khordad [uprising] reactionary, and called the people of Tabriz ruffians during their heroic revolutionary struggle in 1978.

We have always stressed the point that the Tudeh Party's actions have never been the result of their theoretical mistakes, that all of the Party's actions and reactions have been exactly the logical result of their practical tendencies. If we accept that the same conditions necessary for a phenomenon to come into existence, are also necessary to ensure its future growth, many points about the Tudeh Party would be revealed. The formation of the Tudeh Party was not the result of the Iranian masses' internal effort. The Tudeh Pary came into existence with the support of the Red Army and began its growth not in the womb of the masses' movement, but by getting nourishment from the Soviet's foreign policies. Revolutionary organizations always try to be the protector of the people's interest, foremost the proletariat interest. The Tudeh Party has always tried to be the protector of the Soviet Union's interest. A revolutionary organization always tries to guarantee its growth through the process of class struggle and by solidifying itself with the people and relying on the masses power. The Tudeh Party has always tried to guarantee its existence through collusion with the ruling class and for this party it is not important

ABOUT THE EDITOR

Kemal H. Karpat is presently Distinguished Professor of History and Chairman of the Middle East Studies Program at the University of Wisconsin-Madison, and editor of the *International Journal of Turkish Studies*. Dr. Karpat has been a member of the United Nations secretariat and has taught at Montana State University, New York University, Johns Hopkins University, and several universities in Turkey. He was associated as researcher and fellow with Harvard and Princeton Universities.

Dr. Karpat's research has been published in various books, such as *Turkey's Politics* (1959), *Social Foundation of Nationalism in the Ottoman State: From Social Estates to Classes From Millets to Nations* (1974), and *The Gecekondu: Rural Migration and Urbanization* (1976) (just to cite a few), and in nearly 100 articles that have appeared in journals in the United States, Great Britain, France, Italy, Turkey, Austria, Germany, Romania, Yugoslavia, and several Middle Eastern countries.

A graduate of a teachers college in Romania and the Law School in Istanbul, Dr. Karpat received his M.A. from the University of Washington and his Ph.D. from New York University.